IMPORTANT

HERE IS YOUR REGISTRATION CODE TO ACCESS MCGRAW-HILL PREMIUM CONTENT AND MCGRAW-HILL ONLINE RESOURCES

For key premium online resources you need THIS CODE to gain access. Once the code is entered, you will be able to use the web resources for the length of your course.

Access is provided only if you have purchased a new book.

If the registration code is missing from this book, the registration screen on our website, and within your WebCT or Blackboard course will tell you how to obtain your new code. Your registration code can be used only once to establish access. It is not transferable

To gain access to these online resources

1. USE your web browser to go to: **http://www.mhhe.com/bew3e**

2. CLICK on "First Time User"

3. ENTER the Registration Code printed on the tear-off bookmark on the right

4. After you have entered your registration code, click on "Register"

5. FOLLOW the instructions to setup your personal UserID and Password

6. WRITE your UserID and Password down for future reference. Keep it in a safe place.

If your course is using WebCT or Blackboard, you'll be able to use this code to access the McGraw-Hill content within your instructor's online course.

To gain access to the McGraw-Hill content in your instructor's WebCT or Blackboard course simply log into the course with the user ID and Password provided by your instructor. Enter the registration code exactly as it appears to the right when prompted by the system. You will only need to use this code the first time you click on McGraw-Hill content.

These instructions are specifically for student access. Instructors are not required to register via the above instructions.

The premium content of this book includes: **Go To The Web** activities (previously Go To CD) including **Checkpoints and Interactive Exercises** referenced throughout the text.

The McGraw-Hill Companies

McGraw-Hill Irwin

Thank you, and welcome to your McGraw-Hill/Irwin Online Resources.

Jaderstrom/Miller
Business English at Work, 3/e
ISBN 978-0-07-328787-4
MHID 0-07-328787-3

M000087378

ENAT-QTEV-TFKR-Q4A9-

REGISTRATION CODE
REGISTRATION CODE

The McGraw-Hill Companies

McGraw-Hill Irwin

Business English
at Work

Third Edition

Susan Jaderstrom
Santa Rosa Junior College
Petaluma, California

Joanne M. Miller
Business English Consultant
Eau Claire, Wisconsin

 **McGraw-Hill**
Irwin

Boston   Burr Ridge, IL   Dubuque, IA   Madison, WI   New York   San Francisco   St. Louis
Bangkok   Bogotá   Caracas   Kuala Lumpur   Lisbon   London   Madrid   Mexico City
Milan   Montreal   New Delhi   Santiago   Seoul   Singapore   Sydney   Taipei   Toronto

McGraw-Hill
Irwin

BUSINESS ENGLISH AT WORK
Published by McGraw-Hill/Irwin, a business unit of The McGraw-Hill Companies, Inc., 1221
Avenue of the Americas, New York, NY, 10020. Copyright © 2007 by The McGraw-Hill
Companies, Inc. All rights reserved. No part of this publication may be reproduced or distributed
in any form or by any means, or stored in a database or retrieval system, without the prior written
consent of The McGraw-Hill Companies, Inc., including, but not limited to, in any network or
other electronic storage or transmission, or broadcast for distance learning.

Some ancillaries, including electronic and print components, may not be available to customers
outside the United States.

This book is printed on acid-free paper.
Printed in China
3 4 5 6 7 8 9 0 CTP/CTP 14 13 12 11

ISBN-13: 978-0-07-313787-2 (student edition)
ISBN-10: 0-07-313787-1 (student edition)
ISBN-13: 978-0-07-313790-2 (instructor annotated edition)
ISBN-10: 0-07-313790-1 (instructor annotated edition)

Editorial director: *John E. Biernat*
Publisher: *Linda Schreiber*
Senior sponsoring editor: *Doug Hughes*
Developmental editor: *Megan Gates*
Editorial coordinator: *Peter Vanaria*
Marketing manager: *Keari Bedford*
Media producer: *Benjamin Curless*
Lead project manager: *Pat Frederickson*
Senior production supervisor: *Sesha Bolisetty*
Lead designer: *Matthew Baldwin*
Photo research coordinator: *Lori Kramer*
Senior media project manager: *Susan Lombardi*
Cover design: *Jenny El-Shammy*
Interior design: *Jenny El-Shammy*
Cover image: © *Corbis*
Typeface: *10.5/12 Times Roman*
Compositor: *Cenveo*
Printer: *CTPS*

Library of Congress Cataloging-in-Publication Data

Business English at work / Susan Jaderstrom, Joanne M. Miller. — 3rd ed.
       p. cm.
    Includes index.
    ISBN-13: 978-0-07-313787-2 (acid-free paper : student ed.)
    ISBN-10: 0-07-313787-1 (acid-free paper : student ed.)
    ISBN-13: 978-0-07-313790-2 (acid-free paper : instructor annotated ed.)
    ISBN-10: 0-07-313790-1 (acid-free paper : instructor annotated ed.) 1. English
language—Business English—Problems, exercises, etc. I. Miller, Joanne.
    PE1115.J27 2007
    808'.06665—dc22
                                                    2005056113

www.mhhe.com

Table of Contents

Table of Contents

Welcome to *Business English at Work,* Third Edition, and to a journey through the world of English grammar, spelling, and punctuation. Working with these concepts, you will enjoy the activities and the exercises that relate to the Workplace Applications topics—a totally new learning approach relating business English to the world of work.

The third edition of *Business English at Work* is designed to help you meet the challenges of a changing world, one in which the correct usage of English is tantamount to getting and holding a job.

Each chapter opens with relevant Workplace Applications concepts around which the chapter examples and exercises are written. Topics include references, telecommunications, customer service, the World Wide Web, time management, electronic mail, cultural diversity, ergonomics, ethics, decision making, teamwork, computer software, leadership, communication, job skills, and coping strategies.

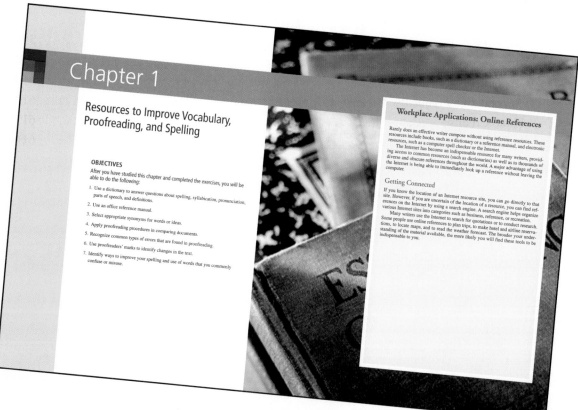

The Objectives provide goals around which you can structure your learning activities and exercises.

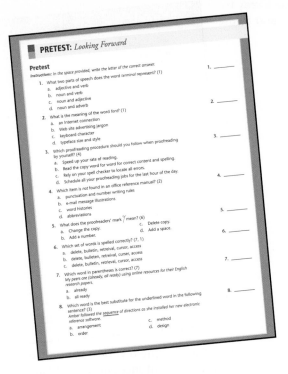

The Looking Forward Pretest gives you the chance to test yourself and see how much you already know. After each question is number or numbers that correlate with the objectives covered in the chapter. Using this information, you can study, review, and practice those concepts that you do not know or that you find most challenging.

Checkpoints provide reinforcement immediately after various concepts are covered. For more practice, go to the student section of the Web site at www.mhhe.com/bew3e to complete checkpoint exercises that correlate to the checkpoint exercises in the text.

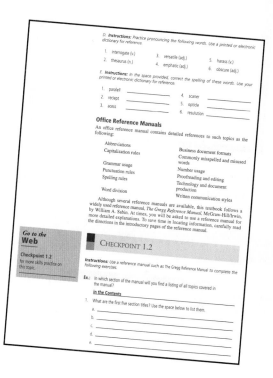

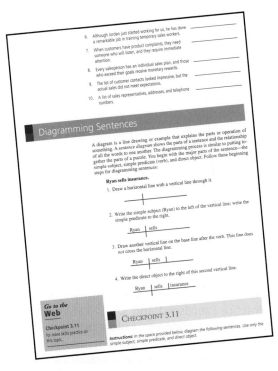

Diagramming Exercises give you a visual opportunity to see how the parts of speech are used and how they interrelate with one other.

Proofreading Exercises offer you a way to check your ability to find errors and to use proofreaders' marks to edit copy.

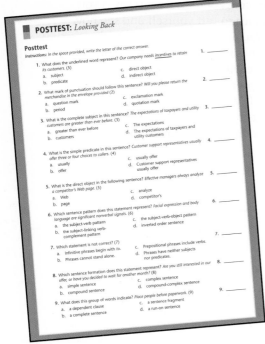

The Looking Back Posttest exercise helps you decide whether you have acquired the concepts and learned the rules that you studied in the chapter.

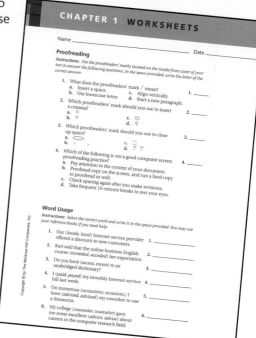

Writing Exercises help you to concentrate on writing simple sentences and short paragraphs about interesting topics while incorporating specific rules of grammar.

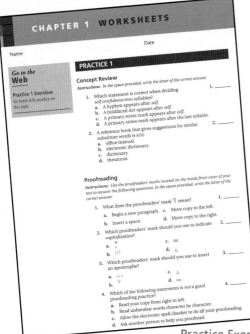

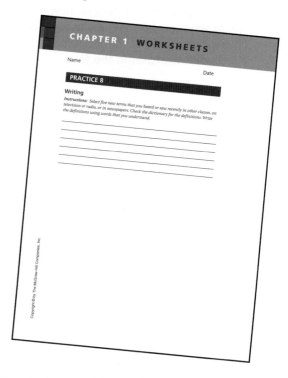

Practice Exercises at the end of each chapter offer ample opportunities for you to increase your skills in the concepts presented in the chapter. Practice Exercises 1–4 are similar to Practice Exercises 5–8. Practice Exercises 2 and 6 are more difficult than Practice Exercises 1 and 5.

For additional reviews of chapter concepts, follow the Go to The Web prompts in the margins of the text to access the **Student Interactive Exercises** located on the student section of the Web site at www.mhhe.com/bew3e.

The **Glossary** presents definitions of workplace terms and grammar concepts as well as usage information. The **Appendixes** contain **Spelling Rules** and **Word Usage** material. In addition, a thorough **Index** is provided to help locate concepts and rules that you may want to review.

Additional features found in the student edition include:

Special margin **NOTES** are provided in appropriate places throughout the text to enhance your learning and emphasize important concepts.

Do This	Do Not Do This
work together	interface
money	monies
features	parameters
happen	transpire

DO THIS/DO NOT DO THIS feature boxes emphasize special grammar or punctuation rules related to the concepts being studied.

PUNCTUATION ALERT!

PUNCTUATION ALERT and **CAPITALIZATION ALERT** icons give you specific information to help you punctuate and use capitalization elements correctly.

Capitalization **ALERT!**

Go to the **Web**

Checkpoint 1.1
for more skills practice on this topic.

GO TO THE WEB reminders direct you to additional exercises on the student section of the Web site at www.mhhe.com/bew3e. These interactive online exercises correlate to the checkpoints and to the practice, proofreading, and writing exercises and provide additional practice on the concepts and rules introduced in the text. We highly recommend that you complete the online exercises as a part of your study plan.

Go to the student section of the Web site at www.mhhe.com/bew3e to find the answers. Answers are not provided for the proofreading or writing exercises.

EDIT PATROL features highlight instances of the misuse of business English. While these may cause a smile, keep in mind that this course is designed to help you avoid such slipups in your workplace communication.

ANSWER KEYS are available for pretests, posttests, checkpoints, and practice exercises online.

This third edition of *Business English at Work* is a complete, well-rounded program that includes the following components:

- **Text-Workbook** with ample examples, checkpoint exercises, and practice exercises to provide a strong foundation in grammar, proofreading, writing, and punctuation. The activities and exercises throughout each chapter are directly related to **Workplace Applications** concepts that offer a realistic view of today's workplace.

- **Web site** with a separate section reserved for you. This student section contains online exercise links, online practice tests, thinking critically exercises, chapter summaries, answers to pretests, checkpoint practice exercises, and posttests, crossword puzzles, flashcards, additional learning exercises, e-mail links to the authors, and other Internet links to stimulate your research efforts. Access to this Web site is gained by entering the following address at your Internet browser location: www.mhhe.com/bew3e.

We enjoyed developing this program for you. Good luck in your studies using the third edition of *Business English at Work*.

Susan Jaderstrom, jaderstrom@comcast.net
Joanne Miller, jmiller34@juno.com

Acknowledgments

The following educators have contributed significantly to the development of this text by their reviews and valuable comments. We thank them for their input.

Lori Brinker
The University of Akron Wayne College
Akron, Ohio

Debbie Brockett
Arkansas Valley Technical Institute
Ozark, Arkansas

Janet Caruso
Briarcliffe College
Bethpage, New York

Gloria Cockerell
Collin County College
Plano, Texas

Veronica Cook
Austin Community College
Austin, Texas

Phyllis J. Donovan
Bryant & Stratton Business Institute
Buffalo, New York

Hazel Emery
Yorktowne Business Institute
York, Pennsylvania

Rebecca C. Ewing
Middle Georgia Technical College
Warner Robins, Georgia

Elizabeth Harbstreit
Manhattan Area Technical College
Manhattan, Kansas

Carolyn K. Hayes
Brevard Community College
Cocoa, Florida

Arlene Iftiger
Victor Valley College
Victorville, California

Eleonore Ingram
Topeka Technical College
Topeka, Kansas

Elizabeth D. Kerbey
San Jacinto College Central
Pasadena, Texas

Joanne M. Landry
Massasoit Community College
Brockton, Massachusetts

William Mark Lewis
Western Business College
Portland, Oregon

Barbara J. Loudon
Lansing Community College
Lansing, Michigan

Carol G. Martin
Chattanooga State Technical Community College
Chattanooga, Tennessee

Diane Penn-Mickey
Northern Virginia Community College
Woodbridge, Virginia

Pat Rajski Lyon
Tomball College
Tomball, Texas

Dean C. Rehm
Skadron College
San Bernardino, California

Carol Ricke
Pratt Community College
Pratt, Kansas

Carolyn Roberts
San Jacinto College
Houston, Texas

Mary Rowe
Miami-Dade Community College
Miami, Florida

Carolyn M. Seefer
Diablo Valley College
Pleasant Hill, California

Alice Smith
Indiana Business College
Lafayette, Indiana

Stephen H. Soucy
Santa Monica College
Santa Monica, California

Tani Theel Stempson
Southeast Community College
Lincoln, Nebraska

Mary Beth VanNess
University of Toledo
Toledo, Ohio

J. M. Vulgan
ECPI Technical College
Roanoke, Virginia

William H. Wray
ECPI Technical College
Roanoke, Virginia

Elizabeth Susan Wright
Weatherford College
Weatherford, Texas

Marilyn Wudarcki
North Idaho College
Coeur d'Alene, Idaho

College English and Communication, 9/e
Sue C. Camp, Gardener-Webb University
Marilyn Satterwhite, Danville Area Community College
ISBN: 007310650X
© 2007

This text is designed to help students achieve success as a professional. It is an educational program designed for college-level business English and business communication courses. The comprehensive products include a student book, a student activity workbook, and a comprehensive Web site. The book offers coverage of reading, listening, speaking, writing, reports, employment communications, ethical communication, and technology, thus providing students with cultural material necessary to keep up with the speed of business today.

Business Communication at Work, 3/e
Marilyn Satterwhite, Danville Area Community College
Judith Olson-Sutton, Madison Area Technical College
ISBN: 0073138312
© 2007

A complete learning package, this text provides the opportunities to learn how to communicate orally, through speaking and listening, as well as by letter, report, and e-mail. The text presents the foundations needed to develop sentences and paragraphs while also explaining how to use the appropriate approach to capture the messages necessary for effective communication.

Business English at Work, 3/e
Susan Jaderstrom, Santa Rosa Junior College
Joanne Miller
ISBN: 0073137871
© 2007

Written in a conversational tone, this text takes a totally new learning approach to relating business English to the workplace. Up-to-date topics of telecommunications, customer service, online references, electronic mail, and a host of other real-world subjects connect directly to an assortment of activities and exercises in grammar, punctuation, and writing. The activities in the text and online accommodate different student learning styles. All students regardless of their previous English background have the opportunity to be successful learning grammar in a business context.

Unit 1

Basic Concepts of Business English

Chapter 1

Resources to Improve Vocabulary, Proofreading, and Spelling

OBJECTIVES

After you have studied this chapter and completed the exercises, you will be able to do the following:

1. Use a dictionary to answer questions about spelling, syllabication, pronunciation, parts of speech, and definitions.

2. Use an office reference manual.

3. Select appropriate synonyms for words or ideas.

4. Apply proofreading procedures in comparing documents.

5. Recognize common types of errors that are found in proofreading.

6. Use proofreaders' marks to identify changes in the text.

7. Identify ways to improve your spelling and use of words that you commonly confuse or misuse.

Workplace Applications: Online References

Rarely does an effective writer compose without using reference resources. These resources include books, such as a dictionary or a reference manual, and electronic resources, such as a computer spell checker or the Internet.

The Internet has become an indispensable resource for many writers, providing access to common resources (such as dictionaries) as well as to thousands of diverse and obscure references throughout the world. A major advantage of using the Internet is being able to immediately look up a reference without leaving the computer.

Getting Connected

If you know the location of an Internet resource site, you can go directly to that site. However, if you are uncertain of the location of a resource, you can find references on the Internet by using a search engine. A search engine helps organize various Internet sites into categories such as business, reference, or recreation.

Many writers use the Internet to search for quotations or to conduct research. Some people use online references to plan trips, to make hotel and airline reservations, to locate maps, and to read the weather forecast. The broader your understanding of the material available, the more likely you will find these tools to be indispensable to you.

Pretest

Instructions: In the space provided, write the letter of the correct answer.

1. What two parts of speech does the word *terminal* represent? (1)
   a. adjective and verb
   b. noun and verb
   c. noun and adjective
   d. noun and adverb

   1. _____

2. What is the meaning of the word *font*? (1)
   a. an Internet connection
   b. Web site advertising jargon
   c. keyboard character
   d. typeface size and style

   2. _____

3. Which proofreading procedure should you follow when proofreading by yourself? (4)
   a. Speed up your rate of reading.
   b. Read the copy word for word for correct content and spelling.
   c. Rely on your spell checker to locate all errors.
   d. Schedule all your proofreading jobs for the last hour of the day.

   3. _____

4. Which item is *not* found in an office reference manual? (2)
   a. punctuation and number writing rules
   b. e-mail message illustrations
   c. word histories
   d. abbreviations

   4. _____

5. What does the proofreaders' mark ⸢ mean? (6)
   a. Change the copy.
   b. Add a number.
   c. Delete copy.
   d. Add a space.

   5. _____

6. Which set of words is spelled correctly? (7, 1)
   a. delete, bulletin, retreival, cursor, access
   b. delete, bulleten, retreival, curser, access
   c. delete, bulletin, retrieval, cursor, access

   6. _____

7. Which word in parentheses is correct? (7)
   My peers are (already, all ready) using online resources for their English research papers.
   a. already
   b. all ready

   7. _____

8. Which word is the best substitute for the underlined word in the following sentence? (3)
   Amber followed the sequence of directions as she installed her new electronic reference software.
   a. arrangement
   b. order
   c. method
   d. design

   8. _____

9. How many words are misspelled in the following sentence? *We have severel catagories*   **9.** _____
of computer software availible for our custumers. (1, 7)

    a.   one   c.   three

    b.   two   d.   four

10. *Our Web site will always give you up to date information about our products.*   **10.** _____
What do the proofreading marks in "up to date mean"? (6)

    a.   Insert an em dash.   c.   Close up space.

    b.   Hyphenate.   d.   Insert an extra space.

11. What is the quickest way to check the pronunciation of a word? (1)   **11.** _____

    a.   Check an office reference manual.

    b.   Look in a dictionary.

    c.   Check your lists of misused words.

    d.   Check a company guide sheet.

12. Which reference provides a writer with the greatest number of synonyms for a   **12.** _____
word? (3)

    a.   thesaurus   c.   office reference manual

    b.   corporate style guide   d.   dictionary

13. Which proofreading procedure should you follow when using a computer to   **13.** _____
produce a lengthy document? (4)

    a.   Rely on your spell checker to locate the errors.

    b.   Scan copy for grammar errors.

    c.   Take short, frequent breaks to rest your eyes.

    d.   Save time by proofing the copy only after completion.

14. Which statement represents a *format* proofreading error? (5)   **14.** _____

    a.   Page numbers are in consecutive order.

    b.   Spacing is consistent between headings throughout the document.

    c.   Labels agree with text references.

    d.   Spacing varies before paragraph indentions.

15. Which of the following references would you use to check a spelling rule? (2)   **15.** _____

    a.   thesaurus   c.   company guide sheet

    b.   office reference manual   d.   dictionary

Everyone appreciates error-free, well-written communications. Aren't you impressed when you can immediately understand a set of instructions? Don't you appreciate receiving mail with your name and address spelled correctly? A company's status, as well as the writer's, increases when documents appear without errors. To produce such error-free documents, an experienced writer never guesses about a writing detail but uses writing aids such as a current dictionary, a thesaurus, and a reference manual to verify the writing choices he or she makes. An experienced writer knows the importance of careful proofreading.

In this chapter, you will explore various reference sources and practice suggested proofreading techniques. You will find that maintaining a "troublesome word list" in which you list difficult spelling words, sound-alike words, and new vocabulary words is helpful. These strategies will get you started and help you develop confidence so that you, too, can produce impeccable documents.

Types of References

To help you develop as a writer, you will want to keep your reference materials where you can access them quickly and easily. Helpful references for studying business English include the dictionary, the thesaurus, and an office reference manual. Electronic references are available on CD-ROMs, on the Internet, or as functions of application software.

Dictionaries

Dictionaries are the most frequently used references. They are regularly revised by highly trained specialists who research and monitor the changes in the English language. Dictionaries vary in size and volume. Pocket dictionaries are easy to carry, but they lack detail. Unabridged dictionaries cover volumes of word entries and information, but they are cumbersome. College-edition (desk) dictionaries with copyright dates of five years or less are satisfactory for most students.

Specialized dictionaries for such fields as medicine, law, and engineering are helpful to the people working in those areas.

Even if you have been using a dictionary for years, you may have neglected to take advantage of all the information provided. In addition to the usual spelling, definitions, pronunciation, and syllabication, a dictionary may include information such as parts-of-speech functions, word usage notes, irregular grammatical forms, word origins, synonyms, and antonyms.

To locate a word in the dictionary, check the spelling of the word letter by letter. Use the two guide words at the top of each dictionary page to save searching time. The guide words represent the first and last words on the page. Each entry, which appears in bold type, is listed in alphabetic order between the two guide words.

To understand the markings and abbreviations in your dictionary, review the introductory pages before the alphabetic entries. You will also want to check the way that your dictionary presents information. Figure 1 illustrates the way that one dictionary presents a word entry. The lettered items correlate with the text descriptions.

doc•u•ment (*n.* dok' yə mənt ; *v.* dok' yə ment'), *n.* **1.** a written or printed paper furnishing information or evidence, as a passport, deed, bill of sale, or bill of lading; a legal or official paper. **2.** any written item, as a book, article, or letter, esp. of a factual or informative nature. **3.** *Archaic.* evidence; proof. --*v.t.* **4.** to furnish with documents. **5.** to furnish with references, citations, etc., in support of statements made: *a carefully documented biography.* **6.** to support by documentary evidence: *to document a case.* **7.** *Naut.* to provide (a vessel) with a certificate giving particulars concerning nationality, ownership, tonnage, dimensions, etc. **8.** *Obs.* to instruct. [1400-50; late ME (<AF)<L *documentum* example (as precedent, warning, etc.), equiv. to *doc-* (s. of *docēre* to teach) + *u-* (var. or -i-ɪ-before labials) + -*mentum* -MENT] -- doc•u•ment•a•ble (dok' y ment t b l, dok' y men' -), *adj.* - doc'u•'ment' er, n. --*Syn.* **6.** corroborate, verify, substantiate, validate.

SOURCE: From *Random House Webster's Unabridged Dictionary* by Random House, Inc. Reprinted by permission of Random House, Inc.

ⓐ Spelling. Pronounce each of the word's syllables and sounds. If an entry has more than one correct spelling, the preferred spelling is listed first in many dictionaries.

ⓑ Syllabication. A boldfaced dot separates an entry into its parts or syllables. If an entry already has a hyphen, that hyphen replaces the boldfaced dot; the dot continues to separate the remaining syllables.

> self-ex • plan • a • to • ry   ed • i • tor-in-chief

If no dot or hyphen appears *between* words, assume that they are two separate words.

> busi • ness card   guide words

ⓒ Stress (Accent) Marks. A bold (primary) accent mark indicates which syllable receives the greatest stress in pronunciation. The lighter (secondary) stress mark indicates less stress. These accent marks help you to pronounce unfamiliar words.

ⓓ Pronunciation. The pronunciation appears in parentheses after the word entry. Use the explanatory notes for pronouncing words. These explanatory notes are found in the introductory pages or at the bottom of every other dictionary page.

ⓔ Parts of Speech. Abbreviations for the parts of speech are in italics and appear after the pronunciation guide. If a word represents more than one part of speech, the correct label appears before *each* definition. Common abbreviation labels include the following:

adj.	=	adjective	*prep.*	=	preposition
adv.	=	adverb	*pron.*	=	pronoun
conj.	=	conjunction	*v.*	=	verb
interj.	=	interjection	*v.i.*	=	verb intransitive
n.	=	noun	*v.t.*	=	verb transitive

Your dictionary may also designate plural (*pl.*) and singular (*sing.*), definite articles (*def.art.*) and indefinite articles (*indef.art.*), and prefixes (*pref.*) and suffixes (*suff.*). You will find these parts-of-speech labels helpful in determining correct word usage.

PUNCTUATION ALERT!

Separating Syllables

Use a hyphen to separate syllables when a word must continue on the next document line.

f Definitions. Many word entries have more than one meaning, and the definitions may be different parts of speech. Definitions appear in consecutive order with the most common part of speech listed first. Within each part-of-speech section, the most frequently used definition is usually listed first.

g Word History (Etymologies). The symbol < designates the source of a word. The symbol means "from" and shows that a word comes from another language or another word. This information often appears in brackets [<] or parentheses at the end of the definition.

h Status Labels. Several labels describe words that are no longer or never were standard English. The introductory pages of your dictionary include such descriptions. Some commonly used status labels include:

obsolete (*obs*): no longer in general use

colloquial dialect (*coll dial*): characteristic of ordinary or familiar conversation or writing rather than formal speech or writing; used by speakers in a specific geographic or social setting

informal (*inf*): not likely to occur in formal, prepared speech or carefully edited writing except when used intentionally to convey a casual tone

slang: very informal usage; used in formal speech and writing only for special effect

archaic: commonly used in an earlier time but rarely used today

nonstandard: not conforming to the speech or grammar of educated persons; often regarded as a mark of low social status

Dictionary information may vary in other dictionaries or reference manuals. Furthermore, all dictionary information does not apply to every entry. For example, the following information does not apply to the entry *document* in Figure 1. Another entry may include these designations as well as those illustrated in Figure 1.

Irregular Grammatical Forms (Inflected Forms). A dictionary lists principal parts for irregular verbs (e.g., *break, broke, broken, breaking*), irregular plurals of nouns (e.g., *child, children*), and irregular adjective and adverb comparatives (e.g., *good, better, best*). The listing may not include the parts for regular forms.

Abbreviations. Abbreviations may appear as normal word entries. Some are capitalized, while others are lowercase. In some dictionaries, abbreviations may appear in a section titled "Abbreviations."

> **USPS**   **p.m.**   **M.B.A.**

Synonyms and Antonyms. Synonyms represent words that mean the same or almost the same as the entry word. Antonyms are words that are opposite in meaning. Synonyms or antonyms, although limited in scope, appear at the end of the word entry.

> A synonym for the adjective *sensitive* is responsive.
>
> An antonym for the verb *appears* is vanishes or disappears.

■ CHECKPOINT 1.1

A. **Instructions:** *Use a dictionary to find the following information for these words: correct syllabication; two guide words that appear at the top of the dictionary page on which* *you locate these terms; and part(s) of speech that each term represents. Write your answers on the lines provided. If you cannot find a word in your dictionary, circle the word.*

Word	Syllabication	Guide Words	Part(s) of Speech
Ex.: dictionary	**dic tio nary**	**dictatorship, diethylcarbamazine**	**N**
1. Internet	_____	_____	_____
2. online	_____	_____	_____
3. search engine	_____	_____	_____
4. reference	_____	_____	_____
5. computer	_____	_____	_____
6. resource	_____	_____	_____

B. **Instructions:** *Use a dictionary (printed or electronic) to locate the definitions of the following words. Write the definitions in the space provided.*

Ex.: reference (n.)

a source of information to which a reader is referred _____

1. ghostwriter (n.)

_____

_____

2. caret (n.)

_____

_____

3. icon (n.)

_____

_____

4. multimedia (n.)

_____

_____

5. pursuance (n.)

_____

_____

C. **Instructions:** *Place the primary accent mark in these words that have been divided into syllables. Use a printed or electronic dictionary.*

Ex.: ad van' tage

1. ref er ence
2. di rec to ry

3. re ferred
4. in dis pen sa ble

5. mil len ni um
6. di verse

D. **Instructions:** *Practice pronouncing the following words. Use a printed or electronic dictionary for reference.*

1. interrogate (v.)
2. thesaurus (n.)
3. versatile (adj.)
4. emphatic (adj.)
5. harass (v.)
6. obscure (adj.)

E. **Instructions:** *In the space provided, correct the spelling of these words. Use your printed or electronic dictionary for reference.*

1. paralell _____
2. reciept _____
3. acess _____
4. scaner _____
5. opticle _____
6. resulution _____

Office Reference Manuals

An office reference manual contains detailed references to such topics as the following:

Abbreviations	Business document formats
Capitalization rules	Commonly misspelled and misused words
Grammar usage	Number usage
Punctuation rules	Proofreading and editing
Spelling rules	Technology and document production
Word division	Written communication styles

Although several reference manuals are available, this textbook follows a widely used reference manual, *The Gregg Reference Manual,* McGraw-Hill/Irwin, by William A. Sabin. At times, you will be asked to use a reference manual for more detailed explanations. To save time in locating information, carefully read the directions in the introductory pages of the reference manual.

Go to the
Web

Checkpoint 1.2
for more skills practice on this topic.

CHECKPOINT 1.2

Instructions: *Use a reference manual such as* The Gregg Reference Manual *to complete the following exercises.*

Ex.: In which section of the manual will you find a listing of all topics covered in the manual?

in the Contents

1. What are the first five section titles? Use the space below to list them.

   a. _____

   b. _____

   c. _____

   d. _____

   e. _____

2. What is the difference in meaning between *desert* and *dessert*?

_____

_____

_____

_____

3. Locate and write the abbreviations of these terms:

   United States Department of Agriculture   _____

   inch   _____

4. Give an example of the correct way to write amounts of money under a dollar.

   _____

5. Identify two functions of a dash.

   _____

   _____

   _____

   _____

Thesaurus and Other References

Careless repetition of words can undermine the effectiveness of your writing. To expand your word choices, use a thesaurus, which is a book of words and their synonyms. A thesaurus gives suggestions for substitute words, indicates their parts of speech, and often provides a brief definition or an example of the word used in context. *Roget's II: The New Thesaurus* and *Bartlett's Roget's Thesaurus* are examples of two such reference books.

Company or personal guide sheets also help you remember words that give you trouble. Differences may exist, however, between your text or reference manual and a guide sheet. For example, you would use the company's guide sheet to determine the preferred style for *workstation* or *work station* and *online* or *on-line*.

Electronic dictionaries and electronic thesauri consist of material that is similar to the printed references. The programs check for the word that you want to change and display the information on the screen; you select a word to substitute by highlighting the word or its appropriate letter.

▮ CHECKPOINT 1.3	*Go to the* **Web**

Instructions: Use a thesaurus to find two synonyms for each of these words.

Checkpoint 1.3
for more skills practice on
this topic.
_____

Ex.: expansive (adj.)   **broad, general, outgoing** _____

1. orientation (n.) _____

2. justify (v.) _____

3. information (n.) _____

4. copy (v.) _____

5. visible (adj.) _____

Proofreading

Proofreading a document is as important as creating it. Documents that are carelessly proofread can result in embarrassment and uncomfortable explanations for companies and individuals. To avoid these situations, use your reference manual and dictionary whenever you have a question about word usage or grammatical accuracy.

Types of Errors

The following list gives you the most common types of errors that you will find in proofreading. Check for these errors as you proofread:

Format Errors

1. Check page numbers. Be sure that they are in consecutive order.

2. Check enumerations. The numbers and letters need to be consecutive with no omissions or double items.

3. Compare labels on illustrations with the text references. They must agree.

4. Review spacing between headings and before paragraph indentions. The spacing should be consistent throughout the document.

Keyboarding Errors

1. Check for transposed letters and figures.

2. Recognize that errors occur in typical spots. Check the following very carefully:
   - long words (Look for missing syllables.)
   - words with double letters
   - titles or proper names
   - headings that use all capital letters
   - addresses
   - quotations, parentheses, and brackets—both beginning *and* ending marks
   - word endings—keying *ing* for *in*

3. Check the number of zeros in figures, and be certain that decimal points are in the correct location. Check all numbers at least twice.

Grammar, Usage, and Style Errors

1. Check capitalization, punctuation, and number usage as well as correct grammatical construction. Use your reference manual or dictionary to clarify a question. *Never guess!*

2. Be sure that all sentences are complete.

3. Eliminate slang or trite expressions in business documents.

4. Change words that are overused. Check your thesaurus to find a replacement for the repeated word.

5. Check the accuracy of words that sound alike but have different meanings. For example, *their* and *there* and *stationery* and *stationary.*

Missing these elementary types of errors in proofreading is a definite sign of carelessness.

Proofreading Procedures

Proofreading on a computer screen is different from proofreading printed copy. In both cases, however, you should proofread your copy at least twice. Here are some proofreading procedures to use when proofreading printed copy:

Proofreading by Yourself

1. Read material from right to left rather than left to right, which is the normal reading pattern. This procedure requires you to concentrate on each word.

2. Read the copy word for word. When you see an unfamiliar word, read the copy character by character.

3. Slow down your rate of reading. To do this, use a ruler and your finger. As you read each word, place the ruler below each line on your final copy; place your finger below each word on your original copy. You cannot proofread carefully by skimming material.

4. Select a time and place to proofread when and where there is little or no noise and activity around you.

5. If possible, proofread copy after you have taken a break from the project. Often you will find that mistakes seem to glare at you when you come back to the project after a break.

Proofreading With Another Person

1. Try to proofread with a coworker when you have technical and legal documents or material that will be published. One person reads aloud from the original document; the second person checks the new copy. Change tasks every 15 minutes to avoid boredom and lack of concentration.

2. Be sure to read aloud all capital letters and marks of punctuation. Be consistent when you read numbers; for example, the number *29,450* is read *two nine comma four five zero.*

3. Ask a coworker to proofread your work. Agree to do the same when your coworker has work that requires proofreading.

Electronic Proofreading

Spell checkers allow you to check for misspelled words in material that has been keyboarded on a computer. Spell checkers check your copy and highlight the words that do not match those in its dictionary. You then choose the appropriate correction in the text from a list of choices.

Grammar and style checkers point out your grammatical usage errors but only within each program's limitations. On the basis of the suggestions made, you must make the corrections. Some of the problem areas covered by style checkers include active/passive voice sentence structures, duplicated words, incorrect possessives, punctuation marks, and overused words. Style checkers do not always pinpoint every error in these categories, however. To use the grammar checkers effectively, you must have a clear understanding of the English language.

Proofreading on a Computer Screen

1. Proofread material in blocks or paragraphs as you proceed through a document. Check that your material makes sense; read it word for word. Proofread the entire document again when you finish it.

2. Use the spell checker. This feature points out the obvious errors; however, a spell checker does not recognize words that are spelled cor-

rectly but used incorrectly in context; for example, *than* for *then* or *an* for *and*.

3. Check references to page numbers within the text, especially if you revise or move copy around in a document. Check for spacing inconsistencies after you make corrections and revisions.

4. Visualize how the finished product will appear on paper.

5. Add words to your software dictionary that are unique to your personal or business communications.

6. Take frequent 60-second breaks to rest your eyes as you proofread lengthy documents.

Many writers recommend a two-step approach to proofreading documents created on the computer. The first step is to proofread the copy on the computer screen using the instructions listed above. The second step is to make a printout of the document, called a hard copy, and to proofread that printed version of the document using the procedures described on the previous page.

Seeing your document presented in two different media, on the computer screen and on paper, will allow you to look at it with a fresh perspective. Errors that you overlook while keyboarding can appear glaringly obvious on paper. Additionally, the person who receives the computer file of your document might very well print it out to read it. It is always a good idea to proofread your work at least once in the format in which it is going to be reviewed by the receiver.

Proofreaders' Marks

Proofreading helps you identify errors that need to be corrected or changes that need to be made to the document. Knowing how to proofread and correct copy is an important skill for writers. You need to know the most efficient way to mark text for corrections. Proofreaders' marks are standardized symbols that allow you to quickly mark errors and changes that are needed. You will find a chart of proofreaders' marks printed on the inside front cover of this textbook.

Go to the
Web

Checkpoint 1.4
for more skills practice on this topic.

CHECKPOINT 1.4

Instructions: Use the proofreaders' marks on the inside front cover of your textbook to answer the following questions in the space provided.

Ex.: / What does this proofreaders' mark mean?   **make a lowercase letter**

1. What do the following proofreaders' marks mean?

    a. _____   c. V _____

    b. # _____   d. ⌐ _____

2. Which proofreaders' mark will you use to correct the following situations?

    a. Capitalize the first letter of a word.   _____

    b. Create a new paragraph.   _____

    c. End a sentence with a period.   _____

    d. Insert a comma.   _____

Spelling

When a workplace communication is not proofread carefully, misspelled words and mistakes in keyboarding usually go unnoticed. The reader sees these errors, loses his or her concentration, and often becomes disinterested in the purpose of the document or transaction. Although the spell checker will catch many errors in spelling, you need to master spelling skills.

In the Appendix of this textbook, you will be introduced to spelling rules and additional words from lists of the most frequently misspelled words.

Spelling Improvement Techniques

If you have not developed your spelling skills, your problems will not disappear overnight or even by the time you finish this course. The following techniques, however, offer suggestions for improvement; your task is to continually practice these techniques.

Frequently Misspelled Words.   Maintain a list consisting of words that you constantly must check in the dictionary. Keep the list on 3 × 5 cards, in a notebook, or in any other convenient format. Use your list of troublesome words regularly to help you master the words. When you master a word, cross it off your list.

Spelling Rules.   Spelling rules are located in the Appendix. Keep in mind that there are exceptions to the rules. Exceptions usually include mispronounced words or confusing spellings of words; for example, *dying* and *dyeing*.

Learning Resource Center.   Your college or school may have a media resource center that offers assistance with individual spelling problem areas. Someone in the center may even assess your skills to determine specific areas of difficulty. Do not be reluctant to ask your instructor for other self-help aids.

Memorization.   Sometimes memorizing words is the best technique for remembering the spelling or definition of troublesome words. Focus on five words a week. Practice the words until you can spell them correctly and also use them accurately in a sentence. A good source for these words is in the Appendix. (See Commonly Confused Words or Phrases.)

Mnemonic Devices.   A mnemonic is a memory device. Here are a few examples to use with troublesome spelling words.

> Think of a goose with a feather loose.
> I want a piece of pie.
> I put the dent in the superintendent's truck.
> Did you attend the dance? (attendance)
> It is never alwrong or never alright; it is always all wrong or always all right.

Pronunciation.   Misspellings often occur because words are not spelled as they sound; for example, in the word *phenomenal*, the *ph* sounds like *f*. If you depend on the pronunciation of words to aid you in spelling, you can expect trouble.

On the other hand, incorrect pronunciation also causes spelling errors; for example, *incidently* (which is not correct) should be pronounced *incidentally*. Sometimes a syllable gets left out of a word; for example, *convenient* becomes *convenent* (which is not correct).

NOTES

Spelling Tip

Listen to a newscast, use online research sources such as magazine article reprints, or obtain words from other classes. Select words from these sources and practice spelling them.

EDIT PATROL

From a student's history paper:

"Christopher Columbus was a great navigator who discovered America while cursing about the Atlantic. His ships were called the Niña, the Pinta, and the Santa Maria."

Dictionary Use. Use a dictionary when you question the spelling of a word. Always use the preferred spelling of the word, which is the one listed first in most dictionary entries (e.g., *judgment*, also *judgement*). Check the meaning of the word and note its pronunciation.

Go to the
Web

Checkpoint 1.5
for more skills practice on
this topic.

CHECKPOINT 1.5

Instructions: Each word below has one missing letter. Write the letter in the space provided. Check your dictionary (printed or electronic).

Ex.: ment**o**r

1. gramm_r
2. man_uver
3. priv_lege
4. li_ense

5. sc_edule
6. curs_r
7. di_gnostic
8. brow_er

9. fa_simile
10. bro_hure

Commonly Misused Words

Words that sound alike but have different spellings and meanings are spell checker demons. An example of commonly confused words is *it's* and *its*. The spell checker checks the spelling of the word but does not highlight the misused word if it is spelled correctly. In addition to commonly confused words, some words are often misused in communications. An example is the confusion between the use of *fewer* and *less*. Understanding the commonly confused and misused words and the way to use them in a document will increase the quality of your proofreading skills.

In the Appendix, you will find examples of commonly confused words or phrases. A reference manual, such as *The Gregg Reference Manual*, will be helpful for the Word Usage Review.

Go to the
Web

Checkpoint 1.6
for more skills practice on
this topic.

CHECKPOINT 1.6

Instructions: In the following sentences, you have a choice of two words that are frequently confused or misused. Select the correct word and write it in the space provided.

Ex.: The revised CD-ROM (*edition, addition*) will be in stores next week.   **edition**

1. Our Internet service provider (*formerly, formally*) had an office on Hastings Avenue. _____

2. My impatience did not (*faze, phase*) the computer repair technician. _____

3. Excessive browsing through unrelated travel information was a (*waste, waist*) of time. _____

4. (*Whether, Weather*) updates and travel information are available on the Internet, but I find the (*latter, later*) more enjoyable.

    _____

5. What (*kind of, kind of a*) dictionary are you using?

    _____

Do This/Do Not Do This

The following **Do This/Do Not Do This** diagram illustrates words or phrases that you should use in the place of those in the second column. This feature, which appears throughout this text, will provide tips in choosing effective words.

Do This	**Do Not Do This**
work together	interface
money	monies
features	parameter
happen	transpire

Name ______________________________ Date ____________________

Go to the
Web

Practice 1 Exercises
for more skills practice on this topic.

PRACTICE 1

Concept Review

Instructions: *In the space provided, write the letter of the correct answer.*

1. Which statement is correct when dividing *self confidence* into syllables? **1.** ______
- **a.** A hyphen appears after *self.*
- **b.** A boldfaced dot appears after *self.*
- **c.** A primary stress mark appears after *self.*
- **d.** A primary stress mark appears after the last syllable.

2. A reference book that gives suggestions for similar substitute words is a(n) **2.** ______
- **a.** office manual.
- **b.** electronic dictionary.
- **c.** dictionary.
- **d.** thesaurus.

Proofreading

Instructions: *Use the proofreaders' marks located on the inside front cover of your text to answer the following questions. In the space provided, write the letter of the correct answer.*

1. What does the proofreaders' mark ¶ mean? **1.** ______
- **a.** Begin a new paragraph. **c.** Move copy to the left.
- **b.** Insert a space. **d.** Move copy to the right.

2. Which proofreaders' mark should you use to indicate capitalization? **2.** ______
- **a.** # ∧ **c.** ≡
- **b.** ∽ **d.** ⁁ (with comma)

3. Which proofreaders' mark should you use to insert an apostrophe? **3.** ______
- **a.** • • • **c.** ⁁ (with comma)
- **b.** ∨ (with apostrophe) **d.** =

4. Which of the following statements is *not* a good proofreading practice? **4.** ______
- **a.** Read your copy from right to left.
- **b.** Read unfamiliar words character by character.
- **c.** Allow the electronic spell checker to do all your proofreading.
- **d.** Ask another person to help you proofread.

Name _____ Date _____

Word Usage

Instructions: Select the correct word and write it in the space provided. You may use your reference books if you need help.

1. My manager was (*formally, formerly*) promoted to vice president in the Global Network Division.

    1. _____

2. (*Never the less, Nevertheless, Never theless*), we bought the CD-ROM dictionary.

    2. _____

3. ExploreNet provides Internet (*access, excess*), networking, consulting, and programming services.

    3. _____

4. I used (*fewer, less*) online reference resources than Susan.

    4. _____

5. We offer our tenants ten free hours of Internet (*access, excess*) time.

    5. _____

6. Many Internet users are (*eager, anxious*) to apply for additional services.

    6. _____

7. The manager (*complimented, complemented*) Makil on her futuristic Web site designs.

    7. _____

8. (*To, Too*) use this program, I need more computer memory.

    8. _____

Definitions

Instructions: Use your dictionary to select the definition for the underlined word. In the space provided, write the letter of the correct answer.

1. A <u>nominal</u> charge for using e-mail seems appropriate.

    1. _____
    a. substantial   c. tentative
    b. small   d. normal

2. Our Internet provider's sales representatives had <u>phenomenal</u> records this month.

    2. _____
    a. fair   c. poor
    b. average   d. extraordinary

3. All the <u>futile</u> attempts to contact Customer Service were irritating.

    3. _____
    a. numerous   c. usual
    b. ineffective   d. speedy

Parts of Speech

Instructions: Select the part of speech that each underlined word represents. In the space provided, write the letter of the correct answer.

1. Which part of speech does the word <u>quickly</u> represent?

    1. _____
    a. noun   c. adjective
    b. verb   d. adverb

Name _____ Date _____

2. Which part of speech does the word <u>suite</u> represent?   2. _____
       a. noun   **c.** adjective
       b. verb   **d.** adverb

Spelling

Instructions: *Check the underlined word. If the word is spelled correctly, write* **Yes** *in the space provided. If it is not correct, write the word using the correct spelling.*

1. You are able to check facts with an electronic   1. _____
dictionary, a <u>thesarus</u>, an atlas, or an almanac.

2. The bill for the Internet installation must be   2. _____
<u>payed</u> within 10 days if you want to receive the
2 percent discount.

3. The last electronic traffic jam prevented me   3. _____
from <u>receiving</u> my e-mail for four hours.

4. I hope that you will find an <u>occasion</u> to use one   4. _____
of the online help forums currently <u>avalable</u>.

5. By browsing the Internet, we found that A.B.   5. _____
Travel <u>offered</u> an <u>excellant</u> air travel discount.

Go to the
Web

Practice 2 Exercises
for more skills practice on
this topic.

PRACTICE 2

Proofreading

Instructions: *Interpret the proofreaders' marks and write the following sentences correctly. If necessary, refer to a reference manual or the inside front cover of your textbook.*

1. Web site design offers a interesting and challenging careers.

_____

2. Your introduction to online classes will begin at 1 PM Friday.

_____

3. PhoneBase includes more than 100 milion telephone listings in five
CD-Roms.

_____

4. Software applications became obsolecsent very quickly.

_____

5. We've found definitions of computer terms through the internet.

_____

Name _____ Date _____

Parts of Speech

Instructions: *Use your dictionary to identify the part or parts of speech that each of these words represents. Use the following abbreviations:* **N** *(noun),* **Pron** *(pronoun),* **VT** *(verb transitive),* **VI** *(verb intransitive),* **Adj** *(adjective),* **Adv** *(adverb),* **Prep** *(preposition),* **Conj** *(conjunction). Write your answers in the space provided.*

1. technique _____
2. function _____
3. demand _____
4. literate _____

5. input _____
6. constructive _____
7. nor _____
8. because _____

Synonyms

Instructions: *Use a thesaurus to substitute simple, commonplace words for those underlined in the sentences below. Write your answers in the space provided. Answers will vary.*

1. We are doing everything possible to <u>expedite</u> the delivery of your computer.

    1. _____

2. CD-ROM drives are <u>standard</u> features on desktop computers.

    2. _____

3. The Internet is a great way to <u>disseminate</u> my product information.

    3. _____

4. Sara and I had <u>dissimilar</u> experiences in using the Internet for medical information.

    4. _____

5. Locating information quickly on the Internet is possible when you <u>utilize</u> the correct search tools.

    5. _____

6. His face was <u>impassive</u> when we told him about the network problems.

    6. _____

PRACTICE 3

Proofreading

Instructions: *The following words and phrases describe printed or online references. Proofread and compare the words and phrases in Column A with those in Column B. If they are the same, write* **Yes** *in the space provided. If they are not the same, write* **No.**

COLUMN A	COLUMN B	
1. forums	forms	1. _____
2. thesaurus	thesarus	2. _____
3. CD-ROMs	CD-Roms	3. _____

Go to the
Web

Practice 3 Exercises
for more skills practice on this topic.

_____

Resources to Improve Vocabulary, Proofreading, and Spelling

Name _____   Date _____

4. subject index	subject index	4. _____
5. latest weather reports	lastest weather report	5. _____
6. service provider	service providor	6. _____
7. toll-free hotline	toll free hot line	7. _____
8. grammar check software	grammer check softwar	8. _____
9. news.announce.newusers	new.announce newusers	9. _____
10. newsgroup services	newsgroup	10. _____

Go to the
Web

Practice 4 Exercises
for more skills practice on
this topic.

PRACTICE 4

Writing

Instructions: *Prepare a list of ten words to describe an ideal business English class. Use a dictionary to check spelling and to determine the part(s) of speech.*

_____

_____

_____

_____

_____

_____

PRACTICE 5

Concept Review

Instructions: *In the space provided, write the letter of the correct answer.*

1. Which of the following statements is *not* a good   1. _____
   electronic proofreading practice?
   a. Read copy word for word.
   b. Take frequent breaks to rest your eyes.
   c. Proofread in blocks.
   d. Increase your rate of reading.

2. Which item is *not* included in an office   2. _____
   reference manual?
   a. capitalization rules   c. business document
                                      formats
   b. number usage   d. status labels

Name _____ Date _____

Proofreading

Instructions: *Use the proofreaders' marks located on the inside front cover of your text to answer the following questions. In the space provided, write the letter of the correct answer.*

1. What does the proofreaders' mark / mean? 1. _____
   a. Insert a space. c. Align vertically.
   b. Use lowercase letter. d. Start a new paragraph.

2. Which proofreaders' mark should you use to insert 2. _____
   a comma?
   a. ∧ c. ⊙
   b. ∨ d. ∜

3. Which proofreaders' mark should you use to close 3. _____
   up space?
   a. ⬯ c. ≖
   b. ∧ ∧ d. ≙ ≙

4. Which of the following is *not* a good computer screen 4. _____
   proofreading practice?
   a. Pay attention to the context of your document.
   b. Proofread copy on the screen, and run a hard copy
      to proofread as well.
   c. Check spacing again after you make revisions.
   d. Take frequent 10-minute breaks to rest your eyes.

Word Usage

Instructions: *Select the correct word and write it in the space provided. You may use your reference books if you need help.*

1. Our (*locale, local*) Internet service provider 1. _____
   offered a discount to new customers.

2. Kari said that the online business English 2. _____
   course (*exceeded, acceded*) her expectation.

3. Do you have (*access, excess*) to an 3. _____
   unabridged dictionary?

4. I (*paid, payed*) my monthly Internet service 4. _____
   bill last week.

5. On numerous (*occassions, occasions,*) I 5. _____
   have (*advised, advized*) my coworker to use
   a thesaurus.

6. My college (*counseler, counselor*) gave 6. _____
   me some excellent (*advice, advise*) about
   careers in the computer research field.

Name _____ Date _____

7. The managing editor (*complemented, complimented*) Jenni on the newest (*addition, edition*) of her online reference guide.

7. _____

8. She (*adapted, adopted*) the online (*course, coarse*) to accommodate (*everyone, every one*) of her students.

8. _____

Definitions

Instructions: Use your dictionary to select the definition for the underlined word. In the space provided, write the letter of the correct answer.

1. Searching for the word on the Internet was <u>ingenious</u>.
   a. not smart   c. difficult
   b. clever   d. time consuming

   1. _____

2. The advertised speed for using that search engine turned out to be <u>hyperbole</u>.
   a. fantastic   c. authentic
   b. exaggeration   d. factual

   2. _____

Parts of Speech

Instructions: Select the part of speech that each underlined word represents. In the space provided, write the letter of the correct answer.

1. Which part of speech does the word *diagnose* represent in the following sentence? *Please <u>diagnose</u> our Internet connection problem.*
   a. noun   c. adjective
   b. verb   d. adverb

   1. _____

2. Which part of speech does the word *expanded* represent in the following sentence? *Our <u>expanded</u> store hours increased sales by 3 percent.*
   a. noun   c. adjective
   b. verb   d. adverb

   2. _____

Spelling

*Instructions: If both words in the following lines are correctly spelled, write **Yes** in the space provided. If a word is spelled incorrectly, write the correction(s) in the space.*

1. occured   enthusiastic   1. _____

2. recommendation   dependable   2. _____

3. goverment   regretted   3. _____

4. enroled   analyze   4. _____

5. prounciation   reviewing   5. _____

Name _____ Date _____

PRACTICE 6

Proofreading

Instructions: Interpret the proofreaders' marks and write the following sentences correctly. If necessary, refer to a reference manual or the inside front cover of your textbook.

1. Ellen is cancelling her subscription to ~~the magazine~~ *BusinessWeek* because she does not have time to read it.

   _____

   _____

2. Even 128 Megabytes of RAM (random access memory) ~~are~~ will not ~~enough to~~ run some of our Graphics Programs.

   _____

   _____

3. Joanne usually arrives at Work at 6 P.M. and checks her e-mail immediately.

   _____

4. He said I will install your software next week.

   _____

5. Internet Service provided by cable is hundreds of times faster then a using phone line.

   _____

   _____

Parts of Speech

Instructions: Use your dictionary to identify the part or parts of speech that each of these words represents. Use the following abbreviations: *N* (noun), *Pron* (pronoun), *VT* (verb transitive), *VI* (verb intransitive), *Adj* (adjective), *Adv* (adverb), *Prep* (preposition), *Conj* (conjunction). Write your answers in the space provided.

1. confident   1. _____   5. barely   5. _____
2. photocopy   2. _____   6. and   6. _____
3. surge   3. _____   7. unhesitating 7. _____
4. domain   4. _____   8. from   8. _____

Name _____ Date _____

Synonyms

Instructions: *Use a thesaurus to substitute simple, commonplace words for those underlined in the sentences below. Write your answers in the space provided.*

1. The directions for installing our latest reference software seemed <u>ambiguous</u> to me.

    1. _____

2. Ben faced <u>innumerable</u> decisions after he completed the online careers course.

    2. _____

3. The virus <u>decimated</u> the hard drive.

    3. _____

4. Joshua found the Internet connection problem <u>enervating</u>.

    4. _____

5. Karen's <u>fulsome</u> comments about computer technicians were irritating.

    5. _____

6. Her <u>perfunctory</u> response to my question regarding online research was disappointing.

    6. _____

PRACTICE 7

Proofreading

Instructions: *The following words and phrases describe printed or online references. Proofread and compare the words and phrases in Column A with those in Column B. If they are the same, write* **Yes** *in the space provided. If they are not the same, write* **No**.

	COLUMN A	COLUMN B	
1.	computer graphics	computer graphic	1. _____
2.	desktop publishing	desk top publishing	2. _____
3.	enhanced keyboard	enhanced key board	3. _____
4.	graphical user interface	graphical use interface	4. _____
5.	groupware	groupware	5. _____
6.	laser printer	lazer printer	6. _____

Name _____ Date _____

PRACTICE 8

Writing

Instructions: *Select five new terms that you heard or saw recently in other classes, on television or radio, or in newspapers. Check the dictionary for the definitions. Write the definitions using words that you understand.*

_____

_____

_____

_____

_____

_____

POSTTEST: *Looking Back*

Posttest

Instructions: In the space provided, write the letter of the correct answer. When necessary, use the appropriate reference materials to obtain your answers.

1. Which Internet addresses are the same? (4)

    a. http://www.tollfree.edu.net/dir800/
       http://www.toll.freeedu.net/dir800/

    b. http://www.tollfree.edu.net/dir800/
       http://www.tollfree.edu.net/dir800/

    c. htp://www.tollfree.edu.net/dir800/
       htp://www.tollfree.educnet/dir800/

    d. http://www.toll.free.ednet.dir800/
       http://www.toll.free.ednet/dir800/

    1. _____

2. What is the meaning of the word *tortuous*? (1)

    a. painful   c. evil
    b. winding   d. unfortunate

    2. _____

3. Which set of words is spelled correctly? (1)

    a. recieve, begining, a lot, creditor, benefitted
    b. recieve, begining, alot, crediter, benefited
    c. receive, begining, a lot, creditor, benefited
    d. receive, begining, a lot, crediter, benefited

    3. _____

4. What does the proofreaders' mark ∪ mean? (5)

    a. Transpose.   c. Add a space.
    b. Capitalize.   d. Delete.

    4. _____

5. What two parts of speech does the word *design* represent? (1)

    a. adverb and verb   c. adverb and adjective
    b. verb and noun   d. adverb and noun

    5. _____

6. Which word is the correct one? (6)

    To update our technological equipment, we invested a considerable amount of (capital, capitol).

    a. capital
    b. capitol

    6. _____

7. Which word is the best substitute for the underlined word in the following sentence? (3)

    Abridged dictionaries are often easier to use.

    a. smaller   c. condensed
    b. online   d. computerized

    7. _____

8. Which of the following items is *not* found in most office reference manuals? (2)

    a. proofreaders' marks   c. word usage
    b. word history   d. word division

    8. _____

9. How many words are misspelled in the following sentence? *I have a boadband conection to acess online refeneces.* (1, 7)

    a. one   c. three
    b. two   d. four

    9. _____

10. *Ian takes classes at barstow college.* What do the proofreading marks in
"barstow college" mean? (6)

    a. Transpose keystrokes.   c. Change keystroke.

    b. Capitalize.   d. Hyphenate.

    10._____

11. What is the quickest way to find words that mean the same as *maneuver*? (3)

    a. Look in a dictionary.

    b. Use a search engine.

    c. Check in an office reference manual.

    d. Use a thesaurus.

    11. _____

12. Which reference would you use to look up the part of speech of the word
incidentally? (1)

    a. thesaurus   c. dictionary

    b. office reference manual   d. corporate style guide

    12._____

13. Which of the following is *not* recommended when proofreading on a computer
screen? (4)

    a. Check references to page numbers within the text.

    b. Check for spacing inconsistencies.

    c. Use spelling and grammar checkers.

    d. Proofread in 30-minute blocks of time.

    13._____

14. You used the word *conscious* when you meant to use the word *conscience*.
What type of proofreading error have you made? (4)

    a. format error   c. keyboarding error

    b. usage error   d. style error

    14._____

15. Which of the following references would you use to determine whether to use
figures with the word *o'clock*? (2)

    a. thesaurus   c. company guide sheet

    b. office reference manual   d. dictionary

    15._____

Chapter 2

Overview of Parts of Speech

OBJECTIVES

After you have studied this chapter and completed the exercises, you will be able to do the following:

1. Recognize the importance of the terminology used in studying grammar.

2. Name and identify the eight parts of speech:

   - Nouns

   - Pronouns

   - Verbs

   - Adjectives

   - Adverbs

   - Conjunctions

   - Prepositions

   - Interjections

Workplace Applications: Telecommunications

Millions of people use electronic devices to keep in touch with family, friends, and business associates. Using technology to transmit text, data, images, and sound over distances is telecommunications. Examples of telecommunications devices include telephones, cell phones, fax machines, handheld computers, pagers, and voice mail.

Because of the growth of the Internet and the wide variety of reasonable telecommunication products, telecommuting is a way of life for many people. Employees can use technology while traveling and at home. New home-based careers are emerging. Virtual assistants are home-based independent contractors who may perform data entry, medical transcription, accounting, graphic design, programming, writing, and marketing for companies around the world. Virtual call centers maintain a network of home-based workers. Calls are forwarded to home-based workers, and those workers can access internal corporate database systems. The telecommuting trend and number of virtual jobs will accelerate with the continued innovation of user-friendly technology designed for mobile employees.

Pretest

Instructions: In the space provided, write the part of speech of each underlined word. Use the following abbreviations:
N *(noun),* **Adv** *(adverb),* **Pron** *(pronoun),* **C** *(conjunction),* **V** *(verb),* **Prep** *(preposition),* **Adj** *(adjective),* **I** *(interjection).*

1. Brian <u>read</u> all the sales <u>literature</u> on <u>wireless</u> voice and data devices. (1, 2) 1. _____

2. <u>We</u> bought our <u>equipment</u> <u>from</u> Cellphone Inc. (1, 2) 2. _____

3. I <u>analyzed</u> the pros <u>and</u> cons <u>of</u> telecommuting. (1,2) 3. _____

4. Callers appreciate quick and <u>courteous</u> responses <u>to</u> their telephone <u>calls</u>. (1, 2) 4. _____

5. Jane <u>thoroughly</u> <u>researched</u> <u>wireless</u> networks. 5. _____

6. Voice recognition systems <u>are</u> popular, <u>but</u> the <u>technology</u> behind them
   is complex. (1, 2) 6. _____

7. I am interested <u>in</u> a <u>multifunction</u> cell phone. (1, 2) 7. _____

8. <u>Oops!</u> I <u>dialed</u> the <u>wrong</u> number. (1, 2) 8. _____

9. <u>Ruiz</u> <u>uses</u> a cell phone <u>headset</u> while driving. (1, 2) 9. _____

10. Virtual assistants benefit <u>immensely</u> from caller ID <u>and</u> call waiting
    telephone services. (1, 2) 10. _____

11. Many employees <u>frequently</u> <u>use</u> their laptops <u>at</u> home and at work. (1, 2) 11. _____

12. The <u>local</u> telephone company <u>has advertised</u> <u>for</u> virtual call center
    employees. (1, 2) 12. _____

13. Our <u>company</u> lost its communication <u>network</u> during the <u>power</u> outage. (1, 2) 13. _____

14. Some vehicle communication systems <u>automatically</u> alert <u>emergency</u>
    centers with the <u>site</u> of an accident. (1, 2) 14. _____

15. The rise <u>in</u> phone bill scams <u>is</u> not unique to <u>Wisconsin</u>. (1, 2) 15. _____

Chapter Preview

As you looked at the chapter title, you probably wondered why you needed to study the parts of speech. Do you need to know how to correctly use nouns, pronouns, conjunctions, etc., in order to write clearly?

Assume that you called a computer hotline operator and received directions such as "Check the 'thingamajig' on the right, press the 'dingathong' a few times, and then move the 'whatchamacallit' over, and you'll be set." You would be confused—perhaps irritated—about the way that your problem was handled.

The same problem exists when you are unaware of the parts of speech and the way that they function in a sentence. A noun is not a "thingamajig"; it's a noun. A noun has the specific function of naming a person, place, thing, activity, idea, or quality in a sentence. The other parts of speech have specific functions as well. If you violate the major rules of the language, you may offend or irritate the reader. A customer, for example, may even lose trust in your information if your writing is unclear and imprecise.

Other fields such as computing, medicine, law, police science, and human services have their respective vocabularies. The English language also has a set of terms, which are called the parts of speech, to organize its many words and groups of words into constructive patterns. The eight parts of speech are the *noun, pronoun, verb, adjective, adverb, conjunction, preposition,* and *interjection.* To identify each part of speech, you must determine the function of each word in a sentence. This understanding of correct grammar leads to clearer writing and gives you confidence when you proofread copy and correct errors. Each of the eight parts of speech will be discussed briefly in this chapter, with more thorough discussions in future chapters.

Parts of Speech

Nouns

Nouns name people, places, things, activities, ideas, or qualities. You will use nouns in almost every sentence that you write. Nouns may be plural or singular.

Proper and Common Nouns.   Some of the nouns in the following list begin with capital letters. These nouns are *proper nouns;* all others are *common nouns.* Proper nouns refer to a *specific* person, place, or thing. Common nouns refer to general names and are not capitalized.

People:	Maria, clients, nurse, salesperson, team
Places:	New Mexico, University of Wisconsin, AT&T, office, hospital
Things:	pager, telephones, dictionary, directory, technology
Activities:	moving, running, calling, formatting, faxing
Ideas or Qualities:	motivation, efficiency, capitalism, promptness, privacy

Examine the common and proper nouns listed below.

Common Nouns	Proper Nouns
woman	Lynn
state	Washington
college	Piedmont College
continent	Africa

In Chapters 4 and 5, you will study other types of nouns and the ways that they function in sentences.

CHECKPOINT 2.1

Instructions: *Identify the underlined noun as a common noun or a proper noun. In the space provided, write* **C** *if the underlined word is a common noun. Write* **P** *if the underlined word is a proper noun.*

1. One <u>employee</u> plans to telecommute to her <u>job</u> in <u>Philadelphia</u>. _____

2. I called a <u>company</u> in <u>New York</u> for price information on cell phone <u>plans</u>. _____

3. *Time* carried several articles on wireless <u>communications</u>. _____

4. <u>Judy</u> contacted a <u>client</u> about a telephone courtesy <u>presentation</u>. _____

5. An <u>instructor</u> gave me the telephone <u>number</u> for a tutor. _____

6. We will attend a telecommunications trade <u>show</u> in <u>Chicago</u>. _____

Pronouns

Pronouns are substitute words for nouns. Like nouns, they may be singular or plural. If you use pronouns correctly, your sentences will be clearer and less cumbersome. You can decrease the repetition of a noun by substituting a pronoun to obtain the same meaning.

Do This	**Do Not Do This**
Jane informed <u>her</u> coworkers that <u>she</u> is retiring.	Jane informed <u>Jane's</u> coworkers that <u>Jane</u> is retiring.

Personal Pronouns. Although there are several other categories of pronouns, the examples in this chapter involve personal pronouns. You will study other pronouns with different functions in Chapter 7. Here are the personal pronouns:

I	me	my	mine				
you	your	yours					
he	she	it	him	her	his	hers	its
we	us	our	ours				
they	them	their	theirs				

Chapter 2

Personal pronouns, with the exception of *it,* can substitute for nouns referring to people. The pronoun *it* can substitute for a thing, a place, an activity, an idea, a quality, or an animal. The following examples show a simple distinction:

Alice answered the telephone.

She answered the telephone.

(The pronoun *She* is a substitute for *Alice*—a person.)

Alice answered the telephone.

Alice answered it.

(The pronoun *it* is a substitute for *telephone*—a thing.)

The following sentences illustrate the use of personal pronouns. Each personal pronoun is underlined.

I finished the telephone usage analysis on Tuesday.

The amount of time to learn the telephone exchange system overwhelmed me.

They used a conference call to plan their telephone survey.

You can buy a telephone from any store that you choose.

The following sentences illustrate the use of nouns and personal pronouns.

As Amy left her office, she reminded the receptionist to transfer calls to her cell phone.

(The pronoun *her* and the pronoun *she* refer to *Amy*.)

When the supervisors requested input concerning the use of the telephone during business hours, they did not expect the large return of responses.

(The pronoun *they* refers to the noun *supervisors*.)

Your study of pronouns will continue in Chapters 7 and 8.

CHECKPOINT 2.2

Go to the
Web

Checkpoint 2.2
for more skills practice on this topic.

Instructions: Identify the personal pronouns in the following sentences. Write your answers in the space provided.

1. The conference call gave him an opportunity to clarify the terms of the contract.   _____

2. I worked the early morning shift, and I spent the afternoon e-mailing my friends.   _____

3. An Internet connection at home allows me to do my work at night. _____

4. Successful telemarketers learn as much as possible about their potential customers before they call.   _____

5. She uses her cell phone to call our customers.   _____

6. We buy computer magazines with telecommunications articles in them.   _____

7. Will you please call me when it is convenient to pick up the order.   _____

Go to the
Web

Checkpoint 2.3
for more skills practice on
this topic.

CHECKPOINT 2.3

Instructions: *Identify the underlined noun as a common noun, proper noun, or pronoun. In the space provided, write **C** if the underlined word is a common noun. Write **P** if the word is a proper noun. Write **Pron** if the word is a pronoun.*

1. I work for a company in Los Angeles from my home in Kentucky.   _____

2. She bought a new cell phone and highly recommended it to her friends.   _____

3. He selected a broadband Internet service for his home office in Houston.   _____

4. My cell phone does not have service in your neighborhood.   _____

5. We used our wireless laptop computer in the Vancouver International Airport to reach our customers in the United States.   _____

Verbs

Verbs are words that show action, show a state of being, or help main verbs. You will use verbs in every sentence that you write. Verbs give your statements power and add meaning.

Action Verbs. Most verbs are action words, and they are usually the main verbs in sentences. Action verbs indicate what someone or something does. Here are some action verbs:

> **think   sell   answer   write   call   retrieve**

When you add a verb to a sentence, you can see the meaning develop. The following noun and pronoun do not mean much when they stand alone, but understanding develops when a verb is added.

> **Bill   (noun)   Bill calls.   (noun and verb)**
>
> **We   (pronoun)   We answer.   (pronoun and verb)**

Linking Verbs. Verbs also can be words that show a *state of being* or a condition. Since this type of verb provides a "link" between the parts of your statements, they are appropriately called *linking verbs*. Linking verbs do not indicate action. The various forms of *to be* are the most commonly used linking verbs.

> **am   is   are   was   were   been   being**

> **Larry is our new telephone installer.**
> **He was too exhausted to attend our final meeting.**
> **Diana and Benson are outstanding employees.**

A discussion of other linking verbs follows in Chapter 9.

Helping Verbs. Helping (auxiliary) verbs help in the formation of another verb. They "assist" and precede the main verb. Here are some examples of helping (auxiliary) verbs:

am	is	are	was	were	been	being	
has	have	had	having	shall	should	will	would
can	could	do	does	did	may	might	must

The form of the main verb may change when you add helping verbs.

Main Verb	Helping Verb	Main Verb With Helping Verb
work	will	Karen will work.
include	might	It might include. . . .
interview	have	We have interviewed.
call	are	They are calling.
receive	had	He had received. . . .

Your study of verbs continues in Chapters 9, 10, and 11.

CHECKPOINT 2.4

Go to the
Web

Checkpoint 2.4
for more skills practice on
this topic.

Instructions: *Check your knowledge of action, linking, and helping verbs by identifying the underlined verbs. Use the following abbreviations:* **A** *(action verb),* **L** *(linking verb),* **H** *(helping verb). Some sentences may have more than one answer.*

1. The combination fax, printer, and copier <u>meets</u> our needs. _____
2. She <u>asked</u> specific questions about the antispam bill. _____
3. Don is <u>writing</u> the original bid for the intercom system, and Carrie <u>will</u> revise it. _____
4. Key locks on cellular phones <u>should</u> <u>discourage</u> unauthorized users. _____
5. Telecommuting <u>is</u> attractive to workers with young families. _____
6. The Federal Communications Commission <u>has</u> <u>established</u> new standards for operations. _____
7. Jacob <u>can</u> <u>retrieve</u> voice mail messages from home. _____
8. The new phone options <u>are</u> necessary for our small firm. _____
9. I <u>entered</u> the incorrect telephone number in my cell phone. _____
10. Some telephone directories <u>list</u> business e-mail addresses. _____

Adjectives

Adjectives modify (describe) nouns and pronouns and often limit their meanings. Adjectives answer these types of questions: *What kind*? *How many*? *Which one*?

What Kind?

<u>potential</u> customers   <u>clear</u> messages

<u>experienced</u> salesperson   <u>large</u> desk

(The question *What kind?* describes a noun or pronoun.)

How Many?

<u>two</u> employees   <u>several</u> copies

<u>numerous</u> responses   <u>frequent</u> interruptions

Which One?

<u>newest</u> machine	<u>incoming</u> call
<u>last</u> report	<u>original</u> proposal

(The questions *How many?* and *Which one?* limit the meaning of nouns.)

Adjectives clarify the meaning of a sentence and make the message more precise and often more interesting. These examples show how adjectives add clarity and preciseness to a sentence. The underlined words are adjectives.

McHenry & Co. shipped the phones.

McHenry & Co. shipped the <u>cordless</u> phones.

(The word *cordless* specifies "the kind" of phones that are being shipped.)

McHenry & Co. shipped the <u>five cordless</u> phones that we ordered.

(Adding the words *five* and *cordless* answers the questions *How many?* and *What kind?* The adjective *five* limits the number of cordless telephones that are being shipped.)

Adjectives With Nouns. Most adjectives that modify nouns appear *before* the nouns; however, some adjectives that modify nouns appear *after* linking verbs.

In the following sentences, the adjectives are underlined.

Our <u>new</u> manager bought an <u>expensive</u> speakerphone.

(The adjective *new* describes "which" manager and *expensive* describes the "kind of" speakerphone.)

A speakerphone is <u>expensive</u>.

(The adjective *expensive,* which follows the linking verb, describes the noun *speakerphone.*)

The workload was <u>heavy</u> last week.

(The adjective *heavy* describes the noun *workload.*)

Adjectives With Pronouns. Adjectives also modify pronouns. When adjectives modify pronouns, they *follow* the linking verb.

They were <u>competent</u> and <u>reliable</u>.

(The adjectives *competent* and *reliable* follow the linking verb *were* and describe the pronoun *they.* The adjectives answer the question *What kind?*)

You were <u>wise</u> to interrupt the abusive caller.

(The adjective *wise* follows the linking verb *were* and describes the pronoun *you.* This adjective indicates "what kind" of person you are.)

Additional information regarding adjectives appears in Chapter 12.

Go to the Web

Checkpoint 2.5
for more skills practice on this topic.

CHECKPOINT 2.5

Instructions: *Underline each adjective in the following sentences. Omit the adjectives a, an, and the.*

1. A blinking light indicates an incoming call. _____

2. A pleasant voice conveys a favorable impression in a company. _____

3. You should answer phone calls by the second ring.   _____

4. Carole writes detailed instructions for telephone procedures.   _____

5. We do not give any information to unknown people over the phone.   _____

6. "Slamming" is an unethical practice of unprincipled companies.   _____

Adverbs

You just learned that adjectives modify nouns and pronouns. Other words may also require description. Adverbs usually give additional information about the main verb, but they also modify adjectives or other adverbs. The following sentences illustrate how adverbs modify main verbs, adjectives, and other adverbs:

We <u>often</u> receive wrong numbers.

(The adverb *often* modifies the main verb *receive*.)

The new telecommunications plan was <u>too</u> expensive.

(The adverb *too* modifies the adjective *expensive*.)

She answers the telephone <u>very</u> efficiently.

(The adverb *very* modifies the adverb *efficiently*.)

Adverbs answer these questions: *In what manner? Where? When? To what extent?* The following examples show the part of speech that the adverb modifies and indicate the type of question that is being answered. All adverbs are underlined.

In What Manner?

Jane analyzed the new phone proposal estimates <u>carefully</u>.

(The adverb *carefully* modifies the verb *analyzed* and answers the question *In what manner?*)

Few organizations <u>effectively</u> control their communication costs.

(The adverb *effectively* modifies the verb *control* and answers the question *In what manner?*)

Where?

Most of our customers live <u>here</u> in the city.

(The adverb *here* modifies the verb *live* and answers the question *Where?*)

We moved our telecommunications workshop dates <u>forward</u>.

(The adverb *forward* modifies the verb *moved* and answers the question *Where?*)

When?

NSP will install a second phone line <u>soon</u>.

(The adverb *soon* modifies the verb *install* and answers the question *When?*)

The president of our company visits each branch office <u>annually</u>.

(The adverb *annually* modifies the verb *visits* and answers the question *When?*)

To What Extent?

Our inventories <u>sharply</u> decreased during the recent Communication Workers of America strike.

(The adverb *sharply* modifies the verb *decreased* and answers the question *To what extent?*)

The buzzer on our phone was <u>too</u> loud.

(The adverb *too* modifies the adjective *loud* and answers the question *To what extent?*).

Do This	Do Not Do This
convert	convert over
cooperate	cooperate together
eliminate	eliminate completely
finish	finish up or finish off
plan	plan ahead
refer	refer back

Do not use an adverb to express a meaning already contained in the verb.

You will study the comparison of adverbs and the ways that adverbs function in sentences in Chapter 13.

Go to the
Web

Checkpoint 2.6
for more skills practice on this topic.

CHECKPOINT 2.6

A. **Instructions:** *Identify the word that each underlined adverb modifies. Write the word and the part of speech that it represents—**V** (verb), **Adj** (adjective), or **Adv** (adverb)—in the space provided.*

1. We had a <u>fairly</u> long discussion about the future of telecommunications.   _____

2. The number of users of BTE Airfones has jumped <u>dramatically</u>.   _____

3. We were <u>completely</u> satisfied with the service from AJ Electronics.   _____

4. We will be marketing voice recognition systems in your area <u>very</u> soon.   _____

5. Customer satisfaction rates decrease when callers cannot get problems solved <u>immediately</u>.   _____

6. We attend communication workshops <u>monthly</u>.   _____

B. **Instructions:** *Identify the underlined word as an **Adj** (adjective) or an **Adv** (adverb). Write your answer in the space provided.*

1. We <u>seldom</u> repair answering machines. _____

2. Our workload is <u>heavy</u> during a new product introduction. _____

3. The <u>appropriate</u> communications system for our business changes each year. _____

4. <u>Angry</u> callers create uncomfortable office situations. _____

5. The client was <u>very</u> interested in purchasing a headset, but Jake was <u>quite</u> disappointed by the poor customer service. _____

6. An ideal telecommuter needs <u>limited</u> supervision. _____

Conjunctions

Conjunctions are connectors. They are not power words and do not add extra meaning to your statements. They simply connect words, phrases, or clauses to make your writing seem less abrupt. This chapter introduces the most frequently used type of conjunction, which is the *coordinating conjunction.* Associate it with coordinating a wardrobe; you want to put similar items together so that they match. When you use coordinating conjunctions, you will join similar items or thoughts of equal rank. You may use more than one conjunction in a sentence. Some common coordinating conjunctions are *and, or, but,* and *nor.* These examples show how the conjunctions join similar ideas.

My fax is old <u>and</u> unreliable.

My fax is old <u>but</u> still reliable.

The staff <u>and</u> management completed <u>and</u> returned their self-evaluation reports.

I must schedule time for my voice recognition training on June 4 <u>or</u> 5.

Neither Sam <u>nor</u> Jane has received training on the wireless data network.

Chapter 15 includes a more detailed discussion of conjunctions.

Prepositions

You just learned that conjunctions are connecting words; now you will be introduced to another part of speech that also connects—the preposition. You will be amazed to see how much you use prepositions as connectors. Here are some frequently used prepositions; there are many more.

about	above	after	among	at
before	behind	by	down	from
in	inside	into	near	of
off	on	over	through	to
under	up	upon	with	

Prepositions appear before a noun or pronoun. The term for the noun or pronoun that follows a preposition is the *object of the preposition.* The following examples show prepositions and the objects of the prepositions:

with me

(*With* is the preposition; the pronoun *me* is the object of the preposition.)

from Hilary

(*From* is the preposition; the proper noun *Hilary* is the object of the preposition.)

for callers

(*For* is the preposition; the noun *callers* is the object of the preposition.)

through Alabama

(*Through* is the preposition; the proper noun *Alabama* is the object of the preposition.)

A group of words that connects nouns and pronouns to other words is a *prepositional phrase.* A prepositional phrase consists of a preposition, the object of the preposition, and the modifiers of the object of the preposition. You may find more than one preposition or prepositional phrase in a sentence. In the following examples, the prepositional phrases are underlined:

The USPS (United States Postal Service) is testing its electronic postmark service <u>in Atlanta.</u>

(In the prepositional phrase *in Atlanta, in* is the preposition, and *Atlanta* is the noun.)

Employees increase communication costs when they use a business phone <u>for excessive personal calls.</u>

(In the prepositional phrase *for excessive personal calls, for* is the preposition, *calls* is the noun, and *excessive* and *personal* are adjectives modifying *calls.*)

Telecommuting is a work alternative, which allows an employee to complete normal work functions <u>at home</u> or <u>in centers</u> <u>in local communities.</u>

(In the prepositional phrases *at home, in centers,* and *in local communities, at, in,* and *in* are prepositions. *Home, centers,* and *communities* are nouns, and *local* is an adjective modifying the word *communities.*)

Chapter 14 includes a detailed list of prepositions and shows how they are used with certain nouns and pronouns.

Interjections

An interjection consists of one or two words and shows an emotion or a strong reaction to something that has occurred. You will use very few interjections in formal communications. Interjections may be appropriate in advertising copy or in informal messages where they express feelings of congratulations, disapproval, or enthusiasm.

An exclamation mark usually follows an interjection.

Good!	**Great job!**	**Ha!**	**Impossible!**
Nonsense!	**No way!**	**Oh, no!**	**Oops!**
Wonderful!	**Ouch!**	**Wow!**	**Yes!**

Great job! Our team efforts resulted in an expanded contract with Telecom.

(*Great job!* is an illustration of a congratulatory reaction.)

NOTES

Prepositional Phrases

Remember that a prepositional phrase begins with a preposition and ends with a noun or pronoun.

PUNCTUATION ALERT!

Exclamation Points

Use an exclamation point after interjections.

Copyright © by The McGraw-Hill Companies, Inc.

Ouch! May's telemarketing contacts were considerably below April's.

(*Ouch!* represents disapproval.)

Wow! I was very impressed with your presentation at the teleconference workshop.

(*Wow!* shows enthusiasm for something that occurs.)

Oh, so that's the answer.

(The interjection *oh* may be followed by a comma.)

CHECKPOINT 2.7

Go to the
Web

Checkpoint 2.7
for more skills practice on this topic.

Instructions: *In the space provided, write the part of speech of each underlined word. Use the following abbreviations:* **C** *(conjunction),* **I** *(interjection),* **Prep** *(preposition or prepositional phrase).*

1. Our telephone system management seminar was well organized, but it did not cover cost control adequately.   _____

2. We research and test every phone that we manufacture.   _____

3. Call accounting gives managers detailed reports about departmental telephone use.   _____

4. Oh, no! Here's another incorrect area code in our company phone book.   _____

5. Neither Sierra nor Rodney returned my calls on Tuesday.   _____

6. We interviewed five candidates for the telemarketing coordinator's position.   _____

7. Wonderful! Our telecommunication system analysts were pleased with the last research findings.   _____

8. Gloria wants her regular phone number, her cell phone number, and the toll-free number on her new business card.   _____

Name _____ Date _____

Go to the
Web

Practice 1 Exercises
for more skills practice on
this topic.

PRACTICE 1

Recognizing Parts of Speech

Instructions: In the space provided, write the letter of the appropriate part of speech that each underlined word represents.

1. My supervisor told <u>her</u> to limit personal e-mail messages at the office.
   - **a.** noun
   - **b.** verb
   - **c.** pronoun
   - **d.** conjunction

   1. _____

2. A fax broadcast feature allows a business to <u>simultaneously</u> send one fax to many customers.
   - **a.** noun
   - **b.** adjective
   - **c.** verb
   - **d.** adverb

   2. _____

3. Costs for cell phone add-on features <u>are</u> beyond my budget.
   - **a.** verb
   - **b.** conjunction
   - **c.** adverb
   - **d.** preposition

   3. _____

4. President Jones addressed the opening <u>session</u> of our teleconferencing workshop.
   - **a.** noun
   - **b.** adjective
   - **c.** verb
   - **d.** adverb

   4. _____

5. The company will ask businesses to pay an <u>extra</u> fee for e-mail listings in telephone directories.
   - **a.** noun
   - **b.** adverb
   - **c.** adjective
   - **d.** preposition

   5. _____

6. Diana uses her cell phone <u>and</u> laptop computer in the airport.
   - **a.** adjective
   - **b.** conjunction
   - **c.** adverb
   - **d.** preposition

   6. _____

7. Travelers use the telephone and <u>the</u> Internet to make reservations and travel plans.
   - **a** pronoun
   - **b.** conjunction
   - **c.** adverb
   - **d.** preposition

   7. _____

8. I attended a telecommunications workshop <u>on</u> June 5.
   - **a.** verb
   - **b.** conjunction
   - **c.** adverb
   - **d.** preposition

   8. _____

9. The upgraded software was less <u>expensive</u> than we had anticipated.
   - **a.** noun
   - **b.** adverb
   - **c.** adjective
   - **d.** preposition

   9. _____

10. Two cable companies <u>reported</u> deficits during the past year.
    - **a.** noun
    - **b.** adjective
    - **c.** verb
    - **d.** adverb

    10. _____

Name _____ Date _____

PRACTICE 2

Identifying Parts of Speech

*Instructions: In the space provided, write the part of speech of each underlined word. Use the following abbreviations: **N** (noun), **Pron** (pronoun), **V** (verb), **Adj** (adjective), **Adv** (adverb), **C** (conjunction), **Prep** (preposition), **I** (interjection).*

Go to the
Web

Practice 2 Exercises
for more skills practice on this topic.

1. When I returned to my office, I immediately saw the message-waiting light flashing on the telephone.　　　1. _____

2. If you plan to upgrade your telephone equipment, obtain several quotes for service and prices.　　　2. _____

3. We need highly motivated telecommuters in our firm.　　　3. _____

4. Fax-on-demand allows you to dial the source, press the desired document code, and key in the number to request documents.　　　4. _____

5. Orders are left at night as voice messages and are retrieved and input the next day.　　　5. _____

6. Debra uses only prepaid calling cards purchased from local companies.　　　6. _____

7. The founders of our telecommunications company had both vision and initiative.　　　7. _____

8. Great! My cellular phone company is providing me with two months of free service.　　　8. _____

9. Because of the mergers of the telecommunication companies, I had difficulty selecting the best telephone service for my home office.　　　9. _____

10. Please send me the catalog on speakerphones, and I will make my purchasing decision very soon.　　　10. _____

Nouns

*Instructions: Underline the common and proper nouns in the following sentences. In the space provided, write **C** if the underlined word is a common noun. Write **P** if the underlined word is a proper noun.*

1. Our phone repair technicians responded to requests for service in Sioux Falls and the surrounding area.　　　1. _____

2. Carrie is a busy virtual employee, but she always has time for her clients in Canada.　　　2. _____

3. Max Phillips from the University of Illinois organized a telecommunications seminar for city employees.　　　3. _____

4. We could not use our cell phones in the patients' rooms at Mercy Hospital.　　　4. _____

Name _____ Date _____

Personal Pronouns

Instructions: Underline the pronouns in the following sentences.

1. Jane responded to her voice mail calls before she left for her meeting.

2. Mr. Sundby thought that he and his assistant, along with a number of their clients, should attend the meeting.

3. I was pleased with the quick phone response from my investment adviser.

4. Will you please leave a message for your telecommunications director to call me.

Verbs

Instructions: Underline the verbs in the following sentence.

1. He called France every day this past week.

2. Carrie's new pager was very inexpensive.

3. She uses her cell phone at work and at home.

4. Tyler will call you this afternoon.

Adjectives

Instructions: Underline the adjectives in the following sentences. Do not underline the adjectives a, an, or the.

1. Kaya left an urgent phone message for the customer service department.

2. You will find a wide variety of telecommunications products to use in business offices.

3. I prefer a prepaid phone card to make long-distance calls.

4. Theresa checked the Internet for recent news about telephone scams.

Adverbs

Instructions: Underline the adverbs in the following sentences.

1. Everyone in our office must be adequately trained in correct telephone etiquette.

2. Patti, our telecommunications expert, is resigning immediately.

3. Prepaid phone cards have become increasingly popular with our employees.

4. We often receive compliments for effectively responding to our callers' concerns.

Name _____ Date _____

Prepositions or Conjunctions

*Instructions: Underline the conjunctions and prepositions. Write **C** if the word is a conjunction. Write **Prep** if the word is a preposition.*

1. New developments in telecommunications will benefit small and large businesses.

   1. _____

2. I went to the telecommunications exhibit, but I could not see everything in one day.

   2. _____

3. We will sponsor a seminar for virtual employees at the Marriott on June 10.

   3. _____

4. The section about cell phones and handheld computers should appear before the information on pagers.

   4. _____

5. Our expense for the new paging system was high, but we expect high efficiency from the system.

   5. _____

6. Kayla always carries her pager or her cell phone with her.

   6. _____

PRACTICE 3

Go to the
Web

Practice 3 Exercises
for more skills practice on
this topic.

Proofreading

*Instructions: Proofread and compare the words and phrases in Column A with those in Column B. If they are the same, write **Yes** in the space provided. If they are not the same, write **No**.*

COLUMN A	COLUMN B	
1. deregulation	deregulation	1. _____
2. numerous accessories	numberous accesories	2. _____
3. toll-free number	toll free number	3. _____
4. distinctive ringing	distinctive ringing	4. _____
5. least-cost routing	least-cost route	5. _____
6. variety of battery options	variety of battery option	6. _____
7. DT-306, DT-326, and DT 346 models	DT-306, DT-336, and DT-346 models	7. _____
8. 1-800-967-5543	1-800-976-5543	8. _____
9. 36 hours of standby time	36 hours of standby time	9. _____
10. Federal Communications Commission (FTC)	Federal Communicatioins Commissioin (FTC)	10. _____

Name _____ Date _____

Go to the
Web

Practice 4 Exercises
for more skills practice on
this topic.

PRACTICE 4

Writing

*Instructions: For each of the following questions, list a common noun and a proper noun. For example, if a friend of yours named Sally Galimba has a cellular phone, **friend** is the common noun and **Sally Galimba** is the proper noun. Answers will vary.*

	COMMON NOUN	PROPER NOUN
1. Who has a cellular phone?	_____	_____
2. Who has a pager?	_____	_____
3. Who has a fax machine?	_____	_____
4. Who uses e-mail?	_____	_____
5. Who telecommutes?	_____	_____

PRACTICE 5

Recognizing Parts of Speech

Instructions: In the space provided, write the letter of the appropriate part of speech that each underlined word represents.

1. Telecommuting <u>helps</u> employers save time and money.
   - **a.** noun
   - **b.** verb
   - **c.** adjective
   - **d.** adverb

   1. _____

2. Your <u>WorldLink</u> card can be used from any phone in the world.
   - **a.** noun
   - **b.** verb
   - **c.** adjective
   - **d.** pronoun

   2. _____

3. The accident rate between using hands-free phones and handheld phones is not <u>statistically</u> significant.
   - **a.** noun
   - **b.** verb
   - **c.** adjective
   - **d.** adverb

   3. _____

4. Brazil, Israel, <u>and</u> Switzerland have banned the use of handheld phones for people who are driving.
   - **a.** noun
   - **b.** conjunction
   - **c.** preposition
   - **d.** adjective

   4. _____

5. Most businesses prefer to hold <u>major</u> negotiations face-to-face instead of through teleconferencing.
   - **a.** noun
   - **b.** adjective
   - **c.** adverb
   - **d.** verb

   5. _____

Name _____ Date _____

6. The long-range impact of teleconferencing <u>on</u>
   business travel is unclear.
       a. noun   **c.** preposition
       b. adjective   **d.** conjunction

6. _____

7. The <u>San Jose Hilton</u> in Silicon Valley has Internet
   access in its guest rooms.
       a. noun   **c.** adverb
       b. adjective   **d.** verb

7. _____

8. TeleCom quickly reacted to <u>customer</u> complaints
   about busy signals.
       a. noun   **c.** adverb
       b. adjective   **d.** verb

8. _____

9. College students <u>rapidly</u> fill telecommunications
   positions.
       a. noun   **c.** adverb
       b. adjective   **d.** verb

9. _____

10. Technological advances have created a demand <u>for</u>
    home-based workers.
        a. noun   **c.** preposition
        b. adjective   **d.** verb

10. _____

PRACTICE 6

Identifying Parts of Speech

Instructions: In the space provided, write the part of speech of each underlined word.
Use the following abbreviations: ***N*** *(noun),* ***Pron*** *(pronoun),* ***V*** *(verb),* ***Adj*** *(adjective),*
Adv *(adverb),* ***C*** *(conjunction),* ***Prep*** *(preposition),* ***I*** *(interjection).*

1. Tens of thousands of technology workers in
   <u>California</u> <u>carry</u> cell phones, and <u>they</u> use them
   <u>frequently</u>.

1. _____

2. Many companies <u>insist</u> that their <u>employees</u> use
   <u>specific</u> software.

2. _____

3. A pager will help <u>you</u> stay <u>in</u> touch when you <u>are</u>
   on the <u>road</u>.

3. _____

4. <u>Amazing</u>! Some of the <u>smartest</u> executives in
   business feel buried by a <u>technology</u> <u>avalanche</u>.

4. _____

5. The best-known computer <u>chip</u> is the one with
   millions of transistors <u>on</u> a <u>silicon</u> wafer.

5. _____

6. Cable TV and phone companies are <u>quickly</u>
   building <u>new</u> capabilities <u>into</u> their <u>networks</u>.

6. _____

7. Some companies <u>need</u> a virtual assistant <u>for</u>
   <u>random</u> projects.

7. _____

Name _____ Date _____

8. Technology <u>users</u> <u>ultimately</u> benefit from fast changes by getting <u>better</u> products and services for less <u>money</u>.

8. _____

9. Telecommuting can be a <u>problem</u> <u>for</u> <u>undisciplined</u> <u>workers</u>.

9. _____

10. The goal <u>of</u> a <u>recently</u> launched Web site <u>is</u> to enable <u>associates</u> to communicate with <u>each</u> other <u>electronically</u>.

10. _____

Nouns

*Instructions: Underline the common and proper nouns in the following sentences. In the space provided, write **C** if the underlined word is a common noun. Write **P** if the underlined word is a proper noun.*

1. The virtual employee attended a specialized seminar in Oklahoma City.

1. _____

2. Jan conducts an ethics check on home-based employees.

2. _____

3. New York bans the use of handheld cell phones for drivers on all public roads.

3. _____

4. The Insurance Institute for Highway Safety monitors highway accidents involving cell phones.

4. _____

Personal Pronouns

Instructions: Underline the pronouns in the following sentences.

1. George Mono provides a company Web site so that he and other employees can download copies of their company contracts.

2. Teresa Herrea takes the bus to the square, and then she checks in at the Boston Telecommuting Center where she works.

3. We differed in opinion with their negative assessment about our response time to our customers.

4. I was annoyed by my inability to change my computer password.

Verbs

Instructions: Underline the verbs in the following sentences.

1. The hotel has a wireless connection in each guest room.

2. We were disappointed by the slow response time of the network.

3. This cell phone is very small.

4. The virtual assistant quickly met our expectations.

Name _____ Date _____

Adjectives

Instructions: Underline the adjectives in the following sentences. Do not underline the adjectives a, an, *or* the.

1. Interpersonal skills, telephone etiquette, and sales skills are needed for the job opening.

2. In-house assistants need office space, an Internet connection, and a quiet work environment.

3. The free newsletter is sent each month and contains practical telecommunications information.

4. A home office should be a pleasant, neat, well-lit, and quiet space.

Adverbs

Instructions: Underline the adverbs in the following sentences.

1. Telecommunication devices are constantly being improved.

2. I completed the voice recognition demonstration quickly but satisfactorily.

3. She often uses her cell phone to talk with customers.

4. Virtual call centers can dramatically reduce company costs.

Prepositions or Conjunctions

Instructions: Underline the conjunctions and prepositions. Write **C** *if the word is a conjunction. Write* **Prep** *if the word is a preposition.*

1. We sent a document by fax to Richard in Galveston. 1. _____

2. Hotel managers in Canada, the United Kingdom, and the United States analyzed the impact of technology on hotel operations. 2. _____

3. Anna works from home with a computer, fax machine, and Internet connection purchased by her company. 3. _____

4. A voice mail system stores messages in the computer memory for later delivery. 4. _____

5. Cell phone companies give consumers many choices in plans, and these choices may be confusing. 5. _____

6. The videoconference had been scheduled for months, but neither Rafe nor Ani remembered the date and time. 6. _____

Name _____   Date _____

PRACTICE 7

Proofreading

*Instructions: Proofread and compare the words and phrases in Column A with those in Column B. If they are the same, write **Yes** in the space provided. If they are not the same, write **No.***

	COLUMN A	COLUMN B	
1.	handheld, battery-run flip-top portable	handheld, battery run flip-top portable	1. _____
2.	e-mail address	email address	2. _____
3.	laptop computers	laptop computors	3. _____
4.	high-speed Internet access	high-speed Internet access	4. _____
5.	wireless personal communications service	wireless personnel communications service	5. _____
6.	www.phonemiser.com	www. phonemiser/com	6. _____
7.	fax-on-demand	fax-on-demand	7. _____
8.	corporate support center	Corporate Support Center	8. _____
9.	palm-size flip variety wireless phone	palm-size flip variety wireless phone	9. _____
10.	1-800-789-4903	1-800-798-4903	10. _____

PRACTICE 8

Writing: Common Nouns and Pronouns

Instructions: Look around the room. List five common nouns and five proper nouns that you see. Answers will vary.

COMMON NOUNS	PROPER NOUNS
_____	_____
_____	_____
_____	_____
_____	_____
_____	_____

Writing: Adverbs

Instructions: Use adverbs to fill in the blanks. Answers will vary.

1. My friends are _____ funny.   1. _____
2. I like to have my questions answered _____ .   2. _____
3. We _____ receive the answers to our questions. 3. _____

POSTTEST: *Looking Back*

Posttest

Instructions: *In the space provided, write the part of speech of each underlined word. Use the following abbreviations:* ***N*** *(noun),* ***Adv*** *(adverb),* ***Pron*** *(pronoun),* ***C*** *(conjunction),* ***V*** *(verb),* ***Prep*** *(preposition),* ***Adj*** *(adjective),* ***I*** *(interjection).*

1. We purchased too many pagers and had to return them to our supplier at a loss. (1, 2)

   1. _____

2. Telephone etiquette is taught over the Internet. (1, 2)

   2. _____

3. People can use digital cameras to view and print photos on their home computers. (1, 2)

   3. _____

4. We strongly communicated our suggestions to our supervisor for a new telephone system. (1,2)

   4. _____

5. The virtual assistant lives in Michigan and communicates by e-mail, fax, and telephone.

   5. _____

6. Cell phone codes identify the phone, the owner of the phone, and the service provider. (1, 2)

   6. _____

7. A "hotspot" is a connection point for a wireless network and is available in restaurants, hotels, libraries, and airports. (1, 2)

   7. _____

8. I reviewed the charges on my phone bill for voice mail, paging, and 800 numbers. (1, 2)

   8. _____

9. Wow! He enthusiastically described his experiences of working from home. (1, 2)

   9. _____

10. Wireless networks connect two or more computers without network cables. (1, 2)

    10. _____

11. Some state governments encourage telecommuting by their employees. (1, 2)

    11. _____

12. The caller to a virtual call center may reach the kitchen of a stay-at-home parent or the dorm room of a university student. (1, 2)

    12. _____

13. You can walk into nearly any big or small office in the United States today, and you will find a fax machine. (1,2)

    13. _____

14. Pagers and pager services are generally less expensive than cell phones. (1, 2)

    14. _____

15. Telephone communication is one of the most crucial skills in work and personal life. (1, 2)

    15. _____

Chapter 3

Sentence Development

OBJECTIVES

After you have studied this chapter and completed the exercises, you will be able to do the following:

1. Demonstrate knowledge of terms used in sentence construction.

2. Use correct ending punctuation for statements, questions, commands, and exclamations.

3. Identify simple, compound, and complete subjects.

4. Identify simple, compound, and complete predicates.

5. Recognize direct objects, indirect objects, and other complements.

6. Identify normal and inverted sentence order patterns.

7. Differentiate between phrases and clauses.

8. Identify simple, compound, complex, and compound-complex sentences.

9. Identify complete sentences, fragments, and run-on sentences.

Workplace Applications: Customer Service

Do you return to a store where the salespeople ignore you? Do you enjoy calling a company that offers only a voice mail option? Do you shop at a store where you cannot return a purchase? If you are like most customers, you want to spend your money with companies that provide the best customer service.

Excellent customer service means that you, the consumer, deserve and expect attention to your needs. You want sales employees to listen to your questions and to respond efficiently and effectively. If you have a problem, you expect courteous, immediate assistance. Because you are a busy person, you desire quality products, convenient store hours, toll-free numbers, liberal return policies, and Web sites.

Making the Best Impression

Customer service is a business's public face, and it is the key to maintaining customers. The way to build a strong client base is to treat customers with respect and to address their concerns and goals as well as their consumer needs.

Effective businesses know that they never get a second chance to make a first impression. These businesses place a high priority on customer service training and have a highly visible commitment to quality service. Their employees are enthusiastic and productive and take pride in helping customers.

Pretest

Instructions: In the space provided, write the letter of the correct answer.

1. What term defines the following? *A group of words arranged in complete thoughts so that the words make sense.* (1)
       a. direct object
       b. complement
       c. sentence
       d. complete predicate

   1. _____

2. What mark of punctuation should follow this sentence? *Will you please contact us tomorrow* (2)
       a. question mark
       b. period
       c. exclamation mark
       d. quotation marks

   2. _____

3. What is the complete subject in this sentence? *Our managers and salespeople must possess outstanding problem-solving skills.* (3)
       a. outstanding problem-solving skills
       b. problem-solving skills
       c. managers and salespeople
       d. Our managers and salespeople

   3. _____

4. What is the simple predicate in this sentence? *I finally received the sales totals.* (4)
       a. received
       b. finally received
       c. I finally received
       d. received the sales totals

   4. _____

5. What is the direct object in the following sentence? *We received numerous requests for information during the last marketing campaign.* (5)
       a. marketing
       b. received
       c. information
       d. requests

   5. _____

6. Which sentence pattern does this statement represent? *Sales letters require strong first paragraphs to attract readers.* (6)
       a. the subject-verb pattern
       b. the subject-linking verb-complement pattern
       c. the subject-verb-object pattern
       d. inverted order sentence

   6. _____

7. Which statement describes a clause? (1, 7)
       a. A clause contains a subject but no verb.
       b. A clause contains a verb but no subject.
       c. A clause contains a subject and a verb.
       d. A clause contains neither a subject nor a verb.

   7. _____

8. Which sentence formation does this statement represent? *Today's customers have limited time to shop, but they require personalized assistance.* (8)
       a. simple sentence
       b. compound sentence
       c. complex sentence
       d. inverted sentence

   8. _____

9. What does this group of words indicate? *We found no problems.* (9)
       a. a dependent clause
       b. a complete sentence
       c. a sentence fragment
       d. a run-on sentence

   9. _____

10. What mark of punctuation should follow this sentence? *I wonder if our new marketing strategy will increase our sales* (2)
        a. period
        b. exclamation point
        c. question mark
        d. quotation mark

    10. _____

11. What is the complete predicate in the following sentence? *My company places a high priority on customer service training.* (4)

    a. places a high priority

    b. My company places a high priority

    c. high priority on customer service training

    d. places a high priority on customer service training

11. _____

12. What does the underlined word represent in this sentence? *Successful <u>companies</u> are concerned about product safety.* (3)

    a. simple subject

    b. compound subject

    c. simple predicate

    d. compound predicate

12. _____

13. What is the indirect object in the following sentence? *The manager told the employees the good news about the sales figures.* (5)

    a. news

    b. figures

    c. employees

    d. manager

13. _____

14. Which statement describes this sentence? *Here are the types of training programs that we offer to our sales associates.* (6, 9)

    a. The sentence is in a normal word pattern.

    b. This is an example of a sentence fragment.

    c. This is an example of a run-on sentence.

    d. The sentence is in inverted word order.

14. _____

15. What does the underlined set of words represent? *When someone recommends a new client to me, I always respond <u>with a thank-you note</u>.* (7)

    a. infinitive phrase

    b. prepositional phrase

    c. independent clause

    d. dependent clause

15. _____

Chapter Preview

If you have tried to set up or have watched someone else set up a computer, you know how important it is to properly connect the monitor and printer to the computer. You have been told or have experienced the need for sufficient memory to run the application software. In other words, all the parts must be considered and correctly put together to make your computer work. This same principle is true with the parts of speech. Each part of speech represents a valuable part of the whole sentence, but the parts must be connected appropriately for the sentence to serve its purpose and make sense.

In Chapter 2, you were introduced to the parts of speech. As you proceed through this chapter, you will see how these parts fit into sentence patterns, and you will learn the definitions of some additional terms. Note how each new term adds to the meaning and clarity of a sentence.

Sentence Identification

Sentences are words arranged to comprise complete statements or ideas that make sense. Each complete sentence begins with a capital letter and ends with an ending mark of punctuation.

Read the Questions for Sentence Identification that follow. With every group of words, you can determine if the words form a sentence by answering all four questions. The answers to all four questions should be "yes." If the answers to Questions 1 and 2 are "no," then you know immediately that the group of words is not a sentence.

Questions for Sentence Identification

1. Do the words make sense?

2. Do the words indicate a complete thought?

3. Does the group of words begin with a capital letter?

4. Does the group of words end with a period, question mark, or exclamation point?

Now look at the following groups of words:

All customers appreciate helpful salespeople.

(Your answers to the four questions should all be "yes." This is a sentence.)

when the sales meeting is over

(All your responses to the four questions should be "no." This is *not* a sentence.)

All salespersons helpful appreciate customer.

(This group of words does not make sense or indicate a complete thought; therefore, it is *not* a sentence.)

NOTES

Sentence Endings

Use an ending mark of punctuation such as a period, question mark, or exclamation point to end a sentence.

CHECKPOINT 3.1

Go to the
Web

Checkpoint 3.1
for more skills practice on
this topic.

*Instructions: In the space provided, write **Yes** if the groups of words that follow are sentences. Write **No** if the words are not sentences. If the answer is No, explain why by writing the number(s) from the **Questions for Sentence Identification** that apply.*

Ex: **and that callers are directed immediately.**   **No (1, 2, 3)**

1. Poor customer service damages a company's reputation.   _____

2. I enjoy shopping.   _____

3. Unconditional service guarantees.   _____

4. Many salespeople seem to enjoy their work.   _____

5. Service can be guaranteed in many ways.   _____

6. the better we get at meeting customers' expectations.   _____

7. Next on the consumer survey.   _____

8. Coupons are available for our latest promotion.   _____

Purposes of Sentences

Sentences have four purposes by which they can be classified:

- Statements (*declarative sentences*)
- Questions (*interrogative sentences*)
- Commands and requests (*imperative sentences*)
- Exclamations (*exclamatory sentences*)

Statements

Statements end with periods. These sentences are explanations or statements of facts and opinions.

> You need a well-prepared sales presentation by the next meeting. (*Explanation*)
> We recently revised our sales manual. (*Fact*)
> I prefer salespeople who are accurate and fast. (*Opinion*)

Questions

Direct questions end with question marks. Direct questions ask for answers. *Indirect questions* may sound like questions, but they are declarative sentences and end with periods. Indirect questions do not ask for answers.

Direct Question

Are your competitors increasing their television advertising?

Indirect Question

She asked whether I planned to send her a copy of the new sales campaign.

Commands and Requests

Command sentences express *direct commands,* or they express *courteous requests* that imply action. Both end with periods. The pronoun *you* is understood even though it is not always stated.

Direct Command

Contact your sales representative if you need assistance.

(The subject of the sentence is *you.* To determine the subject in this sentence, ask the question "To whom is the writer speaking?" The writer wants *you* to contact *your* sales representative if *you* need assistance. The subject of the sentence is *you* even if it is not physically present in the sentence. The subject of the sentence is therefore said to be understood, and this subject is never any word other than *you.* You know *to whom* the writer is addressing his command. The understood subject is then followed by a predicate.)

Courteous Request

May I please have your daily contact summaries by Friday.

(The request sounds like a question but ends with a period.)

To help you decide whether to use a period or a question mark, analyze the response you expect. If you want an answer "in words" to a question, use a question mark. If you want an "action" from the person you are addressing, use a period for a courteous request.

How is your new sales campaign progressing?

(The question needs an answer in words. Use a question mark.)

Will you please send me a report on your new sales campaign.

(You expect to receive the report; you do not expect the response, "Yes, I will send you a report." Use a period to end the sentence.)

Exclamations

Exclamations express strong reactions and end with exclamation marks. Business writers infrequently use exclamatory sentences.

The customer is always right!

You won!

PUNCTUATION ALERT!

End-of-Sentence Punctuation

1. Use a period at the end of statements, indirect questions, commands, and courteous requests.
2. Use a question mark after direct questions.
3. Use an exclamation point at the end of exclamatory sentences.

Go to the
Web

Checkpoint 3.2
for more skills practice on this topic.

CHECKPOINT 3.2

Instructions: *In the space provided, identify the purpose of each of the sentences by writing one of the following abbreviations:* **S** *(statement),* **DQ** *(direct question),* **IQ** *(indirect question),* **DC** *(direct command),* **CR** *(courteous request),* **E** *(exclamatory sentence). Write one of the following punctuation marks at the end of the statement: period (.), question mark (?), exclamation point (!).*

1. Why not take a few minutes to thank your customers for their support _____

2. Some companies offer unconditional service guarantees _____

3. Does your information system tell you which products   _____
    are in great demand

4. Proofread the sales brochure copy, and return it to me   _____
    by Monday

5. What is your reaction to a sales clerk who carries on a   _____
    personal phone conversation while you wait for assistance

6. Will you please contact our marketing manager in Tokyo   _____

7. What a great sales presentation   _____

8. I wonder if our sales commissions will increase   _____

9. Word-of-mouth advertising is an effective way to gain   _____
    new clients

10. Use last year's sales quotas as the basis for comparison   _____

Parts of a Sentence

Sentences have two parts—the *subject* and the *predicate*. The main word in a subject is the noun (person, place, thing, idea, activity, or quality) or the pronoun (noun substitute). The main word in the predicate is the verb (action or *to be* form).

Subject

The subject of a sentence indicates *who is speaking, who is spoken to,* or *who or what is spoken about.* The last category offers the most choices for subjects.

Who Is Speaking?

<u>I</u> plan to contact my customers at least once a month.

<u>We</u> requested copies of the article "The Best Sales Presentation Ideas."

(The subject is typically *We* or *I,* the *person or persons speaking.*)

Who Is Spoken To?

<u>You</u> may try our product in your home for one week.

(The subject is *you,* the *person being spoken to.*)

Who or What Is Spoken About?

<u>Salespeople</u> play important roles in closing sales.

(The subject is *salespeople,* or *who is being spoken about.*)

<u>Guarantees</u> show customers that you respect them and value their support.

(The subject is *guarantees,* or *what is spoken about.*)

Simple and Compound Subjects

A *simple subject* is the main word of the subject. Two or more main words in a subject comprise a *compound subject.* The words *and* and *or* (conjunctions) often connect the main words in a compound subject.

Simple Subjects

We use individualized goal plans to motivate our sales representatives.

(*We* is the main word and the *simple subject,* and the word *We* indicates *who is speaking.*)

Superior service brings customers back for additional purchases.

(*Service* is the main word of the subject. *Service* is the *simple subject* and indicates *what is spoken about.*)

Compound Subjects

Banbury Textiles and McDonough Manufacturing use testimonial letters written by current clients.

(*Banbury Textiles* and *McDonough Manufacturing* are the main words that form the *compound subject* and indicate *who is spoken about.*)

Free consultations and estimates attract customers.

(*Consultations* and *estimates* are the main words that form the *compound subject.* These words indicate *what is spoken about.*)

You may be wondering why it is important to identify the simple and compound subjects. These subject forms determine the verb that you will use in your sentences. Identifying simple and compound subjects first will help you avoid errors in sentence structure later.

Go to the
Web

Checkpoint 3.3
for more skills practice on this topic.

CHECKPOINT 3.3

Instructions: *In each of the following sentences, underline the simple subject once or the compound subject twice.*

1. They are projecting a sales increase of 14 percent.

2. Our representative will demonstrate our newest personal information manager (PIM) software tomorrow.

3. Cameras and film will be on sale for our preferred customers next week.

4. Elizabeth Franson and I would like to discuss the sales position.

5. Customers do not appreciate being kept "on hold" for toll calls to "help" lines.

6. Buying habits are changing as greater numbers of consumers shop from their homes.

7. Good time management is one of the most important skills for customer service representatives to master.

8. You and Julia will answer the hotline calls until 1 p.m.

9. Their employees are enthusiastic and productive.

10. We belong to the world's largest membership association for the service and support industry.

Complete Subjects

Simple or compound subjects plus any of their modifiers comprise the complete subject of a sentence. Modifiers such as adjectives and adverbs describe other words.

Some customers choose products based on service and reliability rather than on price.

(The simple subject is *customers*. The word *some* modifies *customers* and indicates "how many" customers. *Some customers* is the complete subject.)

All objections and product complaints require attention.

(The compound subject is *objections* and *complaints*. The word *all* modifies *objections* and *product complaints;* the word *product* modifies *complaints*. *All objections and product complaints* is the complete subject.)

NOTES

Looking Back
Review adjectives and the questions that they answer (see Chapter 2).

CHECKPOINT 3.4

Go to the
Web

Checkpoint 3.4
for more skills practice on this topic.

*Instructions: In each of the following sentences, place parentheses **( )** around the complete subject. Underline the simple subject once or the compound subject twice.*

Ex.: **(A service guarantee)** informs customers that a firm is serious about doing things right the first time.

1. CRI Technology and TeleVideo Productions produce customer service training films.

2. Most major hotels and airlines reward their loyal customers.

3. CD-ROM phone books provide an inexpensive way to develop lists of prospective customers.

4. A good salesperson listens to a client's needs.

5. Active community support and employee participation help gain exposure for your company.

6. The university and the technical college offer noncredit courses for improving sales techniques.

7. Customer feedback helps you correct problems.

8. One women's apparel shop offers discounts to loyal customers.

Predicates

Once you have found the complete subject, the remainder of the sentence is the predicate. The verb is the easiest part of speech to recognize in the predicate.

The predicate adds meaning and clarity to the subject and tells *what the subject is doing* or *what the subject is.*

NOTES

Locating the Subject
Remember that a subject indicates who is speaking, who is spoken to, and who or what is spoken about.

> **Frequent flier programs encourage passenger loyalty.**
>
> (The complete subject is *Frequent flier programs.* The remainder of the sentence is the predicate.)
>
> **Software companies distribute products to customers for testing in the workplace.**
>
> (The complete subject is *Software companies.* The remainder is the predicate.)
>
> **John developed several effective promotional messages.**
>
> (The complete subject is *John.* The remainder of the sentence is the predicate.)
>
> **Microsoft Corporation sends product-development teams into companies to determine how they use software.**
>
> (The complete subject is *Microsoft Corporation.* The remainder is the predicate.)

Sentence Development

Simple and Compound Predicates

A single verb is the *simple predicate* in a sentence. Two or more verbs form a *compound predicate*.

Simple Predicates

Mary <u>listens</u> carefully.

(The complete subject is *Mary.* The simple predicate is the verb *listens.*)

I <u>sell</u> software and computer supplies.

(The complete subject is *I.* The simple predicate is the verb *sell.*)

Our sales publications <u>are</u> attractive.

(The complete subject is *Our sales publications.* The simple predicate is the verb *are.*)

Compound Predicates

I <u>read</u> the warranty and <u>accepted</u> its provisions.

(The complete subject is *I. Read* and *accepted* are the verbs and the compound predicate.)

Our sales manager and a sales representative <u>listen</u> to our customers' complaints and <u>correct</u> all product deficiencies.

(The complete subject is *Our sales manager and a sales representative. Listen* and *correct* are the verbs and the compound predicate.)

Several companies <u>have eliminated</u> commissions and <u>placed</u> people on salaries.

(The complete subject is *Several companies. Have eliminated* and *placed* are the verbs and the compound predicate.)

NOTES

Compound Subjects and Predicates

A compound subject has two or more subjects. A compound predicate has two or more verbs.

Go to the
Web

Checkpoint 3.5
for more skills practice on this topic.

CHECKPOINT 3.5

Instructions: *In each of the following sentences, underline the simple predicate once or the compound predicate twice.*

1. Customer loyalty is the responsibility of every employee within an organization.

2. Companies with excellent customer service thrive and increase sales.

3. The staff enjoyed the recognition during Customer Service Week.

4. Well-trained customer service representatives are necessary for our company's success.

5. Technical support representatives should record reoccurring customer problems.

6. Rachel and Teresa study marketing materials and learn new products each week.

7. Her presentation focused on customer loyalty.

8. We role-play situations with our manager and receive feedback about our performance.

9. Web-based technologies offer new opportunities and reach more customers.

10. We will require trained retail sales employees for the holiday season.

Complete Predicates

The complete predicate consists of a verb or verbs and all the modifiers that limit or describe the verbs.

Satisfied customers create goodwill for your firm.

(The complete subject is *Satisfied customers*. The simple predicate is *create*. The complete predicate is *create goodwill for your firm*.)

A restaurant trainer may use videos or satellite television programs for training.

(The complete subject is *A restaurant trainer*. The simple predicate is *may use*. The complete predicate is *may use videos or satellite television programs for training*.)

The National Retail Federation offers seminars and conducts workshops in small retail stores.

(The complete subject is *The National Retail Federation*. The compound predicate is *offers* and *conducts*. The complete predicate is *offers seminars and conducts workshops in small retail stores*.)

CHECKPOINT 3.6

Instructions: *In each of the following sentences, place parentheses ( ) around the complete predicate. Underline the simple predicate once or the compound predicate twice.*

1. Timing becomes your greatest advantage in reaching new markets.

2. Large retailers use electronic inventory systems to avoid running out of stock.

3. Lawn Care, Inc. processes all customer communications within 24 hours.

4. Paula plans and rehearses a new product demonstration.

5. Consumers spend more money in strong economic times.

6. Johnson & Johnson rewards new ideas, develops them, and evaluates the end results.

7. Sidewalk sales originated during the early years of retailing.

8. Six hundred field representatives counsel and assist clients in a 12-state area.

Go to the
Web

Checkpoint 3.6
for more skills practice on this topic.

Objects and Complements

You have now identified two parts of a sentence—the subject and the predicate. Another part of the sentence is the object, which is one way to complete the verb. Not all verbs will have objects. You will study additional material about verbs and objects in Chapter 9.

Direct Objects

A direct object is a noun or a pronoun. A direct object provides one way to complete the verb by answering the question *whom* or *what* after the verb. A direct object is *not* the subject of a sentence.

Laurie sells computers for a living.

Verb: *sells*

Sells "what?": *computers*

(Sells "whom" is not appropriate since computers are things.)

Direct object: *computers*

My regional sales manager congratulated <u>me</u>.

Verb: *congratulated*

Congratulated "whom?": *me*

Direct object: *me*

Indirect Objects

A sentence cannot have an indirect object without having a direct object. An indirect object, like a direct object, is a noun or a pronoun and is *not* the subject of a sentence. The indirect object answers the question *To whom?* or *For whom?* Typically, an indirect object precedes the direct object. Verb forms such as *give, offer, wish, ship, make, refuse, present,* or *send* usually precede an indirect object.

The administrative assistant gave the sales <u>staff</u> several messages.

Verb: *gave*

Direct object: *messages*

"To whom" are the messages given?: *staff*

Indirect object: *staff*

We shipped <u>you</u> the new consumer relations book last week.

Verb: *shipped*

Direct object: *book*

"To whom" was the book shipped?: *you*

Indirect object: *you*

Subject Complements

Subject complements are predicate nouns or predicate pronouns that follow linking verbs such as *am, are, is, was,* and *were.* Linking verbs are not action verbs, but they have subjects. Subject complements rename these subjects.

Complements Renaming Subjects (Predicate Nouns)

Karen Daniels is <u>our new regional sales manager</u>.

(The complement *our new regional sales manager* renames *Karen Daniels.*)

We were the <u>top sales winners</u>.

(The complement *top sales winners* renames *we.*)

The last person to contact the customer was <u>she</u>.

(The complement *she* renames *the last person.*)

Predicate Complements

Predicate complements are predicate adjectives that follow linking verbs and modify (describe) the subject in the sentence.

Complements Describing Subjects (Predicate Adjectives)

Billboard advertising is <u>expensive</u>.

(The complement *expensive* describes *billboard advertising.*)

Anonymous survey cards are <u>not useful</u>.

(The complement *not useful* describes *anonymous survey cards.*)

Sales training video use is <u>popular</u>.

(The complement *popular* describes *sales training video use.*)

NOTES

Linking Verbs

Linking verbs do not show action.

Instructions: *Identify the function of the underlined word or words in each sentence. In the space provided, write the abbreviation that identifies the function: direct object (**DO**), indirect object (**IO**), or complement (predicate noun, pronoun, adjective) (**C**).*

1. Database software assists sales <u>representatives</u> in maintaining client addresses and information.   _____

2. Sweetwaters Restaurant sent local food <u>editors</u> news releases of its new menus.   _____

3. Some sales brochures contain <u>testimonials</u> from satisfied customers.   _____

4. R. J. McDermid presented <u>Shermer and Associates</u> the Malcolm Baldrige National Quality Award.   _____

5. The Menominee Chamber of Commerce office processes customer <u>inquiries</u> within two days.   _____

6. I sent <u>her</u> the research about shopping malls in the <u>United</u> States.   _____

7. Our salespeople are <u>intelligent</u> and <u>creative</u>.   _____

8. Service is always <u>excellent</u> at our local antique emporium.   _____

Sentence Order

You have already worked with sentences that are in a normal word pattern. The subject appears first and the predicate follows.

Varying the sentence order is a way to make sentences more interesting. When the predicate or part of the predicate is placed before the subject, the sentence is in inverted order. To identify the subject of a sentence in inverted order, try to change the order of the sentence to the normal subject-verb pattern. When a sentence is in inverted order, the simple subject determines the verb form to use.

There/Here Sentences

The adverbs *here* and *there* are never subjects of sentences. When one of these words begins a sentence, the subject visually follows the verb.

There are several <u>causes</u> for lower customer satisfaction ratings.

Verb: *are*

Simple subject: *causes*

(The subject *follows* the verb.)

Here is my monthly expense <u>report</u>.

Verb: *is*

Simple subject: *report*

(The subject *follows* the verb.)

NOTES

Neither Here nor There
The adverbs *here* and *there* are not subjects of sentences.

Questions

Must we train people to be pleasant to customers?

> (Change the sentence into normal order.)

We must train people to be pleasant to customers.

Verb: *must train*

Simple subject: *We*

How much is a new customer worth?

> (Change the sentence into normal order.)

A new customer is worth how much?

Verb: *is*

Simple subject: *customer*

Sentences Beginning With Prepositional Phrases

On the counter are the most recent customer satisfaction surveys.

> (The subject follows the verb. Change the sentence into normal order.)

The most recent customer satisfaction surveys are on the counter.

Verb: *are*

Simple subject: *surveys*

Within the Target® retail system exist many opportunities for courteous employees to receive promotions.

> (The subject follows the verb. Change the sentence into normal order.)

Many opportunities exist for courteous employees to receive promotions within the Target® retail system.

Verb: *exist*

Simple subject: *opportunities*

Go to the
Web

Checkpoint 3.8
for more skills practice on
this topic.

CHECKPOINT 3.8

Instructions: In the space provided, write **N** if the sentence is in normal order or write **I** if the sentence is in inverted order. Underline the simple subject once and the simple predicate twice.

1. Near the edge of Disney World lie the two visitor relations training centers. _____

2. You know the importance of delivering quality service when it is your own business. _____

3. Here are seven suggestions for improving customer relations. _____

4. What are the sales quotas for next month? _____

5. There are people who prefer to do their shopping in smaller malls. _____

6. Our customers appreciate our lower prices. _____

Phrases and Clauses

Phrases and clauses are sequences of words. Arranging these phrases and clauses in varying patterns makes your writing more interesting and your learning grammar more challenging.

Phrases

A phrase is a sequence of words that has neither a subject nor a predicate. *Prepositional phrases* begin with prepositions such as *of, in, at,* and *for* and end with a noun or pronoun. They do not include a verb. *Infinitive phrases* begin with *to* and include a verb form. Phrases cannot stand alone.

Prepositional Phrases	Infinitive Phrases
of our clients	to cancel the contract
in your move	to share their ideas
at our store	to run these ads
for them	to concentrate

When determining the subject in a sentence, do not consider prepositional or infinitive phrases. You may wish to place parentheses around your phrases as you identify subjects and verbs.

Each (of the managers) gives a brief report (at our district meeting).

Simple subject: *Each*

Verb: *gives*

(Both phrases in parentheses are prepositional phrases. Do not consider the prepositional phrase *of the managers* when selecting the subject.)

A salesperson needs a helpful attitude (to provide quality service).

Simple subject: *salesperson*

Verb: *needs*

(The phrase in parentheses is an infinitive phrase and is not the main verb.)

Clauses

A clause, like a phrase, is a sequence of words, but a clause has *both* a subject and a predicate. A clause that is a complete sentence can stand alone, which makes it an *independent clause*. A *dependent clause* is *not* a complete sentence and cannot stand alone. A dependent clause must be joined to an independent clause to make sense.

Independent Clauses

Point-of-sale (POS) software provides information regarding sales activity by a salesperson.

(The sentence has a subject and a predicate, is a complete thought, and makes sense. When a sentence can stand alone, it is an independent clause.)

All customers appreciate helpful, pleasant salespersons.

(The sentence can stand alone and is an independent clause.)

Dependent Clauses

When we complete our sales training,

(The words cannot stand alone but require an independent clause [complete sentence] to make sense.)

Copyright © by The McGraw-Hill Companies, Inc.

dependent clause | independent clause

When we complete our sales training, we will have a party.

After you have lost an account,

(The words cannot stand alone but require an independent clause to make sense.)

dependent clause | independent clause

After you have lost an account, find out why you lost it.

(The subject *you* is understood in the independent clause.)

When a dependent clause *introduces* an independent clause, place a comma at the *end* of the dependent clause. No comma is necessary when the dependent clause is at the end of the sentence.

If the refrigerator was damaged in moving, our standard guarantee still applies.

(Note the comma at the end of the dependent clause.)

Because they are often the first contacts that customers have with firms, customer service representatives must have excellent communication skills.

(Note the comma at the end of the dependent clause.)

Customer service representatives must have excellent communication skills because they are often the first contacts that customers have with firms.

(No comma is placed before or after the dependent clause when it appears at the end of the sentence.)

Go to the
Web

Checkpoint 3.9
for more skills practice on this topic.

CHECKPOINT 3.9

Instructions: *In the space provided, write **I** if the group of underlined words is an independent clause; write **D** if the group of words is a dependent clause. If the words are phrases, write **P**.*

1. They based award ratings on sales performance. _____

2. The fee is $120 for the sales training workshop. _____

3. Jerry obtained testimonials from people with local community credibility. _____

4. Your service must be superior, or your merchandise must be different from your competitors' goods. _____

5. If Golden Rule Oil Company is late with an oil delivery, the customer gets a discount. _____

6. We have an unstated guarantee that our employees always try to make customers happy. _____

7. Retailers are optimistic about this year's sales. _____

8. Rebecah listened to her clients because she wanted to improve her marketing techniques. _____

Sentence Formations

The number of clauses in a sentence determines whether the formation is a simple sentence, a compound sentence, a complex sentence, or a compound-complex sentence. By using different sentence formations, you can add variety to your writing.

Simple Sentences

A simple sentence has one complete subject and one complete predicate. The subject, the predicate, or both may be compound. Although the subject or verb may be plural in number, it is still only a single subject or a single verb. In the following examples, the subjects are underlined once. The verbs are underlined twice.

Simple Subject, Single Verb

Our advertising **campaigns** usually **succeed**.

Compound Subject, Single Verb

Vicki and **I** **enjoyed** your comments about the new campaign.

Simple Subject, Compound Verb

Professional **salespeople** **listen** to complaints and **find** ways to help.

Compound Subject, Compound Verb

My **realtor** and **banker** **understood** my situation and **worked** for my **benefit**.

Compound Sentences

A compound sentence consists of two independent clauses (simple sentences) connected by a coordinating conjunction. Use a coordinating conjunction to connect two independent clauses of equal importance. Each independent clause has its own subject(s) and its own predicate(s). A comma separates the two independent clauses and appears *before* the coordinating conjunction.

> **Scott did not buy our product, but he recommended our service to several others in his club.**

Independent clause 1: Scott did not buy our product.

Independent clause 2: He recommended our service to several others in his club.

(The two independent clauses are joined by the coordinating conjunction *but* to form a compound sentence. Place a comma *before* the coordinating conjunction.)

```
        independent clause              independent clause
```

We offer 90-minute service training classes, and we always have waiting lists for them.

(The two independent clauses are joined by the coordinating conjunction *and* to form a compound sentence. Place a comma *before* the coordinating conjunction.)

Complex Sentences

A complex sentence consists of an independent clause and a dependent clause. The dependent clause cannot stand alone; it depends on the independent clause for

NOTES

Looking Back

Words such as *and, or, nor,* and *but* are coordinating conjunctions (see Chapter 2).

PUNCTUATION ALERT!

Connectors

Use a comma to separate two independent clauses. The comma appears before the coordinating conjunction.

meaning. When you want to stress one idea more than another, use the complex sentence. The independent clause receives greater emphasis than the dependent clause.

dependent clause	independent clause

When our competition increased, we concentrated on improving our customer service.

(The emphasis is on the independent clause.)

dependent clause	independent clause

Before I called on Northgate Industries, I practiced my sales presentation.

(The emphasis is on the independent clause.)

Compound-Complex Sentences

A compound-complex sentence consists of more than one independent clause and one or more dependent clauses.

dependent clause	independent clause

Because Geoff is rude to customers, he causes problems in our department, and we are getting irritated with his behavior.

independent clause

(The sentence contains two independent clauses and one dependent clause.)

dependent clause	independent clause

After she gave her sales presentation, Dana planned to return to Seattle immediately, but the bad weather delayed her flight.

independent clause

(The sentence contains two independent clauses and one dependent clause.)

Sentence Fragments

Sentence fragments may be words, phrases, or dependent clauses. They cannot stand alone even though some fragments may contain subjects and predicates. You may see fragments written incorrectly with a capital letter and a period. In many cases, you can attach a fragment to a sentence that precedes or follows it.

The next customer appreciation day.

(The fragment does not express a complete thought and does not have a predicate.)

Asked for sales assistance.

(The fragment does not express a complete thought and does not have a subject.)

Run-On Sentences

Run-on sentences are complete sentences with period or comma faults. Two sentences "run" together, which makes it difficult to grasp the meaning of the material. Correcting run-on sentences involves (1) adding a comma and a coordinating conjunction such as *and, or,* or *but;* (2) using a semicolon; or (3) making two separate sentences.

Incorrect: I want to accept the sales job in Porterville the family wants to stay here.

Correct: I want to accept the sales job in Porterville, **but** the family wants to stay here.

(Add a comma and a coordinating conjunction between the two independent clauses.)

Correct: I want to accept the sales job in Porterville; the family wants to stay here.

(Use a semicolon to separate the two independent clauses.)

Correct: I want to accept the sales job in Porterville. The family wants to stay here.

(Use a period to separate the two independent clauses.)

Comma Splice

A comma without a coordinating conjunction between two independent clauses is referred to as a comma splice and results in a run-on sentence.

Incorrect: Every year we conduct a customer survey, our customers tell us what products that they would like to have us offer.

Correct: Every year we conduct a customer survey, **and** our customers tell us what products that they would like to have us offer.

(Add a coordinating conjunction between the two independent clauses.)

Correct: Every year we conduct a customer survey; our customers tell us what products that they would like to have us offer.

(Use a semicolon to separate the two independent clauses.)

Correct: Every year we conduct a customer survey. Our customers tell us what products that they would like to have us offer.

(Use a period to separate the two independent clauses.)

CHECKPOINT 3.10

PUNCTUATION ALERT!

Semicolons
Use a semicolon to separate two closely related sentences.

Go to the
Web

Checkpoint 3.10
for more skills practice on this topic.

Instructions: In the space provided, write one of the following abbreviations to identify each of the sentences listed below: **S** (simple sentence), **D** (compound sentence), **X** (complex sentence), **C** (compound-complex sentence), **F** (fragment), **R** (run-on).

1. Because so much of our business is outside the United States, we need to hire someone with international sales experience. _____

2. Do not focus solely on new customers work to increase sales to old ones. _____

3. The migration to suburbs creates problems for downtown merchants. _____

4. When customers open charge accounts. _____

5. CRI Productions uses videos to train employees, it is expensive. _____

Sentence Development

6. Although Jordan just started working for us, he has done _____
   a remarkable job in training temporary sales workers.

7. When customers have product complaints, they need _____
   someone who will listen, and they require immediate
   attention.

8. Every salesperson has an individual sales plan, and those _____
   who exceed their goals receive monetary rewards.

9. The list of customer contacts looked impressive, but the _____
   actual sales did not meet expectations.

10. A list of sales representatives, addresses, and telephone _____
    numbers.

Diagramming Sentences

A diagram is a line drawing or example that explains the parts or operation of something. A *sentence diagram* shows the parts of a sentence and the relationship of all the words to one another. The diagramming process is similar to putting together the parts of a puzzle. You begin with the major parts of the sentence—the simple subject, simple predicate (verb), and direct object. Follow these beginning steps for diagramming sentences:

Ryan sells insurance.

1. Draw a horizontal line with a vertical line through it.

2. Write the simple subject (Ryan) to the left of the vertical line; write the simple predicate to the right.

3. Draw another vertical line on the base line after the verb. This line does *not* cross the horizontal line.

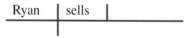

4. Write the direct object to the right of this second vertical line.

Go to the
Web

Checkpoint 3.11
for more skills practice on
this topic.

CHECKPOINT 3.11

Instructions: *In the space provided below, diagram the following sentences. Use only the simple subject, simple predicate, and direct object.*

Chapter 3

1. All product complaints require attention.

2. We will send the sales manual.

3. Customer feedback has caused improvements.

4. I read the warranty.

5. My supervisor congratulated me.

6. Our brochures emphasize service.

7. Teenagers enjoy the shopping malls.

8. Our store offers great discounts.

Name _____ Date _____

Go to the
Web

Practice 1 Exercises
for more skills practice on
this topic.

PRACTICE 1

Word and Sentence Identification

Instructions: In the space provided, write the letter of the item that identifies the underlined word or words in each of the following sentences.

1. We always meet our clients' deadlines our competitors are often late.
    - **a.** dependent clause
    - **b.** inverted sentence order
    - **c.** compound sentence
    - **d.** run-on sentence

    1. _____

2. Please explain to your customers that we are discontinuing these items.
    - **a.** indirect question
    - **b.** direct question
    - **c.** statement
    - **d.** courteous request

    2. _____

3. to the front of the store
    - **a.** phrase
    - **b.** independent clause
    - **c.** inverted sentence order
    - **d.** command

    3. _____

4. Have consumers' buying habits changed with electronic shopping?
    - **a.** indirect question
    - **b.** direct question
    - **c.** simple sentence
    - **d.** complex sentence

    4. _____

5. Your firm cannot afford defensive employee behavior when dealing with an irate customer.
    - **a.** compound subject
    - **b.** direct object
    - **c.** complete subject
    - **d.** complement

    5. _____

6. Because consumer advertising supplements have increased, the average newspaper weighs 50 percent more today than it did ten years ago.
    - **a.** simple sentence
    - **b.** compound sentence
    - **c.** complex sentence
    - **d.** normal sentence order

    6. _____

7. Individual, Inc., delivers news stories to its customers by e-mail or by access to its Web site.
    - **a.** simple subject
    - **b.** compound predicate
    - **c.** complement
    - **d.** simple predicate

    7. _____

8. If a customer has a problem, he or she can call the store, and a service representative will resolve the matter.
    - **a.** independent clause
    - **b.** phrase
    - **c.** dependent clause
    - **d.** complete subject

    8. _____

9. Here are the sales quotas for the next six months.
    - **a.** sentence fragment
    - **b.** normal word pattern
    - **c.** subject complement
    - **d.** inverted word pattern

    9. _____

Name _____ Date _____

10. Top sales performers are <u>ambitious</u> and <u>innovative</u>.   10. _____
     a. indirect object   **c.** compound predicate
     b. complete predicate   **d.** complement

PRACTICE 2

> **Go to the**
> # Web
> ___
> **Practice 2 Exercises**
> for more skills practice on
> this topic.

Parts of a Sentence

Instructions: In each of the following sentences, underline the simple or compound subject once and the simple or compound predicate twice. When appropriate, write an unstated subject in the blank at the beginning of the sentence.

Ex: <u>You</u>   <u>Focus</u> on the value of your product.

1. _____ Our customers demand faster deliveries.

2. _____ The FDA restricted food-labeling procedures to protect consumers.

3. _____ Answer the phone by the second ring.

4. _____ The Better Business Bureau and the U.S. Postal Service are sources for information about unknown clients.

5. _____ What are your sales goals?

Punctuation

Instructions: Place one of the following punctuation marks at the end of the group of words and also in the space provided: period (.), question mark (?), exclamation point (!).

1. Is there a service that I can provide that my competitors are not offering   1. _____

2. Listen more and talk less when you deal with customers   2. _____

3. People do not mind paying more when they know that the product is superior   3. _____

4. A patient asked if I would reschedule her appointment   4. _____

5. Will you please share your most memorable sales experience with our group   5. _____

Objects and Complements

Instructions: In the following sentences, underline a direct object once and an indirect object twice. Circle the predicate nouns or predicate adjectives (complements).

1. Our nine-member team sold products with a value of $6.2 million.

2. Marketing Strategies, Inc., hired me.

3. After reviewing our database entries, we found outdated addresses.

Name _____ Date _____

4. Johnson Printing sends customers monthly satisfaction surveys.

5. First-rate customer service is a prerequisite for any company's success.

Sentence Order

*Instructions: Write **Yes** in the space provided if the sentences that follow are in normal order. Write **No** if they are not in normal order. Underline the simple subject once and the simple predicate twice in all sentences.*

1. Have you built a strong sales team?   1. _____

2. This information system will tell you what your customers want.   2. _____

3. Which new markets will your home business target?   3. _____

4. There are specialized courses for learning creative ways to retain customers. 4. _____

5. Here is an extra bonus for finding all those customer referrals.   5. _____

Independent and Dependent Clauses

*Instructions: If the word groups below are independent clauses, write **Yes** in the space provided. If they are dependent clauses and cannot stand alone, write **No.** Then complete the clause to make it a complete sentence. Answers will vary.*

1. As growing numbers of consumers order from catalogs.

   _____

   _____

2. One of the first divisions that downsizing affects is employee training.

   _____

3. AmericTrend involves current users of its products in new product surveys.

   _____

4. If a company takes its customers for granted.

   _____

5. Shopping malls attract local consumers and tourists.

   _____

Sentence Formation

Instructions: Rewrite the following groups of words correctly. Punctuation marks may be necessary. Answers will vary.

1. Customer service is more than an eagerness to please it is also customer satisfaction.

   _____

   _____

Name _____ Date _____

2. I apologize for the inconvenience our Super Bowl stock disappeared within an hour of delivery.

   _____

   _____

3. We appreciate your business. Whether you are a lifetime customer or a newcomer.

   _____

   _____

4. Bryant and Stoker eliminated commissions, and placed salespeople on salary.

   _____

   _____

5. Business owners may use different training methods but they should make a commitment to improve customer relations.

   _____

   _____

PRACTICE 3

Proofreading

Instructions: Proofread and compare the two sentences in each group. If they are the same, write **Yes** *in the space provided. If they are not the same, write* **No.** *Use the first sentence as the correct copy. If you find errors in the second sentence, underline them.*

Go to the
Web

Practice 3 Exercises for more skills practice on this topic.

1. Ask yourself, "What would make me buy from this company?"

   Ask yourself, What would make me buy from this company?'

   1. _____

2. Prospective clients ignore you or tune you out if your voice is flat and monotonous.

   Prospective clients ignore your or tune out if your voice is flat and monotonous.

   2. _____

3. Here are the complete results of the survey.

   Here are the complete results of the survey.

   3. _____

4. Servicio, Inc., provides translating services to many companies in the United States.

   Servicio, Inc., provides translating services to many companies in the United States.

   4. _____

5. A private sale for our charge account customers only will be held at 7 p.m. Monday.   A private sale for our charge account customers only will be held at 7 a.m. Monday.

   5. _____

Sentence Development

Name _____ Date _____

Go to the
Web

Practice 4 Exercises
for more skills practice on
this topic.

PRACTICE 4

Writing

Instructions: In the space provided, complete the following exercises. Answers will vary.

1. Write a simple sentence describing a company with excellent customer service. Underline the simple subject once and the simple predicate twice.

   _____

2. Write a sentence with a compound subject describing a product or service that you enjoy using. Underline the compound subject once and the simple or compound predicate twice.

   _____

3. Write a question about customer service. Underline the simple subject once and the simple predicate twice.

   _____

4. Write a complex sentence about poor customer service. Underline the simple or compound subject once and the simple or compound predicate twice. Circle the dependent clause.

   _____

PRACTICE 5

Word and Sentence Identification

Instructions: In the space provided, write the letter of the item that identifies the underlined word or words in each of the following sentences.

1. Some businesses may prefer advertising in the newspaper, and others may choose to create Web sites.
       1. _____
   a. simple sentence   c. compound sentence
   b. compound predicate   d. complex sentence

2. We offer customers a money-back guarantee.
       2. _____
   a. indirect object   c. simple subject
   b. direct object   d. compound subject

3. Gump's animated window display received public exposure and enticed customers to shop in the store.
       3. _____
   a. simple and complete predicates   c. compound predicate
   b. simple predicate   d. complete predicate

4. In the lower desk drawer are the lists of prospective clients.
       4. _____
   a. inverted sentence order   c. indirect question
   b. courteous request   d. fragment

Name _____ Date _____

5. Greta asked if we had any customer complaints about   5. _____
   our store hours.
   a. indirect question   c. inverted sentence order
   b. courteous request   d. direct question

6. If they send coupons to satisfied customers   6. _____
   a. phrase   c. dependent clause
   b. independent clause   d. statement

7. Miscommunication frequently occurs in the business   7. _____
   world because of poor message taking.
   a. simple subject   c. complement
   b. simple predicate   d. compound predicate

8. The tone of your voice is especially important when   8. _____
   you are helping a dissatisfied customer.
   a. compound subject   c. direct object
   b. complete subject   d. indirect object

9. Neglect of customers by the average company.   9. _____
   a. simple sentence   c. run-on sentence
   b. fragment   d. compound subject

10. Our marketing representatives are extremely   10. _____
    competent professionals.
    a. indirect object   c. complement
    b. complete predicate   d. compound predicate

PRACTICE 6

Parts of a Sentence

Instructions: In each of the following sentences, underline the simple or compound subject once and the simple or compound predicate twice. When appropriate, write an unstated subject in the blank at the beginning of the sentence.

1. _____ Creativity and originality characterize successful advertising campaigns.

2. _____ Give your full attention to a customer.

3. _____ The sales associate answered my questions and gave me additional sales literature.

4. _____ People often remember only the last point in a sales presentation.

5. _____ An expert initial greeting creates goodwill with your clients.

Name _____ Date _____

Punctuation

Instructions: Place one of the following punctuation marks at the end of each group of words and also in the space provided: period (.), question mark (?), exclamation point (!).

1. If you are friendly, your customers tend to be friendly   1. _____

2. Why do you think it is important to have a positive attitude in a sales management position   2. _____

3. Always be courteous, no matter how busy you are   3. _____

4. Will you please identify the ten essential components of customer satisfaction   4. _____

5. Use voice mail to leave a message if the party you are calling is unavailable   5. _____

Objects and Complements

Instructions: In the following sentences, underline a direct object once and an indirect object twice. Circle the predicate nouns or predicate adjectives (complements).

1. You can show interest in customers by listening to their concerns.

2. Some computer companies send customers software upgrade coupons.

3. Customers appreciate good service.

4. For more information about the products, ask the salesperson.

5. Additional training is available for holiday salespeople.

Sentence Order

Instructions: Write Yes in the space provided if the sentences that follow are in normal order. Write No if they are not in normal order. Underline the simple subject once and the simple predicate twice in all sentences.

1. Have you checked our sales figures for this month?   1. _____

2. Here is the discount coupon that Karen wanted.   2. _____

3. Across from the credit department offices is the customer complaint desk.   3. _____

4. Tim explained why he was unable to attend the sales meeting.   4. _____

5. There are two new sales representatives on the staff at Ryder Technology.   5. _____

Name _____ Date _____

Independent and Dependent Clauses

Instructions: *If the word groups below are independent clauses, write* **Yes** *in the space provided. If they are dependent clauses and cannot stand alone, write* **No;** *then complete the clause to make it a complete sentence. Answers will vary.*

1. If there is an angry customer in your office.

   _____

2. Evaluate and improve your closing in a sales presentation.

   _____

3. When you communicate with customers, match your words with your nonverbal gestures.

   _____

4. When clients are not treated well, they take their business elsewhere.

   _____

5. Before you leave a client.

   _____

   _____

Sentence Formations

Instructions: *Rewrite the following groups of words correctly. Punctuation marks may be necessary. Answers will vary.*

1. If your job involves taking calls from unhappy callers you have a difficult job

   _____

2. Put people before paperwork help the customer first.

   _____

3. When a customer has a problem. Address it quickly.

   _____

4. Your attitude is contagious, and will affect the customer.

   _____

5. Never promise what you cannot deliver honesty is the best policy.

   _____

Name _____ Date _____

PRACTICE 7

Proofreading

*Instructions: Proofread and compare the two sentences in each group. If they are the same, write **Yes** in the space provided. If they are not the same, write **No**. Use the first sentence as the correct copy. If you find errors in the second sentence, underline them.*

1. How does a company create an environment where customer service will flourish?

   How does a company create a environment where customer service will flourish?

   1. _____

2. Nothing makes a customer happier than a follow-up call a few days after a major purchase.

   Nothing makes a customers happier than a follow-up call a few days after a major purchase.

   2. _____

3. A first encounter—whether it is with the gardener, receptionist, or company president—can make or break a sale.

   A first encounter—whether its with the gardener, receptionist or company president—can make or break a sale.

   3. _____

4. Listening to a customer's concern and handling the situation effectively are valuable skills for someone in the retail field.

   Listening to a customer's concern and handling the situation effectively are valuable skills for someone in the retail field.

   4. _____

5. Hewlett-Packard technician Patrick Mufaska has a sign in his workstation that reads, "The job that ate my brain."

   Hewlett-Packard technician Patrick Mufaska has a sign in his workstation that reads, "The job that ate my brain".

   5. _____

PRACTICE 8

Writing

Instructions: In the space provided, complete the following exercises. Answers will vary.

1. Write a simple sentence describing a company with poor customer service. Underline the simple subject once and the simple predicate twice.

   _____

Name _____ Date _____

2. Write a sentence with a compound predicate describing a product or service that you enjoy using. Underline the simple or compound subject once and the compound predicate twice.

   _____

3. Write an exclamatory sentence about customer service. Underline the simple subject once and the simple predicate twice.

   _____

4. Write a compound sentence about good customer service. Underline the simple or compound subject once and the simple or compound predicate twice.

   _____

Posttest

Instructions: In the space provided, write the letter of the correct answer.

1. What does the underlined word represent? *Our company needs incentives to retain its customers.* (5)
   a. subject
   b. predicate
   c. direct object
   d. indirect object

   1. _____

2. What mark of punctuation should follow this sentence? *Will you please return the merchandise in the envelope provided* (2)
   a. question mark
   b. period
   c. exclamation mark
   d. quotation mark

   2. _____

3. What is the complete subject in this sentence? *The expectations of taxpayers and utility customers are greater than ever before.* (3)
   a. greater than ever before
   b. customers
   c. The expectations
   d. The expectations of taxpayers and utility customers

   3. _____

4. What is the simple predicate in this sentence? *Customer support representatives usually offer three or four choices to callers.* (4)
   a. usually
   b. offer
   c. usually offer
   d. Customer support representatives usually offer

   4. _____

5. What is the direct object in the following sentence? *Effective managers always analyze a competitor's Web page.* (5)
   a. Web
   b. page
   c. analyze
   d. competitor's

   5. _____

6. Which sentence pattern does this statement represent? *Facial expression and body language are significant nonverbal signals.* (6)
   a. the subject-verb pattern
   b. the subject-linking verb-complement pattern
   c. the subject-verb-object pattern
   d. inverted order sentence

   6. _____

7. Which statement is not correct? (7)
   a. Infinitive phrases begin with *to.*
   b. Phrases cannot stand alone.
   c. Prepositional phrases include verbs.
   d. Phrases have neither subjects nor predicates.

   7. _____

8. Which sentence formation does this statement represent? *Are you still interested in our offer, or have you decided to wait for another month?* (8)
   a. simple sentence
   b. compound sentence
   c. complex sentence
   d. compound-complex sentence

   8. _____

9. What does this group of words indicate? *Place people before paperwork.* (9)
   a. a dependent clause
   b. a complete sentence
   c. a sentence fragment
   d. a run-on sentence

   9. _____

10. What does the underlined set of words represent? *We decided to contact potential international customers.* (7)

    a. infinitive phrase

    b. prepositional phrase

    c. dependent clause

    d. independent clause

10. _____

11. What is the complete predicate in this sentence? *One or two negative customer service experiences will cause us to lose customers.* (4)

    a. One or two negative customer service experiences

    b. cause us to lose customers

    c. will cause

    d. will cause us to lose customers

11. _____

12. What is the indirect object in the following sentence? *He gave us the statistics about customer satisfaction.* (5)

    a. statistics

    b. gave

    c. us

    d. satisfaction

12. _____

13. What is the simple subject in this sentence? *Brian and Sherri performed well as supervisors of the call center.* (3)

    a. Brian

    b. Sherri

    c. Brian and Sherri

    d. supervisors

13. _____

14. What mark of punctuation should follow this sentence? *She asked whether I wanted to work this weekend* (2)

    a. period

    b. explanation point

    c. question mark

    d. quotation mark

14. _____

15. Which statement describes this sentence? *We have several new products you should learn about them by Friday.* (6)

    a. The sentence is a normal word pattern.

    b. This is an example of a sentence fragment.

    c. This is an example of a run-on sentence.

    d. The sentence is in inverted word order.

15. _____

Unit 2

Reviewing Nouns and Pronouns

Chapter 4
Noun Functions and Plurals

Chapter 5
Compound and Possessive Nouns

Chapter 6
Capitalization

Chapter 7
Pronouns

Chapter 8
Pronoun/Antecedent Agreement

Chapter 4

Noun Functions and Plurals

OBJECTIVES

After you have studied this chapter and completed the exercises, you will be able to do the following:

1. Identify proper and common nouns.

2. Identify functions of nouns in sentences.

3. Recognize the differences between singular, plural, and collective nouns.

4. Apply rules to form plurals of singular nouns, numbers, letters, and abbreviations.

5. Apply rules to form plurals of foreign and irregular nouns.

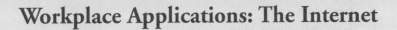

Workplace Applications: The Internet

The Internet is a massive worldwide network of computers. This computer network contains billions of documents, images, and information databases. Through the Internet, you can communicate with other people by using electronic mail. You can also research information, download computer programs, participate in discussion groups, play games, and shop.

Net Growth

Even the most farsighted Internet pioneers did not foresee the enormous growth and the tremendous impact that the Internet has had on global communications. Experts even have difficulty calculating how many billions of people use the Internet daily from either their homes or their workplaces around the world. Entrepreneurial organizations are continuously experimenting with ways to use the Internet, and most companies know that a presence on the Internet is a necessity for competing in business today.

Effectively communicating through the Internet will be an important part of your future. Because virtually anyone can put Web pages on the Internet, the information that is placed there may not always be accurate or reliable. You will need to take special care to evaluate all information sources. In addition, your study of business English will be vital to your ability to communicate effectively through computers and on the Internet.

Pretest

Instructions: In the space provided, write the letter of the correct answer.

1. Which line of nouns represents collective nouns? (3)
   a. boys, store, crews
   b. learn, department, object
   c. books, news, criteria
   d. audience, committee, jury

   1. _____

2. Which line of proper nouns is correct? (1)
   a. TVs, Grand canyon, New York city
   b. january, C's, Adelman Cleaners
   c. CD-ROMs, Dr. Walters, College of the Redwoods
   d. Randy Sabien, university of North Carolina, Pope and Talbot

   2. _____

3. *Both students expressed an interest in the Internet demonstration.* (2)
   In this sentence, the noun *interest* is the:
   a. direct object.
   b. subject of the sentence.
   c. object of a preposition.
   d. indirect object.

   3. _____

4. *Lionel Hawkes, the company's investment counselor, checks several online stock reports daily.* In this sentence, the noun *counselor* is: (2)
   a. the subject of the sentence.
   b. an appositive.
   c. in direct address.
   d. the complement.

   4. _____

5. Which line of nouns is capitalized correctly? (1, 4, 5)
   a. Manila envelope, Carson lake, Nevada
   b. Aspirin, February, Jury
   c. The Ramseys, Integrity, Kilometer
   d. Lake Michigan, No., Google

   5. _____

6. *Tons of statistical data are available on the Internet.* What does the word *Internet* represent in this sentence? (2)
   a. an indirect object
   b. a predicate noun
   c. the object of a preposition
   d. an appositive

   6. _____

7. *Internet users can check the U.S. Postal Service Web site to calculate international and domestic mailing costs.* What does the word *users* represent in this sentence? (2)
   a. a simple subject
   b. a compound subject
   c. a direct object
   d. an indirect object

   7. _____

Instructions: In the space provided, write the letter or letters of the correct plural nouns. (4, 5)

8. a. sketches	b. businesses	c. prefixs	d. waltzs	**8.** _____
9. a. proofes	b. chiefs	c. halfs	d. leaves	**9.** _____
10. a. trolleys	b. vacancys	c. supplys	d. libraries	**10.** _____
11. a. studios	b. concertoes	c. portfolios	d. memoes	**11.** _____
12. a. basis	b. stimuli	c. formulas	d. criteria	**12.** _____
13. a. bldg.	b. bu	c. CPUs	d. Ds	**13.** _____
14. a. organization	b. necessities	c. millions	d. deskes	**14.** _____
15. a. locations	b. programmers	c. provider	d. sentences	**15.** _____

Chapter 2 was an overview of the parts of speech and their functions in sentences. In this chapter, as well as in Chapter 5, you will learn about nouns. Since nouns are highly visible parts of sentences, pay close attention to their many functions. In addition to understanding how nouns are used in sentences, you will learn rules for forming the plurals of nouns.

Classes of Nouns

Nouns name persons, places, and things. Nouns can also identify activities, ideas, and qualities.

Persons

friend	programmer	Queen Elizabeth

Places

city	lake	Glacier National Park

Things

e-mail	desk	software

Activities

printing	talking	filing

Ideas and Qualities

freedom	courage	value

Common and Proper Nouns

All nouns belong to one of two classifications—common nouns or proper nouns. *Common nouns* refer to general persons, places, and things. Do not capitalize common nouns. *Proper nouns* refer to specific persons, places, or things. Capitalize proper nouns.

Common Nouns

magazine	textbook	corporation	dishonesty

Proper Nouns

Microsoft	January	University of West Virginia

Some nouns in trademarks or names of items containing proper nouns were previously capitalized. However, because they have become everyday words, words such as the following no longer require capitalization:

aspirin	e-mail	manila envelope
nylon	magic marker	roman numerals

NOTES

Reference Manual

Refer to a reference manual, such as *The Gregg Reference Manual,* for additional information on common and proper nouns.

CHECKPOINT 4.1

Go to the
Web

Checkpoint 4.1
for more skills practice on this topic.

A. **Instructions:** *Identify the nouns in the following list of words. Underline common nouns once and proper nouns twice. Some words may be used as other parts of speech.*

1. attitude
2. heavy
3. studios
4. Colby
5. Orlando
6. connection
7. years

8. Becker & Associates
9. resign
10. electronic
11. modems
12. achievement
13. Seattle
14. footnote

15. Lake Superior
16. protection
17. shortest
18. Rodriguez
19. directories
20. professional

B. **Instructions:** *Underline the common nouns once and proper nouns twice in the following paragraph.*

Virtual or online classes are prevalent in many educational institutions. Students take online classes with others who share their interests and skills. Some online students meet occasionally, but other students may never meet their classmates or their instructor. Students in one class may be from Japan, Brazil, or Sweden with the common language of English. A benefit of virtual education is that more people have access to college courses.

Functions of Nouns

Nouns appear in different locations in a sentence and assume various roles depending on their positions. In this section, you will learn the uses of nouns and their placement in sentences. You also will see how nouns are used as appositives and in direct address.

Nouns Used as Simple or Compound Subjects

Nouns often appear as *simple* or *compound subjects* of sentences. Their usual placement in the sentence is before the verb.

The number of Web ads has increased tremendously in the last five years.
(The common noun *number* is a simple subject.)

Yahoo! and Google are popular online search engines.
(The proper nouns *Yahoo!* and *Google* represent a compound subject.)

Nouns Used as Direct Objects

A direct object often receives the action of a verb. A direct object appears after the verb. Direct objects may be singular or plural.

Noun Functions and Plurals

My company uses Web-based <u>services</u>.

(The common noun *services* is the direct object.)

Nouns Used as Indirect Objects

An indirect object usually appears before a direct object and directly after a verb in a sentence. Indirect objects usually follow verbs such as *buy, sell, send, ask,* and *give.*

I sent <u>Tony</u> the updated figures for the network configuration.

(The proper noun *Tony* is the indirect object of the verb *sent. Tony* answers the question *To whom?*)

Nouns Used as Objects of Prepositions

A prepositional phrase consists of a preposition, the object of the preposition, which is a noun or pronoun, and its modifiers. More than one prepositional phrase may appear in a sentence.

I send a check <u>to my Internet service provider</u> every month.

(In the prepositional phrase *to my Internet service provider,* the preposition is *to* and the object of the preposition is *provider,* which is a noun.)

Nouns Used as Subject Complements (Predicate Nouns)

A subject complement (predicate noun) follows a linking verb and renames the subject.

Jane White is our technical information <u>specialist</u>.

(The subject complement [predicate noun] *specialist* renames the subject *Jane White.*)

Nouns Used as Appositives

The term *appositive* means that one noun renames another noun or pronoun. The appositive immediately follows the noun it renames.

Jane White, our technical information <u>specialist</u>, recommended that we select a new service provider.

(The common noun *specialist* renames and follows the proper noun *Jane White.*)

Tim Dahill, our <u>programmer</u>, is attending a Web site design workshop this week.

(The common noun *programmer* renames and follows the proper noun *Tim Dahill.*)

Nouns Used as Direct Address

A noun in direct address names the individual being addressed.

<u>Lindsey</u>, please check our Web site for the events scheduled for next week.

(*Lindsey* is the proper noun and the person being addressed.)

You know, <u>Liz</u>, your research on the intranet project was invaluable.

(*Liz* is the proper noun and the person being addressed.)

NOTES

Looking Back

Review the sections on direct objects, indirect objects, objects of prepositions, and subject complements in Chapter 3.

PUNCTUATION ALERT!

Appositive

An appositive is set off from the rest of a sentence by commas when it is not needed to identify the noun that it follows.

PUNCTUATION ALERT!

Direct Address

Set off words in direct address with commas.

CHECKPOINT 4.2

Go to the
Web

Checkpoint 4.2
for more skills practice on this topic.

Instructions: *For each of the underlined nouns in the sentences that follow, select its function from the following:* **Subj** *(subject),* **DO** *(direct object),* **IO** *(indirect object),* **OP** *(object of preposition),* **Comp** *(subject complement),* **App** *(appositive), or* **DA** *(direct address). In the space provided, write the abbreviation for the function.*

1. The new search engine's capabilities improved <u>service</u> *DO* _____
    to our users.

2. Some large companies have investigated the _____
    <u>advantages</u> of intranets, which are basically Internets
    within the firms.

3. Thanks, <u>Beth</u>, for your assistance in organizing the *DA* _____
    <u>demonstrations</u> by our service providers.

4. "This Week on the Internet," a local weekly *APP* _____
    newspaper <u>column</u>, always has good advice.

5. Computers are popular <u>products</u> to purchase online. *OP* _____

6. Our department submitted an <u>analysis</u> of online _____
    financial transactions.

7. Chuck submitted a request for new <u>passwords</u> in his *Comp* _____
    department.

8. <u>Bruce</u>, please check last week's hits and follow up on *DA* _____
    the promising leads.

9. The supervisor gave <u>Carrie</u> the list of related Web sites *IO* _____
    to visit for her research project.

10. Grant Morrison, Mrs. Chin's <u>assistant</u>, maintains our *A* _____
    intranet firewall.

Plural Forms of Nouns

Singular and Plural Nouns

A *singular noun* names one person, place, thing, activity, idea, or quality. A *plural noun* names two or more persons, places, things, ideas, or qualities. To form the plural of most common and proper nouns, add *s* to the singular noun. Use a dictionary when you are not sure about the spelling of a plural noun.

Singular Nouns	Plural Nouns
code	codes
password	passwords
Crawford	the Crawfords

NOTES

Looking for Plurals

Most dictionaries include only those plural noun forms that do not require simply adding an *s* or *es*.

Collective Nouns

A collective noun names a group of persons or things. If a group acts as a unit, the collective noun is singular. If the sentence implies that the members of a team, committee, etc., are acting individually, the collective noun is plural. The following words are collective nouns:

committee	team	department
crew	jury	group
audience	family	

The committee announced <u>its</u> choice of an online leadership course.

(The committee is acting as one group. In this sentence, *committee* is singular and requires the singular pronoun *its*.)

The department received questionnaires concerning online courses and were asked to return <u>their</u> responses by Friday.

(Department members will act individually; therefore, the plural pronoun *their* is required.)

Go to the
Web

Checkpoint 4.3
for more skills practice on this topic.

CHECKPOINT 4.3

Instructions: *Underline each singular noun once and each plural noun twice. Circle each collective noun.*

1. Most employees search for information on the Internet.

2. Carson uses colors in his Web ads and presentations to attract a large audience.

3. An online forum usually covers one topic.

4. The board is expanding its international e-commerce activities.

5. A browser allows users to navigate the Internet and browse the Web.

6. A "flame" is an angry online message.

7. Readers often ignore detailed, lengthy ad copy on an electronic screen.

8. Students search for jobs in health occupations on the Internet.

9. The panel prepared a comprehensive report of privacy issues.

10. Reference librarians provide search services for cardholders.

Nouns Ending in *ch, sh, s, x,* or *z*

If a singular noun or surname (last name) ends in a *ch, sh, s, x,* or *z* sound, form the plural by adding *es.*

Singular Nouns	Plural Nouns
batch	batches
business	businesses
wish	wishes
fax	faxes
waltz	waltzes

Exceptions:

quiz	quizzes
loch	lochs
Surnames	**Plural Surnames**
Gomez	the Gomezes
Fitch	the Fitches
Fox	the Foxes

Nouns Ending in *f*, *fe*, or *ff*

Many singular nouns ending in *f*, *fe*, or *ff* require only adding an *s* for their plural forms. To form the plurals of other singular nouns ending in *f* or *fe*, change the *f* or *fe* to *ve* and add an *s*. Both forms are acceptable for a few nouns. Use the dictionary's preferred spelling, which is the spelling that is listed first.

Singular Nouns	Plural Nouns
proof	proofs
staff	staffs
life	lives
yourself	yourselves
wharf	wharves or wharfs

CHECKPOINT 4.4

Go to the
Web

Checkpoint 4.4
for more skills practice on this topic.

Instructions: In the space provided, write the plural of the following nouns:

1. loss _____
2. inch _____
3. chef _____
4. thief _____
5. virus _____
6. glitch _____
7. Sanchez _____

8. tariff _____
9. tax _____
10. bus _____
11. duplex _____
12. blitz _____
13. scarf _____
14. half _____

Do This

the Wolfs

the Murphys

Do Not Do This

the Wolves

the Murphies

Do not change surname spellings when forming their plurals.

Nouns Ending in *y*

When a noun ends in *y* and the letter before the *y* is a *vowel,* add an *s* to make the noun plural.

Singular Nouns	Plural Nouns
attorney	attorneys
holiday	holidays
Casey	the Caseys

When a noun ends in *y* and the letter before *y* is a *consonant,* change *y* to *i* and add *es* to make the noun plural.

Singular Nouns	Plural Nouns
company	companies
copy	copies
entry	entries
quantity	quantities

Nouns Ending in *o*

When a noun ends in *o* and is preceded by a vowel, add an *s* to form the plural.

Singular Nouns	Plural Nouns
portfolio	portfolios
video	videos
ratio	ratios

When a noun ends in *o* and is preceded by a consonant, add *s* or *es* to form the plural. Add an *s* to a singular musical term that ends in *o.* Some plural forms are acceptable with either *s* or *es.* When in doubt, refer to a dictionary for the preferred spelling.

Singular Nouns	Plural Nouns
logo	logos (add *s*)
memo	memos
macro	macros
veto	vetoes (add *es*)
potato	potatoes
echo	echoes
zero	zeros/zeroes (add *s* or *es*)
cargo	cargos/cargoes

Add an *s* to a singular musical term that ends in *o.*

piano	pianos
alto	altos

Go to the
Web

Checkpoint 4.5
for more skills practice on this topic.

Instructions: *In the space provided, write the plurals of the following nouns. Use a dictionary if you are uncertain about the plural forms. If more than one form is acceptable, write both forms of the plural.*

1. community _____
2. delay _____
3. O'Riley _____
4. photo _____
5. entry _____
6. dictionary _____

7. stereo _____
8. hero _____
9. beneficiary _____
10. ego _____
11. smiley _____
12. solo _____

Irregular Noun Plurals and Special Nouns

Some singular nouns have irregular plurals. The plural forms change within the nouns or at the end of the nouns. Use a dictionary if you are not sure of the correct forms.

Singular Nouns	Plural Nouns
man	men
foot	feet
mouse	mice
goose	geese
child	children

Some nouns have the same singular and plural forms. These nouns do not need an *s* to make them plural.

Singular Nouns	Plural Nouns
sheep	sheep
species	species
Chinese	Chinese
series	series
corps	corps

Do This	**Do Not Do This**
Pronounce the word *corps* as "core" (sing.) or "cores" (pl.).	Pronounce the word *corps* as "corpse."

The spelling is the same for the singular and plural forms of *corps*.

Some nouns that end in *s* look like plurals. Depending on their use, they may have singular meanings.

news	physics	statistics
ethics	politics	economics

Most nouns that represent ideas or qualities have no plural forms.

honesty	patience	integrity

Some nouns are never singular.

proceeds	savings	credentials
earnings	dues	

Go to the
Web

Checkpoint 4.6
for more skills practice on this topic.

 CHECKPOINT 4.6

Instructions: In the space provided, write the plural forms of the following nouns:

1. series _____
2. tooth _____
3. athletics _____
4. trout _____
5. woman _____

6. courage _____
7. gentleman _____
8. decency _____
9. goods _____
10. foot _____

Foreign Nouns

Foreign nouns may use foreign plural forms or English plural forms. Some nouns use both forms, although one form may be preferred over the other, or each form may have its own definition. Different dictionaries have different preferences. Use a dictionary if you are uncertain about a spelling.

Foreign Singular Nouns	Foreign Plurals	English Plurals
syllabus	syllabi (pref.)	syllabuses
analysis	analyses	
appendix	appendices	appendixes (pref.)
index	indices (math)	indexes (books)
criterion	criteria (pref.)	criterions
memorandum	memoranda	memorandums (pref.)
phenomenon	phenomena (pref.)	phenomenons
curriculum	curricula	curriculums (pref.)

Chapter 4

CHECKPOINT 4.7

Go to the
Web

Checkpoint 4.7
for more skills practice on this topic.

Instructions: *In the space provided, write the preferred plural form of the following nouns. If a noun has two acceptable plural forms with different meanings, write both meanings. Use your dictionary if you are uncertain about forming foreign noun plurals.*

1. bureau _____
2. prospectus _____
3. antenna _____
4. formula _____
5. referendum _____
6. matrix _____
7. crisis _____
8. diagnosis _____

Abbreviations

Most abbreviations form their plurals by adding *s* to the singular. Abbreviations should be used sparingly in formal writing.

Singular Abbreviations	Plural Abbreviations
Ave.	Aves.
acct.	accts.
PC	PCs
No.	Nos.
mo.	mos.
yr.	yrs.

Measurements

Most measurement abbreviations are the same in their singular and plural forms. No periods are necessary with measurement abbreviations.

Singular Abbreviations		Plural Abbreviations	
foot	ft	feet	ft
ounce	oz	ounces	oz
pound	lb	pounds	lb
kilometer	km	kilometers	km

Numbers

Numbers expressed in figures form their plurals by adding *s*. Numbers expressed in words form their plurals according to the rules for nouns.

Singular Numbers	Plural Numbers
9	9s
1990	1990s
941	941s
thirty	thirties
four	fours

NOTES

Measurements
Refer to the measurements section in your reference manual.

Letters

Capital letters form their plurals by adding *s*. To avoid confusion, add an apostrophe before the *s* to the plurals of *A, I, M,* and *U*. Without an apostrophe, *A's* would be *As; I's* would be *Is; M's* would be *Ms;* and *U's* would be *Us*. All lowercase letters form their plurals by adding *'s*.

Singular Letters	Plural Letters
D	Ds
CD-ROM	CD-ROMs
I	I's
M	M's
a	a's

Do This

All of the A's in the advertising copy were difficult to read.

Do Not Do This

All of the As in the advertising copy were difficult to read.

Use apostrophes with the capital letters A, I, M, U to avoid confusion in reading copy.

Go to the
Web

Checkpoint 4.8
for more skills practice on this topic.

CHECKPOINT 4.8

Instructions: In the space provided, write the plurals of the following abbreviations:

1. ck. _____
2. C (letter) _____
3. yd _____
4. CPA _____
5. dept. _____
6. HMO _____
7. u (letter) _____
8. 9 (number) _____

Diagramming Sentences

The diagramming format continues with the placement of an appositive and a subject complement (the predicate noun). To diagram a simple sentence with a subject complement (predicate noun), draw a slanted line after the verb. To diagram a simple sentence with an appositive, place the appositive in parentheses after the noun it modifies. In the examples and exercises that follow, diagram only those parts of a sentence that you have worked with in previous chapters or that are introduced in this chapter.

Subject Complement (Predicate Noun)

The Internet is a source of information.

Internet	is \ source

Simple subject: *Internet*
Linking verb: *is*
Subject complement: *source*

He is an experienced programmer.

He	is \ programmer

Simple subject: *He*
Linking verb: *is*
Subject complement: *programmer*

Appositive

DiscoverNet, the Internet service provider company, contacted me.

DiscoverNet (company)	contacted	me

Simple subject: *DiscoverNet*
Simple verb: *contacted*
Direct object: *me*
Appositive: *company*

Mrs. Baird, the Web technician, complimented Tina.

Mrs. Baird (technician)	complimented	Tina

Simple subject: *Mrs. Baird*
Simple verb: *complimented*
Direct object: *Tina*
Appositive: *technician*

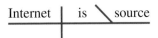

CHECKPOINT 4.9

Go to the
Web

Checkpoint 4.9
for more skills practice on
this topic.

Instructions: *In the space provided, diagram the following sentences. Diagram only the simple subject, simple verb, direct object, subject complement (predicate noun), and appositive.*

1. Laura, the assistant editor of Byte, wrote an article on privacy issues.

Copyright © by The McGraw-Hill Companies, Inc.

Noun Functions and Plurals

105

2. My favorite Internet site is amazon.com.

3. His organizational skills, a requirement for a Web designer, impressed the interviewers.

4. A laser printer, my newest electronic purchase, was a welcome addition in my home office.

5. Business Results, a local Internet consulting firm, obtained ten new clients.

6. The two Internet service provider companies are competitors.

Name _____ Date _____

PRACTICE 1

Identifying Plural Nouns

Instructions: Select the correct plural form from the words in parentheses. Write the word in the space provided.

Go to the
Web

Practice 1 Exercises
for more skills practice on this topic.

1. What are your state legislators' e-mail (*address, addresses*)?

   1. _____

2. We upgraded the (*PCs, PC's*) that were on the second floor.

   2. _____

3. The committee's (*vetos, vetoes*) caused significant (*delayes, delays*) in our new online advertising campaign.

   3. _____
   _____

4. Glen expected more in-depth (*discussiones, discussions*) with (*folks, folkes*) who used the Internet (*chatboxs, chatboxes*).

   4. _____
   _____
   _____

5. Some filtering procedures give parents control over how their (*childs, children*) use online services.

   5. _____

6. Does your e-mail system guarantee (*deliverys, deliveries*) or issue return (*receiptes, receipts*)?

   6. _____
   _____

7. Are you the type of person who calmly handles (*crisis, crises*) such as network downtime?

   7. _____

8. The (*Ruschs, Rusches*) asked for several (*analysis, analyses*) of online provider services.

   8. _____
   _____

9. I need more (*bookshelfs, bookshelves*) to store my (*DVDs, DVD's*).

   9. _____
   _____

10. Digital cameras became popular in the (*1990's, 1990s*).

    10. _____

11. The Yahoo! search engine directory shows thousands of health (*topices, topics*).

    11. _____

12. We discussed several (*hypothesis, hypotheses*), but we could not determine the cause for the network failure.

    12. _____

13. We named Keith and Ben the (*heros, heroes*) of the day because they fixed our network problem so quickly.

    13. _____

14. Her supervisor acknowledged her (*wishs, wishes*) for updated equipment.

    14. _____

15. The (*Bradleys, Bradleyes*) use the Internet to obtain their travel information.

    15. _____

Noun Functions and Plurals

Name _____ Date _____

16. E-mail messages replaced (*memoranda, memorandums*) as the form of interoffice communication.

16. _____

17. Many hospitals make free (*videos, videoes*) of newborn (*babys, babies*) to transmit over Internet e-mail.

17. _____
_____

18. Numerous new Web-based (*companys, companies*) do not make any profits in the first six (*months, monthes*).

18. _____
_____

19. A student designed the (*logos, logoes*) that we selected for our Web pages.

19. _____

20. Multimedia (*portfolioes, portfolios*) are necessary before interviewing with our company.

20. _____

Go to the
Web

Practice 2 Exercises
for more skills practice on this topic.

PRACTICE 2

Plural Forms of Nouns

Instructions: In the space provided, write the plural form of the underlined word or words.

1. Both branch office staff are now on the company network.

1. staves

2. The Bush and the Truax use e-mail to keep in touch during the holiday.

2. Bushes
Truaxes
holidays

3. Successful Internet company concentrate more on serving customers and less on elaborate graphic.

3. Companies
graphics

4. One of the criterion for employment in our company is the ability to be flexible.

4. Criteria

5. Dormitory rooms are equipped with network communications so that student can use their computer at any time.

5. Students
Computers

6. Online opportunities for students include searching other library for materials and registering for class.

6. lib
classes

7. You can obtain payroll tax information from the Internet when you are ready to complete your firm's 940 and 941.

7. 940s
941s

8. Business register their names on the Internet through a Web hosting service.

8. Businesses

Name _____ Date _____

9. Employers generally select nouns as key words in their online employment <u>search</u> for <u>employee</u>.

   9. *Searches*
      employees

10. The best online real estate services usually provide <u>photo</u> of the interiors and exteriors of the <u>property</u>.

    10. *photos*
        properties

11. Internet entrepreneurs find that products such as books, airline tickets, and <u>CD</u> are popular sales items.

    11. *CDs*

12. Only government <u>agency</u>, <u>university</u>, and large companies had Internet access in the <u>eighty</u>.

    12. *agencies*
        universities
        eightys

13. <u>Family</u> buy <u>thousand</u> of <u>DVD</u> to use at home and to entertain their <u>child</u>.

    13. *families*
        thousands
        DVDs
        children

14. Some e-businesses lose over a million <u>dollar</u> a month.

    14. *dollars*

15. Business Internet Services uses the <u>alley</u> behind its <u>factory</u> for <u>delivery</u>.

    15. *alleys*
        factories
        deliveries

16. Kelly found several <u>brand</u> of coffee that were sold only on the Internet.

    16. *brands*

17. I found an interesting Web site on <u>tornado</u>.

    17. *tornados*

18. Drs. Cortez and Ransforth use the Internet to research many of their <u>diagnosis</u>.

    18. *diagnoses*

19. <u>Curriculum</u> are changing because of the research <u>capability</u> on the Internet.

    19. *Curriculums*
        capabilities

20. Pat showed me a Web page displaying pictures of different <u>species</u> of fish.

    20. _____

Noun Functions

Instructions: For each underlined noun in the sentences that follow, select its function from the following: **Subj** *(subject),* **DO** *(direct object),* **IO** *(indirect object),* **OP** *(object of preposition),* **Comp** *(subject complement),* **App** *(appositive), or* **DA** *(direct address). Write the abbreviation of the function in the space provided.*

1. The <u>shelves</u> were not strong enough to hold our technical information manuals.

   1. _____

2. Shoua bookmarks her Web <u>site</u> for quick <u>access</u> later.

   2. _____

3. The Internet has forced cooperation among competing <u>countries</u>.

   3. _____

Name _____ Date _____

4. Lynn, did you know that Internet cafes are common throughout the world?

4. _____

5. Nuo Vang and Paula Olinski are the new language specialists in our Web design division.

5. _____

Noun Usage

Instructions: *Write two sentences using the plural forms of the following nouns. On line **a**, use the noun as the subject of the sentence. On line **b**, use the noun as the direct object of the sentence. Answers will vary.*

1. company

a. _____

b. _____

2. network

a. _____

b. _____

3. survey

a. _____

b. _____

Noun Applications

Instructions: *Correct errors in plural forms and capitalization. Write each sentence correctly in the space provided.*

1. After reviewing many internet sources, I completed two spec and sent them to the companys that met all my criterion.

_____

_____

_____

2. One association for Accountants has partnershipes with several e-learning institutions to offer Online Courses to CPA's.

_____

_____

_____

Name _____ Date _____

PRACTICE 3

Proofreading

*Instructions: Proofread and compare the two sentences in each group. If they are the same, write **Yes** in the space provided. If they are not the same, write **No.** Use the first sentence as the correct copy. If you find errors in the second sentence, underline them.*

1. CDnow Inc. is a cyberstore that can offer every U.S. jazz album as well as thousands of imports.

   CDNow Inc. is a cyberstore that can offer U.S. jazz as well as thousands of imports.

2. Many music companies realize that a presence on the Internet is important for reaching younger customers.

   Many music companys realize that a presence on the Internet is important for reaching younger customer.

3. Online bill-paying services disburse funds within 24 hours.

   Online bill-paying services disburse funds within 24 hours.

4. Amazon, a popular bookstore on the Internet, informs customers via e-mail when new books arrive.

   Amazon, a popular bookstore, on the Internet, informs customer via e-mail when new books arrive.

5. Privacy issues and fraud are major concerns with online banking.

   Privacy issues and fraud are major concerns with online banking.

1. _____

2. _____

3. _____

4. _____

5. _____

Go to the
Web

Practice 3 Exercises
for more skills practice on this topic.

PRACTICE 4

Writing

In the prewriting stage, you choose your topic (what you want to say), your purpose (how to say it), and your audience (to whom you want to say it). The following procedures will help you in the prewriting process:

1. Identify several broad, general topics about which you might like to write. For example, you might identify the following:
   a. The Internet in Business   c. Internet Service Providers
   b. Education and the Internet   d. The Internet's Future

Go to the
Web

Practice 4 Exercises
for more skills practice on this topic.

Noun Functions and Plurals

Name _____ Date _____

2. For this exercise, assume that your selection is "Education and the Internet."

3. Identify several topics that you might write about this general topic. List them under the general topic. For the general topic "Education and the Internet," you might use the following topics:
   a. How your classes have changed because of the Internet
   b. How you use the Internet in class
   c. How you think the Internet will continue to change education
   d. How you think young children will use the Internet to learn

Instructions: In this writing assignment, choose a topic in Step 3 above. Write three statements that express the points that you want to make about this topic. Answers will vary.

_____

_____

_____

_____

_____

_____

PRACTICE 5

Identifying Plural Nouns

Instructions: Select the correct plural form from the words in parentheses. Write the word in the space provided.

1. Max registers for two online Web design (*class, classes*) each semester.

   1. _____

2. My bank offers such services as convenient (*ATM's, ATMs*), easy online banking, and reasonable safe-deposit (*boxs, boxes*).

   2. _____
   _____

3. In our last issue, we gave you (*overviews, overviewes*) that covered the (*basices, basics*) on browsers.

   3. _____
   _____

4. Laurie asked for help using search engines because she had difficulty obtaining (*matchs, matches*) to her (*inquiries, inquirys*).

   4. _____
   _____

5. Do more (*mans, men*) than (*womans, women*) use the Internet?

   5. _____
   _____

6. Many (*citys, cities*) have Web pages linked to local services.

   6. _____

7. We ordered several wireless (*mice, mouses*) for our laptop computers.

   7. _____

Name _____ Date _____

8. The two (*Cortezs, Cortezes*) who work in the online education department are related.

8. _____

9. The manager looked at three (*proofs, proofes*) of his firm's Web page before choosing one.

9. _____

10. The Web did not become popular until the (*1990s, 1990's*).

10. _____

11. We worked with a design team for months to create the right (*icons, icones*) for our Web page.

11. _____

12. Moniji Nursery had five (*criterion, criteria*) for their online order form.

12. _____

13. The quality of sound coming over the Internet is better than our (*stereos, steroes*) at home.

13. _____

14. Our class conducted several Internet (*searchs, searches*) before we found the information that we needed.

14. _____

15. The (*Duncans, Duncanes*) create animated Web pages.

15. _____

16. Rex knew that (*parenthesis, parentheses*) could not be used in a Web address.

16. _____

17. The total amount should have had two (*zeros, zeroes*) instead of three.

17. _____

18. John uses online ratings from Dun and Bradstreet to make financial (*analysis, analyses*) for his clients.

18. _____

19. Both (*CPA's, CPAs*) employed by Business Internet Services graduated from college in the late 1980s, 1980's).

19. _____
   _____

20. (*Multimediums, Multimedia*) collaborations have affected the daily work (*habits, habites*) of office workers.

20. _____
   _____

PRACTICE 6

Plural Form of Nouns

Instructions: In the space provided, write the plural form of the underlined word or words.

1. The <u>sheriff</u> from Sonoma and Napa <u>County</u> are using the Internet in law enforcement.

1. _____
   _____

2. Five <u>city</u> joined to develop a county Web site

2. _____

3. Laurie purchased her <u>dish</u> from the Internet store.

3. _____

Name _____ Date _____

4. Online <u>dictionary</u> are easy to use and provide quick <u>access</u> to words and <u>definition</u>.   4. _____
_____

5. The payroll department files our <u>W2</u> electronically.   5. _____

6. Nonie searched through five <u>batch</u> of printouts before finding the online job-hunting information.   6. _____

7. We use the Internet to find <u>DJ</u> in our area.   7. _____

8. I can find names, telephone numbers, and street <u>address</u> on the Internet.   8. _____

9. I used three search <u>engine</u> to find the perfect graphic image for my <u>Web</u> page.   9. _____

10. The number of <u>fax</u> that we receive today has decreased since the <u>1990</u>.   10. _____
_____

11. We spend several <u>hour</u> using the Internet each day.   11. _____

12. Joe reads about American <u>politics</u> on c-span.org.   12. _____

13. All new employees are required to watch software instructional <u>video</u>.   13. _____

14. Some higher education institutions offer hardware and software discounts in their <u>library</u>.   14. _____

15. Many <u>child</u> have access to the Internet at <u>school</u>.   15. _____

16. Lawrence uses the Internet to buy Alaskan <u>salmon</u>.   16. _____

17. Yvonne defended her <u>integrity</u> when Rich called her cyberphobic.   17. _____

18. You can use two <u>browser</u> and switch back and forth between them.   18. _____

19. My online class has a private chatroom for <u>conversation</u> about the course.   19. _____

20. Our company experienced a tremendous <u>savings</u> by paying yearly for Internet access.   20. _____

Noun Functions

Instructions: For each underlined noun in the sentences below, select its function from the following: **Subj** *(subject),* **DO** *(direct object),* **IO** *(indirect object),* **OP** *(object of preposition),* **Comp** *(subject complement),* **App** *(appositive), or* **DA** *(direct address). Write the abbreviation of the function in the space provided.*

1. <u>Eddie</u> posted three entries on the Web site in an attempt to win a trip to Hawaii.   1. _____

Name _____   Date _____

2. Louis Vucebcui is a food <u>enthusiast</u> who enjoys   2. _____
   participating in food-related newsgroups on
   the Internet.

3. David Granger, a computer security <u>expert</u>, gave   3. _____
   us suggestions on protecting our <u>computers</u>.

4. Today's employers expect their <u>employees</u> to use   4. _____
   the Internet.

5. We added several accessories to the laptop   5. _____
   <u>computer</u>.

Noun Usage

Instructions: Write two sentences using the plural forms of the following nouns. On line *a*, use the noun as the subject of the sentence. On line *b*, use the noun as the direct object of the sentence. Answers will vary.

1. resource

   a. _____

   b. _____

2. community

   a. _____

   b. _____

3. logo

   a. _____

   b. _____

Noun Applications

Instructions: Correct errors in plural forms and capitalization. Write each sentence correctly in the space provided.

1. Larry found databases with thousand of detailes, sketchs, and
   photoes.

   _____

   _____

   _____

2. Check internet sources for information on Product Reviewes,
   Discussion Forums, and Prices for your PDA's.

   _____

   _____

   _____

Name _____ Date _____

PRACTICE 7

Proofreading

*Instructions: Proofread and compare the two sentences in each group. If they are the same, write **Yes** in the space provided. If they are not the same, write **No**. Use the first sentence as the correct copy. If you find errors in the second sentence, underline them.*

1. Womenservices.com covers subjects relating to work, human interest, and self-improvement.

   Women services.com covers subjects relating to work, human interests, and self-improvement.

   1. _____

2. Researchers go online to the Library of Congress, the Smithsonian, and major universities around the world to find the information that they need.

   Researchers go online to the Library of congress, the Smithsonian, and major universities around the world to fine the information that they need.

   2. _____

3. One of the advantages of distance education (online learning) is the opportunity to work at your own pace.

   One of the advantages of distance education (on-line learning) is the opportunities to work at your own paces.

   3. _____

4. Tablet PCs may have considerable impact on e-mail for users who may be away from their desks.

   Tablet PC's may have considerable impact on e-mail for users who may be away from their deskes.

   4. _____

5. Online editions of seminars offer employers greater flexibility in providing training to more workers.

   Online editions of seminars offer employers greater flexibility in providing training to more workers.

   5. _____

Name _____ Date _____

PRACTICE 8

Instructions: After reviewing Chapter 4, consider the new information that you learned about using nouns. Write a paragraph describing a noun or noun plural that you have been using incorrectly. Provide an example. Use simple sentence construction. Answers will vary.

_____

_____

_____

_____

_____

_____

_____

_____

_____

_____

_____

_____

_____

_____

_____

_____

_____

_____

Posttest

Instructions: In the space provided, write the letter of the correct answer.

1. Which word is a collective noun? (3)
   a. dictionary
   b. country
   c. disk
   d. team

   1. _____

2. Which line of proper nouns is correct? (1)
   a. PCs, Great falls, Black Hills
   b. The university of Texas, Pike's Peak, Disneyland
   c. Great America, Pima College, Kansas City
   d. America online, Des Moines, Southern Illinois University

   2. _____

3. *The search engine looks for subjects based upon your criteria.* (2)
   In this sentence, *subjects* is the:
   a. direct object.
   b. complement.
   c. indirect object.
   d. object of the preposition.

   3. _____

4. *Shelley Ling, the district manager, is responsible for our online advertising.* (2)
   In this sentence, *manager* is:
   a. the subject of the sentence.
   b. an appositive.
   c. a direct address.
   d. the complement.

   4. _____

5. Which line of nouns is capitalized correctly? (1, 4, 5)
   a. city, english, french fries
   b. business, internet, CD-ROMs
   c. Cell Phone, Rotary Club, stock
   d. Starbucks, Cobb County, company

   5. _____

6. *Sandra monitors our antivirus software.* What does the word *software* represent in this sentence? (2)
   a. a direct object
   b. an indirect object
   c. the object of a preposition
   d. a subject complement

   6. _____

7. *Spyware is unwanted software on a hard drive.* What does the word *Spyware* represent in this sentence? (2)
   a. a direct address
   b. a singular subject
   c. an appositive
   d. a compound subject

   7. _____

POSTTEST: *Looking Back*

Instructions: *In the space provided, write the letter or letters of the correct plural nouns. (4, 5)*

8. a. matches	b. boxes	c. faxs	d. glasses	**8.** _____
9. a. proofes	b. cliffs	c. yourselfs	d. lives	**9.** _____
10. a. keyes	b. facilitys	c. entries	d. copys	**10.** _____
11. a. pianoes	b. ratios	c. logoes	d. potatoes	**11.** _____
12. a. analyses	b. memorandums	c. indexes	d. diagnosis	**12.** _____
13. a. accts.	b. lbs	c. C's	d. 1990's	**13.** _____
14. a. series	b. men	c. vetos	d. 1970's	**14.** _____
15. a. physics	b. echos	c. attornies	d. PCs	**15.** _____

Chapter 5

Compound and Possessive Nouns

OBJECTIVES

After you have studied this chapter and completed the exercises, you will be able to do the following:

1. Form plurals and possessives of compound nouns.

2. Recognize nominative, objective, and possessive cases of nouns.

3. Differentiate between plural and possessive forms of nouns.

4. Form possessives of singular, plural, and irregular nouns.

5. Identify correct forms of organization, association, and company names.

6. Form possessives of abbreviations, joint or separate ownerships, and understood ownership.

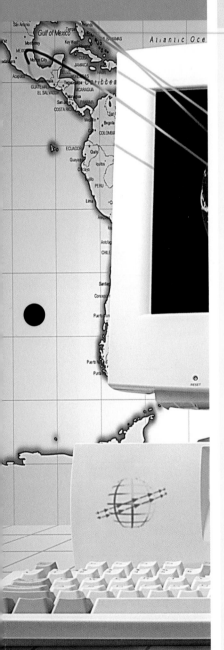

Workplace Applications: The World Wide Web

The World Wide Web is a graphical system on the Internet. A Web site is a location where an individual, a university, a government agency, or a company stores Web pages. Millions of Web sites offer information on everything from government documents to pictures.

The number of users of the World Wide Web is impossible to gauge. Some see the Internet as the world's biggest mall, where users participate in online auctions or shop for clothes or cars. Some spend time chatting, while others use the Internet for research.

Web Browsing

"Surf the Net" applies to browsing the vast storehouse of information on the World Wide Web. Searching the Internet is done by using search engines, which help categorize and find information. Search engines use unique formulas to index and score Web sites. Each search engine works in a different way, and some are more powerful than others. To save time and to use the Web more efficiently, meta search engines can search multiple search engines and combine all the responses on one results page.

The Web has changed forever how we communicate, access information, shop, and do research. In many career fields, a person's future success is enhanced by how effectively and productively he or she can use the extensive resources available on the Internet.

Pretest

Instructions: In the space provided, write the letter of the correct answer.

1. *The firm gave Maria a new password.* In this sentence, what case does the noun *Maria* illustrate? (2)
   a. the nominative case
   b. the possessive case
   c. the objective and nominative cases
   d. the objective case

   1. _____

2. Which statement represents the correct possessive form? (4)
   a. The firm's Internet exposure has steadily increased.
   b. The firms Internet exposure has steadily increased.
   c. The firm Internets' exposure has steadily increased.
   d. The firms Internet exposures' has steadily increased.

   2. _____

3. Which statement represents the correct possessive form? (4)
   a. Mens and women's reactions to technological changes differ.
   b. Men's and women's reactions to technological changes differ.
   c. Mens' and womens' reactions to technological changes differ.
   d. Mens and womens' reactions to technological changes differ.

   3. _____

4. Which statement is written correctly? (3)
   a. Web indexes' are important tools for searching sites' online.
   b. Web indexes are important tools for searching sites' online.
   c. Web indexes are important tools for searching sites online.
   d. Web indexes' are important tools' for searching sites online.

   4. _____

5. Which line of compound words is correct? (1)
   a. print-outs, workstations
   b. postmasters, trademarks
   c. data bases, crossexaminations
   d. driveins, notary publics

   5. _____

6. Which statement represents the correct plural form of a compound noun? (1)
   a. A number of technology firms have been involved in recent takeover's.
   b. A number of technology firms have been involved in recent take overs.
   c. A number of technology firms have been involved in recent take-overs.
   d. A number of technology firms have been involved in recent takeovers.

   6. _____

7. Which statement is written correctly? (1, 3)
   a. Web-based technology firms often yield high stockholders dividends.
   b. Web-based technology firms often yield high stockholder's dividends.
   c. Web-based technology firms often yield high stockholders' dividends.
   d. Web-based technology firms often yield high stock-holders' dividends.

   7. _____

8. *Rodney Scobie, our new editor in chief of Internet Update, has excellent plans for revising our newsletter.* In this sentence, what case does the noun *editor in chief* illustrate? (2)
   a. the possessive case
   b. the objective case
   c. the nominative case
   d. the nominative and possessive cases

   8. _____

9. Which statement is written correctly? (3, 6)

    a. The FTC's (Federal Trade Commission) antifraud statute may soon cover spyware lawsuits.

    b. The FTCs' (Federal Trade Commission) antifraud statute may soon cover spyware lawsuits.

    c. The FTCs (Federal Trade Commission) antifraud statute may soon cover spyware lawsuits.

    d. The FTCs's (Federal Trade Commission) antifraud statute may soon cover spyware lawsuits.

9. _____

10. Which statement is written correctly? (3)

    a. One of our companys' technicians identified several ways to remove viruses from our net work.

    b. One of our company's technicians identified several ways to remove viruses' from our net work.

    c. One of our company's technicians identified several ways to remove viruses from our network.

    d. One of our companies' technicians identified several ways to remove virus's from our network.

10. _____

Instructions: In the space provided, write the letter or letters of the correct possessive or plural forms of nouns.

11. a. write-offs (1, 3)
    b. money's order amount
    c. a company's layoffs
    d. point of views

11. _____

12. a. stockholder's meeting (1, 6)
    b. three CPA's recommendations
    c. Delgado's home
    d. Rob and Kathy's car

12. _____

13. a. Kellogg's® cereals (3, 5)
    b. Pennsylvania Teacher's Association
    c. sale's meeting
    d. savings account balance

13. _____

14. a. AT&T's network (1,4,6)
    b. grandchildren's e-mails
    c. print-outs
    d. accounts payables

14. _____

15. a. a months' accumulation (3)
    b. a company's junk e-mail
    c. a spammer's message
    d. A Webmasters' experience

15. _____

Chapter Preview

You possess or own things; for example, your car, your clothes, your class notes, and your business English textbook. Although you may indicate possession with such words as *own* ("I own"), *belong* ("It belongs to me"), and *of* ("this book of mine"), you may use a quicker and easier way—the apostrophe (') or apostrophe and *s* ('s).

In using the apostrophe to indicate possession, you should follow the rules presented in this chapter. Your knowledge of plural nouns (Chapter 4) will also be useful in recognizing the possessive case.

Because of the changing nature of compound nouns, their plural and possessive features receive special attention in this chapter.

Compound Nouns

Compound nouns consist of two or more words. Some compound nouns are written as one word. Some are written as hyphenated words. Others are written as two words. Sometimes compound nouns go through changes in their forms from two words to hyphenated words to one word.

As compound nouns become more commonly used, they often become one word. Dictionaries may show spellings of compound nouns differently. Be sure to check a current dictionary if you are not certain about the correct forms of compound nouns.

One-Word Compound Nouns

Some compound nouns consist of two or more words combined into one word. To form the plurals of one-word compound nouns, follow the general rules for plurals.

One-Word Compound Nouns	Plural Forms
courthouse	courthouses
workstation	workstations
takeover	takeovers
printout	printouts
handful	handfuls
database	databases

(These compound nouns add *s* to form their plurals.)

businesswoman	businesswomen
chairman	chairmen

(These compound nouns have irregular plural forms.)

Hyphenated Compounds With Nouns

Some hyphenated compounds consist of a noun and another part of speech. To form the plurals of hyphenated compound nouns, make the *most important* word plural.

NOTES

Changing Rules

The word *online* is an example of a word that appears more frequently in current readings as one word rather than in its previous hyphenated form (on-line).

Hyphenated Compounds	Plural Forms
brother-in-law	brothers-in-law
passer-by	passers-by
court-martial	courts-martial (preferred)
cross-examination	cross-examinations
half-truth	half-truths

(The underlined words are the most important ones.)

Hyphenated Compounds Without Nouns

Some hyphenated compounds do not include noun elements. If the hyphenated compound word does not have a noun in it, add the *s* or *es* to the last word.

Compound Nouns	Plural Forms
write-off	write-offs
get-together	get-togethers
stand-in	stand-ins
free-for-all	free-for-alls
drive-in	drive-ins
run-through	run-throughs

(These hyphenated compounds do not have noun elements in them.)

Compound Nouns With Spaces

Some compound nouns consist of two words. To form the plurals of compound nouns separated by spaces, make the most important word plural.

Compound Nouns	Plural Forms
style sheet	style sheets
hard copy	hard copies
printer cartridge	printer cartridges
vice president	vice presidents
editor in chief	editors in chief
post office	post offices
chief of police	chiefs of police
rule of thumb	rules of thumb
account payable	accounts payable

(The underlined words are the most important ones.)

Looking Back

If any plural form is unfamiliar, review the section in Chapter 4 for the rule that you need. You may want to add the word and the plural to your list of difficult words.

CHECKPOINT 5.1

Go to the
Web

Checkpoint 5.1
for more skills practice on this topic.

Instructions: *In the space provided, write the plural form of each word.*

1. clipboard  *Clipboards*

2. cupful  *Cupfuls*

3.	attorney-at-law	_____	10.	department chairperson _____ _____
4.	vice admiral	_____	11.	notary public _____
5.	letterhead	_____	12.	follow-up _____
6.	layoff	_____	13.	paper clip _____
7.	bulletin board	_____	14.	cross-examination _____
8.	disk drive	_____	15.	half-gallon _____
9.	backup	_____		

Cases of Nouns

The term *case* refers to the different functions of words in sentences. For noun and pronoun use, there are three cases: nominative, objective, and possessive. Nouns (or pronouns) that act as subjects of a sentence, as appositives, or as subject complements are in the *nominative* case. Nouns (or pronouns) that act as direct objects, indirect objects, objects of a preposition, or objects of infinitives are in the *objective* case. *Possessive* case nouns do not retain the same forms; therefore, they require special attention.

The new Web site coordinator began work yesterday.

(*Coordinator* [subject] is used in the nominative case.)

Jane is our new Web site coordinator.

(*Coordinator* [subject complement] is used in the nominative case. *Coordinator* follows the linking verb *is* and identifies *Jane.*)

The department manager hired a new Web site coordinator.

(*Coordinator* [direct object] is used in the objective case.)

We still have not had a meeting with the new Web site coordinator.

(*Coordinator* [object of a preposition] is used in the objective case.)

I wanted to meet the new Web site coordinator, but she was in a meeting.

(*Coordinator* is used as the object of the infinitive.)

The new Web site coordinator's job was demanding.

(*Coordinator* changes to *coordinator's,* which is used in the possessive case. An *'s* indicates the possessive form.)

NOTES

Looking Ahead
Further coverage of the nominative and objective cases appears in Chapter 7.

Go to the
Web

Checkpoint 5.2
for more skills practice on this topic.

CHECKPOINT 5.2

A. **Instructions:** *In the space provided, indicate the case of the underlined word or words by writing one of the following abbreviations:* **Nom** *(nominative case),* **Obj** *(objective case), or* **Poss** *(possessive case).*

1. You should address your security <u>complaints</u> directly to the Web site <u>manager</u>. _____

Chapter 5

2. Web <u>users</u> enjoy sophisticated search <u>tools</u>. _____

3. Our <u>client's</u> Web design was unique. _____

4. The online <u>search</u> yielded two different e-mail <u>addresses</u> for Kimberlee Yee. _____

5. <u>Investors</u> can buy and sell hundreds of mutual <u>funds</u> online. _____

B. **Instructions:** *In the space provided, find the incorrect compound nouns and write them correctly.*

1. We use the post-office for bulk mailing. _____

2. Karin discovered many draw-backs to changing browsers. _____

3. The technology economy had many ups-turn this year. _____

4. Our programmers are brother-in-laws. _____

5. My co-workers telecommute one day a week. _____

Possessive Case Nouns

A possessive case noun shows that *someone* owns or possesses something else (another noun). A possessive case noun may also indicate a relationship between two nouns. An apostrophe and *s* (*'s*) or an apostrophe (*'*) indicates the possessive form of a noun.

<u>Gregg's</u> antivirus program requires regular updates.

(Gregg owns the program.)

Most supervisors appreciate their administrative <u>professionals'</u> Internet research skills.

(The administrative professionals possess the skills.)

<u>Sam's</u> friend recommended a successful Web site designer.

(*Sam* and *friend* indicate a relationship. Sam does not own or possess the friend.)

The <u>company's</u> employees quickly adapted to the updated network changes.

(*Company* and *employees* show a relationship. The company does not own or possess the employees.)

Possessive Singular Nouns

Form the possessive of a singular noun (one person, place, activity, thing, idea, or quality) by adding apostrophe and *s* (*'s*). Always look for the possessor of an item. The possessor (a noun) receives the apostrophe and *s* (*'s*) designation, not the item possessed (also a noun). The possessors are underlined in the following examples:

<u>Jack</u> owns a book.

(The possessive form becomes *Jack's book.*)

<u>Jack</u> owns several books.

(Note that it does not make a difference if Jack owns one book or many books, the possessor is Jack. Jack is a singular noun, and the possessive form becomes *Jack's books.*)

EDIT PATROL

In a newspaper headline:
Shot off woman's leg helps Nicklaus to 66.

PUNCTUATION ALERT!

Possessives
Use an apostrophe to form possessive nouns.

A student owns a computer.

(*Student* is a singular noun; the possessive form becomes *student's computer.*)

Charter Online has many customers.

(*Charter Online* is a singular noun; the possessive form becomes *Charter Online's customers.*)

The store owner has a Web site.

(The *store owner's Web site*)

A customer makes several payments.

(The *customer's payments*)

Possessive nouns modify another noun; therefore, they function as adjectives in sentences. The possessive noun usually appears immediately before another noun. In some cases, additional modifiers separate the possessive noun and the item being possessed.

An airline's record concerning on-time and safety information is available on the Internet.

(Two nouns appear consecutively. *Airline* is the possessor, and *record* is the item possessed. The possessive noun *airline* acts as an adjective indicating *what kind* of record.)

You can find out about an airline's on-time and safety records on the Internet.

(The two nouns are separated by the two modifiers, *on-time* and *safety.* The possessive noun *airline's* and the two modifiers act as adjectives indicating *what kind of* records.)

Do not confuse a plural noun ending in *s* with a possessive form. One way to test whether you have a possessive noun is to interchange the two nouns and put the word *of* between them. If the *of* phrase sounds all right in a sentence, you have a possessive case noun. In the following examples, the possessive nouns are underlined:

John's password was a good choice.

(The password of *John* was a good choice.)

When I changed jobs, I lost one week's salary.

(When I changed jobs, I lost the salary *of one week.*)

The college's access to high-tech firms was a major recruiting point.

(The access *of the college* to high-tech firms was a major recruiting point.)

Emily always proofreads a Web site's address.

(Emily always proofreads the address *of a Web site.*)

Go to the
Web

Checkpoint 5.3
for more skills practice on this topic.

CHECKPOINT 5.3

A. **Instructions:** *In the following phrases, underline the nouns that need apostrophes to show possession. Write these nouns correctly in the spaces provided.*

1.   the decision of our committee   _____

2.   the home page of the company   _____

3.   the database of the client   _____

Copyright © by The McGraw-Hill Companies, Inc.

B. **Instructions:** *Write the correct singular possessive noun in the blank line.*

1. Todds Internet service provider provides free antivirus software. _____

2. A customers complaints caused us to reevaluate our online security. _____

3. Jans online bank account is convenient. _____

4. This months online sales are high. _____

5. Microsofts president reported the third-quarter profits last week. _____

6. Many of Idahos colleges have online courses. _____

7. One of our editors comments significantly improved our Web page content. _____

Possessive Plural Nouns

Form the possessive of a plural noun that ends in *s* or *es* by adding only an apostrophe.

Singular Nouns	Plural Nouns	Plural Possessives
girl	girls	girls' books
secretary	secretaries	secretaries' vacations
attorney	attorneys	attorneys' cases
class	classes	classes' requirements

NOTES

Forming Possessive Plurals

To form a possessive plural noun, always make the singular noun plural before you form the possessive. Use the *of* phrase to determine whether you have a possessive noun.

Do This

All e-mail addresses of our clients are current.

Our Web sites have several interesting features.

Do Not Do This

All e-mail addresses' of our clients are current.

Our Web sites' have several interesting features.

Do not use an apostrophe just because you see a word ending in *es* or *s*.

Possessives of Irregular Plural Nouns

Form the possessive of a plural noun that does not end in *s* by adding apostrophe and *s* (*'s*).

Singular Nouns	Plural Nouns	Plural Possessives
woman	women	women's ideas
businessman	businessmen	businessmen's appointments
child	children	children's books

Compound and Possessive Nouns

Do This	Do Not Do This
The new sales figures	The new sales' figures
Our earnings projections	Our earnings' projections
My savings account balance	My savings' account balance
An economics class	An economics' class

Do not use an apostrophe with a descriptive adjective that ends in *s* and that provides identification only. Sometimes only a slight difference in wording will distinguish a descriptive adjective from a possessive.

Go to the
Web

Checkpoint 5.4
for more skills practice on this topic.

CHECKPOINT 5.4

A. **Instructions:** *Write the plural form for each noun on the first blank line. Write the plural possessive form for each noun on the second blank line.*

Singular Nouns	Plural Nouns	Possessive Plurals
1. investor	_____	_____
2. boss	_____	_____
3. browser	_____	_____
4. child	_____	_____
5. designer	_____	_____

B. **Instructions:** *Write the correct plural or plural possessive noun in the blank.*

1. Our programmers were (*heroes, heroes'*) for stopping unwanted e-mail. _____

2. At least two (*committees, committees'*) decisions were overturned by the CEO. _____

3. We uploaded the (*speakers, speaker's*) remarks to our Web page. _____

4. The (*employees, employees'*) passwords are confidential. _____

5. The number of (*visitors, visitors'*) to our Web site increased this month. _____

6. The (*networks, networks'*) in our building frequently have problems. _____

7. The (*administrators, administrators'*) thoroughly answered our questions. _____

Chapter 5

8. We anticipate several (*months, months'*) work to revise our Web page. _____

9. The three (*companies, companies'*) online Web sites look similar. _____

10. The (*womens, women's*) Web site design ideas received positive comments. _____

Forming Possessives

- To form the possessive of a singular noun add *'s*. [boy's]
- To form the possessive of a plural noun that does not end in *s*, add *'s*. [men's]
- To form the possessive of a plural noun ending in *s*, add *'*. [boys']

◼ CHECKPOINT 5.5

Instructions: *Underline plural nouns once and possessive nouns twice in the following sentences. If a possessive noun is required in the sentence, write the noun correctly in the space provided. If a sentence is correct, write **Yes** in the space provided.*

1. Unfortunately, the firms finances were disclosed through a scam referred to as "phishing." _____

2. Jasons Web design planning meeting was rescheduled. _____

3. The Web provides users an inexpensive way to sell products and distribute information. _____

4. The writers words clearly represented his beliefs and convictions about technological changes. _____

5. Lindas Internet search hints save me valuable research time. _____

6. We mailed Aprils Internet transactions report. _____

7. Advertisers should recognize the Webs strength. _____

8. The fourth version of the companys antivirus software will support Macintosh users. _____

9. Intranets were one of the fastest-growing technologies in the 1990s. _____

10. Too many fancy gimmicks in Web site designs often result in turning a viewers attention elsewhere. _____

Go to the
Web

Checkpoint 5.5

for more skills practice on this topic.

Separate and Joint Ownership

Use an apostrophe in all names of persons or companies to indicate *separate ownership* of an item or items. Use an apostrophe in the last of two or more names to show *joint ownership* of an item or items.

Richard's and Lee's e-commerce reports
(Richard had a separate e-commerce report or e-commerce reports, and Lee had a separate e-commerce report or e-commerce reports.)

Richard and Lee's e-commerce reports
(Richard and Lee had e-commerce reports that belonged to them jointly.)

Dell's and Apple's computers
(Both Dell and Apple have their own computers.)

Jean and Andy's Web site design office
(The Web site design office is owned jointly by Jean and Andy.)

Organization, Association, and Company Names

The names of organizations, associations, and companies may contain words that are either possessive or descriptive terms. Use the form that the company, organization, or association displays on its logo, product, or letterhead. Some use an apostrophe and *s* (*'s*); others do not.

Stokely's®

Kellogg's® Frosted Flakes

Bush's® baked beans

Vet's Club

Reader's Digest®

Ladies' Home Journal®

Wisconsin Sheriff's and Deputy Sheriff's Association

American Bankers Association

Citizens Political Committee

Pringles® potato chips

The Greater Madison Convention and Visitors Bureau

Go to the
Web

Checkpoint 5.6
for more skills practice on this topic.

CHECKPOINT 5.6

Instructions: *In the space provided, add the apostrophe or apostrophe s ('s) to show either separate or joint ownership.*

1. Bucholtz and Nardin lawn care company has a clever Web site. _____

2. Thomas and Marcy opinions indicated that they had strong feelings about changing our Web site marketing strategies. _____

3. The Online Education Association dues increased this year. _____

4. Yamika and Nobu online store won an award. _____

5. Symontox eliminated Charles and Liane positions when it merged last year. _____

6. Did you attend the Chamber of Commerce seminar on computer viruses? _____

Compound Nouns

Form the possessive of a singular compound noun by adding an apostrophe and *s* (*'s*) at the end of the word.

stockholder's share

businesswoman's office

chairperson's leadership

underwriter's recommendation

Form the possessive of a plural compound noun that ends in *s* by adding only an apostrophe at the end of the word.

stockholders' dividends

stand-ins' responsibilities

vice presidents' decisions

postmasters' paperwork

Form the possessive of a plural compound noun that does not end in *s* by adding an apostrophe and *s* at the end of the word.

NOTES

Possessive Compound Nouns

All compound nouns are made possessive at the end of the word or words.

sisters-in-law's careers   chiefs of police's duties

editors in chief's columns   businessmen's remarks

Abbreviations

Form the possessive of a singular abbreviation by adding an apostrophe and *s* (*'s*). Form the possessive of a plural abbreviation by adding only an apostrophe (*'*).

FBI's investigation

CEO's decision

William T. Burns Jr.'s question

The Shefley Co.'s promotions

HMOs' restrictions (more than one HMO)

Ph.D.s' speeches (more than one Ph.D.)

Time and Amounts

Form the possessive of a noun expressing time or an amount in the same way as other nouns.

moment's delay   a dollar's worth

a week's vacation   two weeks' pay

Understood Possession

Use an apostrophe and *s* (*'s*) or an apostrophe (*'*) to show possession of a noun that is understood but not stated.

Kathryn's suggestions for domain names were more detailed than Matt's.

(*Suggestions* is the missing but understood noun and refers to *Matt's suggestions*.)

This year's online sales increased 20 percent over last year's.

(*Online sale*s [refers to last year's] is the missing but understood noun.)

CHECKPOINT 5.7

Go to the
Web

Checkpoint 5.7
for more skills practice on this topic.

Instructions: *Underline the incorrect possessive forms in the following sentences. Write the correct forms in the spaces provided. If the sentence is correct, write* **Yes** *in the space provided.*

1. The owner of Werewolf Internet Services has five year's experience with commercial accounts.   _____

2. DRI's financial advice was research-based, but a competitors was not.   _____

3. When our company merged with StarNet, some employees received three months' separation pay.   _____

4. The district attorney's offices in both counties became involved in the online fraud dispute. _____

5. My son-in-law's employer is an experienced Webmaster. _____

6. Matt said that his sites' popularity was due to its unique name. _____

7. This CPAs' online tax advice has received favorable comments. _____

8. The narrative on Cummings Inc.'s Web page was too lengthy. _____

9. This semester's online classes are more difficult than last semesters. _____

10. A proofreaders' corrections are important in producing an error-free Web site. _____

Diagramming Sentences

In Chapter 3, you learned that a direct object appears on the same line as the simple subject and verb in diagrammed sentences. An indirect object appears under the verb. Note the slanted line and the horizontal connecting line under the verbs in the examples. The indirect object is written on the horizontal line. You will be asked to diagram only those parts of a sentence that you have worked with in previous chapters or that are introduced in this chapter.

Betty gave me some online research tips.

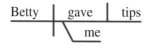

Simple subject: *Betty*

Simple verb: *gave*

Direct object: *tips*

Indirect object: *me*

Place a possessive noun on a slanted line beneath the noun that it modifies. The possessive noun functions as an adjective.

We hired Marty's friend to revise the layouts.

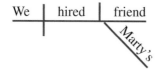

Simple subject: *We*

Simple verb: *hired*

Direct object: *friend*

Possessive noun: *Marty's*

CHECKPOINT 5.8

Go to the
Web

Checkpoint 5.8
for more skills practice on
this topic.

Instructions: *In the space provided, diagram the following sentences. Diagram only the following parts: simple subject, verb, direct object, indirect object, appositive, subject complement, possessive noun.*

1. The company gave the university its unused computer equipment.

2. Did Carole send you an e-mail message?

3. They awarded our company the Web Site Progress designation.

4. Janet's design included additional diagrams.

5. Sheila brought me the preliminary Internet cost figures.

Name _____ Date _____

PRACTICE 1

Compounds, Plurals, and Possessives

Instructions: Select the correct word in parentheses, and write it in the space provided.

1. I have one (*week's, weeks*) time to submit the new Web page.

   1. _____

2. I wanted to check several online (*travelers, travelers'*) sources before I asked for my travel (*agents', agent's*) advice.

   2. _____
   _____

3. Recent Internet scams have attracted the (*worlds, world's*) attention.

   3. _____

4. (*Viruses, Viruses'*) can destroy hard drives or scramble the content of important documents.

   4. _____

5. Web (*advertisers', advertiser's*) messages should not be complicated or lengthy.

   5. _____

6. Unlike some online (*provider's, providers'*) e-mail services, (*Juno's, Junos'*) is inexpensive.

   6. _____
   _____

7. My supervisor always wants a summary of the (*days', day's*) online sales.

   7. _____

8. Hypertext links within the (*news, new's*) article automatically took me to seven related items.

   8. _____

9. Successful companies need to provide different ways for (*feed back, feed-back, feedback*) such as 800 numbers, fax, or e-mail.

   9. _____

10. (*Kelly's and Chuck's, Kelly and Chuck's*) online catalog was a major reason for increased sales.

    10. _____

11. Club Web offers (*childrens', children's*) safety tips, games, and (*kids', kid's*) software.

    11. _____
    _____

12. Most nonprofit (*company's, companies'*) names end with the extension *.org*.

    12. _____

13. Check your (*ISP's, ISPs'*) written policies if you are concerned about invasion of privacy.

    13. _____

14. We have too many (*passwords, passwords'*) and (*PIN's, PINs*) to remember.

    14. _____
    _____

15. Two (*employees, employees'*) answer all (*clients', client's*) e-mail inquiries.

    15. _____
    _____

Name _____ Date _____

Identifying Possessive Forms

Instructions: Write the correct singular possessive form in the first blank, the plural form in the second blank, and the plural possessive form in the third blank.

		Singular Possessive	Plural Form	Plural Possessive
Ex:	assistant	assistant's	assistants	assistants'
1.	witness			
2.	attorney			
3.	agency			
4.	child			
5.	notary public			

Go to the
Web

Practice 2 Exercises
for more skills practice on this topic.

Applying Possessive Rules

Instructions: In the space below each statement, correct the underlined error. Then write the rule that applies in your own words. Answers will vary.

1. I can easily spend an <u>hours</u> time surfing Web sites.

   _____

   _____

   _____

2. Have you seen the Lands' End Web site that advertises <u>womens</u> clothing?

   _____

   _____

   _____

3. The <u>editors' in chiefs</u> responses to Norton's antivirus software were all similar.

   _____

   _____

   _____

Locating Plurals and Possessives

*Instructions: Underline the plural and possessive errors in the words in the following sentences. Write the words correctly in the space provided, inserting or deleting apostrophes as needed. If the sentence is correct, write **Yes** in the space.*

1. *The Complete Idiots Guide to the Internet* was the first book that I used to learn the functions of the Internet.

   1. _____

Name _____   Date _____

2. New Web-based programs' written in the language of Java provide unlimited business applications.

2. _____

3. My sister-in-laws' job as lead programmer in her companies ISP division sounds exciting.

3. _____
  _____

4. I often read the latest computer's magazines to see what is new.

4. _____

5. Our Webmasters major criticism of the Web site concerned the design.

5. _____

6. Entertainment companies may charge subscription fees to users' of online games.

6. _____

7. After four hours' work, she completed her research on firewalls.

7. _____

8. I read an interesting online report about the depletion of some of our nations' natural resources.

8. _____

9. Horn and Harris's Department Store is having a warehouse's clearance sale.

9. _____

10. This weeks' online health tip was more useful than last weeks.

10. _____
   _____

Go to the
Web

Practice 3 Exercises
for more skills practice on this topic.

PRACTICE 3

Proofreading

*Instructions: Proofread and compare the two sentences in each group. If they are the same, write **Yes** in the space provided. If they are not the same, write **No**. Use the first sentence as the correct copy. If you find errors in the second sentence, underline them.*

1. Amazon calls itself the "Earth's biggest bookstore."

1. _____

 Amazon calls itself the "Earths' biggest bookstore.

2. Even though we have an excellent catalog on our Web site, our customers must still dial our 800 number to place orders.

2. _____

 Even though we have an excellent catalog on our Web sight, our customers must still dial our 900 number to place orders.

3. The browser's color graphics were less clear than what I needed for my work.

3. _____

 The browser's color graphics were less clear than what I needed for my work.

Name _____ Date _____

4. This year's trade show was 50 percent larger than last year's.

   This year's trade show was 500 percent larger then last years.

4. _____

5. Alamo's Web site gives its rental car customers suggestions for getting around in a strange city.

   Alamo Web site gives it's rental car customers suggestions for getting around a strange city.

5. _____

6. I like the Web pages that offer prizes or information, but I do not like those that are all pictures.

   I like the Web pages that offer prizes or information, but I do not like those that are all pictures.

6. _____

7. Our lawyers told us that many online legal points are incorrect or incomplete.

   Our lawyer's told us that many online legal points are incorrect and incomplete.

7. _____

8. It's easy to pick up a virus by downloading music from the Internet.

   Its' easy to pickup a virus by downloading music from the internet.

8. _____

PRACTICE 4

The Writing Process: Topic Sentences

Instructions: For each item below, write a topic statement for a paragraph using the topic and purpose provided. Use a complete sentence. Answers will vary.

Ex: **Topic:** Using the Web. **Purpose:** To inform.

   Using our college Web page gives me the opportunity to look up a

   list of classes.

1. **Topic:** A complaint about excessive spam on the Internet.
   Purpose: To persuade.

   _____

2. **Topic:** Online shopping. **Purpose:** To describe.

   _____

3. **Topic:** Your favorite funny Web site. **Purpose:** To entertain.

   _____

Go to the
Web

Practice 4 Exercises
for more skills practice on
this topic.

Compound and Possessive Nouns

Name _____ Date _____

Supporting Statements

Instructions: For each item below, write three related sentences that provide details to support the stated topic sentence. Answers will vary.

1. English grammar is necessary for success in school. (Write at least one sentence using the possessive form of a noun. Underline the possessive noun.)

   _____

   _____

   _____

2. Many students use (or don't use) the Internet in their classes. (Write at least one sentence using a compound noun. Underline the compound noun.)

   _____

   _____

   _____

3. My English grammar has improved since enrolling in this class. (Write at least one sentence including the possessive form of a noun *or* a compound noun. Underline the compound noun once and the possessive noun twice.)

   _____

   _____

   _____

4. Several methods are available for editing and improving your writing. (Write at least one sentence using the possessive form of a compound noun.)

   _____

   _____

   _____

PRACTICE 5

Compounds, Plurals, and Possessives

Instructions: Select the correct word in parentheses, and write it in the space provided.

1. (*Mr. Marcusso's, Mr. Marcussos*) opinion is highly respected in the Web design field.

   1. _____

2. This (*semesters, semester's*) online classes are popular with students.

   2. _____

Name _____ Date _____

3. Several Internet firms are relocating to the Boston (*suburbs, suburbs'*).

3. _____

4. We followed our (*attorney's-at-law, attorney-at-law's*) advice regarding company Internet use by employees.

4. _____

5. Is it practical to do a complete online backup of (*today's, todays*) hard drives?

5. _____

6. Our (*clients, clients'*) connect over the Internet by dialing into (*HP's, HPs*) network.

6. _____
   _____

7. Webcasters have the expertise to identify online (*viewer's, viewers'*) preferences.

7. _____

8. We located an excellent site that included (*mens' and womens', men's and women's*) reactions to online investing.

8. _____
   _____

9. (*Antonio's, Antonio*) and Heather's computers are on different floors of the building.

9. _____

10. The Chicago Board of (*Trade's, Trades'*) Internet Advisory Committee meets monthly.

10. _____

PRACTICE 6

Identifying Possessive Forms

Instructions: Write the correct singular possessive form in the first blank, the plural form in the second blank, and the plural possessive form in the third blank.

	Singular Possessive	Plural Form	Plural Possessive
Ex: assistant	assistant's	assistants	assistants'
1. employee	_____	_____	_____
2. saleswoman	_____	_____	_____
3. M.D.	_____	_____	_____
4. moment	_____	_____	_____
5. post office	_____	_____	_____

Applying Possessive Rules

Instructions: In the space below each statement, correct the underlined error. Then write the rule that applies in your own words. Answers will vary.

1. MSN's search engine as well as <u>Googles</u> finds specific information.

_____

_____

Name _____ Date _____

2. Our company database lists names and e-mail addresses but omits personal information such as <u>employees</u> social security numbers or home addresses.

_____

_____

_____

3. Yahoo! People Search allows searching for phone numbers and <u>addresses.'</u>

_____

Locating Plurals and Possessives

Instructions: Underline the plural and possessive errors in the following sentences. Write the words correctly in the space provided, inserting or deleting apostrophes as needed. If the sentence is correct, write **Yes** in the space.

1. This weeks' spam is about a vitamin supplement.

1. _____

2. David tried to be removed from a senders' mailing list.

2. _____

3. Brad was interested in the Investor's Corner, an online newspaper column.

3. _____

4. The parents section of Nintendos Web site discusses specific question's that parents may have about video games.

4. _____
_____
_____

5. Online businesses' must protect customers transactions such as credit card numbers or e-mail addresses.

5. _____
_____

6. A greeting card Web site e-mails me two days before my mother-in-laws birthday.

6. _____

7. If you want to see detailed descriptions of SAT's and GMAT's, check the Educational Testing Service site.

7. _____

8. We have several eyewitness's testimonies that some employees regularly use the companys' Internet for personal reasons.

8. _____
_____

9. Several chief of police conducted the cross-examinations of the individuals involved in Internet scams.

9. _____

10. The technicians recommendation for avoiding viruses was more informative than my coworker.

10. _____
_____

Name _____ Date _____

PRACTICE 7

Proofreading

*Instructions: Proofread and compare the two sentences in each group. If they are the same, write **Yes** in the space provided. If they are not the same, write **No.** Use the first sentence as the correct copy. If you find errors in the second sentence, underline them.*

1. Net newbies are gravitating to Web sites where they can find friends and feel comfortable.

   Net newbies' are gravitating to Web sites where they can find friends and feel comfortable.

   1. _____

2. If Web sites do not capture Web surfers' interests within eight seconds, the surfers move on to other sites.

   If a Web site do not capture Web surfers interests within eight seconds, the surfers move on to other sights.

   2. _____

3. Numerous online sites include women's issues.

   Numerous online sights include woman's issues.

   3. _____

4. Nearly one-quarter of online users have purchased goods either on the Internet or through an online service.

   Nearly one quarter of on-line users have purchased goods either on the Internet or through an online service.

   4. _____

5. PBS's Computer Chronicles will air a technical trivia game sponsored by Boston's Computer Museum.

   PBS' Computer Chronicles will air a technical trivia game sponsored by Bostons Computer Museum.

   5. _____

PRACTICE 8

Writing Process: Topic Sentences

Instructions: For each item below, write a topic statement for a paragraph using the topic and purpose provided. Use a complete sentence. Answers will vary.

Ex: **Topic:** Chatting at a Web site. **Purpose:** To inform.

   Many Web pages add a way for Web surfers to chat. _____

1. **Topic:** A product that you use and like. **Purpose:** To persuade.

   _____

Name _____ Date _____

2. **Topic:** A happy time in your life. **Purpose:** To entertain.

_____

3. **Topic:** Characteristics of a good teacher. **Purpose:** To describe.

_____

Supporting Statements

Instructions: For each item below, write three related sentences that provide details to support the stated topic sentence. Answers will vary.

1. Knowledge of the Internet is important in my future. (Write at least one sentence using the possessive form of a noun. Underline the possessive noun.)

   _____

   _____

   _____

2. Some students do not take responsibility for their actions. (Write at least one sentence using a compound noun. Underline the compound noun.)

   _____

   _____

   _____

3. Business English will help me succeed at work. (Write at least one sentence including the possessive form of a noun *or* a compound noun. Underline the compound noun once and the possessive noun twice.)

   _____

   _____

   _____

Posttest

Instructions: In the space provided, write the letter of the correct answer.

1. *First Interstate Bank sent Larry to a Web design class.* In this sentence, what does the noun *Larry* illustrate? (2)

    a. the nominative case

    b. the possessive case

    c. the objective and nominative cases

    d. the objective case

    1. _____

2. Which statement represents the correct possessive form? (4)

    a. The Video Store's Web page has 500 hits a day.

    b. The Video Stores' Web page has 500 hits a day.

    c. The Video Store Web's page has 500 hits a day.

    d. The Video Store Web page has 500 hits' a day.

    2. _____

3. Which statement represents the correct possessive form? (6)

    a. Monica and Meg's reactions to Internet research differ.

    b. Monica's and Meg's reactions to Internet research differ.

    c. Monicas' and Megs' reactions to Internet research differ.

    d. Monica and Megs' reactions to Internet research differ.

    3. _____

4. Which statement is written correctly? (3)

    a. Daily e-mails' update our sales figures.

    b. Daily e-mails update our sales figures'.

    c. Daily e-mails update our sales figures.

    d. Daily e-mails' update our sales' figures.

    4. _____

5. Which line of compound words is correct? (1)

    a. multinational, nonjudgmental

    b. news paper, thumbtack

    c. hand shake, eye color

    d. copperwire, newsclip

    5. _____

6. Which statement represents the correct plural form of a compound noun? (1)

    a. Our network had several break downs this week.

    b. Our network had several break-downs this week.

    c. Our network had several breakdowns this week.

    d. Our network had several breakdown's this week.

    6. _____

7. Which statement is written correctly? (1,3)

    a. Several accounting instructor's course materials are online.

    b. Several accounting instructors' course materials are online.

    c. Several accounting instructors course materials are online.

    d. Several accounting instructors' course materials are on-line.

    7. _____

8. Which statement is written correctly? (3, 4) **8.** _____

  a. My sisters-in-law friend works at our companies helpdesk.

  b. My sister-in-laws' friend works at our companies help desk.

  c. My sister-in-law's friend works at our company's help desk.

  d. My sisters-in-laws friend works at our company's help desk.

9. Which statement is written correctly? (3, 6) **9.** _____

  a. The SEC's (Securities and Exchange Commission) Office of Internet
      Enforcement Complaint Center encourages giving tips on potential
      securities law violations.

  b. The SECs (Securities and Exchange Commission) Office of Internet
      Enforcement Complaint Center encourages giving tips on potential
      securitys law violations.

  c. The SECs' (Securities and Exchange Commission) Office of Internet
      Enforcement Complaint Center encourages giving tips on potential
      securities' law violations.

  d. The SECs's (Securities and Exchange Commission) Office of Internet
      Enforcement Complaint Center encourages giving tips on potential
      security's law violations.

10. Which statement is written correctly? (4) **10.** _____

  a. Our company announced the three attorneys' opinions on the legality of
      our Web site disclosure statements.

  b. Our company announced the three attorneys opinions on the legality of
      our Web site disclosure statements'.

  c. Our company announced the three attornies' opinions on the legality of
      our Web site disclosure statements'.

  d. Our company announced the three attornies opinions on the legality of
      our Web site disclosure statements.

Instructions: In the space provided, write the letter or letters of the correct possessive or plural forms of nouns.

11. a. trade-offs (1, 3, 4) **11.** _____

  b. brainstormings ideas'

  c. workers' layoffs

  d. notary's public

12. a. a salesclerk's mistakes (1, 3, 6) **12.** _____

  b. two HMO's doctors

  c. Ms. Lopez's application

  d. a companies' responsibilities

13. a. Levi's jeans (3, 5) **13.** _____

  b. Childrens' Hospital

  c. days notice

  d. business checking account

14. a.   AOL's browser (1, 4, 6)

    b.   brother-in-law's virus protection

    c.   editor in chiefs, passers-by

    d.   weekdays, trade-offs

14. _____

15. a.   two week's pay (3,4,6)

    b.   a CEO's salary

    c.   a man's password

    d.   three childrens' computers

15. _____

Chapter 6

Capitalization

OBJECTIVES

After you have studied this chapter and completed the exercises, you will be able to do the following:

1. Use capitalization rules for proper nouns, first words in sentences, specific organizations, committees, government agencies, boards, and departments.

2. Apply capitalization rules for publications, events and holidays, acts, bills, laws, and titles.

3. Apply capitalization rules for academic degrees, languages, education levels and courses, and ethnic and religious designations.

4. Apply capitalization rules for time periods, seasons, days and months, specific and general locations, and directions.

5. Apply capitalization rules for abbreviations, nouns with numbers, trademarks, brand names, and product names.

6. Apply capitalization rules for direct and indirect quotes, words after colons, and material within parentheses.

7. Identify appropriate items to capitalize in lists, outlines, business letters, and legal documents.

Workplace Applications: Time Management

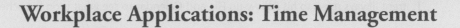

Planning is an important process. Students say that planning helps them reduce stress and keeps them on time. Those students who plan are much more likely to have A and B averages than those who do not plan.

If you know how to plan, you have overcome procrastination and probably have all your paperwork under control. While you are in school, you have an opportunity to develop time management skills, which you can then apply to the workplace.

An Obstacle to Overcome

One of the most common roadblocks to managing time is procrastination. Procrastination means putting off doing tasks until a later time. Procrastination keeps you from starting or seeing a task through to completion and results in overwork, continual crises, and clutter. A procrastinator lacks planning skills and is unable to set priorities. To overcome procrastination, break projects into small tasks, and reward yourself at milestones in the process. Once you start a project, no matter how small the task, you are no longer procrastinating.

Pretest

Instructions: *Underline any capitalization errors in the following sentences. Write the words correctly in the space provided.*

1. trent always refers to his Follow-up File and Calendar to see what is on the schedule. (1)

   _____

2. The Salesperson knew that superintendent Ricci had a busy day; therefore, she outlined her Proposal quickly. (1)

   _____

3. Barbara Hemphill is the author of the Book *Taming The Paper Tiger At Work.* (2)

   _____

4. The Faculty at north central technical college in Rapid city evaluated several Group Calendar systems. (3)

   _____

5. The human resources department asked Nancy Webb, a Professional Speaker and Consultant, to offer a Seminar on Time Management. (3)

   _____

6. After working a 55-hour week, Jay was looking forward to the Fall retreat at the redwood lodge in the Northern part of the State. (4)

   _____

7. We will have to spend some additional time updating health ordinance 502 before memorial day weekend. (2, 5)

   _____

8. Kelly has a Notebook (A three-section spiral) that She uses to record Shortcut ideas, Questions, and Concerns. (6)

   _____

9. Lucas found the following major deterrents in managing his time: Messy desk, Careless file management, and E-mail overload. (6, 7)

   _____

10. She said, "we have an ambitious, time-conscious Staff." (6)

    _____

Instructions: *In the space provided, write the letter of the correct answer.*

11. Which line has items that are all correct? (1, 3)   11. _____
    a. Yavapai community college, Computer Design Course, business English
    b. Yavapai Community College, computer design course, Business English
    c. Yavapai Community college, Computer Design course, business English
    d. Yavapai Community College, computer design course, business English

12. Which line has items that are all correct? (2, 4)　　　　　　　　　　　　**12.** _____

   a.　passover, winter, thursday

   b.　Passover, winter, thursday

   c.　Passover, winter, Thursday

   d.　Passover, Winter, Thursday

13. Which line has items that are all correct? (5)　　　　　　　　　　　　　**13.** _____

   a.　Invoice 2056B, page 95, room 218, Highway 161

   b.　invoice 2056b, Page 95, Room 218, highway 161

   c.　Invoice 2056B, page 95, Room 218, Highway 161

   d.　Invoice 2056B, Page 95, Room 218, highway 161

14. Which line has items that are all correct? (1, 5)　　　　　　　　　　　　**14.** _____

   a.　china plate, Ridgefield park, United States senate

   b.　China Plate, Ridgefield Park, United States Senate

   c.　china plate, Ridgefield Park, United States Senate

   d.　China plate, Ridgefield park, United States senate

15. The correct capitalization usage for the salutation and complimentary closing is: (7)　　**15.** _____

   a.　Dear Manager, Sincerely yours

   b.　Dear Mr. Benton, Sincerely Yours

   c.　dear Mr. Benton, Sincerely Yours

   d.　Dear manager, Sincerely yours

Chapter Preview

What is your reaction to a capitalized word as you are reading? Does it suggest something or someone specific or important? To indicate that importance, writers follow capitalization rules that have evolved through the years.

In this chapter, you will study some of these general rules so that you will know when to capitalize a word and when to use lowercase. Obviously, every rule cannot be studied; therefore, you will need to check your reference manual whenever you are in doubt. In addition, each career field may designate its own important words, and some companies may list their capitalization rules in a company handbook.

Capitalization Rules

These rules cover the major areas that require capitalization. At several points throughout the chapter, you will be advised to refer to a reference manual for more detail.

First Word in a Sentence

Capitalize the first word in a sentence.

> **Time management skills are valuable in any career field.**
> **She managed her time efficiently.**

Proper Nouns

Capitalize proper nouns. Do not capitalize common nouns.

NOTES

Proper Nouns

Proper nouns are specific names of persons, places, and things.

Proper Nouns	**Common Nouns**
Green Bay Unified School District	school district
Laurel Inn	motel
North High School	school
Salt Lake City	city
Tom Carrington	accountant
Yellowstone National Park	park
Germany	country
Putnam Heights Building	building
American Medical Association	association
Pomona Drive	street

Personal Names

Capitalize the names or nicknames of specific persons. Use the capitalization and spelling that the owner of the name designates.

Elizabeth Nelson

Barry McMann

Hoang Duc Hien

Patricia (Trish) Olson

Brandon Jackson (BJ)

Mary Ann, Maryanne, Mary Anne

Luis Salazar, Louis Salazar

Marcia Van Beek, Marcia van Beek

   Marcia VanBeek

Kaitlin (Katie)

Do This	Do Not Do This
Mr. Kauffman specifically asked Anne Wilson to complete the time management report.	Kauffman specifically asked Wilson to complete the management report.

In business writing, refer to individuals by their first and last names, or use a title with the surname.

Pronouns

Always capitalize the pronoun *I*. Do not capitalize other pronouns unless they appear at the beginning of a sentence.

I try to keep my desk organized.

Sherry and I included time-saving hints in our company manual.

Their advice was to handle each piece of paper only once.

They always check their "to do" lists before they leave the office.

Geographic Locations

Capitalize the specific names of geographic locations. Capitalize the names of cities, states, countries, streets, parks, lakes, mountains, rivers, and regions. Do not capitalize general location names.

Specific Locations	General Locations
Kansas City	their country
New York State	our street
Austria	the mountains
Kensington Avenue	the river
Lake Superior	
Grand Canyon National Park	
Himalaya Mountains	
Black River	
Corn Belt	

<table>
<tr><td>Do This</td><td>Do Not Do This</td></tr>
<tr><td>New York City</td><td>New York city</td></tr>
<tr><td>the city of Cincinnati</td><td>the City of Cincinnati</td></tr>
<tr><td>Buckeye State</td><td>Buckeye state</td></tr>
</table>

Do not capitalize the word *city* unless it is part of the city's name. Capitalize the word *state* only when it follows the name of the state or is used as part of an informal name for the state.

Proper Noun Substitutions

Capitalize informal substitutions for proper nouns and shortened versions of proper nouns. These substitutions are often referred to as imaginative names and nicknames.

Informal Substitutions	Shortened Versions
the First Lady	Big Blue (IBM)
Twin Cities (Minneapolis and St. Paul)	the Net (the Internet)
	the Web (the World Wide Web)
the Windy City (Chicago)	Rockies (the Rocky Mountains)
French Quarter (New Orleans)	

Proper Noun Derivatives

Capitalize adjectives formed from proper nouns. Do not capitalize words formed from proper nouns that are now commonly used and that are no longer identified with those nouns.

Slovenian food	china pattern
Spanish language	venetian blinds
European descent	manila folder
Canadian winter	arabic numbers
Bostonians	french fries

Go to the
Web

Checkpoint 6.1
for more skills practice on this topic.

CHECKPOINT 6.1

Instructions: *Underline any capitalization errors in the following sentences. On the lines provided, write the words correctly. If the capitalization is correct, write* **Yes.**

1. jani, kristen, and danielle always keep a Record of the time it takes them to complete a Task.

_____

2. andrew (andy) Wu, barney Mcmillan, and donna parks received Awards for submitting Time-saving Suggestions.

   _____

3. the time management seminars will be held in boston, massachusetts; richmond, virginia; and charleston, south carolina.

   _____

4. I do not like to spend my time working on weekends.

   _____Yes_____

5. Since my time is limited, i walk in owen park during my Lunch Break.

   _____

6. people living in the united states feel more time pressures than people living in many european Countries.

   _____

7. Our next time management conference will be in Mexico City or San Diego.

   _____Yes_____

8. When we attend the Conference in the windy city, we will visit several efficiency experts' Exhibits.

   _____

9. The state of Michigan tried to clarify overtime and compensatory time for its employees.

   _____Yes_____

10. Are Your tasks so time-consuming that you have little time for Planning?

    _____

Companies, Institutions, Organizations, and Clubs

Capitalize the first letters of all major words in names of companies, institutions, organizations, and clubs. Do not capitalize articles (*a, an, the*), conjunctions (*and, but, or, nor*), and prepositions with fewer than four letters (*of, in, on, by*) unless one of these words is the first word of the name. If available, use the official letterhead as a guide.

> Dickman and Rothstein Attorneys (company)
>
> the University of Michigan (institution)
>
> American Association of University Women (organization)
>
> the Girl Scouts of the United States of America (organization)
>
> Future Business Leaders of America (club)

Do not capitalize words such as *company, club, institution,* or *organization* when used as general expressions.

> company profits   the objectives of the institution
>
> our club's membership   the organization's bylaws

Departments, Committees, and Divisions

Capitalize the specific names of departments, committees, project teams, or divisions within the organization with which *you* are associated. Do not capitalize names of departments, committees, project teams, and divisions (1) if the names are used in a general way and you are not sure of the actual name or (2) if the names are not precise.

The Education and Training Department is offering time management courses.

The Policy and Procedures Committee spent hours developing employee time use surveys.

(The writer should know the precise name of the department or committee in the company where he or she works.)

I will check with someone in their advertising department to see if Cole can promote the time management seminar.

Will your advertising division be working on our "Using Your Time Effectively" promotion?

(The words *their* and *your* modify *department* and *division* in a general way.)

Some type of review committee should be appointed to analyze overtime compensation.

Ron does not have time to serve on another board of directors.

(The names of the organizational units are not precise.)

Government Units

Federal, state, county, and city government units should be identified accurately. The telephone directory is a good source for identifying these units. Federal agencies are listed under "United States Government," while state, county, and city government units are listed under the states, counties, or cities in which these units are located. Use a reference manual to locate foreign government designations.

Capitalize specific official names of foreign, national, state, and local government units. Capitalize the names of agencies, divisions, departments, offices, commissions, and boards. Capitalize short forms of the names of government units.

British Empire	Texas Child Welfare Agency
World Health Organization	Wage Hour and Public Contracts Division
United States Senate	Railroad Retirement Board
the Nevada Legislature	Department on Aging
Austin City Council	Office of Consumer Affairs
the House	the Senate

Do This	Do Not Do This
federal offices	Federal offices
federal government	Federal government
Federal Reserve Board	federal Reserve Board

The word *federal* is capitalized only when referred to in a specific organization's name.

CHECKPOINT 6.2

Go to the
Web

Checkpoint 6.2
for more skills practice on
this topic.

Instructions: *Underline any capitalization errors in the following sentences. On the lines provided, write the words correctly. If the capitalization is correct, write* **Yes.**

1. Pat Halsted at people's state bank trains new employees to be especially courteous to clients who have to wait for service.

_____

2. Three employees from our trust department at rohde & samuelson attorneys received time off to attend a three-day workshop.

_____

3. Reviewing federal and state tax regulations is the first item on my "to do" list today.

_____

4. Melanie often must wait when she schedules State Agency appointments, but she brings along work to avoid wasted time.

_____

5. The accounting department knows that it cannot procrastinate with the audit of kerm and associates of Waterloo, Iowa.

_____

6. I entered the deadline date for submitting my nomination papers for the hendersonville city council in my electronic calendar.

_____

7. The future business leaders of america maintained a "to do" list for each Club project.

_____

8. huntington & associates found that the Company could offer two-hour blocks of training time more effectively than all-day training sessions.

_____

Titles

Capitalize a social, professional, religious, academic, political, or military title that precedes a name.

Mrs. Lorna Evans	Professor Lloyd Blake
Dr. Lee Maxwell	Mayor Bob Jeffers
the Reverend Chris Myer	General Overhulzer

High-Ranking Government Officials. Capitalize a title that follows the name of a high-ranking foreign, national, or state government official. Capitalize a title that is used to substitute for the complete name of a high-ranking government official.

Jim Doyle, Governor of Wisconsin

the Prime Minister

the Chief Justice

Company, Institution, or Association Officials. Do not capitalize the title of a company, institution, or association official that follows a name. Likewise, do not capitalize the title of a company, institution, or association official that is used as a substitute for a complete name unless practice or tradition indicates to the contrary.

> Jerome Decker, president of Meridian Press
>
> Lou Ballard, secretary of United Grocers
>
> the president of AMOLCO Corporation
>
> the secretary to the vice president
>
> the treasurer of Teamsters Local 344

General Occupational. Do not capitalize occupational titles (teacher, writer, lawyer) used in a general way.

> **The attorney's comment about being on time embarrassed Warren.**
>
> **The art of delegating tasks effectively is a major attribute of the new chancellor.**

Title Substitutions. Capitalize a title used as a substitute for a complete name in a direct address (except a title such as *sir, madam,* or *miss*). Capitalize a title used in place of a name in minutes or bylaws.

Direct Address

> **When will the bill be introduced, Senator?**
>
> **Commissioner, have you finished your response?**
>
> **Wouldn't you agree, sir, that managing one's time is important?**

Bylaws and Minutes

> **The term of the President will be two years.**
>
> **One duty of the Vice President includes assisting project managers in meeting their task deadlines.**

Family Titles

Capitalize the title of a family member when it is used by itself or when it is used in direct address. Capitalize the title of a family member when it precedes a name.

> **I wondered how Mother managed her time with five children.**
>
> **I will be late to work if I do not leave now, Dad.**
>
> **Did Aunt Marge have her time-saving hints published?**

Do This

my mother

our uncle

her dad

Do not capitalize a family title when it is used with a possessive—*my, your, our, his, her, their.*

Do Not Do This

my Mother

our Uncle

her Dad

CHECKPOINT 6.3

Go to the
Web

Checkpoint 6.3
for more skills practice on this topic.

Instructions: Underline any capitalization errors in the following sentences. On the lines provided, write the words correctly. If the capitalization is correct, write **Yes.**

1. Rex Stout, the Treasurer of Minton Company, wrote a check for the project management software.

   _____

2. Senator Herb Kohl spends his time strategically planning solutions to legislative concerns.

   _____ *yes* _____

3. One point that professor enriquez made was that we should review our long-term objectives periodically.

   _____

4. Since my work at Green Door Graphics required so much overtime, I was not able to be the president of the Meadowview Parent-Teacher Association.

   _____

5. As the Administrative Assistant to Kay Johnson, Manager of Research and Planning, Terri finds that a "to do" list is very important.

   _____

6. George McCann, Author of five time management books, was a former Attorney.

   _____

7. My Mother, aunt Dawn, and aunt Ruth would be excellent role models for outstanding time managers.

   _____ *yes* _____

8. How much time were you planning to spend, Sir, with the President of the AOC?

   _____

Publications

Books, Magazines, and Newspapers.   Capitalize the first letters of all words with four or more letters in the title of a book, magazine, or newspaper. Place these titles in italics. Do not capitalize articles, conjunctions, or prepositions with fewer than four letters unless they are the first or last words in the title.

The Mercury News

USA Today (newspaper)

One-Minute Manager (book)

Travel and Leisure (magazine)

Robert's Rules of Order (book)

The Small Business Encyclopedia (book)

The Delta Pi Epsilon Journal

Do This

Time magazine

The New York Times newspaper

Do Not Do This

Time Magazine

The New York Times Newspaper

Do not capitalize the words *magazine* or *newspaper* unless they are part of the titles of the publications.

Other Published Works. Capitalize the first letters of all the main words in titles of works such as chapters in books, magazine articles, plays, musical productions, movies, documentaries, speeches, radio and television programs, and poems. Do not capitalize articles, conjunctions, or prepositions with fewer than four letters unless they are the first or last words in the title.

"Plural and Possessive Nouns" (chapter in a book)

Anne of Green Gables (play)

Fly Away Home (movie)

Gettysburg Address (speech)

Daffodils (long poem)

"Are You Buying a Business or a Disaster?" (article in a magazine)

Grease (musical production)

The Civil War Years (documentary)

Meet the Press (television program)

Events and Holidays

Capitalize the names of historical and current events, holidays, and special events.

the Great Depression

World War II

Public Safety Week

Save the Railroad Campaign

Fourth of July

Memorial Day

Toys for Tots

Festival in the Pines

Acts, Bills, and Laws

Capitalize specific titles of laws, acts, codes, and amendments. Do not capitalize general names of laws, acts, codes, or amendments.

Specific Titles	General Titles
Child Safety Law 102	the building code
Drug-Free Workplace Act	several environmental bills
Family and Medical Leave Act	a constitutional amendment
Code of Criminal Procedure	
Health and Safety Code 11007	
the First Amendment	
Proposition 13	

CHECKPOINT 6.4

Instructions: *Underline any capitalization errors in the following sentences. On the lines provided, write the words correctly. If the capitalization is correct, write* **Yes.**

1. Keep job and company details, as well as time-saving tips, in your Desk Manual.

   _____

2. Sharon found some excellent time management articles in *The Office Professional* Magazine.

   _____ *yes* _____

3. The first speech was entitled "Identifying Time Wasters."

   _____ *yes* _____

4. The Family and Medical Leave Act allows employees to spend the necessary time with family members who need them.

   _____ *yes* _____

5. Have you read the book *time management for dummies*?

   _____

6. During my free time last evening, I watched the DVD "*million dollar baby.*"

   _____

7. I receive overtime wages when I work on holidays such as thanksgiving and the fourth of july.

   _____

8. Listen to weau-tv *news* at 6 for current events instead of taking time to read the local paper, the *gazette evening news*.

   _____

Academic Degrees

Capitalize a specific academic degree that follows a person's name. Do not capitalize an academic degree used in a general way.

> **Traci Muldoon, <u>Ph.D.</u>, prepared the master schedule of classes for next year.**
> **She received her <u>bachelor's degree</u> from Northern Arizona University.**

Languages

Always capitalize names of specific languages.

Bonnie speaks S̲panish and E̲nglish fluently.

Many of my business clients use F̲rench in their daily transactions.

Education Levels, Subjects, and Courses

Capitalize a specific educational course title. Do not capitalize the general title of a course or area of study unless it is a language.

Specific Title	General Title
Records Management 221	a course in medical terminology
Bus. 201 Word Expert	majoring in accounting

Do This

a course in business English

a major in Spanish history

Capitalize the name of a language in specific and general courses or study areas.

Do Not Do This

a course in Business English

a major in spanish history

Do not capitalize general levels of education.

My daughter will be in kindergarten this fall; therefore, I will have to reschedule my workday.

All members of our team scheduled time to enroll in university courses this semester.

Our community college offers courses at times that appeal to working adults.

Ethnic Designations

Capitalize the names of nationalities, ethnic groups, and races.

Caucasians	African-Americans	Native Americans
Hungarians	Germans	

Religious References

Capitalize the names of specific religious groups, religious days and books, names of churches, and any adjectives derived from religious terms.

Christians	Catholic missionaries
Easter	Judaism
Koran	First Presbyterian Church

CHECKPOINT 6.5

Go to the
Web

Checkpoint 6.5
for more skills practice on this topic.

Instructions: *Underline any capitalization errors in the following sentences. On the lines provided, write the words correctly. If the capitalization is correct, write* **Yes.**

1. I have decided to get a Degree in Business Administration, but first I have to arrange my schedule at the office.

   _____ *yes* _____

2. Jenny majored in human services and worked full-time while she attended the university.

   _____

3. I was too stressed and decided to discontinue taking spanish classes at the college and playing the organ at the first baptist church.

   _____

4. In my Business Communications Class, I completed a research project on time management.

   _____ *yes* _____

5. We needed more time to discuss the plans for revitalizing the downtown area.

   _____ *yes* _____

6. When I started working on my Master's Degree, I found that my free time had disappeared.

   _____ *yes* _____

7. All High School students should be aware of how they spend their time.

   _____

8. George McDonald, ph.d., my instructor for office management 251, is always prompt in returning tests.

   _____

Days and Months

Capitalize days of the week and months of the year.

Tuesday	April
Saturday	September

Seasons

Do not capitalize the name of a season unless it is listed with a specific year or unless it is included in the specific name of an event.

   winter sales

   summers in the South

   registration in the fall and spring

   registration for the Spring 2007 semester

   (*Spring* appears with a specific year.)

Fall Arts and Crafts Fair

Spring Fling

(*Fall* and *Spring* are parts of the names of the events.)

Winter Break

Time Periods

Do not capitalize time periods, decades, or centuries used in a general way.

third-quarter report	the twenty-first century
new millennium	the next century
in the nineties	

Do not capitalize *a.m.* or *p.m.*, *noon* or *midnight*, or general times of the day.

We scheduled the time management workshop for 11 <u>a.m.</u>

The plane landed at <u>noon.</u>

I am not very productive by <u>midafternoon.</u>

Do This	Do Not Do This
He finished the project at <u>12 p.m.</u>	He finished the project at <u>12 p.m. noon.</u>
or	
He finished the project at <u>noon.</u>	The meeting begins at <u>9 a.m. in the morning.</u>
	or
The meeting begins at <u>9 a.m.</u>	The meeting begins at <u>nine a.m.</u>

Use *a.m.* or *p.m.* only when numerals are involved. Do not use *a.m.* or *p.m.* with the words *noon* or *midnight* or with general times of the day.

Compass Directions

Specific Regions.   Capitalize compass directions and derivative words when they designate specific regions of a country.

the <u>Far</u> <u>East</u>	in the <u>East</u>
the <u>Midwest</u>	<u>South</u> Carolina
<u>Midwesterners</u>	a <u>Southerner</u>
(derivative of *Midwest*)	(derivative of *South*)

General Compass Points.   Do not capitalize general compass points or directions.

northern New Mexico	travel north on Wilson Avenue
east side of Cleveland	located east of Highway 12

Street Names. Capitalize compass points when they are part of a street name.

34 <u>North</u> Fulton Street   402 Belview Avenue <u>NW</u>

CHECKPOINT 6.6

Go to the
Web

Checkpoint 6.6
for more skills practice on
this topic.

Instructions: Underline any capitalization errors in the following sentences. On the lines provided, write the words correctly. If the capitalization is correct, write **Yes.**

1. My best hours for completing homework are from 10 P.M. to Midnight.

   _____

2. We completed plans for our annual fall Daze Sale on friday, october 1, the deadline date.

   _____

3. The Annual report is ready weeks ahead of schedule this year.

   _____

4. Because Tews Construction manages multitask jobs well, it was able to complete the office addition before the Winter Snows.

   _____

5. My day planner is filled from 8 A.M. to 5:30 P.M. on tuesday and thursday.

   _____

6. Inevitably when I'm in a rush, I forget about the east elm street detour.

   _____

7. Billie Mae lives North of the city and spends an hour commuting each way.

   _____

8. The work ethic of many Midwesterners includes a respect for time.

   _____

9. Some employees who are asked to spend noon hours in training see this as time theft by management.

   _____

10. Raymond C. Johnson is traveling in the southwest to promote his book *Time Is Money.*

   _____

Abbreviations

Capitalize an abbreviation representing a proper noun. Some common nouns also require capital letters for their shortened forms.

Proper Noun Abbreviations

United States Postal Service	(<u>USPS</u>)
Occupational Safety and Health Administration	(<u>OSHA</u>)
Alaska (on envelope addresses)	(<u>AK</u>)

Common Noun Abbreviations

personal information manager	(PIM)
personal digital assistant	(PDA)
central processing unit	(CPU)
compact disc	(CD)

Do This	**Do Not Do This**
Ask for a demonstration of personal information manager (PIM) software.	Ask for a demonstration of PIM software.
Always identify the abbreviation in full the first time that it is used before allowing it to stand alone in a written communication.	

Nouns With Letters and Numbers

Capitalize nouns when they precede a number or letter. Do not capitalize the first letters of the words *line, paragraph, page, size,* and *verse* when they precede a number.

Volume 10	page 1
Unit 3	size 8
Highway 5	paragraph 2
Invoice 203963	line 75
Flight 925	verse 6
Room 2B	

Do This	**Do Not Do This**
The exhibit booth number is 14D.	The Exhibit Booth Number is 14D.
When a word separates the noun and number, do not capitalize the noun.	

Trademarks, Brand Names, and Product Names

Capitalize trademarks or specific brand names. Generally, do not capitalize the type of product.

Trademarks/Brand Names	**Products**
Magnavox®	stereo system
Maxwell House®	coffee
Dial®	soap

Kleenex®	tissues
Toyota Prius®	car
WordPerfect®	software
Wizard®	personal digital assistant
Parkay®	margarine
Macintosh®	computer

CHECKPOINT 6.7

Go to the
Web

Checkpoint 6.7
for more skills practice on this topic.

Instructions: Underline any capitalization errors in the following sentences. On the lines provided, write the words correctly. If the capitalization is correct, write **Yes.**

1. We thought that we would save time by taking interstate 94 until we reached exit 70.

    _____

2. Rod Stone uses personal information manager (PIM) software for scheduling.

    _____

3. We are trying to meet the deadline that Osha gave us to correct our safety regulations.

    _____

4. To increase my efficiency, I use software that includes Word for my Word Processing work and Excel for my Spreadsheets.

    _____

5. AEC Software's program for project management scheduling is called FastTrack Schedule.

    _____

6. We paid invoice 20968 for the Software that we will use for Contact and Customer Management.

    _____

7. Please check section IX, paragraph 2, for time-saving steps recommended for real estate salespeople.

    _____

8. Felix keeps his personal digital assistant (PDA) in the glove compartment of his car.

    _____

First Words

With Quotations.   Capitalize the first word of a direct quotation that is a complete sentence. Do not capitalize the first word of a quotation that cannot stand as a complete sentence. Do not capitalize the first word of the second part of an interrupted quotation.

Quotation Is Complete Sentence

> When coworkers interrupted Sally, she said, "This project is needed in an hour. Let's get together later for lunch."

> The speaker asked, "How many hours did you waste today?"

Quotation Is Incomplete Sentence

> Do you know how your "free time" disappears?

> Maria's desk was stacked with "unbelievable clutter."

Quotation Is Interrupted

> "Your reservation will be guaranteed," the hotel reservations clerk said, "if you arrive by 6 p.m."

> "I am going to use a 'to do' list," said the office manager, "and I will update it at the end of each day."

With Colons. Capitalize the first word that follows a colon if two or more sentences are involved. Do not capitalize the first word following a colon if the material that follows is not a complete sentence.

> I have two major problems in budgeting my time: My projects need to be divided into smaller tasks. My tasks do not get prioritized.

(The colon is followed by two complete sentences.)

> Ask yourself these time-saving questions: Am I doing the job at the right time? Can I delegate the job to someone else?

(The colon is followed by two complete questions.)

> Time wasters include the following: procrastination, incomplete directions, and interruptions.

(The material following the colon is not a complete sentence.)

> The team project leader requested these items: project objectives, potential problem areas, and time estimates.

(The material following the colon is not a complete sentence.)

Capitalize the first word of a sentence that follows a colon if the sentence states a formal rule (regulation) or needs added emphasis. Do not capitalize the first word of a sentence that follows a colon if the sentence simply expands or completes the first part of the sentence.

> Remember: Divide a large project into manageable subsections.

(The sentence following the colon is one of emphasis. The first word in the sentence requires a capital letter.)

> Here is the policy: All overtime hours must be approved by a supervisor.

(The sentence following the colon is a company regulation. The first word in the sentence requires a capital letter.)

> Helen had one major goal for the week: she wanted to complete the five high-priority items on her "to do" list.

(The sentence following the colon completes the main thought expressed in the first sentence. Do not capitalize the first letter.)

Capitalize the first word in a vertical list following a colon.

> The following time management tools will be helpful:

1. Current work analysis time log

2. Prioritized "to do" lists

3. Tickler file

Within Parentheses.   Capitalize the first word of a complete sentence that stands by itself in parentheses. However, do not capitalize the first word of a sentence in parentheses that is within another sentence.

Sentence Stands Alone

We need major revisions in our proposal for Magic Moments. (All six sections need correction.) Revisions are due by the end of the week.

Sentence Within a Sentence

Major revisions in our proposal for Magic Moments (all six sections need correction) are due by the end of the week.

Outlines

Capitalize the main words in all headings preceded by a roman numeral. Capitalize the first letter in each word in second-level headings. Capitalize the first word and use lowercase for remaining words in third-level headings.

I. TIME MANAGEMENT (all caps)

A. Master Lists (second-level heading)

B. "To Do" Lists

C. Electronic Aids

1. Personal digital assistant (PDA) (third-level heading)

2. Personal information manager (PIM)

CHECKPOINT 6.8

Go to the
Web

Checkpoint 6.8
for more skills practice on
this topic.

Instructions: *Underline any capitalization errors in the following sentences. On the lines provided, write the words correctly. If the capitalization is correct, write* **Yes.**

1. Analyze the following items from your time log: Tasks to simplify, Tasks to modify, and Tasks to delegate.

   _____

2. Use these headings on your weekly master list:

   1. week

   2. activity

   3. starting date

   4. required completion date

   5. estimated amount of time

   _____

Capitalization

3. "This software," the user remarked, "Saves me so much time in contacting potential sales leads."

_____

4. Improvements should be made in our training programs: first, increase the time required for new employee training. second, hire workshop presenters who limit class time to four hours.

_____

5. The speaker asked, "is anyone in the room a procrastinator?"

_____

6. Even more experienced workers need help in handling the "so much to do, no time to do it" problem.

_____

7. Having a quiet work area for your home office (A separate room is preferable) improves efficiency.

_____

8. The first day's lecture for my time management class follows this outline:

   I. Introduction

      A. definition

      B. importance of time

   II. realistic approaches

_____

Business Letters, E-Mail Messages, and Web Site Addresses

Complimentary Closing.   Capitalize only the first letter of the first word in a complimentary closing.

> Very truly yours,
>
> Sincerely yours,

Salutations.   Capitalize the first letter of a salutation or greeting and all nouns that follow. Capitalize the first letters of the main words in a salutation not directed to a specific individual.

> Dear Mrs. Johnston: Dear Selection Committee:
>
> Ladies and Gentlemen: Dear Manager:
>
> Employees: (common e-mail greeting)

Inside Addresses.   Capitalize the first letters of major words in inside addresses.

> Mr. Justin Rand, Treasurer
>
> San Benito County Courthouse
>
> 125 Oak Street
>
> Hollister, CA 99362

E-Mail and Web Site Addresses.   Do not capitalize e-mail and Web site addresses unless specifically indicated. Use the letters and symbols exactly as indicated by the correspondent or company.

NOTES

Open vs. Standard Punctuation

In standard punctuation style, a colon appears after the salutation and a comma appears after the complimentary close. Open punctuation requires no punctuation after those letter parts.

http://167.8.29.7/weather/wfront

BitByte@gnn.com

Addresses on Envelopes. Capitalize all letters in all words in a mailing address on an envelope. Postal guidelines recommend that large mailings be done following this format (including no punctuation marks) to allow electronic equipment to read the addresses and speed mail delivery. Using initial capitals and lowercase letters as in the inside address is also acceptable as long as the font meets the standards of the United States Postal Service.

Preferred	**Acceptable**
MR JUSTIN RAND TREASURER	Mr. Justin Rand, Treasurer
SAN BENITO COUNTY COURTHOUSE	San Benito County Courthouse
125 OAK STREET	125 Oak Street
HOLLISTER CA 99362	Hollister, CA 99362

Legal Documents

Amounts of Money. Capitalize amounts of money written in words in legal documents. Do not capitalize the word after the hyphen in written numbers 21 through 99.

> Nine Hundred Seventy-six Dollars ($976)
>
> Fourteen Hundred Thirty-seven Dollars ($1437)

Resolutions. Capitalize every letter in words such as *RESOLVED* and *WHEREAS.*

> WHEREAS, we the members
>
> BE IT RESOLVED that

Do This

Rydell vs. Bruhn

Rydell versus Bruhn

Do Not Do This

Rydell Vs. Bruhn

Rydell Versus Bruhn

Do not capitalize the words *versus* or *vs.* when referring to legal cases.

CHECKPOINT 6.9

*Instructions: Underline any capitalization errors in the following sentences. On the lines provided, write the words correctly. If the capitalization is correct, write **Yes**.*

1. An e-mail communication does not require the formal salutation of "Ladies And Gentlemen."

Go to the
Web

Checkpoint 6.9
for more skills practice on this topic.

2. I use an online calendar service WWW.CALENDAR.YAHOO.COM that sends me reminders to do tasks at the right times.

_____

3. Omitting the ending punctuation from the salutation "dear Ms. Raymond" is a time-saver for some typists.

_____

4. The rental contract stated that we had to pay Eight hundred dollars ($800) by the first of each month for the project management software.

_____

5. The Simplified Letter Style omits such complimentary closings as *Sincerely Yours* and *Yours Truly*.

_____

6. The last line of the inside address on the letter was Flagstaff, AZ 86001.

_____

Name _____ Date _____

PRACTICE 1

Selecting the Correct Capitalized Words

Instructions: Select the correct item in parentheses, and write your answer in the space provided.

1. Because I procrastinated, I did not mail the order for the (*Fall, fall*) merchandise until (*Tuesday, tuesday*).

   _____

2. The new personal information manager (*PIM, pim*) software from the (*Salt Lake Branch, Salt Lake branch*) arrived today.

   _____

3. Mr. Fredericks, our (*Business Instructor, business instructor*), asked an efficiency expert to speak to our (*Phi Lambda Theta Group, Phi Lambda Theta group*).

   _____

4. "Is it possible," asked my supervisor, "(*That, that*) this report will be finished by (*Noon, noon*)?"

   _____

5. Maintain a (*Time Log, time log*) to record the time that you spend on (*Club, club*) projects.

   _____

6. When (*President, president*) Tom Langdon conducted the meetings, he ended them promptly at 2 (*P.M., p.m.*).

   _____

7. George-Ann Fay, who writes books on time management, was recently quoted by (*The Wall Street Journal, the Wall Street Journal*).

   _____

8. The catalog from (*Highsmith Microcomputer Company, highsmith microcomputer company*) includes many new gadgets for making our work simpler.

   _____

9. We learned to prepare "to do" lists in our classes at the (*Business College, business college*).

   _____

10. During most years, (*Congress, congress*) tries to pass the budget before the (*Fourth of July, fourth of July*) holiday.

    _____

Go to the
Web

Practice 1 Exercises
for more skills practice on this topic.

Capitalization

Name _____ Date _____

11. Jeremy told me that the (*AMA, Ama*) workshop would be held in (*Philadelphia, philadelphia*), the (*City of Brotherly Love, city of brotherly love*), in (*January, january*).

    _____

12. (*I, i*) learned an important bit of philosophy about wasted time from my (*Father, father*).

    _____

13. The (*Department of Public Instruction, department of public instruction*) acknowledged receiving our (*Grant Proposal, grant proposal*) before the deadline date.

    _____

14. A time management tip that (*I, i*) use is labeling a (*Manila, manila*) folder with the project name as soon as I hear about the project.

    _____

15. Traffic delays along (*State Street, state street*) or (*Highway 53, highway 53*) often make me late for appointments.

    _____

16. According to the reminder in my day planner, my note for (*fourteen hundred dollars, Fourteen Hundred Dollars*) is due next Friday.

    _____

17. Bob has a (*Master's, master's*) degree in organizational management from (*Northwestern University, Northwestern university*).

    _____

18. The following activities may be time-wasters: (*Frequent, frequent*) interruptions, (*Tardiness, tardiness*), and (*Lengthy, lengthy*) phone calls.

    _____

19. Our (*Communications, communications*) instructor emphasized (*Time Management, time management*).

    _____

20. We were unhappy when our (*Professor, professor*) scheduled a two-hour test on Valentine's (*Day, day*).

    _____

Name _____ Date _____

PRACTICE 2

Identifying Capitalization Errors

Instructions: Underline any capitalization errors in the following sentences. On the lines provided, write the words correctly.

1. According to a time zone chart, you should send a message by 2 A.M. to reach sydney, australia, by 5 P.M.

2. Many Community Colleges offer Online Training for those who do not have time to attend classes at the local College.

3. In his book *the joy of working*, denis waitley said, "time is an equal-opportunity employer."

4. Eliot Burke, Division Manager for seastrand properties, knows that Project Teams demand more meeting time.

5. Kayling chao asked her group to keep track of all office activities in 15-minute blocks from april 15 to may 1.

6. The Personnel Screening and Review committee at Indiana university spent hours selecting the people whom we wanted to interview.

7. Since Spring vacation is less hectic than other times in the recreation department, I purged the Files.

8. According to professor Sandra Loomis, the "walk and talk" method discourages unnecessary interruptions.

9. After working so many overtime hours this Winter, i took my Family to richland park to hear the u.s. air force jazz band.

10. My Mother-in-Law judi works for a Seminar Bureau and arranges Time Management Workshops.

11. To organize her Customers, our Realtor, Lori Loken, uses access software.

Go to the
Web

Practice 2 Exercises
for more skills practice on this topic.

Name _____ Date _____

12. Pat uses outlook, which has an Alarm Reminder, Address Book, and Calendar.

_____

13. I requested the book *making minutes count* from the office professionals association at 2019 first street sw, seattle, wa 92801.

_____

_____

14. "For a graph showing how executives spend their time," she said, "please see table 4, Page 209."

_____

15. The citizens of rusk county waited more than two Weeks for judge Tobin's decision on the Richmond Versus Wendt Case.

_____

16. We will try to leave New York City after work on friday to travel North to spend a restful weekend at the white briar hotel.

_____

17. After timing her Announcement to coincide with a local political event, the governor of new jersey said that she was seeking a Fourth Term.

_____

18. I recently met Venetta Baker, M.A., the Author of *365 ways for simplifying your work life.*

_____

19. Ben Larson, the Project Manager for scarr properties, inc., says that he schedules an extra 10 percent margin of time on each Project.

_____

20. Here are several ways to avoid wasting time:
    a. discourage lengthy phone calls.
    b. block some quiet working time.
    c. minimize interruptions.

_____

Name _____ Date _____

PRACTICE 3

Proofreading

Instructions: Proofread and compare the two sentences in each group. If they are the same, write **Yes** in the space provided. If they are not the same, write **No.** Use the first sentence as the correct copy. If you find errors in the second sentence, underline them.

Go to the
Web

Practice 3 Exercises
for more skills practice on this topic.

1. When a slowdown occurs, take advantage of that time to do things that you cannot complete during the regular time period.

   When a slow down occurs, take advantage of that time to do things that you cant complete during the regular Time Period.

   1. _____

2. If you follow the suggestions in the book, you will learn to analyze your workload, identify problems, delegate tasks, and reduce time spent working on unnecessary jobs.

   If you follow the suggestions in the book, you will learn to analyse your workload, identify problems, delegate tasks, and reduce time spent working on unecessary jobs.

   2. _____

3. To set up a reminder file, you need 12 folders for the months, 31 folders for the days, and 1 folder for the next year.

   To set up a reminder file, you need 12 folders for the months, 30 folders for the days, and 1 folder for the year.

   3. _____

4. When technological systems do not function properly, we waste time waiting or redoing previous work.

   When Technological Systems do not function properly, We waste time waiting or redoing previous work.

   4. _____

5. If you are pressed for time, let your coworkers know your dilemma.

   If you are pressed for time, let your coworkers know your dilemna.

   5. _____

Capitalization

Name _____ Date _____

Identifying Errors

Instructions: *Compare the keyed version of the "to do" list with the original list. Underline the errors that you find in the second version. In the space provided at the end of the exercise, indicate the number of errors that you found. (The letters A, B, C that you find after each task indicate the urgency of getting a particular task completed. "A" represents the most urgent tasks.)*

JEFF DONOVAN, REALTOR

March 17, 20<year>

1. Compose mass mailing letter (C)
2. Follow up Redmon and Hendrick sales (A)
3. Close Daniels Ave. property (11 a.m.) (A)
4. Show Princeton lots (10 a.m.) (2 p.m.) (A)
5. Call for Kiwanis speakers (B)
6. Organize contracts for monthly report (C)
7. Obtain referrals (B)
8. Check listings (A)
9. Write new biographical sketch (B)
10. Proof brochures (B)

JEFF DONOVAN, rEALTOR

march 17, 20<year>

1. Compose mass mailing letter (C)
2. Follow up Redmon and Hendrick Sales (A)
3. Close Daniels ave. property (1 A.M.) (A)
4. Show Princeton lots (10 A.M.) (2 P.M.) (A)
5. Call for kiwanis speakers (B)
6. Organize contacts for monthly report (C)
7. Obtain referals (C)
8. Check listings (A)
9. Write new Biogaphical sketch (C)
10. Proof brochure (B)

How many errors did you find? _____

Name _____ Date _____

PRACTICE 4

Go to the
Web

Practice 4 Exercises
for more skills practice on
this topic.

Writing Effective Sentences

Use effective sentences to add interest and impact to your writing. As you create and combine sentences, vary the length of the sentences so that some are short and others are longer.

A topic sentence introduces the subject. When writing a topic sentence, make it specific enough to arouse interest. Also, write the topic sentence in a way that will "hook" your readers so that they will want to read further.

Instructions: List three ways that you wasted time this week. Write a sentence for each of the time-wasters indicating how you will avoid wasting time in the future. Vary the sentence length. Answers will vary.

_____

_____

_____

_____

_____

_____

_____

PRACTICE 5

Selecting the Correct Capitalized Words

Instructions: Select the correct item in parentheses and write it in the space provided.

1. The instructor for the (*organizational management, Organizational Management*) class will be Ormando Greco, (*Ph.D., ph.d.*).

   _____

2. Single parents like (*Leslie, leslie*) and (*Kim, kim*) find that job sharing is a solution for spending more time with their (*Children, children*).

   _____

3. To save learning time, I take (*Self-Paced Courses, self-paced courses*) on the (*Internet, internet*).

   _____

4. If you want to see an impressive example of efficiency, go to (*Walt Disney World, walt disney world*) in (*Orlando, Florida; orlando, florida*).

   _____

Capitalization

Name _____ Date _____

5. Time is wasted when mail addressed to Washington, DC, arrives in the (*state, State*) of Washington.

    _____

6. The (*attorney, Attorney*) said, (*"We, "we*) must rush the evidence to the offices of (*judge Ahrens, Judge Ahrens*)."

    _____

7. Voting results in the (*East, east*) are known several hours before they are known in the (*west, West*).

    _____

8. Renee arrives by 7 (*A.M., a.m.*) to plan her workday and to have some quiet work time.

    _____

9. To organize your office, divide it into sections: (*Your, your*) desk, your bookcase, your computer workstation, and your files.

    _____

10. Jerry reserved (*Thursday, thursday*) afternoon, (*September, september*) 9, for a demonstration of the personal information manager (*PIM, pim*) software.

    _____

11. All (*Government, government*) offices close on Memorial (*Day, day*).

    _____

12. On (*Chinese New Year, Chinese new year*), we are unable to do business in (*peking, Peking*).

    _____

13. Cheri Harris, (*president, President*) of the New Jersey (*league of Women Voters, League of Women Voters*), schedules 30 (*minutes, Minutes*) twice a week for reading journal articles.

    _____

14. My (*Mother, mother*) sorts incoming e-mail by subject in order to read and reply to related mail at one time.

    _____

15. Barbara highly recommends the book (*Solutions For Time Management Problems, Solutions for Time Management Problems*).

    _____

Name _____ Date _____

PRACTICE 6

Identifying Capitalization Errors

Instructions: *Underline any capitalization errors in the following sentences. On the lines provided, write the words correctly.*

1. In the book *Managing your Time,* Trevor Boutall recommends reviewing your progress toward your Objectives on a regular basis.

   _____

2. Time is Democratic because we all have exactly the same amount every Day.

   _____

3. I found an interesting article on Procrastination on Page 10 of the april issue of the *Training And Development* magazine.

   _____

4. When posting to a message board, use the Cut and Paste commands just as you would in a Word Processing Document.

   _____

5. Lisa uses the following time management tips:
   a. set aside specific times to check mail.
   b. keep a log of the time spent on tasks.
   c. organize the work area.

   _____

6. If you are most alert and at peak energy in the Morning, do your most difficult or demanding work before 10 A.M.

   _____

7. The Senator from the State of New Jersey used a wall-mounted visual organizer that prominently displayed Her Schedule.

   _____

8. Trisha Mahoney, Secretary of aauw, does not clip newspaper or journal articles but instead does an internet search to find the most up-to-date information quickly.

   _____

9. I worked on labor day, but to avoid interruptions, I let Voice Mail pick up all the Company calls.

   _____

Capitalization

Name _____ Date _____

10. Kevin's car is equipped with a mini clipboard on the car dash so that he can write quick notes while he is making sales calls in the Eastern part of the State.

_____

11. If a company's computers are connected by a Network, a Software Organizer may be used for Electronic Group Scheduling.

_____

12. One of Parkinson's Laws states, "any task expands to fill the time allowed for it."

_____

13. The Manager used these tactics to delay making a decision: Committees, Consultants, and Surveys.

_____

14. Mickey Jordan makes the following observation about organized people: They set deadlines, group similar tasks, and control interruptions.

_____

15. A personal digital assistant (pda) is a handheld Computer with a Calendar and Organizer for personal information.

_____

16. Day-Timer sponsors an Organizational Seminar each Fall and spring.

_____

17. I know that uncle Craig organized his time efficiently while he completed his Master's Degree at the university of arizona.

_____

18. In Office Systems 202, we spent five weeks on Time Management topics.

_____

19. The Yahoo! Search turned up One Million Web sites for the topic, but I finally found a useful URL at zdnet.COM.

_____

20. Karen ended her e-mail messages with *Sincerely Yours,* but She soon learned that those words were wasted keystrokes.

_____

Name _____   Date _____

PRACTICE 7

Proofreading

*Instructions: Proofread and compare the two sentences in each group. If they are the same, write **Yes** in the space provided. If they are not the same, write **No**. Use the first sentence as the correct copy. If you find errors in the second sentence, underline them.*

1. When you have a large project, break it into bite-size tasks to prevent procrastinating and feeling overwhelmed.

   When you have a large project break it into bit-size tasks to prevent procrastinating and feeling overwhelmed.

   1. _____

2. It is often difficult to say "No" to a request, especially if the person asking is in need of help.

   It is often difficult to say No to a request, especially if the person asking is in need of help.

   2. _____

3. To avoid solicitors' calls, place your phone number on the National Do Not Call Registry.

   To avoid solicitor's calls, place your phone number on the National do not Call Register.

   3. _____

4. When organizing your work area, discard the following items: outdated versions of manuals and catalogs, extra copies of documents, and information that you never use.

   When organizing your work area, discard the following items. Outdated versions of manuals and catalogs, extra copies of documents, and information that you never use.

   4. _____

5. Maricela Chavez, treasurer of our Hispanic Club, uses her Palm PDA to keep a database of student members and to manage a calendar of events.

   Maricela Chavez, treasurer of our Hispanic Club, uses her Palm PDA to keep a database of student members and to manage a calendar of events.

   5. _____

Name _____ Date _____

Identifying Errors

Instructions: Compare the keyed version of the "to do" list in the second group with the original list below. Underline the errors that you find in the second version. In the space provided at the end of the exercise, indicate the number of errors that you found. (The letters A, B, C that you find after each task indicate the urgency of getting a particular job completed. "A" represents the most urgent tasks.)

KAREN MACAL, MARKETING MANAGER

February 14

1. Read article about Webcasting in *Newsweek* (C)
2. Call Roberto Gachet about meeting room setup (A)
3. Make arrangements with Jaylie for refreshments on Friday (A)
4. Proofread brochure before sending to printer (B)
5. Call Jane about lunch next week at 11:30 a.m. (B)
6. Make appointment for photograph before March 15 (B)
7. Send e-mail to Doug about budget priorities ($25,000 for new computers) (A)
8. Analyze results of sales incentive program (C)
9. Order a wireless mouse for presentations (C)
10. Write memo to reps about new products (B)

KAREN MACAL, mARKETING mANAGER

February 14

1. Read article about webcasting in *Newsweek* (C)
2. Call Roberto Gachet about meeting room set up (A)
3. Make arrangements with Lydia for refreshments on friday (B)
4. Proofread brochure before sending to Printer (B)
5. Call Jane about lunch next week at 11:30 A.M. (B)
6. Make appointment for photograph before March 25 (B)
7. Send e-mail to Doug about budget priorities ($25,00 for new computers) (A)
8. Analyze results of Sales Incentive Program (C)
9. Order a wireless mouse for presentations (C)
10. Write memo to Reps about new products (B)

How many errors did you find? _____

Name _____ Date _____

PRACTICE 8

Writing

Instructions: *"If you want to get a job done right, you have to do it yourself." Do you agree with this statement? Write three sentences that explain why you agree or why you do not agree with the statement. Vary the sentence length. Answers will vary.*

_____

_____

_____

_____

_____

_____

_____

_____

_____

_____

_____

_____

_____

POSTTEST: *Looking Back*

Posttest

Instructions: Underline any capitalization errors in the following sentences. On the lines provided, write the words correctly.

1. kay feels that dylan wastes time by reading Junk Mail and taking long Breaks. (1)

   _____

2. The Committee was surprised when senator Joe Blake indicated that he would
   speak at the Seminar. (1)

   _____

3. Dr. Charles Hummell wrote the book *Tyranny Of The Urgent,* which is about the
   differences between urgent and important tasks. (2)

   _____

4. She said, "you should use your scheduled work hours for company business." (7)

   _____

5. The Winter retreat for the accounting department is at ravenwood lodge in
   northern New Mexico. (1, 4)

   _____

6. The Managers at asymetrix sponsor the organizational management conference
   at Rohnert park, California. (1)

   _____

7. I enrolled in BGN 71 business english at Central Florida community college to
   improve my grammar and writing skills. (1, 3)

   _____

8. Minimize interruptions by using the following techniques: (1, 6)
   1. arrange your work area so that your back is toward the door.
   2. let Voice Mail answer your telephone calls.
   3. set realistic goals.

   _____

9. Jenny received her Associate's Degree and is majoring in Business
   Communication at a local University. (1, 3)

   _____

10. Shelly uses these four planning tools: a Monthly Planner, a Weekly Objectives
    List, a Weekly Planner, and a Time Log. (1, 6)

    _____

Instructions: In the space provided, write the letter of the correct answer.

11. Which line has items that are all correct? (1, 2)

    a. Martin Luther King day, Family and Medical Leave Act, my Mother, company dividends

    b. father's day, Clear Air act, our aunt, Corporate profits

    c. New Year's Day, Safe Water Drinking Act, her father, the Senate

    d. Independence day, the Fair labor Standards act, my child, our Department

11. _____

12. Which line has items that are all correct? (1, 3)

    a. Golden west college, Multimedia Course, online Tutorial

    b. Golden West College, multimedia course, Online Tutorial

    c. Golden West college, Multimedia course, online Tutorial

    d. Golden West College, multimedia course, online tutorial

12. _____

13. Which line has items that are all correct? (2, 4)

    a. asians, halloween, summer, monday

    b. Asians, Halloween, summer, monday

    c. Asians, Halloween, summer, Monday

    d. Asians, Halloween, Summer, Monday

13. _____

14. Which line has items that are all correct? (5)

    a. Volume X, page 23, room 226, Highway 101

    b. volume X, Page 23, Room 226, highway 101

    c. Volume X, page 23, Room 226, Highway 101

    d. Volume X, Page 23, Room 226, highway 101

14. _____

15. Which line has the correct capitalization for a salutation and a complimentary closing? (7)

    a. Yours very truly, Dear selection committee

    b. Yours Very Truly, Dear Ms. Gronroos

    c. Yours Very Truly, dear ms. Gronroos

    d. Yours very truly, Dear Selection Committee

15. _____

Chapter 7

Pronouns

OBJECTIVES

After you have studied this chapter and completed the exercises, you will be able to do the following:

1. Recognize the function of a pronoun in a sentence.

2. Use nominative (subjective), objective, and possessive case pronouns correctly.

3. Differentiate between personal possessive pronouns and contractions.

4. Use compound personal pronouns correctly.

5. Recognize demonstrative and indefinite pronouns.

6. Recognize differences in the use of and the punctuation with interrogative and relative pronouns.

7. Use *who* and *whom* correctly in sentences.

Workplace Applications: Electronic Mail

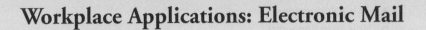

Electronic mail, also known as e-mail, is an online feature that lets you send a message from your computer to another computer, whether the other computer is next door or across the world. You receive messages in an electronic storage space called a mailbox, and each e-mail system has an electronic system administrator (or postmaster) that controls the e-mail.

E-mail is faster, less expensive, more convenient, and more spontaneous than traditional methods of communication. E-mail can be sent to groups of people at the same time, which facilitates collaborative work and efficient dissemination of information. Formatted documents, photos, sound files, and video files can be attached to e-mail messages.

The elements of grammar, punctuation, and spelling are just as important for e-mail as they are for other means of communication. E-mail messages, however, are generally short and concise. Being aware of the proper behavior in sending and receiving your e-mail is called netiquette.

When using e-mail, be aware that deleted messages do not disappear completely. Many computer networks automatically back up all e-mail messages, and these messages may stay in the computer system for years. E-mail messages are not private; therefore, avoid sending sensitive information. An e-mail message is like an electronic postcard—it can be read, forwarded, and even changed by other people without your knowledge.

PRETEST: *Looking Forward*

Pretest

Instructions: In the space provided, write the letter of the correct answer.

1. What is a pronoun? (1)   1. _____
    a. It is a connector.
    b. It is an action word.
    c. It is a noun substitute
    d. It is a modifier of a noun.

2. Which word is *not* a pronoun? (1)   2. _____
    a. anyone   c. it's
    b. what   d. him

3. Which word is not an objective case personal pronoun? (2)   3. _____
    a. them   c. me
    b. she   d. her

4. Which statement is correct? (2, 4)   4. _____
    a. Jack and myself attended the seminar on e-mail legal issues.
    b. Jack and me attended the seminar on e-mail legal issues.
    c. Me and jack attended the seminar on e-mail legal issues.
    d. Jack and I attended the seminar on e-mail legal issues.

5. Which statement is correct? (3)   5. _____
    a. Your asked to provide information before you select your password.
    b. You're asked to provide information before you select your password.
    c. You're asked to provide information before you select you're password.
    d. Your asked to provide information before you select you're password.

6. Which statement is correct? (2)   6. _____
    a. Her mailbox was flooded with e-mail when she and Gretchen returned.
    b. I had answered my e-mail messages by the time her and Sally returned from
        lunch.
    c. The instructor is arranging an e-mail demonstration for we business majors.
    d. The newest e-mail virus concerned our programmers, Wendy and he.

7. Which statement is correct? (4)   7. _____
    a. I taught myself the e-mail software package.
    b. He always expresses hisself very well in his e-mail messages.
    c. The managers theirselves approved the e-mail policies.
    d. Jim and myself checked out the possibility of a virus.

8. Which statement is correct? (5, 6, 7)   8. _____
    a. Everyone whom was hired received information about e-mail procedures.
    b. Everyone who was hired received information about e-mail procedures.
    c. Everyone that was hired received information about e-mail procedures.
    d. Everyone which was hired received information about e-mail procedures.

9. Which statement is correct? (3, 5)   9. _____

    a.   This was the e-mail software program that we needed.

    b.   This here e-mail message is too long.

    c.   Whose review of the e-mail lawsuit is most thorough—his or their's?

    d.   Whose responsible for reviewing those e-mail retention schedules?

10. Which statement is preferred? (6, 7)   10. _____

    a.   To whose did you send the e-mail?

    b.   To whom did you send the e-mail?

    c.   To who did you send the e-mail?

    d.   Who did you send the e-mail to?

11. Which statement is correct? (3)   11. _____

    a.   Its important for employees to know that their e-mail may be subpoenaed in a work-related lawsuit.

    b.   Its important for employees to know that they're e-mail may be subpoenaed in a work-related lawsuit.

    c.   It's important for employees to know that their e-mail may be subpoenaed in a work-related lawsuit.

    d.   It's important for employees to know that they're e-mail may be subpoenaed in a work-related lawsuit.

12. How many pronouns are in this sentence? *Betty scans her supervisor's e-mail for anything that she can handle on her own.* (1)   12. _____

    a.   two   c.   four

    b.   three   d.   five

13. Which statement is correct? (6, 7)   13. _____

    a.   Employees who violate e-mail policies may be terminated.

    b.   Whom will establish the e-mail retention rules?

    c.   Your e-mail policies, that were updated last week, will protect your organization.

    d.   Our e-mail procedures which are relatively lengthy protect us from liability.

14. Which statement is correct? (4, 7)   14. _____

    a.   Whom advised the writers whom wrote our e-mail policies?

    b.   Christine and myself prefer to screen our own e-mail messages.

    c.   From who is this e-mail message?

    d.   I myself reviewed each item in the e-mail policy document.

15. Which word is *not* an indefinite pronoun? (5)   15. _____

    a.   many   c.   each

    b.   this   d.   few

Chapter Preview

Although pronouns are substitutes for nouns, they have special characteristics of their own that require attention. In Chapter 2, you were introduced to personal pronouns, and you saw how pronouns helped you avoid the repetition of nouns. In Chapters 7 and 8, your study of pronouns becomes more challenging as you examine changes in case, gender, number, and person. In addition to studying personal pronouns in greater depth, you will learn about several other classifications of pronouns in this chapter.

Many people struggle with the use of the pronouns *who* and *whom.* In this chapter, you will learn how to determine which form is needed in a sentence. Another pronoun troublespot that you will study is the use of contractions and possessive pronouns such as *it's* and *its.* When this type of error is not corrected, your writing and proofreading skills appear careless.

Cases of Pronouns

NOTES

Looking Back

Review the section on personal pronouns in Chapter 2. See Chapter 5 for a discussion on the cases of nouns.

Pronouns are words that substitute for nouns. Personal pronouns refer to persons or things. Like nouns, pronouns have three cases—*nominative, objective,* and *possessive.* The case of a personal pronoun depends on the function of the pronoun in the sentence. As with nouns, a *first-person* pronoun refers to the one who is speaking, a *second-person* pronoun is the one spoken to, and a *third-person* pronoun is the one spoken about.

Nominative (Subjective) Case Personal Pronouns

Use the nominative case (also called subjective case) when the pronoun is the subject of a verb, when it is a subject complement, or when it is in apposition to a subject. The following pronouns are in nominative case:

	Singular	**Plural**
First Person	I	we
Second Person	you	you
Third Person	he, she, it	they

Subject of Verb.   Use the nominative case when the personal pronoun is the subject of a verb.

He receives at least 50 messages daily.

(*He* is a third-person pronoun and is the subject of the verb *receives.*)

I check my e-mail frequently, but he checks mail only twice a day.

(*I* is a first-person pronoun and is the subject of the verb *check. He* is a third-person pronoun and is the subject of the verb *checks.*)

You reach everyone quickly by sending e-mail messages.

(*You* is a second-person pronoun and is the subject of the verb *reach.*)

It takes only a few minutes to send most e-mail messages.

(*It* is a third-person pronoun and is the subject of the verb *takes.*)

Copyright © by The McGraw-Hill Companies, Inc.

Julie and she have developed new e-mail procedures.

(*She* is a third-person pronoun. *Julie* is a third-person noun. All nouns or pronouns in a compound subject must be in the nominative case.)

Subject Complement.   Use the nominative case when the personal pronoun is a subject complement (predicate noun or predicate pronoun) and follows a linking verb (*am, are, is, was, were, been,* and *being*).

The most experienced online technician is he.

(*He* is the subject complement renaming *technician.* Use the nominative case pronoun *he;* do not use *him.*)

The persons selected to write our e-mail procedures were John and she.

(*John* and *she* are the subject complements for *persons.* Use the nominative case pronoun *she;* do not use *her.* In a sentence with a compound subject complement, both subjects must be in the nominative case.)

Appositive.   Use the nominative case for a personal pronoun that is in apposition to a subject.

The new employees—Danielle and he—received a list of current e-mail addresses.

(*Danielle* and *he* are in apposition to the subject *employees.* The phrase identifies the new employees. The subject *employees* is in the nominative case. *He* must be in the same case as the subject.)

Two nominees—you and she—are featured in our online newsletter.

(*You* and *she* are in apposition to the subject *nominees* and must be in the same case as the subject.)

When an appositive follows a pronoun, choose the case of the pronoun that would be correct if the appositive were omitted.

We employees spend a lot of time contacting customers by e-mail.

(If the appositive *employees* is omitted, the sentence is correct with the word *We* [nominative case]. *We spend a lot of time contacting customers by e-mail.* Do not use *us employees.*)

CHECKPOINT 7.1

Go to the
Web

Checkpoint 7.1
for more skills practice on this topic.

Instructions: *In the space provided, identify the nominative case pronouns in each sentence. Then write the appropriate code or codes to indicate the correct use of these pronouns. Use the following codes:* **S** *(subject of a sentence),* **C** *(complement),* **A** *(appositive).*

1. They use the latest technology for fast, accurate communication. _____

2. You can reduce the number of junk e-mail messages received by _____ contacting your Internet service provider.

3. The person selected to proofread the e-mail etiquette pamphlet _____ was she.

4. The new employees, Robin and she, need clearly written _____ manuals that explain how to use the software.

5. She and I are checking the accuracy of our e-mail addresses. _____

6. We realize that e-mail is the most popular use of the Internet. _____

7. We managers recognize the potential for e-mail abuse. _____

8. Rick and he have developed the company's electronic security plan. _____

Objective Case Personal Pronouns

Use the objective case when the pronoun is a direct or indirect object of a verb or an object of a preposition. In addition, use the objective case when the pronoun is in apposition to a direct or indirect object or to the object of a preposition. The following pronouns are objective case pronouns:

	Singular	**Plural**
First Person	me	us
Second Person	you	you
Third Person	him, her, it	them

Direct or Indirect Object.   Use the objective case of personal pronouns when the pronouns are direct or indirect objects of verbs.

> **Have you asked him for a copy of the message?**
>
> (*Him* is an objective case pronoun used as a direct object.)
>
> **When files are confidential, do not attach them to e-mail messages.**
>
> (*Them* is an objective case pronoun used as a direct object.)
>
> **My supervisor gave her the instructions for sending encrypted e-mail.**
>
> (*Her* is an objective case pronoun used as an indirect object.)
>
> **JadeNet offered us free e-mail service for one month.**
>
> (*Us* is an objective case pronoun used as an indirect object.)
>
> **The e-mail etiquette presentation impressed Todd and me.**
>
> (Use the pronoun by itself as a check. The sentence *The e-mail etiquette presentation impressed me* makes sense. Use the objective case; do not use the nominative case *I*.)

Object of a Preposition.   Use the objective case when a personal pronoun is the object of a preposition.

> **I received two e-mail messages from her today.**
>
> (*Her* is an objective case pronoun that is the object of the preposition *from*.)
>
> **Holly spoke with us about Web-based e-mail accounts.**
>
> (*Us* is an objective case pronoun that is the object of the preposition *with*.)
>
> **My supervisor gave the e-mail guidelines to Sherry and her.**
>
> (In compound objects, use the pronoun by itself as a check. The sentence *My supervisor gave the e-mail guidelines to her* makes sense. Use the objective case; do not use *she*.)
>
> **Please check electronic signatures with Byron or me.**
>
> (The sentence *Please check electronic signatures with me* makes sense. Use the objective case; do not use *I*.)

NOTES

Direct and Indirect Objects

Direct objects answer the questions *What?* or *Whom?* Indirect objects answer the questions *To whom?* or *For whom?*

NOTES

Object of a Preposition

The object of a preposition is the noun or pronoun in a prepositional phrase.

Do This

Everyone except you and me had e-mail training.

The cost of the e-mail installation must be kept between you and me.

Do Not Do This

Everyone except you and I had e-mail training.

The cost of the e-mail installation must be kept between you and I.

Use an objective case pronoun with the prepositions *except* and *between*.

Appositive.   Use the objective case for a personal pronoun that is in apposition to a direct object, an indirect object, or an object of a preposition.

Please call a communication specialist, Hank or me.

(The pronoun *me* is used in apposition to the direct object, *specialist*. The object *specialist* is in the objective case. *Me* must be in the same case as the direct object *specialist*.)

The company offered two clients, Mrs. Riggs and her, free e-mail installations.

(The pronoun *her* [along with *Mrs. Riggs*] is used in apposition to the indirect object *clients*.)

We received requests for e-mail installations from two clients, Mrs. Riggs and her.

(The pronoun *her* is used in apposition to the object of the preposition *clients*.)

When an appositive follows a pronoun, choose the case of the pronoun that would be correct if the appositive were omitted.

Carla sent e-mail messages to us managers.

(If the appositive *managers* is omitted, the sentence is correct with *us*. Use the objective case pronoun; do not use the nominative case pronoun *we*.)

CHECKPOINT 7.2

Go to the
Web

Checkpoint 7.2
for more skills practice on this topic.

Instructions: *Underline the objective case pronouns in each sentence. In the space provided, write the appropriate code or codes to indicate the correct use of these pronouns. Use the following codes:* **DO** *(direct object),* **IO** *(indirect object),* **C** *(complement),* **A** *(appositive),* **OP** *(object of a preposition).*

1. Please send them an updated e-mail address for me.   _____

2. Slow Internet access time irritates him.   _____

3. If you hurt anyone's feelings with a written message, apologize to him or her.   _____

4. I thought that Ed's sarcastic message was meant for me.   _____

5. Mrs. Ludwig gave you the responsibility for distributing new e-mail policies to us. _____

6. The potential for e-mail abuse was evident to the two employees, Lupe and her. _____

7. The supervisor will e-mail you in five minutes. _____

8. She received a message that was intended for me. _____

9. The manager gave her the instruction manual for the new communication system. _____

10. The telecommunications supervisors, John and he, learned how to send video files to us. _____

Possessive Case Personal Pronouns

Possessive pronouns indicate ownership. Possessive pronouns do not have apostrophes. The following pronouns are possessive case pronouns:

	Singular	**Plural**
First Person	my, mine	our, ours
Second Person	your, yours	your, yours
Third Person	his, her/hers, its	their, theirs

Preceding Nouns.   Use the possessive pronouns *my, your, his, her, our,* and *their* to modify the nouns that follow. These possessive pronouns function as adjectives in sentences.

Her explanations for using the e-mail system were excellent.

(*Her* is a possessive pronoun that functions as an adjective modifying the noun *explanations*.)

We must check our grammar and spelling before we send e-mail messages.

(*Our* functions as an adjective modifying the nouns *grammar* and *spelling*.)

He writes clearly; therefore, his messages do not need corrections.

(*His* modifies *messages*.)

To avoid communication misunderstandings, choose your words wisely.

(*Your* modifies *words*.)

Separated From Nouns.   Do not use the possessive pronouns *mine, yours, hers, ours,* and *theirs* as modifiers before nouns. These pronouns stand alone and are separated from the nouns to which they refer.

The responsibility is yours if a document is not transmitted.

(*Yours* is a possessive pronoun that refers to the noun *responsibility*. This possessive pronoun does not precede the noun to which it refers but stands alone.)

Hers was the only message with an attachment.

(*Hers* is a possessive pronoun that refers to the noun *message*.)

Are personal e-mail messages written at work ours or theirs?

(*Ours* and *theirs* are possessive pronouns that refer to the noun *messages*.)

Contractions and Possessive Pronouns

Several contractions and possessive pronouns sound alike and may cause writing difficulties. These pronouns and contractions may be confusing:

its/it's   their/they're   theirs/there's   your/you're

It's/Its.   Do not use the contraction *it's* (a shortened form for *it is*) in place of *its*, the personal pronoun.

<u>It's</u> evident that I prefer using electronic mail rather than voice mail.

(*It's* is a contraction that means *it is*.)

The company announced <u>its</u> budget cuts through an intranet memo.

(*The company announced it is budget cuts* does not make sense. The possessive form *its* is necessary.)

Charline knows that <u>it's</u> important to verify e-mail addresses.

(Contraction)

The USPS continues to examine <u>its</u> role in electronic mail service.

(Possessive case)

You're/Your.   Do not use the contraction *you're* (a shortened form for *you are*) in place of *your*, the personal pronoun.

When attaching files to messages, check that the person to whom <u>you're</u> sending the files can receive them.

(*You're* is a contraction that means *you are*.)

The misuse of e-mail at work can affect <u>your</u> professional image.

(*The misuse of e-mail at work can affect you are professional image* does not make sense. The possessive form *your* is necessary.)

Include <u>your</u> e-mail address on <u>your</u> letterhead and business cards.

(Possessive case)

I understand that <u>you're</u> thinking of becoming an electronic security technician.

(Contraction)

They're/Their.   Do not use the contraction *they're* (shortened form for *they are*) in place of *their*, the possessive pronoun.

<u>They're</u> updating the policy on the proper use of company e-mail.

(*They're* is a contraction that means *they are*.)

A survey showed that women managers prefer to compose <u>their</u> own correspondence.

(If you substitute *they are* for *their*, the sentence does not make sense; therefore, a possessive form is necessary.)

There's/Theirs.   Do not use the contraction *there's* (shortened form for *there is* or *there has*) in place of *theirs*, the possessive pronoun.

There's an attachment to my last e-mail message.

(*There's* is a contraction that means *there is*.)

The attachment with my last e-mail message was theirs.

(*There is* does not make sense in this sentence; therefore, the possessive form *theirs* is necessary.)

The following summary is a guide for using personal pronouns.

	Nominative Case		Objective Case		Possessive Case	
First Person (the one speaking)	I	we	me	us	my mine	our ours
Second Person (the one spoken to)	you	you	you	you	your	yours
Third Person (the one spoken about)	she he it	they they they	her him it	them them them	her(s) his its	their(s) their(s) their(s)
Function	Subject Subject complement Appositive		Direct object Indirect object Object of preposition Appositive		Possessive noun replacement Adjective	

Go to the
Web

Checkpoint 7.3
for more skills practice on this topic.

CHECKPOINT 7.3

Instructions: *Select the correct word in parentheses, and write it in the space provided.*

1. (*It's, Its, Its'*) easier to read printed copy than copy on a screen. _____

2. E-mail communication ignores (*your, you're*) appearance, color, or gender. _____

3. (*They're, There, Their*) casual attitudes toward e-mail communications were not appropriate in our firm. _____

4. I was puzzled by the message in (*my, mine*) e-mail inbox. _____

5. A company may examine (*its, it's, its'*) employees' messages. _____

6. Robin uses (*her, her's*) e-mail service daily. _____

7. (*You're, Your*) probably already familiar with e-mail etiquette in (*your, you're*) office. _____

8. Addie knew that the proofreading error was (*her's, hers*). _____

9. (*There, Their, They're*) investigating the latest virus warning that (*there, their, they're*) department received. _____

10. The option to use the automatic spell and grammar check is (*theirs', there's, their's, theirs*). _____

Miscellaneous Pronouns

In addition to personal pronouns, several other types of pronouns require study. These pronouns have specific classification names that may sound complicated. You will not be required to memorize these names, but you will need to recognize the classifications and use the pronouns correctly in sentences. In the text that follows, these types of pronouns will be presented: compound personal pronouns (intensive and reflexive pronouns), demonstrative pronouns, indefinite pronouns, interrogative pronouns, and relative pronouns.

Compound Personal Pronouns (Intensive and Reflexive Pronouns)

A compound personal pronoun consists of a personal pronoun and the suffix *self* or *selves*. Use a compound personal pronoun to add emphasis (intensive pronoun) or to refer to a previously named noun or pronoun (reflexive pronoun). These pronouns are never used as subjects in sentences. The following pronouns are compound personal pronouns:

myself	himself	ourselves	themselves
yourself	herself	yourselves	
	itself		

Intensive Pronouns.   Use the intensive compound personal pronoun to add emphasis to a noun or to another pronoun.

> **Linda herself assured us that she would limit her use of slang in her messages.**
>
> (The word *herself* is an intensive pronoun that emphasizes the noun *Linda*.)
>
> **I myself never thought that I would screen my supervisor's e-mail messages.**
>
> (The word *myself* is an intensive pronoun that emphasizes the pronoun *I*.)
>
> **We ourselves see no reason for lengthy e-mail messages.**
>
> (The word *ourselves* emphasizes the pronoun *We*.)

Reflexive Pronouns.   Use the reflexive compound pronoun to refer to a noun or pronoun previously used as the subject of a sentence.

> **I allowed myself sufficient time to respond to his message.**
>
> (The reflexive pronoun *myself* refers to the subject *I*.)

NOTES

Pronoun Errors
The words *hisself, ourself(s), theirself, theirselves, yourselfs,* or *themself(s)* are not standard English words.

Copyright © by The McGraw-Hill Companies, Inc.

The students taught <u>themselves</u> the details of blocking unwanted e-mail.

(*Themselves* refers to the noun *students.*)

Do not criticize <u>yourself</u> for mistakes that are beyond your control.

(*Yourself* refers to the pronoun *you*, the understood subject.)

Katherine had already convinced <u>herself</u> that her e-mail policy was not going to be accepted by the other managers.

(*Herself* refers to the noun *Katherine.*)

Do This	Do Not Do This
My supervisor expected Randy Sue and <u>me</u> to finish the mailing.	My supervisor expected Randy Sue and <u>myself</u> to finish the mailing.
Randy Sue and <u>I</u> will finish the mailing.	Randy Sue and <u>myself</u> will finish the mailing.

Before using a compound personal pronoun, be sure that the noun or pronoun to which the compound noun refers is present in the sentence. Do not use a compound personal pronoun if a personal pronoun is adequate.

Go to the
Web

Checkpoint 7.4
for more skills practice on this topic.

CHECKPOINT 7.4

Instructions: *Select the appropriate pronoun in parentheses, and write it in the space provided.*

1. I congratulated (*me, myself*) when I eliminated 90 percent of my junk e-mail. _____

2. The employees (*theirselves, themselves, themselfs*) recommended "netiquette" workshops. _____

3. Give (*yourselfs, yourselves*) a break, and review what you have already learned about "netiquette." _____

4. Please meet with George and (*I, me, myself*) to discuss the plan for improving e-mail communication. _____

5. Terry and (*I, me, myself*) decided to volunteer for the Policies and Procedures Committee. _____

6. They satisfied (*theirselves, themselves, themselfs*) that they could improve internal communications. _____

7. He (*himself, hisself*) thought that the e-mail policy concerning personal use was fair. _____

8. Suzie, MaeLing, and (*I, me, myself*) agreed that we should purchase the software SpamKiller. _____

Chapter 7

Demonstrative Pronouns

Demonstrative pronouns designate specific persons, places, or things. The following pronouns are demonstrative pronouns:

Singular	Plural
this	these
that	those

Use demonstrative pronouns to point out specific persons, places, or things. When these demonstrative pronouns modify nouns, they function as adjectives.

This is an excellent program for tracking e-mail statistics.

(The demonstrative pronoun *This* points out *program,* a thing. The word *this* is the subject of the sentence.)

These are the e-mail statistics for tomorrow's meeting.

(The demonstrative pronoun *These* points out *statistics,* which are things. The word *these* is the subject of the sentence.)

We should have sent these messages yesterday.

(The demonstrative pronoun *these* functions as an adjective and answers the question *Which messages?*)

This company's research team surveyed the users of electronic mail.

(The demonstrative pronoun *This* functions as an adjective.)

Do This

This should be stored in your inbox.

We were not expecting that message until Tuesday.

Do Not Do This

This here should be stored in your inbox.

We were not expecting that there message until Tuesday.

Do not attach words such as *here* and *there* to demonstrative pronouns or to demonstrative pronouns that function as adjectives.

Indefinite Pronouns

Indefinite pronouns refer to persons, places, or things in a general way. They are not precise or exact. Additional information about the use of indefinite pronouns follows in Chapter 8. These pronouns are indefinite pronouns:

all	both	everything	nobody	others
another	each	few	no one	several
any	either	many	none	some
anybody	enough	more	nothing	somebody
anyone	everybody	most	one	someone
anything	everyone	neither	other	something

Use an indefinite pronoun to refer to nouns (persons, places, and things) spoken about in a general way. The nominative and objective cases are the same for indefinite pronouns.

Everyone needs a list of emoticons (shortcut e-mail signs of emotions).

(*Everyone* is an indefinite pronoun referring to people in general. *Everyone* is the subject and is in the nominative case.)

If you plan to use emoticons (shortcut e-mail signs of emotion), give everyone a list of meanings.

(*Everyone* is an indefinite pronoun that refers to people in a general way. In this sentence, *everyone* is an indirect object and is in the objective case.)

Many of our employees use precise subject lines in their e-mails.

(*Many* is an indefinite pronoun that refers to people in a general way. *Many* is the subject and is in the nominative case.)

Some think that they can write anything that they want in an e-mail message, and nobody will ever see it.

(*Some* and *nobody* are indefinite pronouns that refer to persons in general. In this sentence, *some* and *nobody* are in the nominative case. *Anything* is an indefinite pronoun that does not refer to a specific thing. *Anything* is in the objective case.)

Go to the
Web

Checkpoint 7.5
for more skills practice on this topic.

CHECKPOINT 7.5

Instructions: *Draw a line under each indefinite pronoun and circle each demonstrative pronoun. If necessary, refer to the lists for each type of pronoun.*

1. This is my supervisor, Hal Thompson, who proofreads everything for publication in the newspaper.

2. Someone has misinterpreted my e-mail humor, and this concerns me.

3. A few agreed with the newest e-mail policy, but many believed it needed additional review.

4. Be patient with those who are wary of e-mail and technology in general.

5. Most of the e-mail addresses for organizations end with *org.*

6. Some expect the receivers of e-mail messages to respond immediately.

7. E-mail allows users to send messages to anyone in the world in minutes.

8. All of these address lists must be revised.

Interrogative Pronouns

The word *interrogative* relates to forming questions. The following pronouns are interrogative pronouns:

who	which	whoever
what	whom	whomever
whose	whatever	whichever

Use interrogative pronouns to form direct and indirect questions.

Chapter 7

Direct Questions:

<u>Who</u> uses emoticons in e-mail messages?

To <u>whom</u> will you send that message?

<u>What</u> is the name of the e-mail system that you use at home?

<u>What</u> is the best software to control spam?

Indirect Questions:

I wonder <u>what</u> the new e-mail guidelines will be.

(*What* is used in an indirect question. An indirect question does not require a question mark.)

Bob asked <u>which</u> of the legal points related to document retention for e-mail.

(*Which* is used in an indirect question. No question mark is necessary.)

Relative Pronouns

The lists of relative and interrogative pronouns are similar. *That* is the major addition to the list. The most frequently used relative pronouns are *who, whom, that*, and *which*. The following are relative pronouns:

who	which	whoever	whichever
whom	that	whomever	whose

Use a relative pronoun as a reference to a noun in an independent clause. A relative pronoun begins a dependent clause that cannot stand on its own.

We decided to hire Sue, <u>who</u> is an electronic security consultant.

(*Who* is a relative pronoun referring to *Sue*. The relative pronoun introduces the dependent clause *who is an electronic security consultant*.)

Who, Whom, Whose. The relative pronouns *who, whom,* and *whose* relate to people. These pronouns have different forms for each case. See the section "Use of Who, Whom, and Whose" that follows Checkpoint 7.6.

Case	Pronoun
Nominative	who, whoever
Objective	whom, whomever
Possessive	whose

That. The relative pronoun *that* relates to things. Note that the relative pronoun *that* refers to persons *only* when a class or type of person is meant. The word *that* restricts the meaning of the sentence, making the words that follow necessary to the meaning of the sentence.

The firm <u>that</u> installed our intranet provides 24-hour hotline service.

(*That* is a relative pronoun referring to *firm*. The clause beginning with the word *that* is necessary to the meaning of the sentence. It is the firm *that installed our intranet* that provides 24-hour hotline service. No commas are necessary.)

She is the type of employee <u>that</u> answers correspondence promptly.

(*That* refers to a *type* of person. The clause beginning with the word *that* is necessary since it identifies the type of employee. No commas are necessary.)

NOTES

Looking Back

Refer to Chapter 3 for a review of dependent and independent clauses.

PUNCTUATION ALERT!

Essential Clause

Do not use a comma to set aside a clause that is essential to the meaning of a sentence.

EDIT PATROL

From a real estate flyer:

Great home for the city executive that is looking for an easy commute.

Shouldn't the flyer read, "Great home for the city executive who is looking for an easy commute"?

Which. The relative pronoun *which* refers primarily to things. The word *which* introduces nonrestrictive (nonessential) clauses. These clauses are not necessary to the meaning of a sentence.

Besides e-mail, the Internet provides newsgroups, <u>which</u> allow you to discuss shared interests with other users.

(*Which* is a relative pronoun that refers to *newsgroups.* The clause beginning with the word *which* adds interesting material, but it is not necessary to the meaning of the sentence. Commas are necessary to separate the nonrestrictive clause from the rest of the sentence.)

Your service provider, <u>which</u> is your Internet connection, transmits your message to the designated address.

(*Which* refers to *provider.* The clause is not necessary; therefore, it requires commas.)

Go to the
Web

Checkpoint 7.6

for more skills practice on this topic.

CHECKPOINT 7.6

Instructions: *Select the correct pronoun in parentheses, and write it in the space provided. If the pronoun selected is an interrogative pronoun, write* **I** *in the space provided. If the pronoun is a relative pronoun, write* **R.**

1. E-mail information providers gather news and data (*which, that*) directly affect you. _____

2. Tonya Brown is the one (*who, that*) reviews our e-mail subject lines. _____

3. (*Which, That*) software works better—Mail.com or Juno.com? _____

4. My e-mail provider's address, (*which, that*) I had misplaced, was in the folder. _____

5. Tracy Cook is the person (*who, that*) sent her résumé via e-mail. _____

6. (*Whose, Whoevers'*) signature shall I place on this e-mail message? _____

7. Business should establish policies (*which, that*) discourage employees from cluttering their e-mail systems with personal messages. _____

8. (*Who, What*) told you that emoticons were illegal? _____

9. Miranda wondered (*what, who*) the term "netwit" meant. _____

10. (*What, Whichever*) is the correct way to abbreviate "electronic mail"? _____

Use of *Who, Whom,* and *Whose*

When you understand the nominative, objective, and possessive cases of pronouns, you will be able to use *who, whom,* and *whose* correctly in written documents.

Who

Use the relative pronouns *who* or *whoever* to refer to persons. *Who* and *whoever* are nominative case pronouns. Use the nominative case when you can substitute *I, we, he, she,* or *they* in the clause beginning with *who* or *whoever.*

> **Managers <u>who</u> read employees' e-mail messages must be sure that a policy gives them that right.**

(Substitute *they* for *who* in the clause *who read employees' e-mail messages. They read employees' e-mail messages* makes sense; the nominative case pronoun *who* is correct.)

> **Matt Nelson, <u>who</u> is a sales manager for Kirtland Products, submitted his expense report by e-mail.**

(Substitute *he* for *who* in the clause *who is a sales manager. He is a sales manager for Kirtland Products* makes sense. The nominative case pronoun *who* is correct.)

> **<u>Who</u> shall I say is updating the "netiquette" seminar?**

(Rearrange the question to normal order [or a statement] and substitute *he. I shall say he is updating the "netiquette" seminar.* The nominative case *who* is correct.)

> **The person <u>who</u> uses simple words rather than lengthy expressions is usually a good communicator.**

(*He uses simple words rather than lengthy expressions* makes sense. The nominative case *who* is correct.)

> **<u>Whoever</u> needs information about e-mail security issues should contact Karen.**

(*He needs information* makes sense. The nominative case *whoever* is correct.)

Whom

Use the relative pronouns *whom* or *whomever* to refer to persons. *Whom* and *whomever* are objective case pronouns. Use objective case pronouns when you can substitute *me, us, him, her,* or *them* as a direct or indirect object or as an object of a preposition. You can make this simpler by using just *him* and *them* as the substitute words. Both end in *m* as does the word *whom.*

> **Juanita Gomez, <u>whom</u> you met yesterday, left us her e-mail address.**

(*Whom* is the object of the verb *met. You met her yesterday.*)

> **This is the person <u>whom</u> I saw reading e-mail.**

(*Whom* is the object of the verb *saw. I saw him reading e-mail.*)

> **To <u>whom</u> was that last message addressed?**

(*Whom* is the object of the preposition *to. That last message was addressed to him.*)

> **Bob Dawson, for <u>whom</u> we have great respect, was elected to the board of the International Internet Users Association.**

(*Whom* is the object of the preposition *for. We have great respect for him.*)

NOTES

Who and Whom

Who and *whom* are both interrogative pronouns and relative pronouns. *Whose* is the possessive form of *who. Who* is the nominative form, while *whom* is the objective form.

NOTES

Who/Whom Decisions

When deciding to use *who* or *whom,* do not look for the subject of the sentence. Look for the *who* or *whom* clause.

Do This	Do Not Do This
To whom did I send my last e-mail?	Whom did I send my last e-mail to?
From what store should I buy antivirus software?	What store shall I buy antivirus software from?
or	
Where should I buy antivirus software?	
Avoid ending a sentence with a preposition whenever possible.	

Whose and Who's

Use the relative pronoun *whose* to show ownership. Do not use an apostrophe with this possessive form of the pronoun. Do not use the contraction *who's* (*who is, who has*) to show possession.

Do you know whose interpretation of the e-mail policy is correct?

(*Whose* indicates possession.)

We wonder whose technology will change the way that we communicate ten years from now.

(*Whose* indicates possession.)

Who's going to inform the supervisor that his e-mail messages were returned with the wrong addresses?

(*Who's* is the contraction for *who is.*)

Go to the
Web

Checkpoint 7.7
for more skills practice on this topic.

CHECKPOINT 7.7

Instructions: *Select the correct word in parentheses, and write it in the space provided.*

1. Rhonda Patina, (*who, whom, whose*) is the regional sales manager for Lawson Communications, uses e-mail for impersonal messages only. _____

2. By (*who, whom, whose*) were these e-mail procedures written? _____

3. (*Who, Whom, Whose*) installed the intranet at Bentley Industries? _____

4. Dan Dusquene is the service person (*who, whom, whose*) gave us the tip for storing messages. _____

5. (*Who, Whom, Whose*) e-mail address has numbers in it? _____

6. Ron Wilson, with (*who, whom, whose*) you spoke on the phone, can advise us about a company's liability for e-mail. _____

7. (*Who's, Whose*) the presenter for the e-mail organization workshop? _____

8. Is he the person (*who, whom, whose*) is writing the instructions for using Outlook Express? _____

9. Mary, (*who, whom, whose*) I have known since high school, is now an electronic mail network trainer. _____

10. Ann Doyle, (*who, whom, whose*) manages RoyalNet, is the person to (*who, whom, whose*) I refer all my questions. _____

11. We have managers (*who, whom, whose*) do not stop to think about the impact that their messages may have on employees. _____

12. (*Who's, Whose*) the expert in the area of composing clear and accurate messages? _____

13. Usually, there is at least one person in a company (*who, whom, whose*) can access any password. _____

14. E-mail is helpful for salespeople (*who, whom, whose*) want a quick update on new products. _____

15. I wonder (*who, whom*) can assist me in opening my attachments. _____

16. To (*who, whom*) shall I address my concerns about the risks of viruses with e-mail attachments? _____

17. We do not know (*who, whom*) is sending all these unwanted messages. _____

18. To (*who, whom*) shall I send these e-mail attachments? _____

19. (*Whoever, Whomever*) becomes a member of the e-mail policies committee will have to understand legal strategies. _____

20. I open e-mail based on (*who, whom*) the sender is and what the subject line says. _____

Diagramming Sentences

To diagram a sentence with a compound subject, verb, or object, follow the examples below. You will be asked to diagram only those parts of a sentence that you have worked with in previous chapters or that are introduced in this chapter.

Compound Subject:

Clients and employees appreciate e-mail service.

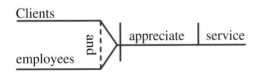

Compound Verb:

Our company purchased and installed an intranet system.

Compound Object:

He uses emoticons and abbreviations in his e-mail messages.

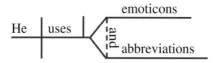

Go to the
Web

Checkpoint 7.8
for more skills practice on
this topic.

 CHECKPOINT 7.8

Instructions: *In the space provided, diagram only the following parts of the sentences: simple and compound subjects and verbs, compound objects, direct and indirect objects, appositives, subject complements, and possessive nouns.*

1. Terry and she misused their e-mail privileges.

2. I use and enjoy my new e-mail software.

3. She gave us the e-mail policy and a list of acceptable emoticons.

4. My instructor and my supervisor emphasized the importance of the subject line in e-mail messages.

5. You can send and receive e-mail to most foreign countries.

Name _____ Date _____

PRACTICE 1

Choosing Pronouns

Instructions: Draw a line under the correct word in parentheses.

1. Computer users can send (*their, there, they're*) commercial ads through (*their, there, they're*) bulk e-mail providers.

2. (*It's, Its, Its'*) inappropriate for (*us, we*) employees to send chain letters on a company's computer network.

3. After (*Todd and he, Todd and him*) made (*their, there, they're*) decision, they gave (*we, us*) the new e-mail policy.

4. (*We, Us*) instructors wanted (*Ethan and her, Ethan and she*) to discuss e-mail etiquette with our students.

5. Everyone received the new e-mail etiquette guidelines except (*me, I*).

6. The instructor asked two former students, (*Juan and I, Juan and me, Juan and myself*), for examples of company e-mail policies.

7. Jason Boyd is the employee (*who, whom, which*) has contributed the best e-mail ad design.

8. Juan Rodriguez, (*who, whom*) you hired last month, is an excellent translator for our foreign e-mail messages.

9. The new advanced electronic mail trainees—Eric, Sue, Beth, and (*I, me*)—will meet next week.

10. (*Them, Those*) employees (*who, whom*) want to discuss controversial issues via e-mail should investigate software with privacy options.

11. (*She, Her*) and other coworkers use descriptive acronyms.

12. (*Whose, Who's*) likely to read (*your, you're*) e-mail messages?

13. The representative (*who, whom*) installed the new electronic mail program was patient with my coworker and (*me, I.*)

14. (*He and I, Him and I, He and myself*) use our e-mail to keep in touch.

15. A firm should have explicit instructions designating the length of time that (*its, its', its*) records must be maintained.

16. (*Sam and I, Sam and me, Sam and myself*) worked on storage procedures for electronic and paper documents.

17. They sent two pages of new e-mail addresses to (*she, her*).

18. (*Her and me, She and I, She and myself*) did not send the attachment until today.

19. Be complete but concise in (*your, you're*) message.

20. (*Whose, Who's*) interpretation of the e-mail report should be submitted first—(*theirs, their's, theirs'*) or mine?

Go to the **Web**

Practice 1 Exercises for more skills practice on this topic.

Name _____ Date _____

Go to the
Web
───

Practice 2 Exercises
for more skills practice on this topic.

PRACTICE 2

Identifying Pronouns and Contractions

*Instructions: In the following sentences, underline all pronouns and contractions. If a pronoun or contraction is used incorrectly, circle it and write the correct word in the space provided. More than one error may appear in a sentence. If the sentence is correct, write **Yes.***

1. Notify the online services that you use, and ask them to remove you're name from their mailing lists.

1. _____

2. I like receiving our company newsletters online because the news is current.

2. _____

3. Both of the assistants are careless in proofreading messages before they send them.

3. _____

4. Several of my coworkers delete all of they're messages when they become overwhelmed by information overload.

4. _____

5. Our instructor taught me to write clear, concise e-mail messages.

5. _____

6. He and myself established the system to monitor our company's passwords.

6. _____

7. Send your message only to them who need a copy.

7. _____

8. He used the abbreviation *FAQ* (frequently asked questions) for his internal correspondence only.

8. _____

9. If you send material to clients whom have multiple e-mail addresses, record the address that they use most frequently.

9. _____

10. We have been warned not to leave messages on our screens when we leave our desks.

10. _____

11. The company owns its' computer system and most of the data in it.

11. _____

12. For them whom work at home, e-mail will save them time and money.

12. _____

13. No one knows whether or not you have expensive envelopes and stationery when you send e-mail messages.

13. _____

14. Her and her supervisor spend at least 45 minutes daily reading their e-mail.

14. _____

15. Some abuse the e-mail system by sending non-work-related messages to they're coworkers.

15. _____

16. Emoticons are symbol combinations that get your emotions across when your using e-mail.

16. _____

Name _____ Date _____

17. We ordered the catalogs that were advertised on   17. _____
the Web site, but mine never arrived; hers' arrived
a week ago.

18. My supervisor expects Ashley and I to produce   18. _____
error-free documents.

19. Who is the speaker at the Internet security   19. _____
workshop?

20. I like to read the headlines from "This Is True," that   20. _____
is a free e-mail service.

Using Correct Pronouns and Punctuation

*Instructions: The sentences below may have usage or punctuation errors. If the sentence is written correctly, write **Yes** in the space provided. If the sentence is written incorrectly, write it correctly in the space provided.*

1. Jon and him used the acronym *RFC* which means a request for
comments at the end of their document.

_____

_____

2. Instead of sending an e-mail message, Jim delivered the
termination notice hisself.

_____

_____

3. E-mail is good for reaching people which live in different time
zones.

_____

_____

4. Somebody has to pay for free e-mail, and its the advertisers whom
pay.

_____

_____

5. Both Joe and myself were late for the electronic security meeting.

_____

_____

6. The e-mail message, that just arrived, was confidential.

_____

7. Usually, theirs at least one person in a company that can access any
password.

_____

_____

Name _____ Date _____

8. Our service provider which Jane and me have used since 2001 is located on Tenth Avenue.

_____

_____

9. Her and me had the responsibility for composing the e-mail to Japan.

_____

10. Between you and I, I think that Jacob and her are the best writers.

_____

Go to the
Web

Practice 3 Exercises
for more skills practice on this topic.

PRACTICE 3

Proofreading

*Instructions: Proofread and compare the two sentences in each group. If they are the same, write **Yes** in the space provided. If they are not the same, write **No.** Use the first sentence as the correct copy. If you find errors in the second sentence, underline them.*

1. Stored electronic documents are viewed by the courts as equivalent to paper, and they're being used in product liability and class action suits.

   Stored electronic documents are viewed by the courts as equivalent to paper, and their being used in product liability and class action suites.

   1. _____

2. The Electronic Communications Privacy Act allows employers the right to read their employees' e-mail messages.

   The Electronic Communications Privacy act allows employers the right to read there employee's e-mail messages.

   2. _____

3. Some companies do not approve of the use of emoticons such as :-) (smiley, when turned on its side) or abbreviations such as *FYI* (for your information).

   Some companies do not approve of the use of emotions such as :-) (smily, when turned on its' side) or abbreviations such a *FYI* (for your information).

   3. _____

4. Before you send your message, double-check the receiver's address because one transposed letter can cause your message to go to someone else.

   Before you send you message, double-check the receivers address because one transposed letter can cause your message to go to someone else.

   4. _____

Name _____ Date _____

5. If administrative assistants send electronic messages   5. _____
    from their computers on behalf of their supervisors,
    who is responsible for the message content—the
    administrative assistants or the supervisors?

    If administrative assistants send electronic messages
    from there computers on behalf of their supervisors,
    whose responsible for the message content—the
    administrative assistants or the supervisors?

Using Proofreaders' Marks

Instructions: Use the following proofreaders' marks to indicate the errors in the company memo below.

delete ⌇   capitalize ≡   insert ∧

lowercase /   change a word ⌇ or _____

    From: Jerry w. Smithfield
    Date: May 31, 20-
    To: All Employees
    Subject: Company Use of Abbreviations

During past month, I have receded many e-mail messages that have
included Abbreviated Terms. In an effort to be be sure that We all
understand and us the same abbreviations, please check the
accepted Company terms listed below:

    FAQ   = frequently asked questions

    RFC   = request for comments

    FYI   = for you're information

    IMO   = in my opinion

    MSgS   = messages

    NLT   = No later than

please use them abbeviations for internal e-mail messages only.

PRACTICE 4

Composing E-Mail Messages

Instructions: After reviewing the following guidelines, respond to the situations presented below. Answers will vary.

Electronic mail is an established method of business and personal communication. The following guidelines help in writing e-mail messages:

- Practice the same rules of writing that you would follow if you were sending the correspondence through traditional channels. Use correct grammar, spelling, and punctuation.

Go to the
Web

Practice 4 Exercises
for more skills practice on
this topic.

Name _____ Date _____

- Include a descriptive subject line, but limit it to 25–35 characters.
- Write concisely and briefly. Eliminate unnecessary phrases and trite expressions.
- Keep line length to 60 characters.
- State important information immediately. Begin with your purpose and include important details.
- Eliminate abbreviations or jargon.
- Avoid using all-capital letters, which have the effect of "screaming" to the reader.
- Omit sarcasm and too much humor.

1. Compose an e-mail message to a friend explaining why it is necessary to have good English skills. Use at least six pronouns in the message. Print a copy of your message for your instructor to evaluate.

2. Compose an e-mail message to your instructor explaining why your good grammar skills will be useful in getting a promotion. Use either *who* or *whom* in one of the sentences.

PRACTICE 5

Choosing Pronouns and Contractions

Instructions: Draw a line under the correct word in parentheses.

1. Advertisers can e-mail (*their, there, they're*) solicitations by using (*their, there, they're*) subscriber lists from PostMaster Direct.

2. (*It's, Its, Its'*) interesting to see the names (*that, which*) people select for (*their, there, they're*) e-mail addresses.

3. After (*Zack and he, Zack and him*) corresponded about Sara's dismissal, they questioned (*we, us*) about privacy issues.

4. (*We, Us*) employees wanted (*Zoe and her, Zoe and she*) to give us e-mail writing tips.

5. Everyone understood the abbreviation *FAQs* (frequently asked questions) except (*me, I*).

6. The supervisor asked two computer technicians, (*Joe and I, Joe and me*), for help with forwarding e-mail messages home.

7. Sherri is the student (*who, whom*) had an internship at Intel last summer.

8. Carolina, (*who, whom*) is originally from El Salvador, is an expert in translating Spanish correspondence.

9. The most recently hired employees—Bianca, Jack, and (*I, me*)—need e-mail training this week.

Name _____   Date _____

10. Companies (*who, that*) do not have e-mail policies should immediately put them in place.

11. If Richard is ill again today, we will need to ask (*him, he*) for (*his, he*) e-mail password.

12. (*Whose, Who's*) responsibility is it to delete (*your, you're*) e-mail messages?

13. The programmer (*who, whom*) wrote our e-mail software was happy to explain it to my office mate and (*me, I*).

14. (*He and I, He and myself, Him and I*) receive at least 100 e-mail messages a day.

15. (*It's, Its, Its'*) unlikely that I will respond to every e-mail message.

16. (*Abby and I, Abby and me*) began working at Adobe Systems on the same day.

17. Teresa gave several Web addresses to (*she, her*).

18. (*Him and me, He and I, He and myself*) asked how to advertise by e-mail without spamming.

19. (*Your, You're*) message should include only one topic.

20. (*Whose, Who's*) address directory did you consult—(*theirs, their's, theirs'*) or mine?

PRACTICE 6

Identifying Pronouns and Contractions

*Instructions: In the following sentences, underline all pronouns and contractions. If a pronoun or contraction is used incorrectly, circle it and write the correct word in the space provided. More than one error may appear in a sentence. If the sentence is correct, write **Yes.***

1. These small stack of messages is mine, but the big stack is his.

   1. _____

2. Barb was careless, and she missed correcting the errors in several of her documents.

   2. _____

3. You should not use e-mail to send confidential information to someone.

   3. _____

4. They're messages were so general; there was nothing specific in them.

   4. _____

5. We thought that e-mail technology would give we paralegals time for researching cases.

   5. _____

6. As you receive messages, scan them and respond to them immediately if possible.

   6. _____

Name _____ Date _____

7. She overuses the boring line "First the good news,   7. _____
   then the bad" in her messages.

8. You're password on our e-mail system expires in   8. _____
   a month, and its time for you to choose another.

9. I tried attaching a file to your e-mail message, but   9. _____
   it did not work.

10. We do not want Sandy or he to have access to   10. _____
    our passwords.

11. After the manager and him agreed, they told us   11. _____
    about monitoring our e-mail messages.

12. A subject for each of your e-mail messages is   12. _____
    necessary for Roberto and I.

13. It must have been her who left her password next   13. _____
    to my computer.

14. The employees whom use the Internet must use   14. _____
    it for business purposes only.

15. Today we expected to receive you're e-mail about   15. _____
    our online order.

16. You should not compose a message when your   16. _____
    angry.

17. If you need confidential advice from someone,   17. _____
    talk to him or her in person about it.

18. Will you please contact them people whom repair   18. _____
    our computers.

19. He left a message in my voice mailbox instead of   19. _____
    e-mailing me.

20. Was it him whom developed our international   20. _____
    communication guidelines?

Using Correct Pronouns and Punctuation

Instructions: The sentences below may have usage or punctuation errors. If the sentence is written correctly, write **Yes** *in the space provided. If the sentence is written incorrectly, write it correctly in the space provided.*

1. When asked for her suggestions, Katy used the acronym *IMO* which
   means "in my opinion."

   _____

   _____

Name _____ Date _____

2. If you wish to keep you're correspondence confidential, do not use e-mail.

_____

3. People which live outside the United States have difficulty understanding our sarcasm.

_____

_____

4. Somebody left me hundreds of unwanted messages, and its not any of my friends, which left me these messages.

_____

_____

5. Both Kara and myself were annoyed by the announcement.

_____

_____

6. International students—Kaydrah and her—use e-mail to keep in touch with relatives that live in India.

_____

_____

7. Several colleagues asked Mandy and I why we used EOM at the end of our documents.

_____

_____

8. Please give this list of emoticons to Phillip and she.

_____

_____

9. I tried to contact Elise and he for their comments about MSN® Messenger.

_____

_____

10. My supervisor refers questions regarding the attachment of photographs to Kay or myself.

_____

_____

Name _____ Date _____

PRACTICE 7

Proofreading

Instructions: Proofread and compare the two sentences in each group. If they are the same, write **Yes** in the space provided. If they are not the same, write **No.** Use the first sentence as the correct copy. If you find errors in the second sentence, underline them.

1. According to the employee handbook, the corporation's electronic mail system is business property, and it's to be used for business purposes.

   According to the employee handbook the corporation's electronic mail system is business property and its to be used for business purposes.

   1. _____

2. E-mail can be a creative and social tool that should be used to tell workers about important events.

   E-mail can be a creative and social tool which should be used to tell worker's about important events.

   2. _____

3. Because of the way e-mail is transmitted through the Internet, parts of it may remain on every intermediate host computer through which it passes.

   Because of the way e-mail is transmitted through the Internet, parts of it it may remain on every intermediate host computer through which it passes.

   3. _____

4. E-mail does not have the same legal right to privacy as a letter in an envelope that is sent through the postal service.

   E-mail does not have the same legal right to privacy as a letter in an envelope that is sent through the postal service.

   4. _____

5. E-mail is a useful tool for researchers, academicians, and government employees who need to share documents quickly.

   E-mail is a useful tool for researchers, acadmicians, and government employees whom need to share documents quickly.

   5. _____

Name _____ Date _____

Using Proofreaders' Marks

Instructions: Use the following proofreaders' marks to indicate the errors in the meeting reminder notice below.

delete ↟   insert ∧

capitalize ≡   change a word / or ⎯⎯⎯

lowercase /

The first meeting of the E-Mail policies committee will be on Friday, April 21, at 2:30 P.M. The purpose of this meeting is to identify the guidelines for managing company e-mail. Please clear you're calendars a two-hour meeting.

As a starting point, be be prepared with suggestions in the folllowing areas:

1. what type of written policy will be necessary to identify the rules for employee use of company e-mail?

2. how will this company educate all its employes about complying with the rules?

3. How will Company Supervisors enforce the policy once it has been established.

Since I need to know whom will be attending, please e-mail your response by April 17.

PRACTICE 8

Composing E-Mail Messages

Instructions: Write five sentences including the proper use of the following. Answers will vary.

1. *Who* or *whom*
2. *Its* and *it's*
3. Two pronouns (*he, her, him,* etc.)
4. Reflexive pronoun
5. *That* or *which* used at the beginning of a clause

_____

_____

_____

_____

_____

_____

Pronouns

POSTTEST: *Looking Back*

Posttest

Instructions: In the space provided, write the letter of the correct answer.

1. Which of the following is *not* a pronoun? (1)
   a. its
   b. her
   c. for
   d. whomever

1. _____

2. Which statement is correct? (2, 4)
   a. Molly and myself researched international e-mail netiquette.
   b. Molly and me researched international e-mail netiquette.
   c. Me and Molly researched international e-mail netiquette.
   d. Molly and I researched international e-mail netiquette.

2. _____

3. Which statement is correct? (2)
   a. Lisa sends e-mail computer virus alerts to Luke and I once a week.
   b. Lisa sends e-mail computer virus alerts to I and Luke once a week.
   c. Lisa sends e-mail computer virus alerts to Luke and myself once a week.
   d. Lisa sends e-mail computer virus alerts to Luke and me once a week.

3. _____

4. Which statement is correct? (3)
   a. Your asked to verify you're password before you use e-mail.
   b. You're asked to verify your password before you use e-mail.
   c. You're asked to verify you're password before you use e-mail.
   d. Your asked to verify your password before you use e-mail.

4. _____

5. Which statement is correct? (2)
   a. Her password had expired when she and Stan returned from vacation.
   b. Taylor had to answer an e-mail message before her and Stan went to lunch.
   c. The instructor is assigning e-mail accounts for we communication students.
   d. The lack of computer time concerned the managers, Denny and he.

5. _____

6. Which statement is correct? (4)
   a. I taught myself how to attach e-mail documents.
   b. He becomes irritated with hisself when he forgets an e-mail address.
   c. The students theirselves recognized the importance of using e-mail.
   d. Melissa and myself are experts in searching for e-mail addresses.

6. _____

7. Which statement is correct? (5, 6, 7)
   a. Everyone whom was enrolled in the class knew how to use e-mail.
   b. Everyone who was enrolled in the class knew how to use e-mail.
   c. Everyone that enrolled in the class knew how to use e-mail.
   d. Everyone which enrolled in the class knows how to use e-mail.

7. _____

8. Which statement is correct? (3, 5)
   a. This was the e-mail policy that we signed.
   b. This here e-mail policy needs to be signed.
   c. Whose password do you think is better—his or hers'?
   d. Who's e-mail message shall I respond to first?

8. _____

9. Which statement is correct? (6, 7)

    a.   To whose did you e-mail the memo?

    b.   To whom did you e-mail the memo?

    c.   To who did you e-mail the memo?

    d.   Who did you e-mail the memo to?

9. _____

10. Which of the following is a possessive pronoun? (2)

    a.   her's   c.   there's

    b.   they're   d.   its

10. _____

11. Which statement is preferred? (7)

    a.   To who do I address this e-mail?

    b.   Who forwarded this attachment?

    c.   Whom will be the new director of communications?

    d.   In who does Jane have the most confidence?

11. _____

12. Which statement is correct? (6)

    a.   Janie is a person that needs a quiet office.

    b.   He is the technician that can answer your questions about attachments.

    c.   This wireless mouse, that we purchased last week, is not working properly.

    d.   This e-mail, which arrived yesterday, should be answered immediately.

12. _____

13. Which statement is correct? (3)

    a.   Its time to upgrade our software.

    b.   Our company announced it's new e-mail policy.

    c.   It's easier to read reports electronically.

    d.   The company updated it's e-mail address.

13. _____

14. Which statement is correct? (2, 4, 6)

    a.   Cindy and me answer all the technical e-mail questions.

    b.   Its difficult to read this lengthy e-mail.

    c.   He and myself will attend the e-mail writing seminar.

    d.   Please forward this e-mail to John and her.

14. _____

15. Which statement is correct? (2, 4, 6)

    a.   You answered that e-mail better than me.

    b.   He told myself and Gayle about the computer virus.

    c.   Their responsible for maintaining our firewall.

    d.   Karen is the person who forwarded a video file.

15. _____

Chapter 8

Pronoun/Antecedent Agreement

OBJECTIVES

After you have studied this chapter and completed the exercises, you will be able to do the following:

1. Determine pronoun/antecedent agreement with reference to person, number, and gender.

2. Determine the correct use of singular or plural pronouns with compound subject antecedents.

3. Use the correct pronoun references with collective antecedents.

4. Use appropriate singular and plural pronoun references with indefinite pronoun antecedents.

5. Correct unclear or dual pronoun references.

6. Identify explanatory phrases in determining antecedents.

7. Use correct pronoun forms with *than* and *as*.

8. Differentiate between one- and two-word indefinite pronouns.

Workplace Applications: Cultural Diversity

One factor leading to success in school or at work is the acceptance of those who are "different" from you. *Cultural diversity* is the term used to name these differences. Cultural diversity is more than race or ethnicity, however. Cultural diversity also includes gender, age, religion, political orientation, physical size, and appearance. All these factors influence the cultural experiences and backgrounds of individuals and groups.

Increasing Awareness

As life and work become more intertwined, people need a greater awareness of the ways that cultural heritage and background influence values, assumptions, and relationships. Some people do not realize that they exhibit biased behavior and may not be aware that their own behavior is offensive. Other people are aware of their biases and prejudices and know that their behavior offends others but still continue with derogatory jokes, comments, and actions. Still other people are willing to take action when they encounter inappropriate words or behaviors.

A good way to achieve an understanding of cultural diversity is to develop relationships with individuals who are culturally different. The more informed you are about different perspectives and lifestyles, the more marketable you will be in an increasingly diverse society and world. By appreciating the differences in others, you will be more successful in the diverse global workplace.

Pretest

Instructions: In the space provided, write **Yes** if the pronoun and antecedent in the sentence are in agreement. If the pronoun is used incorrectly, underline the pronoun, and write the correction in the space provided.

1. Even though we have different backgrounds, we still have the same goals. (1)   1. _____

2. Whenever a diversity issue arises, a supervisor must look at their own attitudes. (1)   2. _____

3. Educators and curriculum directors should develop new courses to help their students survive in a global market. (2)   3. _____

4. The American Association of Affirmative Action is holding their meeting in April. (3)   4. _____

5. Many poorly educated women obtain low-skilled service jobs to support her families. (4)   5. _____

6. If we laugh at racial or gender jokes, you give our children the idea that this is acceptable behavior. (5)   6. _____

7. My coworkers said that they had trouble communicating with international clients especially when they didn't know the language. (5)   7. _____

8. Kristen, as well as Maria, was concerned about their equal opportunity rights. (6)   8. _____

9. I think that Ray still receives more money than me. (7)   9. _____

10. Every one should be present for his or her cultural diversity orientation. (8)   10. _____

11. Libby and William consider cultural differences when she and he plan company activities. (2)   11. _____

12. Gini or Maddy will recommend purchasing a video on diversity issues to their supervisor. (2)   12. _____

13. Neither of the two men asked their supervisor for special treatment or extra training. (4)   13. _____

14. All of the pending workplace discrimination reports have been categorized into their appropriate files. (4)   14. _____

15. The team completed their summary of the employee survey. (3)   15. _____

Chapter Preview

Now that you have been introduced to pronouns, you should use them correctly in sentences. Pronouns are not always specific in their meaning; therefore, they may cause problems when it is unclear as to whom or to what these pronouns are referring. You have probably experienced this frustration in following printed instructions such as those found in computer manuals or in assembling children's toys or furniture. Even when the parts are all there, you may not be sure to what the words *it* and *them* refer.

Your readers should not have to second-guess your intent or take a chance on what you actually mean by your pronoun references. In this chapter, you will determine ways to make these references clear. You will also study several additional pronoun troublespots.

Pronoun/Antecedent Agreement

An *antecedent* is the word or group of words to which a personal pronoun refers or that a personal pronoun replaces. A pronoun must give accurate and unmistakable reference to the noun or other pronoun that it replaces. In other words, the pronoun must agree with its antecedent in *number* (singular, plural), *gender* (masculine, feminine, neuter), and *person* (first, second, third).

Noun as Antecedent

Strong <u>individuals</u> recognize <u>their</u> biases.

(The antecedent is *individuals,* a third-person plural noun. The third-person plural pronoun *their* refers to this antecedent.)

<u>Janet</u> remarked that <u>she</u> had benefited from affirmative action.

(The antecedent is *Janet,* a third-person singular noun. The third-person singular pronoun *she* refers to this antecedent.)

Pronoun as Antecedent

<u>We</u> need a clear idea of what is expected of <u>us</u> under the ADA Act.

(The antecedent is *we,* a first-person plural pronoun. The first-person plural pronoun *us* is necessary when referring to this antecedent.)

<u>He</u> expects to have <u>his</u> harassment case considered by the board.

(The antecedent is *he,* a third-person singular pronoun. The third-person singular pronoun *his* is necessary when referring to this antecedent.)

Steps for Determining Antecedent Agreement

When locating the antecedents and the referenced pronouns, follow the steps below to be sure that these two areas are in agreement:

1. Identify the pronoun.

2. Decide to whom or to what the pronoun refers or what it replaces—the antecedent.

3. Identify the person (first, second, third); gender (masculine, feminine, neuter); and number (singular, plural) of the antecedent.

NOTES

First, Second, and Third Persons
First person refers to the one speaking, second person refers to the one spoken to, and third person refers to the one spoken about.

4. Identify the person, gender, and number of the referenced pronoun.

5. Determine if the person, gender, and number are the same for the pronoun and the antecedent. If they are, you have agreement. If they are not the same, you have a correction to make.

6. Continue the process with any remaining pronouns in the sentence.

Person

The three persons are *first, second,* and *third.* Follow the preceding steps to be sure that you have pronoun and antecedent agreement in person.

First Person.   Use a first-person pronoun if you have an antecedent that refers to the *person* or *persons speaking.*

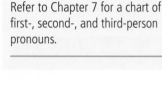

NOTES

Looking Back

Refer to Chapter 7 for a chart of first-, second-, and third-person pronouns.

I become angry when people laugh at my accent.

Identify the pronoun: *my*

Reference to: *I*

Antecedent: *I*—first person

Pronoun: *my*—first person

Agreement: yes

We perceive situations from our cultural backgrounds.

(The pronoun *our* refers to the antecedent *we* [another pronoun]. Both are first-person pronouns. They are in agreement.)

Second Person.   Use a second-person pronoun if you have an antecedent that refers to the *person* or *persons spoken to.*

You may want to discuss your plans for decreasing employee tensions in the workplace.

Identify the pronoun: *your*

Reference to: *you*

Antecedent: *you*—second person

Pronoun: *your*—second person

Agreement: yes

When you show signs of insecurity, your credibility lessens in some people's eyes.

(The pronoun *your* refers to the pronoun *you.* Both are second-person pronouns. They are in agreement.)

Third Person.   Use a third-person pronoun if you have an antecedent that refers to the *person* or *thing spoken about.*

Affirmative action is not so effective as it was in earlier years.

Identify the pronoun: *it*

Reference to: *affirmative action*

Antecedent: *affirmative action*—third person

Pronoun: *it*—third person

Agreement: yes

The women's movement focuses on the career woman and her status in the workplace.

(The pronoun *her* refers to the antecedent *career woman.* Both are third-person. They are in agreement.)

Many <u>managers</u> are sensitive to <u>their</u> employees' problems.

(The pronoun *their* refers to the antecedent *managers.* Both are third-person. They are in agreement.)

CHECKPOINT 8.1

Go to the
Web

Checkpoint 8.1
for more skills practice on this topic.

Instructions: Underline each antecedent once and its personal pronoun twice.

1. Connie indicated that employers appreciated her attitude about her disability.

2. You will have an opportunity to share your views on cultural diversity at tomorrow's workshop.

3. Women sometimes experience more pay discrimination than their male coworkers.

4. People should concentrate on what they have in common.

5. Terry resists change as well as the methods to bring it about.

6. David Wing earns his living explaining American customs to international businesspeople.

7. We have increased the Hispanic enrollments in hospitality management classes at our college.

8. John tries to hire the best-qualified workers that he can find.

9. Elia wanted to brush up on his language skills.

10. Discrimination against people with disabilities is not so evident as it was 25 years ago.

Gender

In the study of grammar, the three genders are *masculine* and *feminine* (referring to persons) and *neuter* (referring to things). Follow the steps listed previously to ensure pronoun and antecedent agreement in gender.

Feminine and Masculine Gender. Use a *feminine* pronoun (*she, her, hers*) when the pronoun definitely refers to a feminine antecedent. Use a *masculine* pronoun (*he, his, him*) when the pronoun definitely refers to a masculine antecedent.

> **<u>Carol</u> preferred to work alone on <u>her</u> research about benefits for part-time workers.**
>
> Identify the pronoun: *her*
> Reference to: *Carol*
> Antecedent: *Carol*—third person, feminine gender
> Pronoun: *her*—third person, feminine gender
> Agreement: yes
>
> **<u>Marita</u> will begin to trust the system when <u>she</u> begins to feel included.**
>
> (The pronoun *she* refers to the antecedent *Marita.* Both are third-person, feminine gender. They are in agreement.)
>
> **<u>Dennis</u> decided that <u>his</u> negative stereotypes of immigrants were inaccurate.**
>
> (The pronoun *his* refers to the antecedent *Dennis.* Both are third-person, masculine gender. They are in agreement.)

What did <u>he</u> mean by <u>his</u> statement that Mary has an attitude problem?

(The pronoun *his* refers to the antecedent *he*. Both are third-person, masculine gender. They are in agreement.)

Neuter Gender. Use a neuter gender pronoun (*it, its*) to refer to an antecedent that represents things rather than persons.

The best way to solve a <u>problem</u> is to identify <u>its</u> cause.

Pronoun: *its*

Reference to: *problem*

Antecedent: *problem*—third person, neuter gender

Pronoun: *its*—third person, neuter gender

Agreement: yes

<u>Diversity training</u> is a waste of time if <u>it</u> is done hurriedly with no follow-through sessions.

(The pronoun *it* refers to the antecedent *diversity training*. Both are third-person, neuter gender. They are in agreement.)

A harassment <u>issue</u> often escalates over time; therefore, handle <u>it</u> immediately.

(The pronoun *it* refers to the antecedent *issue*. Both are third-person, neuter gender. They are in agreement.)

Unknown Gender. Use both masculine and feminine pronouns (*he or she, his or her*) when you do not know the gender of the antecedent or when you want to refer to a common gender antecedent such as *instructor* or *student.* Do not overuse these combinations. If a sentence sounds awkward using both the masculine and feminine pronouns, rephrase it by making the pronouns and antecedents plural.

A <u>manager</u> should provide diversity training for <u>his or her</u> administrative office professionals.

Pronouns: *his, her*

Reference to: *manager*

Antecedent: *manager*—third person, common gender

Pronouns: *his or her*—third person, masculine and feminine genders

Agreement: yes

Do you believe that how a <u>person</u> acts is how <u>he or she</u> wants to be treated?

(The pronouns *he* and *she* refer to the common gender antecedent *person.* All are third-person. The antecedent *person* may be masculine or feminine. The pronouns *he* and *she* are appropriate. They are in agreement.)

Do you believe that how <u>people</u> act is how <u>they</u> want to be treated?

(Compare this sentence to the one above. The pronoun *they* refers to the antecedent *people.* Both are third-person pronouns. The sentence is less awkward, and it expresses the same message.)

The average <u>salesperson</u> is not successful unless <u>he or she</u> understands the customer's culture.

(The pronouns *he* and *she* refer to *salesperson.*)

Average <u>salespeople</u> are not successful unless <u>they</u> understand the customer's culture.

(The pronoun *they* refers to *salespeople.* Rephrasing the sentence eliminates the awkwardness of the *he or she* combination.)

Number

In addition to person and gender, you must be aware of pronoun number. The two options are *singular* and *plural*. Follow the steps listed previously to be sure that you have pronoun and antecedent agreement in number.

Singular and Plural.   Use a singular pronoun (*he, she, him, her, his, it*) if you use a singular antecedent. Use a plural pronoun (*they, their, them*) if you use a plural antecedent.

> **Heather claimed that management's failure to listen to her harassment complaint caused her to file a lawsuit.**

Pronoun: *her, her*

Reference to: *Heather*

Antecedent: *Heather*—third person, singular form

Pronoun: *her*—third person, singular form

Agreement: yes

(The pronoun *her* refers to the antecedent *Heather.* Both are third-person singular forms. They are in agreement.)

> **Most employees expect to have their views considered and respected.**

(The pronoun *their* refers to the antecedent *employees.* Both are third-person plural forms. They are in agreement.)

> **Young workers may not realize the seriousness of their early drug abuse until they are older.**

(The pronouns *their* and *they* refer to the antecedent *workers.* All are third-person plural forms. They are in agreement.)

CHECKPOINT 8.2

Go to the
Web

Checkpoint 8.2
for more skills practice on this topic.

Instructions: *Complete each sentence by adding a personal pronoun that agrees with the antecedent. Underline the antecedent.*

1. Sue Chin knows that _____ analytical skills will be helpful to _____ team members as they tabulate the diversity questionnaire results.

2. Diversity does not refer to race and ethnicity only; _____ also includes age, gender, religion, and education.

3. Each employee should be able to maintain _____ own culture and lifestyle.

4. The first step was to ask employees to share _____ feelings about diversity.

5. Several managers said that _____ found the book *Working With Diversity* helpful in _____ understanding of different cultures.

6. Laura looked for traits that _____ had in common with _____ diverse group of friends.

7. Armando wrote about cultural diversity in _____ research paper for _____ sociology class.

8. Diversity training is not an event; _____ is an ongoing process.

---

9. When we stereotype individuals, we expect _____ to act according to those characterizations.

10. Companies are finding that _____ must share _____ goals and expectations with _____ employees.

Compound Antecedents

A compound subject consists of two or more persons, places, things, activities, ideas, or qualities. When the antecedent is a compound subject, the connecting word (*and, or, nor*) determines whether the pronoun is singular or plural.

Joined by *And.* Use a plural pronoun to refer to two or more antecedents (compound subject) joined by the word *and.*

> **Massachusetts and Missouri allow their state employees to work four 10-hour days.**

(The plural pronoun *their* refers to two antecedents joined by *and.*)

> **David and Inez consider their diverse backgrounds to be an advantage in their working relationship.**

(*David* and *Inez* are third-person antecedents joined by *and.* These antecedents require the plural pronoun *their* for agreement.)

> **Molly and Denise are presenting their diversity awareness workshop tomorrow.**

(*Molly* and *Denise* are third-person antecedents joined by *and.* These antecedents require the plural pronoun *their* for agreement.)

Do This	Do Not Do This
The diversity management director and trainer scheduled his or her presentations.	The diversity management director and trainer scheduled their presentations.
The diversity management director and the trainer scheduled their presentations	The diversity management director and the trainer scheduled his or her presentations.

Use a singular pronoun reference when one person holds two positions. Note that the article *the* appears before the first title only. Use a plural pronoun when there are two positions held by two different people. Note that the article *the* appears before both titles. The repetition of the article indicates that two people and two positions are involved.

Joined by *Or* or *Nor.* Use a singular pronoun to refer to two singular antecedents joined by *or* or *nor.* Use a plural pronoun to refer to two plural antecedents joined by *or* or *nor.*

> **Katie or Wanda will discuss the unfair treatment with her supervisor.**

(Two third-person singular feminine antecedents joined by *or* require a third-person singular feminine pronoun reference.)

Chapter 8

Neither Dawn nor Simone seemed motivated by an increase in her paycheck.

(Two singular antecedents joined by *nor* require a singular pronoun reference.)

Neither diversity training classes nor social occasions accomplished their purpose of lessening racial tensions.

(Two plural antecedents joined by *nor* require a plural pronoun reference.)

Closed minds or unfair stereotypes take their toll on workers.

(Two plural antecedents joined by *or* require a plural pronoun reference.)

Joined by *Or* or *Nor*—Special Cases. Use a pronoun that agrees in number with the closer antecedent when a singular antecedent and a plural antecedent are joined by *or* or *nor*. Reword the sentence to make it sound less awkward when necessary.

Neither Cassie nor her coworkers were aware of their prejudices.

(The pronoun must agree with the closer antecedent, which is *coworkers*. *Coworkers* is plural; therefore, the pronoun must also be plural.)

The division manager or the team leaders had to devise their strategies for hiring additional handicapped personnel.

(The pronoun *their* is closer to the antecedent *team leaders*.)

Neither the project workers nor the project leader was aware that his or her problems were caused by cultural differences.

(Even though this sentence is correctly written according to the *or/nor* rule, the sentence sounds awkward. Rewrite the sentence to place the plural antecedent closer to the pronoun.)

Neither the project leader nor the project workers were aware that their problems were caused by cultural differences.

(The rewritten sentence places the plural antecedent closer to the pronoun.)

CHECKPOINT 8.3

Go to the
Web

Checkpoint 8.3
for more skills practice on this topic.

Instructions: *Check the underlined word(s) for pronoun usage. If the pronoun is used correctly, write **Yes** in the space provided. If it is not used correctly, write the correct pronoun.*

1. Neither the supervisor nor the employees wanted to see their cultural diversity training opportunities discontinued. _____

2. Mr. Brown and a student will be participating in his college's Cultural Awareness Day. _____

3. Sue and her classmates misinterpreted their instructor's comments about cultural differences. _____

4. Either June or Carolyn will be available to assist the new employee in any way that they can. _____

5. Randy or Hank will speak about their experiences growing up in a segregated community. _____

6. Neither the cultural diversity author nor the trainers were able to identify the sources for his statistics. _____

7. Rosa and Margaret were concerned about <u>her</u> promotion opportunities.   _____

8. Either Ted or James will answer discrimination questions for <u>their</u> employees.   _____

9. Neither Ismael nor his friends felt that <u>his</u> remarks were biased.   _____

10. Prejudice and discrimination have <u>their</u> negative influence on the workplace.   _____

Collective Antecedents

A collective antecedent refers to a group of people such as a committee, class, board, or jury. A collective antecedent is neuter in gender.

With Groups. Use a singular pronoun reference when the collective antecedent is acting as a group. Use a plural pronoun reference when the members within the group are acting individually.

> **At <u>its</u> meeting, the <u>Cultural Awareness Committee</u> will make <u>its</u> recommendations.**
>
> (The collective antecedent, *Cultural Awareness Committee,* is acting as one group.)
>
> **Every <u>group</u> has a culture that identifies <u>its</u> values.**
>
> (The collective antecedent *group* is acting as one body.)
>
> **After the diversity awareness <u>team</u> finished <u>its</u> project, <u>it</u> celebrated.**
>
> (The team is acting as a group in its celebration.)
>
> **The <u>faculty</u> were not unanimous in <u>their</u> voting to offer a program in cultural diversity.**
>
> (The members of the faculty acted individually in voting; therefore, the pronoun reference is plural.)

NOTES

Collective Agreement

A collective antecedent requires an analysis of the intent of the sentence. Is the antecedent acting as a group, or are the members of the group acting individually?

Do This

If <u>members of a diverse team</u> are to perform successfully, they must develop trust and cooperation.

Reword a sentence if the plural pronoun sounds awkward. Instead use <u>members of</u> such groups as *faculty, team, firm,* or *board.*

Do Not Do This

If a <u>diverse team</u> are to perform successfully, they must develop trust and cooperation.

With Companies and Organizations. In most cases, use a singular pronoun reference with antecedents that are companies and organizations.

> **<u>Stride Rite</u> has a center that cares for the children as well as the elderly relatives of <u>its</u> workers.**
>
> (The company *Stride Rite* requires a singular pronoun.)
>
> **<u>Firstar International</u> sent <u>its</u> managers to Switzerland for a trial work period.**
>
> (The company *Firstar International* requires a singular pronoun.)

The Museum of Black Inventors displays its photographs and documents in an interesting manner.

(The organization *The Museum of Black Inventors* requires a singular pronoun.)

Do This

The institute is offering its cultural survey without charge. It hopes to receive useful feedback.

Be consistent with the pronoun used. Do not change from singular to plural from one sentence to the next.

Do Not Do This

The institute is offering its cultural survey without charge. They hope to receive useful feedback.

CHECKPOINT 8.4

Go to the
Web

Checkpoint 8.4
for more skills practice on this topic.

*Instructions: Check the underlined word(s) for correct pronoun usage. If the pronoun is used correctly, write **Yes** in the space provided. If it is not used correctly, write the correct pronoun.*

1. The Firefly Acts Company will present their interactive sessions on stereotypes and conflict. _____

2. TFC Corporation will provide additional parking space for their handicapped clients. _____

3. Several members of the Cultural Awareness Committee completed its tasks before the designated deadline. _____

4. The department demonstrated its ability to recover after several unfortunate multicultural incidents. _____

5. The firm realized how much their employees appreciated the diversity training workshops. _____

6. How successful are the staff in its relationships with older workers? _____

7. REACH, Inc., offers their training services to developmentally disabled individuals in the community. _____

8. The members of the management team completed its cultural growth and development training sessions. _____

Indefinite Pronoun Antecedents

Some indefinite pronouns are always singular; others are always plural. Several are either singular or plural depending on their context in the sentences. Indefinite pronouns are third-person pronouns. When indefinite pronouns are used as antecedents, appropriate third-person pronouns must be used in reference to them.

Indefinite Pronouns
(always singular)

another	either	many a	one
anybody	enough	much	other
anyone	every	neither	somebody
anything	everybody	no one	someone
each	everyone	nobody	something
each one	everything	nothing	

Indefinite Pronouns
(always plural)

both	others
few	several
many	

Indefinite Pronouns
(singular or plural)

all	most
any	none
more	some

NOTES

Third-Person Pronouns

Third-person pronouns are *he, she, it, they, them, his, her, him, hers, their, theirs, its.*

Singular Indefinite Pronouns. Use a singular personal pronoun reference when the antecedent is a singular indefinite pronoun. Ignore an intervening prepositional phrase when locating the antecedent. The words *each* and *every* often function as adjectives in sentences.

Everyone should appreciate <u>his or her</u> ethnic values.

(*Everyone* is a singular pronoun antecedent that requires the singular pronoun reference *his or her.*)

Neither of the two women testified against <u>her</u> supervisor in the discrimination hearing.

(*Neither* is a singular indefinite pronoun that requires the singular pronoun reference *her.* Remove the prepositional phrase *of the two women* to determine the antecedent.)

No one should ever feel that <u>his or her</u> heritage is unimportant.

(*No one* is a singular indefinite pronoun that is always two words. *No one* requires the singular pronoun reference *his or her.*)

Every <u>company</u> needs legal advice when writing <u>its</u> harassment policy.

(The singular indefinite pronoun *every* functions as an adjective in this sentence. *Company* is the antecedent, and it requires the singular reference pronoun *its.*)

Plural Indefinite Pronouns. Use a plural personal pronoun reference when the antecedent is a plural indefinite pronoun. Ignore intervening prepositional phrases when locating the antecedent.

Both of the new workers handle <u>their</u> disabilities without problems.

(*Both* is a plural pronoun antecedent and requires the plural pronoun reference *their.* To locate the antecedent, eliminate the prepositional phrase *of the new workers.*)

Several of the new ethnic groups want to share <u>their</u> cultural traditions with <u>their</u> coworkers.

(To locate the antecedent, eliminate the prepositional phrase *of the new ethnic groups. Several* is a plural pronoun antecedent and requires the plural pronoun reference *their.*)

Chapter 8

Many of the foreign-born workers have done similar work in **their** home countries.

(*Many* is a plural pronoun antecedent and requires the plural pronoun reference *their.*)

Only a few of the applicants listed their ethnic backgrounds on the employment forms.

(*Few* is the plural pronoun antecedent and requires the plural pronoun reference *their.*)

Do This

<u>Each</u> cultural diversity program has <u>its</u> strong and weak points.

Do Not Do This

<u>Each</u> cultural diversity program has <u>their</u> strong and weak points

Do not use a plural pronoun reference with a singular indefinite pronoun used as an adjective.

Singular or Plural Indefinite Pronouns.   Use an appropriate personal pronoun when the antecedent may be singular or plural. Determining whether the antecedent is singular or plural depends on the context of the sentence.

All of the legal material from the discrimination case is in its appropriate folder.

(*All* is an indefinite pronoun used as a singular antecedent. *All* refers to *legal material* [singular] and requires a singular pronoun [*its*] reference.)

All of the managers working outside the United States received their employment instructions.

(*All* is an indefinite pronoun used as a plural antecedent. *All* refers to *managers* [plural] and requires a plural pronoun [*their*] reference.)

Most of the article is written, but it requires a thorough review for gender bias.

(*Most* is an indefinite pronoun used as a singular antecedent. *Most* refers to *article* [singular] and requires a singular pronoun [*it*] reference.)

Most of the authors writing today have carefully checked their articles to avoid gender bias.

(*Most* is an indefinite pronoun used as a plural antecedent. *Most* refers to *authors* [plural] and requires a plural pronoun [*their*] reference.)

NOTES

Singular or Plural
The six indefinite pronouns that may be singular or plural are *all, any, more, most, none,* and *some.*

CHECKPOINT 8.5

Go to the
Web

Checkpoint 8.5
for more skills practice on this topic.

A. **Instructions:** *Underline each antecedent once and its personal pronoun reference twice in each of the following sentences. In the space provided, identify the antecedent as being singular or plural. Use **S** for singular antecedents or **P** for plural antecedents.*

1. All of the workers have to understand basic instructions from _____
   their supervisors.

2. Everyone can learn to improve his or her interpersonal skills. _____

3. Several of my coworkers have requested specific time off for their religious holidays. _____

4. Both of the men hesitated to report their health-related problems to their supervisors. _____

5. A few of the smaller companies are recognizing that they need alternative work schedules for their employees. _____

6. Some of the managers recommended a multicultural social event for their employees. _____

B. **Instructions:** *In the following sentences, underline the antecedent once. If the underlined pronoun reference is not correct, write the correct pronoun in the space provided. If the underlined pronoun is correct, write* **Yes.**

1. Most of the book on disability training is thorough, but <u>it</u> needs a list of additional resources. _____

2. No one wanted to file a harassment complaint because <u>they</u> dreaded the mental stress that would be involved. _____

3. Neither of the two men had received diversity training at <u>their</u> previous place of employment. _____

4. One of the counselors may be willing to explain the Family and Medical Leave Act when we talk with <u>them</u>. _____

5. Most of our managers follow the fair hiring and promotion policies established by <u>their</u> firm. _____

6. If someone would like to share <u>their</u> view on ethnic diversity, I would appreciate the input. _____

7. All of the employees have made <u>their</u> recommendations about the new fair practices policy. _____

8. A few had the opportunity to express <u>his or her</u> opinions about the changes in the employees' grievance policy. _____

C. **Instructions:** *In the space provided, rephrase the sentences to avoid the use of* **he or she** *and* **his or her.**

1. No one should feel that his or her contribution to the project is unimportant.

_____

2. Someone with a disability may need his or her workstation adjusted.

_____

3. Everyone should review his or her copy of the diversity policy in the handbook.

_____

4. If anybody would like to serve on the Cultural Diversity Committee, he or she should see Barb Johnson.

_____

_____

5. If he or she wants his or her passport stamped, the line starts at the front desk.

_____

6. Each one of the participants in the diversity discussion group was encouraged to analyze the implications of his or her own attitudes.

_____

_____

Reference Pronoun Clarity

If you want your writing to be clear, you must make sure that the antecedent of a pronoun is clear and that a pronoun cannot possibly refer to more than one antecedent.

Use of *They, You, It*

Avoid the use of the pronouns *they, you,* and *it* unless you are very specific in identifying the antecedent. The following sentences are examples of faulty construction:

> **We never discuss religion because <u>they</u> become very opinionated.**
>
> (Substitute *my coworkers* or *my friends* for *they.*)
>
> **Before the meeting, <u>they</u> decided to picket the area.**
>
> (Substitute *union members* or *the employees* for *they.*)
>
> **The newer groups of immigrants often seek jobs where <u>you</u> do not need to speak English.**
>
> (Substitute *they, workers,* or *employees* for *you.*)
>
> **<u>It</u> says that the costs of cultural awareness training are going to increase.**
>
> (*It* is not specific. Substitute *the article* or *the report* to which you are referring for the pronoun *it.*)

Explanatory Phrases

Do not consider such explanatory phrases as *in addition to, as well as,* or *together with* when identifying an antecedent.

> **<u>Support staff</u>, as well as managers, can work in <u>their</u> homes rather than commute to their offices.**
>
> (The antecedent is *support staff*. The members of the support staff are acting individually. The phrase *as well as managers* is not considered.)
>
> **<u>Managers</u>, in conjunction with a trainer, should develop interactive diversity sessions for <u>their</u> project leaders.**
>
> (The antecedent is *managers*. The phrase *in conjunction with a trainer* is not considered.)
>
> **<u>Toni</u>, as well as her sister, is working in <u>her</u> home rather than commuting to the office.**
>
> (The antecedent is *Toni*. The phrase *as well as her sister* is not considered.)

Unclear Reference

Reword a sentence if a pronoun seems to refer to more than one antecedent.

Pronoun/Antecedent Agreement

237

Unclear:

> **Supervisors who observe certain drug-related symptoms in their employees should report <u>them</u> to trained professionals.**
>
> (Are the supervisors reporting the symptoms, or are the supervisors reporting the employees?)

Rewritten:

> **Supervisors who observe certain drug-related symptoms in their employees should report <u>these employees</u> to trained professionals.**
>
> *or*
>
> **Supervisors who observe certain drug-related symptoms in their employees should report <u>the symptoms</u> to trained professionals.**

Unclear:

> **The city of Cleveland publishes its multicultural guidebook every year. <u>It</u> has several ethnic points of interest.**
>
> (Does *it* refer to the city of Cleveland or to the guidebook?)

Rewritten:

> **The <u>multicultural guidebook</u> that is published every year by the city of Cleveland includes several ethnic points of interest.**
>
> *or*
>
> **The <u>city of Cleveland</u> has several ethnic points of interest that are included in its yearly multicultural guidebook.**

Unclear:

> **Companies send workers all over the world, but they give little thought to how <u>they</u> will make adjustments.**
>
> (Are the companies making the adjustments, or are the workers going to be making the adjustments?)

Rewritten:

> **Companies send workers all over the world, but they give little thought to how <u>these workers</u> will adjust.**
>
> *or*
>
> **Companies send workers all over the world, but <u>these companies</u> give little thought to how they will help their workers adjust.**

Unclear:

> **Lea had to keep reminding her boss that <u>she</u> had a Cultural Awareness Committee meeting this afternoon.**
>
> (Who had the meeting—Lea or her boss?)

Rewritten:

> **<u>Lea</u> had a Cultural Awareness Committee meeting this afternoon and had to keep reminding her boss that she would be leaving to attend the meeting.**
>
> *or*
>
> **<u>Mrs. Ruiz</u>, Lea's boss, had a Cultural Awareness Committee meeting this afternoon, and Lea had to keep reminding her about this meeting.**

Go to the
Web

Checkpoint 8.6
for more skills practice on this topic.

Instructions: *In the space provided, rewrite the sentences that are vague or unclear or that have incorrect reference pronouns. If the sentence is correct, write* **Yes.** *Answers may vary.*

1. Adruf's emotional outburst and Tom's objections made me realize that he had a point.

   _____

2. MCI, in conjunction with the International Institute of Minnesota, started a training course for their newest Spanish-speaking bank tellers.

   _____

   _____

3. The manager told Jerry that he was not focusing on this particular problem.

   _____

   _____

4. They said that the number of working women with children under one year had increased.

   _____

   _____

5. Conflict occurred because Jamie thought that Shelley should do her share of the work.

   _____

   _____

6. The general managers, as well as the union president, voiced their objections about the gender job title discrepancies.

   _____

   _____

7. The members of the Cultural Diversity Committee made several recommendations, and management is seriously considering them.

   _____

   _____

8. Three sections of the company-sponsored child care proposal will contain illustrations, but they must be carefully reviewed.

   _____

   _____

   _____

   _____

Pronouns Requiring Special Attention

Several pronoun areas require special consideration.

Pronouns After *Than* and *As*

In an incomplete adverb clause using *than* or *as*, choose the case of the pronoun that you would use if the missing word were present.

I do not have the same language pronunciation difficulties as you.

(I do not have the same language pronunciation difficulties as you *have*.)

The employees at our European branch office are much more relaxed than we.

(The employees at our European branch office are much more relaxed than we *are*.)

In spite of her handicap, she can complete the work faster than I.

(In spite of her handicap, she can complete the work faster than I *can complete it*.)

My manager likes me better than her.

(My manager likes me better than *he likes* her.)

Biased practices affected Juan more than me.

(Biased practices affected Juan more than *they affected* me.)

One or Two Words

Write the words *every one* and *any one* as two words when they precede an *of* phrase. At all other times, write them as one word (*everyone, anyone*). *No one* is always two words.

Everyone is invited to hear Marshall speak about his year of work in Russia.

(There is no *of* phrase following *everyone*. *Everyone* is one word.)

Every one of the attendees enjoyed hearing Marshall speak about his experiences while working in Russia.

(*Every one* is two words. Note that these words precede an *of* phrase.)

If anyone has a concern with the gender equity policy, he or she should contact me by Friday.

(There is no *of* phrase following *anyone*. *Anyone* is one word. Note the singular pronoun reference *he or she*.)

Any one of these concerns will require attention by management.

(*Any one* is two words. Note that these words precede an *of* phrase.)

Each Other/One Another

Use *each other* when you refer to two persons or things. Use *one another* when you refer to more than two persons or things.

Before team members with diverse interests can work on the team's objectives, they must get to know one another.

Did it take time for the French and American workers to get to know one another?

Matt and I discovered that our biases interfered with our ability to listen to each other effectively.

Go to the
Web

Checkpoint 8.7
for more skills practice on this topic.

 CHECKPOINT 8.7

Instructions: Select the correct word in parentheses, and write it in the space provided.

1. Stereotypes and prejudices cause many of us to have _____ distorted visions of (*each other, one another*).

2. A trait displayed by one person in a group does not mean that it is indicative of (*every one, everyone*) in the group.

_____

3. Excessive bragging bothers my Asian friends as much as (*I, me*).

_____

4. (*Anyone, Any one*) of several employees could have reported the drug use problem to the supervisor.

_____

5. Robin is as capable as (*I, me*), but she did not receive the promotion.

_____

6. You understand the Americans With Disabilities Act better than (*her, she*).

_____

7. (*Everyone, Every one*) of my colleagues enrolled in the Spanish course.

_____

8. After their argument, the two women seldom spoke to (*each other, one another*).

_____

Diagramming Sentences

Adjectives describe nouns or pronouns. Some pronouns function as adjectives in a sentence. Possessive nouns and pronouns also function as adjectives.

To diagram a sentence with an adjective, place the adjective on a slanted line beneath the noun or pronoun that it modifies. The words *a, an,* and *the* also function as adjectives.

Different customs can create some awkward social situations.

CHECKPOINT 8.8

Go to the
Web

Checkpoint 8.8
for more skills practice on this topic.

_____

Instructions: *In the space provided, diagram the following sentences. Use all words in these sentences for diagramming.*

1. All college business majors take one cultural diversity course.

2. The negotiating committee disagreed and tabled the controversial material.

3. The company's sexual harassment policy was fair.

4. Most new employees accept the company's benefit package.

5. Some committee members expressed their frustrations and angry feelings.

CHAPTER 8 WORKSHEETS

Name _____ Date _____

PRACTICE 1

Identifying Antecedents and Pronoun References

A. Instructions: In each of the following sentences, underline the antecedents once and the pronoun references twice.

1. Charles Brown received one of the community service awards for his leadership in ethnic diversity forums.

2. Tamiko appreciated having her supervisor greet her in Japanese.

3. You should learn at least 500 words in several languages if you get a job that requires interaction with international clients.

4. J. J. Lewis, director of human resources, submitted his report on promotion and attrition rates.

5. We enjoyed our overseas work experience.

B. Instructions: Select the correct word in parentheses, and write it in the space provided. Underline the antecedents once.

1. Either the St. Louis Museum or the Washington Museum keeps (*their, its*) black history week activities online.

    1. _____

2. One survey indicates that Missouri, along with 12 other states, finds that (*they, it*) must provide remedial education for (*their, its*) government workers.

    2. _____

3. A supervisor should create an environment in which people can freely express (*their, its*) diverse opinions.

    3. _____

4. The U.S. Immigration and Naturalization Service released (*their, its*) statistics about immigrants.

    4. _____

5. A trainer should understand the type of disabilities that (*he or she, they*) will likely find in the workplace.

    5. _____

6. Neither John nor the other cultural trainers have seen (*his, their*) paychecks increase for two years.

    6. _____

7. Someone who is overweight may feel that (*he or she, they*) did not get promoted because of appearance.

    7. _____

8. Role models are important because (*he or she, they*) promote positive images.

    8. _____

9. Each of the employees should complete (*his or her, their*) diversity survey.

    9. _____

10. The team finished (*their, its*) project under budget.

    10. _____

Go to the
Web

Practice 1 Exercises
for more skills practice on this topic.

Copyright © by The McGraw-Hill Companies, Inc.

CHAPTER 8 WORKSHEETS

Name _____ Date _____

Go to the
Web

Practice 2 Exercises
for more skills practice on
this topic.

PRACTICE 2

Pronoun Antecedent Agreement

Instructions: Complete each sentence by adding a personal pronoun that agrees with the antecedent. Underline the antecedent or antecedents in each sentence.

1. Most of the employees stated that _____ had taken additional courses in _____ fields.

2. Before receiving the company's sexual harassment policy, each employee had to sign for _____ copy.

3. The Texas Hotel and Motel Association, in partnership with two colleges, is promoting _____ international hospitality training program.

4. The United States, from _____ very beginnings, has been proud of _____ diversity.

5. How do you persuade _____ coworkers to change _____ negative attitudes toward different racial and ethnic groups?

6. Tim had experience working with Native Americans, and it prepared _____ for interacting with other ethnic groups.

7. Andy or Joe Yang will share _____ feelings about adjusting to U.S. culture.

8. The board of directors decided to review _____ diversity policies.

9. How could diversity training help Randy and his brothers conduct _____ business more effectively?

10. Delia, along with several friends, joined the group because it cared about the values of the community in which _____ was raising _____ children.

11. Some trainees will say that _____ understand the directions even when _____ do not.

12. Any company with an on-site exercise program tries to emphasize healthy lifestyles for _____ employees.

13. People from cultural backgrounds communicate _____ opinions in a very direct fashion.

14. Lance or several selected committee members will prepare _____ final list of specific behaviors that are not permitted at work.

15. Employment Learning Specialists emphasized the value of a diverse and multicultural workforce in _____ seminars.

Name _____ Date _____

Unclear Reference Pronouns

*Instructions: In the space provided, correct those sentences that are vague or unclear or that have incorrect reference pronouns. If the sentence is satisfactory, write **Yes**. Answers may vary.*

1. They should provide counseling to all workers so that the workers can do their best work.

   _____

   _____

2. If a good worker has consistent gender-based problems with a coworker, offer him or her the option of a transfer.

   _____

   _____

3. A friend of mine told his supervisor that he needed to see a psychiatrist.

   _____

   _____

   _____

4. When I requested a transfer, they asked me for my reasons.

   _____

   _____

5. Toby saw the harassment file on the desk and picked it up.

   _____

   _____

6. Our teaching methods may not work for adults from other countries. It may even lead to conflict in our literacy classes.

   _____

   _____

7. Some companies provide cultural training for their employees who are assigned to work in other countries.

   _____

   _____

8. Robert has more seniority than me.

   _____

9. The affirmative action plan has the approval of every one.

   _____

10. Kara felt that Renee was overreacting to the discrimination concerning her disability.

    _____

    _____

    _____

    _____

Name _____   Date _____

Go to the
Web

Practice 3 Exercises
for more skills practice on
this topic.

PRACTICE 3

Proofreading

*Instructions: Proofread and compare the two sentences in each group. If they are the same, write **Yes** in the space provided. If they are not the same, write **No**. Use the first sentence as the correct copy. If you find errors in the second sentence, underline them.*

1. Businesspeople in some countries prefer lengthy business meetings, but those in other countries want quick closures to their transactions.

   Businesspeople in some counties prefer lengthly business meetings, but those in other countries want quick closures to their transactions.

   1. _____

2. Workers who are able to function cooperatively increase productivity, boost morale, and promote their company's goals.

   Workers who are able to function cooperatively increase productivity, boost morale, and promote its company's goal.

   2. _____

3. For you to qualify as disabled under the Americans With Disabilities Act (ADA), you must have a physical or mental condition that limits a major life activity.

   For you to qualify as disabled under the Americans With Disabilities Act (ADA), one must have a physical or mental condition that limit a major life activity.

   3. _____

4. Small business owners can learn about diversity issues if they attend seminars at the community college or if they participate in company-sponsored workshops.

   Small Business Owners can learn about diversity issues if they attend seminars at the community college or if they participate company-sponsered workshops.

   4. _____

Name _____ Date _____

Using Proofreaders' Marks

Instructions: Your work with a cultural diversity workshop presenter gives you an opportunity to proofread instructional materials. Proofread the following section of a cultural diversity pretest. (You may want to rate yourself on these points.) Make the necessary corrections using the proofreaders' marks that follow:

delete ⸓	make lowercase /
insert ∧	move to the left [
transpose ∽	move to the right]
capitalize ≡	space #

CULTURAL DIVERSITY AWARENESS SURVEY (DRAFT)

Directions: Use the scale that follows to respond to the questions below:

A = Always   S = Sometimes   N = Never

1. I am a role model of hard work and open-mindedness for my staf.   1. _____
2. I can see things from other worker's points of veiw.   2. _____
3. I handle conflict and job stresses well inmy departmnet.   3. _____
4. i speak clearly and slowly when I'm explaining a task to a new employee.   4. _____
5. I do not use slang and jargon when I speak to a visitor from another country.   5. _____
6. I am able too motivate people through employee empowerment.   6. _____
7. I am able to resolve problems with Employees from different backgrounds.   7. _____
8. I listen carfully to my Employees and coworkers.   8. _____
9. I tolerate changes well and initiate it when it appears to be the best solutions.   9. _____
10. I am aware of International Events and customs.   10. _____

PRACTICE 4

Writing

Instructions: Write five sentences containing each of the following. Answers will vary.

1. *Each other*

   _____

   _____

2. A pronoun after the word *than*

   _____

   _____

Go to the
Web

Practice 4 Exercises
for more skills practice on this topic.

Name _____ Date _____

3. *Everyone*

_____

_____

4. A singular pronoun reference when the collective antecedent is acting as a group

_____

_____

5. A company name that has a singular pronoun reference

_____

_____

PRACTICE 5

Identifying Antecedents and Pronoun References

A. Instructions: In each of the following sentences, underline the antecedents once and the pronoun references twice.

1. Jun Minorikawa was promoted because of her skills in negotiating Pacific Rim trade agreements.

2. You should know that every large city provides you an opportunity to work with people from all over the world.

3. Tonya and Will realized that they were competing for the same promotion.

4. An employee needs to communicate effectively with all customers whom he or she is likely to encounter.

5. Neither of the two men could understand why his ethnic jokes were not appreciated.

B. Instructions: Select the correct word in parentheses, and write it in the space provided. Underline the antecedents once.

1. The Society of Women Engineers and Women in Technology International offer (*its, their*) encouragement to women who have careers in science and technology.

1. _____

2. Project HIRED released (*their, its*) report on clients with disabilities who had secured full-time jobs.

2. _____

3. San Francisco, as well as Singapore, provides (*their, its*) businesses with excellent locations for global ventures.

3. _____

Name _____ Date _____

4. Everyone should list (*his or her, their*) suggested interview questions.

4. _____

5. Jill Adamson, Maple's CEO, released (*her, their*) plan to provide better jobs for women.

5. _____

6. Most of the larger companies have outstanding facilities for accommodating (*its, their*) disabled employees.

6. _____

7. Neither Auturo nor his colleagues have changed (*his, their*) attitudes about working for a female supervisor.

7. _____

8. Someone who is handicapped may feel that (*he or she, they*) was not hired because of discrimination.

8. _____

9. Some of the discrimination survey results, as well as the statistics, were distributed before (*it, they*) were verified.

9. _____

10. The class finished (*their, its*) final project on workplace diversity.

10. _____

PRACTICE 6

Pronoun/Antecedent Agreement

Instructions: Complete each sentence by adding a personal pronoun that agrees with the antecedent. Underline the antecedent or antecedents in each sentence.

1. Most of the Chinese employees stated that _____ speak Mandarin.

2. During the past month, several employees resigned _____ positions.

3. The Capital Training Foundation, along with the Township Chamber of Commerce, is promoting _____ occupational path program for high school students.

4. Tokyo is proud of _____ reputation as a center of technological innovation.

5. The extra travel took _____ toll on Kara's health.

6. Vera Esponda-Foster is director of diversity affairs and is widely recognized as a leader in _____ efforts to develop sensitivity workshops.

7. Some scientists say that _____ know how to write computer programs, but _____ often struggle with office politics.

8. The cultural diversity coordinator said, "I want people to change _____ hearts, _____ perspectives, and _____ behaviors."

9. Lee Vyenielo or Kevin Vuong will speak with us about _____ work exchange experiences.

10. Motorola used the Quick Start program to staff _____ manufacturing facility in Georgia.

11. Neither of the women realized that _____ was being considered for a promotion.

12. If somebody needs translation assistance, send _____ to me.

13. Tina is the chairperson of the Cultural Diversity Committee; therefore, direct all your questions to _____.

14. Alisa or the other office professionals will share _____ plans for entertaining the Japanese visitors.

15. Because of new legislation, the Board of Directors agreed to evaluate _____ affirmative action goals again.

Unclear Reference Pronouns

*Instructions: In the space provided, correct those sentences that are vague or unclear or that have incorrect reference pronouns. If the sentence is satisfactory, write **Yes**. Answers may vary.*

1. They should offer sensitivity workshops to all employees so that the employees can change their behaviors.

_____

_____

2. Aghee has been in the United States longer than me.

_____

3. Anyone of those suggestions should improve office morale.

_____

4. When I refused to share an office with her, everyone wanted to know my reasons.

_____

_____

5. Several sensitivity trainers shared their experiences with each other.

_____

6. Racial slurs, ethnic jokes, and unkind remarks are demoralizing to employees, and they must not be allowed in the workplace.

_____

_____

7. A new manufacturing plant in Spain will require a great amount of work, but this will greatly increase our productivity.

_____

_____

Name _____ Date _____

8. If your workers have suggestions for improving working conditions, send them to me.

_____

_____

_____

_____

9. Everyone of her ideas for improving the diversity training film was outstanding.

_____

_____

10. Nina found the Spanish dictionary on the bookshelf and picked it up for Monika.

_____

_____

PRACTICE 7

Proofreading

*Instructions: Proofread and compare the two sentences in each group. If they are the same, write **Yes** in the space provided. If they are not the same, write **No.** Use the first sentence as the correct copy. If you find errors in the second sentence, underline them.*

1. Most people want to be part of an organization in which they believe that they are making a difference.

   Most people want to be part of an organzation in which they believe that they our making a difference.

   1. _____

2. Hans resented being asked to behave like an American, to dress and groom like an American, to eat and drink like an American, and to speak the same language as an American.

   Hans resented being asked to behave like an American, to dress and groom like an American, to eat and drink like an American, and to speak the same languages as an American.

   2. _____

3. The U.S. Census Bureau predicts that by the year 2050 only half of the population will be non-Hispanic whites. Hispanics and Asians will account for over half of the population growth.

   The U.S. Census Bureau predicts that by the year 2040 only one-half of the population will be non-Hispanic whites. Hispanics and asians will account for over half of the population growth.

   3. _____

Name _____ Date _____

4. SHPE is a nonprofit association that promotes the development of Hispanics in engineering, science, and other technical professions to achieve educational excellence and social equity.

    4. _____

SHPE is a non-profit association that promotes the development of hispanics in engineering, science, and other technical professions to acheive educational excellence and social equity.

Using Proofreaders' Marks

Instructions: *What does cultural diversity include? Here are some suggestions from a workshop group. The workshop trainer asked a student to proofread the following list of workshop suggestions. Use these proofreaders' marks to correct the copy.*

delete ⌒   make lowercase /

insert ∧   move to the left [

transpose ∽   move to the right]

capitalize ≡   space #

cultural diversity awareness

1. Age.
2. Male or female
3. Raciaal
4. experience work
5. education And training
6. Gender
7. Sex orientation
8. Economic Status
9. Birthplace
10. Homtown
11. Socialactivitis
12. Religion
13. Disability
14. Political beleifs

PRACTICE 8

Writing

Instructions: *Write five sentences containing each of the following words: Answers may vary.*

1. *Every one*

_____

_____

Name _____ Date _____

2. A pronoun after the word *as*

   _____

   _____

3. An organization with a singular pronoun reference

   _____

   _____

4. A plural pronoun reference when the members within a committee are acting individually

   _____

   _____

5. *Neither* joined by *nor* and followed by a pronoun

   _____

   _____

Posttest

Instructions: *In the space provided, write* **Yes** *if the pronoun and antecedent in the sentence are in agreement. If the pronoun is used incorrectly, underline the pronoun, and write the correction in the space provided.*

1. Even though we speak different languages, we should still be able to communicate effectively. (1)

   1. _____

2. Whenever a disagreement occurs, a manager must review their method of solving conflicts. (1)

   2. _____

3. The Affirmative Action Committee and the Diversity Committee work together to help their members appreciate people of various cultures. (2)

   3. _____

4. Phillips Aluminum plans to review their affirmative action policy. (3)

   4. _____

5. Someone should bring their conflict resolution manual to the meeting. (4)

   5. _____

6. If we do not know about other cultures, you may offend others and not realize that your behavior is offensive. (5)

   6. _____

7. Many of our employees are proud of their diverse workforce. (4)

   7. _____

8. Some of my coworkers, as well as my friend Selena, were concerned about their ability to speak English. (6)

   8. _____

9. I think that Bill has a better understanding of the Chinese culture than me. (7)

   9. _____

10. Every one of the employees attended the diversity workshop. (8)

    10. _____

11. People clapped his or her hands at the end of the speaker's presentation on diversity. (1)

    11. _____

12. The Western Group designed their diversity Web page last year. (2)

    12. _____

13. The committee unanimously reached their decision on a new chairperson. (4)

    13. _____

14. Neither Judee nor Jackie agreed on their definition of discrimination. (2)

    14. _____

15. All of the customer service employees received their evaluations on Friday.

    15. _____

UNIT 3

Reviewing Verbs

Chapter 9
Verb Types and Parts

Chapter 10
Verb Tense, Voice, and Mood—Verbals

Chapter 11
Subject-Verb Agreement

Chapter 9

Verb Types and Parts

OBJECTIVES

After you have studied this chapter and completed the exercises, you will be able to do the following:

1. Use action, linking, and helping verbs correctly.

2. Recognize the difference between transitive and intransitive verbs.

3. Recognize the parts of verbs—present, past, past participle, and present participle.

4. Identify regular and irregular verb forms.

5. Recognize spelling changes in parts of regular verb formations.

6. Use verb forms for *lie, lay; raise, rise;* and *set, sit* correctly.

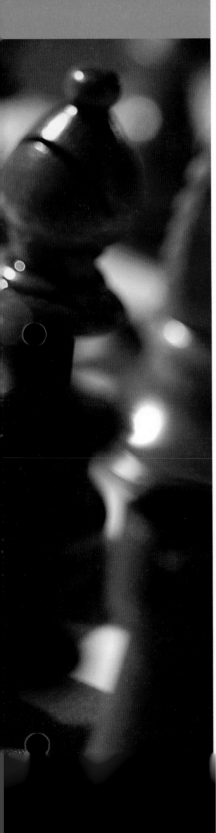

Workplace Applications: Problem Solving and Decision Making

Each day you make hundreds of decisions. Today you decided when to get up, what to wear, what to eat, and whether or not to read this book. You started a decision-making pattern when you were young and probably use that same pattern today. For most people, this decision-making process is successful. Poor decision makers, however, usually do not realize that their decision-making processes may be inadequate.

A popular process for making decisions involves identifying the problem, gathering information, listing and selecting the best solution, and evaluating the results. Your effectiveness in solving problems increases if you include opinions of others and generate multiple alternatives. Generating these alternatives is called *brainstorming*.

Making the Right Decision

Some people avoid making decisions because they are afraid that they will make mistakes. Their goal is to make the perfect decision, not realizing that there is no such thing as the perfect decision. Every decision is a risk. Good decision makers know that almost any decision can be changed or adjusted.

Because of the complexity of business decisions, more managers are relying on decision-making software to simplify the process. This software helps the decision maker organize thoughts, analyze multiple options, and make the best choice. One of the advantages of using decision-making software is documentation of the decision-making steps, which makes it easy to explain the process and decision to others. Using decision-making software is just one of the ways that businesses are taking advantage of the power of their computers.

PRETEST: *Looking Forward*

Pretest

Instructions: In the space provided, write the letter of the correct answer.

1. In the sentence *Mr. Danson encouraged project teams to solve their own problems,* the verb *encouraged* is: (1)
   a. a linking verb.
   b. a helping verb.
   c. an action verb.
   d. an intransitive verb.

   1. _____

2. In the sentence *First impressions of a decision are important,* the verb *are* is: (1)
   a. a linking verb.
   b. a helping verb.
   c. an action verb.
   d. a transitive verb.

   2. _____

3. In the sentence *We have solved complex problems by doing online research,* the verb *have* is: (1)
   a. a linking verb.
   b. a helping verb.
   c. an action verb.
   d. an intransitive verb.

   3. _____

4. In the sentence *Computer programs help managers with their complex decisions,* the verb *help* is: (2)
   a. a linking verb.
   b. a helping verb.
   c. a transitive verb.
   d. an intransitive verb.

   4. _____

5. Which line consists of only irregular verb forms? (4)
   a. require, identify, attempt
   b. become, build, choose
   c. form, outline, wish
   d. communicate, check, delay

   5. _____

6. Which sentence is written correctly? (4, 5)
   a. They have went to all the brainstorming sessions.
   b. Our team identifyed three possible solutions to the problem.
   c. We will be stopping our discussion in one hour.
   d. Our instructor refered to an interesting case study today.

   6. _____

7. Which sentence is written correctly? (4, 5, 6)
   a. I seen a decrease in the number of employee conflict complaints.
   b. Jerome has always exceled in brainstorming sessions.
   c. She copyied Carrie's notes from the last employee relations meeting.
   d. He planned to lie down to rest between meetings.

   7. _____

8. Which statement is correct about the following sentence? *We are analyzing the possible solutions, and we will make our final decision by Thursday.* (1, 2)
   a. The sentence has two action verbs and one helping verb.
   b. The sentence has one transitive verb and one intransitive verb.
   c. The sentence has two helping verbs and two action verbs.
   d. The sentence has two intransitive verbs.

   8. _____

9. Which statement is correct about the following sentence? *This conflict resolution article has lain in my in-basket for several days.* (2, 6)
   a. The word *lain* is a transitive verb.
   b. The word *lain* is an action verb.
   c. The word *lain* is an intransitive verb.
   d. The word *lain* is a helping verb.

   9. _____

10. Which sentence is written correctly? (3, 4, 5)   10. _____

    a.   The committee has chose two solutions to the problem.

    b.   He payed slight attention to the speaker's suggestions on problem solving.

    c.   Nancy has recommended several solutions for us to consider.

    d.   The problem occured too late in the day for me to review.

11. Which sentence is written correctly? (4)   11. _____

    a.   "We have always did it that way before."

    b.   "We have always done it that way before."

    c.   I have drew a schematic of the way that a decision is processed.

    d.   I have drawed a schematic of the way that a decision is processed.

12. Which sentence is *not* written correctly? (4)   12. _____

    a.   She seen the results that were gained from carefully analyzed decisions.

    b.   Todd is making the final decision about the site for the next meeting.

    c.   The group should avoid the criticism of any individual's brainstorming idea.

    d.   Carly went to her supervisor with a solution for the department's problem.

13. Which line of verbs represents correct past participle forms? (3)   13. _____

    a.   fallen   laid   rung   built

    b.   began   tried   occurred   requiring

    c.   taught   spoke   done   paid

    d.   went   said   written   choosing

14. How many verbs are in the following sentence? *You can solve most of your own job*   14. _____
problems, but some may require the help of your supervisor. (1)

    a.   two   c.   four

    b.   three   d.   five

15. Which sentence contains a linking verb? (1)   15. _____

    a.   Colleen will outline a decision-making proposal for her team.

    b.   Tio defined the problem succinctly and accurately.

    c.   Sam has devised a systematic decision-making process.

    d.   Roberta always remains calm in controversial discussions.

Chapter Preview

A verb is an integral part of a sentence. You cannot write a clear, complete sentence without using a verb since the verb states what the subject does or is. Good writers select their verbs carefully and use them correctly.

A verb involves more form changes than any other part of speech; therefore, you have some new terms to learn in Chapter 9. In this chapter, you will identify several kinds of verbs and also work with the four parts of verbs. Before you begin the study of verbs, you will find it helpful to review the parts of speech and the parts of a sentence that were introduced in Chapters 2 and 3.

Verb Identification

Verbs are words that express action or a state of being. In order to write effective sentences, you must use verbs correctly. The first step in your study of verbs is to identify the type of verb and its purpose in a sentence. The three types of verbs are *action, linking,* and *helping* (auxiliary) verbs.

Action Verb

Use an action verb to tell what someone or something (the subject) does. The action may be physical or mental.

NOTES

Looking Back

Review subjects in sentences in Chapter 3.

> **We <u>solved</u> the problem.**
>
> (The subject is *We. Solved* is an action verb that indicates what the subject *We* did.)
>
> **Gerta <u>summarized</u> the committee's brainstorming ideas.**
>
> (*Summarized* is an action verb that indicates what the subject *Gerta* did.)
>
> **Always <u>weigh</u> the consequences of your decisions.**
>
> (*Weigh* is an action verb that indicates what the subject *you* [understood] should do.)

Action verbs include *transitive* and *intransitive* verbs. Your dictionaries identify verbs as transitive (*v.t.*) and intransitive (*v.i.*). Understanding the differences between transitive and intransitive verbs will also help you later in the chapter as you work with several frequently misused words.

Transitive Verb. A transitive verb is an action verb that needs an object to complete the thought. The words following the verb answer the questions *What?* or *Whom?*

NOTES

Looking Back

Review direct objects in Chapter 3.

> **Joe Bjiong <u>assessed</u> his competitor's products early in the decision-making process.**
>
> (*Assessed* is a transitive verb that requires an object to complete the thought. The object *products* answers the question *What is assessed?*)
>
> **We <u>analyzed</u> Solutions 1, 3, and 6 very carefully.**
>
> (*Analyzed* is a transitive verb that requires an object to complete the thought. The object *Solutions 1, 3, and 6* answers the question *What?*)

His legal firm often <u>refers</u> its paralegals to our decision-making seminars.

(*Refers* is a transitive verb in this sentence. The object *paralegals* is a direct object that completes the thought and answers the question *Whom?*)

Intransitive Verb.   An intransitive verb is an action verb that does not require an object to complete the thought.

The managers <u>listened</u> carefully to the employees' concerns.

(*Listened* is an intransitive verb. The intransitive verb *listened* does not require an object to complete the thought.)

Analytical thinking <u>refers</u> to an individual's problem-solving ability.

(*Refers* is an intransitive verb in this sentence. No object is necessary to complete the thought.)

CHECKPOINT 9.1

Go to the
Web

Checkpoint 9.1
for more skills practice on this topic.

Instructions: *Underline the transitive verbs once and the intransitive verbs twice. Write any direct objects in the space provided.*

1. The technique of brainstorming often generates unique solutions to problems.   _____

2. Conflict occurs in every relationship.   _____

3. Some managers encounter difficulties with employee personality conflicts in the workplace.   _____

4. Our approach to decision making usually works.   _____

5. Employees need information about management's decisions.   _____

6. We examined the problem and developed an action plan.   _____

7. A committee recommended a solution for a persistent problem.   _____

8. Union officials responded favorably to the mediator's suggestions.   _____

Linking Verb

Linking Verb—State of Being.   Use a linking verb to connect the subject of the sentence with a subject complement (predicate noun, predicate pronoun) or with a predicate adjective. A linking verb does not indicate action. Some common state-of-being linking verb forms are forms of the verb *to be: am, is, are, was, were, be, been, being.*

Maria LaCosta <u>was</u> the principal speaker at the artificial intelligence conference.

(*Was* is a linking verb that connects the subject *Maria LaCosta* and the subject complement *the principal speaker.* The subject complement renames the subject. *Was* is not an action verb.)

Verb Types and Parts

Brainstorming sessions <u>are</u> usually eventful and lively.

(*Are* is a linking verb that links the subject *brainstorming sessions* and the predicate adjectives *eventful* and *lively.* The predicate adjectives describe the subject.)

Linking Verb—Other. Use a verb associated with the senses (*feel, look, smell, sound, taste*) in the same way that you use a linking verb. Additional linking verbs are *appear, become, grow, remain, stay,* and *seem.* Some of these linking verbs function as action verbs as well. To test whether a verb is a linking verb, use a *to be* verb form (*is, was*) in place of one of the 11 verbs just listed. If the sentence makes sense with the substitute *to be* form, the verb is a linking verb.

She <u>remained</u> skeptical of the value of brainstorming sessions.

(Substitute the word *was* for *remained. She was skeptical of the value of brainstorming sessions.* The sentence makes sense with the substitution. In this sentence, *remained* is a linking verb. *Skeptical* describes the subject *she.*)

The problem <u>appeared</u> very complicated.

(Substitute *is* or *was.* In this sentence, *appeared* is a linking verb.)

All the possible solutions <u>looked</u> good for our needs.

(Substitute *are* or *were.* In this sentence, *looked* is a linking verb.)

We <u>looked</u> at all the possible solutions to the absenteeism problem.

(Substitute *are* or *were.* The sentence does not make sense with the substitution. In this sentence, *looked* is an action verb.)

Go to the
Web

Checkpoint 9.2
for more skills practice on this topic.

CHECKPOINT 9.2

Instructions: Underline action verbs once and linking verbs twice.

1. Decision making is often a team experience.

2. Poor decisions result from vague objectives.

3. Mr. Larvik encouraged our open and frank discussions.

4. These decision-making steps sound complicated.

5. Carrie knew that her problem-solving approach was too costly.

6. I identified my goals and set my priorities.

7. Jackie understood the importance of effective communication in conflict resolution.

8. Your decision appears sound.

9. Brainstorming helped our radio station personnel in their new ad campaign.

10. The group looked at several different solutions to the problem.

Helping Verb and Verb Phrase

Use a helping (auxiliary) verb with a main verb to form a verb phrase. The main verb in a verb phrase is always the last word in the phrase. Some helping verbs can function as main verbs and are used alone in such cases.

The following list of helping verbs will be useful in the remainder of this chapter and also in Chapter 10.

Helping Verbs

am	be	have	do	may
is	being	has	does	might
are	been	had	did	must
was	can	shall	will	
were	could	should	would	

Success <u>may depend</u> on an individual's timely decision-making ability.

(*May* is the helping verb used with the main verb *depend* to form the verb phrase *may depend.*)

I <u>have</u> several decisions that I <u>must make</u> by Friday.

(*Have* is used alone as a main verb. *Must* is the helping verb used with the main verb *make.*)

Do This

We <u>used to be able to</u> discuss our problems rationally.

or

We <u>once could</u> discuss our problems rationally.

Do Not Do This

We <u>used to could</u> discuss our problems rationally.

We <u>use to</u> discuss our problems rationally.

Do not use the dialect form *use to* or *used to could* for *once could* or *used to be able.*

CHECKPOINT 9.3

Go to the
Web

Checkpoint 9.3
for more skills practice on this topic.

Instructions: *Draw a line under each verb phrase and circle each helping verb.*

1. Work teams must resolve their problems promptly.

2. Sometimes a problem can be viewed in several different ways.

3. We were asked for a problem solution by the end of the week.

4. He has developed an effective action plan for union members.

5. Most people in work environments have encountered problem situations.

6. We may suggest several alternatives for the solution of the problem.

7. Sheila was asked for her evaluation of the critical thinking seminar.

8. You will make many types of decisions every day.

Verbs are either *regular* or *irregular.* All regular and irregular verbs, with the exception of *be,* have four principal parts—the *present,* the *past,* the *past participle,* and the *present participle.* These principal parts are used to form verb tenses. An error in tense often occurs because of a failure to choose the correct principal part of the verb.

Definitions

Present. The first principal part of a verb is the present form, which refers to now or the present time.

> Expert systems <u>require</u> a knowledge base of rules and facts.
>
> (*Require* refers to the present time.)
>
> Members of our family business <u>discuss</u> the issues and then <u>take</u> a vote.
>
> (*Discuss* and *take* refer to the present time.)

Past. The second principal part of a verb refers to the past. The past verb part indicates that the action already took place. For most usage, this verb part is formed by adding *d* or *ed* to the present form of the verb. No helping verb is used with this principal part of the verb.

> We <u>discussed</u> many solutions to the problem.
>
> (*Discussed* is a verb that indicates the discussion already took place.)
>
> I <u>compared</u> the alternatives and <u>selected</u> the best solution.
>
> (*Compared* and *selected* are verbs that indicate the comparison and selection already took place.)

Past Participle. The third principal part of a verb is the past participle. To form the past participle of most verbs, add *d* or *ed* to the present part of the verb. The past participle requires a helping verb (*have, has,* or *had*). A past participle combined with a helping verb indicates that the action was completed. In a verb phrase, the past participle is always the last word of the phrase.

> We <u>have struggled</u> through many problem situations without a clear plan.
>
> (The past participle *struggled* and the helping verb *have* indicate that the subject has already completed the action.)
>
> Our committee members <u>have reached</u> a deadlock, and both sides <u>have refused</u> to negotiate.
>
> (The past participles *reached* and *refused* along with the helping verb *have* indicate that the members have completed the actions.)

Present Participle. The fourth principal part of a verb is the present participle. A present participle is formed by using the present form of a verb plus *ing.* This verb form requires the use of a helping verb and indicates that there is continuing action involved. Some helping verbs are *is, are, was, were, can, could, have, has, had, should, would,* and *shall* or *will.*

NOTES

Verb Tenses

Tense refers to the time (present, past, and future) indicated by a verb. You will work with verb tenses in greater depth in Chapter 10.

We are considering an Executive Support System (ESS) for accessing relevant decision-making information.

(*Considering* is the present participle and consists of the present form *consider* plus *ing*. The required helping verb in this sentence is *are*. The combination *are considering* suggests a continuing action.)

John is outlining improvements for the next brainstorming session.

(*Outlining* is the present participle and consists of the present form *outline* plus *ing*. The combination *is outlining* suggests an ongoing action.)

Regular Verbs

Most verbs are regular verbs. If you check your dictionaries, you probably will not find the past, past participle, or present participle of a regular verb listed. In such cases, form these parts by adding *d, ed,* or *ing* to the present part of the verb.

Regular Verbs—General Formations. Add *d* or *ed* to the present part of most verbs to form the past or past participle. Add *ing* to the present part of most verbs to form the present participle.

Present Part	Past Part	Past Participle	Present Participle
assess	assessed	assessed	assessing
contribute	contributed	contributed	contributing
fail	failed	failed	failing
hang (death)	hanged	hanged	hanging
listen	listened	listened	listening
review	reviewed	reviewed	reviewing
solve	solved	solved	solving
support	supported	supported	supporting

Regular Verbs—Y Endings. Change the final *y* to *i* and add *ed* to form the past or the past participle of a verb that ends in *y* preceded by a consonant. The present participle retains the *y* before adding *ing*. Even though spelling changes occur with these verbs, they are regular verbs.

Present Part	Past Part	Past Participle	Present Participle
carry	carried	carried	carrying
identify	identified	identified	identifying
try	tried	tried	trying

Regular Verbs—One Syllable. Double the last consonant of a one-syllable verb that ends in one consonant preceded by *one* vowel before you add *ed* to form the past and past participle or *ing* to form the present participle. Even though spelling changes occur with these verbs, they are regular verbs.

Present Part	Past Part	Past Participle	Present Participle
plan	planned	planned	planning
stop	stopped	stopped	stopping
wrap	wrapped	wrapped	wrapping

NOTES

Spelling Review
Refer to the spelling section of the Appendix for more spelling tips.

Regular Verbs—Accented Syllables.   Double the final consonant of a two-syllable verb accented on the *last* syllable that ends in a *single* consonant preceded by a *single* vowel when you add the suffix *ed* or *ing*. Even though spelling changes occur with these verbs, they are regular verbs.

Present Part	Past Part	Past Participle	Present Participle
ex cel´	excelled	excelled	excelling
oc cur´	occurred	occurred	occurring
pre fer´	preferred	preferred	preferring
re fer´	referred	referred	referring

CHECKPOINT 9.4

A. **Instructions:** *In the blank spaces, write the appropriate forms of the following regular verbs. The present part of the verb is given. Use a dictionary if you are not certain of a spelling or verb form.*

Present Part	Past Part	Past Participle	Present Participle
1. accept	_____	_____	_____
2. ship	_____	_____	_____
3. label	_____	_____	_____
4. require	_____	_____	_____
5. control	_____	_____	_____
6. copy	_____	_____	_____
7. attempt	_____	_____	_____
8. impel	_____	_____	_____

B. **Instructions:** *Select the correct part of the verb indicated in parentheses, and write it in the space provided.*

1. Tyjha (past—*defend*) her point of view very effectively.   _____

2. Critical thinking exercises (past participle—*help*) in on-the-job confrontations.   _____

3. She (past—*classify*) our concerns into three specific categories.   _____

4. I (present participle—*refer*) John's decision to resign to the Human Services Department.   _____

5. I especially (present—*enjoy*) the brainstorming step involved in problem solving.   _____

Irregular Verbs

Irregular verbs do not form their past parts or past participles by adding *d* or *ed* to the present parts of the verb. The spellings and forms of irregular verbs do not follow a consistent pattern. To use these verbs correctly, memorize the forms, or check a dictionary whenever you are in doubt.

Although there are more regular verbs than there are irregular verbs, many of the irregular verbs are commonly used. Here is a list of many of the irregular verbs:

Present Part	Past Part	Past Participle	Present Participle
be (am, is, are)	was, were	been	being
become	became	become	becoming
begin	began	begun	beginning
blow	blew	blown	blowing
break	broke	broken	breaking
bring	brought	brought	bringing
build	built	built	building
catch	caught	caught	catching
choose	chose	chosen	choosing
come	came	come	coming
do	did	done	doing
draw	drew	drawn	drawing
drive	drove	driven	driving
eat	ate	eaten	eating
give	gave	given	giving
go	went	gone	going
grow	grew	grown	growing
hang	hung	hung	hanging
have	had	had	having
hear	heard	heard	hearing
know	knew	known	knowing
lead	led	led	leading
leave	left	left	leaving
lose	lost	lost	losing
mean	meant	meant	meaning
pay	paid	paid	paying
ring	rang	rung	ringing
say	said	said	saying
see	saw	seen	seeing
show	showed	shown	showing
speak	spoke	spoken	speaking
spend	spent	spent	spending
take	took	taken	taking
teach	taught	taught	teaching
tell	told	told	telling
think	thought	thought	thinking
wear	wore	worn	wearing
write	wrote	written	writing

Verb Types and Parts

Go to the
Web

Checkpoint 9.5
for more skills practice on this topic.

CHECKPOINT 9.5

A. **Instructions:** *In the blank spaces, write the appropriate forms of the following irregular verbs. The present part of the verb is given. Use a dictionary if you are not certain of a spelling or form.*

	Present Part	Past Part	Past Participle	Present Participle
1.	fall	_____	_____	_____
2.	bind	_____	_____	_____
3.	sing	_____	_____	_____
4.	run	_____	_____	_____
5.	withdraw	_____	_____	_____
6.	feel	_____	_____	_____
7.	quit	_____	_____	_____
8.	strike	_____	_____	_____
9.	bend	_____	_____	_____
10.	tell	_____	_____	_____

B. **Instructions:** *Select the correct part of the verb indicated in parentheses, and write it in the space provided.*

1. Her suggestions for solving problems (past—*make*) an impact on her coworkers. _____

2. Annette (past participle—*sell*) several thousand copies of her book on critical thinking. _____

3. He (present participle—*go*) to enroll in the decision-making course at the community college next semester. _____

4. Kevin (past participle—*do*) the research on the status of artificial intelligence. _____

5. Mae Ling (past—*see*) the advantages of using decision-making software. _____

Special Verbs

Several pairs of verbs cause confusion. These verbs require special practice—*lay, lie; raise, rise;* and *set, sit.* To avoid misuse, remember that within each pair of the verbs just listed, one is transitive and the other is intransitive.

Definitions

lay: to put or place an item somewhere (*Requires an object*)

Substitute the words *put (put, putting)* to determine if *lay* is the correct form to use.

lie: to recline; to be located in a spot; to tell an untruth (*No object required*)

raise: to lift up or bring something up (*Requires an object*)

rise: to get up (*No object required*)

set: to put or place something (*Requires an object*) *exception:* the sun *sets*

sit: to be seated (*No object required*)

NOTES

Intransitive Verbs

The verbs that have *i* as their second letter are intransitive and do not require an object.

Special Verb Forms

The following table will help you determine the correct use of these irregular verbs:

	Present	Past	Past Participle (uses *have, had, has*)	Present Participle
Transitive **Requires an object**	raise set lay	raised set laid	raised set laid	raising setting laying
Intransitive **No object required**	lie sit rise	lay sat rose	lain sat risen	lying sitting rising

Verb Types and Parts

Go to the
Web

Checkpoint 9.6

for more skills practice on this topic.

The prioritized solutions <u>lay</u> on her desk for weeks.

(*Lay* is the past form of *lie*. *Lie* is an intransitive verb and does not require an object.)

Do you remember <u>laying</u> the critical thinking book on my desk?

(*Laying* is the present participle of *lay*. *Lay* is a transitive verb and requires an object [*book*].)

I <u>laid</u> the recommendations for resolving the conflict next to Sandy's evaluation.

(*Laid* is the past form of *lay*. *Lay* is a transitive verb and requires an object [*recommendations*].)

I will <u>set</u> the rules before we begin our brainstorming session.

(*Set* is a transitive verb that requires an object [*rules*].)

The meeting will be long; therefore, <u>sit</u> in a comfortable chair.

(*Sit* is an intransitive verb and does not require an object.)

Did you <u>raise</u> the question, or was it Jack who started the discussion?

(*Raise* is a transitive verb and requires an object [*question*].)

The discussion was controversial and voices often <u>rose</u>.

(*Rose* is the past form of *rise*. *Rise* is an intransitive verb and does not require an object.)

I had <u>risen</u> at 5:30 a.m. because I thought that we had an early morning negotiations meeting.

(*Risen* is the past participle of *rise*. *Rise* is an intransitive verb and requires no object.)

CHECKPOINT 9.6

Instructions: Select the correct word, and write it in the space provided.

1. Let's (*set, sit*) down to discuss the complaint. _____

2. I had (*laid, lain*) the groundwork for our problem-solving session very carefully. _____

3. Our morale level (*raised, rose*) when the president indicated that the company had solved its financial problems. _____

4. You should (*set, sit*) goals before you brainstorm. _____

5. Please (*lay, lie*) your evaluations of the expert system software on my desk. _____

6. The instructor plans to (*raise, rise*) several controversial issues in his critical thinking class. _____

7. Please get the conflict resolution manuals that are (*laying, lying*) on my desk. _____

8. I (*lay, laid*) the magazine article about brainstorming on the shelf in your office. _____

9. Dean (*sets, sits*) quietly and listens to his coworkers' concerns. _____

10. Annie will (*raise, rise*) the parking issue at the meeting. _____

Diagramming Sentences

The sentences in this diagramming section will be a review of the areas covered in other diagramming sections in Chapters 3, 4, 5, 7, and 8. The numbers in parentheses indicate the chapters for your reference.

Simple subject (3)

Simple predicate—verb (3)

Direct object (3)

Appositive (4)

Subject complement (4)

Indirect object (5)

Possessive noun (5)

Compound subjects (7)

Compound verbs (7)

Compound objects (7)

Adjectives (8)

CHECKPOINT 9.7

Go to the
Web

Checkpoint 9.7
for more skills practice on this topic.

Instructions: *In the space provided, diagram the following sentences. Remember that a, an, and* the *function as adjectives.*

1. Our group leader set a discussion time limit.

2. Child care and elder care are two major employee problems.

3. The committee's decision affected employee morale and job loyalty.

4.   Caroline, my supervisor, sent me the negotiation team's minutes and a new agenda.

5.   Rod and I discussed and evaluated Jane's recommended solutions.

6.   Most artificial intelligence systems are expensive.

7.   Successful salespeople reach the right decision makers.

Name _____ Date _____

PRACTICE 1

Choosing Verb Forms

Instructions: *At the beginning of each sentence is a verb part. Select the correct verb from those in parentheses and write it in the space provided.*

Go to the
Web

Practice 1 Exercises
for more skills practice on this topic.

1. past participle — Les has (*gone, went*) to a seminar on decision making for health technicians.

    1. _____

2. past — The manager (*forgot, forgotten*) to include Ray's solutions in the final report.

    2. _____

3. past — Our delayed decision (*cost, costed*) the company unnecessary expense.

    3. _____

4. past participle — I thought that I had (*became, become*) more tolerant of my coworkers' disorganization.

    4. _____

5. present participle — He is (*raising, rising*) some important issues for us to consider.

    5. _____

6. past — Our present managers (*notified, notifyed*) us about the final decision through e-mail.

    6. _____

7. present participle — She is (*sitting, setting*) the dates and times for the brainstorming sessions.

    7. _____

8. present — Write your solutions on cards, and (*lay, lie*) the cards in three piles— workable, possible, not workable.

    8. _____

9. past — An unexpected conflict (*ocured, occurred*) in a negotiation meeting.

    9. _____

10. past — He (*plan, planned*) to discuss the issue of excessive overtime.

    10. _____

Identifying Verbs and Verb Phrases

Instructions: *Underline the verbs or verb phrases in each of the following sentences.*

1. He ignored the problems among the members of his staff.

2. A positive work environment improves worker morale and increases production.

3. Russ is making the problem more complex than necessary.

4. Some workers are not comfortable in confrontations with coworkers whose actions have upset them.

5. My favorite problem-solving technique involves "what if" questions.

Name _____ Date _____

Selecting Special Verbs

Instructions: Select the correct verb, and write it in the space provided.

1. Her report (*laid, lay*) on the manager's desk for a week.   1. _____

2. Please (*lay, lie*) your report on the desk.   2. _____

3. Our conflict resolution workshops have (*growed, grown*) steadily.   3. _____

4. She had expertly (*laid, lain*) the groundwork for the brainstorming session.   4. _____

5. We followed the problem-solving steps, but we (*drawed, drew*) an illogical conclusion.   5. _____

Go to the
Web

Practice 2 Exercises
for more skills practice on this topic.

PRACTICE 2

Identifying Types of Verbs

*Instructions: In the space provided, identify the underlined verb or verbs by writing the appropriate code or codes. **A-T** (action—transitive verb), **A-I** (action—intransitive verb), **L** (linking verb), **H** (helping verb), **VP** (verb phrase).*

1. My supervisor <u>is</u> an expert in leading brainstorming sessions.   1. _____

2. Mr. Norvik <u>informed</u> his employees about the firm's decision-making process.   2. _____

3. We reached a consensus and immediately <u>announced</u> our decision.   3. _____

4. In emotional confrontations, sensitivity <u>seems</u> more important than the issues.   4. _____

5. Kate <u>apologized</u> to the group for her hasty decision.   5. _____

6. One rule for brainstorming sessions <u>is</u> the elimination of the statement "That will never <u>work</u>."   6. _____

7. Their solution to the problem <u>will</u> involve no extra cost to our department.   7. _____

8. I often <u>talk</u> with other managers about problem-solving techniques.   8. _____

9. Sometimes office conflicts <u>are</u> caused by reactions to workplace changes.   9. _____

10. Children <u>recognize</u> adult indecision and use it to their advantage.   10. _____

Name _____ Date _____

Forming Verb Parts

Instructions: Each of the lines below includes one verb form. Fill in the remaining verbs in the spaces provided under each heading.

	Present Part	Past Part	Past Participle	Present Participle
1.			done	
2.		controlled		
3.				meeting
4.		dropped		
5.	sink			
6.	modify			
7.			inferred	
8.				keeping
9.		froze		
10.	send			

Selecting Correct Verbs

Instructions: Select the correct verb and underline it.

1. He (*did, done*) the preparation work for the meeting.
2. Our manager slightly (*modified, modifyed*) our recommendations.
3. We (*infered, inferred*) disappointment from our manager with the results of our decision.
4. Teresa has (*chose, chosen*) a new meeting date.
5. We (*laid, lay*) our ballots on the table for Marsha to tally.

PRACTICE 3

Proofreading

Instructions: Proofread and compare the two sentences in each group. If they are the same, write **Yes** in the space provided. If they are not the same, write **No.** Use the first sentence as the correct copy. If you find errors in the second sentence, underline them.

1. Conflicts result when workers complain to their coworkers rather than to the person who can do something about the problem.

   Problems result when workers complain to their coworkers rather than to the persons who can do something about the problem.

1. _____

Name _____ Date _____

2. One of the best ways to get employee support is to give away the credit and ownership of your ideas.

   One of the best ways to get employee's support is to give the credit and ownership of your ideas.

   2. _____

3. The major parts of a rule-based expert system are an expert knowledge base, a user interface, and an inference engine.

   The mayor parts of a rule based expert system are an expert knowledge base, a user interface, and an inferance engine.

   3. _____

4. As you progress through the steps of problem solving, ask the question, "What is the best solution to the problem based on costs and feasibility?"

   As you progress through the steps of problem solving, ask the question, "what is the best solution to the problem based on costs and feasability?"

   4. _____

5. The New York Center for Critical Thinking at 618 Washington Street in New York provides workshops to businesses in the United States and Canada.

   The New York Center for Critical Thinking at 681 Washington Street in New York provides workshops to businesses in the United States and Canada.

   5. _____

Using Proofreaders' Marks

Steps in Problem Solving

1. Define the problem.

   Be certain that the symptoms of the problem do not overshadow the causes. This step is the most difficult.

2. Identify solutions.

   Gather as many ideas as possible. Brainstorming is a method that often works because it encourages participants to be creative and spontaneous in their solutions.

3. Select the best solution.

   List and rank the points that you use to evaluate each idea. Each solution will have strengths and weaknesses.

4. Evaluate the solution.

   Record the results of selecting your solution. If a similar problem occurs, you will have some of your work already accomplished.

Name _____ Date _____

Instructions: Use the following proofreaders' marks to make corrections in the copy
that follows. Use the correct copy above as your guide.

Lowercase /   Move left ⌐   Insert letter ∧

Capitalize ≡   Move right ⌐   Insert comma ⋏

Delete ⌁   Insert space #∧   Transpose ∽

Delete and close up ⌇

Steps In Problem Solving

1. Define the Problem.

    Be certain that the symtoms of the problem do not overshadow
    the causes. This step isthe most difficult.

2. identify solutions.

    Gather as many ideas as possible. Brainstorming,
    isa method that often works because it encouragees participants to
    be creative and spontaneous in thier solutions.

3. Select the best solution.

    List and rank the points that you use to evaluate each idea.
    Each solution will have strenths and have weaknesses.

4. Evaluate the solution.

    Record the results of selecting your solution. If a similar
    problem occurs you will have some of your work
    allready accomplished.

PRACTICE 4

Writing

Instructions: Write sentences using the following verbs. Unless specified, you may use
any forms of these verbs. Answers will vary.

1. *lay* (use the form that means to put or place an item)

    _____

    _____

2. *lie* (use the form that means to recline or to be located in a spot)

    _____

    _____

3. *raise*

    _____

    _____

Go to the
Web

Practice 4 Exercises
for more skills practice on
this topic.

NOTES

Phrases Defined
An infinitive phrase is the word *to*
and a verb form. The main verb in
a sentence is never an infinitive.

Name _____ Date _____

4. *rise*

_____

_____

5. *set*

_____

_____

6. *sit*

_____

_____

7. *seen*

_____

_____

8. *done*

_____

_____

PRACTICE 5

Choosing Verb Forms

Instructions: At the beginning of each sentence is a verb part. Select the correct verb from those in parentheses, and write it in the space provided.

1. past participle   She has (*gave, given*) several excuses for not attending our planning meetings.   1. _____

2. past participle   Ross has (*drew, drawn*) the wrong conclusions about our postponement of the decision deadline.   2. _____

3. past   We (*paid, payed*) a high price for making a quick decision.   3. _____

4. present   I noticed that Greg always (*sits, sets*) next to Karen at meetings.   4. _____

5. past   The software engineer (*teached, taught*) us how to use the decision-making software.   5. _____

6. present participle   She is (*raising, rising*) some positive support for two of the alternative solutions.   6. _____

Name _____ Date _____

7. past   Shelly (*began, begun*) the discussion   7. _____
with a clear statement of the
problem.

8. present   We (*use, used*) many resources in   8. _____
our critical thinking case studies.

9. present participle Heinrich is (*becoming, become*) an   9. _____
outstanding lecturer on artificial
intelligence.

10. past   I (*modified, modifyed*) the cost   10. _____
estimates for our decision-making
software.

Identifying Verbs and Verb Phrases

Instructions: Underline the verbs or verb phrases in each of the following sentences.

1. Good decisions are based on sound goals and objectives.

2. Hank Larson is a strong, independent decision maker.

3. We must evaluate the credibility of the information.

4. We knew that our employees needed additional decision-making
   practice.

5. Rianna's final choices were obvious to her, but her explanation to
   her supervisor was difficult.

Selecting Special Verbs

Instructions: Underline the correct verb or verb phrase in each of the following sentences:

1. I (*raised, rose*) hurriedly and left the personnel meeting.

2. She (*has gone, has went*) to an outstanding workshop on conflict
   resolution.

3. Perhaps we should (*set, sit*) a date and time for our next
   brainstorming session.

4. You will find the book on problem solving (*lying, laying*) on the
   table in the staff lounge.

5. The flight instructor (*teached, taught*) the pilots to prioritize their
   responses to emergencies.

Name _____ Date _____

PRACTICE 6

Identifying Types of Verbs

Instructions: In the space provided, identify the underlined verb or verbs by writing the appropriate code or codes. A-T (action—transitive verb), A-I (action—intransitive verb), L (linking verb), H (helping verb), VP (verb phrase).

1. The Chinese <u>developed</u> I Ching in 3000 BC to provide a more systematic process of decision making.

    1. _____

2. A poor decision <u>is</u> reversible.

    2. _____

3. Michelle <u>was</u> appointed our group leader.

    3. _____

4. Your coworkers always <u>speak</u> very highly of your decisions.

    4. _____

5. Todd <u>adjusted</u> the rules to keep peace in the group.

    5. _____

6. Our work team rarely <u>misses</u> a deadline.

    6. _____

7. Your information <u>appears</u> inaccurate.

    7. _____

8. We <u>had</u> hoped for more time to gather our data.

    8. _____

9. Brainstorming <u>encourages</u> group participation.

    9. _____

10. After stressful meetings, I <u>walk</u> around the company parking lot.

    10. _____

Forming Verb Parts

Instructions: Each of the lines below includes one verb form. Fill in the remaining verbs in the spaces provided under each heading.

	Present Part	Past Part	Past Participle	Present Participle
1.	begin	_____	_____	_____
2.	_____	drove	_____	_____
3.	_____	flew	_____	_____
4.	_____	_____	_____	making
5.	_____	wore	_____	_____
6.	_____	clarified	_____	_____
7.	solve	_____	_____	_____
8.	_____	_____	_____	flying
9.	_____	_____	written	_____
10.	lose	_____	_____	_____

Name _____ Date _____

Selecting Correct Verbs

Instructions: Select the correct verb and underline it.

1. We have already (*began, begun*) our decision-making seminars for managers this year.

2. Tom (*has went, went*) to every brainstorming meeting this month.

3. We are (*planing, planning*) to resolve this conflict before Friday afternoon.

4. Helen (*preferred, prefered*) to avoid all types of conflict at work.

5. I (*saw, seen*) the final draft of the recommendations for solving the parking problem.

PRACTICE 7

Proofreading

*Instructions: Proofread and compare the two sentences in each group. If they are the same, write **Yes** in the space provided. If they are not the same, write **No**. Use the first sentence as the correct copy. If you find errors in the second sentence, underline them.*

1. In business, 80 percent of decisions should be made immediately, 15 percent should take more time and thought, and 5 percent should not be made at all.

   In business, 80 percent of decisions should be made imediately, 10 percent should take more time and thought, and 5 percent should be made at all.

   1. _____

2. When making decisions, avoid the impossible task of "getting all the facts."

   When making decisions, avoid the impossible task of "getting all the facts."

   2. _____

3. When asking others for their opinions, just present the facts and issues, and let them tell you what they would do.

   When asking others for thier opinion, just present the facts and issues, and let them tell you what they would have done.

   3. _____

4. Brainstorming involves listing every solution, no matter how far-out or crazy, that comes to mind.

   Brainstorming involves listing every solution, no matter how farout or crazy, that comes to mind.

   4. _____

Verb Types and Parts

Name _____ Date _____

5. People who think carefully about what they are being told before taking action are more likely to make effective decisions.

    5. _____

People who think carefully about what they are being told before taking acktion are more likely to make effective decisions.

Using Proofreader's Marks

Suggestions for Decision Making

- Do not waste time trying to "gather all the facts."
- Consult with your supervisor, your coworkers, and others before the problem becomes unmanageable.
- Respect your intuition.
- Use brainstorming to generate ideas.
- Think of the best and worst possible outcomes of the decision.
- Strive for acceptance of the decision by group members.
- Inform others who will be affected by the decision.
- Change plans if a decision does not work.

Instructions: You are the recorder for a brainstorming session on suggestions for decision making. Use the following proofreaders' marks to make corrections in the copy that follows. Use the correct copy above as your guide.

Delete ⌐	Delete and close up ℉
Insert letter ∧	Lowercase /
Transpose ∽	Move left ⌐
Capitalize ≡	Move right ⌐
Insert comma ∧	Insert space #∧

Sugestions for Decision Making

- Don't waste time trying to "gather all teh facts."
- Consult with your supervisor, your co-workers and others before the problem becomes unmanageible.
- Respect yourintuition or "gut feelings."
- Use brainstorming ot generate ideas.
- think of the best and worst possible outcomes of the decision.
- Strive for acceptance of the decision by gruop members.
- Enform others who will be affected by the decision.
- Change plans if a decision does not work.

Name _____ Date _____

PRACTICE 8

Writing

Instructions: *Write sentences using the following verbs. Answers will vary.*

1. *lain*

    _____
    _____
    _____

2. *laying*

    _____
    _____
    _____

3. *lying*

    _____
    _____
    _____

4. *risen*

    _____
    _____
    _____

5. *raised*

    _____
    _____
    _____

6. *gone*

    _____
    _____
    _____

7. *went*

    _____
    _____
    _____

Posttest

Instructions: In the space provided, write the letter of the correct answer.

1. In the sentence *Decision-making software helps users make decisions quickly,* the verb *helps* is: (1)

   a. a linking verb.

   b. a helping verb.

   c. an action verb.

   d. an intransitive verb.

   1. _____

2. In the sentence *Brainstorming is a method to increase your creativity,* the verb *is* is: (1)

   a. a linking verb.

   b. a helping verb.

   c. an action verb.

   d. a transitive verb.

   2. _____

3. In the sentence *Many software programs are devoted to decision making,* the verb *are* is: (1)

   a. a linking verb.

   b. a helping verb.

   c. an action verb.

   d. an intransitive verb.

   3. _____

4. In the sentence *Good decision makers identify possible solutions to problems,* the verb *identify* is: (2)

   a. a linking verb.

   b. a helping verb.

   c. a transitive verb.

   d. an intransitive verb.

   4. _____

5. Which line consists only of irregular verb forms? (4)

   a. succeed, consider, assess

   b. carry, result, try

   c. confer, wrap, stop

   d. leave, hear, pay

   5. _____

6. Which sentence is written correctly? (5)

   a. We done a good job in describing our job functions.

   b. Our company will be droping "Inc." from our name.

   c. John has forgoten our monthly planning meeting.

   d. The supervisor issued new guidelines for the distribution of meeting minutes.

   6. _____

7. Which sentence is written correctly? (4, 5, 6)

   a. I have set next to Michelle in every meeting.

   b. We have forgiven John for his outburst of dissatisfaction about the new computer system.

   c. We tryed to give each committee member an opportunity to speak.

   d. Our workforce has shrank in the last month.

   7. _____

8. Which statement is correct about the following sentence? *We are writing guidelines for customer request procedures.* (1)

   a. The verbs are *writing* and *procedures.*

   b. The linking verb is *are* and the action verb is *request.*

   c. The verb phrase is *are writing* and the direct object is *guidelines.*

   d. The verb is *writing* and the direct object is *customer.*

   8. _____

9. Which statement is correct about the following sentence? *We lay incoming mail on Erica's desk for distribution.* (2, 6)

  a. The verbs are *lay* and *incoming.*
  b. The verb is *lay* and the direct object is *mail.*
  c. The verb is *incoming* and the direct object is *desk.*
  d. The verb is *lay* and the direct objects are *desk* and *distribution.*

9. _____

10. Which sentence is written correctly? (1, 4, 6)

  a. Writing often help me make a decision.
  b. I open my e-mail inbox and finds an e-mail from Jason.
  c. Our supervisor lain down the ground rules for our decision-making meeting.
  d. We are reviewing the proposal for another week.

10. _____

11. Which statement is correct about the following sentence? *He hurriedly made a poor decision.* (1, 2)

  a. The verb is *made* and is an irregular verb.
  b. The helping verb is *hurriedly.*
  c. The verb is *made* and is a linking verb.
  d. The verb is *made* and is an intransitive verb.

11. _____

12. Which statement is correct about the following sentence? *I lay down at the end of the day and reviewed my decisions* (1, 6)

  a. The verb is *down.*
  b. The verb is *lay.*
  c. The verbs are *lay* and *reviewed.*
  d. The verbs are *down* and *reviewed.*

12. _____

13. Which sentence is written correctly? (6)

  a. We will sit the deadline for our project for Tuesday.
  b. Our landlord rises rent each year.
  c. I laid the report on Jerri's desk.
  d. I layed the summary on your desk.

13. _____

14. Which sentence is written correctly? (4)

  a. Janis payed the programmer for revising our software.
  b. I seen a solution to Kate's problem.
  c. Someone snuck into my office last night and read my e-mail.
  d. We meant to revise our Web page last week.

14. _____

15. Which sentence is written correctly? (4)

  a. I have broke my promise to arrive on time to meetings.
  b. Jerry brung me the report yesterday.
  c. We set high standards for our committee.
  d. The number of meetings have rose again.

14. _____

Chapter 10

Verb Tense, Voice, and Mood—Verbals

OBJECTIVES

After you have studied this chapter and completed the exercises, you will be able to do the following:

1. Use the irregular verbs *be, have,* and *do* correctly.

2. Use the present, past, and future tenses of verbs correctly.

3. Recognize the use of the perfect tenses, progressive tenses, and emphatic tenses of verbs in sentences.

4. Differentiate between active and passive voices of verbs.

5. Identify the three ways to express verb mood.

6. Demonstrate the functions of verbals—gerunds, participles, and infinitives—in sentences.

Workplace Applications: Computer Software

Software is a set of electronic instructions that enables a computer to perform certain tasks. Most software is classified into two major categories: system software and application software. One type of system software is operating system software such as Windows®. Application software tells the computer how to accomplish specific tasks such as word processing.

Operating system software exists primarily for the benefit of the computer. Application software does almost every task imaginable. Thousands of applications—from business to entertainment—are available. Commercial software firms range in size from a single, self-employed programmer to huge corporations like Microsoft and IBM.

The biggest legal problem affecting the computer industry is software piracy, which is the illegal copying or use of programs. Using pirated software is a felony. Many people who use the Internet think that all the data available on it is free; however, downloading software or reference materials may violate someone else's copyright. Because of the difficulty in developing effective antipiracy schemes, software developers rely on the law and on people's respect for the law to use computer programs and other materials legally.

Pretest

Instructions: In the space provided, write the letter of the correct answer.

1. Which statement is written correctly? (1)

    a. You was correct in your evaluation of our file management needs.

    b. You were correct in your evaluation of our file management needs.

    1. _____

2. Which statement is written correctly? (2)

    a. Accounting programs save small business owners time and money.

    b. Accounting programs saves small business owners time and money.

    2. _____

3. Which statement is written correctly? (2)

    a. We done the promotion for the new software well in advance of its release.

    b. We did the promotion for the new software well in advance of its release.

    3. _____

4. Which statement is written correctly? (2)

    a. I am certain that software prices will rise soon.

    b. I am certain that software prices rise soon.

    4. _____

5. Which tense is represented by the underlined words in this statement?
    I had used an outdated database package for several years before I received an updated version. (3)

    a. past

    b. past perfect

    5. _____

6. Which tense is represented by the underlined words in this statement?
    I have sent you a corrected copy of the manuscript, which was completed using Microsoft Word. (3)

    a. future

    b. present perfect

    6. _____

7. Which of the following statements is written using active voice? (4)

    a. Our company produces many software programs.

    b. Many software programs are produced by our company.

    7. _____

8. Which statement is written correctly? (5)

    a. I move that this software design meeting is adjourned.

    b. I move that this software design meeting be adjourned.

    8. _____

9. Which statement is written correctly? (6)

    a. We appreciate you advising us to keep a record of our software expenses for tax purposes.

    b. We appreciate your advising us to keep a record of our software expenses for tax purposes.

    9. _____

10. Which statement involves a gerund? (6)

    a. Writing a weekly software column keeps Maggie busy.

    b. Knowing the difficulty of the program, I allowed myself extra learning time.

    10. _____

11. Which statement is correct? (2)

    a. Craig and Jordan use several different types of software daily.

    b. Craig and Jordan uses several different types of software daily.

11. _____

12. Which statement involves an infinitive? (6)

    a. To enroll in an Excel class at the community college, I completed a registration form.

    b. I took my registration form for the Excel class to the business office at the college.

12. _____

13. Which statement is true? (4)

    a. Active voice means that the subject of a sentence performs the action.

    b. Active voice means that the subject of a sentence receives the action.

13. _____

14. Which statement is written correctly? (5)

    a. Fletcher and I do appreciate the new computer technology.

    b. Fletcher and I does appreciate the new computer technology.

14. _____

15. Which statement is written correctly? (5)

    a. If I were a software manual writer, I would keep my instructions simple.

    b. If I was a software manual writer, I would keep my instructions simple.

15. _____

Chapter Preview

Now that you have studied the principal parts of regular and irregular verbs, you are ready to apply this knowledge to form the present, past, and future tenses of verbs.

You have probably heard the saying "It's the small things that make a difference." This saying can be applied to verbs as well. Knowing how to use the "small" verbs—*be, do,* and *have*—correctly is especially important.

You will see why many writers prefer active voice rather than passive voice in writing documents. Verbs also have moods. You are familiar with your own moods and how they affect what you do and feel. Mood also refers to the way verbs express their actions.

Some verb forms known as *verbals* look like verbs, but they function as nouns, adjectives, or adverbs in sentences. You will study gerunds, participles, and infinitives and learn to use these forms correctly.

Irregular Verbs: *Be, Do,* and *Have*

As you learned in Chapter 9, irregular verbs require extra study since there are no specific guidelines to follow when forming their parts. Three of the irregular verbs—*be, do,* and *have*—require special attention. You will find it helpful to memorize the parts of these three frequently used verbs.

Verbs	Present	Past	Past Participle	Present Participle
(be)	am, is, are	was, were	been	being
(have)	have, has	had	had	having
(do)	do, does	did	done	doing

The following charts indicate the singular and plural verb forms of *be, do,* and *have* for first, second, and third persons. The present form of the verb is in the first parentheses (*am*). The past form is in the second parentheses (*was*).

NOTES

Looking Back
Review regular and irregular verb forms in Chapter 9. Keep a list of those verbs with which you have difficulty.

Be
Singular

First Person:	I (am) (was)
Second Person:	you (are) (were)
Third Person:	he, she, it (is) (was)
	Mary (is) (was)

Plural

First Person:	we (are) (were)
Second Person:	you (are) (were)
Third Person:	they (are) (were)
	Mary and Tom (are) (were)

Chapter 10

I was correct in the way that I changed my password.

(*Was* is a linking verb used with *I,* a singular subject in first person.)

They were lab partners in the computer courses at Corinthian College last quarter.

(*Were* is a linking verb used with *they,* a plural subject in third person.)

She is experimenting with several new software programs.

(The verb phrase *is experimenting* consists of a present participle *experimenting* and a helping verb *is.* The verb phrase is used with *she,* a singular subject in third person.)

Do
Singular

First Person:	I (do) (did)
Second Person:	you (do) (did)
Third Person:	he, she, it (does) (did)
	Mary (does) (did)

Plural

First Person:	we (do) (did)
Second Person:	you (do) (did)
Third Person:	they (do) (did)
	Mary and Tom (do) (did)

The software technicians did the corrections for our program.

(*Did* is the main verb used with *software technicians,* a third-person plural subject.)

We do the software preview tests in our Lexington plant.

(*Do* is the main verb used with *we,* a first-person plural subject.)

Sherry did not memorize her password.

(*Memorize* is the main verb, and *did* is the helping verb. *Sherry* is a third-person singular subject.)

Have
Singular

First Person:	I (have) (had)
Second Person:	you (have) (had)
Third Person:	he, she, it (has) (had)
	Mary (has) (had)

Plural

First Person:	we (have) (had)
Second Person:	you (have) (had)
Third Person:	they (have) (had)
	Mary and Tom (have) (had)

We have partnerships with several leading independent software vendors.

(*Have* is the main verb used with *we,* a plural subject in first person.)

She has a new password.

(*Has* is the main verb used with *she*, a singular subject in third person.)

They have ordered another copy of the software instructions.

(The verb phrase *have ordered* consists of a past participle *ordered* and the helping verb *have*. The phrase is used with *they*, a plural subject in third person.)

Go to the
Web

Checkpoint 10.1
for more skills practice on this topic.

CHECKPOINT 10.1

Instructions: *Select the correct verb, and write it in the space provided. Circle the simple subject in each sentence.*

1. We (*was, were*) at the computer products exhibition on Saturday. _____

2. They (*do, does*) the programming research in the Dallas office. _____

3. Nick (*had, have*) Quicken® installed on his home computer. _____

4. Gina (*did, done*) the artwork for the advertisement for our new database package. _____

5. You (*was, were*) in the software design department for many years. _____

6. He (*has done, done*) a virus check on our software several times. _____

7. It (*is, are*) easy to forget lengthy software instructions. _____

8. You (*did, done*) the evaluation of the three software packages very quickly. _____

9. We (*has, have*) not received the updated documentation yet. _____

10. She (*was, were*) learning two software programs concurrently. _____

Verb Tense

In addition to describing "what happens" to a subject in a sentence, a verb indicates "when it happens." The tense of a verb helps to identify the time of an action or a state of being. Although a verb has several tenses, its principal ones are referred to as the simple tenses—the *present*, the *past*, and the *future*.

Present Tense

Use the present tense to express a general truth or an action that is occurring now. Also, use the present tense to express an action that occurs regularly or habitually.

Dana completes software competency questionnaires quickly.

(*Completes* is a verb in the present tense that indicates an action is occurring now.)

The new software program costs $900.

(*Costs* is a verb in the present tense that expresses a general truth.)

My supervisor <u>makes</u> all the decisions about software training.

(*Makes* is a verb in the present tense that indicates a regularly occurring action.)

With Singular Subjects. Add *s* to a verb in present tense when the subject is a third-person singular noun (*student*) or a third-person singular pronoun (*he*, *she*, or *it*). Add *es* to the verb if it ends in *o*, *ch*, *s*, *sh*, *x*, or *z*.

<u>Mark</u> knows	**<u>he</u> know<u>s</u>**

(*Mark* is a third-person singular noun; *he* is a third-person singular pronoun. The present tense of the verb *know* requires an *s*.)

<u>company</u> produces	**<u>it</u> produces**

(The subject *company* is a third-person singular noun; *it* is a third-person singular pronoun. The present tense of the verb *produce* requires an *s*.)

The sound <u>echoes</u>	**<u>it</u> echo<u>es</u>**
Mr. <u>Lawton</u> teaches	**<u>he</u> teach<u>es</u>**
the <u>student</u> misses	**<u>he or she</u> miss<u>es</u>**
a <u>programmer</u> finishes	**<u>he or she</u> finish<u>es</u>**
the <u>accountant</u> faxes	**<u>he or she</u> fax<u>es</u>**
the <u>phone</u> buzzes	**<u>it</u> buzz<u>es</u>**

(Add *es* to verbs that end in *o*, *ch*, *s*, *sh*, *x*, or *z*.)

With Plural Subjects. Do not add *s* or *es* to a verb in the present tense when the subject is a plural noun or a compound subject.

we <u>know</u>	**Mark and Lynn <u>teach</u>**
sounds <u>echo</u>	**accountants <u>fax</u>**
they <u>plan</u>	**programmers <u>finish</u>**

Do This   Do Not Do This

Wade <u>does</u> not <u>know</u>   Wade <u>don't know</u> the
the cost of the software   cost of the software.

Use the singular form of *do* (*does*) with a singular third-person noun or pronoun.

Two examples of present tense verbs with first-, second-, and third-person subjects follow:

Present Tense Regular Verb: *Work*

	Singular Subject	Plural Subject
First Person:	I (work)	we (work)
Second Person:	you (work)	you (work)
Third Person:	he, she, it (works)	they (work)
	Kim (works)	

NOTES

Changes in Verb Forms

Be aware of the changes in verb forms when subjects are third-person singular.

NOTES

More Practice

Use other verbs from the lists of regular or irregular verbs in Chapter 9 to practice forming present verb tenses.

Present Tense Irregular Verb: *Build*

	Singular Subject	Plural Subject
First Person:	I (build)	we (build)
Second Person:	you (build)	you (build)
Third Person:	he, she, it (builds)	they (build)
	Ron (builds)	

Go to the
Web

Checkpoint 10.2
for more skills practice on this topic.

CHECKPOINT 10.2

Instructions: Complete each sentence by writing the correct present tense of the verb in parentheses. Circle the simple subject in each sentence.

1. I (*spend*) several hours each week installing software updates. _____

2. A user's concern with a new program (*deserve*) a response from the manufacturer. _____

3. Va Maoa (*miss*) her old version of word processing software. _____

4. This example (*show*) how the software can be applied to your operations. _____

5. Popular software often (*come*) with work-group features. _____

6. You (*receive*) excellent online tutorials with all our programs. _____

7. The managers (*support*) a new software piracy policy. _____

8. We (*recommend*) that you evaluate at least three tax software packages. _____

Past Tense

Use verbs in past tense to express an action or condition that was started and completed in the past. Regular verbs require *d* or *ed* endings for their past tenses. Irregular verbs form their past tenses in various ways. Do not use a helping verb with a main verb to form the past tense.

> **Last week Mr. Sullivan <u>interviewed</u> ten candidates for the hotline technician's position.**
>
> (*Interviewed* is a regular verb in past tense that indicates Mr. Sullivan already completed the action.)
>
> **He <u>found</u> several clip art images and <u>used</u> them in the last issue of the newsletter.**
>
> (*Found* is an irregular verb and *used* is a regular verb. Both are in past tense and indicate that the actions took place in the past.)

Two past tense verbs in first, second, and third person appear below.

Past Tense Regular Verb: *Assist*

	Singular Subject	Plural Subject
First Person:	I (assisted)	we (assisted)
Second Person:	you (assisted)	you (assisted)
Third Person:	he, she, it (assisted)	they (assisted)
	Jon (assisted)	

<table>
<tr><td>

Do This

The intranet <u>cost</u> several thousand dollars to install.

</td><td>

Do Not Do This

The intranet <u>costed</u> several thousand dollars to install.

</td></tr>
</table>

Costed is not a verb form and is never used. Use the past tense *cost*. The present and past tenses for the verb *cost* are the same.

Past Tense Irregular Verb: *Forget*

	Singular Subject	Plural Subject
First Person:	I (forgot)	we (forgot)
Second Person:	you (forgot)	you (forgot)
Third Person:	he, she, it (forgot)	they (forgot)
	Jon (forgot)	

<table>
<tr><td>

Do This

They <u>saw</u> the newest contact management software.

</td><td>

Do Not Do This

They <u>seen</u> the newest contact management software.

</td></tr>
</table>

Do not use the past participle form when you need a past tense verb. *Seen* always requires a helping verb.

CHECKPOINT 10.3

Go to the
Web

Checkpoint 10.3
for more skills practice on this topic.

Instructions: *In the space provided, write the tense of the verb indicated in parentheses. Circle the simple subject in each sentence.*

1. We (*buy,* past) the software on the basis of its outstanding rating. _____

2. Our firm (*complete,* past) its analysis of accounting software packages. _____

3. Project management software (*allow,* present) the user to break any job into smaller tasks. _____

4. Leslie (*give,* past) some professional pointers on desktop publishing. _____

5. I (*be,* past) positive that my mailing labels (*be,* past) appropriate for my printer. _____

6. PowerPoint presentations *(be, present)* helpful to speakers and lecturers. _____

7. Accounting software *(do, present)* not replace a good accountant or a knowledge of basic bookkeeping. _____

8. A header *(appear, present)* at the top of a page, and a footer _____
(appear, present) at the bottom of a page. _____

Future Tense

Use future tense to indicate an action or condition that will occur in the future. To form the future tense, use the helping verb *will* or *shall* before the present part of the verb.

He will explain the integration of the two programs.

(*Explain* is the present part of the verb; *will* is the helping verb. *Will explain* is the verb phrase that indicates the explanation will be done in the future.)

Our software will arrive by FedEx.

(*Arrive* is the present part of the verb; *will* is the helping verb. *Will arrive* is the verb phrase that indicates the software has not arrived but will arrive in the future.)

Go to the
Web

Checkpoint 10.4
for more skills practice on this topic.

 CHECKPOINT 10.4

*Instructions: Check the underlined words for future tense use. If the word or words indicate future tense, write **Yes** in the space provided. If the words do not indicate future tense, write your corrections in the space provided. Circle the simple subject in each sentence.*

1. The Software Publishers Association will educate users about laws regarding computer software. _____

2. We used our desktop publishing program to produce brochures and newsletters. _____

3. We will investigate several project management software programs. _____

4. Our computer users' group reviewed its objectives. _____

5. The software checked other users' calendars for free dates and times. _____

6. The new software makes the payroll easier to prepare. _____

7. Newer versions of mailing software will improve our overall service and productivity. _____

8. Several human resource managers experimented with the latest skills testing. _____

Perfect Tenses

In addition to the present, past, and future tenses (the simple tenses), there are three perfect tenses—the *present perfect*, the *past perfect*, and the *future perfect*.

Present Perfect Tense.   Use the present perfect tense to show that an action or condition that started in the past has just been completed or continues to take place up to the present. Use *has* or *have* with the past participle of a verb to form the present perfect tense.

> **Our firm <u>has finished</u> the testing of the software.**
>
> (*Has finished* is a verb phrase that consists of the past participle *finished* and the helping verb *has*. The verb phrase shows that the action has recently been completed.)
>
> **We <u>have found</u> the instructions for installing the software difficult to understand.**
>
> (*Have found* is a verb phrase that consists of the past participle *found* and the helping verb *have*. The action in present perfect tense indicates that the firm found the directions difficult to understand in the past and continues to find them difficult up to the present time.)

Do This

She <u>could have taken</u> a course in Excel at the business college.

Do Not Do This

She <u>could of taken</u> a course in Excel at the business college.

Do not use the preposition *of* as a substitution for the verb *have.*

Past Perfect Tense.   Use the past perfect tense to show that one action or condition began and was completed *before* another past action. Use the helping verb *had* with the past participle of a verb to form the past perfect tense.

> **She <u>had prepared</u> her demonstration before the programmers <u>made</u> some major software changes.**
>
> (The action of preparing the demonstration was started and completed *before* another past action [that of the programmers].)
>
> **By the time the firm <u>published</u> its evaluation, the manufacturer <u>had increased</u> the cost.**
>
> (The action by the manufacturer was started and completed before another past action [that of the firm].)

Future Perfect Tense.   Use the future perfect tense to indicate an action or condition that will begin and end before a specific future time. Use the helping verbs *shall have* or *will have* before the past participle of a verb to form the future perfect tense.

> **He <u>will have learned</u> the software before next weekend.**
>
> (*Will have learned* is a verb phrase that consists of the past participle *learned* and the helping verbs *will* and *have*. The action of learning begins and ends before the future time of *next weekend.*)
>
> **By next year, all my software statistics <u>will have become obsolete</u>.**
>
> (*Will have become* is a verb phrase that consists of the past participle *become* and the helping verbs *will* and *have*. The action begins and ends before the future time of *next year.*)

Verb Tense, Voice, and Mood—Verbals

An example of the perfect tense verbs—present, past, future—in first, second, and third person appears below.

Present Perfect Tense: *See*

	Singular Subject	Plural Subject
First Person:	I (have seen)	We (have seen)
Second Person:	you (have seen)	you (have seen)
Third Person:	he, she, it (has seen)	they (have seen)
	Tom (has seen)	

Past Perfect Tense: *See*

	Singular Subject	Plural Subject
First Person:	I (had seen)	we (had seen)
Second Person:	you (had seen)	you (had seen)
Third Person:	he, she, it (had seen)	they (had seen)
	Tom (had seen)	

Future Perfect Tense: *See*

	Singular Subject	Plural Subject
First Person:	I (will [or shall]) have seen	we (will [or shall] have seen)
Second Person:	you (will have seen)	you (will have seen)
Third Person:	he, she, it (will have seen)	they (will have seen)
	Tom (will have seen)	

Go to the
Web

Checkpoint 10.5
for more skills practice on this topic.

NOTES

Looking Back
Review the present participles listed in Chapter 9.

CHECKPOINT 10.5

A. **Instructions:** *Fill in the blanks with the verb tense indicated. The first column gives you the present part of the verb with the subject in parentheses. Use your text if you are uncertain about a form.*

	Present Part	Present Perfect	Past Perfect	Future Perfect
1.	begin (I)	_____	_____	_____
2.	cover (it)	_____	_____	_____
3.	do (she)	_____	_____	_____
4.	break (you)	_____	_____	_____
5.	use (company)	_____	_____	_____
6.	carry (we)	_____	_____	_____
7.	see (Ryan)	_____	_____	_____

Chapter 10

*B. **Instructions:*** *Underline the perfect tense verbs in the following sentences. Using the codes below, indicate the number of the verb tense in the space provided. Circle the simple subject in the sentence.*

1 = present perfect
2 = past perfect
3 = future perfect

1. Project management software has become popular with administrative _____
   professionals.

2. By Friday, Mary will have trained me on the file management software. _____

3. I had shown Phil the PDF file procedures before I left the office. _____

4. Rachel will have completed the database management course by the end _____
   of the month.

5. We have ordered another copy of Excel for our Denver office. _____

Progressive Tenses

The six progressive tenses follow the patterns of the simple and perfect tenses. These progressive tenses show continuing actions or conditions. The progressive tenses consist of the present participle (main verb ending in *ing*) and appropriate tenses of *to be* (*am, is, are, was, were, will be, shall be, have been, has been, had been,* or *will have been*).

Present Progressive Tense.   Use the present participle plus the helping verb *am, is,* or *are* to form the present progressive tense. This tense involves an action or condition that is in progress at the present time.

> **I am using a personal finance software program.**

Past Progressive Tense.   Use the present participle plus the helping verb *was* or *were* to form the past progressive tense. This tense involves an action or condition that was in progress at a time in the past.

> **I was using a personal finance software program.**

Future Progressive Tense.   Use the present participle plus the helping verbs *will be* or *shall be* to form the future progressive tense. This tense involves an action or condition that will continue in the future.

> **I will be using a personal finance software program.**

Present Perfect Progressive Tense.   Use the present participle plus the helping verbs *have been* or *has been* to form the present perfect progressive tense. This tense describes a continuous action up to the present time.

> **I have been using a personal finance software program since 1997.**

Past Perfect Progressive Tense.   Use the present participle plus the helping verbs *had been* to form the past perfect progressive tense. This tense describes an action that was being completed at a specific time in the past.

> **I had been using a personal finance software program until I learned an accounting program.**

Future Perfect Progressive Tense.   Use the present participle plus the helping verbs *will (shall) have been* to form the future perfect progressive tense. This tense describes an action that will continue to be in progress at a specified time in the future.

> **By the end of this month, I will have been using a personal finance software program for at least three years.**

Emphatic Tense

The present and past tenses have additional forms, called emphatic tenses, that add emphasis to the verb. Use the verb *do* or *does* with the present part of a verb to form the present emphatic tense. Use the verb *did* to form the past emphatic tense.

> **I do make an effort to read the ads for new software products.**
>
> (*Do* gives extra emphasis to the verb *make* and indicates present emphatic tense.)
>
> **She does place an emphasis on software security.**
>
> (*Does* emphasizes *place* and indicates present emphatic tense.)
>
> **My manager did show me how to improve the formatting of the newsletter.**
>
> (*Did* emphasizes *show* and indicates past emphatic tense.)

Go to the
Web

Checkpoint 10.6
for more skills practice on this topic.

 CHECKPOINT 10.6

Instructions: Underline the progressive or emphatic tense verbs in the following sentences. Using the codes below, indicate the number of the verb tense in the space provided. Refer to your text if you are uncertain about a form. Circle the simple subject in each sentence.

> 1 = present progressive tense
> 2 = past progressive tense
> 3 = future progressive tense
> 4 = present perfect progressive tense
> 5 = past perfect progressive tense
> 6 = future perfect progressive tense
> 7 = present emphatic tense
> 8 = past emphatic tense

1. Tracey is considering the purchase of scheduling software for her catering business. _____

2. They will be doing a software satisfaction survey throughout the week. _____

3. We did try to obtain everyone's input concerning additional software needs. _____

4. I was reading a computer magazine when my supervisor called. _____

5. Selena has been learning several new software packages. _____

6. They do provide excellent software training videos. _____

7. Until this summer, the firm had been hiring computer software specialists. _____

8. By the end of the summer, I will have been working as a database manager for a year. _____

Voice

An action verb may be in *active* or *passive* voice. Active voice means that the subject of a sentence performs the action. Passive voice means that the subject receives the action. Use the *active* voice for most business writing. Use the *passive* voice if you want to draw attention to an act rather than to the person or thing performing the act. The passive voice consists of a past participle of the verb and one or more forms of the helping verb *be*.

We <u>tested</u> several new pieces of software.

(The subject *We* is performing the action. The verb *tested* is in active voice.)

Several new pieces of software <u>were tested</u> by us.

(*Pieces* is the subject being acted upon; *pieces* are not performing the action. The verb phrase *were tested* is in passive voice.)

Some computer applications <u>require</u> considerable computer memory.

(The subject *applications* is performing the action. The verb *require* is in active voice.)

Considerable computer memory <u>is required</u> for some computer applications.

(The verb is in passive voice.)

Business managers frequently <u>use</u> event planning software.

(The subject *managers* is performing the action. The verb *use* is in active voice.)

Event planning software <u>is used</u> frequently by business managers.

(The subject *software* is being acted upon. The verb phrase *is used* is in passive voice.)

Several inappropriate software purchases <u>were made</u> in the past.

(Use the passive voice when you do not wish to identify the person who made the inappropriate purchases.)

The awards <u>were announced</u> at the annual Software Users' Association Conference.

(Use the passive voice. The awards are more important than the person who announced them.)

CHECKPOINT 10.7

Go to the
Web

Checkpoint 10.7
for more skills practice on this topic.

A. Instructions: *Underline the verb or verb phrase in each sentence. In the space provided, write **A** if the action verb is in the active voice. Write **P** if the verb is in the passive voice. Circle the simple subject in each sentence.*

1. A simple accounting package was recommended by my CPA. _____

2. We needed software for payroll and inventory control. _____

3. Our firm paid $500 per person for project management training last year. _____

4. The CEO appreciated Hunter's security software recommendation. _____

5. Her presentation was supported by interesting graphics. _____

*B. **Instructions:** Change the voice in the following sentences from passive to active. Write the corrected sentence in the space provided.*

1. The new client's software was quickly learned by the virtual assistant.

   _____

2. The office suite software was purchased by Barbara.

   _____

3. One of the largest collections of shareware is held by the Public Software Library in Houston.

   _____

   _____

4. The new accounting software was highly recommended by Steve.

   _____

5. The software consultants were hired by Ashley.

   _____

Mood

The mood of a verb indicates whether the sentence is intended to make a statement, give a command, ask a question, express necessity, or express a wish or a statement contrary to fact. The three moods are *indicative, imperative,* and *subjunctive.*

Indicative Mood

Use the indicative mood to state facts or to ask direct questions.

> **We distributed the brochures to all the stores where our software is sold.**
>
> (The sentence makes a statement of fact.)
>
> **Are you familiar with personal information manager (PIM) software?**
>
> (The sentence is a question.)

Imperative Mood

Use the imperative mood to give instructions and commands or to make courteous requests. The subject of a verb in the imperative mood is *you,* which is usually omitted.

> **Return this software to the accounting department.**
>
> (*You,* the subject, is understood. *You* represents the person to whom the instruction is given. The sentence expresses a command.)
>
> **Will you please return this software to the accounting department.**
>
> (The instruction, *Will you please,* is a courteous request. The sentence requires action, not words, and needs a period rather than a question mark.)

Chapter 10

Subjunctive Mood

To Express Conditions Contrary to Fact. Use a subjunctive verb to express a condition that is contrary to fact or subject to an element of doubt. The verb *were* is used for *was*.

If I were you, I would not revise the original document.

(*If I were you* [I am not you] is contrary to fact. Do not use *If I was you.*)

If I were the purchasing agent, I would pay attention to the employees' suggestions about software.

(*If I were* indicates a phrase contrary to fact. You are not the purchasing agent.)

To Express a Wish. Use a subjunctive verb in sentences that begin with an expression of a wish.

I wish that I were more skilled in using my word processing software.

(The sentence expresses a wish. Do not use *I wish that I was.*)

He wishes that he were going to the demonstration workshop.

(The sentence expresses a wish. Do not use *He wishes that he was.*)

To State Motions. Use the subjunctive form in a clause beginning with *that* which states a motion or formal proposal.

He moved that the meeting be adjourned.

(This is a motion, and it requires the subjunctive form of the verb *be* in the *that* clause. Do not use the verb *is.*)

CHECKPOINT 10.8

A. Instructions: *Identify the mood of the sentence by writing* **IN** *(indicative mood) or* **IM** *(imperative mood) in the blank. Underline the verb or verb phrase.*

1. Are you aware of the legal implications in copying software? _____

2. Please call our toll-free number about information on the newest accounting software. _____

3. Our desktop publishing software is not suitable for full-color documents. _____

4. Check the software installation procedures carefully. _____

B. Instructions: *Underline the correct subjunctive mood verb.*

1. If I (*was, were*) the project leader, I would ask management for more sophisticated project management software.

2. We wish that we (*was, were*) able to answer your questions concerning NetWare systems.

3. If I (*was, were*) you, I would enroll in an Excel class at the community college.

4. He proposed that the vote to purchase file management software (*is, be*) postponed until the next meeting.

NOTES

If Clauses

When a clause begins with the word *If*, you can be fairly certain that the clause is going to be contrary to the actual facts. In this case, use the verb *were*. If the sentence is true, this rule does not apply. Use the verb *was*.

Go to the Web

Checkpoint 10.8
for more skills practice on this topic.

Sometimes words that look like verbs function instead as nouns, adjectives, or adverbs. These verb forms are called verbals. The three verbals are *gerunds, participles,* and *infinitives.*

Gerunds

A gerund is a verb form ending in *ing* that functions as a noun. A *gerund phrase* includes a gerund and any modifiers that are needed to make the meaning complete. Every word that ends in *ing* is not a gerund. Many words that end in *ing* are parts of verb phrases; others are participles. (See the section on participles that follows.)

Gerund Use.   Use a gerund as a subject (noun), object of a verb (noun), or object of a preposition (noun). When a gerund or gerund phrase is used as the subject of the sentence, do *not* use a comma after the gerund or the gerund phrase.

> **Using reputable software** saves new business owners money in the short run.

> (*Using reputable software* is a gerund phrase that functions as the complete subject of the sentence. No comma is necessary after the gerund phrase.)

> Carla enjoyed **designing software programs.**

> (*Designing software programs* is a gerund phrase that functions as the object of a sentence. The phrase answers the question "Carla enjoyed what?")

> Small companies often have unanticipated problems with **handling software changes.**

> (*Handling software changes* is a gerund phrase that functions as the object of the preposition *with.*)

Dangling Constructions—Prepositional Gerund Phrases.   When you *begin* a sentence with a gerund phrase that starts with a preposition, be sure that the phrase agrees with the subject of your sentence. (The subject must perform the action in the gerund phrase.) If no agreement exists, you have a dangling sentence construction. As with other introductory prepositional phrases, use a comma after the introductory prepositional gerund phrase.

Correct:

> **After using the new software manual, I found several errors.**

> (The subject [*I*] performed the action [*using*] in the gerund phrase. The preposition *After* begins the gerund phrase. Use a comma after the introductory gerund phrase.)

Dangling:

> **After using the new software manual, several errors were found.**

> (The subject [*errors*] did not perform the action of *using* the software manual. This is an example of a dangling construction.

Gerund Modifiers.   Use the possessive case of a noun or pronoun to modify a gerund.

We appreciated your teaching the introduction to computers course.

(*Teaching* is a gerund that functions as a direct object. In this sentence, the gerund *teaching* requires the possessive pronoun *your* before it. Do not use the pronoun *you.*)

I questioned his bringing the controversial topic of software theft into the discussion.

(Use the possessive case *his* to modify the gerund *bringing;* do not use *him bringing.*)

CHECKPOINT 10.9

Go to the
Web

Checkpoint 10.9
for more skills practice on this topic.

Instructions: In the following sentences, underline the gerund phrase once. Underline the main verb or verb phrase twice.

1. Backing up software requires only a few minutes of time.

2. Maria enjoys designing integrated office suite programs.

3. Training new employees in the use of our groupware program requires time.

4. Small businesses should try using contact management.

5. Reviewing sales literature is giving me some good ideas for buying software.

6. Records management software involves tracking active and inactive records.

7. By downloading software from the Internet, you may have violated someone else's copyrighted material.

8. Our new employee has experience in using Microsoft Word.

9. After determining the glitch in the software, the programmers continued their work.

10. Designing software programs requires patience and concentration.

Participles

A participle is a verbal that functions as an adjective. A *participial phrase* consists of a present, past, or perfect participle, additional modifiers, and an object; it also functions as an adjective. A *present participle* ends in *ing.* A *past participle* ends in *ed* for regular verbs and changes for irregular verbs. A *perfect participle* includes the word *having* before the past participle.

Use a participle or participial phrase as an adjective to modify a noun or a pronoun. Do not confuse a participle with a gerund that functions as a subject or an object of a sentence or with a prepositional gerund phrase. Use a comma to set off an introductory participle or participial phrase.

PUNCTUATION ALERT!

Participles
Use a comma after an introductory participial phrase.

Finding the software difficult to use, I selected another program.

(*Finding the software difficult to use* is a participial phrase that modifies the subject *I. Finding* is a present participle. Use a comma after the word *use* in the introductory participial phrase.)

Assisted by the hotline operator, she was able to solve her problem in a few minutes.

(The participial phrase modifies *she,* the subject of the sentence. *Assisted* is a past participle. Use a comma after the participial phrase.)

Verb Tense, Voice, and Mood—Verbals

Having reviewed the surveys, I decided to purchase the software.

(The participial phrase modifies *I*, the subject. *Having reviewed* is a perfect participial phrase. Use a comma after the participial phrase.)

We bought some used software for our children.

(*Used* is a past participle that modifies software.)

The software cost $1000 plus handling charges.

(*Handling* is a present participle that modifies charges.)

Dangling Constructions—Participial Phrases. When you begin a sentence with a participial phrase, be sure that the phrase agrees with the subject of your sentence. (The subject must perform the action in the participial phrase.) If no agreement exists, you have a dangling sentence construction.

Correct:

Having analyzed the reviews, we approved the project management software purchase.

(The subject [*we*] performed the action [*having analyzed*] in the participial phrase.)

Dangling:

Having analyzed the reviews, the project management software purchase was approved.

(The subject [*purchase*] did not perform the action [*having analyzed*] in the participial phrase.)

Go to the
Web

Checkpoint 10.10
for more skills practice on this topic.

CHECKPOINT 10.10

Instructions: Underline the participial phrase in the following sentences. In the space provided, write the noun or pronoun that the participle or participial phrase modifies. Underline the verb or verb phrase twice.

1. Using her spell checker feature, Carla completed the daily crossword puzzle quickly. _____

2. The interview team considering my application was impressed with my computer skills. _____

3. Putting aside my personal preferences, I accepted the group's recommendation to change spreadsheet programs. _____

4. Having heard that the firm was downsizing, she made plans to upgrade her computer skills. _____

5. Concerned about the illegal copying of software, the vice president wrote a new company policy. _____

6. Knowing my supervisor's previous reactions, I hesitated to ask for contact management software. _____

7. Reviewing my difficulties in using Excel, I decided to enroll in a two-day review course. _____

8. Satisfied with his expertise in WordPerfect, Glen listed this skill on his résumé. _____

9. Using ideas from previous PowerPoint presentations, we saved a considerable amount of preparation time. _____

10. The word processing class scheduled for January is offered again in the summer session. _____

Infinitives

An infinitive is a verbal that consists of the present part of a verb plus the word *to*. An *infinitive phrase* is the infinitive and its modifiers.

Use an infinitive or infinitive phrase as a noun, an adjective, or an adverb. Do not confuse an infinitive phrase with a prepositional phrase. The infinitive phrase has the word *to* preceding the verb. Use a comma to set off an introductory infinitive phrase. Do *not* use a comma if the infinitive phrase is the subject of the sentence.

To make a decision about a software purchase requires a careful evaluation of each product.

(*To make a decision about a software purchase* is an infinitive phrase. The infinitive consists of the present tense of *make* plus the word *to*. The infinitive phrase in this sentence functions as a noun and is the subject of the sentence. This phrase does not require a comma.)

I wanted to buy the least expensive word processing package available.

(*To buy the least expensive word processing package available* is an infinitive phrase used as a noun—the direct object of the verb *wanted*. The phrase provides the answer to the question [*Wanted what?*].)

If you will wait, I will give you a software hotline number to call.

(*To call* is an infinitive used as an adjective modifying the noun *number*.)

Jackie called to order her new project management software.

(*To order* is an infinitive used as an adverb modifying the verb *called*.)

Dangling Construction—Infinitive Phrases.   When you begin a sentence with an infinitive phrase, be sure that the phrase agrees with the subject of your sentence. (The subject must perform the action in the infinitive phrase.) If no agreement exists, you have a dangling sentence construction.

Correct:

To reserve a place at our software preview workshop, please send us your registration fee today.

(The subject [*you* is understood] should perform the action of *reserve* in the infinitive phrase. Use a comma to set off the introductory infinitive phrase.)

Dangling:

To reserve a place at our software preview workshop, a registration fee should be sent in today.

(The subject [*fee*] did not perform the action [*reserve*] in the infinitive phrase.)

Do This

Our supervisor asked us to <u>proofread</u> our documents <u>carefully</u>.

Acceptable

To <u>deliberately evade</u> the issue of copying software is unwise.

Do Not Do This

Our supervisor asked us to <u>carefully proofread</u> our documents.

Awkward

To <u>evade</u> the issue of copying software <u>deliberately</u> is unwise.

Do not split an infinitive unless it sounds awkward or loses meaning in the process. A split infinitive means that an adverb appears between *to* and *the verb*.

Go to the
Web

Checkpoint 10.11
for more skills practice on this topic.

 # CHECKPOINT 10.11

Instructions: *In the following sentences, underline the infinitive phrase once. Underline the main verb or verb phrase twice.*

1. Our company's accountants advised us to buy accounts receivable, accounts payable, and billing modules.

2. It is not difficult to get different software programs to "talk" to each other.

3. She used a full-featured desktop publishing program to produce the 200-page documentation.

4. Our CPAs examined the software and decided to install Personal Tax Edge.

5. This software permits us to streamline our ordering processes.

6. Without our groupware installation, we would have to hire an additional employee.

7. To use the new software means additional training for our staff.

8. I prefer to use Quicken for my personal finance records.

9. To become a software technician, she attended classes for two years.

10. To retain good software technicians is difficult for many employers.

Diagramming Sentences

A *gerund* functions as a noun and may be a subject or an object. To diagram a gerund, place it on a step. Place the gerund so that it curves along the lines. If the gerund is a subject, position it in the subject location. If the gerund is an object, position it in the object location.

They considered <u>selecting the most expensive program</u>. (object)

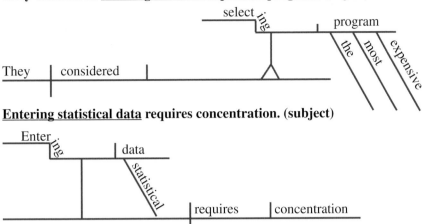

<u>Entering statistical data</u> requires concentration. (subject)

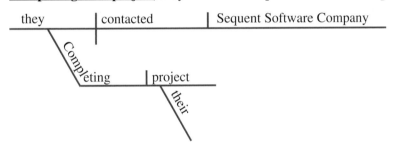

A *participle* functions as an adjective in a sentence. To diagram a participle or participial phrase, place it under the noun or pronoun it modifies. The participle curves along the line.

<u>Completing their project</u>, they contacted Sequent Software Company.

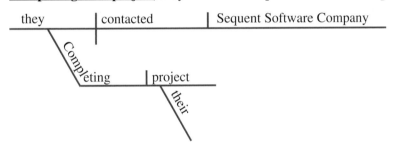

CHECKPOINT 10.12

Go to the
Web

Checkpoint 10.12
for more skills practice on this topic.

Instructions: *Diagram the following sentences in the space provided.*

1. She denied copying Excel and Peachtree.

2. Using the Microsoft Word thesaurus, I checked several synonyms.

3. My supervisor approved subcontracting the software bid.

4. Using accounting software helps small business owners.

5. Working long hours, Sam finished the network installation.

Name _____   Date _____

PRACTICE 1

Word Choice

Instructions: Select the correct word, and write it in the space provided. Circle the simple subject in each sentence.

1. I (*did, done*) the spreadsheet exercises during my lunch hour.

    1. _____

2. The latest version of our accounting software (*cost, costed*) more than $325.

    2. _____

3. The salesperson encouraged (*me, my*) asking questions about the online banking software.

    3. _____

4. All of our spreadsheet work requires (*concentrate, concentrated*) attention.

    4. _____

5. He (*does, do*) try to provide online answers to software questions.

    5. _____

6. If I (*were, was*) the instructor, I would stress the importance of learning several software packages.

    6. _____

7. Nate (*don't know, doesn't know*) how to install his new software.

    7. _____

8. They (*should have, should of*) approved the purchase of new accounting software last week.

    8. _____

Describing Verbs and Verbals

Instructions: In the space provided, write the letter of the item that describes or identifies the underlined verb or verbal. Circle the simple subject in each sentence.

1. *The CPA Software News* has always <u>prepared</u> excellent reviews of new accounting products.
    - a. present tense
    - b. past tense
    - c. perfect tense
    - d. progressive tense

    1. _____

2. I learned <u>to use</u> a database program in a college computer class.
    - a. verb phrase
    - b. gerund
    - c. infinitive
    - d. participle

    2. _____

3. My instructor <u>explains</u> the steps in a software application very clearly.
    - a. present tense
    - b. past tense
    - c. perfect tense
    - d. future tense

    3. _____

4. Most software outlets <u>will stock</u> the most popular programs.
    - a. present tense
    - b. future tense
    - c. emphatic tense
    - d. progressive tense

    4. _____

Go to the
Web
_____

Practice 1 Exercises
for more skills practice on this topic.
_____

Verb Tense, Voice, and Mood—Verbals   **311**

Name _____ Date _____

5. The computer information systems department will be issuing its first newsletter this week.
   a. present
   b. past tense
   c. progressive tense
   d. future tense

   5. _____

6. Reviewing my computer background, I knew that I needed more software training.
   a. infinitive phrase
   b. verb phrase
   c. participial phrase
   d. gerund phrase

   6. _____

7. Noreen had completed the Excel worksheets before the instructor assigned them.
   a. past tense
   b. past perfect tense
   c. emphatic tense
   d. future tense

   7. _____

8. Learning the database management software was easy for me.
   a. infinitive phrase
   b. verb phrase
   c. participial phrase
   d. gerund phrase

   8. _____

Active or Passive Voice

*Instructions: In the space provided, write **A** if the action verb is in the active voice. Write **P** if the verb is in the passive voice. Circle the simple subject in each sentence. Underline the verb or verb phrase in each sentence.*

1. Lyndsay uses a new keyboard that is immune to dust, crumbs, and spills.

   1. _____

2. A voice recognition system is being investigated by Keyword Technology.

   2. _____

3. Britain's largest telephone company has experimented with eye point recognition databases.

   3. _____

4. The term "blogging" was used by my computer tutor.

   4. _____

PRACTICE 2

Go to the **Web**

Practice 2 Exercises
for more skills practice on this topic.

Verb Tenses

Instructions: At the beginning of each sentence is a verb form. In the space provided, write the tense of the verb indicated in parentheses. Circle the simple subject in each sentence.

1. present perfect — He (*master*) a variety of business software.

   1. _____

2. present — I (*need*) to import a spreadsheet into a document.

   2. _____

3. past — Larry (*bring*) the training videotapes to the last department meeting.

   3. _____

Name _____ Date _____

4. past

By offering rebates and discounts, we (*decrease*) the prices of desktop publishing software.

4. _____

5. past perfect

He (*prepare*) a list of the advantages of each piece of software that our firm was considering.

5. _____

6. future

The videotapes (*show*) Jeff how the software works.

6. _____

7. past perfect

I (*see*) an advertisement for VoiceType, but I could not remember the source.

7. _____

8. present

Foreign-currency management (*be*) a helpful feature for companies in international sales.

8. _____

9. present progressive

Many software trainers (*use*) computer-based programs in their classes.

9. _____

10. future progressive

SRC Graphics (*hire*) two new technical trainers next month.

10. _____

Tense, Voice, Mood, Verbals

*Instructions: In the space provided, correct the sentences containing incorrect verb forms or follow the instructions in parentheses. Some sentences may also have punctuation or other errors. If a sentence has no errors, write **Yes.***

1. She wrote software instructions and designs advertising brochures for a major computer firm.

   _____

   _____

   _____

   _____

2. Abe's Muffler Company has began to depend on billing software in its collection procedures.

   _____

   _____

3. Will you please select spreadsheet software that are compatible with other software packages?

   _____

   _____

Name _____   Date _____

4. This accounting software is used by many home business owners.
   (*Change this sentence to active voice.*)

   _____

5. Keying statistical data hurriedly often causes errors in my
   spreadsheets.

   _____

6. I was surprised at him learning the new version of the software so
   quickly.

   _____

7. The broke printer made it impossible to produce the labels for the
   mass mailing project.

   _____

   _____

8. Having reviewed the various course descriptions I decided to enroll
   in a word processing class.

   _____

   _____

9. I wish that I was being considered for the database manager's
   position.

   _____

10. Decisions to upgrade software are made by our office managers.
    (*Use active voice.*)

    _____

Go to the
Web

Practice 3 Exercises
for more skills practice on
this topic.

_____

PRACTICE 3

Proofreading

*Instructions: Proofread and compare the two sentences in each group. If they are the same, write **Yes** in the space provided. If they are not the same, write **No.** Use the first sentence as the correct copy. If you find errors in the second sentence, underline them.*

1. Off-the-shelf accounting packages usually include   1. _____
   accounts receivable, accounts payable, and general
   ledger functions.

   Off-the-shelf-accounting packages usualy include account
   recievable, accounts payable, and general ledger functions.

2. Microsoft's "office assistant" consists of action icons   2. _____
   that provide suggestions and tips.

   Microsofts' 'office assistant' consists of action icons
   that provides suggestions and tips.

Name _____ Date _____

3. SystemWizard is a diagnostic program that analyzes
   the peripherals attached to a PC.

   SystemWizard are a diagnostic program that analyzes
   the peripherals attached to a PC.

   3. _____

4. When someone copies software illegally, other
   consumers pay the price.

   When someone copies software illegally, other
   consumers will pay the prices.

   4. _____

5. Randy uses videos to learn how to take advantage of
   the newest software in the automotive repair business.

   Randy uses videos to learn how to take advantage of
   the newest software in the automotive repair business.

   5. _____

Using Proofreaders' Marks

If you are thinking about purchasing additional software, give the task careful consideration. The following material gives some suggestions for selecting software:

SOFTWARE SELECTION GUIDELINES

List the tasks that you need to perform now or need to perform in the future.

Make a list of the features that you want your software to have.

Review the sales literature, trade magazines, and consumer reports.

Discuss advantages of various programs with software dealers.

Determine the ease of learning the software.

Find out about user support. Is there an 800 hotline number to call?

Identify the computer hardware that you are currently using. Will the software work on the equipment that you now have?

Know your printer requirements and limitations.

Instructions: Use the following proofreaders' marks to make corrections in the copy below. Use the above copy as your correct guide.

lowercase /	move left ⌐
capitalize ≡	move right ⌐
delete ϒ	insert space ∧#
transpose ∽	insert letter ∧
delete space ⌣	insert comma ∧
insert period ⊙	delete and close up ϒ

Name _____ Date _____

SOFTWARE SELECTOIN GUIDELINES

List the tasks that you need to perform orneed to perform in the future.

Make a list of the features that you want your software to have.

Review the sales literature Trade magazines, and consumer reports

Discuss the advantages of various programs with software dealers

Determine the ease of learning the software.

Find out about user support. is there an 800 hot line number to call.?

Identify the computer hard ware that you are curently using. Will the software work on the equipment that you now have?

Know your printer requirements and limitations.

Go to the
Web

Practice 4 Exercises
for more skills practice on this topic.

PRACTICE 4

Writing

Instructions: Write a paragraph describing the advantages of using word processing software to compose documents. Use action verbs, active voice, and correct punctuation. Sentences must include the following. Answers will vary.

subjunctive mood using the verb *were*

gerund phrase

participial phrase

infinitive

_____

_____

_____

_____

_____

_____

_____

_____

_____

_____

_____

_____

_____

_____

Name _____ Date _____

Word Choice

Instructions: Select the correct word, and write it in the space provided. Circle the simple subject in each sentence.

1. The manager (*expect, expected*) to receive a multiuser discount on software.

   1. _____

2. He moved that the decision to purchase new software (*is, be*) tabled.

   2. _____

3. We disliked (*his, him*) complaining about using the old version of the desktop publishing program.

   3. _____

4. Suzanne (*does, do*) ask our opinion on page layout.

   4. _____

5. She (*has seen, seen*) demonstrations on patient billing software.

   5. _____

6. If I (*was, were*) you, I would upgrade the billing software program.

   6. _____

7. Adelina appreciated (*you, your*) demonstrating the shortcuts in Windows.

   7. _____

8. We could (*has, have*) ordered a trial version of the software.

   8. _____

Describing Verbs and Verbals

Instructions: In the space provided, write the letter of the item that describes or identifies the underlined verb or verbal. Circle the simple subject in each sentence.

1. This computer <u>is</u> no longer powerful enough for our software.

   1. _____
   - a. present tense
   - b. past tense
   - c. future tense
   - d. perfect tense

2. Janey learned <u>to pay</u> her bills with an online banking program.

   2. _____
   - a. verb
   - b. gerund
   - c. infinitive
   - d. participle

3. <u>Recognizing the errors in the program</u>, we checked all the payroll figures again.

   3. _____
   - a. verb phrase
   - b. infinitive phrase
   - c. gerund phrase
   - d. participial phrase

4. <u>Organizing our customer database</u> has increased our efficiency.

   4. _____
   - a. verb phrase
   - b. infinitive phrase
   - c. gerund phrase
   - d. participial phrase

Verb Tense, Voice, and Mood—Verbals

Name _____ Date _____

5. *PC Magazine* <u>will be offering</u> a free CD with a subscription renewal.
   a. present
   b. past tense
   c. progressive tense
   d. future tense

5. _____

6. <u>To determine the appropriate accounting software,</u> we asked Judi to prepare an analysis of two popular programs.
   a. verb phrase
   b. infinitive phrase
   c. gerund phrase
   d. participial phrase

6. _____

7. We <u>spent</u> three days learning how to use Access software.
   a. present tense
   b. past tense
   c. future tense
   d. perfect tense

7. _____

8. <u>Preparing for his six-month leave of absence,</u> Josh developed written instructions for updating the Web page.
   a. verb phrase
   b. infinitive phrase
   c. gerund phrase
   d. participial phrase

8. _____

Active or Passive Voice

Instructions: In the space provided, write A if the action verb is in the active voice. Write P if the verb is in the passive voice. Circle the simple subject in each sentence. Underline the verb or verb phrase in each sentence.

1. Jane enrolled in our classes to receive training on the latest software programs.

1. _____

2. All of the news releases about the new desktop publishing software were faxed by us today.

2. _____

3. As a summer promotion, free updates of software programs were released by several companies.

3. _____

4. The workshop speaker thoroughly covered the topic of software piracy.

4. _____

PRACTICE 6

Verb Tenses

Instructions: In the space provided, write the tense of the verb indicated in parentheses. Circle the simple subject in each sentence.

1. Rob (*design;* present perfect) our spreadsheet templates.

1. _____

2. Our video store (*offer;* present) multimedia software that rates movies.

2. _____

3. I (*need;* future) a new operating system by next year.

3. _____

Name _____   Date _____

4. Kim (*leave;* past) her backup disks at home.   4. _____

5. My supervisor (*order;* past perfect) group videoconferencing software while I was on vacation.   5. _____

6. Analog telephone lines (*seem;* present emphatic) slow for using the Internet.   6. _____

7. Our company (*advertise;* past) our new software during the Super Bowl.   7. _____

8. We (*wait;* present perfect progressive) for the upgrade for six months.   8. _____

9. Elementary science teachers (*recommend;* present progressive) The Magic School Bus as home enrichment.   9. _____

10. _____

10. They (*promote;* future progressive) multimedia software during the holiday season.

Tense, Voice, Mood, Verbals

*Instructions: In the space provided, correct the sentences containing incorrect verb forms or follow the instructions in parentheses. Some sentences may have punctuation errors. If a sentence has no errors, write **Yes.***

1. Some network software is priced according to the number of users. (*Change to active voice.*)

   _____

2. He has went to the national computer exhibition in Minneapolis for the past five years.

   _____

   _____

3. Analyzing our current software needs, gave us an idea for planning future budgets.

   _____

4. I wish that I was able to feel comfortable using this database program.

   _____

5. Will you please recommend a keyboarding program that I can use at home?

   _____

6. I done the research on the newest PowerPoint presentation software.

   _____

Verb Tense, Voice, and Mood—Verbals   **319**

Name _____ Date _____

7. Assisted by our computer technician I was able to retrieve my 30-page document.

_____

_____

8. At some point, everyone have experiences with viruses or other software problems.

_____

_____

9. A detailed description of Outlook was presented by Andrew. (*Use active voice.*)

_____

10. The Software Purchaser's Index help managers make decisions about upgrading software.

_____

_____

PRACTICE 7

Proofreading

*Instructions: Proofread and compare the two sentences in each group. If they are the same, write **Yes** in the space provided. If they are not the same, write **No**. Use the first sentence as the correct copy. If you find errors in the second sentence, underline them.*

1. With SelectPhone, you can find, count, locate, download, call, and mail anyone or any group of business or residential listings.

   With SelectPhone, you can find, count, locate, download, call and mail anyone or any group of business or residential listings.

   1. _____

2. Claris HomePage is designed for novices to build a basic but professional-looking Web site.

   Claris HomePage is designed for novices to build a basic but professional looking Web site.

   2. _____

3. McAfee provides a list of recent virus threats on its Web page.

   McFee provides a list of recent virus threats on its Web page.

   3. _____

4. FileMaker Server allows the sharing of database files with clients running FileMaker Pro on their workstations.

   FileMaker Server allows the sharing of database files with clients running FileMaker Pro on their workstations.

   4. _____

Name _____ Date _____

5. Avery designed preset labels to work in Microsoft Word, WordPerfect, and hundreds of other software programs.

     Avery designed preset lables to work in Microsoft Word, Wordperfect, and hundreds of other softwear programs.

5. _____

Using Proofreaders' Marks

The following material gives some preparation steps to follow before calling a software company for help:

Calling for Software Support

When you call for support, be at your computer, and have the appropriate product documentation available. Be prepared to give the following information:

The version number of the product that you are using.

The type of hardware that you are using, including network hardware, if applicable.

The exact wording of any messages that appeared on your screen.

A description of what happened and what you were doing at the time.

A description of how you tried to solve the problem.

Instructions: Use the proofreaders' marks to make corrections in the copy below. Use the above copy as your correct guide.

lowercase /	move left ⌐
capitalize ≡	move right ⌐
delete ∤	insert space #
transpose ∽	insert letter ∧
delete space ⌣	insert comma ⋀
insert period ⊙	delete and close up ℘

Calling for software Support

When you call for support be at your computer and have the appropriate product documentation available. Be prepared to give the following information:

The Version number of the product that you are using

    The type of hardware that you are using including netowrk hard ware, if applicable.

The exact wording of any messsages that apeared on your screen.

A description of what happened and what you were doing at the time.

    A description ofhow you treid to solve the problem

Verb Tense, Voice, and Mood—Verbals

Name _____ Date _____

PRACTICE 8

Writing

Instructions: *Write a paragraph describing the types of software that you use. Use active voice. Use correct punctuation. Sentences must include the following. Answers will vary.*

subjunctive mood using the verb *were*

gerund phrase

participial phrase

infinitive

_____

_____

_____

_____

_____

_____

_____

_____

_____

_____

_____

_____

_____

_____

_____

Posttest

Instructions: In the space provided, write the letter of the correct answer.

1. Which statement is written correctly? (1)

    a. You was accurate in analyzing our data recovery needs.

    b. You were accurate in analyzing our data recovery needs.

1. _____

2. Which statement is written correctly? (2)

    a. Manufacturers of PC operating systems design newer, more capable versions each year.

    b. Manufacturers of PC operating systems designs newer, more capable versions each year.

2. _____

3. Which statement is written correctly? (2)

    a. He done the linking of Word with PowerPoint.

    b. He did the linking of Word with PowerPoint.

3. _____

4. Which statement is written correctly? (2)

    a. She is certain that a new version of the word processing software will be released soon.

    b. She is certain that a new version of the word processing software will release soon.

4. _____

5. Which statement is written correctly? (6)

    a. We were amazed by him volunteering to develop our database queries.

    b. We were amazed by his volunteering to develop our database queries.

5. _____

6. Which tense is represented by the underlined word in this sentence? (3)

He <u>updates</u> the antivirus software on our network.

    a. future

    b. present

6. _____

7. Which tense is represented by the underlined word in this sentence? (3)

I <u>had used</u> Word for several years before I learned Access.

    a. past

    b. past perfect

7. _____

8. Which statement is written correctly? (5)

    a. I wish that I were able to write HTML codes.

    b. I wish that I was able to write HTML codes.

8. _____

9. Which statement is written using the active voice? (4)

    a. The new brochure was designed by several team members.

    b. Several team members designed the new brochure.

9. _____

10. Which statement is written correctly? (6)

    a. Ruben appreciated you thanking him for designing the Excel spreadsheet.

    b. Ruben appreciated your thanking him for designing the Excel spreadsheet.

10. _____

11. Which statement involves a gerund? (6)

    a. Using virus protection software is mandatory in our office.

    b. Realizing our mistake, we immediately corrected the Web page.

11. _____

12. Which statement involves a participial phrase? (6)   **12.** _____

    a.   Calling customer support is not an option with this software.

    b.   Completing our research, we made a software recommendation to our manager.

13. Which statement involves an infinitive? (6)   **13.** _____

    a.   To use this software, we must purchase a license.

    b.   We e-mailed our software questions to the company.

14. Which statement is written correctly? (5)   **14.** _____

    a.   If I was you, I would scan the computer for viruses every day.

    b.   If I were you, I would scan the computer for viruses every day.

15. Which statement is written in active voice? (4)   **15.** _____

    a.   Software instructions have been developed in the past by Julie.

    b.   We took several days to install the new software.

Chapter 11

Subject-Verb Agreement

OBJECTIVES

After you have studied this chapter and completed the exercises, you will be able to do the following:

1. Select single verbs that agree with single subjects, plural verbs that agree with plural subjects, and linking verbs that agree with subjects.

2. Identify phrases between subjects and verbs that do not affect the choice of the verb.

3. Use verbs that agree with subjects joined by *and, or*, and *nor* correctly.

4. Select verbs that agree with indefinite pronouns used as subjects.

5. Use verbs that agree with collective nouns.

6. Use verbs that agree with money, time periods, numbers, and measurements.

7. Use correct verbs with subjects in inverted sentences.

8. Use verbs that agree with plural nouns and gerund phrases.

Workplace Applications: Teamwork

Change is redefining the workplace. Factors such as global competition, information technology, and rising customer expectations are affecting businesses of all sizes. One of the ways that organizations are responding to change is by focusing on teams and teamwork.

Groups, committees, and task forces have existed for years. Within these organizations, individuals come together for a specific purpose—to produce a product or service.

A team, on the other hand, is a designation for people who manage themselves. Team members clearly understand the tasks, and their top priority is getting the job done. A climate of trust and understanding exists because open communication takes place. Team members share power and authority when possible, and much of the decision making is by consensus. The team evaluates its own effectiveness.

People on a team feel a strong bond with others on the team. Team members appreciate one another's differences and take pride in the contributions that they make to the organization. The businesses using the team model feel that teams produce an energetic and satisfying work climate.

PRETEST: *Looking Forward*

Pretest

Instructions: *In the sentences below, underline the simple subject. Then select the correct verb, and write it in the space provided.*

1. Mike (*teach, teaches*) team development classes for the American Management Association. (1)

1. _____

2. Multimedia collaborations (*allow, allows*) organizations to share individual knowledge more efficiently. (1)

2. _____

3. The survey, along with the employees' comments, (*provide, provides*) a starting point for the safety committee. (2)

3. _____

4. Either Nancy or Brandon (*plan, plans*) to take my place on the search team for the new dean. (3)

4. _____

5. A vital link in a team's success (*are, is*) the professional level of support staff. (1)

5. _____

6. Most of the work group leaders (*schedule, schedules*) the times for meetings. (4)

6. _____

7. The committee (*know, knows*) that its recommendations must be based on reliable data. (5)

7. _____

8. In most teams, three-fifths of the time (*are, is*) spent in planning strategies. (6)

8. _____

9. Here (*are, is*) 35 additional surveys for our committee to tabulate. (7)

9. _____

10. The economics of the team's proposals (*was, were*) realistic. (8)

10. _____

11. The most important work in organizations today (*take, takes*) place in teams. (2)

11. _____

12. Every business instructor and business manager (*recommend, recommends*) teamwork. (4)

12. _____

13. Everyone (*seem, seems*) to prefer short and well-organized committee meetings. (4)

13. _____

14. Berrett-Koehler Publishers Inc. (*publish, publishes*) books on time management and collaboration in business. (5)

14. _____

15. Five hundred dollars (*was, were*) the team's bonus for completing the project ahead of schedule. (6)

15. _____

Chapter Preview

As you identified subjects in Chapter 3, you were reminded that if you selected the correct subject you would find verb identification easier when you studied verbs. You will find this to be true as you study this chapter.

The verb in a sentence must be in agreement with its subject. In Chapter 10, you saw the changes that occurred in a verb with first-, second-, and third-person subjects. A verb must also agree with its subject in number. A singular subject requires a singular verb. Likewise, a plural subject needs a plural verb. Not all sentences are that simple. Certain words or phrases are trouble spots in subject-verb agreement. In this chapter, you will analyze some of these more troublesome agreement areas.

Good writers are very aware of subject-verb agreement. They know that errors of this type can distract their readers.

Subject-Verb Agreement

A verb must agree with its subject in person (first, second, third) and number (singular, plural).

Singular Subject—Singular Verb

Use a singular verb with a singular subject. Add *s* or *es* to the present part of a verb when the subject is third-person singular. Use the simple subject to determine the correct verb form.

a manager supports	experience brings	she says
a team player shares	John agrees	he decides

(All the subjects are third-person singular and require singular verbs. The verbs require an *s* ending.)

he reaches	time passes	Shelly misses
Carri finishes	it taxes	telephone buzzes

(The subjects are third-person singular and require singular verbs. Verbs that end with the sounds of *ch*, *o*, *s*, *sh*, *x*, and *z* require *es* endings.)

Plural Subject—Plural Verb

Use a plural verb with a plural subject. A noun forms its plural by adding *s* or *es*, but this is not true with the plural form of a verb. Use the simple subject to determine the correct verb form.

the departments cooperate	members agree	we decide
the managers confer	they say	
team members compromise	they analyze	

(All the subjects are plural and require plural verbs. The plural verbs do not end in *s* or *es*.)

NOTES

Looking Back
Do not confuse the plurals of nouns and verbs. Plural verbs do not end in *s* or *es*. Refer to Chapter 10 for a review of singular and plural verb formations.

Pronoun *You*—Plural Verb

Use a plural verb with both the second-person singular *or* second-person plural subject *you*.

you <u>acknowledge</u>	you <u>learn</u>	you <u>are</u>
you both <u>enjoy</u>	you <u>are</u> all <u>invited</u>	

Subject Complement—Linking Verb

A linking verb should agree with its subject, not its subject complement (predicate noun or pronoun).

Four new members <u>seem</u> a large number to add to this committee.

(The plural verb *seem* is a linking verb that must agree with the plural subject *members*, not with the subject complement *number*.)

NOTES

Linking Verbs

taste	grow	stay
smell	look	seem
remain	feel	become
appear	sound	

The forms of *to be*

Go to the **Web**

Checkpoint 11.1

for more skills practice on this topic.

CHECKPOINT 11.1

Instructions: *In the sentences below, underline the simple subject. Then select the correct verb, and write it in the space provided.*

1. Our supervisor (*take, takes*) the time to explain the value of teamwork in an organization. _____

2. Teamwork success (*depend, depends*) on keeping the lines of communication open. _____

3. The first item on the team's agenda (*was, were*) introductions. _____

4. Jason Rowe (*serve, serves*) as our project coordinator. _____

5. Social gatherings (*are, is*) a good opportunity to meet other team members. _____

6. Our project leader (*know, knows*) his own communication style. _____

7. As a member of the executive team, you (*need, needs*) effective time management skills. _____

8. Twenty team members (*remain, remains*) a hindrance for effective group discussions. _____

9. Many companies (*stress, stresses*) the importance of teams. _____

10. Employees' opinions (*seem, seems*) to count in group interactions. _____

11. The job advertisements (*emphasize, emphasizes*) working as members of a team. _____

12. Agendas for all group meetings (*are, is*) an excellent way to stay on schedule. _____

Subject-Verb Agreement—Special Cases

In addition to the basic principles, subject-verb agreement also applies to numerous special cases. These cases involve intervening phrases; compound subjects;

linking verbs; indefinite pronouns; collective nouns; amounts of money, numbers, and fractions; inverted sentences; and special nouns.

Intervening Words—Prepositional Phrases

The verb must agree with the subject, *not* with the object of a prepositional phrase that appears between the subject and the verb.

> **Five <u>members</u> of our team <u>work</u> in their home offices.**
>
> (*Members* is the plural subject; *team* is the object in the prepositional phrase *of our team.* The plural verb *work* agrees with the subject, not the object of the preposition.)
>
> **The <u>notes</u> from our supervisor <u>keep</u> our team motivated.**
>
> (*Notes* is the plural subject; *supervisor* is the object in the prepositional phrase *from our supervisor.* The plural verb *keep* agrees with the subject, not the object of the preposition.)

Intervening Words—Other Modifying Phrases

When determining which verb to use, disregard modifying phrases such as *along with, in addition to, together with, accompanied by, as well as,* and *in conjunction with.* These phrases modify the subject, but they do not change the subject in number and do not form a compound subject.

> **<u>Zana</u>, along with several other members, <u>presents</u> good ideas.**
>
> (*Zana* is the subject that must agree with the singular verb *presents.* The modifying phrase *along with several other members* does not make the subject plural, nor does it form a compound subject.)
>
> **The project <u>leader</u>, together with his or her administrative assistants, <u>assumes</u> the responsibility for the final group report.**
>
> (*Leader* is the subject that must agree with the verb *assumes.* The modifying phrase *together with his or her administrative assistants* does not make a compound subject.)

PUNCTUATION ALERT!

Essential Phrases

Do not use commas to set aside essential prepositional phrases from the rest of the sentence.

PUNCTUATION ALERT!

Intervening Words

Use commas to set aside modifying phrases such as *in addition to, accompanied by,* and *in conjunction with* when they are placed between the subject and the verb.

Do This

Group interaction, not personal egos, <u>is</u> important in teamwork.

Do Not Do This

Group interaction, not personal egos, <u>are</u> important in teamwork.

In a sentence where you find both a positive and a negative subject, use a verb that agrees with the positive subject.

CHECKPOINT 11.2

Go to the Web

Checkpoint 11.2

for more skills practice on this topic.

Instructions: *In the sentences below, underline the simple subject. Then select the correct verb, and write it in the space provided. Identify the verb as singular (**S**) or plural (**P**).*

1. Robert, as well as Joan, (*collect, collects*) facts and figures _____
   before making contributions to the group.

Copyright © by The McGraw-Hill Companies, Inc.

2. The members of our team (*is, are*) more idea-oriented than action-oriented. _____

3. Group disagreements of any kind (*make, makes*) me uncomfortable. _____

4. Our company, in conjunction with the local technical college, (*offer, offers*) workshops in teamwork and conflict resolution. _____

5. Owners of small businesses in our country (*understand, understands*) the value of teamwork. _____

6. My interest in management topics (*include, includes*) teamwork. _____

7. Hank, as well as several other team members, (*believe, believes*) that the decision needs more in-depth review. _____

8. His knowledge of group dynamics always (*amaze, amazes*) me. _____

Compound Subjects Joined by *And*

Use a plural verb with a compound subject joined by *and* or *both . . . and*.

The project leader and group members need time to plan their strategies.

(The compound subject *leader* and *members* joined by *and* requires the plural verb *need*.)

Both Ann and Lindsay listen carefully to their colleagues' recommendations.

(The compound subject *Ann* and *Lindsay* joined by *both . . . and* requires the plural verb *listen*.)

Use a singular verb with a compound subject that refers to the same person or thing.

My colleague and mentor has an article on teamwork in our next company newsletter.

(The subjects *colleague* and *mentor* refer to one person; therefore, the sentence requires the singular verb *has*.)

Compound Subjects Joined by *Or* or *Nor*

Make the verb agree with the subject nearer the verb when a compound subject is joined by *or* or *nor* or by *either . . . or* or *neither . . . nor*.

Lynn or Dan usually prepares the committee assignments.

(*Dan*, a singular subject, is the part of the compound subject nearer the verb. The singular verb *prepares* must agree with this singular subject.)

Neither the chairperson nor the ad hoc committee members were available after the meeting.

(*Members*, a plural subject, is the part of the compound subject that is nearer the verb. The plural verb *were* must agree with this plural subject.)

Acceptable:

Either the managers or the group leader explains the goals to the group.

(The verb *explains* agrees with the nearer subject *leader*.)

NOTES

Compound Subject Reminder

Remember that a compound subject that refers to the same person or thing must have a singular verb.

Copyright © by The McGraw-Hill Companies, Inc.

Chapter 11

Less Awkward:

Either the group leader or the <u>managers</u> <u>explain</u> the goals to the group.

(Sentences with singular and plural subjects usually sound better with plural verbs. Therefore, rearrange the subjects so that the plural subject *managers* is closer to the verb)

Compound Subjects Preceded by *Many a, Many an, Each, Every*

Use a singular verb when the words *many a, many an, each*, and *every* immediately precede a compound subject connected by *and*. The subject that follows one of these four expressions is considered singular; the verb must agree.

Every team member and project leader <u>needs</u> a sense of commitment toward the team's goals.

(*Every* precedes the compound subject *team member* and *project leader*. The combination of *every* and a compound subject requires the singular verb *needs*.)

Many a committee meeting and negotiation session <u>has resulted</u> in a waste of my time.

(*Many a* precedes the compound subject *committee meeting* and *negotiation session*. The combination of *many a* and a compound subject requires the singular verb *has*.)

NOTES

***Every* With Compound Subjects**

When you use *every* before a compound subject, remember that you are saying *every single*. This will remind you that *every* is a singular verb.

CHECKPOINT 11.3

Go to the
Web

Checkpoint 11.3
for more skills practice on this topic.

Instructions: Select the correct verb, and write it in the space provided. Underline the simple subject in each sentence.

1. Jeff and Rick (*find, finds*) the group process challenging. _____

2. Each group project and job assignment (*need, needs*) direction. _____

3. Neither Ellen nor Marty (*are, is*) cooperating with the other team members. _____

4. Every team leader and team member (*has, have*) access to the groupware network. _____

5. Three mentors and a master teacher (*work, works*) with teams of student teachers at several middle schools. _____

6. Both the project team members and the executive board (*agree, agrees*) that the first recommendation is too expensive. _____

7. Many a supervisor and team member (*has, have*) requested more productive meetings. _____

8. Either the project leader or the support staff personnel (*prepare, prepares*) the agendas for the meetings. _____

9. My supervisor and team leader (*tries, try*) to encourage me to participate in the group discussions. (Note: The supervisor and team leader is one person.) _____

10. Every manager and first-level supervisor (*is, are*) responsible for summarizing weekly goals. _____

11. Many an inquiry and investigation (*has, have*) required hours of preparation time for me. _____

12. Evaluation and feedback (*provide, provides*) ways to improve your communication skills within a group. _____

13. Neither the observation nor the evaluations by management (*intimidate, intimidates*) our team. _____

14. Each agenda and set of minutes (*need, needs*) proofreading before distribution. _____

15. Yanbo or Crystal (*reserve, reserves*) the meeting room every Monday. _____

Indefinite Pronouns That Require Singular Verbs

Use a singular verb when the subject of a sentence is one of the following singular indefinite pronouns:

anybody	either	neither	one
anyone	everybody	no one	somebody
anything	everyone	nobody	someone
each	everything	nothing	something

NOTES

Looking Back

Review indefinite pronouns in Chapter 8. Do not confuse an indefinite pronoun used as a subject with one used as an adjective.

Someone in our group has a copy of the notes from our last meeting.

(The singular indefinite pronoun *Someone* is the subject and requires the singular verb *has*.)

Everyone develops his or her own style of leading a work group.

(The singular indefinite pronoun *Everyone* is the subject and requires the singular verb *develops*.)

Indefinite Pronouns That Require Plural Verbs

Use a plural verb when the subject is one of the following plural indefinite pronouns: *both, few, many, others,* and *several.*

Several of our committees meet twice a month.

(The plural indefinite pronoun *Several* is the subject and requires the plural verb *meet*.)

Many of our firm's best decisions are the result of teamwork.

(The plural indefinite pronoun *Many* is the subject and requires the plural verb *are*.)

Indefinite Pronouns That Require Singular or Plural Verbs

Use a singular *or* plural verb when the indefinite pronouns *all, any, more, most, none,* and *some* are used as subjects. The form of the verb depends on whether the pronoun refers to something singular or something plural.

Most of our players are more successful when they are free from stress.

(The indefinite pronoun and subject *Most* refers to *players,* which is plural. For agreement, the verb *are* must be plural.)

Some of our decisions <u>were</u> based on advice from outside experts.

(The indefinite pronoun and subject *Some* refers to *decisions,* which is plural. For agreement, the verb *were* must be plural.)

Some of our work <u>depends</u> on the research done by a team of experts.

(The indefinite pronoun and subject *Some* refers to *work,* which is singular. For agreement, the verb *depends* must be singular.)

CHECKPOINT 11.4

Go to the
Web

Checkpoint 11.4
for more skills practice on this topic.

Instructions: In the sentences below, underline the simple subject. Then, in the space provided, write the correct present tense form of the verb indicated in parentheses.

1. Each of the project members (*possess*) strengths that will benefit the final outcome.   _____

2. Some of the team's dissension (*result*) from inaccurate information.   _____

3. Both of my friends (*attend*) the accounting study group meeting every day at 8 a.m.   _____

4. One of the team's policies (*be*) to keep the communication free of sexist or profane remarks.   _____

5. Either of the two locations (*seem*) satisfactory for a group retreat.   _____

6. Most of the options presented by team members (*appear*) workable.   _____

7. All of our team members (*enjoy*) working together.   _____

8. Everyone (*plan*) to attend the picnic to celebrate the completion of the project.   _____

9. Several of our group's projects (*be*) already completed.   _____

10. Nothing (*keep*) Sadie from attending her team meetings.   _____

Collective Nouns That Require Singular Verbs

Use a singular verb to refer to a group as one unit.

This particular project <u>team</u> <u>seems</u> very result-oriented.

(The subject *team* refers to a group that is acting as one unit. Therefore, *team* requires the singular verb *seems.*)

Our work <u>group</u> <u>spends</u> several sessions discussing new ways to approach our assignment.

(The subject *group* refers to one unit and requires the singular verb *spends.*)

Collective Nouns That Require Plural Verbs

Use a plural verb to refer to group members acting as individual members of the group. To avoid the awkward construction of a collective noun with a plural verb, reword the sentence. Use phrases such as *members of the team (group)* or *team (group) members.*

Acceptable:

The <u>team</u> <u>are</u> checking their calendars for available meeting dates.

(*Team,* the subject, is a collective noun. In this sentence, the team members are acting individually rather than as one group. The plural verb *are* is necessary.)

Less Awkward:

The (<u>members of the team</u>, <u>team members</u>) are checking their calendars for available meeting dates.

Acceptable:

At S & C Graphics, the <u>support group</u> <u>assist</u> workers with drug or alcohol problems.

(*Support group,* the subject, is a collective noun. In this sentence, the support people are acting individually to assist workers rather than as one group. The plural verb *assist* is necessary.)

Less Awkward:

At S & C Graphics, (<u>members of the support group</u>, <u>support group members</u>) assist workers with drug or alcohol problems.

Publications

Use a singular verb when the name of a publication such as a book, magazine, software application, or newspaper is used as a subject.

<u>*Team News*</u> <u>is</u> the publication that our company uses to share information among its 12 teams.

(*Team News* is a publication and requires the singular verb *is.*)

<u>*Management Review*</u>, a business publication, often <u>runs</u> a column on teamwork.

(*Management Review* is a publication and requires the singular verb *runs.*)

Companies, Institutions, and Organizations

Use a singular verb when the name of a company, an institution, or an organization is used as a subject of a sentence.

<u>Northwestern University</u> <u>makes</u> teamwork a key issue in its curriculum.

(*Northwestern University* is a singular subject that requires the singular verb *makes.*)

<u>Lutheran Hospital Counseling Services</u> <u>recommends</u> the formation of employee support groups to prevent staff burnout.

(*Lutheran Hospital Counseling Services* is a singular subject that requires the singular verb *recommends.*)

Go to the
Web

Checkpoint 11.5
for more skills practice on this topic.

CHECKPOINT 11.5

Instructions: In the sentences below, underline the simple subject. Then select the correct verb, and write it in the space provided.

1. Our work group (*meet, meets*) every Friday. _____

2. Silicon Logic Engineering (*has, have*) two work teams that design computer chips for Synopsys. _____

3. Our task force (*include, includes*) members of all ages. _____

4. The personnel screening committee (*are, is*) recommending four candidates. _____

5. North Central Technical College (*encourage, encourages*) its staff to organize support groups for students. _____

6. Microsoft Word (*allow, allows*) a group of people to review and edit word processing and graphics files. _____

7. Members of the team (*need, needs*) to share their ideas with one another. _____

8. *How to Make Collaboration Work* (*stress, stresses*) five principles that can be applied to work groups. _____

Money, Time Periods, Numbers, and Measurements

Use a singular verb with money, measurements, time periods, or numbers when referring to one total amount or unit.

> **Twenty minutes is all that I can spend at the project meeting today.**
>
> (*Twenty minutes* is a time period that refers to a total unit of time. Therefore, the singular verb *is* is required.)
>
> **One hundred dollars is the registration fee for the leadership training workshop.**
>
> (*One hundred dollars* is one total amount and requires the singular verb *is.*)
>
> **Twenty square feet is the size of our committee's meeting room.**
>
> (*Twenty square feet* is a total measurement and requires the singular verb *is.*)

Fractional Amounts—Singular Verbs

Use a singular verb with expressions such as *the majority of, a part of, a portion of, a percentage of,* or *one-half of* when the noun that follows the word *of* is singular.

> **The majority of the report concerns the committee's recommendations.**
>
> (The singular noun *report* follows the word *of.* The subject *majority* requires the singular verb *concerns.*)
>
> **A large portion of our work session is set aside for questions.**
>
> (The singular noun *session* follows the word *of.* The subject *portion* requires the singular verb *is.*)

Fractional Amounts—Plural Verbs

Use a plural verb with expressions such as *a majority of, a part of, a portion of, a percentage of,* or *one-half of* when the noun that follows the word *of* is plural.

> **A large percentage of the questionnaires were not returned to the task force chairperson by the requested date.**
>
> (The plural noun *questionnaires* follows the word *of.* The subject *percentage* requires the plural verb *were.*)
>
> **One-half of the group facilitators have difficulties with setting goals.**
>
> (The plural noun *facilitators* follows the word *of.* The subject *one-half* requires the plural verb *have.*)

A Number/The Number

Use a plural verb with the subject *a number* when *of* follows. Use a singular verb with the subject *the number* when the word *of* follows.

> **A number of the members of our work team are new to the group process.**
>
> (The subject *a number* followed by *of* requires the plural verb *are*.)
>
> **The number of women in project leadership roles is increasing.**
>
> (The subject *the number* requires the singular verb *is*.)

Go to the
Web

Checkpoint 11.6
for more skills practice on this topic.

CHECKPOINT 11.6

*Instructions: In the space provided, write **Yes** if the subject and verb agree in the sentence. Write the correct verb in the space if the subject and verb do not agree.*

1. Twenty dollars per team member are too much. _____

2. The number of survey responses were helpful in our team's decision. _____

3. Three-fourths of the union members agree with the committee's suggestions. _____

4. A majority of our team members work in their homes and go to the office only for scheduled meetings. _____

5. A large percentage of the final report still need to be checked by the project leader. _____

6. Two months to complete the project demonstrate the power of teamwork. _____

7. A number of our team members dislikes the leader's communication style. _____

8. The majority of our team members is punctual to all meetings. _____

9. A large portion of research have already been completed. _____

10. Only one-half of the funds for the group's expenses was approved by management. _____

Inverted Sentences

In an inverted sentence, the subject appears after the verb.

Sentences Beginning With *Here* and *There*.   Locate the subject in a sentence that begins with *here* or *there*. The verb should agree with the subject.

> **There are six people on our interview team.**
>
> (The subject is *people*. *People* is plural and requires the plural verb *are*.)
>
> **Here are five additional points for the team to consider.**
>
> (The subject is *points*, which is plural and requires the plural verb *are*.)
>
> **In teamwork, there is no guarantee that you will receive personal credit for your ideas.**
>
> (The subject is *guarantee*, which is singular and requires the singular verb *is*.)

EDIT PATROL

Quote from a newspaper article:

"There are no national temperatures today due to transmission difficulties."
Note: How is it possible to have no temperatures?

Questions.   Locate the subject in a question, and make the verb agree with the subject.

Was <u>anyone</u> from our team absent from the last meeting?

(The subject is *anyone*, which is singular and requires the singular verb *was*.)

Is <u>groupware</u> considered to be a useful communication tool for work groups?

(The subject is *groupware*, which is singular and requires the singular verb *is*.)

Why <u>are you</u> concerned about a change in the team's personnel?

(The subject is *you*. *You* always requires the plural verb *are*.)

NOTES

Here/There

If the subject is difficult to find, delete *here* or *there* and turn the statement around. Remember that *here* and *there* are never subjects.

CHECKPOINT 11.7

Go to the

Web

Checkpoint 11.7
for more skills practice on this topic.

*Instructions: In the sentences below, underline the simple subject. In the space provided, write **Yes** if the subject and verb agree. In the space provided, write the correct verb if the subject and verb do not agree.*

1. There are a considerable amount of dissension between the   _____
    old and new team members.

2. Do you enjoy solitary work more than you enjoy teamwork?   _____

3. Here is some ideas to motivate people who work in groups.   _____

4. There are different team members writing various sections   _____
    of the report.

5. How do companies show their appreciation for the efforts of   _____
    outstanding individual team members?

6. Has Conrad and Blaine reviewed our proposed changes?   _____

Special Nouns/Gerund Phrases

Nouns Ending in *ics*.   Use a singular verb with a noun that ends in *ics* when the noun refers to one topic of study or body of knowledge. Use a plural verb with a noun that ends in *ics* when the noun refers to more than one idea or item such as qualities or activities.

<u>Statistics</u> <u>is</u> a course that helps me analyze some of our work group's surveys.

(The subject *statistics* refers to one topic of study and requires the singular verb *is*.)

The <u>statistics</u> from employee surveys <u>are</u> important in our group's informal research.

(The subject *statistics* refers to numerous items and requires the plural verb *are*.)

<u>Economics 301</u> <u>is</u> a required course for marketing students.

(The subject *Economics 301* refers to one topic of study and requires the singular verb *is*.)

The economics of third-world countries require some review by our consulting team.

(The subject *economics* refers to more than one situation and requires the plural verb *require*.)

Plural Nouns. Use a plural verb with nouns ending in *s* such as *assets, dues, earnings, goods, grounds, odds, proceeds, savings,* and *thanks* when these nouns are used as subjects.

The grounds upon which the teams' policies were formulated are the result of months of work.

(*Grounds* is the subject and always requires the plural verb *are*.)

The odds were against us, but we tried to get additional support staff for the project team.

(*Odds* is the subject and always requires the plural verb *were*.)

Gerund Phrases. Use a singular verb when a gerund phrase is the subject of a sentence.

Establishing outstanding teams requires time and commitment.

(*Establishing outstanding teams* is a gerund phrase and is the complete subject in this sentence. This phrase requires the singular verb *requires*.)

Sharing decision-making responsibilities with employees is a difficult change for some managers.

(*Sharing decision-making responsibilities with employees* is a gerund phrase, is the complete subject in this sentence, and requires the singular verb *is*.)

NOTES

Gerunds as Subjects

The simple subject is the gerund itself. The complete subject is the entire gerund phrase.

Go to the
Web

Checkpoint 11.8
for more skills practice on this topic.

CHECKPOINT 11.8

Instructions: *Select the correct verb, and write it in the space provided. Underline the complete subject in each sentence.*

1. Learning to handle conflicts (*are, is*) a sign of professionalism. _____

2. Earnings (*has, have*) increased since the teams have been organized. _____

3. Office politics (*seem, seems*) to be ignored in this committee. _____

4. Disagreeing with someone's comment (*do, does*) not mean that you are angry with this person. _____

5. The goods (*was, were*) late in arriving; therefore, our production team started three days late. _____

6. His leadership tactics (*concern, concerns*) management. _____

7. Business Statistics 302 (*was, were*) a course that involved many small study groups. _____

8. Dues for our new professional group (*was, were*) very low. _____

Diagramming Sentences

The sentences in this section involve the infinitive (a verb preceded by the word *to*). To diagram the infinitive phrase used as a noun, place the word *to* on a diagonal line that extends slightly below the connecting horizontal line. Write the verb in the infinitive phrase on the horizontal line that connects to the diagonal line.

Then place the infinitive phrase on a "stilt" in the appropriate position.

Laura prefers to ask thought-provoking questions. (infinitive phrase used as a direct object)

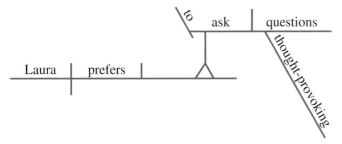

To become a project manager requires good communication skills. (infinitive phrase used as a subject)

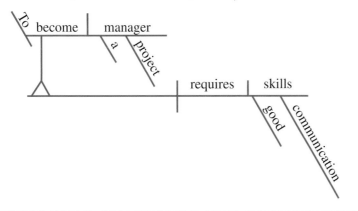

CHECKPOINT 11.9

Go to the
Web

Checkpoint 11.9
for more skills practice on this topic.

Instructions: *Diagram each sentence in the space provided.*

1. To complete the assignment will take ten people.

2. Our team expects to make a difference.

3. A team member needs to understand the team's purpose.

4. To rebuild team rapport will take a long time.

Name _____ Date _____

PRACTICE 1

Singular and Plural Verbs

Instructions: Select the correct verb, and write it in the space provided. Identify the verb as being singular (S) or plural (P).

1. If you are in the hospitality industry, you really (*has, have*) to operate as a team.

   1. _____

2. No decision or recommendations (*was, were*) made.

   2. _____

3. Each of the work team leaders (*submit, submits*) a plan of action to his or her supervisor.

   3. _____

4. Harvey Robbins (*include, includes*) some interesting points in his book *Why Teams Don't Work.*

   4. _____

5. Our work group (*participate, participates*) in Casual Day on Fridays.

   5. _____

6. Jane and David (*was, were*) team leaders of a task force to improve customer satisfaction ratings.

   6. _____

7. Some of our work (*depend, depends*) on the research done by the team of experts.

   7. _____

8. She (*enjoy, enjoys*) working on team projects when all members are dependable workers.

   8. _____

9. A team member, through his or her contributions, (*gain, gains*) a feeling of personal accomplishment.

   9. _____

10. RDC Plastics (*has, have*) a policy that allows only two strategic team members to fly on the same flight.

    10. _____

11. Three-fifths of the articles written about teamwork (*are, is*) outstanding.

    11. _____

12. Checking your understanding by repeating someone's comments (*help, helps*) you grasp this person's meaning correctly.

    12. _____

13. There (*are, is*) 22 quality control teams in our company.

    13. _____

14. Differences of opinion (*are, is*) a normal occurrence in the beginning stages of a group project.

    14. _____

15. A number of our busy committee members (*does not, do not*) appreciate long meetings.

    15. _____

Go to the
Web

Practice 1 Exercises
for more skills practice on this topic.

Subject-Verb Agreement

Name _____ Date _____

16. A large percentage of the employees (*attend, attends*) meetings online.

16. _____

17. Thirty minutes (*is, are*) the longest time for any of our weekly meetings.

17. _____

18. *Productive Meetings* (*are, is*) my favorite time management book.

18. _____

19. Most of our decisions (*are, is*) made by a consensus vote of attendees.

19. _____

20. Many a conflict and disagreement (*has, have*) been negotiated after communication with both parties.

20. _____

PRACTICE 2

Go to the
Web

Practice 2 Exercises
for more skills practice on this topic.

Subject-Verb Agreement

*Instructions: In the sentences below, underline the simple subject. In the space provided, write **Yes** if the subject and verb are in agreement. Write the correct verb in the space if the subject and verb are not in agreement.*

1. Sometimes members of a workgroup makes unintentional remarks that later become exaggerated.

1. _____

2. Neither the project manager nor the supervisors has been informed of the cancellation of the job.

2. _____

3. Everyone on the team are cross-trained.

3. _____

4. Our psychology instructor organizes discussion groups at least once a week.

4. _____

5. Some of our work center around group projects.

5. _____

6. A team of financial analysts manage my mutual fund.

6. _____

7. Disagreements, as well as progress, were communicated.

7. _____

8. Their careful analyses of the situations was appreciated by other team members.

8. _____

9. Every team member and project leader are recognized for his or her efforts.

9. _____

10. A large percentage of the group's discussions were positive.

10. _____

11. Having access to technical personnel and support are a major concern for our project work group.

11. _____

Name _____ Date _____

12. Florence, as well as Connie, support my position on starting meetings on time.

12. _____

13. The statistics regarding on-time shipments supports Tom's recommendation.

13. _____

14. A self-managing team, unlike a traditional group, improves the quality of planning.

14. _____

15. Some unions and some union members suspects the values of teamwork.

15. _____

16. There are several approaches to use in resolving conflicts.

16. _____

17. All of the committee members have some skill to contribute to the efficiency of the group.

17. _____

18. Trimedics bring key people together and make them responsible for specific customers or for certain product lines.

18. _____

19. The number of team members opposed to the changes surprise me.

19. _____

20. Brainstorming was the major source for our team's solution to the problem.

20. _____

PRACTICE 3

Proofreading

*Instructions: Proofread and compare the two sentences in each group. If they are the same, write **Yes** in the space provided. If they are not the same, write **No**. Use the first sentence as the correct copy. If you find errors in the second sentence, underline them; insert any omitted words or marks of punctuation.*

Go to the
Web

Practice 3 Exercises
for more skills practice on this topic.

1. Management has formed a team of supervisors to study the issues of employee turnover and training.

   Management have formed a team of supervisors to study the issue of employee turnover and training.

1. _____

2. Our international sales team is experiencing an increase in sales in Poland, Hungary, and the Czech Republic.

   Our international sales team are experiencing a increase in slaes in Poland, Hungery, and the Czech Republic.

2. _____

3. The best team leaders are self-starters who are enthusiastic about their responsibilities.

   The best team leaders are self-starters whom are enthusastic about their responsibilities.

3. _____

Subject-Verb Agreement

Name _____ Date _____

4. George Russell Jr., chairman of Frank Russell Co. in Tacoma, Washington, supports mountain climbing as a team-building exercise.

   George Russell Sr., chairman of Frank Russell Corp. in Seattle, Washington supports mountain climbing as a team-building experience.

4. _____

5. The concept of teamwork de-emphasizes individual achievement and encourages workers to learn from one another.

   The concept of teamwork de-emphasises individual achievement and encourages workers to learn from each other.

5. _____

Using Proofreaders' Marks

Instructions: Review the proofreaders' marks listed below. Use these marks to make corrections in the copy that follows:

Make lowercase /	Move left ⌐	Insert letter ∧
Capitalize ≡	Move right ⌐#	Insert comma ∧
Delete ϒ	Insert space ∧	Transpose ∽
Delete space ⌣	Insert period ⊙	
Delete and close up ϙ		

TO: Anita Gregg Manager
        Benefits Division

FROM: Richard Chen, Vice president
         Human Services

DATE: April 21, 20—

SUBJECT: Emplooyee Benefits Review

Please organize a team of employees(approximately 10–12) too review the current package of employee's benefits. The president has given our office the approval to send questionnaires to all employees to identify thier needs and concerns

The team will be responsible for reviewing the questionnaires, tabulating the results, researching the the benefit options, and preparing recomendations for change. You should asses the strengths of each potential team member for his or her computer skills, analytical capabilities, or communication skills. Team members should be aware of a six- month time commitment to this project.

Please let me know the names of the team Members by May 1. I will then schedule a planing meeting with you and the team before May 15.

cg

Name _____ Date _____

PRACTICE 4

Writing

Instructions: *Write the following sentences with subject and verb agreement. Answers will vary.*

1. A sentence with a prepositional phrase between the subject and the verb. Identify the subject, verb, and prepositional phrase.

   _____

   _____

2. A sentence with an intervening word or phrase between the subject and the verb. Identify the subject, verb, and intervening word or phrase.

   _____

   _____

3. A sentence with a compound subject joined by *and.* Identify the subjects and the verb.

   _____

   _____

4. A sentence with a compound subject joined by *nor.* Identify the subjects and the verb.

   _____

   _____

5. A sentence beginning with the word *each.* Identify the subject and the verb.

   _____

   _____

Go to the
Web

Practice 4 Exercises
for more skills practice on this topic.

PRACTICE 5

Singular and Plural Verbs

Instructions: *Select the correct verb, and write it in the space provided. Identify the verb as being singular (S) or plural (P).*

1. You (*determine, determines*) your own work schedule on our team.

   1. _____

2. Either Sandy or Louis (*coordinate, coordinates*) our workshop.

   2. _____

3. Each of the employees (*have, has*) a job with interrelated tasks.

   3. _____

Subject-Verb Agreement

Name _____ Date _____

4. Lead workers (*coordinate, coordinates*) activities of their peers.   4. _____

5. Our participation in "gainsharing" (*give, gives*) us a part of the increase in organization profits.   5. _____

6. Samantha and Erin (*is, are*) on the employee involvement committee.   6. _____

7. Many (*suggest, suggests*) the evaluation of a team's effectiveness periodically.   7. _____

8. He (*feel, feels*) responsible and committed to our team's decisions.   8. _____

9. Group behaviors (*remains, remain*) a challenge to many meeting planners.   9. _____

10. All members of the team (*participate, participates*) in the problem-solving process.   10. _____

11. Here (*are, is*) the list of interpersonal skills necessary for success in our group.   11. _____

12. Over 50 percent of our team leaders (*take, takes*) seminars in conflict resolution.   12. _____

13. Sheila, in addition to others from our group, (*leave, leaves*) for a meeting in Los Angeles tomorrow.   13. _____

14. Wolfe Builders (*use, uses*) scheduling software to analyze the status of the construction team's progress.   14. _____

15. Listening to "respond" rather than listening to "understand" frequently (*cause, causes*) misunderstandings among our team members.   15. _____

16. One-third of the employees (*has, have*) attended a leadership workshop.   16. _____

17. *How to Make Meetings Work* (*include, includes*) tips on facilitating a meeting.   17. _____

18. Most of our work-related problems (*are, is*) easily solved.   18. _____

19. Statistics from the survey (*are, is*) important to the managers.   19. _____

20. All of the group members (*develop, develops*) a sense of commitment to solve problems.   20. _____

Name _____ Date _____

Subject-Verb Agreement

Instructions: In the sentences below, underline the simple subject. In the space provided, write **Yes** *if the subject and verb are in agreement. Write the correct verb in the space if the subject and verb are not in agreement.*

1. The number of women on management teams are increasing.

    1. _____

2. Neither Luis nor Pamela was able to attend the first task force meeting.

    2. _____

3. Others on our committee disagree with Richard and Charles.

    3. _____

4. Because of our success, Jennifer wants to be on our team.

    4. _____

5. Elizabeth Wilson, one of our vice presidents, communicate clearly and precisely.

    5. _____

6. Statistics indicates that large businesses are increasing their number of teams.

    6. _____

7. Many of the group's morale problems results from just a few disgruntled employees.

    7. _____

8. Patricia, Mary, and Tom makes decisions by consensus.

    8. _____

9. Getting to know employees as individuals are important for every supervisor.

    9. _____

10. Approximately 90 percent of our employees belongs to a union.

    10. _____

11. Technology resources remain an important factor in our success.

    11. _____

12. The project team have completed setting group goals.

    12. _____

13. Was you offended by the lack of consideration shown for opposing ideas at the last council meeting?

    13. _____

14. Both of the consultants suggest smaller work groups.

    14. _____

15. *In the Age of the Smart Machine,* the author describes the psychology of self-management in organizations.

    15. _____

16. Nick or Dan were responsible for informing team members of the meeting time.

    16. _____

Name _____   Date _____

17. Every leader and manager in our firm appreciate the work of our teams.

17. _____

18. Dade Community College encourage the formation of student study groups.

18. _____

19. Fifteen minutes seem like a long time to wait for a meeting to begin.

19. _____

20. There is several methods for organizing teams of workers.

20. _____

PRACTICE 7

Proofreading

*Instructions: Proofread and compare the two sentences in each group. If they are the same, write **Yes** in the space provided. If they are not the same, write **No**. Use the first sentence as the correct copy. If you find errors in the second sentence, underline them; insert any omitted words or marks of punctuation.*

1. Self-managing teamwork is known by names such as autonomous work groups, work teams, self-directed teams, self-maintaining teams, business teams, self-leading teams, semiautonomous work groups, self-regulating groups, and many others.

   1. _____

   Self-managing teamwork is known by names such as autonomous work groups, work teams, self directed teams, self-maintaining teams, business teams, self-leading teams, semi-autonomous workgroups, self-regulating groups and many others.

2. Quality Circles, a movement started by the Japanese, are groups of employees who voluntarily meet for an hour or more each week to solve a specific work problem.

   2. _____

   Quality Circles, a movement started by the Japanese, are groups of employees who voluntarily meet for an hour or more each week to solve a specific work problems.

3. In a recent study of supervisors' attitudes toward employee involvement programs of all types, 72 percent of the supervisors viewed the programs as being good for their companies; 60 percent, good for the employees; but only 31 percent, beneficial to themselves.

   3. _____

   In a recent study of supervisors' attitudes toward employee involvement programs of all types, 72 percent of the supervisors viewed the programs as being good for their companies; 60 percent, good for the employees; but only 31 percent, beneficial to themselves.

Name _____ Date _____

4. A controlling person with superior knowledge and
ability may have an attitude that does not invite
new ideas, challenge people, or stimulate a
cooperative, supportive spirit.

    A controling person with superior knowledge and
ability may have an attitude that does not invite
new ideas, challenge people, or simulate a
cooperative, supportive spirit.

4. _____

5. Drucker has suggested that 20 years from now the
typical large business will have only half of the levels of
management and a third of the number of managers
that organizations have today.

    Drucker has suggested that 12 years from now a
typical large business will have only half of the levels of
management and a third of the number of managers
that organizations has today.

5. _____

Using Proofreaders' Marks

Instructions: Review the proofreaders' marks listed below. Use these marks to make corrections in the copy that follows.

Make lowercase /	Move left ⌐	Insert letter ∧
Capitalize ≡	Move right ⌐#	Insert comma ∧
Delete	Insert space ∧	Transpose ∽
Delete space ⌣	Insert period ⊙	
Delete and close up		

CHARACTERISTICS OF A SELF-MANAGING TEAM

The team perform a distint task.

    Team members possesss a variety of skills related tothe task.

Team members are interdependent.

The teams' focus are on the group ratherthan Individuals.

Team members may rotate through the tasks.

    the team have clear boundaries in terms of space and
task responsi bilities.

The Team monitors and controls its work quantity and quality

Name _____ Date _____

PRACTICE 8

Writing

Instructions: *Write the following sentences with subject and verb agreement. Answers will vary.*

1. A subject that is a singular indefinite pronoun. Identify the subject and the verb.

    _____

    _____

2. A subject that has an indefinite pronoun that can be plural. Identify the subject and the verb.

    _____

    _____

3. A sentence with a collective noun that is acting together as a group. Identify the subject and the verb.

    _____

    _____

4. A sentence with the name of a company as the subject. Identify the subject and the verb.

    _____

    _____

5. An inverted sentence. Identify the subject and the verb.

    _____

    _____

Posttest

Instructions: In the sentences below, underline the simple subject. Then select the correct verb, and write it in the space provided.

1. Carmen (*analyze, analyzes*) statistics on workplace trends. (1)

   1. _____

2. Task force members (*present, presents*) recommendations to our company every week. (1)

   2. _____

3. The article, as well as the Web resources, (*stimulate, stimulates*) our thinking about reorganizing our teams. (2)

   3. _____

4. Neither Stanley nor Julia (*suggest, suggests*) changing the title of the report. (3)

   4. _____

5. Self-managing team evaluations (*is, are*) difficult to develop. (1)

   5. _____

6. Many of the managers (*like, likes*) the productivity benefits of teamwork. (4)

   6. _____

7. The team (*understand, understands*) that the sales brochure must be completed by Friday. (5)

   7. _____

8. A large percentage of our employees (*enjoy, enjoys*) working in teams. (6)

   8. _____

9. There (*is, are*) numerous names to describe teamwork. (7)

   9. _____

10. Randy's politics (*have, has*) splintered the group. (8)

    10. _____

11. Solving problems (*take, takes*) time and effort by everyone involved. (8)

    11. _____

12. The agenda for our meetings (*give, gives*) the meeting location and the start and end times. (2)

    12. _____

13. Every facilitator and participant on our team (*keep, keeps*) our meetings productive and interesting. (2, 4)

    13. _____

14. Everyone (*seem, seems*) to enjoy our weekly meetings. (4)

    14. _____

15. Reynolds Stationers (*sell, sells*) flip chart paper with grids. (5)

    15. _____

Unit 4

Reviewing Modifiers and Connectors

Chapter 12

Adjectives

OBJECTIVES

After you have studied this chapter and completed the exercises, you will be able to do the following:

1. Identify the function of an adjective in a sentence.

2. Identify limiting, descriptive, possessive, proper, and demonstrative adjectives in sentences.

3. Use the articles *a, an,* and *the* correctly.

4. Hyphenate compound adjectives when appropriate.

5. Use the positive, comparative, and superlative degrees of adjectives correctly.

6. Identify nouns modified by adjectives, adjective phrases, and adjective clauses.

7. Determine the correct usage of commonly misused adjectives.

Workplace Applications: Ergonomics

Ergonomics is the study of the relationship between the worker and the work environment. Ergonomic planners adjust the surrounding working conditions to meet the needs of the individual worker. Ergonomic planning includes an analysis of all workplace risk factors such as lighting, workstations, seating, monitors, work-rest cycles, and temperatures.

Work-Related Injuries

When a mismatch occurs between the worker and the physical requirements of the job, cumulative trauma disorder (CTD) or musculoskeletal disorder (MSD) sometimes occurs. Additional terms for CTD are repetitive motion injury or illness, repetitive strain injury or illness, or repetitive stress injury or illness (RSI). Usually CTDs occur when workers repeat the same motion each day, work in awkward positions, lift heavy objects, or use force to perform their jobs. CTDs comprise more than 100 different types of job-induced injuries and illnesses. Symptoms of CTD vary widely from minor aches and pains to crippling impairment such as carpal tunnel syndrome.

Work-related injuries cost employers billions of dollars in workers' compensation claims. Simple and inexpensive ergonomic solutions such as adjusting the height of a workstation or encouraging short breaks often will prevent needless CTDs from affecting workers. The Occupational Safety and Health Administration (OSHA) is responsible for providing education, research, and enforcement as well as for making rules to combat CTDs in the workplace. OSHA sponsors conferences, tracks ergonomic programs, reviews scientific literature, and investigates ergonomic cases.

Pretest

Instructions: In the space provided, write the letter of the correct answer.

1. Which question is *not* answered by an adjective? (1)

    a. What kind?   c. How?

    b. How many?   d. Whose?

1. _____

2. Which parts of speech are modified by adjectives? (1)

    a. verb and noun   c. noun and adverb

    b. verb and pronoun   d. noun and pronoun

2. _____

3. In the sentence *Our office furniture showroom was messy and crowded,* the adjectives are: (2)

    a. Our, office, showroom, messy, crowded.   c. office, furniture, messy, crowded.

    b. office, furniture, showroom.   d. Our, office, furniture, messy, crowded.

3. _____

4. In the sentence *European decor has a definite charm,* the word *European* functions as a: (1)

    a. proper noun.   c. possessive adjective.

    b. proper adjective.   d. limiting adjective.

4. _____

5. Which phrase represents the incorrect use of an article? (3)

    a. an universal appeal   c. a blueprint

    b. an office window   d. an hour

5. _____

6. In the sentence *Julia selected those colors for the employees' break room,* the function of *those* is that of: (2)

    a. an interrogative adjective.   c. a demonstrative adjective.

    b. a possessive pronoun.   d. a demonstrative pronoun.

6. _____

7. Which compound adjective is *not* hyphenated correctly? (4)

    a. first-class service   c. short term solution

    b. point-of-sale transaction d. real estate office

7. _____

8. The superlative for *stunning* is: (5)

    a. stunninger   c. more stunning

    b. stunning   d. most stunning

8. _____

9. In the sentence *We preferred the building blueprints that Lancaster Builders submitted,* which of the following is modified by the adjective phrase? (6)

    a. building   c. blueprints

    b. Lancaster Builders   d. We

9. _____

10. Which sentence is *not* written correctly? (7)

    a. I am experiencing less stress on my job this year.

    b. We sold fewer office furniture this year than we sold last year.

    c. Our firm now has fewer employees with musculoskeletal disorders.

    d. Dane pays less attention to the construction of his office chair than he should.

10. _____

11. Which sentence is *not* written correctly? (4)

    a. My occupational physician's office is located just a one-mile drive from here.

    b. Our self-study showed a lack of awareness about CTDs.

    c. My high school business instructor told me about carpal tunnel syndrome.

    d. Brantley Incorporated ordered 4, 5, and 6 foot tables to accommodate programmers' demands.

11. _____

12. Which sentence is *not* written correctly? (7)

    a. We ordered further tests for radon detection.

    b. We ordered farther tests for radon detection.

    c. The latest test for radon detection was not satisfactory.

    d. The last test for radon detection was not satisfactory.

12. _____

13. Which sentence is *not* written correctly? (3, 4)

    a. I am concerned about the ever-increasing costs of office furniture.

    b. Displaying an up-to-date-career award adds a personal touch to your office cubicle.

    c. A chair that is customized to fit you is an excellent long-term health investment.

    d. I was fortunate to locate an end-of-the-year sale on office furniture.

13. _____

14. Which sentence is *not* written correctly? (3)

    a. I wanted to create an office image that was professional.

    b. He found that his monitor stand gave him an unexpected benefit in eliminating eyestrain.

    c. Hank selected a unique design for his office shelves.

    d. We were fortunate to work with a honest furniture manufacturer.

14. _____

15. Which sentence is *not* written correctly? (5)

    a. Kathy's office is more warm because it is located on the sunny side of the building.

    b. Which of the two office chairs is better for you?

    c. My corner office has the best view of any office on the third floor.

    d. If clients never visit your office, you can be more casual with your office decor.

15. _____

Nouns and verbs provide the substance of a sentence, but writing would be very dull and vague without adjectives. Adjectives are the words that add the interesting details and descriptive color to sentences.

Wouldn't you be pleased if your supervisor wrote a letter of recommendation that described you as a dependable, intelligent, and energetic employee? These adjectives certainly provide a favorable "picture" for a prospective employer. In this chapter, you will learn to create "pictures" in your writing by using adjectives that add variety, descriptive details, and specificity to your sentences.

Types of Adjectives

An adjective modifies (describes) a noun or a pronoun. Several adjectives often appear in one sentence. More than one adjective may describe one noun. An adjective answers these questions:

What kind?	red, new, exciting, durable
Which one?	this, that, these, those
How many?	one, few, 200, one-half, all, some
Whose?	his, Ryan's, companies'
	(Possessive pronouns and possessive nouns function as adjectives.)

Several types of adjectives, including limiting, descriptive, possessive, proper, and demonstrative, will be discussed in this chapter.

Limiting Adjectives

Limiting adjectives are numbers or words that indicate *how many*. Use a limiting adjective to limit the scope of the noun or pronoun.

We still need <u>three</u> workstations for the office on State Street.

(The adjective *three* indicates *how many* workstations are needed.)

<u>All</u> safety programs require the commitment of management.

(The adjective *all* indicates *how many* safety programs require commitment.)

Descriptive Adjectives

Descriptive adjectives answer the question *What kind?* They usually precede nouns or follow linking verbs.

Before Nouns.   Use a descriptive adjective to tell something about (describe) a noun or a pronoun. Place a descriptive adjective as close as possible to the noun or pronoun that it modifies.

The heating system caused problems.

(The descriptive adjective *heating* tells *what kind* of system. *Heating* appears before the noun that it modifies.)

I knew that the office furniture was a good bargain.

(The descriptive adjective *office* tells *what kind* of furniture. The adjective *good* tells *what kind* of bargain. Both adjectives appear before the nouns that they modify.)

After Linking Verbs. Use a descriptive adjective after a linking verb to modify a noun or pronoun used as a subject. A descriptive adjective that follows a linking verb is one type of complement (predicate adjective).

Excessive noise in the workplace is annoying.

(The linking verb *is* connects the descriptive adjective *annoying* to the noun *noise*.)

The total amount for the new carpeting seems high.

(*Seems* is a linking verb connecting the descriptive adjective *high* to the noun *amount*.)

CHECKPOINT 12.1

Go to the
Web

Checkpoint 12.1
for more skills practice on this topic.

Instructions: Underline each descriptive adjective once. Circle each limiting adjective. Ignore a, an, and the. In the space provided, write the noun or nouns that are modified.

1. The upholstery came in four different colors. _____

2. Tendinitis is one common type of workplace injury. _____

3. Workers need education about proper posture and lifting techniques. _____

4. The new furniture for the office is sturdy and functional. _____

5. A thorough investigation of worksites is important. _____

6. If you plan to order some furniture through a catalog, expect to wait six weeks for delivery. _____

7. We reviewed several office catalogs for unique, functional furniture. _____

8. Green plants give an office a pleasant ornamental touch. _____

9. Poor-quality chairs can mean painful backaches or circulation problems. _____
_____

10. Sheila looks for four basic features in office chairs. _____

Possessive Adjectives

Possessive pronouns such as *my, her, his, your, its,* and *our* function as adjectives and are called possessive adjectives. Possessive nouns such as *Jack's* or *firm's* function as possessive adjectives also. Possessive adjectives answer the question *Whose?* Use a possessive adjective to modify a noun or pronoun.

Adjectives

Jane buys used furniture in good condition for <u>her</u> office at home.

(*Her* functions as a possessive adjective that answers the question *Whose office?*)

The <u>decorator's</u> hints about lighting showed us how to create some striking effects.

(*Decorator's* answers the question *Whose hints?*)

<u>Ron's</u> college major was ergonomic design.

(*Ron's* functions as a possessive adjective that answers the question *Whose major?*)

Proper Adjectives

Proper nouns or words derived from proper nouns also function as adjectives and are referred to as proper adjectives. Capitalize most proper adjectives as you would proper nouns. Do *not* capitalize proper adjectives when they lose their connections with the proper nouns from which they were derived. Proper adjectives answer the question *Which?*

The <u>January</u> office products catalog included several types of ergonomic chairs.

(*January* requires capitalization. *January* is a proper adjective that modifies *catalog*. *January* answers the question *Which catalog?*)

Several <u>Canadian</u> firms sell furniture that meets <u>OSHA</u> standards.

(*Canadian* modifies *firms* and *OSHA* modifies *standards*. Both *Canadian* and *OSHA* require capitalization.)

<u>Shelly's</u> second color choice for the <u>venetian</u> blinds was light blue.

(*Venetian blinds* are common items; therefore, the word *venetian* does not need to be capitalized.)

Demonstrative Adjectives

The words *this, that, these,* and *those* are demonstrative pronouns, but they also function as demonstrative adjectives when they modify nouns. Demonstrative adjectives answer the question *Which one?* or *Which ones?*

Use the demonstrative adjectives *this, that, these,* and *those* to point out *which one* or *which ones*. Use *this* or *that* with singular nouns. Use *these* or *those* with plural nouns.

Ramsey Rehab designed <u>this</u> chair for workers with back problems.

(*This* is a singular demonstrative adjective that indicates *which* chair.)

Many of <u>these</u> motions cause hand and wrist strains.

(*These* is a plural demonstrative adjective indicating *which* motions.)

NOTES

Looking Back

Review Chapter 5 for the use of possessive nouns and Chapter 7 for the use of possessive pronouns.

NOTES

Looking Back

Refer to Chapters 4 and 6 for examples of proper nouns. Note those nouns that are no longer capitalized.

EDIT PATROL

Published in the *Soviet Weekly:*

"There will be a Moscow Exhibition of the Arts by 15,000 Soviet Republic painters and sculptors. These were executed over the past two years." Were the painters and sculptors executed?

Do This	Do Not Do This
<u>Those</u> furniture containers are good packing boxes.	<u>Them</u> furniture containers are good packing boxes.

or

<u>These</u> furniture containers are good packing boxes.

Them, which is a pronoun, is never used as an adjective.

Chapter 12

Go to the
Web

Checkpoint 12.2
for more skills practice on this topic.

Instructions: *Underline the possessive adjectives once and the proper adjectives twice. Circle the demonstrative adjectives. In the space provided, write the noun or nouns that are modified by possessive, proper, or demonstrative pronouns.*

1. Mitch's desk had limited work surface space for his reference materials. _____

2. Those computer tables were expensive for our firm. _____

3. I hope to purchase some hand-carved Mexican furniture for my home office. _____

4. These rules provide work environment guidelines for American companies. _____

5. He studied British architecture in his ergonomics class. _____

6. Several building committee members stated that this carpeting was best for heavily used areas. _____

7. The oriental rug was the focal point of Ruth's office. _____

8. We will have our difficulties in complying with that regulation concerning safety. _____

9. You should always buy a chair that fits your height. _____

10. I will need that list of the CEO's requirements for office furniture. _____

11. Those colors are the most effective for his office. _____

12. Sheila checked a manufacturer's Web site for the description of an adjustable chair for her office. _____

Articles

Although the articles *a, an,* and *the* are less descriptive than words such as *strong* or *dull,* these articles are some of the most frequently used words in the English language. Articles always modify nouns.

A and An

Use *a* and *an* with singular nouns, not with plural nouns. Place *a* or *an* before any other adjective if two or more adjectives precede a noun.

> **We plan to place <u>an</u> order for new furniture that will meet ergonomic standards.**

> (The article *an* refers to *order,* a singular noun.)

> **<u>A</u> large company cannot buy one type of chair for all its workers.**

> (The article *a* refers to *company,* a singular noun.)

Guidelines for Using *A* or *An*

The initial sound (not the first letter) of the word that follows an article determines whether you will use *a* or *an*.

Before Sounded Consonants.   Use *a* before words beginning with a consonant that is sounded.

<u>a</u> room   <u>a</u> hobby   <u>a</u> designer   <u>a</u> computer table

---

Do This

<u>a</u> one-time offer

<u>a</u> once-in-a-lifetime chance

Use *a* before words beginning with *o* that have a *w* sound.

Do Not Do This

<u>an</u> one-time offer

<u>an</u> once-in-a-lifetime chance

Before Long *u*.   Use *a* before words beginning with the long sound of *u*.

<u>a</u> university   <u>a</u> union

<u>a</u> unique design   <u>a</u> unilateral decision

Before *a*, *e*, *i*, *o*, and Short *u*.   Use *an* before words beginning with the vowel sounds *a*, *e*, *i*, and *o* and the short sound of *u*.

<u>an</u> oblong table   <u>an</u> unusual design

<u>an</u> interior designer   <u>an</u> accident

<u>an</u> X-ray   <u>an</u> f.o.b. order

(*X* is pronounced *ex.*)   (The letter *f* is pronounced *ef.*)

Before Silent *h*.   Use *an* before words beginning with silent *h*.

<u>an</u> hour ago   <u>an</u> honest sales staff

<u>an</u> honor   <u>an</u> honorarium

The

Use the article *the* with singular or plural nouns. Place *the* before any other adjective when two or more adjectives precede a noun.

Our consultants evaluate your needs on <u>the</u> basis of <u>the</u> information sheet that you complete.

(The first *the* refers to *basis* and the second *the* refers to *sheet*. Both *basis* and *sheet* are singular nouns. *The* precedes *information*, a descriptive adjective that also modifies *sheet*.)

<u>The</u> offices seem to have high noise levels.

(*The* refers to *offices*, a plural noun.)

Repetition of Articles

Repeat an article before *each* noun when two persons, places, or things are involved. Do not repeat an article when only one person, place, or thing is intended.

The facilities manager and <u>the</u> space planner proposed an open-office environment.

(Two people—*the* facilities manager and *the* space planner—proposed an open-office environment.)

The facilities manager and space planner proposed an open-office environment.

(The same person [*the* facilities manager is also the space planner] proposed the open-office environment. *The* is not repeated.)

Our designer thought that <u>the</u> store and showroom was beyond our budget.

(The combined store and showroom refers to one area. *The* is not repeated before *showroom*.)

CHECKPOINT 12.3

Go to the
Web

Checkpoint 12.3
for more skills practice on this topic.

A. **Instructions:** *In the space provided, write a or an, whichever is correct.*

1. OSHA report   _____
2. showroom   _____
3. eye-catching design   _____
4. hour ago   _____
5. uniform color scheme   _____
6. hundred dollars   _____

B. **Instructions:** *Select the correct word, and write it in the space provided.*

1. We need advice on (*a, an,*) wide variety of ergonomic issues.   _____
2. The company adds (*a, an, the*) extra charge if you want (*a, an, the*) furniture delivered tomorrow.   _____
3. We have seen (*a, an, the*) dramatic increase in injuries at our workplace.   _____
4. (*A, An*) union member should be on (*an, the*) building committee.   _____
5. (*An, The*) number one priority is (*a, an,*) adjustable chair.   _____
6. We hired (*a, an*) consultant to advise us about our lighting concerns.   _____
7. Our company received (*a, an*) honor for our injury-free workplace.   _____
8. (*A, An*) university professor serves as our ergonomics consultant.   _____
9. Tracey immediately filed (*a, an*) accident report after the injury.   _____
10. Amanda's proposed workstation has (*a, an*) unusual plan.   _____

Compound implies a combination of two or more parts. Compound adjectives combine two or more words to form *one* thought when they modify nouns. These words may be nouns, adjectives, participles, verbs, or adverbs. Many compound adjectives require hyphens.

Always use an up-to-date dictionary or reference manual to determine whether a compound adjective is two words or hyphenated. A dictionary entry showing a hyphenated compound adjective does *not* mean that the adjective is always hyphenated. This type of entry means that the compound adjective is hyphenated before a noun.

Compound Adjectives—Hyphenated Before and After Nouns

Use a hyphen when these compound adjective combinations appear before or after a noun or in other locations in a sentence.

year-round	(noun + adjective)
price-conscious	(noun + adjective)
decision-making	(noun + participle)
work-related	(noun + participle)
high-ranking	(adjective + participle)
long-standing	(adjective + participle)
fast-paced	(adjective + noun + *ed*)
open-ended	(adjective + noun + *ed*)

Our water-repellent furniture for the lobby should last many years.

(*Water-repellent* is a noun plus an adjective that modifies *furniture.* The compound adjective *water-repellent* requires a hyphen.)

Our new furniture for the lobby was advertised as water-repellent.

(*Water-repellent* [noun plus adjective combination] appears after the noun and requires a hyphen.)

In this fast-paced office, employees should be receptive to stress-reducing suggestions.

(*Fast-paced* [adjective plus noun plus *ed* combination] and *stress-reducing* [noun plus participle combination] appear before nouns. Both of these compound adjectives require hyphens.)

Compound Adjectives—Hyphenated Only Before Nouns

Use a hyphen when these compound adjective combinations appear before a noun. Do not use a hyphen when these combinations appear in other locations in a sentence.

low-cost	(adjective + noun)
long-range	(adjective + noun)
well-known	(adverb + participle)
ever-increasing	(adverb + participle)

scaled-down	(participle + adverb)
make-or-break	(verb + verb)
drive-through	(verb + adverb)
up-to-date	(phrase)
state-of-the-art	(phrase)
end-of-the-year	(phrase)
off-the-shelf	(phrase)

We hope to receive some <u>low-cost</u> bids from local interior designers.

(*Low-cost* combines two separate words—an adjective and a noun—to form one compound adjective that modifies *bids*. The compound adjective *low-cost* requires a hyphen.)

We were surprised that the bid was submitted at such a <u>low cost</u>.

(In this sentence, the compound adjective *low cost* [adjective and noun] appears after the noun and does not require a hyphen.)

A <u>well-known</u> safety expert identified the principal causes of factory accidents.

(*Well-known* [adverb plus participle] appears before a noun and requires a hyphen.)

We needed <u>up-to-date</u> statistics verifying our safety record at the <u>end of the year</u>.

(*Up-to-date* is a phrase that appears before a noun and requires hyphens. *End of the year* is a phrase that does not appear before a noun and does not require hyphens.)

Our <u>end-of-the-year</u> report showed a decrease in the number of employee accidents.

(*End-of-the-year* is a phrase that appears before a noun and requires hyphens.)

Common Compound Adjectives

Do not use a hyphen when an adjective plus a noun combination is widely recognized as a concept or institution. Here are some common compound adjectives that do not require hyphens:

accounts receivable	high school	real estate
branch office	income tax	social security
free trade	post office	word processing

Decorators, Inc., recently completed designing the interior of a local <u>real estate</u> office.

(*Real estate* is a recognized adjective and noun combination and does not require a hyphen.)

To become a facilities planner, you need more than a <u>high school</u> education.

(*High school* is a recognized adjective and noun combination and does not require a hyphen.)

Numbers With Nouns

Use a hyphen to connect a number (words or figures) and a noun to form a compound adjective before a noun. The second element is always singular. Do *not*

---

use a hyphen when the expression consisting of a number and noun *follows* the noun. This unit of measurement is singular or plural depending on the intent of the sentence.

> **a 6-foot acoustical panel**
>
> (The second element *foot* is singular. The combination number and noun appears before a noun and requires a hyphen.)
>
> **an acoustical panel that is 6 feet (plural)**
>
> (The number and noun follow the noun. No hyphen is necessary. The unit of measurement, *feet*, is plural.)
>
> **an eight-point proposal (*point* is singular)**
>
> **a proposal that has eight points (plural)**

Numerical Compound Adjectives

Use hyphens in the numbers between 21 and 99 when the numbers are written as words.

> **Thirty-two construction projects are in the Builders Exchange tour.**
>
> **Our note to Inside Designs is for Eighteen Thousand Two Hundred Twenty-three Dollars ($18,223).**

Series of Compound Adjectives

Use a hyphen in a series of compound adjectives even though the base noun does not follow each adjective.

> **The supervisors found the one-, two-, and four-hour tapes helpful for the employee safety workshops.**
>
> (The base noun *tapes* is not needed after each word in the series, but the hyphen after each word is necessary.)
>
> **We were warned to anticipate a two-, three-, or four-week delay of our ergonomic chair order.**
>
> (The base noun *delay* is not needed after each word in the series, but the hyphen after each word is necessary.)

"Self" Words

Use a hyphen when *self* is connected to another word to form a compound adjective.

> **self-help** **self-management** **self-evaluation**

Go to the Web

Checkpoint 12.4
for more skills practice on this topic.

CHECKPOINT 12.4

Instructions: *In the following sentences, place the proofreaders' mark for inserting a hyphen (⊼) in the correct location. If a hyphen is incorrect, use the proofreaders' mark for delete (⌒). Use a dictionary or reference manual if necessary.*

1. The ergonomics consultant did a first class analysis of our furniture needs.

2. Betty suggested curvilinear tables for the work related conference rooms.

3. Some showrooms have 20,000 square foot areas to display complete workstations.

4. If you are trying to find a short term solution, rent or lease your office furniture.

5. KD Carpets was selling its fire resistant carpet at a low-price.

6. After reading a recent branch-office agenda, I noticed that you were having a discussion on safety.

7. Twenty five employees complained about the office temperatures this month.

8. Are you attending the one, two, or three day ergonomic training session?

9. We completed a self evaluation of our working conditions.

10. The accounts-payable office calculates the social-security taxes for our ergonomic adviser.

Adjective Comparisons

Most descriptive adjectives have three degrees of comparison—positive (*long*), comparative (*longer*), and superlative (*longest*). Absolute adjectives such as *round* and *square* are not capable of realistic comparison. Dictionaries provide information about adjective comparisons.

Positive Degree

Use the positive degree as the base form of the adjective to describe one person, place, thing, quality, idea, or activity or one group of things.

light color   **large office**   **wide selection**

Daley's Office Products carries a wide selection of office furniture.

I have a large office.

Comparative Degree

Use the comparative degree to compare two people, places, ideas, qualities, activities, or things.

lighter color   **larger office**   **wider selection**

Daley's Office Products carries a wider selection of office furniture than Dunn's Furniture.

My office is larger than yours.

Do This	Do Not Do This
The offices in the executive suite are larger than the offices downstairs.	The offices in the executive suite are larger than downstairs.

State comparisons precisely. The offices are not larger than the downstairs.

Superlative Degree

Use the superlative degree to compare more than two persons, places, qualities, activities, or things.

<u>lightest</u> color   <u>largest</u> office   <u>widest</u> selection

Daley's Office Products carries the <u>widest</u> selection of office furniture that I have ever seen.

My office is the <u>largest</u> one in the building.

Guidelines for Forming Comparisons

One-Syllable Adjectives.   Add *er* to the positive form of a one-syllable adjective to form its *comparative* degree. Add *est* to the positive form of a one-syllable adjective to form its *superlative* degree.

Comparative			Superlative		
warm	+ <u>er</u>	warmer	warm	+ <u>est</u>	warmest
short	+ <u>er</u>	shorter	short	+ <u>est</u>	shortest
big	+ <u>er</u>	bigger	big	+ <u>est</u>	biggest

Two-Syllable Adjectives.   Add *er* to the positive form of a two-syllable adjective, or add the word *more* or *less* before the positive form of a two-syllable adjective to form its *comparative* degree. Add *est* to the positive form of a two-syllable adjective, or add the word *most* or *least* before the positive form of a two-syllable adjective for its *superlative* degree. The sound often determines the choice.

Positive	Comparative	Superlative
narrow	narrow<u>er</u> *or* <u>more</u> narrow	narrow<u>est</u> *or* <u>most</u> narrow
quiet	quiet<u>er</u> *or* <u>more</u> quiet	quiet<u>est</u> *or* <u>most</u> quiet
painful	<u>more</u> painful (*not* painfuler)	<u>most</u> painful (*not* painfulest)
awkward	<u>less</u> awkward	<u>least</u> awkward

Three-Syllable Adjectives.   Add the word *more* or *less* before the positive form of a three-syllable adjective for its *comparative* degree. Add the word *most* or *least* before the positive form of a three-syllable adjective for its *superlative* degree.

Positive	Comparative	Superlative
attractive	more attractive	most attractive
essential	more essential	most essential
efficient	less efficient	least efficient

Words Ending in y.   Change the *y* to *i* and add *er* or *est* to form the *comparative* and *superlative* degrees.

Positive	Comparative	Superlative
friendly	friendlier	friendliest
busy	busier	busiest
heavy	heavier	heaviest

Special Forms.   Some irregular adjectives do not form their comparatives and superlatives in the normal way.

Positive	Comparative	Superlative
good	better	best
bad	worse	worst
little	less, lesser	littlest, least
many	more	most
much	more	most

Absolute Adjectives

The positive degree may be the only degree necessary for an adjective if it already expresses the highest degree. For example, if a table is oblong, it cannot become more oblong or most oblong. A list of some absolute adjectives follows:

circular	horizontal	straight
complete	ideal	supreme
correct	instantaneous	unanimous
dead	perfect	unique
empty	single	vertical
final	square	wrong

CHECKPOINT 12.5

Go to the
Web

Checkpoint 12.5
for more skills practice on this topic.

Instructions: In the spaces provided, fill in the missing degree forms. One of the three adjective forms is already in correct order. All forms may not have missing degree forms.

	Positive	Comparative	Superlative
Ex.:	**active**	**more active**	**most active**
1.		more stressful	
2.		worse	
3.	high		
4.	reputable		
5.	difficult		
6.	easy		
7.			tallest
8.	quiet		
9.			most supportive
10.	wrong		

Go to the
Web

Checkpoint 12.6
for more skills practice on
this topic.

CHECKPOINT 12.6

Instructions: *Select the correct word or words and write them in the space provided.*

1. To lower the noise levels, we purchased (*taller, more tall*) acoustical panels. _____

2. Which of these carpet samples is the (*more, most*) practical for a lobby area? _____

3. Of the two architects, who is (*better, best*)? _____

4. Your layouts are the (*more appealing, most appealing*) of any others in the display. _____

5. The best way to decrease equipment noise is to buy (*quieter, more quieter*) equipment. _____

6. My office is always (*more warm, warmer*) than yours. _____

7. The architect recommended a (*circular, more circular*) lobby area. _____

8. Some people strike keyboards (*harder, more hard*) than necessary. _____

9. Since the first floor of our building is the (*busiest, most busiest*), we have concentrated on noise reduction strategies. _____

10. The storage room on the third floor is the (*most narrow, narrower*) space in the entire building. _____

Adjective Clauses and Phrases

NOTES

Looking Back

Refer to Chapter 7 for a review of the correct use of *that, which,* and *who.*

Sometimes clauses and phrases modify nouns or pronouns. When a phrase modifies a noun or pronoun, it is an *adjective phrase.* An adjective phrase does not have a subject or a predicate and cannot stand by itself. When a clause modifies a noun or pronoun, it is an *adjective clause.* An adjective clause is a dependent clause that has a subject and predicate, but it is not a sentence and cannot stand by itself.

Adjective Clauses

Use the relative pronouns *who, whose, which,* and *that* to connect an adjective clause to the noun or pronoun that is modified. Place the adjective clause immediately after the noun that is described. Use commas to set aside the clause when it does not add to the meaning of the sentence (nonrestrictive clause). Do not use commas to set aside the clause when the clause is necessary (restrictive) to the meaning of the sentence.

> **The employee <u>who designs the best workstation</u> will receive a prize.**
>
> (*Who* connects the adjective clause to the noun *employee.* The adjective clause *who designs the best workstation* describes the specific employee receiving the prize. The clause is necessary to the meaning of the sentence. No commas are necessary.)

The firm's main office, which is in South Carolina, compiled statistics on workplace injuries.

(*Which* refers to *office*. The clause is not necessary to the meaning of the sentence. Commas set the clause aside from the rest of the sentence.)

Adjective Phrases

When infinitive, participial, or prepositional phrases function as modifiers of nouns or pronouns, they are called adjective phrases.

Having heard the statistics on carpal tunnel syndrome, I became more aware of this disorder's effects.

(*Having heard the statistics on carpal tunnel syndrome* is a participial phrase. In this sentence, it functions as an adjective phrase modifying the pronoun *I*.)

We highly recommend the consultant from Acme Lighting.

(*From Acme Lighting* is a prepositional phrase. In this sentence, it tells *which* consultant and functions as an adjective phrase.)

The ergonomics report to be proofread immediately is on Kathy's desk.

(In this sentence, the infinitive phrase to be proofread immediately modifies the noun report and functions as an adjective.)

EDIT PATROL

On the Internet:
We bought a bushel of apples from a roadstand farmer that was rotten.
Note: Are the apples or the farmer rotten?

PUNCTUATION ALERT!

Nonessential Phrases
Use a comma to set aside nonrestrictive phrases or clauses.

Do This

Coming into the building, <u>we saw the spectacular artwork.</u>

Do Not Do This

Coming into the building, <u>the artwork was spectacular.</u>

The adjective phrase *coming into the building* modifies the pronoun *we*. The artwork is not *coming into the building.*

CHECKPOINT 12.7

Go to the Web

Checkpoint 12.7
for more skills practice on this topic.

Instructions: In the space provided, write the word that is modified by the underlined adjective phrase or clause.

1. I did not agree with the ergonomics consultant <u>who evaluated our facilities.</u> _____

2. The OSHA report <u>that I must review</u> is 55 pages. _____

3. Richley Furniture, <u>whose president is Dave Richley,</u> specializes in furniture for the physically handicapped. _____

4. My new chair, <u>which I just purchased last week,</u> does not support my lower back. _____

5. Lu Cheng, <u>who is my team leader,</u> is concerned about employees taking sufficient rest breaks. _____

Adjectives

6. Several executives in our company think that interior design is an expensive luxury. _____

7. Offices in disarray create unfavorable impressions that distract visitors. _____

8. Having analyzed my office space requirements, I ordered two multifunctional work tables. _____

Special Adjectives

Several adjectives require special attention.

Fewer/Less

Use *fewer* with plural nouns. *Fewer* refers to number. Use *less* with singular nouns that refer to degree or amount. Use *less than* before nouns that express money, percentage, time, distance, and measurements.

We noticed less noise since the construction workers left the area.

(*Less* modifies *noise,* a singular noun. *Less* refers to degree.)

Langley Telemarketers had fewer cumulative trauma disorders last year than it had in the previous year.

(*Fewer* modifies *disorders,* a plural noun. *Fewer* refers to number.)

Jason keeps the temperature in his office set for less than 70 degrees.

(*Less than* is used when referring to a measurement.)

We bought used furniture for less than $100.

(*Less than* is used when referring to money.)

Farther/Further

Use *farther* to refer to physical distance. Use *further* to mean additional.

Your architectural firm is farther from our office than I had anticipated.

Our Bloomington office is farther from office furniture stores than our Joliet office.

(In both sentences, *farther* refers to distance.)

Further help is available for workers suffering from repetitive motion injuries.

We will give the equipment survey further attention at the board meeting.

(In both sentences, *further* means additional.)

Latter/Later/Last/Latest

Use *latter* to refer to the second of two persons, places, or things mentioned. Use *later* to refer to time. Use *last* to refer to whatever follows everything else in a series. Finally, use *latest* to refer to time (as in *most recent*).

The latter set of statistics referred to work-related injuries.

The later time for the safety committee meeting was not suitable for me.

The last time that we attended an ergonomics training class was two years ago.

We just submitted the latest landscape plan for the front grounds.

CHECKPOINT 12.8

Instructions: *Select the correct word, and write it in the space provided.*

1. Jill announced that no (*farther, further*) lighting options would be considered. _____

2. After looking at the (*later, latest*) designs, I selected the one that seemed the most conservative. _____

3. We have had (*fewer, less*) accidents resulting from assembly line carelessness since we instituted safety workshops. _____

4. The (*last, latter*) book that I read on interior design was impressive. _____

5. We purchased adjustable chairs for all our employees (*less than, fewer than*) ten years ago. _____

6. I thought that the (*later, latter*) of the two building plans was creative and unique. _____

7. He spends (*fewer, less*) hours at the office because he finds the environment depressing. _____

8. The furniture that was recommended by our ergonomics specialist will cost (*less, fewer*) money than we had anticipated. _____

9. The office of the cumulative trauma disorder specialist is (*farther, further*) down the block. _____

10. (*Less than, Fewer than*) 10 percent of our employees complain about cumulative trauma disorders. _____

Go to the
Web

Checkpoint 12.8
for more skills practice on this topic.

Diagramming Sentences

In a sentence with an adjective clause, place the main clause in one diagram and the adjective clause beneath it in another diagram. Use a dotted line to connect the relative pronoun in the adjective clause to the modified noun or pronoun in the main clause.

Kathryn, who is our supervisor, plans to order new file cabinets.

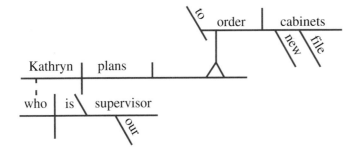

Copyright © by The McGraw-Hill Companies, Inc.

Adjectives

375

The carpet colors that I like are available.

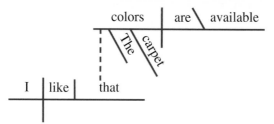

Go to the
Web

Checkpoint 12.9
for more skills practice on this topic.

CHECKPOINT 12.9

Instructions: *Diagram the following sentences in the space provided. All words in the sentences may be diagrammed.*

1. I need a new computer table that accommodates my height.

2. We bought a VDT screen that had low radiation emissions.

3. Those employees who have team responsibilities need some private space.

4. My supervisor is the person who orders the firm's office furniture.

5. A good workstation needs lighting that the workers can control.

Name _____   Date _____

Go to the
Web

Practice 1 Exercises
for more skills practice on this topic.

PRACTICE 1

Adjective Selection

Instructions: Select the correct word or words, and write them in the space provided.

1. Have you received (*a, an*) application from Clarke Watson for the position of facilities coordinator?

   1. _____

2. (*These, Them*) computer tables seem (*more sturdy, most sturdy*) than the ones at the discount stores.

   2. _____
   _____

3. We offer our employees (*a, an*) (*one hour, one-hour*) ergonomics training session.

   3. _____
   _____

4. This (*well designed, well-designed*) chair is ideal for our employees.

   4. _____

5. I know that Blakely Decorators will give us the (*better, best*) design plan for our money.

   5. _____

6. I prefer the (*more light, lighter*) of the two fabrics for the lobby furniture.

   6. _____

7. (*Thirty six, Thirty-six*) workers complained about the poor lighting in the file storage area.

   7. _____

8. To assist me in learning more about ergonomics, I purchased a (*self help, self-help*) guide.

   8. _____

9. (*Further, Farther*) evaluations of our ergonomic policies will be necessary before (*OSHA's, osha's*) visitation.

   9. _____
   _____

10. Since we installed new computer desks, we have had (*less, fewer*) complaints about fatigue.

    10. _____

Nouns and Adjectives

Instructions: In the following sentences, a noun or pronoun is underlined once. Place two lines under each adjective, adjective phrase, or adjective clause that modifies the underlined words.

1. Sometimes <u>lighting</u> is overlooked in improving work environments.

2. The company safety <u>brochure</u> to be printed tomorrow needs several changes.

3. We have received five sealed <u>bids</u>.

4. Jane buys used office <u>furniture</u> in good condition.

5. Henry's poor <u>posture</u> causes his <u>fatigue</u>.

6. These back <u>complaints</u> are painful and irritating.

7. The decorator's <u>suggestions</u> included several major decor <u>changes</u>.

8. Several American <u>manufacturers</u> produce high-quality office furniture.

Name _____ Date _____

9. Most open-office <u>environments</u> have movable <u>panels</u>.

10. Our safety <u>procedures</u> will meet OSHA's <u>standards</u>.

PRACTICE 2

Go to the
Web

Practice 2 Exercises
for more skills practice on
this topic.

Identifying Adjectives

Instructions: Underline the adjectives, adjective phrases, and adjective clauses in the following sentences. Ignore the articles a, an, *and* the.

1. Our company requires mandatory employee rest breaks.

2. After Franco uses my computer, the contrast control always needs some adjustments.

3. The building acoustics are excellent.

4. Wood lateral files give an office a professional, elegant appearance.

5. This facility's heating and cooling system has individual worker temperature controls.

6. Even though Jennifer's office space is small, she has floor-to-ceiling windows.

7. Experts suggest that an in-house facilities manager should identify potential repetitive stress risk factors.

8. Inappropriate food smells, which are often the remains of lunch, give clients a negative impression.

9. Erin's plan to study ergonomics requires additional college-level physiology and anatomy courses.

10. Both the keyboard and the mouse should be placed on the same level.

Using Adjectives Correctly

Instructions: In the space provided, correct the following sentences. These sentences will have punctuation or grammatical errors.

1. A 6 foot man requires a more different workstation than a petite woman.

   _____

2. The later of the two workers' compensation claims resulted in farther research on CTDs.

   _____

   _____

3. Chris Novelski who is our ergonomics coordinator recommended them chairs.

   _____

   _____

Name _____ Date _____

4. Thirty six percent of the employees with repetitive motion injuries lost at least 31 days of work.

_____

_____

5. Companies can improve employee performance by shifting the angle between an computer screen and the user's eyes to eliminate glare.

_____

_____

6. The supervisor at the post-office reported the injury within one-hour.

_____

_____

7. The personnel in our branch-office prefer more brighter colors.

_____

_____

8. The Department of Labor's latest report shows less injuries caused by repetitive workplace tasks.

_____

_____

Go to the
Web

Practice 3 Exercises
for more skills practice on this topic.
_____

PRACTICE 3

Proofreading

*Instructions: Proofread and compare the two sentences in each group. If they are the same, write **Yes** in the space provided. If they are not the same, write **No**. Use the first sentence as the correct copy. If you find errors in the second sentence, underline them; insert any omitted words or marks of punctuation.*

1. OSHA's ergonomics program covers four major areas—worksite analysis, prevention, medical management, and training and education.

   OSHAs ergonomics program covers major four areas—worksite analysis, prevention, medical management, and training education.

   1. _____

2. Employers and employees should understand the work patterns that may cause cumulative trauma disorders (CTDs) or repetitive motion disorders.

   Employers and employees should understand the work patterns that cause cumulative trauma disorders (CDT's) or repetitive motion disorders.

   2. _____

Name _____   Date _____

3. Ergonomics centers on such work environment areas
    as workstation design, safety devices, and lighting to
    fit the employee's physical requirements.

    Ergonomics center on such work environment areas
    as workstation design, safty devises, and lighting to
    fit the employees' physical requirements.

4. Anyone whose job demands excessive repetitive wrist
    and hand motion is a potential candidate for CTS
    (carpal tunnel syndrome).

    Anyone whose job demands excessive repetitive wrist
    and hand motions is a potential candidate for CTS
    (carpol tunnel syndrome).

5. Many companies consider the design of physical
    work spaces to be an important health and safety issue.

    Many companies consider the design of physical
    work spaces to be an important health and safety issue.

3. _____

4. _____

5. _____

Using Proofreaders' Marks

The following list identifies some of the characteristics of an ergonomically
correct workstation.

ERGONOMIC WORKSTATIONS

1. Adjustable chairs.

2. Stable chairs with 5-leg bases.

3. Adjustable backrests.

4. Task lighting for reading printed copy.

5. Adequate space for equipment.

6. Adjustable working surfaces.

7. Antiglare screens on computer monitors.

8. Adequate wiring and cabling installations for electronic
   equipment.

9. Adequate storage space for supplies, backup tapes, and personal
   items.

10. Soothing colors on large wall areas.

11. Acoustic fabrics for noise reduction.

12. Clean ventilation system.

Adjectives

Name _____ Date _____

Instructions: Use these proofreaders' marks to correct the copy that follows. Use the previous copy as your correct guide.

Make lowercase /   Move left ⌐   Insert letter ∧

Capitalize ≡   Move right ⌐   Insert comma ∧

Delete ϒ   Insert space ∧#   Transpose ∪

Delete and close up ϒ   Delete space ⌒   Insert period ⊙

Double space ds⌐   Insert hyphen ⹀

ERGONOMIC WORK STATIONS

1. Adjustable chairs
2. Stable chairs with 5 leg bases.
3. Adjustable backrests.
4. Task-lighting for reading copy.
5. Adequate space for equipment.
6. Adjustable working surfaces.
7. Anti-glare screens on computermonitors.
8. Adequate wiring and cabling installations for electronic equipment.
9. Adequate storeage space for supplies, back-up tapes and personal items.
10. Soothing colors on large wall areas.
11. Acuostic fabrics for noise reduction.
12. clean air ventilation system.

Go to the
Web

Practice 4 Exercises
for more skills practice on this topic.

PRACTICE 4

Writing

Instructions: Write a paragraph about your favorite activity that you do in your spare time. Identify all adjectives. Identify all articles. Include the following:

- At least one adjective comparison
- A series of compound adjectives
- *Fewer* or *less*
- *Farther* or *further*

Answers will vary.

Name _____ Date _____

_____

_____

_____

_____

_____

_____

_____

PRACTICE 5

Adjective Selection

Instructions: Select the correct word or words, and write them in the space provided.

1. The new safety manager seems (*most friendly, friendlier*) than Robert.

   1. _____

2. The meeting had a (*two-hour, two hour*) agenda.

   2. _____

3. You are fortunate if you have (*a, an, the*) adjustable chair and (*a, an, the*) nonglare work surface.

   3. _____

4. Privacy acoustical panels were not feasible because of the (*high-cost, high cost*).

   4. _____

5. Joan has the (*best, most best*) office.

   5. _____

6. Frank developed a (*self-imposed, self imposed*) length of time to work at his computer.

   6. _____

7. Of the two printers, we believe that this one is (*most quiet, quieter*).

   7. _____

8. Your document holder should have (*a, an, the*) dull matte finish to avoid glare.

   8. _____

9. (*Farther, Further*) assistance with ergonomics issues is necessary.

   9. _____

10. (*Ninety five, Ninety-five*) employees responded to our survey about back pain.

    10. _____

Nouns and Adjectives

Instructions: In the following sentences, a noun or pronoun is underlined once. Place two lines under each adjective, adjective phrase, or adjective clause that modifies the underlined words.

1. Peter's dark <u>office</u> seems dreary and cold.

2. Working environments shape our <u>moods</u> and <u>performances</u>.

3. I still have one additional ergonomics <u>workshop</u> to organize.

Name _____ Date _____

4. CDR Furniture sells only American-made office <u>products</u>.

5. Should I use these <u>standards</u> to determine the durability of our office products?

6. I had two work-related <u>injuries</u> last year.

7. The task lighting suggestions included Chee's latest <u>preferences</u>.

8. This new adjustable office <u>chair</u> is comfortable.

9. Waverly Interiors has the most reliable reputation of all our local design <u>studios</u>.

10. Her Brazilian fabric <u>samples</u> created a sense of warmth in our offices.

PRACTICE 6

Identifying Adjectives

Instructions: Underline the adjectives, adjective phrases, and adjective clauses in the following sentences. Ignore the articles a, an, *and* the.

1. Crown Delivery Services failed to provide a safe and hazard-free workplace; therefore, they had to pay a $12,000 compliance fine.

2. Dr. Myer's firm is a full-service ergonomics consulting company.

3. After work-site modifications, compensation claims dropped 78 percent.

4. A flat light-touch keyboard may increase hand and arm injuries.

5. We reviewed Jason Woo's work-related complaint last month.

6. The Medical Multimedia Group's Web page offered the latest information on CTD.

7. Some computer operators use T'ai Chi yoga to combat job-related injuries.

8. Excessive stress may increase blood pressure as well as the risk of cumulative trauma disorders.

9. We wanted to read further research before we adopted the alternative keyboard.

10. These well-trained OSHA investigators checked our work premises thoroughly.

Using Adjectives Correctly

Instructions: In the space provided, correct the following sentences. These sentences will have punctuation or grammatical errors.

1. OSHA which is located in Washington, D.C. has a ergonomic Web page.

_____

Name _____ Date _____

2. If I had a choice, I would select the most largest office available.

   _____

3. The long range safety committee recommended that employees receive farther training in ergonomics issues.

   _____

   _____

4. Fifty five percent of the poultry workers in the oklahoma plant have repetitive stress injuries.

   _____

   _____

5. The computer operator's monitor should be tilted to a 90 degree angle.

   _____

6. Barbara Silverstein's book about musculoskeletal symptoms will be released at the end-of-the-year.

   _____

   _____

7. We hope to see less claims for on the job injuries submitted this year.

   _____

8. The price for an U-shaped table is the lower that I have ever found.

   _____

PRACTICE 7

Proofreading

*Instructions: Proofread and compare the two sentences in each group. If they are the same, write **Yes** in the space provided. If they are not the same, write **No.** Use the first sentence as the correct copy. If you find errors in the second sentence, underline them; insert any omitted words or marks of punctuation.*

1. California became the first state in the nation to develop regulations to prevent work-related ailments such as carpal tunnel syndrome and other repetitive stress injuries.

   California became the first State in the Nation to develop regulations to prevent work related ailments such as Carpal Tunnel Syndrome and other repetitive stress injuries.

1. _____

Name _____ Date _____

2. Assembly-line workers, meat cutters, sewing machine operators, supermarket cashiers, carpenters, pianists, violinists, bank tellers, and baseball pitchers are just a few of the American workers plagued by job-related aches, pains, and nerve damage.

    Assembly-line workers, meat cutters, sewing machine operators, supermarket cashiers, carpenters, pianists, violinists, bank tellers, and baseball pitchers are just a few of the American workers plagued by job-related aches, pains, and nerve damage.

2. _____

3. Cumulative trauma disorders (CTDs) are not always caused on the job but can develop based on individual factors such as obesity, diabetes, pregnancy, and physical stresses occurring away from work.

    Cumulative trauma disorders (CTD) are not always caused on the job, but can develop based on factors such as obesity, diabetis, pregnancy, and physical stresses occuring away from work.

3. _____

4. The National Aeronautics and Space Administration (NASA) recommends the following plants to improve indoor-air quality (IAQ): thin-leafed spider plant, Chinese evergreen, peace lily, philodendron, golden pothos, ficus, mother-in-law's tongue, and English ivy.

    The National Aeronautics and Space Administration NASA recommends the following plants to improve indoor air quality (IAQ): thin-leafed spider plant, Chinese evergreen, Peace lily, philodendron, golden pothos, ficus, mother-in-laws tongue, and english ivy.

4. _____

5. Coverage for chiropractic care—considered a viable alternative therapy by many in the medical community—is not provided by all health insurance policies.

    Coverage for chiropractic care—considered a viable alternative therapy by many in the medical community—is not provided by all health insurance policies.

5. _____

Name _____ Date _____

Using Proofreaders' Marks

The following list contains workstation components and their estimated costs:

COMPUTER WORKSTATION

60-inch Computer Desk—Radius-edge Design	$404
48-inch Computer Desk	250
Corner Desk	470
Peninsula Top—Connects With Computer Desk	279
Support Column Kit—Peninsula Top	105
Peninsula Leg Kit—Peninsula Top	35
Hutch With Doors—Fits on Top of Computer Desk, 48"	335
Hutch With Doors—Fits on Top of Computer Desk, 60"	420
Articulating Keyboard Platform With Mouse Pad	198

Instructions: Use the proofreaders' marks below to correct the copy that follows. Use the previous copy as your correct guide.

Make lowercase /	Move left ⌐	Insert letter ∧
Capitalize ≡	Move right ⌐	Insert comma ∧
Delete ϙ	Insert space # ∧	Transpose ∽
Delete and close up ℓ	Delete space ◡	Insert period ⊙
Double space ds⌐	Insert hyphen = ∧	

COMPUTER WORKSTATIONS

60-inch Computer Desk—Radius Edge Design	$404
48 inch ComputerDesk	250
Corner Desk	470
Peninsula Top—Conects With Computer Desk	279
Support Column Kit—Peninsula Top 105	
Penninsula Leg Kit—Peninsula Top	35
Hutch With Doors—Fits On Top of Computer Desk, 48"	353
Hutch With Doors—Fits on Top of Computer Desk, 60"	420
Articulating Key board Platfrom With Mouse pad	198

Adjectives

Name _____ Date _____

PRACTICE 8

Writing

Too much stress is related to increased blood pressure and increased risk of cumulative trauma disorders. Here are several events that can cause stress:

1. Death of a family member
2. Personal illness
3. Illness of a family member
4. Divorce or separation
5. Relocation
6. Addition to the family
7. Marriage
8. Change in working conditions
9. Job change
10. Financial problems
11. Company layoffs
12. Job termination

Instructions: Describe a stressful situation that may have occurred to you during the last year. This situation may be an event other than one from the above list. Describe the steps that you took to cope with your stress. Identify all adjectives. Identify all articles. Include the following. Answer will vary.

- At least one adjective comparison
- A series of compound adjectives
- *Fewer* or *less*
- *Farther* or *further*

_____
_____
_____
_____
_____
_____
_____
_____
_____
_____
_____

Posttest

Instructions: *In the space provided, write the letter of the correct answer.*

1. Which parts of speech are not modified by adjectives? (1)

   a. nouns

   c. verbs

   b. pronouns

   d. adverbs

   1. _____

2. In the sentence *Tendon inflammation often results from repetitive work such as prolonged keyboarding,* the adjectives are: (2)

   a. Tendon, inflammation, repetitive, prolonged.

   b. Tendon, inflammation, work, prolonged.

   c. Tendon, repetitive, prolonged.

   d. Tendon, repetitive, work.

   2. _____

3. In the sentence *OSHA conference speakers present solutions to ergonomic problems,* the word *OSHA* functions as a: (2)

   a. proper noun.

   c. possessive adjective.

   b. proper adjective.

   d. limiting adjective.

   3. _____

4. Which phrase does *not* represent the correct use of an article? (3)

   a. a safety hazard

   c. an unusual request

   b. a honest mistake

   d. a short rest break

   4. _____

5. In the sentence *We use those checklists to analyze workstation comfort,* the function of *those* is that of: (2)

   a. a descriptive adjective.

   c. a demonstrative adjective.

   b. a possessive pronoun.

   d. a demonstrative pronoun.

   5. _____

6. Which compound adjective is *not* hyphenated correctly? (4)

   a. long-term commitment

   c. well-known cause

   b. office support function

   d. fast paced environment

   6. _____

7. The superlative for *complicated* is: (5)

   a. complicater.

   c. more complicated.

   b. complicated.

   d. most complicated.

   7. _____

8. In the sentence *Businesses implement ergonomic programs that reduce rates of injuries and illnesses,* which of the following is modified by the adjective phrase? (6)

   a. businesses

   c. rates

   b. programs

   d. ergonomic

   8. _____

9. Which sentence is *not* written correctly? (7)

   a. We had fewer work-related injuries than we had last year.

   b. We had less work-related injuries than we had last year.

   c. The ergonomics company earned less money this year.

   d. Sandi purchased fewer ergonomic keyboards last month.

   9. _____

10. Which sentence is *not* written correctly? (4)

    a. Twenty five employees complained about the temperature.

    b. We completed a self-evaluation.

    c. The one-day injury prevention seminar was informative.

    d. Did you distribute the branch office agenda?

    10. _____

11. Which sentence is *not* written correctly? (7) 11. _____

    a.   A further observation established a problem with Jerry's keyboarding technique.

    b.   Moving the file cabinets a farther distance from her desk gave Cindi more opportunities for exercise.

    c.   The latter meeting time gave me a much-needed break from my computer.

    d.   I answered the ergonomic questionnaire late last night.

12. Which sentence is *not* written correctly? (3, 4) 12. _____

    a.   Please choose among a one, two, or three hour ergonomics seminar.

    b.   The latest workplace analysis is up to date.

    c.   Last year we hired a well-known ergonomics consultant.

    d.   The one-day training session on selecting office equipment was excellent.

13. Which sentence is *not* written correctly? (5) 13. _____

    a.   December is the most accident-prone month of the year.

    b.   Taking on five new clients this month makes our workplace more hectic.

    c.   This workstation analysis seems more final.

    d.   The offices on the second floor are warmer than the offices downstairs.

14. Which sentence is *not* written correctly? (3, 6) 14. _____

    a.   Knowing that I was experiencing wrist pain, I contacted a union official.

    b.   To answer questions about ergonomics Jim did an Internet search.

    c.   The ergonomics workshop, which is next month, will be about injury prevention.

    d.   Our company will reward employees who have perfect attendance records.

15. Which sentence is *not* written correctly? (4) 15. _____

    a.   Workplace injuries usually occur in a fast-paced environment.

    b.   The end-of-year survey provided statistics on reasons for absences.

    c.   The free-trade agreement affected the delivery date of our office furniture.

    d.   I requested a 3-foot acoustical panel to reduce noise.

Chapter 13

Adverbs

OBJECTIVES

After you have studied this chapter and completed the exercises, you will be able to do the following:

1. Identify adverbs and the words they modify.

2. Differentiate between the use of adjectives and adverbs.

3. Recognize the importance of the placement of adverbs.

4. Form the comparative and superlative degrees of regular and irregular adverbs.

5. Recognize and correct double negatives and other incorrect uses of negative words.

6. Use special adverbs correctly.

Workplace Applications: Ethics and Etiquette

As children, we developed many of our basic morals and values. We continue to reevaluate and readjust our value systems throughout our lives. As Dr. Albert Schweitzer said, "Ethics is the name we give to our concern for good behavior. We feel an obligation to consider not only our own personal well-being, but also that of others and of human society as a whole." The principles of right and wrong that guide our decisions affecting others are called *ethics*.

Surrounding us, however, is evidence of good people choosing to do what they know is wrong. Students cheat on tests or claim the work of others as their own. Employees manipulate budgets and expenses or steal office supplies for their personal use. People gossip, "play politics," or lie to customers.

Developing Codes of Conduct

All of us routinely face ethical dilemmas. Sometimes a clear choice exists between right and wrong. In other cases, we know what is right or wrong but feel concern for ourselves or our future when challenging the wrong action. We then compromise our values and justify our actions.

To help employees with ethical decision making, the majority of businesses provide frameworks for making ethical decisions. Ethical frameworks may include developing codes of conduct or sets of standards, supporting people in making ethical decisions, and training employees for their ethical responsibilities.

As employees carefully make decisions in an ethical environment, they take comfort in knowing how rightness, fairness, and goodness are defined within their organization. Ethical employees apply the rules of proper business etiquette and always treat their colleagues and customers with respect. An ethical business operates consistently and predictably with committed employees.

Pretest

Instructions: In the space provided, write the letter of the correct answer.

1. In the sentence *Dishonest behavior has ramifications in virtually every society,* the adverb *virtually* modifies: (1)

   a. a verb.   c. a noun.

   b. an adjective.   d. an adverb.

1. _____

2. In the sentence *Vance Motors always resolves its sales negotiations in a professional manner,* the adverb is: (1)

   a. professional.   c. always.

   b. resolves.   d. manner.

2. _____

3. In the sentence *If you must leave a meeting, do so quietly,* the adverb answers the question: (1)

   a. How?   c. Where?

   b. When?   d. To what extent or degree?

3. _____

4. In the sentence *Emotionally disturbed people may have very distorted views of ethical behavior,* you will find: (2)

   a. four adjectives and one adverb.   c. four adjectives and no adverbs.

   b. two adjectives and three adverbs.   d. three adjectives and two adverbs.

4. _____

5. Which one of the following sentences is correct? (2)

   a. Lois felt badly after she took the office supplies home.

   b. Once the ethical issue was solved, we carefully outlined our next project.

   c. Some managers act ethical at home, but they cheat at work.

   d. We looked close at the company's code of ethics.

5. _____

6. Which of the following lines correctly represents the *comparative* degree of adverbs? (4)

   a. more frequently; more slower   c. calmlier; more widely

   b. more likely; most strongly   d. more precisely; sooner

6. _____

7. Which of the following sentences is *not* correct? (5)

   a. I could not hardly believe such deceitful merchandising.

   b. I have never understood the term *situational ethics.*

   c. I will have no difficulty locating a current book on etiquette.

   d. Separating personal ethics from business ethics is not easy.

7. _____

8. Which one of the following sentences is *not* correct? (6)

   a. Michaela works very well in an atmosphere of open communication.

   b. Is low morale really a problem in your firm?

   c. Yolanda was sure surprised with her appointment to the ethics committee.

   d. Almost all difficult choices require an analysis of values.

8. _____

9. In the sentence *Bruce always remembers his clients' names and sincerely appreciates their business,* you will find: (2)

   a. three adverbs and two adjectives.

   b. two adverbs and three adjectives.

   c. one adverb and four adjectives.

   d. three adverbs and no adjectives.

9. _____

10. Which sentence is written correctly? (3)   10. _____
    a. Lindsey schedules a meeting only when she has a purpose for one.
    b. Lindsey schedules a meeting when she has a purpose for one only.
    c. Lindsey schedules a meeting when she only has a purpose for one.
    d. Lindsey schedules only a meeting when she has a purpose for one.

11. Which sentence is written correctly? (3, 4)   11. _____
    a. Her new ethics book is exceptionally informative.
    b. Carolyn always answers customers' questions quick.
    c. Clint is very, very courteous to his clients.
    d. Padeo phrased the question more precise the second time.

12. Which sentence is written correctly? (3, 4)   12. _____
    a. The latest ethics survey results dramatically are different from the results five years ago.
    b. The ethics section in our policies manual is the most longest of all sections.
    c. Studies show that workplace disagreements affect employee morale more fast than anything else.
    d. Cyndi eventually changed jobs because of incivility in her former workplace.

13. Which sentence is *not* written correctly? (6)   13. _____
    a. We almost completed the final plans for our ethics workshop.
    b. She was real pleased with the number of employees who completed the ethics survey.
    c. Was the lack of courtesy the real reason for the customer's complaint?
    d. Most employees understand the formal rules of dining etiquette.

14. Which sentence is *not* written correctly? (6)   14. _____
    a. Sometimes ethical dilemmas are difficult to solve.
    b. We should review the firm's code of ethics some time.
    c. I felt good when the members of the identity theft gang were convicted.
    d. Our formal ethics training workshops work well for our employees.

15. Which sentence is *not* written correctly? (2, 3)   15. _____
    a. Ethical decision making results in mutually-beneficial relationships between management and staff.
    b. A former client calls repeatedly with comments about the discourteous treatment that he received from our sales associates.
    c. Gil reacted badly to the false rumors about his personal problems.
    d. Properly conducted meetings are based on good manners and respect for everyone in attendance.

Chapter Preview

Adjectives and adverbs have some similarities. Both modify other parts of speech, and both have degrees of comparison. Many adverbs have adjective bases. Sometimes making a choice between using an adverb or an adjective is confusing.

An adverb adds specificity to a sentence. Correct adverb use will help you express your thoughts more precisely and clearly. The different placements of an adverb such as *only* can change the meaning of a sentence. Using a double negative makes a sentence sound child-like or unintelligent. In this chapter, your study of adverbs will include the general use of adverbs as well as several adverbs that require special attention.

Identification of Adverbs

An adverb makes a sentence more precise. An adverb answers the questions *how, when, where,* and *to what extent or degree.* In addition to these questions, an adverbial clause often answers the question *why.* A later section covers adverbial clauses.

How? In what manner?	carefully, quickly, loudly, proudly, neatly, well
When?	yesterday, immediately, often, now, again, then, formerly
Where?	outside, there, down, forward, upward, away
To what extent? Degree?	very, too, greatly, quite, gradually, rather, extremely

Go to the
Web

Checkpoint 13.1
for more skills practice on this topic.

CHECKPOINT 13.1

*Instructions: In the space provided, identify the type of question answered by each underlined adverb. Use the following codes: **A** (How?), **B** (When?), **C** (Where?), **D** (To what extent?).*

1. If someone is having trouble opening a door, move <u>quickly</u> to assist the individual. _____

2. Company personnel must go <u>outside</u> if they want to smoke. _____

3. If you ever lose your temper, apologize <u>immediately</u>. _____

4. The workers have <u>very</u> high morals and adhere to strict ethical standards. _____

Copyright © by The McGraw-Hill Companies, Inc.

5. If you borrow something, return it <u>promptly</u>. _____

6. My colleagues suggested that I step <u>forward</u> to report a policy violation. _____

7. A company's code of ethics must be <u>correctly</u> enforced. _____

8. My supervisor treats all company personnel <u>considerately</u>. _____

Functions of Adverbs

Both adjectives and adverbs are modifiers. Adjectives modify only nouns and pronouns. Adverbs modify verbs, adjectives, and other adverbs. Adverbs *never* modify nouns and pronouns.

Modify Verbs

Use an adverb to modify a verb. Place the adverb before or after the verb that is modified.

> **The law <u>generally</u> <u>sets</u> the minimum acceptable rules for measuring ethical behaviors.**

> (*Generally* is the adverb that modifies the verb *sets*. The adverb appears before the verb.)

> **In some countries, businesspeople will <u>bow</u> <u>slightly</u> and shake hands as an indication of good manners.**

> (*Slightly* is the adverb that modifies the verb *bow*. The adverb appears after the verb.)

Modify Adjectives

Use an adverb to modify an adjective. Place the adverb immediately before the adjective.

> **In some cases, it is <u>truly</u> <u>difficult</u> to separate individual ethics from business ethics.**

> (*Difficult* is an adjective that follows the linking verb *is*. *Difficult* modifies the subject *it*. *Truly* is an adverb that modifies the adjective *difficult*.)

> **We are <u>extremely</u> <u>suspicious</u> of any person who misuses his or her authority.**

> (*Extremely* is an adverb that appears before the adjective *suspicious* and modifies it.)

Modify Other Adverbs

Use an adverb to modify another adverb. Place the adverb immediately before the adverb being modified.

> **Several employees wanted to have the discrimination issue outlined <u>very</u> <u>precisely</u>.**

> (*Very* is an adverb that modifies the adverb *precisely*. *Precisely* modifies the verb *outlined*.)

> **The speaker at the ethics seminar spoke <u>too</u> <u>rapidly</u>.**

> (*Too* is an adverb that modifies the adverb *rapidly*. *Rapidly* modifies the verb *spoke*.)

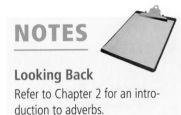

NOTES

Looking Back
Refer to Chapter 2 for an introduction to adverbs.

NOTES

Looking Back
Refer to Chapter 9 for a review of linking verbs.

Copyright © by The McGraw-Hill Companies, Inc.

Do This	**Do Not Do This**
Mary Jo is <u>polite</u>.	Mary Jo is <u>very</u>, <u>very</u> polite.
or	
Mary Jo is <u>very</u> polite.	

Do not use the phrase *very very*. This is redundant usage that adds nothing more to the meaning.

Go to the
Web

Checkpoint 13.2
for more skills practice on this topic.

 ## CHECKPOINT 13.2

Instructions: Underline the adverb(s) in each of the following sentences. In the space provided, write the word that is being modified by the underlined adverb. Then write the part of speech of the word being modified. Use the following codes: **V** *(verb),* **Adj** *(adjective),* **Adv** *(adverb).*

1. The ethics of our colleagues may strongly affect our behavior at work. _____

2. The Social Venture Network (SVN) is a national organization of socially conscious business leaders. _____

3. A receptionist who understands confidentiality issues is vitally important to a firm. _____

4. Many businesses' community contributions reflect positively on their reputations. _____

5. When supervisors handle sensitive issues, they need to proceed very cautiously. _____
_____

6. The ethics workshop was rather long. _____

7. When businesses knowingly deceive customers, they are violating ethical standards. _____

8. Greeting colleagues within your firm is a universally acceptable courtesy in the United States. _____

Formation of Adverbs

You can form many adverbs from adjective root words. The following guidelines will help you identify adjectives and adverbs. These guidelines will also help you spell adverbs correctly.

Adjective Base Used to Form Adverbs

Add *ly* to an adjective root to form the majority of adverbs.

Adjective	Adverb	Adjective	Adverb
cautious	cautiously	honest	honestly
clear	clearly	polite	politely
extreme	extremely	skillful	skillfully

Noun Base Used to Form Adjectives Ending in *ly*

Use root words to identify words ending in *ly* as adjectives or adverbs. Although many adverbs end in *ly,* some adjectives also end in *ly.* Most of these adjectives are formed by adding *ly* to a noun root.

Noun	Adjective	Noun	Adjective
cost	costly	love	lovely
elder	elderly	neighbor	neighborly
friend	friendly	world	worldly

Adverbs Formed From Adjectives Ending in *y*

Change the *y* to *i* and add *ly* to an adjective ending in *y* to form an adverb.

Adjective	Adverb	Adjective	Adverb
angry	angrily	heavy	heavily
busy	busily	ordinary	ordinarily
easy	easily	satisfactory	satisfactorily

Adverbs Formed From Adjectives Ending in *ible* or *able*

Drop the final *e* on adjectives that end in *able* or *ible* before adding the *y* to form the adverb.

Adjective	Adverb	Adjective	Adverb
acceptable	acceptably	horrible	horribly
considerable	considerably	sensible	sensibly
forcible	forcibly	terrible	terribly

Adverbs Formed From Adjectives Ending in *ic*

Add *ally* to adjectives ending in *ic* to form the adverb.

Adjective	Adverb	Adjective	Adverb
automatic	automatically	drastic	drastically
basic	basically	logic	logically
chronic	chronically	specific	specifically

Other Adverbs

Although there are many adverbs that may be identified with the *ly* ending, there are other adverbs that do *not* end in *ly.* Following is a list that includes some of these other adverbs:

again	how	not	seldom	too
almost	inside	now	since	up
always	just	often	sometimes	very
down	more	once	soon	well
far	much	quite	then	when
here	near	rather	there	where

NOTES

Adverb Questions

Remember to ask the questions *how* or *in what manner, when, where,* and *to what extent or degree* when you identify any adverb.

Do This	**Do Not Do This**
The ethics report is <u>nowhere</u> in the room.	The ethics report is <u>nowheres</u> in the room.

Do not use *anywheres* or *nowheres*. Neither word is correct English. Use *anywhere* or *nowhere*.

Do Not Hyphenate Adverbs Ending in *ly*

Do not hyphenate an expression made up of an adverb ending in *ly* and an adjective. These expressions are not compound adjectives (which often require hyphens) but adverbs followed by adjectives.

   an <u>extremely</u> loud environment

   a <u>universally</u> acceptable greeting

Go to the
Web

Checkpoint 13.3
for more skills practice on this topic.

CHECKPOINT 13.3

A. **Instructions:** *If a word in the following list is an adverb, write* **Yes** *in the space provided. If a word is not an adverb, write the correct adverb form.*

1. short _____
2. always _____
3. intense _____
4. now _____
5. particularly _____
6. inside _____
7. specific _____
8. cautious _____

9. horrible _____
10. hasty _____
11. seldom _____
12. immediate _____
13. again _____
14. quite _____
15. unfair _____

B. **Instructions:** *Underline each adverb in the following sentences.*

1. We are constantly reviewing our policy manual, and we will soon be writing a code of ethics.

2. We must determine here and now to make this a safe workplace.

3. Our presenter emphatically stated that good table manners were very important at business functions.

4. The CEO often mentioned that a decrease in ethical behavior would definitely have a negative impact on a business.

5. Grumpy people may truly not realize that their negativity affects others.

Use of Adverbs or Adjectives

Making the correct choice of an adjective or an adverb is important in writing sentences. In most cases, the type of verb in the sentence indicates the need for an adjective or an adverb.

Verbs—Action Versus Linking

Use an adverb to modify action verbs. Use an adjective, not an adverb, after a linking verb to describe the subject.

Interest in the social responsibilities of businesses increased considerably this past year.

(The action verb *increased* requires the adverb *considerably* as a modifier. Do not use the adjective *considerable*.)

The malicious rumors badly damaged the supervisor's reputation.

(The action verb *damaged* requires the adverb *badly* as a modifier.)

The supervisor felt bad about the lack of an internal hiring practice.

(The adjective *bad* follows the sense verb *felt* and describes the subject *supervisor.* Do not use the adverb *badly*.)

The firm's pollution control options seem limitless.

(The linking verb *seem* requires the adjective *limitless*. *Limitless* describes the subject *options*.)

Verbs—Both Linking and Action

Clarify the intent of the sentence before making a decision about such verbs as *look, taste,* or *feel*. These verbs may be either action verbs or linking verbs. Use adverbs when these verbs are action verbs. Use adjectives when these verbs function as linking verbs.

She looked frantically for another lawyer to handle her age discrimination suit.

(The verb *looked* functions as an action verb and requires the adverb modifier *frantically*.)

Things looked bad for our company during the time of the harassment hearings.

(The verb *looked* functions as a linking verb and does not indicate action. The adjective *bad* describes the subject *things*. Do not use the adverb *badly*.)

He appeared briefly at the preliminary hearing for a former employee.

(The verb *appeared* functions as an action verb and requires the adverb modifier *briefly*.)

She appeared relieved after she talked to her supervisor about a colleague's action.

(The verb *appeared* functions as a linking verb and does not indicate action. The adjective *relieved* describes the pronoun *she*.)

Adjectives and Adverbs With the Same Form

Some adverbs and adjectives that have the same form include *fast, first, last, early,* and *right.* Use an adjective to modify a noun or pronoun. Use an adverb to modify verbs, adjectives, and other adverbs.

Kim arrived early for the business etiquette seminar.

(*Early* is an adverb that modifies the verb *arrived.*)

I prefer an early hour for attending the business etiquette seminar.

(*Early* is an adjective that modifies the noun *hour.*)

Go to the
Web

Checkpoint 13.4
for more skills practice on this topic.

CHECKPOINT 13.4

Instructions: Select the correct word, and write it in the space provided.

1. The human resources department monitors fair hiring practices (*close, closely*). _____

2. Corporate donations (*definite, definitely*) improve the cultural life of a community. _____

3. Krogan Insurance responded (*quick, quickly*) to its workers' concerns. _____

4. The mission statement that included a section on the firm's social responsibilities is (*perfect, perfectly*). _____

5. His argument for more company responsibility for a clean environment was (*powerful, powerfully*). _____

6. When you receive an invitation, respond to it (*prompt, promptly*). _____

7. She felt (*bad, badly*) about the misunderstanding. _____

8. Sam realized that the sales managers needed etiquette training (*bad, badly*). _____

Comparisons of Adverbs

Adverbs form comparisons in ways that are similar to those of adjectives. Adverbs also have three degrees of comparison—*positive, comparative,* and *superlative.* Some adverbs (*absolute*) do not allow comparisons. With the comparative degree, you compare two persons or things; with the superlative degree, you compare three or more persons or things.

Guidelines for Using Comparisons

One-Syllable Adverbs. Add *er* to the positive form of a one-syllable adverb to form its comparative degree. Add *est* to the positive form of a one-syllable adverb to form its superlative degree.

Positive	Comparative	Superlative
fast	faster	fastest
slow	slower	slowest
soon	sooner	soonest

I must leave soon.

(*Soon* modifies the verb *leave*. *Soon* is the positive form and indicates that there is no comparison involved.)

Rick works faster than Gary.

(*Faster* modifies *works* and indicates the comparison of the two people, *Rick* and *Gary*. In this sentence the verb *works* does not appear with the subject *Gary* but is understood.)

Two-Syllable Adverbs. Some two-syllable adverbs form their comparative and superlative degrees by adding *er* or *est* to their positive forms. Other two-syllable adverbs form their comparative and superlative degrees by placing *more* (*less*) or *most* (*least*) before the adverb. Sometimes, either method is correct.

Positive	Comparative	Superlative
often	more (or less) often	most (or least) often
smoothly	more smoothly	most smoothly
quickly	more quickly	most quickly
early	earlier	earliest

The complaint that we hear most often involves impolite employees.

(*Most often* modifies *hear* and implies a comparison of many complaints.)

Three-Syllable Adverbs. Add the word *more* or *less* before the positive form of a three-syllable adverb to form its comparative degree. Add the word *most* or *least* before the positive form of a three-syllable adverb to form its superlative degree.

Positive	Comparative	Superlative
carefully	more carefully	most carefully
hurriedly	more hurriedly	most hurriedly

This safety device operates more reliably than the one that I used yesterday.

(*Reliably* modifies the verb *operates*. *More* modifies *reliably* and indicates the comparison of two items.)

The third ethics policy is the most accurately documented.

(*Accurately* modifies the adjective *documented*. *Most* modifies *accurately* and implies a comparison of many policies.)

Irregular Adverbs

Use irregular comparisons for some adverbs.

Positive	Comparative	Superlative
well	better	best
badly	worse	worst

Janine works <u>well</u> under pressure, but she is often abrupt with her team members.

(*Well* modifies the verb *works*. *Well* is the positive form and indicates that there is no comparison involved.)

Can you think of a time that I behaved <u>worse</u> than I did today?

(*Worse* is the comparative form of *badly*. In this sentence, *worse* compares a time in the past with today.)

Absolute Adverbs

Some adverbs do not allow for comparisons. The list includes such adverbs as *no, now, past, there, here, too, very, partly, annually, basically,* and *sometimes.*

Some agree that we need additional ethics courses <u>now</u>.

(*Now* is absolute; you do not refer to *more now* or *most now* or *less now* or *least now*. *Now* tells when we need additional courses.)

Global Concepts gives ethics awards <u>annually</u>.

(*Annually* is absolute; you do not refer to *more annually, most annually, less annually,* or *least annually*. *Annually* tells when.)

Go to the
Web

Checkpoint 13.5
for more skills practice on this topic.

CHECKPOINT 13.5

A. **Instructions:** *In the spaces provided, fill in the missing adverb degree forms.*

	Positive	Comparative	Superlative
Ex.:	sweetly	more sweetly	most sweetly
1.		more casually	
2.	late		
3.	efficiently		
4.			soonest
5.		more accurately	

B. **Instructions:** *Complete each sentence by writing the correct comparative or superlative form of the modifier indicated in parentheses.*

1. Some companies keep track of office supplies (*close*) than others. _____

2. The revised hiring practices went into effect (*soon*) than we had expected. _____

3. We finally completed the (*careful*) constructed set of ethical guidelines that we have ever written. _____

4. Try putting a smile in your voice to make it (*lively*). _____
   _____

5. She thinks that today's business students respond (*ethical*) _____
   than the students did five years ago. _____

6. Theresa answers the telephone the (*courteous*) of all the _____
   sales associates in the office.

7. Fraud occurs (*frequent*) when the economy is poor than _____
   when the economy is good.

8. The company's policy on confidentiality was (*wide*) _____
   accepted than we had anticipated.

9. Understanding the fine print is the (*difficult*) aspect of _____
   this job. _____

10. Listening to my coworker's angry tirade was one of the _____
    (*badly*) situations that occurred this week.

Cautions for Using Adverbs

Several adverbs require special attention. This includes the use of negative words such as *never* and *not,* contractions, double negatives, and the placement of such adverbs as *nearly, merely,* and *only.*

Negative Words

A number of negative words are adverbs. These include *barely, hardly, never, no, not, nowhere,* and *scarcely.* The contraction *n't,* which means *not,* is also an adverb. A contraction is a word with one or more letters omitted.

Not and ***Never.*** Use *not* in a negative statement. In most cases, place the word *not* between the helping verb and the main verb in a sentence. Use *never* as a stronger word than *not* to mean "at no time." If *not* will suffice, refrain from using *never.*

Some people simply do <u>not</u> use good judgment in making decisions.

(*Not* is an adverb that modifies the verb phrase *do use.*)

Proper sales etiquette <u>never</u> goes out of style.

(*Never* is an adverb that modifies the verb *goes. Never* means "at no time" in this sentence.)

Contractions. Use an apostrophe to take the place of the missing letter or letters in such words as *aren't, doesn't, can't, wouldn't, hasn't, don't,* and *isn't.*

She <u>doesn't</u> expect support from management regarding her harassment claim.

(*Doesn't* is a contraction for *does not.*)

They <u>didn't</u> apologize for their rude behavior.

(*Didn't* is a contraction for *did not.*)

Double Negatives

A double negative is a sentence construction in which two negative words are used when one is sufficient. This combination gives the clause a positive meaning rather than the intended negative meaning.

Avoid double negatives in the same clause if the intent of the clause is supposed to be negative. Correct a double negative by deleting one of the negative words.

Incorrect

I have **not** seen **no** evidence of unethical sales tactics in this store.

Corrected

I **have seen** no evidence of unethical sales tactics in this store.

I **have not seen any** evidence of unethical sales tactics in this store.

Incorrect

She **couldn't hardly** believe the statistics about white-collar crime.

Corrected

She **could hardly** believe the statistics about white-collar crime.

She **could not** believe the statistics about white-collar crime.

Placement of *Only, Merely,* and *Nearly*

Place the adverb *only* immediately before the word or group of words that it modifies. Place the adverbs *merely* and *nearly* as close as possible to the words modified. Clarify the intent of the sentence before using these adverbs. Sentence meanings may change with different placements.

Only Barry wants the code of ethics in the policies and procedures manual.

(Barry is the only person who wants the code of ethics in the policies and procedures manual.)

Barry wants only the code of ethics in the policies and procedures manual.

(Barry wants the code of ethics to be the one and only item in the policies and procedures manual.)

Barry wants the code of ethics in the policies and procedures manual only.

(Barry does not want the code of ethics to appear anywhere else but in the policies and procedures manual.)

Tony proofread nearly every line of the new ethics code.

(*Nearly* is an adverb that modifies *every.*)

Go to the Web

Checkpoint 13.6
for more skills practice on this topic.

CHECKPOINT 13.6

Instructions: *In the space provided, correct the following sentences. If the sentence is correct, write* **Yes.**

1. The company insists that it never did nothing illegal with its price structuring.

_____

_____

2. It is'nt always easy to make a decision that will benefit the most people.

   _____

   _____

3. Human resources personnel knew that the firm did not have a clear-cut process for
   reporting harassment.

   _____

4. I can't hardly believe that she was so rude to a client.

   _____

   _____

   _____

5. I don't have no contact with colleagues involved in office politics.

   _____

   _____

   _____

6. Illegal insider trading couldn't never happen here.

   _____

   _____

7. After the lecture on ethical behavior in corporations, the students didn't ask no
   questions.

   _____

   _____

   _____

   _____

8. You can't expect to make no sales if you are discourteous to customers.

   _____

   _____

CHECKPOINT 13.7

Go to the
Web

Checkpoint 13.7
for more skills practice on
this topic.

Instructions: *In the space provided, write the word that is modified by the underlined
word.*

1. She used a PowerPoint presentation that <u>only</u> those people   _____
   in the front rows could read.

2. Ethical behavior should be the <u>only</u> acceptable behavior.   _____

3. We know that it is <u>only</u> good manners to introduce new   _____
   employees to the rest of the staff.

4. He heard <u>only</u> positive viewpoints from his coworkers.   _____

5. By putting our customers first, we gained <u>nearly</u> 50 accounts.   _____

6. In our firm, <u>only</u> top-level executives receive stock options. _____

7. <u>Nearly</u> every employee has picked up the new ethics guidelines. _____

8. I <u>merely</u> was delayed ten minutes, but I apologized to the _____ group anyway.

Adverb Clauses

When a clause modifies a verb, an adjective, or an adverb, it is an adverb clause. An *adverb clause* is a dependent clause that has a subject and a predicate. A dependent clause is not a sentence and cannot stand by itself.

Adverb Clauses

In addition to answering the question of *How? In what manner? When? Where?* or *To what extent or degree?* an adverb clause often answers the question *Why?* Use subordinating conjunctions such as *after, although, before, because, if, unless, when,* and *while* to introduce dependent adverb clauses. Place the adverb clauses as closely as possible to the words modified. Use commas after introductory adverb clauses that precede independent clauses. Generally, do not use commas to set aside adverb clauses that follow independent clauses.

Kayla always greets the guests <u>before a meeting begins</u>.

(*Before* connects the dependent adverb clause *before a meeting begins* to the independent clause *Kayla always greets the guests.* No comma is necessary since the adverb clause *follows* the independent clause.)

<u>When you answer the telephone</u>, ask for the name of the caller politely.

(*When you answer the telephone* is a dependent adverb clause that introduces the independent clause. Use a comma after the introductory adverb clause.)

PUNCTUATION ALERT!

Introductory Adverb Clause

Use a comma after an introductory adverb clause. Generally, do not use a comma when the adverb clause follows an independent clause.

Go to the
Web

Checkpoint 13.8
for more skills practice on this topic.

CHECKPOINT 13.8

Instructions: In the following sentences, underline the adverb clauses once.

1. Do not allow others to read the company's confidential materials while you are away from your desk.

2. She organized her notes as soon as the ethics workshop was completed.

3. I prefer to work where ethics guidelines are clearly defined.

4. You must respect yourself before you can accept others' differences and opinions.

5. Because she was such a detail-oriented person, we expected her to find our errors.

6. Several of my coworkers voiced their approval when the manager announced the decision to offer ethical decision-making seminars.

7. I did not return her e-mail because I was upset.

8. Carlos has flown over 5000 miles since he started offering etiquette training workshops.

Special Adverbs

In Chapter 12, you learned the differences between the adjectives *farther* and *further*. In this chapter, you will study these words as adverbs. You will also study several other adverbs that require special attention.

NOTES

Further, Farther

The definitions for the adverbs *further* and *farther* are the same as those for the adjectives *further* and *farther*, but their functions in sentences are different.

Farther/Further (Adverbs)

Use *farther* to refer to physical distance. Use *further* to mean additional or additionally.

To conduct business today, salespeople must travel <u>farther</u> from their homes. (adverb)

(*Farther* is an adverb that modifies the verb *travel*.)

We explained <u>further</u> our decision to move the production plant to South America. (adverb)

(*Further* is an adverb that modifies the verb *explained*.)

Good/Well

Use *good* as an adjective. Use *well* as an adverb. Use *well* as an adjective in reference to the state of someone's health.

I always feel <u>good</u> after I have helped someone.

(*Good* is an adjective that means "in good spirits." *Good* modifies the pronoun *I*.)

The firm's family-leave proposal has worked very <u>well</u>.

(*Well* is an adverb that modifies the verb *has worked*.)

She knew that her child was not <u>well</u> but felt that she had to be at work.

(*Well* is an adjective that indicates the state of someone's health. *Well* modifies the noun *child*.)

Most/Almost

Use *almost* as an adverb to mean "nearly." Use *almost* if the word *nearly* can be substituted. Use *most* as a limiting adjective to modify a noun. Also, use *most* as the superlative degree in a comparison.

Joan is <u>almost</u> finished with the ethics survey.

(*Almost* is an adverb that may be interchanged with the word *nearly*.)

<u>Most</u> managers treat employees fairly.

(*Most* is an adjective that modifies the noun *managers*.)

The union members liked the profit-sharing plan <u>most</u>.

(*Most* is an adverb that modifies the verb *liked* and indicates the superlative degree of comparison.)

Real/Really

Use *real* as a descriptive adjective to mean "genuine." Do not use *real* to modify another adjective. Use *really* as an adverb to modify a verb or an adjective. *Really* used as an adverb to modify a verb means *genuinely* or *actually*. When *really* is used as an adverb to modify an adjective, substitute *very* for the word *really* to determine if *really* is the correct word.

I never understood Penny's <u>real</u> reason for lying to her supervisor.

(*Real* is an adjective that modifies the noun *reason*.)

Ben gave a <u>really</u> good summary of his liberal views regarding the social responsibilities of business.

(*Really* is an adverb that modifies the adjective *good*. Substitute *very* for *really*. *Very* sounds satisfactory, which indicates *really* is the correct word.)

What does civility in the office <u>really</u> mean?

(*Really* is an adverb that modifies the verb phrase *does mean*. Substitute the word *actually* to determine if *really* is the correct word.)

Sometime/Sometimes/Some Time

Use *sometime* as an adverb to mean "at some unscheduled time" or "in the future." Use *sometimes* as an adverb to mean "on some occasions." Use *some time* as a phrase in which the adjective *some* modifies the noun *time*. *Some time* designates an "amount of time."

We are going to review the basics of telephone etiquette <u>sometime</u> next week.

(*Sometime* is an adverb that modifies the adjective *next*.)

<u>Sometimes</u> we make inaccurate snap judgments.

(*Sometimes* is an adverb that modifies the verb *make*.)

To recover the stolen computer equipment will require <u>some time</u>.

(*Some time* is two words—the adjective *some* and the noun *time*.)

Sure/Surely

Use *sure* as an adjective. Use *surely* as an adverb to mean "without a doubt."

They thought that a child-care center on-site was the <u>sure</u> solution for high absenteeism rates.

(*Sure* is an adjective modifying *solution*.)

Mary Ellen <u>surely</u> makes every attempt to be courteous to all clients.

(*Surely* is an adverb that modifies the verb *makes*.)

Go to the
Web

Checkpoint 13.9
for more skills practice on this topic.

CHECKPOINT 13.9

Instructions: *Select the correct word, and write it in the space provided.*

1. Northwestern Community College will offer students an ethics workshop (*some time, sometime, sometimes*) next month. _____

2. Scott (*sure, surely*) investigated appropriate manners for conducting business in the eastern European countries. _____

3. (*Almost, Most*) employees face tough ethical choices regularly. _____

4. The employees were (*real, really*) pleased with the CEO's statement about the importance of ethics. _____

5. The safety figures looked (*good, well*) after the company added new equipment. _____

6. No one commented (*farther, further*) about incivility in the workplace. _____

7. We will have to discuss policy violations at (*some time, sometime, sometimes*) in the future. _____

8. Rhonda handles her many responsibilities (*good, well*). _____

9. We were (*real, really*) determined to improve our voice mail system. _____

10. Shall we speak (*farther, further*) about your concerns tomorrow at 2 p.m.? _____

Diagramming Sentences

In sentences with adverbs, place the adverb on a slanted line below the word it modifies. In diagramming contractions, place the *n't* on a slanted line below the verb.

Adverb Modifying a Verb

Our receptionist greets clients professionally.

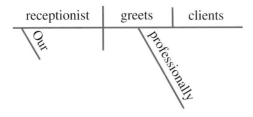

Adverb Modifying an Adjective

The clearly marked copy was our legal proof.

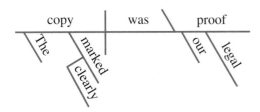

Adverb Modifying Another Adverb

Good manners very clearly reflect your company's image.

Contraction

Royalton Plastics didn't win the ethics award.

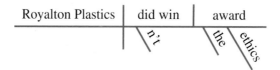

Go to the
Web

Checkpoint 13.10
for more skills practice on
this topic.

 CHECKPOINT 13.10

Instructions: *Diagram each sentence in the space provided. Use all words in the sentences.*

1. The company finally stopped its negative advertisements.

2. We can discuss the etiquette issue rather quickly.

3. Linda uses the office telephone excessively.

4. Socially responsible companies that treat their employees fairly are successful.

5. Senn Industries generously supports local charities.

Name _____ Date _____

PRACTICE 1

Go to the
Web
_____

Practice 1 Exercises
for more skills practice on
this topic.
_____

Choosing Adverbs and Adjectives

Instructions: Select the correct word or words, and write them in the space provided.

1. When someone is introduced to you, shake hands
   (*firm, firmly*).

   1. _____

2. I felt (*bad, badly*) about the company's unethical
   investment tactics.

   2. _____

3. We rely on the integrity of (*almost, most*) everyone
   with whom we work.

   3. _____

4. I took a (*real, really*) interesting class called
   Business Ethics and Social Responsibility.

   4. _____

5. Those who attended the Etiquette in Global
   Business lectures (*sure, surely*) enjoyed them.

   5. _____

6. Hope responded to the company picnic invitation
   (*quickly, more quickly*) than Melanie.

   6. _____

7. We (*do'nt, don't*) want our business to make a
   profit at the expense of our employees.

   7. _____

8. She (*couldn't hardly, could hardly*) believe the
   positive feedback that she received from the
   Minding Your Manners workshop.

   8. _____

9. The employee dispute has been (*further, farther*)
   complicated by the stringent production schedule.

   9. _____

10. The ethics training program is progressing very
    (*well, good*).

    10. _____

11. The supervisor acted (*responsible, responsibly*)
    when I needed assistance with a personal matter.

    11. _____

12. I think that it will take (*some time, sometime,
    sometimes*) before political campaign reform
    becomes noticeable.

    12. _____

13. Jim responded to my request for foreign etiquette
    tips (*faster, more fast*) than I expected.

    13. _____

14. We (*readily, more readily*) show respect by using
    polite expressions such as "please" and "thank you."

    14. _____

15. Only 40 percent felt (*comfortable, comfortably*)
    about reporting a breach of ethics.

    15. _____

Adverbs

Name _____   Date _____

Locating Adverbs

Instructions: In the following sentences, a word or phrase is underlined once. Place two lines under each adverb that modifies the underlined word or phrase.

1. Elizabeth is always courteous even when she is extremely busy.

2. Some unethical people want things now and are not willing to wait.

3. With proper checks and balances, it becomes very difficult to hide unethical acts.

4. Supervisors can greatly influence subordinates' ethical behavior.

5. We often judge people too harshly.

Go to the
Web

Practice 2 Exercises
for more skills practice on this topic.

PRACTICE 2

Identifying Adverbs and Adjectives

Instructions: Underline each adverb once. Draw two lines under each adjective. Ignore the articles a, an, *and* the. *Do not underline adjective or adverb clauses or phrases.*

1. The speaker described ethical problems that he had experienced firsthand.

2. Sometimes we are too quick to judge people.

3. Courteous receptionists speak directly into the phone and articulate clearly.

4. Do not ask callers to hold unless it is absolutely necessary.

5. We knew that the evidence against the devious client was largely circumstantial.

6. We inadvertently told Karen about the potential criminal investigation.

7. Administrative assistants should not discuss confidential company business.

8. I am frequently asked to contribute money for office celebrations that I never attend.

9. The newly devised environmental plan will be released quite soon.

10. Your employees are always crucial to the success of your firm.

Using Adverbs

Instructions: In the space provided, correct the following sentences. If the sentence is correct, write **Yes.**

1. Ethics issues nearly exist in every workplace.

_____

Name _____ Date _____

2. This book only deals with international customs and etiquette.

_____

_____

3. Kendra was sure pleased to be asked to join the ethics committee.

_____

4. Lee was real disturbed with the firm's false advertising.

_____

5. This company has always served us good; therefore, I will not change suppliers.

_____

6. If we receive poor merchandise from a company, we do'nt order from that company no more.

_____

_____

7. You acted exceptionally fast in reporting the theft of the office supplies.

_____

8. I feel badly about my rude reaction to my supervisor's criticism.

_____

9. We were able to settle the discrimination suit more soon than we had anticipated.

_____

10. We have not asked no one for his or her opinion on our revised code of ethics.

_____

PRACTICE 3

Proofreading

Instructions: Proofread and compare the two sentences in each group. If they are the same, write **Yes** *in the space provided. If they are not the same, write* **No.** *Use the first sentence as the correct copy. If you find errors in the second copy, underline them; insert any omitted words or marks of punctuation.*

1. Businesses, of course, must make profits, but they don't have to make these profits at the expense of their employees, customers, or society in general.

   1. _____

   Businesses, of course, must make profits, but they do'nt have to make these profits at the expense of their employees, customers, or society in general.

Go to the
Web

Practice 3 Exercises
for more skills practice on this topic.

Adverbs

Name _____ Date _____

2. Diversity programs, family-leave policies, local community projects, and enforced safety regulations can simultaneously benefit employees as well as a company's bottom line.

    Diversity programs, family-leave policies, local community projects, and enforced safty regulations can simultaneous benefit employees as well as and a company's bottom line.

2. _____

3. We readily show respect by using such polite expressions as "please," "thank you," and "I appreciate your prompt response."

    We readly show respect by using such polite expressions as "please," "thank you," and "I appreciate you prompt response."

3. _____

4. Levi Strauss & Co. bases its approach to ethics upon six principles—honesty, promise-keeping, fairness, respect for others, compassion, and integrity.

    Levi Strauss and Co. bases their approach to ethics on six principals—honestly, promise-keeping, fairness, respect for others, compassion, and integrity.

4. _____

5. The Ethics Resource Center in Washington, D.C., reports that almost all large corporations today have organized ethics programs.

    The Ethics Resource Center in Washington, D.C., reports that most all large corporations today have organized ethics programs.

5. _____

Interpreting Proofreaders' Marks

Instructions: Key the document below and make the corrections that are indicated by the proofreaders' marks. If you are not certain about the use of a proofreaders' mark, use your reference manual or the chart on the inside front cover.

MINDING yOUR VOICE MAIL MANNERS

To use Voice Mail to your advantage, here are some good manners and businesslike behaviors to follow:

1. Plan your message in advance. Write it out if necessary.

2. Identify yourself before you record your message. Do not assume that the receiver of the message can recognize your voice.

3. Do not use voice mail for messages that should be delivered in person such as evaluations, h iring decisions or disagreeable news.

4. Recognize the time limits on recorders. State the purpose of your call succinct.

Name _____ Date _____

5. Indicate the type of response that you need. State a time when the receiver can reach you.

6. Don't speak too fast. Spell names correctly and repeat numbers slow.

7. Try to time your messages for periods during the day when the receiver is likely to be avialable. Do not leave messages on Mon. mornings since there maybe a backup from the week end.

8. Keep a written log of the messages that you leave and when you leave them.

PRACTICE 4

Writing

Occasionally, you are involved in situations where ethics are a concern. In the classroom, you may see others cheating on tests or copying work from others and turning the work in as their own. On the job, you may notice others taking home office supplies or using a work phone for lengthy personal phone calls.

*Instructions: Write a paragraph describing a specific ethical situation that you have encountered at school or work. Write at least five sentences. As you are writing, put (**adj**) after an adjective and (**adv**) after an adverb. Do not identify articles. Answers will vary.*

The following is an example:
The harried (adj) student suddenly (adv) decided to cheat on the difficult (adj) quiz.

_____
_____
_____
_____
_____
_____
_____
_____
_____
_____
_____
_____
_____
_____

Go to the
Web

Practice 4 Exercises
for more skills practice on this topic.

Name _____ Date _____

PRACTICE 5

Choosing Adverbs and Adjectives

Instructions: Select the correct word or words, and write them in the space provided.

1. Criticizing a competitor's product to a customer makes you look (*bad, badly*).

   1. _____

2. Rick said that he would have to be (*real, really*) sick before he would miss the awards banquet.

   2. _____

3. (*Sometimes, Some times*) I feel that my supervisor does not trust my judgment.

   3. _____

4. You (*sure, surely*) were aware that our company has an indoor smoking ban.

   4. _____

5. We could not decide which of the three alternatives would be the (*better, best*).

   5. _____

6. The ethics committee completed its analysis of the complaint (*quick, quickly*) and (*fair, fairly*).

   6. _____
   _____

7. Michael Josephson, a noted ethics expert, was an (*extreme, extremely*) knowledgeable speaker.

   7. _____

8. Please do not send (*any, no*) e-mail messages to employees after 5 p.m. on Fridays.

   8. _____

9. Of the two socially responsible projects, the first is (*less costly, less costlier*).

   9. _____

10. The difficult downsizing decisions for Munyon Lumber are (*most, almost*) over.

   10. _____

11. Rosie (*isn't never, is never*) going to stop her gossiping about other employees.

   11. _____

12. We responded (*quickly, more quickly*) to the customer's complaint.

   12. _____

13. The etiquette seminar (*didn't, did'nt*) draw a large crowd.

   13. _____

14. To be effective, a code of ethics must be enforced (*correct, correctly*).

   14. _____

15. Codes of ethics often make decision making (*easier, more easier*).

   15. _____

Name _____ Date _____

Locating Adverbs

Instructions: In the following sentences, a word or phrase is underlined once. Place two lines under each adverb that modifies the underlined word or phrase.

1. Unethical managers view safety and health as strictly <u>financial</u> decisions.

2. She vaguely <u>remembered</u> the incident that involved tax evasion.

3. Jake and Peter <u>argued</u> heatedly about the proposed layoffs.

4. Ethical decisions <u>are</u> sometimes overly <u>influenced</u> by financial considerations.

5. What are the really <u>important</u> things in the operation of our business?

PRACTICE 6

Identifying Adverbs and Adjectives

Instructions: Underline each adverb once. Draw two lines under each adjective. Ignore the articles, a, an, *and* the. *Do not underline adjective or adverb phrases or clauses.*

1. Managers in essentially authoritarian organizations often find little latitude to question policies.

2. The personal characteristics of managers greatly influence their reactions to moral standards.

3. Ethical codes are laws, regulations, and rules that have been carefully studied, interpreted, and recorded for easy reference.

4. Performance appraisals and product quality have ethical implications but frequently have few clear-cut answers.

5. We should examine all dilemmas objectively.

6. These documents are strictly confidential—for my boss's eyes only.

7. Today's employees increasingly are recognizing their responsibilities in ethical matters.

8. People who make mistakes (especially serious ones) often need help to move forward.

9. Do you really believe that rudeness and bad manners are common behavior in our office?

10. Your well-delivered presentation was very helpful to me professionally.

Name _____ Date _____

Using Adverbs

Instructions: *In the space provided, correct the following sentences. If the sentence is* *correct, write* **Yes**.

1. Our Ethics Committee almost comprises members from every department.

   _____

2. Disruption caused by conflict between groups nearly happens in every business.

   _____

3. Our manager only loses his temper with overseas shippers.

   _____

4. We were sure surprised when we heard about the incorrect reports.

   _____

5. Holly was real sad when she learned about the sexual harassment of Yolanda.

   _____

   _____

6. We still have not notified no one about the missing office supplies.

   _____

7. We should treat everyone in our company respectful.

   _____

8. Although she did not feel good, she attended a portion of the ethics workshop.

   _____

   _____

9. Codes of ethics are vital important documents for successful firms.

   _____

   _____

10. We more constantly need to analyze the consequences of our actions.

   _____

Name _____ Date _____

PRACTICE 7

Proofreading

*Instructions: Proofread and compare the two sentences in each group. If they are the same, write **Yes** in the space provided. If they are not the same, write **No**. Use the first sentence as the correct copy. If you find errors in the second sentence, underline them; insert any omitted words or marks of punctuation.*

1. One of the missions of the United States Office of Government Ethics is to prevent and resolve conflicts of interest and to foster high ethical standards.

   One of the misssions of The United States Office of Government Ethics is to prevent and resolve conflicts of interest and to foster high ethical standards.

   1. _____

2. The Jefferson Center for Character Education has identified ten "universal values," which are honesty, integrity, promise keeping, fidelity, fairness, caring for others, respect for others, responsible citizenship, pursuit of excellence, and accountability.

   The Jefferson Center for Character Education has identified ten "universal values," which are honesty, integrity, promise keeping, fidelity, fairness, caring for others, respect for others, responsible citzenship, pursuit of excelence, and accountability.

   2. _____

3. Unethical behavior among North American companies costs about $100 billion a year to investigate allegations, to resolve activities in question, and to put mechanisms in place to ensure that problems do not reoccur.

   Unethical behavior among North American companys cost about $100 billion a year to investigate allegations, to resolve activities in question, and to put mechanisms in place to insure that problems do not reoccurr.

   3. _____

4. Elements of an effective business ethics environment may include codes of conduct, mission statements, training and awareness programs, frequent communication meetings, and an ethics office.

   Elements of an effective business ethics environment may include codes of conduct, mission statements, training and awareness programs, frequent communication meetings, and an ethics office.

   4. _____

Name _____ Date _____

5. The fairness or justice approach to ethics originated in the teachings of the Greek philosopher Aristotle, who said that "equals should be treated equally and unequals unequally."

5. _____

The fairness or justice approach to ethics originated in the teachings of the Greek Philosopher Aristotle, who said that "Equals should be treated equal and unequals unequal".

Interpreting Proofreaders' Marks

You participated in a brainstorming session on determining ethical mistakes that employees make. The draft that follows is a list of reasons generated from the brainstorming.

Instructions: Key the document and make the corrections that are indicated by the proofreaders' marks. If you are not certain about the use of a proofreaders' mark, refer to the chart on the inside front cover.

EXAMPLES OF UNETHICAL BEHAVIOR

1. Falsifying expense reprots
2. Taking long breaks,
3. Misrepresenting Issues to others
4. Withholding information to "Protect" others
5. Covering up drug or alcohol abuse
6. Permitting sub/standard quality in product or service
7. covering up on the job accidents
8. Taking home officesupplies
9. Blaming my supervisor for for my mistakes
10. Divulging personal or confidential information

Name _____ Date _____

Writing

Instructions: *Write a paragraph describing the kind of person whom you consider unethical. Use a variety of sentence structures. You may use any of the behaviors in the previous proofreading exercise in your paragraph. You may add any other unethical behaviors that you think should be emphasized. Write at least five sentences. As you are writing, put (**adj**) after an adjective and (**adv**) after an adverb. Do not identify articles. Answers will vary.*

The following is an example:
I once (adv) worked with an inconsiderate (adj) person who was always (adv) late (adj) for work.

_____

_____

_____

_____

_____

_____

_____

_____

_____

_____

_____

_____

_____

_____

Posttest

Instructions: In the space provided, write the letter of the correct answer.

1. In the sentence *Joanne respectfully listened to Stephanie's concerns about her heavy workload,* the adverb *respectfully* modifies: (1)

    a. a verb.   c. a noun.

    b. an adjective.   d. an adverb.

1. _____

2. In the sentence *Most customer service representatives patiently answer all questions,* the adverb is: (1)

    a. most.   c. patiently.

    b. answer.   d. all.

2. _____

3. In the sentence *Our manager carefully analyzes ethical situations,* the adverb answers the question: (1)

    a. How?   c. Where?

    b. When?   d. To what extent or degree?

3. _____

4. In the sentence *Extremely disgruntled employees often undermine work environments,* you will find: (2)

    a. four adjectives and one adverb.

    b. two adjectives and two adverbs.

    c. four adjectives and no adverbs.

    d. five adjectives and two adverbs.

4. _____

5. Which one of the following sentences is correct? (2, 3, 4)

    a. Tom felt badly when he realized the extent of the customer's anger.

    b. The manager clearly insisted that employees be accountable for their actions.

    c. Howard spoke about ethical responsibility but acted unethical.

    d. We analyzed careful the cash report to find the shortage.

5. _____

6. Which of the following lines represents the *comparative* degree of adverbs? (4)

    a. more hurriedly; best   c. quicklier; more narrowly

    b. more cautiously; most immediately   d. more persistently; better

6. _____

7. Which of the following sentences is *not* correct? (3, 5)

    a. Rick could not hardly decide on the best solution for the problem.

    b. She had nothing to say about the gossip in the office.

    c. We claim overtime only if we work on Sunday.

    d. Eliminating motives for unethical behavior is not easy.

7. _____

8. Which one of the following sentences is *not* correct? (2, 5)

    a. I do not work very good in an isolated environment.

    b. Are you really trying to understand your manager's motivations?

    c. We were surely amazed by the theft of the computers.

    d. Almost all employees support our code of ethics.

8. _____

9. In the sentence, *Accountable people do not blame others for their own mistakes,* you will find: (2)

    a. two adjectives and two adverbs.

    b. two adjectives and one adverb.

    c. two adjectives and no adverbs.

    d. three adjectives and one adverb.

9. _____

10. Which sentence is written correctly? (2)

    a. We respond ethical when helping customers.

    b. Some actions are perfectly legal but not very ethical.

    c. He speaks careless about company payroll information.

    d. Marie adapts quick to customer feedback.

10. _____

11. Which sentence is written correctly? (2, 3)

    a. Karen is very, very thorough when answering customer inquiries.

    b. Jake responded appropriate to customers' questions about returning merchandise.

    c. The attorneys strictly enforced the terms of the legal contract.

    d. This situation should have been managed different.

11. _____

12. Which sentence is written correctly? (3, 4, 5)

    a. A contract is typically in writing and usually enforceable by law.

    b. I felt badly about missing the ethical standards workshop.

    c. Our company's code of conduct is real good in answering common ethics questions.

    d. The trainer explained farther about the difference between laws and ethics.

12. _____

13. Which sentence is *not* written correctly? (3, 4, 6)

    a. Ethical standards usually provide a framework for handling difficult situations.

    b. We surely will have an opportunity to review the revisions in the code of ethics.

    c. The ethics survey is due some time next week.

    d. The real reason for hiring the ethics consultant was unclear.

13. _____

14. Which sentence is *not* written correctly? (4, 5, 6)

    a. We described further our objections to the new policy.

    b. The lawyer explained good the conflict of interest problems.

    c. We have seen no evidence of fraud.

    d. He appeared relieved with the outcome of the court case.

14. _____

15. Which sentence is *not* written correctly? (4, 5)

    a. Julie couldn't hardly believe the excuse that Rex gave.

    b. The shipper didn't apologize for the late arrival of our order.

    c. Of all companies in Indiana, Hammond Inc. performs most reliably.

    d. The mediator resolved the conflict of interest sooner than we had expected.

15. _____

Chapter 14

Prepositions

OBJECTIVES

After you have studied this chapter and completed the exercises, you will be able to do the following:

1. Identify prepositions.

2. Recognize prepositional phrases, objects of prepositions, and compound prepositions.

3. Differentiate between infinitive phrases and prepositional phrases.

4. Recognize the functions of prepositional phrases as adjectives and adverbs.

5. Determine inclusion, exclusion, and placement of prepositions.

6. Differentiate between commonly confused prepositions.

7. Use the correct idiomatic prepositional combinations.

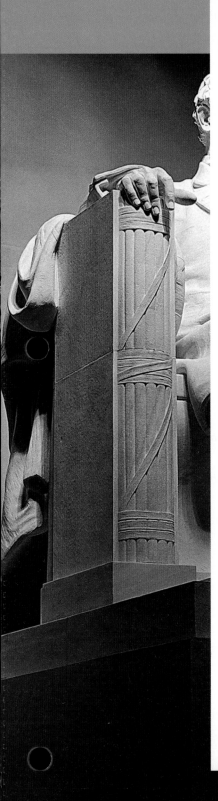

Workplace Applications: Leadership

A leader does not need to be a high-ranking person or a president of a company. A leader may sometimes be a follower at work yet a leader in the community. A person may not work but still show leadership ability by volunteering in an elementary classroom, teaching in a local literacy program, or helping with the organization of community events.

Decades of research have produced hundreds of definitions of leadership and thousands of research studies on leaders. Despite the attention on leadership, no specific formula exists that can distinguish leaders from nonleaders. Leaders may be outgoing or reserved, charismatic or boring, male or female, young or old.

Rising to the Top

One characteristic all leaders do possess, however, is that they have followers. People follow leaders because leaders have a clearly understood vision or direction. Leaders inspire others to commit to a vision by encouraging teamwork. Leaders are aware of their own strengths and compensate for their weaknesses. This capacity to inspire and to improve their own personal weaknesses is one characteristic that distinguishes leaders from followers.

Debate about whether leadership skills can be taught continues. Much of the current thinking about leadership contends that it can be divided into behaviors and abilities and taught with some degree of success. Most companies that undertake leadership training usually train all levels of employees and hope that employees become inspired to reexamine themselves, the organization, and other people in the organization.

PRETEST: *Looking Forward*

Pretest

Instructions: In the space provided, write **T** if the statement is true and **F** if the statement is false.

1. The sentence *The American Management Association sponsors seminars on leadership in several cities throughout the United States* has four prepositions. (1)

    1. _____

2. In the sentence *Some chief executive officers (CEOs) receive bonuses based on the company's profits,* the object of the preposition is *company's.* (2)

    2. _____

3. In the sentence *Unfortunately, he used threats instead of education to motivate his subordinates, instead of* is a compound preposition. (2)

    3. _____

4. In the sentence *Some leaders refuse to change course once they begin a project,* the phrase *to change course* is a prepositional phrase. (3)

    4. _____

5. The preposition *at* is placed correctly in the sentence *Where is the job description for the sales manager at?* (5)

    5. _____

6. Prepositional phrases modify nouns, pronouns, and verbs. (4)

    6. _____

7. The word *among* is used correctly in the sentence *Hiring a professional family-business consultant may ease conflicts among family members.* (6)

    7. _____

8. The sentence *My supervisor had no reason to be angry at me* is written correctly. (7)

    8. _____

9. In the sentence *The book that I ordered on leadership strategies arrived by UPS,* the prepositional phrase *by UPS* functions as an adverb. (4)

    9. _____

10. The sentence *The leadership conference will be held in Detroit near to the airport* is written correctly. (5)

    10. _____

11. The sentence *Employees will work hard for their supervisors if the supervisors are appreciative of completed projects* has two prepositions. (1)

    11. _____

12. The sentence *This year's group of management trainees is quite different than last year's group* is written correctly. (6)

    12. _____

13. The sentence *The CEO knew that not everyone was going to agree with every one of his decisions* is written correctly. (7)

    13. _____

14. In the sentence *Marni asked her assistant to reserve a room for team leaders,* the phrase *to reserve a room* is an infinitive phrase. (3)

    14. _____

15. The sentence *We are going over to the leadership workshop* is written correctly. (5)

    15. _____

Chapter Preview

You have studied nouns and pronouns that identify persons, places, activities, ideas, and things, as well as verbs that indicate action. You learned that adjectives and adverbs modify various parts of speech. Now you will learn about the words that make the connections between all of these various parts of speech. In this chapter, you will see how prepositions function as connectors in sentences.

Certain words and prepositions always appear together. Usage rather than rules determines these combinations. In order to make your writing indicate your precise intentions, you should pay particular attention to these combinations, as well as to several other prepositions that are often misused. Once you see how frequently prepositions are used, you will realize how indispensable they are in your writing.

Identification of Prepositions

A preposition is a word that connects a noun or a pronoun (the *object* of the preposition) to another word or set of words in a sentence. A preposition shows the relationship between the object of the preposition and these other words.

Commonly Used Prepositions

about	behind	during	on	throughout
above	below	except	onto	to
across	beneath	for	opposite	toward
after	beside	from	out	under
against	besides	in	outside	underneath
along	between	inside	over	until
among	beyond	into	past	up
around	by	like	pending	upon
as	concerning	near	regarding	with
at	despite	of	since	within
before	down	off	through	without

Prepositions and Prepositional Phrases

A prepositional phrase begins with a preposition and ends with a noun or pronoun called the object of the preposition. A prepositional phrase consists of a preposition, the noun or pronoun object, and any modifiers of the noun or pronoun object. A prepositional phrase cannot stand alone. More than one prepositional phrase often appears in a sentence.

Use a preposition to connect the object of the preposition (noun or pronoun) to another word or set of words in a sentence.

Prepositions

These managers know the risks of leadership.

(The preposition is *of.* The prepositional phrase is *of leadership.* The noun *leadership* is the object of the preposition.)

Self-awareness often helps people understand the leadership style that works best for them.

(The preposition is *for.* The prepositional phrase is *for them.* The pronoun *them* is the object of the preposition.)

The speed of communication is a leadership challenge that will continue into the next century.

(This sentence contains two prepositional phrases. In the prepositional phrase *of communication,* the preposition is *of* and the object of the preposition is *communication.* In the prepositional phrase *into the next century,* the preposition is *into,* and the object of the preposition is *century.* *The* and *next* are modifiers of the noun *century.*)

Phil did not change his leadership style when he moved from a military career to business.

(Each of the two consecutive prepositional phrases has objects. The object of the preposition *from* is *career.* The object of the preposition *to* is *business.*)

CHECKPOINT 14.1

Instructions: In the following sentences, circle each preposition and draw one line under each prepositional phrase.

1. Dundee Research hired managers with listening and nurturing skills.

2. Leadership is more what you do for other people than what you do to them.

3. Employees may feel uncomfortable under the leadership of a "Type A" personality.

4. She needs a four-year degree and an internship for a management position.

5. For information about the International Directory of Young Entrepreneurs, call (617) 555-4690.

6. Without integrity, a leader will have a difficult time obtaining loyalty from followers.

7. I have improved my supervisory skills through the use of training tapes and videos.

8. Leaders must work with many different personalities within their organizations.

Compound Prepositions

A compound preposition consists of a combination of words that is often considered as one preposition. A compound preposition connects the object of a preposition to another word or set of words.

Compound Prepositions

according to	in accordance with	instead of
ahead of	in addition to	next to
along with	in front of	on account of
apart from	in place of	on behalf of
because of	in regard to	out of
by means of	in spite of	with reference to

Good managers give sufficient, positive feedback <u>instead of</u> only constant criticism.

(The prepositional phrase is *instead of only constant criticism.* The compound preposition is *instead of.* The object of the compound preposition is *criticism.*)

She completed her computer classes <u>in spite of</u> home and family pressures.

(The prepositional phrase is *in spite of home and family pressures.* The compound preposition is *in spite of.* The object of the compound preposition is *pressures.*)

CHECKPOINT 14.2

Go to the
Web

Checkpoint 14.2
for more skills practice on this topic.

Instructions: In the following sentences, circle the object of the preposition and draw one line under each prepositional phrase.

1. Because of job security, many people are uncomfortable with changes in the management of a firm.

2. According to our records, Charles became president in 1989.

3. In place of Jerri, you will represent the department at the next staff meeting.

4. In most cases, putting your goals on paper bridges a gap between thought and action.

5. In accordance with our supervisor, we requested extra time for completing the project.

6. Rikki is sending an e-mail about the leadership seminar on behalf of Miranda.

7. The president of the board accepted the award in addition to a check for $10,000.

8. All of the team members spoke in support of the team leader's recommendation.

Considerations in Identifying and Using Prepositions

Making a distinction between prepositional phrases and infinitive phrases is necessary. Some prepositions may also function as other parts of speech; for example, the adverb. The use of a pronoun as an object of a preposition also requires review.

Infinitive Phrases/Prepositional Phrases

An infinitive phrase consists of the word *to* followed by a verb. Examples of infinitive phrases include the following: *to drive, to calculate, to work, to finish, to win, to enjoy, to understand.* A prepositional phrase has a noun or pronoun as its object. A prepositional phrase *does not* contain a verb.

The assistant <u>to the president</u> decided <u>to investigate expert system software.</u>

(*To the president* is a prepositional phrase. A verb does not follow the word *to. To investigate expert system software* is an infinitive phrase. A verb follows the word *to.*)

Prepositions

Listen to yourself to learn how clearly you present ideas.

(*To yourself* is a prepositional phrase. No verb follows the word *to*. *To learn* is an infinitive phrase. A verb follows the word *to*.)

Prepositions and Adverbs

The words *by, through,* and *in* can be used as adverbs without objects. When these same words take objects, they are prepositions.

My order for the book *Great Leaders See the Future First* finally came in.

(*In* is an adverb that answers the question *Where?* No object follows the word *in*.)

Andersen Consulting is establishing a "thought leadership" center in Palo Alto.

(*In* is a preposition. In this sentence, it takes the object *Palo Alto*.)

Objects of Prepositions and Pronouns

Objective case pronouns include *her, him, you, me, us, them, it,* and *whom*. Use the objective case of a pronoun as the object of a preposition.

The team leader gave the netware research material to Yolanda and her for processing.

(Omit *Yolanda* to see if the sentence sounds correct with the pronoun *her*. If it does, use the objective case pronoun *her*. The nominative case *she* is not a satisfactory substitution. *Yolanda* and *her* are the objects of the preposition.)

Between you and me, I would not wish to be a manager in that company.

(The objective case *you* and *me* is necessary after the preposition *between*. *You* and *me* are the objects of the preposition.)

A writer about whom few people have heard has written a book on leadership.

(Use the objective case pronoun *whom* as the object of the preposition.)

NOTES

Looking Back
Refer to Chapter 7 for a review of the objective case of pronouns.

EDIT PATROL

Newspaper headline:
"Astronauts Practice Landing on Laptops."
Note: How difficult is it to land on a laptop computer?

Go to the Web

Checkpoint 14-3
for more skills practice on this topic.

CHECKPOINT 14.3

*Instructions: In the space provided, identify the underlined word or words in each of the sentences. Use the following codes: **Prep** (preposition), **PP** (prepositional phrase), **I** (infinitive or infinitive phrase), **Adv** (adverb), **OP** (object of preposition).*

1. A new CEO needs to understand the goals of the major stockholders. _____

2. My supervisor said that he would wait outside for me. _____

3. People need to know that they are doing a good job for the company. _____

4. If you let society place you in a role, you will never go beyond that role. _____

5. During the past few decades, the autocratic style of management has not been popular. _____

6. When you are finished with the book on values, please return it to <u>Jane</u> or <u>me</u>. _____

7. Hiring a manager from outside the company <u>to lead</u> a department might cause resentment with some employees. _____

8. A supervisor should immediately step <u>in</u> to resolve customer complaints. _____

9. You need <u>to complete</u> the online leadership questionnaire by Friday. _____

10. All vacation requests go <u>to the manager</u> for approval. _____

Functions of Prepositional Phrases

Prepositional phrases function as modifiers. A prepositional phrase that modifies a noun or pronoun functions as an adjective. A prepositional phrase that modifies a verb, adjective, or adverb functions as an adverb.

Adjective Function

Use a prepositional phrase as an adjective to modify a noun or a pronoun. In most cases, place the prepositional phrase after the word or words being modified or after a linking verb.

Once you have lost the trust <u>of your employees</u>, you will have a difficult time regaining it.

(*Of your employees* modifies the noun *trust* and answers the question *Whose trust?*)

The woman <u>with the president</u> is a leadership consultant.

(*With the president* describes the noun *woman* and answers the question *Which one?*)

Linda was <u>under considerable pressure</u> last week.

(*Under considerable pressure* describes the noun *Linda* and follows the linking verb *was.*)

Adverb Function

Use a prepositional phrase as an adverb to modify a verb, an adjective, or another adverb.

He was a good leader who will be judged <u>by his effective leadership record</u>.

(*By his effective leadership record* modifies the verb *judged* and answers the question *How?*)

Benjamin Franklin rarely spoke <u>in public</u> but worked <u>behind the scenes</u> to accomplish his goals.

(*In public* and *behind the scenes* are prepositional phrases that modify the verbs *spoke* and *worked.* The phrases answer the question *Where?*)

The supervisor's compliment was important <u>to me</u>.

(*To me* is a prepositional phrase that modifies the adjective *important.*)

NOTES

Prepositional Phrases Modify Nouns and Pronouns

Prepositional phrases that modify nouns and pronouns answer such questions as *Who? How many?* and *What kind?*

NOTES

Prepositional Phrases Modify Verbs

Prepositional phrases that modify verbs answer the questions *How? In what manner? When? Where? Why?* and *To what extent or degree?*

Go to the
Web

Checkpoint 14.4
for more skills practice on this topic.

CHECKPOINT 14.4

Instructions: *In the space provided, write the word or phrase modified by the underlined prepositional phrase. All prepositional phrases may not be underlined in this exercise.*

1. None <u>of their children</u> wanted to assume a leadership role in the family business. _____

2. Make a list <u>of the drawbacks and benefits</u> of your decision. _____

3. Within many organizations, risk is not greeted <u>with enthusiasm.</u> _____

4. A positive outlook moves you <u>toward a problem-solving mode</u> of thinking. _____

5. Power, like any other mark <u>of authority,</u> can be used in a negative way. _____

6. Some employees consistently make negative remarks <u>about their leaders.</u> _____

7. The team's final project received intense scrutiny <u>by the management staff.</u> _____

8. The workshop on collaboration in the workplace will begin <u>at 8 a.m.</u> _____

Placement of Prepositions

General Placement

Although it is not incorrect to end a sentence with a preposition, you should try to place the preposition before its object in the majority of sentences. If a sentence sounds awkward with this pattern, revise the sentence. An exception to this general placement of a preposition is with some short questions or sentences.

Awkward

Allison had a clear-cut goal to strive <u>for</u>.

Revised Sentence

Allison had a clear-cut goal <u>for</u> which to strive.

Awkward

Mission statements often become too complicated for employees to relate <u>to</u>.

Revised Sentence

Mission statements often become too complicated for employees to relate <u>to them</u>.

What is a leadership analysis good for?

(*For what is a leadership analysis good?* or *For what good is a leadership analysis?* are awkward questions. The example, which is a short question ending in a preposition, is acceptable. The revised question *Of what benefit is a leadership analysis?* is also satisfactory.)

Inclusion of Necessary Prepositions

Do not omit a preposition when it is needed. Use separate prepositions when words cannot be related to one object by the same preposition.

A family emergency prevented Harry <u>from</u> going to the leadership institute.

(Do not use *prevented Harry going*. The preposition *from* is necessary.)

What style <u>of</u> management do you prefer—participative or autocratic?

(Do not use *What style management*. The preposition *of* is necessary.)

Executives must <u>plan for</u> and <u>win acceptance of</u> new operations in the production department.

(Separate prepositions are necessary. Do not use *Executives must plan and win acceptance of new operations in the production department*.)

Omission of Unnecessary Prepositions

Omit prepositions that do not add clarity to the meaning of a sentence. Do not repeat a preposition in a sentence if phrases make sense by using the same preposition.

The president's office is <u>near</u> the lobby.

(Do not use *near to the lobby*. The preposition *to* is not necessary.)

Our team leader would like <u>us</u> to finish the project before the holidays.

(Do not use *like for us to finish*. The preposition *for* is not necessary.)

Our president frequently speaks <u>at</u> Kiwanis and Rotary meetings.

(The preposition *at* does not need to be repeated before *Kiwanis* and *Rotary* since the same preposition [*at*] applies to both phrases.)

CHECKPOINT 14.5

*Instructions: In the space provided, correct those sentences that are written incorrectly. Write **Yes** if the sentence is correct.*

1. She asked what leadership activities he was involved in.

   _____

2. Honeywell's goal is to get more employees to think like and act like leaders.

   _____

3. The human resources director hires only those applicants who have graduated college.

   _____
   _____

EDIT PATROL

From a local newspaper:
Senator Barnes was quoted as saying, "I like to shop for guns and presents for my grandchildren in the small towns in the North Woods."
Note: We hope that the Senator is not buying the guns *for* his grandchildren.

***Go to the* Web**

Checkpoint 14.5
for more skills practice on this topic.

NOTES

More Prepositions
Refer to a reference manual such as *The Gregg Reference Manual* for additional examples of unnecessary prepositions.

4. A leader must have a clear understanding and a caring attitude toward employee needs.

   _____

   _____

5. Where can I get a copy of the policies and procedures manual at?

   _____

6. How much middle management support can we count on?

   _____

7. I could not understand why my supervisor was asking the question for.

   _____

8. Bonnie took the book on leadership off of Tom's desk.

   _____

Cautions in Using Special Prepositions

Some prepositions cause confusion. The following pairs require special consideration:

Beside/Besides

Use *beside* as a preposition to mean "by the side of" or "not connected with something." Use *besides* as a preposition to mean "in addition to" or "other than."

The person taking minutes should sit <u>beside</u> the chairperson.

(*Beside* means "by the side of" or "next to.")

The discussion on leadership values was <u>beside</u> the point at this time.

(*Beside* means the discussion was not connected with the material currently being discussed.)

<u>Besides</u> Maria, the manager appointed two other women to the restructured team.

(*Besides* means "in addition to.")

Our team leader had several possible solutions <u>besides</u> the one that we agreed upon.

(*Besides* means "other than.")

Among/Between

In general, use the preposition *between* to refer to two persons, places, qualities, activities, ideas, or things. Use the preposition *among* to refer to more than two persons, places, qualities, activities, ideas, or things.

In our family business, my mother and father share decision-making responsibilities <u>between</u> them.

(*Between* refers to two persons.)

He is <u>among</u> those who believe that leadership requires a futuristic attitude.

(*Among* suggests that more than two people are involved.)

Chapter 14

Different From

Use the word *different* followed by the preposition *from* when *from* connects an object to another word or set of words in a sentence.

> **To some, a leader is <u>different from</u> a manager.**
>
> (Use the preposition *from* after *different*. In this sentence, *from* connects the object *manager* to the rest of the sentence. Do not use *different than*.)
>
> **His leadership style is quite <u>different from</u> mine.**
>
> (Use the preposition *from* after *different*. In this sentence, *from* connects the object *mine* to the rest of the sentence. Do not use *different than*.)

Like/As

Use the preposition *like* to mean "similar to" or "resembling." Do not use a verb after the preposition *like*. Do not use *like* to join clauses. Use the conjunction *as* or *as if* to join clauses.

> **Jeremy acts <u>like</u> a leader.**
>
> (The preposition *like* is not followed by a verb and takes the object *leader*.)
>
> **Adam wants to be the president of the family's company just <u>like</u> his father.**
>
> (The preposition *like* is not followed by a verb and takes the object *father*.)
>
> **Jeremy acts <u>as if</u> he wants to be a leader.**
>
> (The words *as if* introduce the clause *he wants to be a leader*. The clause includes a subject and a verb. Do not use *like*.)
>
> **The negotiation process worked <u>as</u> it should.**
>
> (The word *as* introduces a clause, *it should*. The clause includes a subject and a verb. Do not use *like*.)

NOTES

Like Rules

Like takes an object (noun or pronoun) and is not followed by a verb.

Off/From

Do not use *off of* in prepositional phrases. Do not substitute *off* for *from* in certain phrases.

> **The supervisor had to keep reminding people to keep beverages <u>off</u> their computer desks.**
>
> (Do not use *off of* their computer desks.)
>
> **I got the leadership meeting notes <u>from</u> her.**
>
> (Do not use *off of* her as the prepositional phrase.)
>
> **The board of directors decided to borrow $1 million <u>from</u> the local bank.**
>
> (Do not use *off the local bank* as the prepositional phrase.)

In/Into

Use *in* to indicate a "location or position within a place." Use *into* to indicate "movement or direction from outside to inside" or a "change of condition or form."

> **Ironically, those who avoid risks often seem to end up <u>in</u> leadership positions.**
>
> (*In* indicates a "position within someplace.")
>
> **Much of a leader's time is spent <u>in</u> meetings.**
>
> (*In* indicates a location.)

Would everyone please move <u>into</u> the lecture hall for Juan's presentation on motivation.

(*Into* indicates movement from outside the hall to the inside.)

To achieve a goal, break it down <u>into</u> small, concrete actions.

(*Into* indicates a change of form.)

To/Too/Two

Use the preposition *to* to indicate "toward." Also use *to* as an infinitive or as part of an infinitive phrase. Use *too* as an adverb to indicate an "excessive amount" or "also." Use *two* as an adjective to indicate the number (how many).

How do you react <u>to</u> setbacks and difficult situations?

(*To* is a preposition. No verb follows.)

Does he have the time and energy <u>to</u> develop the international markets?

(*To* is part of an infinitive phrase. A verb follows the word *to*.)

Many people in leadership positions speak <u>too</u> quickly.

(*Too* indicates excessively.)

Ryan was selected for leadership training, <u>too</u>.

(*Too* means "also.")

I am one of the <u>two</u> people to be selected for the management training program.

(*Two* is the number.)

Go to the
Web

Checkpoint 14.6
for more skills practice on this topic.

 ## CHECKPOINT 14.6

Instructions: *Select the correct word, and write it in the space provided.*

1. Chairing a meeting is different (*from, than*) anything that I have ever done. _____

2. His leadership style is (*as, like*) mine. _____

3. You will be able to find several similar characteristics (*between, among*) the leaders of today's large companies. _____

4. Few people knew as much about leadership (*as, like*) Peter Drucker did. _____

5. Workers want to know how their jobs fit (*in, into*) the overall picture. _____

6. We find leadership in many places (*beside, besides*) the CEO's office. _____

7. Allen had (*to, too, two*) many other commitments when he became our team leader. _____

8. The finance director took my budget proposal (*off, off of*) today's agenda. _____

9. These guidelines are different (*from, than*) the ones discussed last week. _____

10. Tom's office assistant always sits (*beside, besides*) him at _____ staff meetings.

11. He did not solve the problem (*like, as*) I would have. _____

12. Our CEO is moving (*to, too, two*) New Hampshire next year. _____

Identification of Idiomatic Expressions

An idiom refers to an expression that has evolved from general usage through the years but which has no established rule for this usage. Many idioms involve a verb and preposition combination. Notice carefully that a pattern develops as you read the idiomatic expressions. When the word following the expression is a person, generally the preposition *with* is preferred. You agree *with* a person, you get angry *with* a person, you argue *with* a person, you concur *with* a person, and you talk *with* a person.

In contrast, you do not get angry *at* a person. You do not talk *to* a person unless you are giving a speech in front of a large audience, in which case you are talking to the audience.

Following are some examples of these verb and preposition combinations along with brief definitions. Since the same verb may precede different prepositions, it is necessary to select the correct combination to express the meaning intended.

NOTES

Additional Idioms

Refer to the sections on prepositions or word usage in your reference manual to determine the correct idiomatic expression to use.

The supervisor <u>accompanied by</u> his boss went to the meeting.

(accompanied *by a person*)

We noticed that the check was <u>accompanied with</u> a letter of appreciation.

(accompanied *by* or *with an item*)

They knew his management techniques were <u>adapted from</u> those that he used in England.

(adapted *from another source*)

Anna soon <u>adapted to</u> her new leadership role.

(adapted *to* or *adjusted to a situation*)

We all <u>agreed in</u> principle that a leader has to be open-minded about changing technology.

(agree *in principle*)

The committee <u>agreed on</u> the need to increase the number of leadership seminars.

(agree *on a plan*)

Kent <u>agreed with</u> me about some new ways to motivate employees.

(agree *with a person* or *viewpoint*)

I am still <u>angry about</u> the board's decision to limit overtime hours.

(angry *at* or *about a situation*)

When Lucy is <u>angry with</u> someone, she delays her actions until she can think more clearly.

(angry *with a person*)

Several committee members <u>argued about</u> the wording of the mission statement.

(argue *about a situation*)

Our team leader <u>argued for</u> additional support staff assistance.

(argue *for something*)

I do not like to <u>argue with</u> my supervisor.

(argue *with a person*)

I will <u>arrive at</u> the university to speak about leadership issues in the new millennium.

(arrive *at a time, specific location, conclusion*)

We plan to <u>arrive by</u> plane although we have scheduled our executives on different flights.

(arrive *by a type of transport*)

Hank plans to <u>arrive in</u> Tucson for a meeting with the Arizona branch managers.

(arrive *in a general location*)

Everybody on the board <u>concurred in</u> hiring Robin Malloy.

(concur *in an opinion*)

The owner of the firm <u>concurred with</u> us regarding our request for a refund.

(concur *with a person*)

Go to the
Web

Checkpoint 14.7
for more skills practice on this topic.

 CHECKPOINT 14.7

Instructions: Select the correct idiomatic expression, and write it in the space provided.

1. Team members could not (*agree with, agree to, agree on*) the person who should be the team leader. _____

2. We were (*angry with, angry about*) the lack of leadership training opportunities. _____

3. I adapted my goals (*from, to*) those that I outlined last year. _____

4. The chairman of the board will arrive (*at, by, in*) the airport (*at, by, in*) 12:35 p.m. _____

5. Although both plans had merit, I (*argued about, argued for, argued with*) the least expensive plan to implement. _____

6. The manager (*concurred in, concurred with*) Betsy in her request for a salary increase. _____

7. Most world leaders are (*accompanied by, accompanied with*) trusted advisers when they visit other countries. _____

8. We quickly (*adapted from, adapted to*) our new manager's leadership style. _____

9. I usually (*agree in, agree on, agree with*) my team leader's recommendations. _____

10. Kelsey is (*angry at, angry about, angry with*) the shipper for not informing her about the delay. _____

Other Idiomatic Expressions

Review the following idiomatic expressions carefully.

Even in the executive offices, <u>correspondence by</u> mail is decreasing.

(correspond *by a specific means*)

Fran's plan <u>corresponded to</u> the one management had envisioned.

(correspond *to show similarity*)

<u>Corresponding with</u> international businesspeople requires careful use of the language.

(correspond *with a person by writing*)

Our insecure manager <u>enters</u> every infraction of the rules <u>in</u> a log book.

(enter *in* or *on a record*)

The two recruitment coordinators <u>entered into</u> a reciprocal agreement concerning the hiring of employees.

(enter *into an agreement* or *a discussion*)

Sometimes his family thinks that he <u>lives</u> at the office.

(live *at an address, place*)

Our firm encourages all managers to <u>live in</u> the city.

(live *in an area*)

Union leaders tried to convince management that workers cannot <u>live on</u> a minimum wage.

(live *on an amount*)

I am <u>reconciled to</u> the fact that I will not be promoted this year.

(reconciled *to* or *accept*)

Our auditor insists on the <u>reconciliation</u> of our checkbook <u>with</u> the ledgers.

(reconciled *with* or *brought into agreement*)

At our fall meeting, the superintendent <u>talked about</u> the enrollment patterns for community colleges.

(talk *about something*)

We <u>talked for</u> some time about the impending merger.

(talk *for a time period*)

Have you <u>talked to</u> your manager about a leadership training program?

(talk *to tell something to someone* or *to an audience*)

Our telecommunications network allows our branch managers in Akron and Waterloo to <u>talk with</u> each other.

(talk or converse *with an individual* or *small group*)

Please <u>wait at</u> the information desk for the human services director.

(wait *at a location*)

She <u>waited for</u> an answer to her leave request.

(wait *for a person, thing*)

Never appear too busy to <u>wait on</u> a customer.

(wait *on a customer*)

Prepositions

Go to the
Web

Checkpoint 14.8
for more skills practice on
this topic.

CHECKPOINT 14.8

Instructions: *Select the correct idiomatic expression, and write it in the space provided.*

1. I (*waited at, waited for, waited on*) Terry to contact me _____
   about the leadership training meeting.

2. Has the checkbook been (*reconciled to, reconciled* _____
   with) the bank statement this month?

3. Our CEO (*entered in, entered into*) merger negotiations _____
   with another firm last March.

4. Many of our managers (*live at, live in*) Cedarburg or Port _____
   Washington.

5. We (*correspond by, correspond with*) our three branch _____
   managers through e-mail.

6. The board chairman asked the CEO to (*talk about, talk* _____
   to, talk with) the stockholders at the annual meeting.

7. Tri Dec's final merger plan (*corresponded to, corresponded* _____
   with) the one that it had proposed to the CEO a month ago.

8. Leslie (*talked to, talked with, talked for*) the leadership _____
   development class at UWEC.

Diagramming Sentences

To diagram a prepositional phrase, place the preposition on a diagonal line under
the word that it modifies. Place the object of the preposition on a horizontal line
that extends from the diagonal.

Prepositional Phrase as an Adjective

A leader must have a vision of the future.

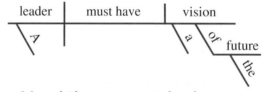

Prepositional Phrase as an Adverb

She completed an internship at Sacred Heart Hospital.

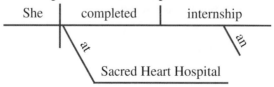

Copyright © by The McGraw-Hill Companies, Inc.

CHECKPOINT 14.9

Go to the
Web

Checkpoint 14.9
for more skills practice on this topic.

Instructions: *In the space provided, diagram the following sentences.*

1. The workforce of the next decade will require a new type of leadership.

2. Leaders require extra energy in crisis situations.

3. Our managers consider all sides of a controversy.

4. The supervisor disliked any criticisms of his plans.

5. Participative leaders appreciate input from their employees.

Name _____ Date _____

PRACTICE 1

Preposition Identification

*Instructions: In the space provided, identify the underlined word or words in each of the sentences. Use the following codes: **Prep** (preposition), **PP** (prepositional phrase), **I** (infinitive or infinitive phrase), **OP** (object of a preposition), **CP** (compound preposition).*

1. My long-term goal is <u>to become</u> the president of a small company.

    1. _____

2. We completed a leadership survey in the engineering <u>businesses</u> of Tulsa.

    2. _____

3. He thought of <u>himself</u> as a manager, not as a leader.

    3. _____

4. When employees care <u>about</u> company goals as much as the leader does, the company will prosper.

    4. _____

5. <u>To lead</u>, try focusing on positive ways that you can make changes.

    5. _____

6. We convinced our team leader that this was the best solution <u>in spite of</u> the many alternatives.

    6. _____

7. Max, who thrives <u>on</u> competition, received a promotion to lead technician.

    7. _____

8. To improve the way in which you interact with people, try to change your attitude <u>toward them</u>.

    8. _____

9. What leadership literature have you read <u>in the past few months</u>?

    9. _____

10. <u>In addition to</u> moving expenses, our company paid our new manager's rent for two months.

    10. _____

Special Prepositions and Idiomatic Expressions

Instructions: Select the correct word or words, and write them in the space provided.

1. Sometimes it is difficult to tell the difference (*between, among*) a manager and a leader.

    1. _____

2. (*To, Too, Two*) some managers, style is more important than anything else.

    2. _____

3. My manager seems to be prejudiced against me and people (*as, like*) me.

    3. _____

4. Management finally (*agreed in, agreed with*) the union negotiators.

    4. _____

Name _____ Date _____

5. My (*anger with, anger about*) the injustice of the CEO's decision seemed justifiable at the time.

5. _____

6. When making decisions, leaders always prefer to have a (*couple of, couple*) options.

6. _____

7. Our president chose this office because it is (*near, near to*) the conference room.

7. _____

8. Is there anyone (*beside, besides*) Miguel who wants to become the team leader?

8. _____

9. Successful leaders have quickly (*adapted to, adapted from*) technological changes.

9. _____

10. The president (*accompanied with, accompanied by*) a supervisor attended the exit interviews of two managers.

10. _____

PRACTICE 2

Identifying Prepositions and Objects of Prepositions

Instructions: Draw one line under each prepositional phrase. Circle the object of each preposition.

1. He is the CEO of a company with millions of dollars in annual sales.

2. Employees need a sense of control over their working environments.

3. Do not try to reason with people when they are in the middle of their outbursts.

4. The CEO Institute provides solutions to management problems through peer involvement and discussions.

5. A family business owner needs to work on the development of leadership qualities in the next generation.

Using Prepositions

*Instructions: In the space provided, correct those sentences that are written incorrectly. Write **Yes** if the sentence is correct.*

1. How well do you listen and communicate with your subordinates?

_____

2. To whom do promotions go to in your firm?

_____

3. They kept asking for and bargaining for additional safety measures.

_____

4. The leadership development team met over at the restaurant.

_____

Go to the
Web

Practice 2 Exercises
for more skills practice on this topic.

Prepositions

Name _____ Date _____

5. We could not arrive by a conclusion; therefore, we agreed with another course of action.

_____

_____

6. Running the family business requires dividing leadership responsibilities among the three of us.

_____

7. Where are my books on leadership development at?

_____

8. We had to little time too complete the leadership style questionnaire.

_____

9. I have always felt that Mac did not listen to his workers like he should.

_____

10. Antonio plans to arrive at Cheyenne to talk at a large audience of corporate executives.

_____

_____

Go to the
Web

Practice 3 Exercises
for more skills practice on this topic.

PRACTICE 3

Proofreading

*Instructions: Proofread and compare the two sentences in each group. If they are the same, write **Yes** in the space provided. If they are not the same, write **No**. Use the first sentence as the correct copy. If you find errors in the second sentence, underline them; insert any omitted words or marks of punctuation.*

1. Cargill, Inc., the country's largest privately held firm, has had a nonfamily CEO twice in the past 30 years.   1. _____

   Cargill, Inc., the countries' largest privately-held firm, had a nonfamily CEO twice in the past 30 years.

2. He interviewed for the position of manager of the executive development program at the University of St. Thomas in Minneapolis.   2. _____

   He interviewed for the position of manager for the executive development program in the University of St. Thomas in Minnesota.

Name _____ Date _____

3. The Hugh O'Brian Youth Foundation (HOBY) helps high
   school sophomores learn leadership skills by allowing
   them to interact with those who run today's businesses.

   3. _____

   The Hugh O"Brian Youth Foundation (HOBY) help high
   school sophmores learn leadership skills by allowing
   them to interact with those who run todays businesses.

4. Business Cents Resources in Pittsburgh offers "day-
   camp" programs for children ages 3 through 16 to
   teach them about money, leadership, and other
   business topics.

   4. _____

   Business Cents Resource in Pittsburgh offers "day-
   camp" programs for children ages 3 to 16 to teach
   them about money, leadership, and other business topics.

5. One-fourth of the participants in a national family-
   business survey indicated that their next CEO may be
   a woman.

   5. _____

   One-fifth of the participants in a national family-
   business survey indicated that their next CEO may be
   a woman.

Interpreting Proofreaders' Marks

Your employer, Dr. Fred Tyler, asks you to prepare a final copy of a suggested
reading list for his management classes. The draft that follows requires
corrections.

Instructions: Key the document and make the corrections that are indicated by the
proofreaders' marks. If you are not certain about the use of a proofreaders' mark, use
your reference manual or the proofreaders' marks listed on the inside front cover of
this textbook.

SUGGESTED READING LIST
MANAGEMENT 310
DR FRED B. TYLER

Warren Bennis and Patricia Ward Beiderman, *Organizing Genius: Secrets*
of Creative Collaboration, Addison-Wesley, New York.

David L. Bradford and Allan R. Cohen, *Managing For Excellence,* John
Wiley & Sons, New York.

Paul Hershey, *The Situational Leader,* Warner Books, Inc., New York.

John P. Kotter, *the Leadership Factor,* The Free Press, New York.

☐ James Lundy, *Lead, Follow, or Get Out of the Way,* Pfieffer &
Company, San Diego.

James Miller with Paul Brown, *The Corporate Coach,* Harper Business,
New York.

Prepositions

Name _____ Date _____

Patricia Pitcher, *The Dramas of Leadership*, John Wiley & Sons, ~~NY~~ New York.

Joseph Quigley, *Vision: How Leaders Develop It, Share It, and Sustain It*, McGraw-Hill Inc., New York.

Perry M. Smith, *Taking Charge*, Avery Publishing Group Inc., Garden City ~~Park~~, New York.

Go to the
Web

Practice 4 Exercises
for more skills practice on this topic.

PRACTICE 4

Writing

Instructions: Write a paragraph describing a person whom you believe to be a good leader. Describe the qualities that make this person a good leader. Write at least five sentences. Put parentheses around each prepositional phrase. Answers will vary.

The following is an example:
My favorite kind (of leader) is one who leads (by example).

_____

_____

_____

_____

_____

_____

_____

PRACTICE 5

Preposition Identification

Instructions: In the space provided, identify the underlined word or words in each of the sentences. Use the following codes: **Prep** *(preposition),* **PP** *(prepositional phrase),* **I** *(infinitive phrase),* **OP** *(object of a preposition),* **CP** *(compound preposition).*

1. My goal is to become the best leader possible, both on the job and <u>in</u> my personal life.

    1. _____

2. I am leading the meeting <u>on behalf of</u> Terry.

    2. _____

3. Margaret will not be accepted as a leader until she learns <u>to communicate clearly and directly</u>.

    3. _____

4. Virtually every organization is looking for women with strong leadership <u>abilities</u>.

    4. _____

5. Support your supervisor or staff <u>through difficult times</u>, and your loyalty likely will be reciprocated.

    5. _____

Name _____ Date _____

6. Karl took a battery <u>of psychological tests</u> before he entered a leadership development training program.

6. _____

7. Peter Drucker claims that leadership is identified <u>by</u> results.

7. _____

8. <u>Because of</u> his leadership, production quality increased.

8. _____

9. If leaders want to succeed, they must look for ways <u>to cut</u> costs and improve service.

9. _____

10. How can I integrate leadership skills into my day-to-day <u>actions</u>?

10. _____

Special Prepositions and Idiomatic Expressions

Instructions: Select the correct word or words and write them in the space provided.

1. We always place the recorder (*beside, besides*) the president's chair.

1. _____

2. If I had to choose (*among, between*) the two candidates, I would prefer Margaret's leadership style.

2. _____

3. The final report on leadership styles is (*different from, different than*) the draft that I submitted to Cynthia.

3. _____

4. Patricia is taking several university courses to help her move (*in, into*) a leadership position.

4. _____

5. All of these committee meetings are taking up (*to, too, two*) much of my time.

5. _____

6. To build morale, senior managers (*agreed in, agreed on, agreed with*) a plan to survey workers for their opinions.

6. _____

7. Just (*as, like*) he promised, our CEO kept us informed about budget negotiations.

7. _____

8. A successful leader makes a commitment to the organization, and this commitment often fosters the same (*kind, kind of*) loyalty from other employees.

8. _____

9. The winter storms prevented Jim (*from going, going*) to the leadership seminar in Duluth.

9. _____

10. If John becomes (*angry with, angry at*) a staff member, he does not show his anger in front of others.

10. _____

Name _____ Date _____

PRACTICE 6

Identifying Prepositions and Objects of Prepositions

Instructions: Draw one line under each prepositional phrase. Circle the object of each preposition.

1. In spite of the delayed shipment, our vice president of sales still managed to retain the business of the largest customer in Canada.

2. Our managers encourage leadership development among employees at all levels of the organization.

3. The president hired Michael Wilson to establish the identity of a new division that is separate from the parent company.

4. Burt Nanus and Warren Bennis base their definition of leadership on five competencies or strategies.

5. We need to obtain the support of the board in addition to the approval of our department manager.

Using Prepositions

*Instructions: In the space provided, correct those sentences that are written incorrectly. Write **Yes** if the sentence is correct.*

1. A successful leader makes a commitment to the organization and fosters that same kind commitment in other employees.

   _____

   _____

2. The president is always accompanied by her assistant when traveling in Japan.

   _____

3. It looks like Tom will be promoted before the end of the month.

   _____

4. Beside the manager, no one has access to the master list of computer passwords.

   _____

   _____

5. Janie should plan for and decide the speakers for our annual meeting.

   _____

   _____

Copyright © by The McGraw-Hill Companies, Inc.

Name _____ Date _____

6. I found many similarities in leadership styles among the two managers.

_____

7. The leadership trainer panicked when she noticed that someone had removed her course materials off of her desk.

_____

_____

8. Where is the interview for the senior manager at?

_____

9. To many businesses fail too make a profit because the owners do not have adequate organizational skills.

_____

_____

10. My mentor talked at me about leadership qualities such as optimism, accessibility, and sensitivity to others.

_____

_____

PRACTICE 7

Proofreading

*Instructions: Proofread and compare the two sentences in each group. If they are the same, write **Yes** in the space provided. If they are not the same, write **No.** Use the first sentence as the correct copy. If you find errors in the second sentence, underline them; insert any omitted words or marks of punctuation.*

1. Johnson & Johnson articulates its business principles in a document called "Our Credo," which clearly describes the company's responsibilities to customers, employees, communities, and stockholders.   1. _____

   Johnson & Johnson articlates it's business principals in a document called "Our Credo," which clearly describes the company's responsibilities to customers, employees, communities and stockholders.

2. The management team distributed two brief surveys: one to employees and one to a sample of current clients.   2. _____

   The management team distributed two brief surveys: one for employees and one for a sampling of current clients.

Prepositions   **451**

Name _____ Date _____

3. An important leadership skill is the ability to mentor, which means helping an employee to improve his or her job performance.

3. _____

An important leadership skill is the ability to mentor, which means helping an employee to improve his or her job performance.

4. Some strategies for motivating employees include listening to complaints and ideas objectively, finding ways to recognize and reward good work, praising good performance in public, and counseling poor performers privately.

4. _____

Some strategys for motivating employees include listening to complaints and ideas objectivly, finding ways to recognize and award good work, praising good performance in public, and counsoling poor performers privately.

5. Difficult people can be negative, irritating, and impossible to manage, but a good leader always tries to analyze challenging behavior.

5. _____

Difficult people can be negative, iritating, and impossible to manage, but a good leader always tries to analyse challenging behavor.

Interpreting Proofreaders' Marks

Your manager is preparing a list of leadership quotations. The following draft of quotes requires corrections.

Instructions: Key the document and make the corrections that are indicated by the proofreaders' marks. If you are not certain about the use of a proofreaders' mark, use your reference manual or the proofreaders' marks listed on the inside front cover of this textbook.

LEADERSHIP QUOTATIONS

"You cannot push anyone up the ladder ~~unless he is willing to climb himself~~." Andrew Carneige.

stet "The buck stops here." Harry S. Truman *stet*

"You can only make others better by being good yourself." Hugh R. Hanels

"treat people as if they were what they ought to be and you help them become what they are capable of being." Johann Wolfgang Von Goethe

"Managers are people who do things right, and leaders are people who do the right thing." Warren Bennis

"If you can dream it, you can do it." Walt Disney

"If we don't change our direction, we're likely to endup where we're headed." Chinese proverb

Name _____ Date _____

PRACTICE 8

Writing

Instructions: Write a paragraph describing a successful leadership experience that you have had. Include your role and the results of your experience. Write at least five sentences. Put parentheses around each prepositional phrase. Answers will vary.

The following is an example:
My successful leadership experience occurred (during the past summer).

_____

_____

_____

_____

_____

_____

_____

_____

_____

_____

_____

_____

_____

_____

_____

Posttest

*Instructions: In the space provided, write **T** if the statement is true and **F** if the statement is false.*

1. The sentence *Most managers who understand participatory management techniques look for opportunities to apply the principles and practices within their own units* has three prepositions. (1)

   1. _____

2. In the sentence *Our company understands the importance of leadership,* the object of the preposition is *importance.* (2)

   2. _____

3. In the sentence *Leaders need persistence and a willingness to take risks,* the phrase *to take risks* is an infinitive phrase. (3)

   3. _____

4. In the sentence *The manager's parking space is located in the underground parking lot beneath the building,* the phrase *beneath the building* is a prepositional phrase. (2)

   4. _____

5. The sentence *The promotion to vice president is between Betty and me* is written correctly. (6)

   5. _____

6. Prepositional phrases modify adjectives. (4)

   6. _____

7. The word *like* is used correctly in the sentence *My manager said that he wanted to hire another conscientious worker like me.* (6)

   7. _____

8. The idiomatic expression *agree in* is used correctly in the sentence *I agree in principle with my supervisor's decision.* (7)

   8. _____

9. The sentence *Please keep confidential memos off of your desk* is written correctly. (5)

   9. _____

10. The sentence *Where is my telephone directory at?* is written correctly. (5)

    10. _____

11. The sentence *A great leader is aware of the strong need for actions to match words* has three prepositions. (1, 3)

    11. _____

12. The sentence *Your understanding of leadership is different than mine* is written correctly. (6)

    12. _____

13. The sentence *Patti reacted too slowly to the supervisor's suggestions for improvement* is written correctly. (6)

    13. _____

14. The sentence *Our manager encourages us to talk to each other to solve our differences* is written correctly. (7)

    14. _____

15. The sentence *Jamie would like for us to finish the report by Friday* is written correctly. (5)

    15. _____

Chapter 15

Conjunctions

OBJECTIVES

After you have studied this chapter and completed the exercises, you will be able to do the following:

1. Identify conjunctions.

2. Identify types of clauses and sentences.

3. Use coordinating and correlative conjunctions correctly.

4. Use subordinating conjunctions and conjunctive adverbs correctly.

5. Use correct punctuation in sentences containing coordinating, correlative, or subordinating conjunctions, or conjunctive adverbs.

6. Identify correct parallel structure in sentences.

7. Distinguish between conjunctions and prepositions.

8. Use commonly confused conjunction expressions correctly.

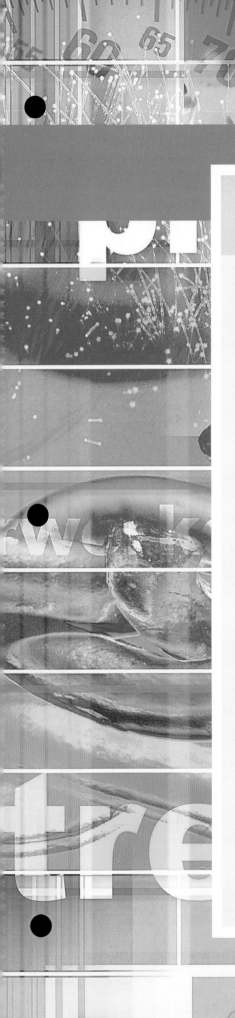

Workplace Applications: Stress and Coping Strategies

Stress is emotional tension caused by everyday events in our lives. Certain occupations cause more stress than others, but most Americans feel that their jobs cause them stress. Researchers are showing links between stress and physical symptoms like tension, pain, and irritability. Stress may also be a cause of illnesses such as headaches, high blood pressure, and cancer.

Stress can be a negative force in our lives if we do not have adequate coping resources. Coping strategies involve exercise, healthful eating, and relaxation techniques. For many people, developing coping strategies means making lifestyle changes.

Managing Stress

Exercise not only releases frustrations but also makes you feel better about yourself. Many working people say that they do not have time to exercise, but exercise opportunities are all around us. You can get off the bus a stop early or park your car in the farthest space available and then walk to your workplace. You can take the stairs or walk briskly around the office. You can use an exercise bike while you watch television, or you can take a walk during the half time of a televised sports event.

Proper nutrition helps stabilize your moods. By reducing your intake of caffeine, sugar, nicotine, and alcohol, you can reduce stress. Even though candy or soft drinks help increase your energy temporarily, they cause your blood sugar to drop, making you feel fatigued. Sources of long-lasting energy are fruits, vegetables, and whole grains.

Relaxation techniques involve activities that you like to do but do not take the time to do. Some people relax by listening to music, reading, or doing deep-breathing exercises. Others find it uplifting to be around positive people who like to laugh.

Pretest

Instructions: In the space provided, write the letter of the correct answer.

1. In the sentence *When you feel overwhelmed and overloaded with work, talk with your manager or a trusted coworker about your concerns,* how many conjunctions do you find? (1)

   a. one   c. three

   b. two   d. four

   1. _____

2. The sentence *Things went well initially, but soon I was spending too much time at work* is an example of a: (2)

   a. simple sentence.   c. complex sentence.

   b. compound sentence.   d. compound-complex sentence.

   2. _____

3. In the sentence *We encourage our employees to leave the office at 5 p.m. or as close to 5 as possible,* the conjunction *or* is a: (3)

   a. coordinating conjunction.   c. subordinating conjunction.

   b. correlative conjunction.   d. conjunctive adverb.

   3. _____

4. Which sentence is written correctly? (3)

   a. Either Lisa will contact a psychologist or participate in group counseling.

   b. Lisa will either contact a psychologist or participate in group counseling.

   c. Lisa will either contact a psychologist and either participate in group counseling.

   d. Either Lisa will contact a psychologist and either participate in group counseling.

   4. _____

5. In the sentence *Since I work from my home, I can set a routine that is comfortably paced,* the conjunction *since* is a: (4)

   a. coordinating conjunction.

   b. correlative conjunction.

   c. subordinating conjunction.

   d. conjunctive adverb.

   5. _____

6. Which of the following is an example of a conjunctive adverb? (4)

   a. neither . . . nor   c. when

   b. nevertheless   d. like

   6. _____

7. Which sentence is punctuated correctly? (5)

   a. Work, family relationships and financial problems are three leading causes of stress.

   b. Companies may offer anxiety, or depression treatments for their employees.

   c. Most managers think that they delegate effectively, but often fail to release their challenging projects.

   d. Neither Aaron nor Larry has been at work the past week.

   7. _____

8. Which sentence is punctuated correctly? (5)

   a. If you have been a victim in the downsizing of a company, you have experienced stress.

   b. I worked at CT Labs, until I retired in 2004.

   c. To relieve stress, I take a short break, furthermore; I exercise whenever I can.

   d. Most workers are health-conscious therefore; our firm offers stress reduction activities.

   8. _____

9. Which sentence is written correctly? (6)

    a. Walking is exercise that is healthy, easy, and energizes you.

    b. I have considered taking a stress management workshop and to apply for a new job.

    c. Janet relaxes by recording her innermost thoughts, observations, and emotions in a daily journal.

    d. Our firm will terminate either a third of its workers or merge with Software Solutions, Inc.

9. _____

10. Which sentence is written correctly? (8)

    a. To maintain your health, be sure and contact your doctor for yearly physicals.

    b. To maintain your health, be sure to contact your doctor for yearly physicals.

    c. I can't help but think that I need to delegate more of my work.

    d. I can't but help think that I need to delegate more of my work.

10. _____

11. Which statement applies to the sentence *Betty and Jean go on their breaks after I do*? (1, 7)

    a. The sentence has two conjunctions and two prepositions.

    b. The sentence has one conjunction and one preposition.

    c. The sentence has two conjunctions and one preposition.

    d. The sentence has one conjunction and two prepositions.

11. _____

12. Which sentence is *not* written correctly? (8)

    a. Being an office worker can be just as stressful as being a doctor.

    b. I read in a magazine where laughter has a positive effect on mental health.

    c. My workload is not so heavy as Ivo's.

    d. I read in my nutrition textbook that skipping meals should be avoided.

12. _____

13. Which statement applies to the sentence *After a stressful day at work, I wanted to relax and read a good book*? (2)

    a. The sentence has two dependent clauses and two independent clauses.

    b. The sentence has one dependent clause and one independent clause.

    c. The sentence has two dependent clauses and one independent clause.

    d. The sentence has one dependent clause and two independent clauses.

13. _____

14. Which statement applies to the sentence *Keeping up with my daily schedule and learning new software make my days stressful*? (5)

    a. The sentence requires a comma after the word *schedule.*

    b. The sentence includes a dependent and independent clause.

    c. The sentence is written in a parallel format.

    d. The sentence is an example of a compound sentence.

14. _____

15. Which sentence is written correctly? (7, 8)

    a. I don't know but what my volunteer work adds too much stress in my life.

    b. I must create a balance between my work responsibilities and the time that I spend with my family.

    c. Furthermore: Al works out daily and maintains his weight.

    d. Shelly acted like she did not have time for lunch out today.

15. _____

You will often find a need to connect your thoughts rather than present them in short choppy sentences. Within a sentence, you can join nouns, pronouns, verbs, adjectives, and adverbs. You can also join phrases, clauses, and even sentences.

In this chapter, you will learn how to form these connections. You will also learn that the expressions you connect must be grammatically equal; for example, nouns must be connected with other nouns or adjectives with other adjectives. This principle, parallelism, is a requisite for clear writing.

Before you begin your work with conjunctions, you will have an opportunity to review dependent and independent clauses as well as the types of sentence structures. When you complete this chapter, you will have finished your intensive study of basic grammar principles.

Review of Clauses and Sentences

A brief review of the types of clauses and sentence formations is appropriate before you study the connecting function of conjunctions.

Clauses

Independent Clauses.   An independent clause (or main clause) can stand alone as a complete sentence. A clause has a complete subject and predicate.

independent clause

Stress-related symptoms vary.

(*Stress-related symptoms* is the complete subject, and *vary* is the complete predicate. These words make a complete sentence and can stand alone.)

Dependent Clauses.   A dependent clause (or subordinate clause) also contains a subject and a predicate; however, a dependent clause is not a complete sentence and cannot stand alone. A dependent clause requires an independent clause to make sense. A dependent clause may appear before or after an independent clause.

| dependent clause | independent clause |

After I received my promotion, I began to delegate more of my work.

(*After I received my promotion* is the dependent clause and has a subject and a predicate, but it cannot stand alone. The clause is not a complete thought, and it must depend on the independent clause *I began to delegate more of my work* to make sense. In this sentence, the dependent clause comes before the independent clause.)

| independent clause | dependent clause |

I began to delegate more of my work after I received my promotion.

(In this sentence, the dependent clause comes after the independent clause.)

Sentences

Simple Sentence.   A simple sentence consists of one complete subject and one complete predicate. The subject, the predicate, or both may be compound.

Company leaders often set the workaholic pace in their firms.

(The sentence has a complete subject, *company leaders,* and a complete predicate, *often set the workaholic pace in their firms.*)

independent clause

Work and worry create tension and cause headaches.

(The sentence has a compound subject, *work* and *worry,* and a compound simple predicate, *create* and *cause.* The complete predicate is *create tension and cause headaches.*)

Compound Sentence.   A compound sentence consists of two simple independent clauses connected by a conjunction such as *or, and, nor,* or *but.*

independent clause

Work pressures often cause stress, but

independent clause

family and financial concerns are additional causes.

(The conjunction *but* connects the two independent clauses.)

independent clause

Nick spends time with his family, and

independent clause

he never fails to attend his children's scheduled events.

(The conjunction *and* connects the two independent clauses.)

Complex Sentence.   A complex sentence contains an independent clause and one or more dependent clauses.

dependent clause

Although his team was ahead in its production goal,

independent clause

Bryan worried about the final outcome.

(The sentence contains an independent clause, *Bryan worried about the final outcome,* and a dependent clause, *Although his team was ahead in its production goal.*)

dependent clause   dependent clause

Because our supervisor challenges us and because he sets short-

independent clause

range goals, he decreases the tension involved in doing new tasks.

(The sentence contains an independent clause, *he decreases the tension involved in doing new tasks.* The sentence also contains two dependent clauses—*Because our supervisor challenges us* and *because he sets short-range goals.*)

Compound-Complex Sentence.   A compound-complex sentence contains more than one independent clause and one or more dependent clauses.

dependent clause

If managers do not develop time management techniques,

independent clause | independent clause

their stress levels will increase; furthermore, their personal

time will decrease.

(The sentence contains two independent clauses—*their stress levels will increase* and *furthermore, their personal time will decrease*. The sentence contains one dependent clause, *If managers do not develop time management techniques*.)

dependent clause | independent clause

After he recovered from his heart attack, he continued his same

independent clause

stressful routine; moreover, he failed to exercise.

(The sentence contains two independent clauses—*he continued his same stressful routine* and *moreover, he failed to exercise*. The sentence contains one dependent clause, *After he recovered from his heart attack*.)

Go to the **Web**

Checkpoint 15.1
for more skills practice on this topic.

CHECKPOINT 15.1

Instructions: *Use the following codes to identify the sentences listed below:* **S** *(simple sentence),* **D** *(compound sentence),* **X** *(complex sentence),* **C** *(compound-complex sentence). Underline each independent clause once and each dependent clause twice.*

1. The supervisor was a patient teacher, and Angie felt very comfortable during her initial training.   _____

2. While many workers experience stress in their lives, some people cope with the stress more effectively than others.   _____

3. A job loss causes a stressful situation.   _____

4. Everyone is subject to burnout unless he or she recognizes the early symptoms.   _____

5. Jane's daughter did not like her mother's hectic schedule, and she vowed to live her life differently.   _____

6. When I became the department manager, I had to learn to delegate; otherwise, I would have become a frustrated workaholic.   _____

7. My job interview was a stressful event for me.   _____

8. Stress and tension cause productivity delays; furthermore, they are detrimental to the health of employees if they are ignored.   _____

Types of Conjunctions

Conjunctions join words, phrases, and clauses. Like prepositions, they show relationships. Conjunctions, however, do not have objects; prepositions do. All conjunctions are either *coordinating, correlative,* or *subordinating.* One function of the *conjunctive adverb* is that of a connector; therefore, it appears in this section.

Coordinating Conjunctions

A coordinating conjunction such as *and, or, but,* or *nor* joins words, phrases, or clauses that are equal in grammatical construction and importance.

Use *but* to express a contrasting idea. Use *and* to show an addition. Use *or* to indicate a choice. Use *nor* to make a second choice negative.

Telemarketers and others who work alone are potential stress victims.

(The conjunction *and* joins the noun *telemarketers* and the pronoun *others.* The conjunction shows an addition to the noun *telemarketers.*)

Owners of small businesses make or break their companies with their reactions to unexpected events.

(The conjunction *or* joins the verb *make* and the verb *break.* The conjunction indicates a choice between *make* or *break.*)

One employee sees the project as an exciting challenge, but another sees the project as an impossible task.

(The conjunction *but* joins two independent clauses. The conjunction indicates a contrasting idea.)

Jon and Kara did not view the conflict as a threat to their working relationship, nor did they discuss the issue.

(The conjunction *nor* joins the two independent clauses. The conjunction *nor* makes the second choice negative.)

Insert a comma before a coordinating conjunction that separates two independent clauses.

Burnout does not necessarily come from hard work, but it may result from a lack of enjoyment of the work.

(This compound sentence has two independent clauses. A comma is necessary before the coordinating conjunction *but.*)

People prefer to work with mature individuals, and one indication of maturity is self-control.

(This compound sentence has two complete clauses. A comma is necessary before the coordinating conjunction *and.*)

Do not use a comma before a coordinating conjunction that links two words or two phrases. Do not use a comma before a conjunction if the material following the conjunction is not a complete sentence.

Sometimes the appointments on my personal calendar and on my daily planner are in conflict.

(No comma is necessary before the coordinating conjunction *and* that links two words—*calendar* and *planner.*)

Her job is to analyze office stress patterns and to conduct seminars on stress management.

(No comma is necessary before the coordinating conjunction *and* that links two infinitive phrases.)

Sherry did not enjoy new assignments but preferred her regular routine of work.

(No comma is necessary before the coordinating conjunction *but.* The phrase *but preferred her regular routine of work* is not a complete sentence.)

Gordy praises his employees in public <u>but</u> reprimands them in private.

(No comma is necessary before the coordinating conjunction *but*. The phrase *but reprimands them in private* is not a complete sentence.)

Use commas to separate three or more words, phrases, or clauses in a series. Do not place a comma after the last item in a series. Include a comma before the coordinating conjunction.

Much of a manager's stress comes from the board of directors, shareholders, employees, <u>or</u> the media.

(This is a series of four items. Each item must be separated from the other with a comma. A comma is necessary before the coordinating conjunction *or.*)

The arguments, accusations, <u>and</u> inaccurate information created a stressful situation.

(This is a series of three items. Each item must be separated from the others with a comma. A comma is necessary before the coordinating conjunction *and.* Do not use a comma after the last item, *inaccurate information.*)

Go to the
Web

Checkpoint 15.2
for more skills practice on this topic.

CHECKPOINT 15.2

Instructions: Underline the coordinating conjunctions. Use the proofreaders' mark ∧ to insert a comma where it is appropriate.

1. Meetings, paperwork and downsizing create the most stress for managers.

2. My manager delegates vendor and customer inquiries to Holly or me.

3. An organized work area increases your productivity and reduces your stress.

4. Kay always felt apprehensive about a new assignment but tried to cover her fears with a display of enthusiasm optimism and calmness.

5. Signs of burnout are chronic fatigue and disinterest in things that you once enjoyed.

6. A project may not be done your way but you must learn to delegate.

7. The trainees are well-educated and perform well under pressure.

8. We did not realize our coping skills were inadequate nor did we understand the consequences.

Correlative Conjunctions

Correlative conjunctions join words, phrases, and sentences of equal importance. Correlative conjunctions appear in pairs, and both parts receive the same attention. The common pairs used as correlative conjunctions are as follows:

both/and	neither/nor
either/or	not only/but also
whether/or	

Use correlative conjunctions to join words, phrases, and clauses that are equal in construction and importance. Place the paired conjunctions as near as possible to the words that they connect.

Neither he nor she causes your reactions; you do.

(The paired conjunctions *neither* and *nor* are of equal importance and work together. They appear next to the words that they connect, *he* and *she*.)

A company focuses on stress not only because of a concern for its employees' health but also because of the effects of employee stress on its profit.

(The paired conjunctions *not only* and *but also* work together and appear next to the phrases that they connect.)

Whether personal problems or work difficulties cause you stress, recognize the early burnout signs.

(The paired conjunctions *whether* and *or* are of equal importance and work together. They appear next to the words that they connect, *personal problems* and *work difficulties*.)

CHECKPOINT 15.3

Go to the
Web

Checkpoint 15.3
for more skills practice on this topic.

Instructions: *In the space provided, write the appropriate missing conjunction.*

1. Either walking _____ exercising helps relieve tension and stress.   _____

2. Kelly's aggressive behavior caused problems not only with her coworkers _____ with the customers.   _____

3. To decrease the amount of time spent reading communications, employees were asked to streamline both e-mail _____ voice mail messages.   _____

4. My new venture is not only time-consuming _____ satisfying.   _____

5. If Lou does not organize her time, neither the survey results _____ the analysis of the information will be completed on schedule.   _____

6. I have not decided whether to ride the bus _____ to drive my car to the meeting.   _____

7. Our company suggests that we use either our sick leave _____ a floating holiday if we are experiencing stress.   _____

8. Kristen not only did the research _____ prepared the final report.   _____

Subordinating Conjunctions

Another way to join expressions is with a subordinating conjunction. A subordinating conjunction introduces a dependent clause and links it to an independent clause. A dependent clause does not make sense by itself; it depends on the independent clause for meaning.

Following are some subordinating conjunctions grouped according to their meanings in sentences. Several appear in more than one column.

Looking Back

Refer to Chapter 13 for an introduction to subordinating conjunctions.

Time	Reason	Place	Condition	Concession
after	as	where	as if	although
as long as	because	wherever	except	even though
as soon as	for		if	though
before	in order that		otherwise	
since	inasmuch as	**Manner**	unless	**Comparison**
until	since	as		as much as
when	so that	as if		than
whenever	whereas	as though		
while				

Use a subordinating conjunction to introduce a dependent clause. Place a comma after a dependent clause that begins a sentence. Generally, do not use a comma before a dependent clause that appears at the end of a sentence.

<u>Although I lost money</u>, I handled the stress of the cycles in the real estate market very well.

(*Although I lost money* is a dependent clause that cannot stand alone. The dependent clause appears at the beginning of the sentence and introduces an independent clause [*I handled the stress of the cycles in the real estate market very well*]. A comma is necessary after the dependent clause.)

<u>When you think that someone is overstressed</u>, show your concern and understanding.

(*When you think that someone is overstressed* is a dependent clause that indicates time and introduces an independent clause [*show your concern and understanding*]. The dependent clause cannot stand alone. A comma is necessary after the dependent clause.)

Too many of us become ill <u>before we decide to change our habits.</u>

(*Before we decide to change our habits* is a dependent clause and indicates time. The dependent clause cannot stand alone. The dependent clause appears at the end of the complete sentence and does not require a comma before it.)

EDIT PATROL

From an article in the *Pittsburgh Press:*

American primitive painter Grandma Moses produced much of her work before she died at 101.

Note: Did she really produce the rest of her work *after* she died?

Do This

I <u>can't help worrying</u> that my job will be eliminated after the merger.

I <u>think that perhaps</u> I should discuss this move with my family.

Do Not Do This

I <u>can't help but worry</u> that my job will be eliminated after the merger.

I <u>don't know but what</u> I should discuss this move with my family.

Avoid the expressions *can't help but* and *but what.*

CHECKPOINT 15.4

Go to the
Web

Checkpoint 15.4
for more skills practice on
this topic.

Instructions: In each of the following sentences, underline the dependent clause. Circle the subordinating conjunction.

1. Since Taylor was unhappy with her hectic 55-hour workweek, she opened her own business.

2. Employees should know where they can go to get help.

3. Flextime makes it easier for employees to be home when their children get out of school.

4. As recent statistics indicate, the need to manage time is more urgent than ever.

5. Some companies do not lay off workers because they value their employees' loyalty and trust.

6. If these suggestions help you cope, let me know.

7. Even though I plan each day carefully, stressful interruptions often occur.

8. I enjoy a long walk after I have had a stressful day at work.

Conjunctive Adverbs

A conjunctive adverb shows a relationship between two independent clauses of equal weight. The words are adverbs, but they also function as connectors. Some common conjunctive adverbs are as follows:

consequently	nevertheless
furthermore	otherwise
hence	similarly
however	still
indeed	therefore
instead	thus
likewise	yet
moreover	

Use a semicolon before a conjunctive adverb when it joins two independent clauses. Use a comma after a conjunctive adverb of two or more syllables.

Most businesses take three to six months to recover from a major disaster; however, some businesses never recover their losses.

(The word *however* is a conjunctive adverb that connects the two independent clauses. In this sentence, a semicolon precedes the conjunctive adverb *however*, and a comma follows it.)

Our speaker suggested that we should not avoid stress; instead, we should let it work for us.

(In this sentence, the word *instead* functions as a conjunctive adverb that connects the two independent clauses. A semicolon precedes the conjunctive adverb *instead*, and a comma follows it.)

PUNCTUATION ALERT!

Punctuation With Conjunctive Adverbs
Use a semicolon before a conjunctive adverb when it joins two independent clauses. Use a comma after a conjunctive adverb of two or more syllables.

Conjunctions

A supervisor's words are powerful; <u>therefore,</u> they can cause an employee some anxious moments.

(*Therefore* is a conjunctive adverb that connects the two independent clauses. A semicolon precedes the conjunctive adverb *therefore,* and a comma follows it.)

Go to the
Web

Checkpoint 15.5
for more skills practice on this topic.

CHECKPOINT 15.5

Instructions: Underline each conjunctive adverb. Add commas or semicolons using the proofreaders' marks ⋀ and ⋏ where necessary.

1. Most businesses will not have to deal with serious disasters nevertheless managers need plans that will keep their firms operating during emergencies.

2. Avoid negative situations by associating with workers who provide stimulating conversation similarly refrain from joining the gossip enthusiasts.

3. My supervisor always comments on our work furthermore she knows how to make the work environment pleasant.

4. Jack's intention was to relieve the tense moment however his words did just the opposite.

5. Travel can be a major source of stress at any time moreover it is especially traumatic during the holidays.

6. I felt isolated and stressed working at home consequently I requested a transfer to a local branch office.

Go to the
Web

Checkpoint 15.6
for more skills practice on this topic.

CHECKPOINT 15.6

Instructions: Underline all conjunctions and all conjunctive adverbs in the following sentences. In the space provided, identify each conjunction as a coordinating conjunction (**Co-ord**), a correlative conjunction (**Corr**), a subordinating conjunction (**SC**), or a conjunctive adverb (**CA**). Add commas or semicolons using the proofreaders' marks ⋀ and ⋏ where necessary.

1. The mark of a great CEO is how he or she handles stress. _____

2. Workers are beginning to take steps to make their lives simpler and less stressful however these are not easy tasks. _____

3. Whether you delegate work or you do it yourself allow sufficient time for completing the tasks. _____

4. Employees who are mentally and physically drained are not productive workers. _____

5. If you find Monday mornings especially stressful you have plenty of company. _____

6. Satisfied workers and productivity seem to correlate however some studies show no strong connection between satisfaction and performance. _____ _____

7. When you experience a stressful experience take a deep breath and react calmly. _____

8. Although Carl completed the project under stressful conditions his supervisor neither acknowledged the work nor complimented Carl. _____

Parallelism

Parallelism is the linking together of similar grammatical parts in a sentence. To have parallel sentence structure, similar constructions should be connected, such as nouns to other nouns, verbs to other verbs, or clauses to other clauses. Use coordinating conjunctions or correlative conjunctions to join parallel parts of a sentence.

Correct: **To relieve work stress, Sylvia exercises daily, gets physical checkups yearly, and plays tennis several times a week.**

(The three present tense verbs *exercises, gets,* and *plays* are parallel in construction.)

Incorrect: **To relieve work stress, Sylvia exercises daily, gets physical checkups yearly, and is playing tennis several times a week.**

(The phrase *is playing tennis several times a week* is not parallel to the verbs *exercises* and *gets.*)

Correct: **Having a home-based business eliminates rush-hour traffic hassles and department meetings.**

(The two nouns *hassles* and *meetings* are parallel.)

Incorrect: **Having a home-based business eliminates rush-hour traffic hassles and going to department meetings.**

(The phrase *going to department meetings* is not parallel to the noun *hassles.*)

Correct: **Jason is overworked, irritable, and demanding.**

(The three adjectives are parallel in construction.)

Incorrect: **Jason is overworked, irritable, and demands too much from his staff.**

(The phrase *demands too much from his staff* is not parallel to the adjectives *overworked* and *irritable.*)

Correct: **Stress took its toll both on her health and on her family.**

(The two phrases *on her health* and *on her family* connected by correlative conjunctions are parallel in construction.)

Correct: **She thought that the coping strategies were working and that the department was decreasing its turnover rate.**

(If necessary, repeat an introductory word. The word *that* introduces the two dependent clauses and makes the parallel construction clear.)

Go to the
Web

Checkpoint 15.7
for more skills practice on
this topic.

CHECKPOINT 15.7

Instructions: *The following sentences are not parallel in construction. In the space provided, write the sentence correctly.*

1. Workers derive satisfaction from feeling valued and to be in control of their work.

   _____

   _____

2. My interests away from the office include reading, hiking, and I like to swim.

   _____

3. Workers with high-stress levels respond not only in ways that may be harmful to the company but also to themselves.

   _____

   _____

4. After starting his own company, Andy had less stress, more flexible schedules, and spent more time with his family.

   _____

   _____

5. Policies for using e-mail and how to reduce paperwork can relieve the tension from information overload.

   _____

   _____

   _____

   _____

6. The stress management counselor either advised spending less time at the office or finding another job.

   _____

   _____

7. To keep up with family demands and maintaining my management position create a great deal of stress for me.

   _____

   _____

8. The new stress reduction program is helpful, enjoyable, and it costs nothing.

   _____

Cautions in Using Conjunctions

A number of words may be used as conjunctions and as prepositions; therefore, it is important to understand the functions of the conjunction. Several uses of confusing conjunctions also require clarification and special attention.

Conjunctions and Prepositions

Determine the appropriate function of a word in a sentence. Some words may be both prepositions and conjunctions; for example, *before, after, until, for, than,* and *since.* Use a conjunction to connect clauses. Use a preposition when an object is expressed or understood; conjunctions do not have objects.

She will not accept the promotion <u>until</u> she discusses it with her family.

(In this sentence, *until* is a conjunction. *Until* connects the clause *she discusses it with her family* with the clause *She will not accept the promotion.*)

She will not accept the promotion <u>until</u> next month.

(In this sentence, *until* is a preposition and takes the object *month.* No verb follows the preposition.)

Tom always leaves the office <u>after</u> I do.

(*After* is a conjunction that connects the clause *I do* with the clause *Tom always leaves the office.* Both clauses have a subject and a predicate.)

Tom always leaves the office <u>after</u> 5 p.m.

(*After* is a preposition. *After* takes the object *5 p.m.*)

Try To, Be Sure To, Go To

Do not use expressions such as *try and, go and,* and *be sure and* when the infinitive form is needed. Use *try to, go to,* and *be sure to.*

I'd like some time alone to <u>try to determine</u> why I'm feeling so stressed.

(Use *try to,* not *try and.*)

<u>Be sure to inform</u> your supervisor if you need some time off because of personal problems.

(Use *be sure to,* not *be sure and.*)

As, As If, As Though, Like

Use the conjunctions *as, as if,* or *as though* to introduce a subordinate clause. The clause will have a verb in it. Use the preposition *like* to introduce a prepositional phrase. The prepositional phrase will not contain a verb.

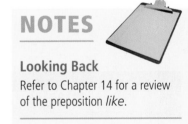
Megan acts <u>as if</u> she does not want help with the project.

(*As if* is a subordinating conjunction that introduces the clause *she does not want help with the project.* Note that the verb is *does want.*)

Many companies are aware of work/life issues and provide employee services <u>like</u> child care and on-site shopping.

(*Like* is a preposition that takes the objects *child care* and *shopping.* Note that there is no verb expressed after *like.*)

As . . . As, So . . . As

Use *as . . . as* in positive comparisons. Use *so . . . as* in negative comparisons. Do not use *equally as,* which is a redundant phrase.

My coping strategies are <u>as effective as</u> yours.

(*As effective as* indicates a positive comparison. Do not use the phrase *equally as effective as.*)

My coping strategies are <u>not so effective as</u> yours.

(*Not so effective as* indicates a negative comparison.)

Where, That

Do not use the conjunction *where* instead of *that* to introduce a clause that includes a reference to a location.

> **I read in the newspaper <u>that</u> a stress management expert would be speaking at the college.**
>
> (Do not use *I read in the newspaper where . . . .*)

Go to the
Web

Checkpoint 15.8
for more skills practice on this topic.

CHECKPOINT 15.8

Instructions: Check the underlined word(s) for correct usage. If the word is correct, write **Yes** *in the space provided. If it is not correct, write the word correctly.*

1. Our new manager is not <u>as</u> demanding as her predecessor.   _____

2. Some companies provide workers with tickets to functions <u>as</u> the symphony or sport events.   _____

3. Try <u>and</u> exercise before leaving for work each morning.   _____

4. He always acts <u>as</u> if he really enjoys his job.   _____

5. Her supervisor suggested that she go <u>and</u> see a depression therapy counselor.   _____

6. I saw in *Time* magazine <u>where</u> research is being done on the effects of stress on heart disease.   _____

7. Good nutrition habits are <u>as</u> important <u>as</u> sufficient exercise for workers with stressful jobs.   _____

8. When you have a fast-paced job, be sure <u>and</u> schedule some relaxation time for yourself.   _____

Diagramming Sentences

You have already learned to use the conjunctions *and, or, nor,* and *but* in diagramming sentences with compound subjects, verbs, and objects.

Matt and Al organized a stress reduction seminar.

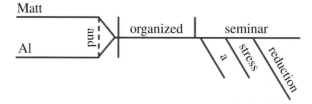

Matt developed and presented a stress reduction seminar.

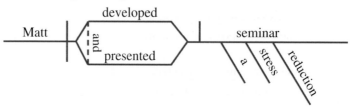

472   Chapter 15

Matt presents stress reduction seminars and workshops.

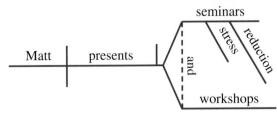

In addition to reviewing the diagramming of a conjunction used with nouns, verbs, and objects, you will learn to diagram sentences with compound adjectives and adverbs. Use a dotted line to connect two adjectives or two adverbs.

A heavy but steady workload challenges some workers.

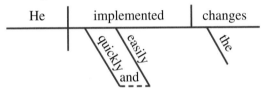

He implemented the changes quickly and easily.

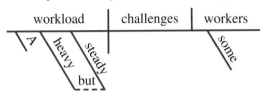

CHECKPOINT 15.9

Go to the
Web

Checkpoint 15.9
for more skills practice on this topic.

Instructions: *In the space provided below, diagram the following sentences. All words may be diagrammed.*

1. Most healthy and successful people are Type A and Type B personalities.

2. Work pressures and personal problems often cause stress-related illnesses.

3. Pam eats carbohydrates in times of stress or work anxiety.

4. People with low self-esteem are comfortable with familiar and undemanding tasks.

5. She has an enthusiastic but realistic work attitude.

6. She outlined her concerns about overtime hours clearly but emphatically.

Name _____ Date _____

PRACTICE 1

Choosing Conjunctions

Instructions: Select the correct word or words, and write them in the space provided.

1. She neither asked for help (*or, nor*) confided in her coworkers.

   1. _____

2. You do not always get to choose what happens to you, (*but, and*) you can choose how to handle each situation.

   2. _____

3. When she discovered her management style was (*like, as*) her supervisor's, she decided to change it.

   3. _____

4. Should I sell the business or (*try and, try to*) restructure the way I operate it?

   4. _____

5. Diane neither participates in office functions (*nor, or*) socializes with her coworkers.

   5. _____

6. I heard on the news (*where, that*) a stress management speaker was scheduled to speak at the paralegals' monthly meeting.

   6. _____

7. (*As, Like*) I indicated in my application letter, I am interested in a challenging job.

   7. _____

8. (*Be sure and, Be sure to*) let me know when you plan to attend the stress workshop.

   8. _____

9. Brett apologized to Kathy (*as, like*) I suggested.

   9. _____

10. The stress that I feel at work is not (*as, so*) great as the stress that I have at home.

    10. _____

Identifying Types of Conjunctions

*Instructions: In the space provided, identify the type of conjunction represented by the underlined word. Use the following codes: **Coord** (coordinating conjunction), **Corr** (correlative conjunction), **SC** (subordinating conjunction), **CA** (conjunctive adverb). If the underlined word is* not *a conjunction, write **No**.*

1. Some stress keeps us alert, <u>but</u> too much stress can be disastrous.

   1. _____

2. Family expectations sometimes cause people to work at jobs that they really do not <u>like</u>.

   2. _____

3. These managers will not survive this high-stress environment <u>unless</u> they change their attitudes about managing their time.

   3. _____

4. Indications of burnout include a loss of interest <u>not only</u> in activities outside the business <u>but also</u> in family events.

   4. _____

Go to the
Web

Practice 1 Exercises
for more skill practice on this topic.

Name _____ Date _____

5. Job security is not a sure thing for today's workers; <u>nevertheless</u>, those who can adjust to the insecurity do move ahead.

5. _____

6. <u>Although</u> she worked well with people, she could not adjust to the fast pace of the office.

6. _____

7. We know the importance of rest, proper nutrition, <u>and</u> exercise in managing stress.

7. _____

8. When I arrive home, I leave "work problems" at the office; <u>therefore</u>, I can concentrate on my family's activities.

8. _____

9. <u>Whether</u> you meditate <u>or</u> schedule your quiet time, you will find that 15 minutes a day will help manage stress.

9. _____

10. <u>If</u> I feel overly stressed, I say "no" to unnecessary commitments.

10. _____

Go to the
Web

Practice 2 Exercises
for more skills practice on this topic.

PRACTICE 2

Identifying Conjunctions and Conjunctive Adverbs Correctly

Instructions: Underline the conjunctions and the conjunctive adverbs in the following sentences. Insert any missing commas or semicolons by using the proofreaders' marks ⋀ or ⋏.

1. Flextime, job sharing and work-at-home arrangements are ways to help employees balance work and other parts of their lives.

2. Self-esteem is the way that you think and feel about yourself but it is not the way that someone else thinks or feels about you.

3. She is unreceptive to emotional appeals however she will listen to facts and reason.

4. Caring for your pet will calm you and prevent the buildup of stress.

5. Low self-esteem is the cause of hostility and cynicism furthermore these two traits are factors in Type A–related heart disease.

6. After you have taken a vacation ease into your old routine and activities slowly.

7. Unless home-based entrepreneurs make an effort to meet people they can feel isolated and stressed.

8. Not only economic pressures but also time pressures create stress for real estate agents.

9. Even though I will have to work all weekend I am going to complete the report.

10. Neither the working conditions nor the tasks are enjoyable.

Name _____ Date _____

Correcting Conjunctions and Sentence Structure

Instructions: In the space provided, correct the following sentences. Check for errors in word usage, punctuation, and appropriate sentence structure. If the sentence is correct, write **Yes.**

1. Ways to reduce stress include yoga, meditation and exercising.

   _____

2. After working at such a fast pace for years I began to experience stress insomnia and I was constantly tired.

   _____

   _____

3. Whether an early riser or a night owl or not, maintain your high energy level by eating properly, and exercise.

   _____

   _____

4. When people know that they are valued they are more secure and produce more.

   _____

5. Some workers said that bad management was the cause of their stress however others blamed their stress on the difficulties in balancing their professional and personal lives.

   _____

   _____

   _____

6. Audrey often acts like she were bored, when she trains new employees.

   _____

7. Socially responsible businesses must try and make an effort to involve their employees in community service activities.

   _____

   _____

8. My work does not seem to be so stressful as yours.

   _____

9. I read in a health magazine where you should talk with a professional if you constantly feel angry disappointed or frustrated.

   _____

   _____

10. Some managers are skilled decision makers, but are not effective trainers.

    _____

Name _____ Date _____

Go to the
Web

Practice 3 Exercises
for more skills practice on
this topic.

PRACTICE 3

Proofreading

*Instructions: Proofread and compare the two sentences in each group. If they are the same, write **Yes** in the space provided. If they are not the same, write **No**. Use the first sentence as the correct copy. If you find errors in the second sentence, underline them.*

1. When the International Survey Research Corporation completed a recent study, it found that 44 percent of the employees felt that their workloads were excessive.

    As the International Survey Research Corporation completed a recent study, it found that 45 percent of the employees felt that their workloads were excessive.

    1. _____

2. Dr. Stephen Rechtschaffen is a pioneer in the wellness movement and the author of the book *Time Shifting*.

    Dr. Stephen Rechtschaffen is a pioneer in the wellness movement, and the the author of the book *Time Shifting*.

    2. _____

3. According to a recent study, a majority of the 185,000 people interviewed experienced some feelings of depression on the first business day of the month.

    According to a recent study, a majority of the 185,000 people interviewed experienced some feelings of depression on the first business day of the month.

    3. _____

4. Perhaps I could manage my stress more effectively if I read *The Overwhelmed Person's Guide to Time Management* by Ronni Eisenberg.

    Perhaps I could manage my stress more effectively as I read *The Overwhelmed Person's Guide to Time Management* by Ronnie Eisenberg.

    4. _____

5. Rob Krakovitz, author of *High Energy,* says that the sound of an alarm clock "starts your day in distress by blaring you awake and putting your system into a panic."

    Rob Krakovitz, author of *High Energy,* says that the sound of a alarm clock "starts your day in distress by blaring you awake or putting your system in a panic."

    5. _____

Name _____ Date _____

Interpreting Proofreaders' Marks

Instructions: *The draft that follows requires corrections. Key the list of coping strategies below and make the corrections that are indicated by the proofreaders' marks. If you are not certain about the use of a proofreaders' mark, use your reference manual or the proofreaders' marks listed on the inside front cover of this textbook.*

COPEING STRATEGIES

1. Exercise

   Remember that the exercise needs to be consistent but it does not have to be strenuous.

2. Visualization

   Think of positive solutions or of ways that successful

   people would solve the problem.

3. Diet

   Eat a low fat breakfast and watch your wt.

4. Meditation and yoga

   Try to get in touch with your inner self. *stet*

5. Asertiveness

   Learn to say "No" some times.

6. Luaghter

   learn to laugh at yourself.

7. Outside activities

   Learn a new skill and task, volunteer at an interesting location, or become involved with community activities.

8. Friendships

   Confide in a trusted friend away from the office.

PRACTICE 4

Writing

Instructions: *Write a paragraph describing the most stressful time that you have had at work, school, or home during the past month. Write at least five sentences. Place parentheses around all conjunctions. Include the following conjunctions. Answers will vary.*

- A series
- At least one subordinating conjunction
- One correlative conjunction

> **Go to the**
> ## Web
>
> **Practice 4 Exercises**
> for more skills practice on this topic.

Name _____ Date _____

The following is an example:
Wearing a Halloween costume was (not only) enjoyable (but also) necessary to alleviate stress.

_____

_____

_____

_____

_____

_____

_____

PRACTICE 5

Choosing Conjunctions

Instructions: Choose the correct word or words, and write them in the space provided.

1. Loreen lost her temper (*because, as*) her manager called her during the weekend.

   1. _____

2. If you are frustrated with someone, write your grievances in a letter, (*and, but*) do not mail the letter.

   2. _____

3. Neither excess anger (*or, nor*) stress is good for one's mental health.

   3. _____

4. (*As, When*) she realized that she was trying to be perfect all the time, she was better able to handle her stress.

   4. _____

5. I am going to (*try and, try to*) arrive at work early tomorrow.

   5. _____

6. I heard from my supervisor (*where, that*) the company is planning to downsize its operations again.

   6. _____

7. (*Be sure to, Be sure and*) register for the health workshops sponsored by Midelfort Clinic.

   7. _____

8. Ken always acts (*as if, like*) a difficult project is an exciting challenge.

   8. _____

9. Although this exercise plan looks (*as, like*) yours, it is less strenuous.

   9. _____

10. My workload this month is not (*so, as*) heavy as it was last month.

    10. _____

Name _____ Date _____

Identifying Types of Conjunctions

Instructions: In the space provided, identify the type of conjunction represented by the underlined word. Use the following codes: **Coord** *(coordinating conjunction),* **Corr** *(correlative conjunction),* **SC** *(subordinating conjunction),* **CA** *(conjunctive adverb). If the underlined word is not a conjunction, write* **No.**

1. Anger can ruin relationships <u>or</u> destroy careers.   1. _____

2. <u>If</u> you are feeling blue, wear a particularly comfortable shirt or bright scarf to brighten your spirits.   2. _____

3. One of the best cures <u>for</u> frustration is exercise.   3. _____

4. <u>Whenever</u> you exercise outdoors, carry personal identification.   4. _____

5. Stretching before a workout increases aerobic capacity; <u>therefore</u>, you should stretch 5 to 7 minutes before exercising.   5. _____

6. Men with higher fitness levels live longer <u>even though</u> they may be overweight.   6. _____

7. Tap water contains <u>not only</u> calcium and magnesium <u>but also</u> other trace elements that protect the heart.   7. _____

8. <u>Because</u> anger is cumulative, it can break down your immune system.   8. _____

9. If you refuse to compromise <u>or</u> to modify your ideas, you are destined to fail at your job.   9. _____

10. A fad diet requires you to eat huge quantities of only one food <u>or</u> type of food.   10. _____

PRACTICE 6

Identifying Conjunctions and Conjunctive Adverbs Correctly

Instructions: Underline the conjunctions and the conjunctive adverbs in the following sentences. Insert any missing commas or semicolons by using the proofreaders' marks ⋀ or ⋀̧.

1. When Ken travels for business he finds that he suffers from separation stress encounters language differences and experiences travel-related sleep disorders.

2. Women who report high levels of job-related stress are often depressed anxious and socially isolated.

3. A large number of people are using alternative medicines such as acupuncture massage therapy or megavitamins however these alternatives could worsen some medical problems.

Conjunctions

4. Since Lou's heart attack he avoids stressful situations.

5. If you have a low degree of control over your job you have nearly twice the risk of developing heart disease.

6. The wellness consultant suggested that we either develop a stress prevention program or offer seminars in coping strategies.

7. While many factors determine a person's tendency to exercise recent research indicates genetic factors may play a role.

8. Cigarette smoking excessive body fat and lack of exercise may be the predominant causes of stroke in people under the age of 75.

9. Stress is caused not only by work problems but also by home pressures.

10. Jenny enjoys her work but finds the pace hectic at times.

Correcting Conjunctions and Sentence Structure

Instructions: *In the space provided, correct the following sentences. Check for errors in word usage, punctuation, and appropriate sentence structure. If the sentence is correct, write* **Yes.**

1. Rachel stopped eating candy bars and cola.

_____

2. Reducing your stress load and exercise help you sleep better at night.

_____

3. Confidence is a valuable ally in combating stress and it helps you feel that you will be successful.

_____

_____

4. Ruth was experiencing not only difficult times at work but also increased demands at home.

_____

5. Healthful lifestyle habits and to have proper nutrition help build your energy reserves.

_____

6. Try and spend a limited amount of time with people who have a considerable amount of negative energy.

_____

_____

Name _____ Date _____

7. Thinking about the past or worrying about the future causes stress therefore focus on current situations.

_____

_____

8. Nancy always acts like her life is completely under her control.

_____

9. Since Kim moved to corporate headquarters she has been working 10-hour days.

_____

_____

10. Meditation and relaxation exercises help relieve tension but they do not eliminate the source of the tension.

_____

_____

PRACTICE 7

Proofreading

*Instructions: Proofread and compare the two sentences in each group. If they are the same, write **Yes** in the space provided. If they are not the same, write **No**. Use the first sentence as the correct copy. If you find errors in the second sentence, underline them; insert any omitted words or marks of punctuation.*

1. Dr. Randal Beaton, research associate professor at the University of Washington School of Nursing, says, "People who work in offices are stressed because their jobs offer little in the way of creativity, control, or satisfaction."   1. _____

   Dr. Randle Beaton, research associate professor at the University of Washington School of Medicine, says, "People who work in offices are stressed because their jobs offer little in the way of creativity, control, or satisfaction."

2. The U.S. Centers for Disease Control (CDC) designed a federal campaign to encourage more Americans to participate in regular exercise programs, and information on this campaign can be found at http://www.cdc.gov/nccdphp/dnpa/readyset.   2. _____

   The U.S. Center for Disease Control (CDC) designed a Federal campaign to encourage more Americans to participate in regular exercize programs, and information on this campagn can be found at http://www.cdc.gov/nccdphp/dnpa/readyset.

Name _____ Date _____

3. A new study concludes that working women with one
    or more children tend to have higher levels of the stress
    hormone cortisol than working women with no children;
    consequently, working women with children have an
    increased risk of cardiovascular disease.

    A new study concludes that working women with one
    or more children tend to have higher levels of the stress
    hormone cortisle than working women with no children;
    consequently, working women with children have an
    increased risk of cardiovasculor disease.

3. _____

4. Researchers at the University of California—Davis,
    School of Medicine, report that working more than
    25 hours a week in the first trimester of pregnancy is
    associated with a threefold increase in the risk of
    miscarriage compared with working fewer hours.

    Researchers at the University of California—Davis,
    School of Medicine, report that working more than
    25 hours a week in the first trimester of pregnancy is
    associated with a threefold increase in the risk of
    miscarriage compared with working fewer hours.

4. _____

5. Chronic stress may accelerate cell aging according to
    research from doctors at the University of California at
    San Francisco. This groundbreaking finding in the field
    of stress research may help explain why the immune
    response is altered by chronic stress.

    Chronic stress may acellerate cell ageing according to
    research from doctors at the University of California at
    San Francisco. This ground-breaking finding in the field
    of stress research may help explain why the immune
    response is altered by chronic stress.

5. _____

Interpreting Proofreaders' Marks

*Instructions: The draft that follows requires corrections. Key the anger coping
strategies below, and make the corrections that are indicated by the proofreaders'
marks. If you are not certain about the use of a proofreaders' mark, use your reference
manual or the proofreaders' marks listed on the inside front cover of this textbook.*

Managing Anger

1. Be aware of situations that make you angry at work, at home, or in
    your car.

2. Put yourself in the other person's place, and try to see his or her pt.
    of view.

3. Resist the urge to get into Name-calling.

4. Speak quietly, and calmly to keep the situation from escalating.

Name _____ Date _____

5. Practice relaxation techniques by focusing on something pleasant.

6. Write out what is bothering you, but don't give to the other person.
the list

7. Walk away if you can't get your feelings under control.
emotions

8. Don't take anger out on yourself by overeating or drinking.

PRACTICE 8

Writing

Instructions: *Write a paragraph describing the person in your life who gives (or gave) you the most stress. Write at least five sentences. Place parentheses around all conjunctions. Include the following conjunctions. Answers will vary.*

- A series
- At least one subordinating conjunction
- One correlative conjunction

The following is an example:
Leon (neither) set goals (nor) determined priorities.

_____

_____

_____

_____

_____

_____

Posttest

Instructions: *In the space provided, write the letter of the correct answer.*

1. The sentence *Jan's job is very stressful, but she uses relaxation techniques to help her cope with her stress* is an example of a: (2)

    a. simple sentence.
    c. complex sentence.
    b. compound sentence.
    d. compound-complex sentence.

1. _____

2. In the sentence *If you speak quietly and calmly, other people are likely to lower their voices,* the conjunction *and* is a: (3)

    a. coordinating conjunction.
    c. subordinating conjunction.
    b. correlative conjunction.
    d. conjunctive adverb.

2. _____

3. Which sentence is written correctly? (3)

    a. She was either late or I was early.
    c. She either was late or I was early.
    b. Either she was late or I was early.
    d. She was late or either I was early.

3. _____

4. In the sentence *Although I arrive early at work, I still do not finish my work,* the conjunction *although* is a: (4)

    a. coordinating conjunction.
    c. subordinating conjunction.
    b. correlative conjunction.
    d. conjunctive adverb.

4. _____

5. Which of the following is an example of a conjunctive adverb? (4)

    a. not only/but also
    c. if
    b. furthermore
    d. but

5. _____

6. Which sentence is punctuated correctly? (5)

    a. Anger may break down your immune system and cause heart disease, ulcers and depression.

    b. Focus your thoughts on something pleasant during boring meetings, or a slow-moving checkout line.

    c. If you are a workaholic you should reduce the energy drain that you are placing on your body.

    d. Overstressed people often complain about being tired, and they frequently make mistakes in their work.

6. _____

7. Which sentence is written correctly? (6)

    a. Julie is a bank teller, a business student, and her daughter is in kindergarten.

    b. I read where 10 percent of the American people inherited a low tolerance for stress.

    c. Try to eat a healthy breakfast each day.

    d. Neither Luis or Sam attended the stress management seminars.

7. _____

8. Which sentence is written correctly? (3, 4, 7)

    a. Stress is a major contributing factor for disease, and many office visits to physicians are for stress-related illnesses.

    b. Some people exercise with equipment as a stationary bicycle or a rowing machine.

    c. Be sure and leave yourself time each day to relax.

    d. After I returned from my vacation I felt rested and eager to start working.

8. _____

9. Which sentence is punctuated correctly? (5)   9. _____

    a. Disorganization, unclear goals and too many personal phone calls often result in stress.

    b. If people pay attention to time management they will discover their time wasters.

    c. Jane said that time management is really simple but she never has enough time to leave work by 5 p.m.

    d. Workers have to stay flexible and adaptable to the unexpected; otherwise, unplanned situations will cause stress.

10. Which sentence is written correctly? (6)   10. _____

    a. Stress may be considered as any physical, chemical, or emotional factor that causes bodily or mental tension.

    b. The degree of stress in our lives depends upon factors such as our physical health, the quality of our interpersonal relationships, and receiving support from others.

    c. Sleep disorders are one of the most common symptoms of stress and to control high-quality sleep is difficult.

    d. Removing clutter is not only more visually relaxing but also you will avoid the stress of searching for important items.

11. Which sentence is written correctly? (8)   11. _____

    a. To reduce background and unwanted noise, try and create quiet rooms for important tasks.

    b. I read where copy machines contribute to poor air quality in the office.

    c. Try to get more physical exercise by taking the stairs instead of the elevator.

    d. Be sure and work next to a window, which provides natural light.

12. Which sentence is *not* written correctly? (8)   12. _____

    a. My job description is not so complicated as yours.

    b. Joshua acts like he is tired all of the time.

    c. Be sure to get a headset, which allows walking while talking on the phone.

    d. I usually walk after I eat dinner.

13. Which statement applies to this sentence? *If you have your own office, consider keeping a resistance band or ankle weights in your desk drawer.* (2)   13. _____

    a. The sentence has two dependent clauses and two independent clauses.

    b. The sentence has one dependent clause and one independent clause.

    c. The sentence has two dependent clauses and one independent clause.

    d. The sentence has one dependent clause and two independent clauses.

14. Which statement applies to this sentence? *Designing your computer workstation to be comfortable and adhering to good ergonomic principles result in less stress and increased productivity.* (5)   14. _____

    a. The sentence requires a comma after the word *comfortable.*

    b. The sentence requires a comma after the word *principles.*

    c. The sentence requires a comma after the word *stress.*

    d. The sentence is written in parallel format.

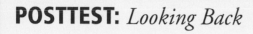

15. Which sentence is written correctly? (7, 8)   **15.** _____

    a.   I read where low-level noise can increase stress and decrease employee motivation.

    b.   Junko makes her small cubicle relaxing and welcoming by adding plants, displaying photos, or anything that makes her feel good.

    c.   Jerri acts as if she does not want to participate in the stress management seminar.

    d.   Try and identify things that cause you stress, and then you should develop a plan to change your life.

Unit 5

Reviewing Punctuation and Number Use

Chapter 16
The Period and the Comma

Chapter 17
Other Punctuation

Chapter 18
Numbers

Chapter 16

The Period and the Comma

OBJECTIVES

After you have studied this chapter and completed the exercises, you will be able to do the following:

1. Use periods correctly at the end of declarative and imperative sentences, courteous requests, and indirect questions.

2. Identify miscellaneous uses of the period.

3. Use commas correctly between items in a series and in compound sentences.

4. Use commas correctly with independent adjectives.

5. Use commas correctly to set off appositive and parenthetical expressions.

6. Use commas correctly with introductory expressions.

7. Use commas correctly with nonrestrictive clauses.

8. Identify miscellaneous uses of the comma.

Workplace Applications: Job Search and Career Development

Most people dread a job search because they dislike the feeling of not being in control. While you cannot control the economy or the hiring policies of companies, you can control your own job search.

The majority of jobs, as many as 80 percent by most estimates, are filled by networking. Networking involves asking friends and relatives for job leads and using sources available through college placement offices.

Job Search Tools

A résumé, a cover letter, and the interview are factors that enter into a hiring decision. The résumé must be well organized and error free; it must include concrete examples of achievements. The cover letter gives new information that is not included on the résumé, shows how well you know the company, and demonstrates your knowledge of the English language. The cover letter asks for the interview and makes it easy for the interviewer to contact you.

The interview is the final step in the employment process—and the most crucial. Most interviewers make a judgment within the first three to five minutes of an interview. The best way to prepare for an interview is to find out as much as possible about the company and the person interviewing you. Companies are looking for well-prepared candidates with positive attitudes who can show how they will fit into an organization.

Pretest

Instructions: Use the proofreaders' mark ⊙ to insert periods where necessary. Use the proofreaders' mark ⋀ to insert commas. Use the proofreaders' mark ⋎ to delete a mark of punctuation.

1. Kaitlin wanted to know the questions that most interviewers ask during interviews (1)

2. My most recent supervisor was K R Stonefield, CPA of Baker Strong & Lester Wilmington DE 19804. (2, 8)

3. A healthy economy creates more jobs but qualified people are still scarce (1, 3)

4. The interviewer expressed an interest in the types of training, seminars or workshops that I had attended. (3)

5. Several temporary agencies in our area offer computerized self-paced training programs for their employees (1, 4)

6. Lynn Davis a career transition specialist reminded us about the importance of learning new skills. (5)

7. Before Ken hired a new employee he prepared a list of detailed job qualifications. (6)

8. Firstar Bank encourages all of its employees regardless of age to take advantage of training opportunities. (5)

9. Do not forget to check the public library for career information which is readily available and easily accessed (1, 7)

10. You remember when I began working at the Thompson store on December 1 2000 in the city of Marshfield Wisconsin don't you? (8)

11. To obtain a promotion emphasize the positive reasons for a change not the negative concerns. (6, 8)

12. Rumors and gossip seem to escalate, when employees are worried about job security. (6)

13. Job seekers, who are late to interviews, create negative impressions with employment managers. (7)

14. Jennie left her last, professional administrative position two months ago. (4)

15. The employment manager said "We require well-trained workers, who are Certified Microsoft Office Specialists." (7, 8)

Chapter Preview

You have learned to place words in a logical and meaningful order, and you are familiar with the grammatical terms used in the process of putting a sentence together. You are now ready to take the next step, which involves using the proper marks of punctuation. Punctuation marks often determine the exact meaning of a sentence; therefore, they cannot be placed whenever you pause for a breath or at your individual whim. Imagine this entire page without a mark of punctuation. Of course, you would agree that no one would understand the material. The same concept applies to each sentence. Punctuation details are essential in making your words flow smoothly and in clarifying the intent of your writing.

Many of the rules in this chapter have already been identified in the Punctuation Alert features throughout the previous chapters. In this chapter, you will review these marks of punctuation and also learn several new rules.

The Period

The period is the most frequently used punctuation mark. The period usually appears at the end of a sentence, but it has several other uses within a sentence.

Declarative Sentences

Use a period at the end of a declarative sentence. A declarative sentence states a fact, an idea, or an opinion.

> **Our company is an equal-opportunity employer.**

> (The sentence states a fact; a period is necessary.)

Imperative Sentences

Use a period at the end of an imperative sentence. An imperative sentence indicates a command or makes a strong suggestion.

> **Do not be late for an interview.**

> (The sentence is a command and requires a period. *You* is the understood subject.)

> **Make a positive point in your cover letter about the recent training that you have received.**

> (The sentence is a suggestion and requires a period. *You* is the understood subject.)

Courteous Requests

Use a period at the end of a sentence that makes a courteous request. A courteous request requires an action rather than an answer in words.

> **Will you please show me how to organize my résumé.**

> (The type of response requested, *show me*, is one of action, not words. The person making the request wants someone to *act*. The *action* desired is to show the person how to organize a résumé.)

PUNCTUATION ALERT!

Spacing with Periods
In general, use one space after a period at the end of a sentence.

EDIT PATROL

Source: A courteous request in a Paris hotel
Please leave your values at the desk.
Note: You may leave your *valuables* but preferably not your *values*.

Copyright © by The McGraw-Hill Companies, Inc.

The Period and the Comma

Indirect Questions

Use a period after an indirect question. An indirect question does not require an answer.

I wonder how many applications have been submitted for the medical records technician position.

(This indirect question requires no specific answer. A period is necessary at the end of the sentence.)

Decimal Points

Use a period to separate dollars and cents. Do not place a period after a dollar amount if there are no cents involved. Use a period as a decimal point to express whole numbers and fractional amounts.

$3.99   **$156.28**   **$11,928.32**

(A decimal point is necessary between the dollar amount and the cents.)

$2   **$900**   **$62,300**

(No decimal point is necessary after a dollar amount without cents.)

0.005   **0.05**   **2.5**   **37.8**

(A period functions as a decimal point in fractional amounts.)

Abbreviated Words and Measurements

Use a period at the end of an abbreviated word. Do not use a period after a measurement that is abbreviated on most business or technical forms. Spell out measurements when they are used in general or nontechnical writing.

assn.	= association	**intl.**	= international
asst.	= assistant	**mfg.**	= manufacturing
bldg.	= building	**pd.**	= paid

(Periods are necessary after abbreviated words.)

ft	= foot, feet	**oz**	= ounce, ounces
gal	= gallon, gallons	**qt**	= quart, quarts
hr	= hour, hours	**yr**	= year, years

(No periods are necessary after abbreviations for measurements on invoices or other business forms.)

Small and Capital Letters

Use a period after each letter in abbreviations that consist of small letters. Do not use a period after each letter in most abbreviations that consist of all capital letters.

a.k.a. = also known as

c.o.d. = collect on delivery

f.o.b. = free on board (within sentences)

(Periods are necessary with abbreviations made up of small letters.)

CEO = chief executive officer

IRS = Internal Revenue Service (government)

ASAP = as soon as possible

HMO = health maintenance organization

PIN = personal identification number

PDA = personal digital assistant

Exceptions:

P.O. = post office

U.S. = United States

A.A. = Associate in Arts

M.D. = Doctor of Medicine

D.C. = District of Columbia

(Use periods after each capital letter in abbreviations for certain academic degrees and other abbreviations.)

NOTES

Abbreviations

Refer to the sections on abbreviations in your reference manual for additional examples of abbreviations with or without periods.

CHECKPOINT 16.1

Go to the
Web

Checkpoint 16-1
for more skills practice on this topic.

Instructions: *Use the proofreaders' mark ⊙ to insert periods where needed. Use the proofreaders' mark ⌿ or ℘ to delete unnecessary periods.*

1. I was not sure whether the abbreviation for the word *association* was *assoc* or *assn*.

2. I wonder how long it will take to find out if the position is mine

3. I budgeted $400. for my job search activities.

4. Jamie said that I should call about the paralegal position A.S.A.P.

5. Will you please send rejection letters to these 30 job applicants

6. The human resources manager indicated that there would be a 2.5. percent C.O.L.A. after the second year of employment

7. Do not bring a friend or relative along with you on an interview

8. I am going to apply for a position at the US Department of Transportation (D. O. T.)

Personal Names and Corporate Names

Use a period after the initials or with abbreviations of most names. Do not use a period with a nickname. Use the same format that an individual uses in a signature or that a company uses on its letterhead as its official designation.

T. C. Robbins   **Thos. C. Robbins**   **Brown Bros.**

(A period is usually necessary after initials or with an abbreviation of a personal or company name.)

Tom Robbins   **Buzz Carey**

(A period is not necessary with a nickname.)

Harry S Truman   **AAA Travel Agency**

(Periods after initials are not necessary if the official signature or the name on the company letterhead does not include them.)

Titles, Academic Degrees, Professional Identification

Use a period after an abbreviation of a person's title.

Mrs. **Ms.** **Mr.** **Dr.**

Dr. Peter Sandford applied for a position as a college curriculum director.

Use a period after each element in the abbreviation of an academic degree or professional identification.

B.A. **Ph.D.** **M.B.A.** **M.D.**

(Periods are necessary after an abbreviated title.)

Helen Wing, M.D., spoke to our classes on Career Day.

(Periods are necessary after letters in professional designations.)

Anthony Doneli, M.B.A., explained ways to use a Web page for hiring employees.

(Periods are necessary after letters in academic degrees.)

Do This

Miss Reilley included a unit on finding a job in our keyboarding class.

Do Not Do This

Miss. Reilley included a unit on finding a job in our keyboarding class.

Do not use a period after *Miss* because it is not an abbreviation.

Seniority Designations

Use a period after an abbreviated seniority designation.

Jerome Madson Jr. is planning a career in tourism and hospitality.

(*Jr.* is a seniority designation and requires a period.)

James Redman III reviewed the top four recommendations of the interview committee.

(The seniority designation *III* does not require a period; it is not an abbreviation.)

Geographic Locations

Use a period after an abbreviation of a country, state, or province unless the abbreviation appears in ZIP Code format.

State or Province	ZIP Code Abbreviation	Standard Abbreviation
Alabama	AL	Ala.
New Jersey	NJ	N.J.
Ontario	ON	Ont.

(Periods are necessary with standard state and province abbreviations. Periods are not necessary after the abbreviations in ZIP Code format.)

Shortened Forms of Words

Do not use periods after shortened words or foreign words that are not abbreviations.

info = information	**rep = representative**
specs = specifications	**temp = temporary**

(Periods are not necessary after shortened words that are not abbreviations.)

ad hoc = for a particular purpose

in re or re = concerning

(Periods are not necessary with foreign words that are not abbreviations.)

NOTES

Write It Out
Use shortened forms of words for informal writing only.

Outlines and Lists

Use a period after the numbers or letters that identify items in an outline or list unless the numbers or letters are in parentheses.

   I. CAREER PLANNING

       A. Job Resources

          1. Classified ads

             a. Advantages

                (1) Accessibility

(In this abbreviated outline, periods are necessary after all letters and numbers except the last item [(1)], which is enclosed in parentheses.)

Use periods after complete sentences, dependent clauses, and long phrases in a list or outline. Do not use periods after short phrases unless the phrases are necessary to complete the introductory statement.

Follow these basic interview rules:

1. Do not complain about a former employer.

2. Demonstrate a positive attitude.

3. Avoid discussing personal problems.

(Periods are necessary after these complete sentences.)

These characteristics will impress an interviewer:

1. A genuine smile

2. A sincere greeting

3. An interest in the company

4. A display of enthusiasm

(Periods are not necessary after short phrases listed on separate lines. The lead-in statement is complete.)

NOTES

Parallel Structure
Remember to write lists using parallel structure—all beginning words should begin with the same part of speech.

Before going on an interview, be sure to check on:

a. Time and date of interview.

b. Pronunciation of interviewer's name.

c. Location of interview.

(Each lettered item is necessary to complete the introductory statement. Periods at the end of each phrase are necessary.)

Go to the
Web

Checkpoint 16.2
for more skills practice on
this topic.

Instructions: *Use the proofreaders' mark ⊙ to insert periods where needed. Use the proofreaders' mark ϒ or ℒ to delete unnecessary periods.*

1. My interview is at 9 am with Dr Martin B Stein

2. Willard Kline Jr was one of the finalists who returned for a second interview.

3. I addressed the thank-you note to Roger D Bennet, 3460 Third Avenue, Topeka, K.S 91303.

4. Mrs Liz. Alldred told me about a job opening at the T.V. station W.E.A.Q.

5. Mr D T Garcia organized an ad. hoc. committee to improve the firm's outdated application forms.

6. Record the following information for each job contact:

    a Name, address, and phone number.

    b Contact person.

    c Position and responsibilities.

7. Jen Carey PhD, will be interviewing applicants for the scheduling manager's position.

8. These suggestions are helpful in getting promotions:

    1 Assume additional responsibilities

    2 Improve your communication skills

    3 Become involved with team projects.

The Comma

NOTES

Looking Back
Refer to Chapter 15 for a review of compound sentences. For a more thorough review, refer to your reference manual section on commas.

The comma ranks second only to the period in use. A comma shows a division or an interruption in a sentence. The comma is a versatile mark of punctuation and appears in different locations within a sentence.

Compound Sentences

Use a comma to separate two independent clauses in a compound sentence. Place the comma before the coordinating conjunction (*and, or, nor, but*) that joins the two clauses.

> **An employee's interest in continuing education impresses employers, and they will often pay the worker's tuition.**

(The sentence contains two independent clauses separated by the conjunction *and*. The comma appears before the conjunction.)

> **Our company's education opportunities are available to everyone but must be job-related.**

(The subject *they* is missing from the expression following the conjunction *but*. *But must be job-related* cannot stand alone. No comma is needed before the conjunction.)

Omit the comma before the coordinating conjunction in a compound sentence if either or both of the two independent clauses are very short (four words or fewer). Do not omit the comma if it is necessary for clarity.

Make your objective realistic <u>or</u> eliminate this section of the résumé.

(The first clause is short. No comma is necessary before the coordinating conjunction *or.*)

Stevenson's offers high salaries <u>but</u> we offer better benefits.

(Both independent clauses are short [four words or fewer]. No comma is necessary before the coordinating conjunction *but.*)

John interviewed me, <u>and</u> Sara explained my tasks.

(Even though both independent clauses are short, the comma before the conjunction *and* is necessary to avoid confusion about the number of people John interviewed. Without the comma, the reader could misunderstand and assume that John interviewed "me and Sara.")

Use a comma before the coordinating conjunction when a subject is not expressed (but implied) in one or both clauses in an imperative sentence. Do not use a comma if one of the independent clauses is very short.

Online résumé postings are popular ways to search for a job, <u>but do</u> not forget the value of direct company contacts.

(The second clause is a command with the implied subject *you.* A comma before the coordinating conjunction is necessary to separate the two clauses.)

Complete the application and return it by September 20.

(The first imperative clause is very short; therefore, no comma is necessary to separate the two clauses.)

Do not use a comma before a coordinating conjunction that joins a compound subject, predicate, object, or subject complement.

Lucy finds it difficult to ask character questions <u>or</u> to question the accuracy of a résumé.

(*Or* is the coordinating conjunction that joins the two phrases *to ask character questions* and *to question the accuracy of a résumé.* No comma is necessary with two phrases.)

An expert interviewer is a good listener <u>and</u> a perceptive evaluator of responses.

(*And* is the coordinating conjunction that joins the two subject complements *listener* and *evaluator.* No comma is necessary.)

The interviewers verified that candidates had the necessary work experience <u>and</u> that they had the licenses they claimed to have.

(The subject of this sentence is *interviewers.* The compound object of the sentence is *that candidates had the necessary work experience* and *that they had the licenses they claimed to have.* No comma is necessary before the conjunction *and.*)

CHECKPOINT 16.3

Instructions: *Use the proofreaders' mark ∧ to insert commas where needed. Use the proofreaders' mark ⅄ to delete unnecessary commas.*

EDIT PATROL

Source unknown:

He slipped into a comma and died. Note: This comma must have been powerful!!!

NOTES

Identifying Clauses

If the second clause does not have *both* a subject and a verb, it is not an independent clause; therefore, no comma is necessary between the clauses.

Go to the Web

Checkpoint 16.3
for more skills practice on this topic.

---

1. Job hunting is often hard work and it can be very frustrating when no interviews result.

2. Many employers realize the need to give references but they fear retaliation if the person fails to get the job.

3. Janie always researches a company, and then completes the application.

4. Be sure that your nails and hair are neat, and that your attire is conservative.

5. Fred upgraded his skills, but failed to receive the desired promotions.

6. Address your thank-you letter to the interviewer and include a statement about your continued interest in the job.

7. Our new job service board allows human resource managers to list jobs, or review applicants' résumés.

8. Give proper termination notice, and exit a job gracefully.

Series

Use commas to separate words, phrases, or clauses in a series (three or more items). Be sure to include the comma before the coordinating conjunction.

A good résumé includes information about your education, skills, and experience.

(Commas separate words in a series. A comma is necessary before the coordinating conjunction *and.*)

This job requires knowledge of the insurance business, a community college degree, and previous office experience.

(Commas separate phrases in a series. A comma is necessary before the coordinating conjunction *and.*)

Prepare a list of questions, organize the questions according to priority, and take the list with you to the interview.

(Commas separate clauses in a series. The subject *you* is understood. A comma is necessary before the coordinating conjunction *and.*)

Do not use commas to separate items when each item is connected by a conjunction.

Are you looking at new career options or hoping for a promotion or thinking about a lateral move for more experience?

(No commas are necessary to separate the items since conjunctions [*or*] already separate them.)

Use commas in a series of names in an organization exactly the way that the organization uses the commas on its letterhead or on another verifiable source. Do not use a comma before the ampersand (&) in the name of an organization unless the company itself does.

Gavin, Lokken, Holbrook, and Elkins interviewed five applicants for its administrative assistant position.

(In this example, the comma appears before the coordinating conjunction. A company's letterhead is the best format guide to use in punctuating names of organizations.)

Reinhart, Reynolds & Steinberg has a list of standard questions for its interviewers to ask potential employees.

(Do not use a comma before the ampersand [&] unless the company includes it on its letterhead.)

Use a comma before and after the abbreviation *etc.* When *etc.* appears at the end of a sentence, use a comma before the abbreviation only. The abbreviation *etc.* means "and so forth" or "and others." Do not use the phrase *and etc.*

Most people use classified advertisements, personal contacts, college listings, employment agencies, etc., as their basic sources of job-hunting information.

(*Etc.* implies that there are other sources. *Etc.* is a vague ending because it does not indicate the additional sources available. A comma is necessary before and after *etc.*)

To enhance our job hunting, we use classified advertisements, personal contacts, college listings, etc.

(A comma is needed before *etc.* but not after it.)

Do This

In preparing a résumé, avoid items such as past or desired salaries, reasons for leaving past positions, and health status.

or

In preparing a résumé, avoid past or desired salaries, reasons for leaving past positions, health status, etc.

Do not use *etc.* if the expression *such as* has already been used in the sentence.

Do Not Do This

In preparing a résumé, avoid items such as past or desired salaries, reasons for leaving past positions, health status, etc.

CHECKPOINT 16.4

Go to the
Web

Checkpoint 16.4
for more skills practice on this topic.

Instructions: *Use the proofreaders' mark ∧ to insert commas where needed. Use the proofreaders' mark ⸿ to delete unnecessary commas or words. Treat company names as normal items in a series.*

1. The firm sent its job announcement to the high schools, and to the community colleges, and to the newspapers.

2. Questions about age race sex religion national origin etc. are prohibited on job application forms.

3. We have placed online ads for administrative assistants sales associates sales managers etc.

4. Perrin Van Kleef Smith and Lowry requires that each job candidate sign a reference check waiver.

5. More and more companies are providing elder care, adoption benefits and child care options as a part of their benefits package.

6. Working as a temporary employee gave me an opportunity to keep my schedule flexible to learn new skills and to find a permanent job.

7. Lyndon keeps a list of names of former supervisors, current managers, coworkers etc. in his personal employment folder.

8. Will you emphasize your current job duties your current skills or your past work experience in your cover letter?

Independent Adjectives

Place a comma between independent adjectives that precede a noun unless they are already separated by a coordinating conjunction. To determine whether adjectives are independent, reverse their order or place the word *and* between the two adjectives. If both revisions sound satisfactory, place a comma between the two adjectives.

NOTES

Looking Back

Refer to Chapter 12 for additional information on independent adjectives.

We need <u>competent, courteous</u> employees to serve our customers.

(Reverse the order of the two adjectives. *Courteous, competent employees* sounds satisfactory. Insert the word *and* between the two adjectives. *Competent and courteous employees* sounds satisfactory. A comma between the two adjectives is necessary.)

We need competent <u>and</u> courteous employees to serve our customers.

(A comma is not needed because *competent* and *courteous* are separated by the coordinating conjunction *and*.)

Finding the ideal employee in a <u>dynamic, fast-paced</u> industry is a challenge.

(Reverse the order of the adjectives. *Fast-paced, dynamic* industry sounds satisfactory. Insert the word *and* between the two adjectives. *Dynamic and fast-paced industry* sounds satisfactory. A comma between the two adjectives is necessary.)

Job enrichment can expand boring work into <u>several new</u> roles and responsibilities.

(Reverse the order of the adjectives. *New several* does not sound satisfactory. Insert the word *and* between the two adjectives. *Several and new* does not sound satisfactory. No commas are necessary.)

Go to the
Web

Checkpoint 16.5
for more skills practice on this topic.

CHECKPOINT 16.5

Instructions: *Use the proofreaders' mark* *to insert commas where needed. Use the proofreaders' mark* ⁊ *to delete unnecessary commas.*

1. Read the local newspaper for information about the fastest-growing most profitable companies in your area.

2. Dennis has a self-assured confident attitude about his future.

3. Some temporary workers prefer the freedom of temporary work to the requirements of consistent permanent employment.

4. I had never worked on the two, outdated, computer programs that they gave me to use in my business, skills test.

5. Serious job hunters search for a job at a steady well-planned pace.

6. Wendy bought an attractive, new suit to wear for her job interviews.

7. Ames Ltd. wants to hire several, mature individuals with computer skills.

8. The Human Resources Director shared his most, unusual, interview, stories.

Appositives

Use commas to set off an appositive if it is not essential to the meaning of a sentence. An appositive explains or identifies the noun or pronoun that it follows.

> **Rob McClellan, <u>chief executive officer of McClellan and Associates</u>, looks for candidates with international experience.**

(*Rob McClellan* is the subject of the sentence. The appositive *chief executive officer of McClellan and Associates* adds information that is not necessary for the meaning of the sentence. The appositive requires commas to set it aside from the rest of the sentence.)

> **America's Job Bank, <u>a job search site on the Web</u>, gave me some insights into the national job market.**

(The appositive *a job search site on the Web* is an explanation that is not necessary for the meaning of the sentence. The appositive requires commas to set it aside from the rest of the sentence.)

Do not use commas to set off an appositive that explains or clarifies the noun preceding it.

> **The book *Finding a Job on the Internet* contains practical advice about preparing résumés for online use.**

(The appositive indicates *which* book and is essential for the meaning of the sentence. No commas are necessary to set off the appositive from the rest of the sentence.)

> **My business instructor Len Halvorsen wrote an excellent letter of recommendation for me.**

(You may have more than one business instructor. *Len Halvorsen* identifies the specific instructor and is necessary for the meaning of the sentence. No commas are necessary to set off the appositive from the rest of the sentence. If Len Halvorsen is the only business instructor you have, his name should be set aside with commas.)

CHECKPOINT 16.6

Go to the
Web

Checkpoint 16.6
for more skills practice on
this topic.

Instructions: *Use the proofreaders' mark ⋀ to insert commas where needed. Use the proofreaders' mark ⅄ or ⅃ to delete unnecessary commas.*

1. Some hiring committees select a compromise applicant one who neither totally pleases nor displeases anyone.

2. Emmett Lowry president of a Trenton outplacement firm carefully checks all business and professional references of job applicants.

3. I was not able to define the term, "functional résumé," in my introductory careers course.

4. Ted's brother, Dan, is also applying for a job at the Memorial Surgery Center.

5. Lori Robbins the receptionist introduced me to the members of the interviewing team.

6. Victory Medical Center the largest employer in our city always has openings for nurses.

7. One of my career mentors Angie Shaw has given me several sources for locating work in my field.

8. The search agency, Career Locators Inc., supplied me with five outstanding job leads.

Parenthetical Expressions

Parenthetical expressions interrupt a sentence. These side remarks do not add to the clarity of a sentence, and they are set aside by commas. Parenthetical words and phrases act as connectors, or they express a writer's opinion or explanation about the statement. Here is a partial list of parenthetical expressions:

after all	consequently	it would seem
as a consequence	for example	of course
as a matter of fact	however	on the contrary
as a result	I believe	therefore
as you know	if any	to be exact
believe me	in fact	unfortunately

Set off a nonessential parenthetical expression with commas.

There is, <u>I am sure</u>, an explanation for the delay in informing me of my employment test results.

(The parenthetical expression *I am sure* that appears within the sentence is not necessary for the meaning of the sentence. The parenthetical expression requires commas to set it aside from the rest of the sentence.)

<u>Actually</u>, I have always been satisfied with my temporary work assignments.

(The parenthetical expression *actually* is not necessary for the meaning of the sentence. The parenthetical expression requires a comma to set it aside from the rest of the sentence.)

A college degree, <u>as you know</u>, does not guarantee a job.

(The parenthetical expression *as you know* appears in the middle of the sentence, but it is not necessary for the meaning of the sentence. The parenthetical expression requires commas to set it aside from the rest of the sentence.)

NOTES

Parenthetical Expressions

Refer to your reference manual for additional examples of parenthetical expressions. They may be called transitional expressions or independent comments in your reference manual.

Go to the
Web

Checkpoint 16.7

for more skills practice on this topic.

CHECKPOINT 16.7

Instructions: *Underline the parenthetical expressions. Use the proofreaders' mark* ∧ *to insert commas where needed.*

1. Several major newspapers in fact post their "Help Wanted" ads online.

2. Interviews in most cases last 30 to 45 minutes.

3. Many job hunters have little if any knowledge of the best ways to discuss the salary issue.

4. You realize I am sure that company Web pages can be valuable recruitment tools.

5. Videoconferencing by the way is a low-cost way to review many candidates.

6. This job candidate no doubt has good computer and communication skills.

7. Unfortunately our first choice for city manager had already accepted another position.

8. It is imperative as you know that all information concerning job candidates be kept confidential.

Introductory Expressions

Introductory expressions may be words, phrases, or clauses. Dependent clauses have subjects and verbs but cannot stand alone. Other introductory expressions include prepositional, infinitive, and participial phrases.

Dependent Clauses. Use a comma to separate an introductory dependent clause from the independent clause.

> **If you lost your job tomorrow, would you be able to get another job without too much trouble?**

(The dependent clause *If you lost your job tomorrow* introduces the independent clause *would you be able to get another job without too much trouble.* A comma is necessary after the dependent clause.)

> **Although he was not hired for the information systems manager position, he was told about another opening in computer operations.**

(The dependent clause introduces an independent clause. A comma is necessary after the dependent clause since it comes at the beginning of the sentence.)

Generally, do not use a comma when the dependent clause follows the independent clause or when it is necessary for the meaning of the sentence.

> **Be sure to request a letter of recommendation before you leave a job.**

(The dependent clause *before you leave a job* appears at the end of the sentence. A comma is not necessary to separate the dependent clause from the rest of the sentence.)

> **Many people stay in their mediocre jobs because they are afraid of failure.**

(The dependent clause appears at the end of the sentence. A comma is not necessary.)

Prepositional Phrases. Use a comma to set off an introductory prepositional phrase from the independent clause that follows.

> **Within ten months, she received a promotion to the position of office manager.**

(The short prepositional phrase *Within ten months* introduces the independent clause *she received a promotion to the position of office manager.* A comma follows the prepositional phrase.)

> **From a job hunter's standpoint, online newsgroups are a good way to learn about a specific profession.**

(*From a job hunter's standpoint* introduces the independent clause. A comma follows the prepositional phrase.)

Looking Back

Refer to Chapter 3 to review clauses and to Chapter 15 to review subordinating conjunctions.

Looking Back

A prepositional phrase consists of a preposition and its object. Refer to Chapter 14 for a review of prepositional phrases.

Infinitive Phrases.   Use a comma to set off an introductory infinitive phrase from the rest of the sentence. Do not use a comma when an infinitive phrase is the subject of a sentence.

> **To find qualified job applicants, more companies are using online services.**
>
> (*To find qualified job applicants* is the infinitive phrase that introduces the independent clause *more companies are using online services*. A comma is necessary after the introductory infinitive phrase.)
>
> **To find qualified applicants is a competitive task faced by most companies.**
>
> (In this sentence, *To find qualified applicants* is the subject of the sentence followed by the verb *is*. No comma is necessary after the word *applicants*.)

Participial Phrases.   Use a comma to set off an introductory participial phrase from the rest of the sentence.

> **Disappointed about the lack of jobs in his field, Darrin decided to return to the community college for retraining.**
>
> (*Disappointed about the lack of jobs in his field* is the participial phrase that introduces an independent clause. The participial phrase modifies the subject *Darrin*. A comma is necessary after the participial phrase.)
>
> **Reviewing the job qualifications, I realized that I needed additional skills to obtain the position.**
>
> (*Reviewing the job qualifications* is the participial phrase that introduces an independent clause. The participial phrase modifies the subject *I*. A comma is necessary after the participial phrase.)

Go to the Web

Checkpoint 16.8
for more skills practice on this topic.

CHECKPOINT 16.8

Instructions: In the following sentences use the proofreaders' mark ∧ to insert commas where needed. Use the proofreaders' mark ⸘ to delete unnecessary commas.

1. When you are introduced to the interviewer greet him or her with a firm handshake.

2. After you are employed proof of immigration status will be necessary.

3. To highlight your problem-solving ability use action words such as *initiated* and *created*.

4. You probably will not be happy in an autocratic environment, if you are a "free spirit."

5. Throughout your job search follow these steps to market your skills and attributes.

6. Surprised by the large number of job applicants Edie decided to allow the committee extra time to review applications.

7. After the first few interview questions I finally began to relax.

8. Working as a temporary employee I have flexibility in setting my work hours.

Nonrestrictive and Restrictive Adjective Clauses

A *nonrestrictive* (nonessential) adjective clause is not necessary for the meaning of the word it modifies. A nonrestrictive adjective clause usually begins with the word *which.* A *restrictive* (essential) adjective clause is necessary for the meaning of the word it modifies. A restrictive adjective clause usually begins with the word *that.* The words *who* and *whose* introduce either restrictive or nonrestrictive clauses.

Nonrestrictive Adjective Clauses.
Use commas to set off a nonrestrictive adjective clause from the rest of the sentence. A nonrestrictive clause is not necessary for the meaning of the sentence.

His personality test indicated that he had high empathy, <u>which is a strong attribute for social workers.</u>

(The nonrestrictive adjective clause *which is a strong attribute for social workers* modifies the noun *empathy.* The clause is not necessary for the meaning of the sentence and must be set aside with commas.)

Some temporary agencies use self-paced CD-ROM job search materials, <u>which include workbooks and videotapes,</u> for training purposes.

(The nonrestrictive adjective clause modifies the noun *materials.* The clause is not necessary for the meaning of the sentence and must be set aside with commas.)

Restrictive Adjective Clauses.
Do not set off restrictive adjective clauses from the rest of the sentence. A restrictive adjective clause is necessary or essential for the meaning of the word it modifies. A *who* clause may or may not be set off by commas. The determining factor is whether the *who* clause is necessary to the meaning of the sentence. Never put commas around a clause that begins with *that.*

Job applicants <u>who indicate that they have spent more than nine months looking for a job</u> are carefully checked and evaluated.

(The restrictive adjective clause *who indicate that they have spent more than nine months looking for a job* modifies the noun *applicants.* The clause restricts the meaning of the sentence by identifying *which* job applicants are being checked. No commas are necessary to set off the restrictive clause.)

Companies <u>that continue to offer a wide array of benefit options</u> attract high-caliber workers.

(The clause restricts the meaning of the sentence by clarifying *which* companies attract high-caliber workers. No commas are necessary to set off the restrictive clause.)

CHECKPOINT 16.9

Go to the
Web

Checkpoint 16.9
for more skills practice on this topic.

Instructions: *In the following sentences, underline the restrictive or nonrestrictive adjective clauses. Use the proofreaders' mark ⋀ to insert commas where needed. Use the proofreaders' mark ⍀ to delete unnecessary commas.*

1. People, who are 40 years and older, will comprise more than half of our workforce in the next few years.

2. Some firms are now producing employment tests, that evaluate an applicant's reactions in a real job.

3. My brother Stan who works at a temporary agency gave me some job-hunting tips.

4. At my second interview which was held at Colby's Grille the interviewer discussed many advantages of working for the firm.

5. We did not hire the job applicant, who sent us an outdated résumé.

6. I read Grant Parkinson's latest job search book which outlined several ways to write a résumé for online use.

7. Jamie decided to apply for a job in the health care industry which is one of the growth areas for employment.

8. Jobs, that require bilingual abilities, can increase opportunities for advancements.

Miscellaneous Comma Usage

Contrasting Expressions. Use commas to set aside a contrasting expression from the rest of the sentence. A contrasting expression often begins with the word *not* or *never.* A contrasting expression contradicts the noun or idea that it follows.

> **The résumé, not the cover letter, is the place for job experience and education details.**

(*Not the cover letter* is a contrasting expression. The contrasting expression requires commas to set it aside from the rest of the sentence.)

> **The position for which I am interviewing is a new position, not an existing one.**

(*Not an existing one* is a contrasting expression that is not necessary for the meaning of the sentence. The contrasting expression requires a comma to set it aside from the rest of the sentence.)

Direct Address. Use commas to set off the names of individuals who are being addressed directly.

> **We are happy to inform you, Taylor, that you have been selected as our new technical services representative.**

(*Taylor* is the person being addressed. The individual's name requires commas to set it aside from the rest of the sentence.)

> **Kimberly, do you have any questions that you would like to ask the members of the committee?**

(*Kimberly* is the person being addressed. The individual's name requires a comma to set it aside from the rest of the sentence.)

Tag Questions. Use a comma to separate a tag question from the rest of the sentence.

> **He has already reserved the conference room for interviews on Tuesday, hasn't he?**

(The tag question *hasn't he?* requires a comma before it to separate the question from the rest of the sentence.)

> **We do not have to answer questions about our marital status, do we?**

(The tag question *do we?* is separated by a comma from the rest of the sentence.)

Quotations. Use a comma to introduce a direct quotation or set it off from other parts of a sentence. Do not use a comma to set off an indirect quotation.

> **She said, "Honesty on an application form is imperative."**

(The comma after the word *said* is necessary before a direct quotation.)

Chapter 16

"Honesty," she said, "is imperative on an application form."

(The commas are necessary to set aside a direct quotation from the other parts of a sentence.)

She said that honesty on an application form is imperative.

(No commas are necessary for this indirect quotation.)

CHECKPOINT 16.10

Go to the
Web

Checkpoint 16.10
for more skills practice on this topic.

Instructions: Use the proofreaders' mark ∧ to insert commas where needed. Use the proofreaders' mark ꝗ to delete unnecessary commas.

1. Thank you for interviewing me Mr. Decker.

2. Our firm has always had excellent results never unfavorable with preemployment psychological tests.

3. Jenni said, that Suyon Yee is planning to begin work on November 1.

4. You have never been fired from a job have you?

5. The receptionist said "Mrs. Barstow, the personnel manager, will be interviewing you."

6. Meghan why are you interested in working for this firm?

7. The division manager not the department supervisor will be leading the interview team.

8. "Project coordinators" said the industry analyst "must be skilled in database management software."

Dates. Use a comma before and after the year when a date includes a month, day, and year. Do not use a comma if only the month and day or only the month and year are in a sentence.

I hope to have my first promotion by June 30, 2007, or at the latest December 31, 2008.

(Commas are necessary before and after the year *2007*. The month, day, and year are included in the sentence.)

Mrs. Melendez indicated that she would inform me by November 10 about my job status.

(No commas are necessary. Only the month and day are included.)

My last job interview was in October 2004 for a data entry position.

(No commas are necessary. Only the month and year are included.)

EDIT PATROL

On a résumé:
"Instrumental in *ruining* entire operation for a Midwest chain operation."
Will he or she ruin our business as well?

Addresses. Use commas to separate parts of an address or geographical location. Do not place a comma between a state name or a two-letter state abbreviation and the ZIP Code within a document or on an envelope. Within a document, use a comma after the ZIP Code to separate it from the material that follows.

I ordered two career books from McGraw-Hill Irwin, 1333 Burr Ridge Parkway, Burr Ridge, IL 60527, last week.

(Each part of the address is set off by commas except the state and ZIP Code. A comma follows the ZIP Code to set it aside from the remainder of the sentence.)

Stratten Technology is opening a new plant in Raleigh, North Carolina, and plans to hire 750 new employees.

(The city *Raleigh* is set off from the state *North Carolina*. The comma after *North Carolina* sets the state off from the rest of the sentence.)

Occupational Designations, Academic Degrees.   Use commas to set off occupational designations or academic degrees when they follow a person's name. Do not use both a personal or job title before a name and a job or academic degree designation after the name.

Austin Hugo, M.D., was one of the speakers at the new employee orientation.

(The occupational designation *M.D.* is set aside with commas. Do not use *Dr. Austin Hugo, M.D.*)

I enjoy my job with Leslie Perko, M.B.A.

(Do not use *Mrs. Leslie Perko, M.B.A.*)

Seniority Designations.   Do not use commas to separate seniority designations from the name unless the person being referenced prefers to use commas.

Thomsen Electronics promoted Nathan Snyder Jr. to the position of manager of its South American operations.

(*Jr.* is a seniority title and does not require commas to separate it from the name.)

Thomsen Electronics promoted Nathan Snyder II to the position of manager of its South American operations.

(*II* is a seniority title and does not require commas to separate it from the name.)

Company Names.   Do not use commas to separate *Inc.* or *Ltd.* from the rest of the company name unless the company's letterhead or other official source indicates that commas are necessary.

Career Associates Inc. helps displaced workers find jobs.

(No commas are necessary to set off *Inc.* unless a company indicates a preference to include commas. You should check correspondence, letterheads, or other reference sources to determine this preference.)

Numbers.   Use a comma in a whole number with *more than* four figures. However, some still prefer to insert a comma in a number such as 3,482. Do not use a comma in a policy, account, page, serial, model, or check number or in a house number in an address.

A research firm surveyed 30,500 businesses to determine future hiring practices.

(The number has more than four figures and requires a comma for ease in reading.)

We charge all expenses for hiring employees to Account No. 6930.

(No commas are used in account numbers.)

CHECKPOINT 16.11

Instructions: *Use the proofreaders' mark ∧ to insert commas where needed. Use the proofreaders' mark ⸔ to delete unnecessary commas.*

Go to the
Web

Checkpoint 16.11
for more skills practice on this topic.

1. I was a part-time student at the community college between September, 2001, and June, 2003.

2. Evergreen Rehabilitation, Inc., hired Elizabeth Michaels Ph.D. as its staff psychologist.

3. Please contact me at 69,150 Admiral Way Bend OR 97702.

4. On January 1 2003 Douglas Seward, Jr., became the CEO of Bartingale, Inc.

5. The hospital administrator recommended that Alison Whitby R.N. and Mike Ramos M.D. become members of the hospital's interview committee.

6. From research for my interview, I knew that the firm had produced 12325 units last month.

7. William will be traveling to Denver Colorado for his on-site interview.

8. I will always remember the date of November 15 2005 since that was the date of my first interview.

Diagramming Sentences

Each independent clause in a compound sentence receives separate attention in diagramming. Use vertical dotted lines separated by a solid horizontal line to connect the verbs in each independent clause. Write the conjunction on the solid horizontal line.

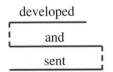

Jeanne is the chairperson of the interview committee and Antonio is the recorder.

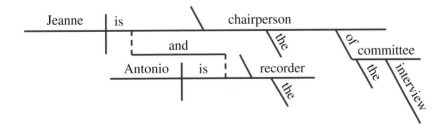

Go to the
Web

Checkpoint 16.12
for more skills practice on
this topic.

CHECKPOINT 16.12

Instructions: *In the space provided below, diagram the following sentences. All words may be diagrammed.*

1. I can juggle a complicated schedule, and I handle pressure situations well.

2. Lynn plans to attend college, but she needs a part-time summer job.

3. You can post your résumé online, or you can send us a copy.

4. An interview is not an everyday event, and feelings of fear or unease are normal.

Name _____ Date _____

PRACTICE 1

Using Periods and Commas Correctly

*Instructions: If the sentence is punctuated correctly, write **Yes** in the space provided. If the sentence is not punctuated correctly, write **No**.*

1. During the course of your career, you can expect to change employers a number of times.

    1. _____

2. To gauge an applicant's ability to solve problems, interviewers ask questions that require some analysis.

    2. _____

3. You are the one who must sell your skills, experience, and education

    3. _____

4. Basing hiring decisions on IQ tests, which some say are unfair leaves a company open to lawsuits.

    4. _____

5. No one can guarantee you a job, no matter how well you perform at school.

    5. _____

6. An untrained, inexperienced interviewer must not let preconceived ideas cloud his or her judgment.

    6. _____

7. She asked "What did you do when a coworker missed a deadline that caused your work to be late?"

    7. _____

8. Knowledge of market trends, and new skills is important if you want to look for a job.

    8. _____

9. You do know if an organization is democratic or autocratic don't you.?

    9. _____

10. I have worked for Noland and Nichols, Inc. since December 1 1998.

    10. _____

Working with Commas

Instructions: Use the proofreaders' mark ⋀ to insert commas where needed. Use the proofreaders' mark ꝗ to delete unnecessary marks of punctuation. In the space provided, write the letter of the appropriate reason for each of the marks that you inserted. Some sentences may not require commas.

> A = *Set off a nonrestrictive clause.*
> B = *Set off an introductory phrase or clause.*
> C = *Set off a parenthetical expression.*
> D = *Set off an appositive.*
> E = *Separate a series.*
> F = *Separate compound sentences.*
> G = *Separate independent adjectives.*
> H = *No commas are necessary.*

1. To find the position that you want approach your job hunt with a plan.

    1. _____

The Period and the Comma

Name _____ Date _____

2. The job search workshop showed me how to develop a complete comprehensive plan to approach the job market.

    2. _____

3. Maggie for instance should have left her boring job months ago.

    3. _____

4. The interviewer asked every applicant to sign a comprehensive waiver a form allowing the employer to contact all references.

    4. _____

5. Job hunters, who fail to follow directions, will have trouble finding a job.

    5. _____

6. Some applicants ask no questions which makes interviewers think that the job is of no interest to these interviewees.

    6. _____

7. Should you accept the first salary figure that is offered or should you negotiate salary during the job interview?

    7. _____

8. She worked in a comfortable environment received good benefits and enjoyed her coworkers.

    8. _____

9. Most professional associations conduct annual salary surveys, that they send to their members, or that they publish in special brochures.

    9. _____

10. Attempting to meet the deadline for submitting her application Sandra neglected to proofread her résumé carefully.

    10 _____

Go to the
Web

Practice 2 Exercises
for more skills practice on this topic.

PRACTICE 2

Using Correct Punctuation

Instructions: Use the proofreaders' marks ⋀ and ⊙ to insert commas and periods where needed. Use the proofreaders' mark ⌇ or ⌇ to delete unnecessary marks of punctuation.

1. Are you looking for a new job, or just exploring additional careers?

2. Few management opportunities are available for investment representatives commercial bankers or consultants, without college degrees.

3. In recent years it has become easier to change jobs, because health benefits and pensions are simpler to transfer.

Name _____ Date _____

4. A company is interested primarily in your ability to improve the company's operation not in your former job titles.

5. To deduct job-hunting expenses on your income taxes you will need itemized detailed accounts and receipts.

6. Holly encourages applicants to talk about themselves which gives them an opportunity to discuss more than their skills.

7. As you prepare your résumé be sure that your objective refers to your contribution to the company

8. Use titles such as Mr   Ms   Mrs   Miss etc   in a salutation for an employment cover letter.

9. Dunbar Peterson and Edwards has a paralegal position available in its office at 1206 Union Street Alexandria Minnesota.

10. Ben Collins, Jr., had limited experience in leading, and managing in the new team-based business environment.

11. The best references, usually, are those from past supervisors

12. Sam wondered how many questions the interviewer would ask in his 30-minute, videoconference interview

13. Will you please write N.A. (not applicable) in the blank, if a question does not apply to you.

14. Employers by the way report a lack of proficiency in written and oral communication skills.

15. Barbara knew what she enjoyed doing but she had problems describing her strengths in a concise positive way.

16. A friend of mine Kerry Williams MD transferred to Lexington Kentucky in August 2005

17. Having researched the company I knew its reputation in the community.

18. The best time to visit a temp. agency is Monday at 10 am, or Friday at 3 pm

19. You have read the book, *Finding a Job on the Internet,* haven't you.?

20. Temporary agencies usually divide jobs into these employment groups:
    1   Office.
    2   Industrial.
    3   Medical.
    4   Technical.

Name _____   Date _____

Go to the
Web

Practice 3 Exercises
for more skills practice on
this topic.

PRACTICE 3

Proofreading

Instructions: *Proofread and compare the two sentences in each group. If they are the same, write* **Yes** *in the space provided. If they are not the same, write* **No.** *Use the first sentence as the correct copy. If you find errors in the second sentence, underline them; insert any omitted words or marks of punctuation.*

1. A recent Gallup poll shows that one-third of college-educated people who are employed would select a different career if they could begin again.

   A recent Gallup pole shows that one-third of college-educated people, who are employed, would select a different career, if they could begin again.

   1. _____

2. The Job Web at http://www.jobweb.org has job listings and links to job recruiters and professional associations.

   The Job Web at http://www.jobweb.org has job listings, and links for job recruiters and professional associations.

   2. _____

3. Development Dimensions Intl., which is headquartered in Pittsburgh, Pennsylvania, prepares tests that simulate activities on the real job.

   Development Dimensions Internl., which is headquartered in Pittsburgh, Pennsylvania, prepares tests that stimulate activities on the real job.

   3. _____

4. Some employers think that applicants who hold part-time jobs and participate in several extra-curricular activities while maintaining good grades make excellent employees.

   Some employers think that applicants that hold part-time jobs and participate in several extra-curricular activities while maintaining good grades make excellent employees.

   4. _____

5. Twenty-six states have laws that offer varying degrees of protection to employers who provide "good-faith" references and release truthful information about their former employees.

   Twenty-six states have laws that offer varying degrees of protection to employers that provide good-faith references, and release truthful information about their former employees.

   5. _____

Name _____ Date _____

Editing Copy

Instructions: Use proofreaders' marks to correct the following copy. If you are not certain about the use of a proofreaders' mark, use your reference manual or the proofreaders' marks listed on the inside front cover of this textbook.

PERSONAL PLANING GUIDE LINES

1. What things are improtant to me?

2. What makes my current job meaningfull to me?

3. What do I want to be doing one year form now? three years from now?

4. What am I doing <u>now</u> to prepare myself to reach these goals.

5. What must I do by a year from now to prepare myself to reach these goals

6. What negative things are occurring at work, or in my personal life now?

6. What positive things are occuring at work or in my personal life now?

8. What are my mayor attributes?

9. What skills do I need.

10. what type of competition will I encounter in the field in which I am most interested?

11. WHere can I obtain the training or up-grade the skills that I need?

12. What is the future forthe field in which I am most interested?

PRACTICE 4

Writing

Instructions: Write a paragraph describing the characteristics of your ideal job. Include the type of work performed, the skills needed, the pay and fringe benefits, and the ideal working conditions. Use the punctuation rules that you already have learned to punctuate the sentences correctly. Answers will vary.

Go to the
Web

Practice 4 Exercises
for more skills practice on this topic.

_____

_____

_____

_____

_____

_____

_____

Name _____ Date _____

PRACTICE 5

Using Periods and Commas Correctly

*Instructions: If the sentence is punctuated correctly, write **Yes** in the space provided. If the sentence is not punctuated correctly, write **No**.*

1. Lateral movement, not upward movement, may be a way to develop new skills.   1. _____

2. She wondered how he passed the computer proficiency test without studying?   2. _____

3. Gary's yearly salary is between $30,000 and $40,000.   3. _____

4. My last interview for the position is with the C.E.O.   4. _____

5. Dr. Larry Kliner teaches a career class at Santa Barbara City College.   5. _____

6. Jason Navarro III applied for a position in Colorado Springs, Colorado.   6. _____

7. To sell yourself inform the employer about your qualifications in the cover letter.   7. _____

8. If you prepare for an interview you will sound more professional during your actual presentation.   8. _____

9. During an interview, do not test a new hairstyle, break in new shoes, or wear new clothes for the first time.   9. _____

10. Over 25 percent of major U.S. corporations use lie-detector tests for some employees, and 50 percent of all supermarket chains require them.   10. _____

Working With Commas

Instructions: Use the proofreaders' mark ∧ to insert commas where needed. Use the proofreaders' mark ⌖ to delete unnecessary marks of punctuation. In the space provided, write the letter of the appropriate reason for each of the marks that you inserted. Some sentences may not require commas.

A = Set off a nonrestrictive clause.
B = Set off an introductory phrase or clause.
C = Set off a parenthetical expression.
D = Set off an appositive.

E = Separate a series.
F = Separate compound sentences.
G = Separate independent adjectives.
H = No commas are necessary.

1. Some job applicants unfortunately are not prepared for their interviews.   1. _____

2. Employers say that they want employees who are loyal energetic and reliable.   2. _____

3. If you belong to a job club you will receive emotional support from other job seekers.   3. _____

Name _____ Date _____

4. Elizabeth McCarthy, assistant vice president wants every interviewee to leave thinking that he or she did well in the interview.

4. _____

5. Some companies interview outsiders only to compare them with workers within the firm which does not seem fair.

5. _____

6. Conservative professional clothing is always appropriate attire for a job interview.

6. _____

7. Written job descriptions can be helpful but they may fail to stress what you will be expected to do most of the time.

7. _____

8. You will probably be unhappy in your job, if your working environment is unpleasant.

8. _____

9. A lack of opportunities can dampen interest in the work, and result in frustration and boredom.

9. _____

10. If you are considering the salary and benefits for a job in another geographic area make an allowance for differences in the cost of living.

10. _____

PRACTICE 6

Using Correct Punctuation

Instructions: Use the proofreaders' marks ⋀ and ⊙ to insert commas and periods where needed. Use the proofreaders' mark ╱ or ℒ to delete unnecessary marks of punctuation.

1. Networking is speaking out meeting new people and sharing professional job information.

2. Leaving a job with "class," creates good feelings, and makes your supervisor think well of you.

3. Please complete the application, and return it to our office at 6,309 Adams Street, Anchorage AK 99516.

4. Randolph McRay, II, has a reputation for expecting precise prompt responses from his employees.

5. Shirley please contact Terri Herndon MD, for an interview on Monday October 5 in Kansas City, K.S.

6. The cover letter should use descriptive detailed sentences not general statements.

7. On the other hand if you want your résumé to look professional use a laser printer.

8. An effective job search method is to contact every friend and I mean every friend about any job vacancies.

9. Will you please describe your strengths and also your weaknesses

The Period and the Comma

Name _____ Date _____

10. Jorin Smyth Ubach and Gallen usually hires one employee a month, doesn't it?

11. You may prefer full-time work but you may be able to find part-time work only.

12. Anne Von Sund is a friendly personable interviewer.

13. Some interview questions, that employers ask, determine your ability to think through a typical realistic job situation.

14. Before going on a job interview use the following methods to find out about the company:
    a. Read newspaper clippings articles etc at a library
    b. Ask everybody you know, if he or she knows anyone who works there
    c. Sign up with a local temp. agency and ask to be placed in the organization

15. The American Accounting Association in Sarasota Florida publishes *Accounting Review* a journal describing trends in the accounting profession.

16. A new form of health coverage one that may increase in popularity involves a corporate medical center which, is on-site and staffed by the company.

17. If you prefer bureaucratic management you might be very unhappy in a small entrepreneurial company.

18. In some cases however the interviewer will insist on discussing salary early in the interview.

19. Having been interviewed by a group I realize the importance of thinking about the answers before verbalizing them.

20. Job application cover letters addressed to a C.E.O. are usually discarded, or sent to the human resources department.

PRACTICE 7

Proofreading

*Instructions: Proofread and compare the two sentences in each group. If they are the same, write **Yes** in the space provided. If they are not the same, write **No**. Use the first sentence as the correct copy. If you find errors in the second sentence, underline them; insert any omitted words or marks of punctuation.*

1. Richard Nelson Bolles, author of *What Color Is Your Parachute?*, believes that all of us have handicaps; consequently, we must find employers who will overlook our handicaps and hire us.

   1. _____

   Richard Nelson Bolles, author of *What Color Is Your Parachute?*, believes that all of us have handicaps; consequently, we must find employees, who will overlook our handicaps and hire us.

Name _____ Date _____

2. The three basic résumé styles include the chronological, **2.** _____
    which focuses on time and job continuity; the functional,
    which is organized by functions, skills, and responsibilities;
    and the combination, which uses elements of both the
    chronological and functional styles.

    The three basic résumé styles include the chronologicle,
    which focuses on time and job continuity; the functional,
    which is organized by functions, skills, and responsibilities;
    and the combination, which is eliments of both the
    chronological and functional style.

3. Some action verbs that you might use on your résumé **3.** _____
    to emphasize efficiency and problem-solving skills include
    expedited, improved, reorganized, revised, simplified, and
    streamlined.

    Some action verbs that you might use on your résumé
    to emphasize efficency and problem solving skills include:
    *expedited, improved, re-organized, revised, simplified, and
    streamlined.*

4. *Standard & Poor's Register of Corporations, Directors,* **4.** _____
    and Executives (a.k.a. S&P) is a directory available on
    CD-ROM covering more than 50,000 firms.

    Standard & Poor's Register of Corporations, Directors,
    and Executives (a.k.a. S&P) is a directory available on
    CD-ROM covering more than 50,000 firms.

5. Unfortunately, most college graduates do not have the **5.** _____
    proper interview attire. A college student should be
    doing the talking, not the clothes. One or two well-
    chosen business suits will serve a student all the way
    to the first day on the job and beyond.

    Unfortunately most college graduates do not have the
    proper interview attire. A college student should be
    doing the talking not the clothes. One or two well-
    chosen business suits will serve a student all the way
    to the first day on the job, and beyond.

Editing Copy

*Instructions: Use proofreaders' marks to correct the following copy. If you are not
certain about the use of a proofreaders' mark, use your reference manual or the
proofreaders' marks listed on the inside front cover of this textbook.*

INTERVIEWING.

1. Prepare for the interview. Learn about the company, the position and
    the salary range.

2. Dress appropriately. Wear professional conservative clothing.

The Period and the Comma

Name _____ Date _____

3. Arrive at least 15 minutes early. If you arrive earlier than 15 min. before the interview use the time to relax and collect your thoughts.

4. Arrive alone. Never bring any body with you to the interview.

5. BE aware of your behavoir in the reception area. Do not smoke or eat or apply cosmetics or use a cellular-phone or exhibit nervous mannerisms.

6. Do not criticize former employers. critical statements indicate that you may be difficult to work with and may raise questions about your discretion

7. Be truthful about your accomplishments. Employers appreciate honesty, and you will be discovered sooner or later if you exaggerate.

8. Avoid talking aboutsensitive subjects. Sensitive subjects involve religion, politics and sex.

PRACTICE 8

Writing

Instructions: *Identify an achievement that you have accomplished. Use one of the following suggestions: paid work experience; volunteer work; school, classroom, or extracurricular activity; hobby; recreational activity; or a social relationship. Write a paragraph detailing how you made the achievement happen. Answers will vary.*

_____
_____
_____
_____
_____
_____
_____
_____

Posttest

Instructions: *Use the proofreaders' mark ⊙ to insert periods where necessary. Use the proofreaders' mark ⋀ to insert commas. Use the proofreaders' mark ⌉ or delete and close up ℒ to delete a mark of punctuation.*

1. Roger wondered whether he would be asked to return for a second interview (1)

2. Carolyn Lock PhD is a well-known career counselor and can be reached at 4893 Mountain Road Phoenix AZ 85674 (2, 8)

3. Finding a job does not begin with writing a résumé but it does begin with self-analysis. (3)

4. Managers who are looking for work find newspaper advertisements private employment agencies and contacts with friends to be more productive than other job search methods. (3)

5. During the interview Ken used examples that indicated he was a creative original problem solver. (4, 6)

6. The majority of jobs as many as 80 percent by most estimates seem to be filled by people who hear about the openings informally. (5)

7. If you do informational interviews you will have the knowledge to competently negotiate salaries. (6)

8. Employment firms particularly the smaller ones will keep your résumé and cover letter on file won't they? (5)

9. Job clubs which are support groups sponsored by community groups and government agencies provide encouragement and reinforcement for those looking for jobs. (7)

10. I applied for a job at HLR Technology and I was finally hired on June 1 2005 in Carbondale Illinois. (3, 8)

11. To determine a salary range for the account clerk position Kristina read the want ads and searched the Internet. (6)

12. Kirsta wrote a thank-you note to her interviewer, after the job interview. (6)

13. Jessie Ruff who recommended me for a promotion has been with the company for over 10 years. (7)

14. For his job interviews Jim purchased a thin, leather portfolio. (4, 6)

15. My teacher said "You should treat every interview as if it were the only one you will ever get with that company and you must convince the employer, that you are the right candidate for the position". (3, 7, 8)

Chapter 17

Other Punctuation

OBJECTIVES

After you have studied this chapter and completed the exercises, you will be able to do the following:

1. Use semicolons and colons correctly.

2. Use quotation marks and apostrophes correctly.

3. Differentiate between the uses of hyphens and dashes.

4. Use parentheses and italics correctly.

5. Identify uses for ellipses, brackets, and asterisks.

6. Use capital letters with other punctuation marks correctly.

Workplace Applications: Business Communication

Studying business English builds a foundation for your written and spoken communications. No matter what career you choose or how technologically advanced your workplace may be, the basic skills of writing, speaking, and listening remain essential. You increase your likelihood of on-the-job success by communicating effectively.

Workplace communication depends in part upon the written word. While you may not write formal reports or letters, you probably will join the ranks of millions of workers worldwide who use e-mail for quick and fast communication. Your choice of written words makes either a positive or a negative impression on your reader and is a permanent record of your abilities.

Speaking and Listening

Oral communication is another part of workplace communication. Most people fear public speaking. Even though your job may not require speaking in front of large groups, you definitely will communicate every day with customers and other employees. You probably will make presentations in small-group meetings. You must use proper grammar and be aware of not only what you are saying but also how you are saying it. The right choice of words enhances your ability to get along with others.

On the job, you will spend more of your time listening than you do reading, writing, or speaking; yet the average person remembers only about 25 percent of what he or she hears. In the workplace, avoiding distractions and listening for information such as dates, names, prices, and explanations are valued communication skills.

PRETEST: *Looking Forward*

Pretest

Instructions: *Check the following sentences for punctuation and capitalization errors. Write the sentences correctly in the space provided. If the sentence is punctuated and capitalized correctly, write* **Yes.**

1. The letter is too curt, there is nothing personal about it. (1)

   _____

2. "The five Cs of writing, said the instructor, are in the textbook in three places; Chapter 2, chapter 7, and Chapter 9. (1, 2, 6)

   _____

   _____

3. Transparencies and slides do not hold a viewer's attention today. (2)

   _____

4. Lisa knew the importance of communicating any job related concerns to her project coordinator. (3)

   _____

   _____

5. Discuss three or four major points five at the very most in your oral presentations. (3)

   _____

6. Include the subject of your message in your e-mail correspondence. (you will get a better response with a specific subject line. (4, 6)

   _____

   _____

7. I read several good suggestions about maintaining communication among workers in an article that appeared in The San Antonio Business Journal. (4)

   _____

   _____

8. We played a communication game in which we had to complete the sentence, "Say it like a pro and listen. . . . " (5)

   _____

9. Employees communicate with each other in different ways therefore we are conducting a survey to identify these practices. (1)

   _____

   _____

10. Several areas covered in the book Write to the Point are: Punctuation and capitalization, Grammar, and Often-confused words. (1, 6)

_____

_____

_____

_____

_____

_____

_____

11. I could not believe that a manager misspelled the word excellent in a letter that promoted the firms description of its service. (2)

_____

_____

12. Each sentence should consist of one thought "and one thought only" to make it easier for your reader to understand. (3)

_____

_____

13. At least three fourths of my day is spent in writing emails and reports. (3)

_____

14. Karen had to adjust her writing to adhere to the requirements of the Food and Drug Administration—FDA. (4)

_____

_____

15. Her online job request included the statement "I recieved (sic) my Microsoft Specialist certificate in May." (5)

_____

_____

Chapter Preview

Punctuation is more than knowing where to place a period and a comma. Although the other marks of punctuation presented in this chapter are not so frequently used as the period and comma, they can add variety and clarity to your sentences.

Semicolons and colons are additional ways to indicate pauses in your writing. Dashes, parentheses, and italics set off or emphasize information. Quotation marks, apostrophes, and hyphens provide clarity. Ellipses, brackets, and asterisks have specific uses also. By adding these marks of punctuation to your knowledge of using periods, commas, and proper grammatical structure, you will have a sound foundation for writing.

The rules for these other punctuation marks provide consistency and standardization in their use; therefore, this area of punctuation requires study and practice.

The Semicolon

A semicolon (;) is a mark of punctuation that indicates a pause. The semicolon is not so strong as a period, but it is stronger than a comma.

Independent Clauses

Use a semicolon to separate two closely related independent clauses that are not joined by a coordinating conjunction (*and, or, nor, but*).

> **Indicate the specific action that you expect the reader of your memo to take; suggest only one action.**

(The two closely related clauses are not separated by a coordinating conjunction. A semicolon is necessary to separate the two clauses.)

Conjunctive Adverbs

Use a semicolon to separate two independent clauses joined by a conjunctive adverb such as *however, nevertheless, therefore, moreover,* and *furthermore*. A comma usually follows a conjunctive adverb of two or more syllables.

> **The speaker arrived late; nevertheless, he had an effective multimedia presentation.**

(The two independent clauses are joined by the conjunctive adverb *nevertheless*. A semicolon is placed before the word *nevertheless*, and a comma follows the word. This sentence could also be separated into two sentences: *The speaker arrived late. Nevertheless, he had an effective multimedia presentation.* The second sentence has a conjunctive adverb, *nevertheless,* followed by a comma and an independent clause.)

> **We take great care in writing letters to make good impressions; however, we are very informal in writing e-mail messages and often leave poor impressions.**

(A semicolon is placed before *however* to separate the two independent clauses. A comma follows the conjunctive adverb *however*.)

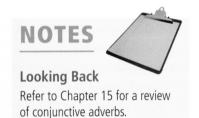

NOTES

Looking Back

Refer to Chapter 15 for a review of conjunctive adverbs.

Copyright © by The McGraw-Hill Companies, Inc.

Enumerations and Explanations

Use a semicolon before such introductory expressions as *for example* (e.g.), *that is* (i.e.), or *namely* when they introduce enumerations, explanations, or examples that are *not* essential to the sentence. Place a comma after the expressions. (Refer to the section on colons for enumerations, explanations, or examples that are essential to the sentence.)

> **We are changing our direct sales campaign; for example, we are sending out several gift catalogs rather than just one.**

(The expression *for example* introduces an explanation that is not necessary for the meaning of the first independent clause. A semicolon is necessary before the words *for example,* and a comma follows.)

> **A manager should communicate his or her expectations to the teams; namely, his or her deadlines for reports to management and the format for the reports.**

(*Namely* suggests an enumeration that is not necessary for the meaning of the independent clause. A semicolon is necessary before *namely,* and a comma follows.)

Series

Use a semicolon to separate items in a series if any of the items already contain commas.

> **People have inquired about the communication workshops that will be held in Cleveland, Ohio; Pensacola, Florida; Springfield, Illinois; and Little Rock, Arkansas.**

(Each city and state combination already contains a comma. A semicolon after each state name makes the sentence easier to understand.)

> **I will be judging students' speeches for Tina Kendall's business communication class on Monday, May 15; Wednesday, May 17; and Wednesday, May 24.**

(Each day and month combination already contains a comma. A semicolon after each of the days makes it easier to read the dates.)

CHECKPOINT 17.1

Go to the
Web

Checkpoint 17.1
for more skills practice on this topic.

Instructions: *Use the proofreaders' mark ⋀ to insert semicolons and the proofreaders' mark ⋀ to insert commas where necessary.*

1. Skimming a report gives you the essential meaning the remaining sentences clarify these major ideas.

2. Something always seemed to block Amy's success namely her lack of communication skills.

3. I tried to explain the delay to my supervisor she seemed too busy to listen.

4. The price for the communication texts did not include shipping costs consequently we must add this amount to your order.

5. His itinerary to present seminars on listening techniques includes Joliet Illinois Terre Haute Indiana and Grand Rapids Michigan.

6. Both high schools have students who may be finalists in the citywide essay contest for example students in the advanced-level writing classes enjoy opportunities to compete.

7. Some of my coworkers proofread their own writing others ask colleagues to assist them.

8. Quinn thought that he had selected clever headings for the sections of his report however his supervisor did not agree.

The Colon

A colon (:) is a stronger mark of punctuation than a comma. The colon is not so strong as a period. The main function of a colon is to introduce lists.

Introduction to Lists

Use a colon to introduce lists after expressions such as *the following, as follows, these,* and *thus.* Capitalize the word following the colon when items begin on separate lines in a list. Capitalize the word after the colon when two or more complete sentences follow the colon. Do not capitalize the word after the colon when the material (other than an enumerated list) cannot stand alone or when the material explains the first clause.

NOTES

Capitalization After Colons

Refer to a reference manual such as *The Gregg Reference Manual* for additional guidelines for the capitalization of material following colons.

PUNCTUATION ALERT!

Do not space *before* a colon. Space once *after* a colon.

A business letter consists of <u>the following</u> parts<u>:</u>
1. **Date line**
2. **Inside address**
3. **Salutation**
4. **Message**
5. **Closing**
6. **Writer's name and title**
7. **Reference initials**

(The expression *the following* suggests that a list will appear. A colon is necessary after the introductory clause. The first word in each line requires a capital letter.)

Before you begin to write copy for a Web site, ask <u>these</u> questions: What aspect of my service or product will benefit <u>the</u> viewer most? How will it benefit the viewer?

(A colon is necessary between the introductory clause and the two questions. The statement contains two complete sentences following the colon; therefore, the first word in each sentence requires a capital letter.)

My basic references for writing are <u>as follows</u>: a dictionary, a thesaurus, and an office reference manual.

(The expression *as follows* indicates a list will follow. A colon is necessary after the introductory clause. The items listed do not require capital letters because they cannot stand alone as a complete sentence.)

Incomplete Introductory Clauses

Do not use a colon after an incomplete introductory clause that introduces a list.

The office assistants attending the writing workshop are Ann Avery, Mary O'Neill, and Nelson Clark.

Copyright © by The McGraw-Hill Companies, Inc.

(The introductory clause *The office assistants attending the writing workshop are* preceding the list cannot stand on its own. No colon is necessary to introduce the list.)

Use a colon if the items in the list appear on separate lines.

The office assistants attending the writing workshop are:

Ann Avery

Mary O'Neill

Nelson Clark

(The introductory clause cannot stand on its own; however, since the individuals' names appear on separate lines, a colon is necessary after the word *are.*)

Illustrations and Explanations

Use a colon before expressions such as *namely, for example,* or *that is* when these expressions introduce explanations that are *essential* to the meaning of the sentence.

> **Three communication minicourses will be offered at our college: namely, punctuation, grammar, and proofreading.**

(The introductory clause suggests that an essential explanation is still to appear. The word *namely* identifies the specific courses. A colon precedes the word *namely,* and a comma follows it.)

> **Several types of lists will help you communicate your ideas: for example, bulleted lists, numbered steps, and modified bulleted lists.**

(The introductory clause suggests that an illustration of the lists [essential material] is still to appear. A colon is necessary before the words *for example,* and a comma follows the words.)

Sentence Interruptions

Do not use a colon before a list if another sentence separates the introductory clause and list.

> **The basic items listed below are suggestions for writing a new product advertisement. All copy for product advertisements requires the marketing director's approval.**
>
> **• Benefits**
>
> **• Features**
>
> **• Service**
>
> **• Ordering information**

(A sentence interrupts the introductory clause and the list. No colon is necessary after the introductory clause or after the interrupting sentence.)

> **The following newsletter suggestions work for me. I have a more detailed explanation for each one if you are interested.**
>
> **1. Know your objectives.**
>
> **2. Make it easy and quick to read.**
>
> **3. Concentrate on content.**

(No colon is necessary because a sentence interrupts the introductory clause and the list.)

Time

Use a colon between the hour and minutes expressed in figures.

My business communication class begins at 10:30 a.m.

(A colon is necessary between the hour *10* and the minutes *30*.)

Salutations

Use a colon after the salutation in a business letter with mixed punctuation (a colon after the salutation and a comma after the complimentary close). Do not use a colon with open punctuation (no punctuation after the salutation or complimentary close).

Dear Manager:

(A colon is necessary after *Manager* in a letter using mixed punctuation.)

Dear Mr. Ramirez

(No colon is necessary after Ramirez if the letter uses open punctuation.)

CHECKPOINT 17.2

Instructions: *Use the proofreaders' marks ⊙ and ⊙ to insert colons and periods where necessary. Use the proofreaders' mark ≡ to capitalize letters when necessary. Use the proofreaders' mark ⌿ to delete unnecessary punctuation.*

1. The last speech class that I took gave me the confidence to do these two things give a speech without notes and handle questions with ease.

2. In a letter with mixed punctuation, a salutation for a U.S. senator is as follows Dear Senator Feingold

3. These businesses responded to our communication survey

   legal offices

   medical and health facilities

   financial institutions

   nonprofit organizations

4. You may call the television station with your response to our viewers' questions anytime between the hours of 630 p.m. to 930 p.m.

5. Check the following paragraphs in *The Gregg Reference Manual* for suggestions on letter placement: The suggestions should be followed for all future assignments.

   top margins

   side margins

   bottom margins

   lengthening a short letter

   shortening a long letter

6. The survey indicates two trends first, presentation software is replacing the overhead projector. second, companies are investing money in training employees to use the software.

7. Reporters rely on several questions in their writing, namely; Who? What? When? Where? Why? How?

8. The steps in the writing process include: planning, organizing, writing, revising, and rewriting.

Quotation Marks

Quotation marks (" ") identify someone else's words. Quotation marks also set aside parts of published works as well as special words or phrases.

Direct Quotations

Use quotation marks around a direct quotation. A direct quotation includes the exact words spoken or written by someone. Place periods and commas inside the closing quotation mark.

> **O. R. Mahmud said, "I want our brochure to show that our products are different from the others out there."**

(The words between the pair of quotation marks are the exact words of the speaker. The period goes inside the closing quotation mark.)

> **"I have never analyzed my communication style," she said.**

(This is a direct quotation. The comma goes inside the closing quotation mark.)

Indirect Quotations

Do not use quotation marks in an indirect quotation. An indirect quotation is a restatement of the original material. The word *whether* or *that* often introduces an indirect quotation.

> **I was very pleased when my supervisor told me that I had excellent writing skills.**

(The clause *I had excellent writing skills* is not a direct quote by the supervisor and does not need quotation marks around it. The word *that* introduces the indirect quotation.)

> **The supervisor asked whether we had all completed our survey forms.**

(*Whether we had all completed our survey forms* is not a direct quote. No quotation marks are necessary.)

Separated Quotations

Use two sets of quotation marks when a quotation is separated by intervening expressions such as *he said.* Do not capitalize the first word of the second part of the quoted material.

> **"Business correspondence," says Werner, "must be clearly written and interesting to read."**

(The intervening expression [*says Werner*] separates the two parts of the quotation. Both parts require a pair of quotation marks. The word *must* does not require a capital letter.)

Parts of Published Works

Use quotation marks around the names of articles in newspapers and magazines. Use quotation marks around the titles of chapters in books.

> **I found an interesting article entitled "Communication Games" in one of my business magazines.**

(The title *Communication Games* requires quotes to indicate that it is part of a larger publication—a magazine.)

NOTES

Commas and Quotes

Commas separate the direct quote from the rest of the sentence.

EDIT PATROL

From an M-Law contest for silly warning labels:
The label on a bottle of drain cleaner warns that if you do not understand or cannot read all directions, cautions, and warnings, you should not use the product. Note: If you cannot read, the warning is of little assistance.

NOTES

Quotes in Titles
Refer to a reference manual such as *The Gregg Reference Manual* for a discussion on using quotation marks with the titles of literary and artistic works.

Our business English instructor assigned the exercises in Chapter 17, "Other Punctuation Marks."

(The chapter title *Other Punctuation Marks* requires quotes around it to designate that it is part of a larger publication—a book. The period goes inside the closing quotation mark.)

Technical or Unusual Expressions

Use quotation marks around technical or unusual expressions.

Leave enough "white space" on each page of your newsletter.

(The technical term *white space* requires quotation marks around it for emphasis.)

Do not use the expression "Thanking you in advance for your cooperation" because it is an obsolete phrase.

(The outdated expression *Thanking you in advance for your cooperation* requires quotation marks around it.)

Special Effect Words

Use quotation marks around slang words or special effect words and phrases.

I think that the newsletter column featuring different employees each month is "awesome."

(The slang word *awesome* requires quotation marks around it.)

Darrin's e-mail messages are rude, and I would like to suggest that he apply some "netiquette" to his writing.

(The use of the word *netiquette* is intended for special effect and requires quotation marks.)

Instructions

Use quotation marks to highlight instructions introduced by the words *signed, entitled, marked, labeled,* and *headed.* Capitalize the first letter of the word or phrase.

I returned the files to Dan in an envelope marked "Confidential."

(The word *marked* introduces *Confidential,* an instruction that requires quotation marks around it.)

Please place all messages that must be answered by 4 p.m. in a folder labeled "Urgent."

(The word *labeled* introduces *Urgent,* an implied instruction. *Urgent* requires quotation marks around it.)

Quotation Marks With Other Marks of Punctuation

Place a question mark or exclamation point inside the closing quotation mark when the question mark or exclamation point applies only to the quoted material.

The office assistant asked, "Did you want the e-mail addresses before noon?"

(The question applies to the direct quote; the question does not apply to the entire sentence. The question mark goes inside the closing quotation mark.)

"What a surprise!" exclaimed Mary when she heard that she had placed first in the speech contest sponsored by Kiwanis.

(The exclamation point refers to the direct quote; the explanation point does not apply to the entire sentence. The exclamation point goes inside the closing quotation mark.)

NOTES

Quotes for Emphasis

Refer to a reference manual such as *The Gregg Reference Manual* for information on using quotation marks to emphasize expressions.

EDIT PATROL

Tech Service

An exasperated caller to Technical Support couldn't get her new computer to turn on. After ensuring that the computer was plugged in, the technician asked the caller what happened when she pushed the power button. Her response was "I pushed and pushed on this foot pedal and nothing happens." The "foot pedal" turned out to be the computer's mouse.

Place a question mark or exclamation point outside the closing quotation mark when the exclamation point or question mark applies to the entire sentence.

Are you sure that she said, "The PowerPoint workshop will be on Friday, not Thursday"?

(The question refers to the entire sentence. The question mark goes outside the closing quotation mark.)

Place semicolons and colons after the closing quotation mark.

Our instructor repeated, "Periods and commas go inside the closing quotation mark"; however, some of us had trouble remembering this rule.

(The semicolon goes after the closing quotation mark.)

The envelope containing the following items should be marked "Priority": budget committee minutes and agenda for Friday's meeting.

(The colon goes after the closing quotation mark.)

CHECKPOINT 17.3

Go to the
Web

Checkpoint 17.3
for more skills practice on this topic.

Instructions: Use the appropriate proofreaders' mark ⱽ to insert quotation marks where necessary. Use the proofreaders' mark ≡ to capitalize letters where necessary. Use the proofreaders' mark ⸋ to delete unnecessary quotation marks.

1. The team leader said "that the team's report would be used as the basis for improving communication."

2. I told my assistant that an envelope marked personal should not be opened.

3. Speaking before large audiences, said our speech instructor, is a skill that you can practice by listening to these motivational tapes at home.

4. Did Mary say, I think that listening skills are as important as speaking skills?

5. My supervisor tends to hit the ceiling every time that I misunderstand his directions.

6. I really do not like these smileys that everyone seems to be placing on e-mail messages.

7. She distributed the article Listening Is an Art to the people attending the seminar.

8. I asked, don't dashes and parentheses have similar functions in sentences?

9. My mechanic gets this look of spare me however, I attempt to communicate by mimicking the noises that my car makes when I start it.

10. The news release must be on the editor's desk by this afternoon, said Gloria.

The Apostrophe

An apostrophe (') is used to indicate a missing letter in a contraction or a possessive. An apostrophe is also used in some plural forms.

Contractions

Use an apostrophe to show the omission of a letter or letters in a contraction.

I'm	=	I + am	isn't	=	is + not
couldn't	=	could + not	we're	=	we + are
they'll	=	they + will	it's	=	it + is

Possessives

To form the possessive of a singular noun or an irregular plural noun, add an apostrophe and *s* (*'s*) to the noun. (An irregular plural noun does not end in *s*.) To form the possessive of a regular plural noun that ends in *s* or *es*, add an apostrophe only.

Singular Possessive	**Plural Possessive**
Jane's speech	students' speeches
speaker's message	employees' newsletter
writer's ideas	proofreaders' marks

Irregular Plural Possessive

women's issues

children's essays

salespeople's body language

NOTES

Looking Back

Refer to Chapter 5 for information about forming possessives.

Plurals

Do not use an apostrophe to form the plurals of words from other parts of speech used as nouns unless the word would be easily misread.

His most recent newsletter article generated some <u>pros</u> and <u>cons</u> among the readers.

(The words *pros* and *cons* do not require an apostrophe and *s* (*'s*) for their plural forms. Their meanings are not likely to be misconstrued.)

She uses too many <u>so's</u> in her writing.

(The word *so's* requires an apostrophe to avoid a misreading.)

Lowercase Letters and Abbreviations

To form the plurals of lowercase letters and abbreviations with letters, add an apostrophe and *s* (*'s*). The apostrophe is used so that the resulting plurals are not confused with other words.

crossing <u>t</u>'s and dotting <u>i</u>'s	two letter <u>a</u>'s
several <u>c.o.d.</u>'s	registering <u>d.b.a.</u>'s

Numbers

To form the plurals of numbers expressed in figures, add an *s*. Adding an apostrophe and *s* (*'s*) is not necessary.

in the 1990<u>s</u>	size 10<u>s</u>	four 4<u>s</u>
several 5<u>s</u>	two Form 941<u>s</u>	two No. 942<u>s</u>

Capital Letters and Abbreviations

To form the plurals of the single capital letters *A, I, M,* and *U,* add an apostrophe and *s* (*'s*) to avoid misunderstandings in meanings.

A<u>'s</u>	I<u>'s</u>	M<u>'s</u>	U<u>'s</u>

Do not add an apostrophe and *s* (*'s*) to form the plurals of other single capital letters.

      four Ns   **two Ks**

To form plurals of abbreviations ending with capital letters, add *s* only.

      CPAs   **HMOs**   **PCs**   **M.A.s**   **Ph.D.s**

Quotations Within Quoted Material

Use apostrophes (single quotation marks) around a quotation within a quotation. Place the period inside the closing apostrophe.

> **John M. Mora wrote, "A sentence longer than 30 words usually needs a 'brevity check.'"**

(The words *brevity check* require single quotation marks to set them aside from the rest of the sentence. The period goes inside the single closing quotation mark.)

CHECKPOINT 17.4

Go to the
Web

Checkpoint 17.4
for more skills practice on this topic.

Instructions: *Use the proofreaders' mark* ⱽ *to add an apostrophe where needed. Use the proofreaders' mark* ℒ *to delete unnecessary apostrophes.*

1. Margies address is easy to remember; it has two 5's followed by two 4's.

2. The speaker said, "Theres always a danger of getting too folksy in your business correspondence."

3. The plant secretaries English review class meets at 6:45 a.m. on Friday's.

4. Dora uses too many "you know's" in her conversations.

5. My supervisors handwriting is difficult to read because she doesnt cross her ts.

6. I have completed the registration packets for all the Ms.

7. Our CPA's have excellent handwriting skills.

8. The writers handwriting was difficult to read because of the way he forms his As and Is.

The Hyphen

A hyphen (-) has a variety of uses in compound words and in numbers. A hyphen also indicates syllabication. Changes in word hyphenation sometimes occur over time. For example, in the past, *on-line* was the preferred spelling. Now *online* (no hyphen) is preferred. Use a current dictionary as a helpful reference.

Compound Numbers

Use a hyphen with compound numbers from *twenty-one* through *ninety-nine*.

> **Thirty-five messages arrived yesterday.**
> **Two hundred seventy-five registrations have been received.**

Other Punctuation

Fractions

Use a hyphen to separate the numerator (top number in a fraction) from the denominator (bottom number) of a fraction written in words.

> **three-fourths** of the page
> **two-fifths** majority

Compound Adjectives

Use a hyphen in a compound adjective (two or more words) that precedes a noun. In most situations, do not hyphenate a compound adjective that follows the noun modified.

> He summarized the sensitive issue in a **well-written** memo.
> The memo is **well written**.
> She made a number of **off-the-record** comments.
> She asked that her comments be kept **off the record**.
> The **up-to-date** report contains many illustrations.
> The report is **up to date** and contains many illustrations.

Numbers and Nouns

Use a hyphen in an adjective consisting of a number and a noun that precedes the noun modified.

> **first-rate** job   the **two-letter** state abbreviation
> a **$25-a-month** charge   a **30-minute** presentation

Suspending Hyphens

When two or more hyphenated adjectives have a common element and this element is shown only with the last term, use a suspending hyphen after each of the incomplete adjectives to show a relationship with the last term.

> **12-** to **15-hour** project
> **two-** or **three-column** newsletter
> **large-** and **small-scale** drawings
> **long-** and **short-term** assignments

Compound Nouns

Do not hyphenate well-known compound nouns acting as adjectives. If the compound noun does not appear as one word or as a hyphenated word in a dictionary, assume that the word is written as two words.

> **public relations** consultant
> **high school** newsletter
> **accounts receivable** aged report
> **real estate** description

Adverbs

Do not place a hyphen after an adverb ending in *ly* that is combined with a present or past participle.

> an **extremely interesting** speaker
> **hastily prepared** speech
> **clearly documented** manuscript
> **carefully edited** copy

NOTES

Looking Back
Refer to Chapter 10 for a review of participles.

Copyright © by The McGraw-Hill Companies, Inc.

Self Prefixes

Use a hyphen after the word *self* when it acts as a prefix.

self-confidence   **self-paced**

Range of Numbers or Letters

Use a hyphen to indicate a range of numbers or letters. The hyphen takes the place of the word *to*.

10-12 years   March **12-16**   Letters **A-C**

One Person With Two Functions

Use a hyphen to indicate dual functions performed by one person.

owner-manager   **director-producer**

secretary-treasurer   **teacher-counselor**

CHECKPOINT 17.5

Go to the
Web

Checkpoint 17.5
for more skills practice on
this topic.

Instructions: *Use the proofreaders' mark ₌∧ to insert hyphens where needed. Use the proofreaders' mark ꟼ or ꟾ to delete unnecessary hyphens.*

1. That long three hour meeting of the Budget Committee created friction between the chairperson and the secretary treasurer.

2. You will find the e mail policies on pages 34 40 of the employee handbook.

3. We specialize in developing presentation materials for minority and women-owned businesses.

4. At its last meeting, the Budget Committee authorized one eighth of the total budget for a communications lab.

5. His well organized illustrations and easily-understood directions made the exercises simple to complete.

6. Marie purchased a self study book that contained a step by step guide to improve listening effectiveness.

7. Mae Ling summarized a three year research project in a 90 minute speech.

8. Writing a three or four page newsletter each month is a time consuming task.

The Dash

A dash (—) may be substituted for a comma, a semicolon, a colon, or parentheses only if there is a noticeable break in a sentence or if a word, phrase, or clause needs to be emphasized. Dashes may enclose essential as well as nonessential material. Do not use a dash just because you are not sure which mark of punctuation is correct.

Change of Thought

Use a dash to indicate a break or a change of thought in a sentence.

Listen attentively—with your eyes as well as your ears—so that people recognize your interest in their remarks.

(Dashes set aside a break *with your eyes as well as your ears.*)

Andrew's business plan—50 pages long—included his plans for the future of his company.

(Dashes set aside a change of thought.)

Parenthetical Comment

Use a dash to set off a parenthetical comment or an afterthought from the rest of the sentence.

Either during the first or second week in October—I cannot remember exactly—I wrote to you about our change of address.

(Dashes set aside *I cannot remember exactly,* which is a nonessential parenthetical expression.)

They agreed on all the final recommendations—every one of them!

(*Every one of them* is an afterthought and requires a dash to set it apart from the rest of the sentence.)

Repetitions and Reminders

Use a dash to set off repetitious statements or to emphasize a reminder.

Words left out of letters or misspelled names are common errors made by writers—errors that could be avoided.

(The word *errors* is repeated. A dash sets the word *errors* off from the rest of the sentence.)

Don't forget the orientation meeting—January 2 at 4 p.m.—with our new employees.

(*January 2 at 4 p.m.* is a reminder set off by dashes from the rest of the sentence.)

Summary Words

Use a dash before the words *these, they, any, all,* and *each* when these words are used as subjects to summarize a preceding list.

Accuracy, completeness, clarity, and conciseness—these are the goals that I try to remember when I am writing.

(The dash precedes the subject *these.*)

Listening, speaking, and writing—each represents a skill that managers and supervisors need.

(The dash precedes the subject *each.*)

CHECKPOINT 17.6

Instructions: *In the following sentences, use the proofreaders' mark* *to insert dashes where needed.*

1. Terry had to give a sales presentation on a new product a presentation that required detailed diagrams and examples.

Copyright © by The McGraw-Hill Companies, Inc.

2. Sally wasted much of her time too much of it trying to write a perfect first draft of a report.

3. After the meeting, I had nothing to say nothing at all.

4. We have more than one hundred inquiries all in response to our Web page advertisement that we must answer.

5. The objective, the outline, and the format these need to be determined before you begin to write the report.

6. The chairperson's next tactic no one should be offended is to limit each individual's discussion time at our meetings.

7. The book illustrated every step of the writing process every step from planning through the final draft.

8. My mentor views writing as a skill an extraordinarily important one that will help me obtain a promotion.

Parentheses

Parentheses (( )), like dashes, enclose interruptions in sentences. However, parentheses set off only nonessential information. Using parentheses does not appear so abrupt as using dashes. Parentheses de-emphasize material; dashes emphasize material.

Nonessential Material

Use parentheses to set off nonessential material that is not intended to be part of the main statement. Do not capitalize the first word of material within the parentheses if the material is a short complete sentence. Capitalize the first word of material within the parentheses if the sentence is lengthy.

Lindsay Dotson (she was a Mansfield graduate) is now the public relations director for IPAL.

(The parentheses set aside *she was a Mansfield graduate,* which is nonessential material. The word *she* is not capitalized since it begins a short sentence that appears within a sentence.)

The director chose Marty as the team leader for the Crawford project. (His communication skills surpass those of the other members on the team.)

(The sentence in parentheses is lengthy. The first word *his* requires a capital letter.)

Lists

Use parentheses around numbers or letters that identify a list of items in the text copy.

The school referendum failed for these reasons: (1) lack of communication with the voters, (2) cost of computer facilities, and (3) increase in taxes.

(Parentheses make it easier to read numbered lists included in the text copy.)

1. Evaluate your presentation by asking these questions: (a) How did your audience react? (b) Were the visual aids effective? (c) What were

the strengths of the presentation? (d) What were the weaknesses of the presentation?

(Use letters if a number is already used in the sentence context.)

Outlines

Use parentheses for sections of an outline.

> **I. VISION AND MISSION**
>   **A. Set Target Dates**
>   **1. Status reports**
>   **a. Organizational**
>   **(1) Format**
>   **(a) Written outline**
>   **(b) Formal report**
>   **(2) Frequency**

(The parentheses around (1) and (2) and around (a) and (b) include the fifth and sixth subdivisions in this outline.)

Nonessential References and Directions

Use parentheses to enclose a nonessential reference or set of directions.

> **This article includes three samples of correct formats for business letters (Figures 6, 7, and 8).**

(The material in parentheses is a nonessential reference notation.)

> **Please send the e-mail to all branch offices. (Be sure to use today's date.)**

(The material in parentheses is a direction.)

Explanations

Use parentheses to enclose explanatory words or phrases.

> **The Association for Business Communication (ABC) met in San Antonio for the fall meeting.**

(The letters in parentheses are the abbreviation of the *Association for Business Communication.*)

> **At our last meeting, the chairperson assigned accountabilities (who is responsible for each job) and established tentative due dates.**

(*Who is responsible for each job* explains the meaning of the word *accountabilities.*)

Numbers in Formal Documents

Use parentheses around figures that follow amounts written in words in legal or formal business documents.

> **In the last collection letter that I received, you indicated that I owed Three Thousand Two Hundred Dollars ($3,200).**

NOTES

Parentheses

Parentheses should not be used too frequently, or their importance will be minimized.

Go to the
Web

Checkpoint 17.7
for more skills practice on this topic.

CHECKPOINT 17.7

Instructions: *Use the proofreaders' mark* ⧵ ⧸ *to insert parentheses where necessary. Use the proofreaders' mark* ≡ *to capitalize letters where necessary. Use the proofreaders' mark* ⧸ *to delete unnecessary parentheses.*

1. The terms of the contract give employees retroactive pay for (ninety) 90 days.

2. My former business communication instructor had high standards she required correct grammar, which helped me become a good newspaper reporter.

3. Avoid these redundant expressions in your correspondence: 1 each and every, 2 consensus of opinion, 3 refer back, and 4 true facts.

4. Pressing the palms of your hands together tightly relieves tension. try this the next time you give a speech.

5. Companies hiring new graduates rated communication skills see Table 10 high on their lists of employment requisites.

6. WYSIWYG what you see is what you get was a significant computer design feature that improved the communication process.

7. Selena Taylor my mentor at KDC has recently written a communications textbook for corporate executives.

8. My supervisor asked me to correct the following section of the document:

   VI. REVISING YOUR DOCUMENT

     (A). Check Paragraphs

       (1.) Organizational pattern

         (a.) Topic sentences

           (1) Clarity

             (a.) Active voice

             (b) Positive tone

Italics

Use italic type to emphasize words and phrases and to indicate titles of complete published works.

Definitions and Word Emphasis

Use italics to identify words that are being defined or highlighted.

The number of *fantastics* and *terrifics* in William's speech reflected a somewhat limited vocabulary.

(Italics are used to highlight the words *fantastics* and *terrifics*.)

The term *at-will* means that an employer can fire an employee as long as the reason is not illegal.

(Italics are used to identify the term *at-will* that is being defined.)

Published Materials

Use italics to identify complete published works such as titles of books, newspapers, magazines, and pamphlets. Use italics for titles of movies, plays, television and radio series, paintings, and sculptures. When you proofread, underline the phrase or word to be italicized.

The *Leader Telegram*, our local newspaper, featured several articles on public speaking.

(Italics are used to identify the newspaper *Leader Telegram,* which is a complete published work.)

The chapter "Oral Presentations" appears in the book *Communication Systems.*

(Italics are used to identify the book *Communication Systems,* which is a complete published work.)

Ellipsis Marks

Ellipsis marks (. . .) indicate that part of a quoted sentence is omitted.

Omissions

Use ellipsis marks to indicate omissions in quoted material. Use three spaced periods to designate omissions at the beginning or in the middle of a sentence. Use four spaced periods (or other ending punctuation) at the end of a sentence. Do not use more or fewer periods.

Barry advised, "Audiovisual aids enhance a speech . . . but require careful planning."

(Three spaced periods are necessary to identify the omission because it falls in the middle of the sentence.)

Barry advised, "Audiovisual aids enhance a speech . . . . To be effective, the visuals must be dynamic."

(Four spaced periods are necessary to identify the omission because it falls at the end of the sentence. One of the periods is the ending mark of punctuation.)

Brackets

Brackets ([ ]) are used when a separation is necessary in a sentence already enclosed in parentheses, when an error occurs in quoted material, or when an editorial comment is made in a quotation. Brackets are not used frequently in business documents.

Errors

Insert the word *sic* in brackets immediately after a misspelled word, grammatical error, or factual error made by the person quoted. *Sic* means "so" or "thus" and points out that the error was not made by the present writer but was present in the original version.

The job advertised in the Tuesday evening *Tribune* was for someone "with computer knowledge and good grammer [sic] skills."

(The word *grammar* is misspelled. The word was misspelled by the person who submitted the ad.)

Editorial Comments

Insert editorial comments or interpretations of situations being reported in brackets. This designates that the material within the brackets is not the original writer's.

The speaker ended his presentation by saying, "Listening skills are the key to effective management." [Applause indicated agreement.]

(The material in the bracket is not part of the quoted material but is the reviewer's interpretation of the applause.)

Parenthetical Expressions Within Parentheses

Use brackets to enclose a parenthetical expression within a statement that is already within parentheses. Place the shorter parenthetical expression in brackets, and place the longer parenthetical statement in parentheses.

(Review Chapter 16 [commas] before you rewrite your report.)

(The parenthetical word *commas* is enclosed in brackets to set it aside from the rest of the material already in parentheses.)

The Asterisk

The main purpose of the asterisk (*) is to refer the reader to another location for a more detailed explanation or reference.

Use an asterisk to indicate that a footnote or explanation appears in a table or at the bottom of the page. Place an asterisk after a comma, semicolon, colon, or period.

The average manager spends 10 percent of his or her time writing and 15 percent reading.*

(The asterisk indicates that the percentage is explained in another location. The asterisk is placed after the period.)

CHECKPOINT 17.8

Go to the Web

Checkpoint 17.8
for more skills practice on this topic.

*Instructions: Insert italics (underline), ellipsis marks, brackets, or asterisks where necessary. Use the proofreaders' mark ⸆ or ⸅ to delete unnecessary punctuation marks. If the sentence is correct, write **Yes** in the space provided.*

1. The word grammar is often misspelled in job advertisements. _____

2. Please check the last newsletter I wrote the communications article see page 4 and e-mail your suggestions for additional subjects for the next issue. _____

3. The *Book of Lists** identifies speaking before a group as the top human fear in the United States. _____

4. The following books are useful in writing a business plan: How to Write a Clear, Effective Business Plan and Business Plans That Win. _____

5. Gossip flourishes when employees lose faith in administration . . . , or when employees feel helpless. _____

6. (Please use 3- by 5-inch notes [Post-it Notes] to list agenda items.) _____

7. Kevin's e-mail message states, "The listning [sic] workshop that I attended yesterday was extremely informative." _____

8. In each issue, OfficePRO includes an ongoing column about English style and grammar. _____

Other Punctuation

The following sentences for diagramming practice are a review of the rules that you have studied in the past 16 chapters.

Go to the
Web

Checkpoint 17.9
for more skills practice on this topic.

 CHECKPOINT 17.9

Instructions: *In the space provided, diagram the following sentences. All words may be diagrammed.*

1. Supervisors need training in the communication of goals to front-line workers.

2. At the end of a meeting, identify those items that need future consideration.

3. People often receive the nonverbal message and do not hear the words.

4.	Corporate executives use factual reports for policy or action decisions.

5.	My supervisor requires fact-based written and verbal communication from everyone.

Name _____   Date _____

Go to the
Web

Practice 1 Exercises
for more skills practice on
this topic.

PRACTICE 1

Using Correct Punctuation

Instructions: *Check the following sentences for punctuation errors. Rewrite the sentences correctly in the space provided. If a sentence is punctuated correctly, write* ***Yes.***

1. The intranet carried an employee information announcement concerning up to date communication procedures.

   _____

   _____

2. To improve your writing, obtain a copy of *The Elements of Style* by Strunk and White.

   _____

   _____

3. In your next report, omit some of the I's.

   _____

   _____

4. I checked out several books all on the topic of nonverbal communication from the public library.

   _____

   _____

5. "Public speaking is uncomfortable for many people, says Bill Menard, because it was never taught properly."

   _____

   _____

6. Most people are not good listeners they are too busy thinking about what they are going to say next.

   _____

   _____

7. Nonverbal communication consists of the following; (1) eye contact, (2) gestures, (3) mannerisms, and (4) body movement.

   _____

   _____

8. Heather's last email message was a reminder to attend the seminar on womens issues.

   _____

   _____

Name _____ Date _____

9. Proofread your outgoing correspondence for the correct use of numerals versus words (or vice versa).

_____

_____

10. My communications design instructor said, "Brochures should be easy to read ... Select a font that is businesslike."

_____

_____

Choosing Correct Punctuation

Instructions: *In each of the following sentences, a mark or marks of punctuation are missing. In the space provided, write the code for the missing mark(s) of punctuation. Then use proofreaders' marks to indicate the correct placement of the punctuation in the sentence. Use underlining to indicate italics.*

Semi = Semicolon	**Hy** = Hyphen
Col = Colon	**Dash** = Dash
QM = Quotation Marks	**Paren** = Parentheses
Apos = Apostrophe	**Ital** = Italics

1. Write a simple, straightforward document use declarative sentences. 1. _____

2. Did you know that many words used in formal report writing such as sic and ibid are Latin words? 2. _____

3. Most labor-law experts agree that a business needs an employee handbook one that clearly identifies policies, rules, and benefits. 3. _____

4. Liquid crystal display LCD portable projectors are perfect for speakers who enjoy making dynamic presentations. 4. _____

5. The clients name was misspelled again, said John. 5. _____

6. I thought that her cover letter sounded self centered and arrogant. 6. _____

7. The term layout refers to the process of making a page look the way that you want it to be. 7. _____

8. She thought that my well intended compliment was insensitive. 8. _____

9. Every meeting has three stages planning, conducting, and evaluating. 9. _____

10. Deb uses desktop publishing software to create newsletters she prints them on a color laser printer. 10. _____

Other Punctuation

Name _____ Date _____

Go to the
Web

Practice 2 Exercises
for more skills practice on this topic.

PRACTICE 2

Punctuation and Capitalization

Instructions: Use proofreaders' marks to make the necessary corrections in punctuation and capitalization. Use underlining to indicate italics. More than one correction in a sentence may be needed.

1. Use the exact format of the company name as it appears in the companys letterhead for example Sean McQuinn & Sons.

2. These are questions that are often asked what is the role of the annual meeting in attracting investors? is the annual report a successful recruitment device for new investors?

3. Some on the move executives need light-weight equipment to deliver their high-impact multi-media presentations.

4. The supervisors responsibility is to write an evaluation of the interns progress in meeting his or her on the job learning objectives.

5. Almost three fourths of our high-school students attend a community or four-year college however the number is less nationwide.

6. Although its possible to create an all purpose brochure, its more difficult to write copy for a general audience. (If budgets allow, create different brochures for different customers.

7. Betty is a self taught writer its quite evident in her reporting.

8. Bon asked Is the equipment available for a presentation on Friday?

9. The officers of our family business include the following Rod Cole, president Maggie Cole, vice president Donna Weins, secretary treasurer.

10. Richard Koonce stated, too many managers practice mushroom management these managers control their employees by keeping them in the dark.

11. Words left out of letters or misspelled names are common errors errors that could be avoided.

12. The audience will appreciate a speakers remarks if its clear that he or she enjoys the subject matter.

13. Small teams four or fewer members are the best for editing copy.

14. In her newsletter Communication Insights, Priscilla Richardson emphasizes the importance of writing for quick reading.

15. In the article Benefits of Effective Listening, the author said To become an effective listener, we have to stop talking.

Name _____ Date _____

PRACTICE 3

Proofreading

Instructions: Proofread and compare the two sentences in each group. If they are the same, write **Yes** in the space provided. If they are not the same, write **No.** Use the first sentence as the correct copy. If you find errors in the second sentence, use proofreaders' marks to correct the copy.

Go to the
Web

Practice 3 Exercises
for more skills practice on this topic.

1. NEC Technologies Inc. has a new LCD (liquid crystal display) projector line that weighs less than 16 pounds and has a built-in carrying handle.

   NEC Technologies Inc. has a new L. C. D. (liquid crystal display) projector line that weighs less than 6 pounds and has a builtin carrying handle.

   1. _____

2. Three courses in our administrative assistant program—Business English 140, Written Communications 40, and Report Writing 70—stress the importance of communication skills.

   Three courses in our Administrative Assistant program—Business English 140; Written Communications 40; and Report Writing 70—stress the importance of communication skills.

   2. _____

3. David Quigley of the advertising agency Quigley and Mather says that the headlines are read five times more than the material beneath them.

   David Quigley of the advertising agency Quigley and Mather said that headlines are read five times more than the material beneath them.

   3. _____

4. Over 1300 readers (over the age of 18) were tested on editorial and ad copy, and the results showed that 98 percent of the readers misunderstood some part of the material that they had read.

   Over 1300 readers (over the age of 18) were tested on editorial and ad copy and the results showed that 95 percent of the readers mis-understood some part of the material that they had read.

   4. _____

5. Mark Twain said, "My idea of a good conversation is someone who will listen to me."

   Mark Twain said "My idea of a good conversation is someone who will listen to me.

   5. _____

Name _____ Date _____

Editing Copy

Instructions: Use proofreaders' marks to edit the following information about listening skills. If you are not certain about the use of a proofreaders' mark, use your reference manual or the proofreaders' marks on the inside front cover of this textbook.

LISTENING TECHNIQUES

1. Give the speaker your undivided attention. Concentrate onthe message or instructions being given not on the speakers appearance or mannerisms.

2. Do not become so engrossed in taking notes that you miss the important concepts. (if you have good notes, you will be able to ask appropriate questions for clarification of a point or direction.)

3. Avoid letting your preconcieved ideas about a topic interfer with the message. You may not agree with message, but you should not tune it out.

4. Ask appropriate questions after a Presentation or a set of Instructions been given. Save your questions ask them at one time rather than interrupting periodically.

5. Review your notes at once. (Much of the message is lost immediately after hearing it. Going over a set of notes helps re-inforce what has been said and helps you remember the material.

Go to the
Web

Practice 4 Exercises
for more skills practice on this topic.

PRACTICE 4

Writing

Instructions: Observe the interactions among your classmates as they talk and sit together in different places like the classroom, library, cafeteria, etc. Notice the space that they maintain and how it differs from one person to another. Make notes on your observations. Write a paragraph or two on your observations, and include what you believe are the reasons for the different space allocations that you observe. Punctuate all sentences correctly. Answers will vary.

_____

_____

_____

_____

_____

_____

_____

_____

_____

Name _____ Date _____

PRACTICE 5

Using Correct Punctuation

*Instructions: Check the following sentences for punctuation errors. Rewrite the sentences correctly in the space provided. If a sentence is punctuated correctly, write **Yes.***

1. Some refer to caring about office ethics as taking the high road.

    _____

2. Here is a copy of an actual—no kidding!—memo that my supervisor sent last week.

    _____

    _____

3. Some people leave their pagers on beep instead of vibrate, which is annoying during meetings.

    _____

    _____

4. John has the habit of saying, "That reminds me . . . "

    _____

5. I am exhausted because I worked a 12-hour day yesterday.

    _____

6. Our performance evaluation has a number of categories (creativity, initiative, teamwork, etc.) with spaces to indicate "strengths" and "growth opportunities."

    _____

    _____

7. Anna was too self absorbed to actively participate in our conversation.

    _____

8. This three to four month research project is more interesting than I thought that it would be.

    _____

    _____

9. Jack feels that it is unfair for people to suggest (As many have) that engineers are antisocial.

    _____

    _____

Other Punctuation

Name _____ Date _____

10. Becoming a good listener means overcoming listening barriers; for example, not concentrating, becoming distracted, and talking instead of listening.

_____

_____

Choosing Correct Punctuation

Instructions: In each of the following sentences, a mark or marks of punctuation are missing. In the space provided, write the code for the missing mark(s) of punctuation. Then use proofreaders' marks to indicate the correct placement of the punctuation in the sentences. Use underlining to indicate italics.

Semi = *Semicolon*	***Apos*** = *Apostrophe*
Col = *Colon*	***Hy*** = *Hyphen*
QM = *Quotation Marks*	***Dash*** = *Dash*
Paren = *Parentheses*	***Ital*** = *Italics*

1. The book Woe Is I is a survival guide for those who want a sensible, modern introduction to grammar usage.

1. _____

2. When taking notes, concentrate on the key points for example, do not write everything that the speaker says.

2. _____

3. ASAP as soon as possible appears on just about every e-mail that Lora sends.

3. _____

4. The following months have only 30 days April, June, September, and November.

4. _____

5. Immediately and I mean immediately call 911 for every emergency that occurs.

5. _____

6. When companies collect opinions of people who care about a decision, they are involved in a process that some call getting buy-in.

6. _____

7. Ralph is a strong willed, opinionated manager.

7. _____

8. Frauka's manager replied, "Thats why we need you to proofread all outgoing correspondence."

8. _____

9. Please use the term businessperson instead of businessman.

9. _____

10. When it is 930 in San Francisco, it is 1230 in New York City.

10. _____

Name _____ Date _____

PRACTICE 6

Punctuation and Capitalization

Instructions: Use proofreaders' marks to make the necessary corrections in punctuation and capitalization. Use underlining to indicate italics. More than one correction in a sentence may be needed.

1. To emphasize an idea, place it first or last in your correspondence letter, memo, email, or report.

2. Scott said that his coworkers are not in his opinion busy enough.

3. The videoconference takes advantage of these types of media Audio, Graphics, and Video.

4. The term spamming refers to the sending of unwanted email.

5. Keep your written messages simple dont use more than two or three typefaces.

6. Many email messages do not need to be saved therefore delete electronic messages after reading them.

7. To improve the quality of our written correspondence, we are purchasing new printers consequently please notify Sally if you do not have a laser printer.

8. Our products have higher than average sales in Seattle Washington Portland Oregon and Monterey California.

9. To make a form letter more personal, try the following hints

   1. use personalized envelopes instead of labels.

   2. spell names correctly.

   3. use high grade paper and a laser printer.

10. In the article Understanding Foreign Correspondence, the writer stated that the French prefer a formal salutation such as Very Honored Mr. Professor Hermann.

11. Avoid overusing words that may irritate your listener, said Devron, such as you know or sort of.

12. Joy wondered "Whether we found her five page handout on voice mail too detailed."

13. Please read Chapter 3 in The Art of Communicating before 130 p.m. next Tuesday.

14. At the end of the staff meeting, our new manager said, Do not forget to cross your ts and dot your is.

15. During the 1990's, several HMO's underwent massive restructuring.

Name _____ Date _____

PRACTICE 7

Proofreading

*Instructions: Proofread and compare the two sentences in each group. If they are the same, write **Yes** in the space provided. If they are not the same, write **No**. Use the first sentence as the correct copy. If you find errors in the second sentence, use proofreaders' marks to correct the copy.*

1. When brainstorming ideas for a presentation, write one idea on a 3- x 5-inch index card or Post-it Note.

    When brainstorming ideas for a presentation, write one idea on a 3 x 5 inch index card or Post-It Note.

    1. _____

2. Research studies indicate that people who cannot "read" another person's body language have difficulty adjusting their behaviors to improve relationships; consequently, these people are not always socially adaptable or popular.

    Research studies indicate that people who cannot read another persons body language have difficulty adjusting their behaviors to improve relationships; consequently these people are not always socially adaptable or popular.

    2. _____

3. Although you cannot change your features (without the benefit of plastic surgery), you can control your attractiveness and social acceptance by establishing your own "style" of grooming, clothing, and accessories.

    Although you cannot change your features (without the benefit of plastic surgery, you can control your attractiveness and social acceptance by establishing your own style of grooming, clothing and accessories.

    3. _____

4. The advertising slogan "Come alive with Pepsi" was translated in one country as "Bring your ancestors back from the dead."

    The advertising slogan "come alive with Pepsi" was translated in one country as "Bring your ancestors back from the dead".

    4. _____

5. Our human resources specialist often says, "If I receive a résumé or cover letter with a typographical error or if it smells like cigarette smoke, I throw it away."

    Our human resources specialist often says, "If I receive a résumé or cover letter with a typographical error or if it smells like cigarette smoke, I throw it away."

    5. _____

Name _____ Date _____

Editing Copy

Instructions: Use proofreaders' marks to edit the following information about conducting effective meetings. If you are not certain about the use of a proofreaders' mark, use your reference manual or the proofreaders' marks on the inside front cover of this textbook.

MEETING MANAGEMENT

1. Determine meeting objectives. What are you trying to accomplish? If their is know clear reason to meet, dont call a meeting.

2. Develop an agenda. If possible (And it generally is), see that every one receives an agenda before the meeting.

3. Appoint an facilitator. The facilitator does not necessarily have to be the person of the highest rank; he or she may be the person who 'owns' the discussion issue or issues.

4. Establish ground rules. Ground rules encourage "straight" talk with no "dancing around the issues."

5. Establish the meeting length. Avoid the tendency to get "hung up" on trivial points and never feel obligated to fill an alloted meeting time period, after the goals have been accomplished.

6. Prepare written minutes. Allways have someone take notes onthe key points of the discussion, and distribute the minutes to the meeting participants (and other concerned parties within 24-hours.

PRACTICE 8

Writing

Instructions: Stereotyping means judging in a positive or negative way based upon an individual's perceptions. Examples of stereotyping include classifying all homeless people as lazy or people with poor grammar as dumb. Have you ever been stereotyped? Write about a personal experience when you felt that someone stereotyped you. Punctuate all sentences correctly. Answers will vary.

_____
_____
_____
_____
_____
_____
_____
_____
_____

Posttest

Instructions: *Check the following sentences for punctuation and capitalization errors. Write the sentences correctly in the space provided. If the sentence is punctuated and capitalized correctly, write **Yes.***

1. Nonverbal cues are especially important in conveying feelings, some researchers maintain that a nonverbal message contributes more to the message than the spoken words. (1)

_____

_____

_____

_____

2. "Quadico strives for effective communication, said the speaker, and uses the following techniques when introducing a new employee benefits plan; written summaries, face to face training meetings, and videos." (1, 2, 3)

_____

_____

_____

3. Your receiver's feedback lets you know if you have not communicated accurately. (2)

_____

4. Many businesses offer in house training programs in communications. (3)

_____

5. Spanish, Japanese, Chinese, Italian, and French these are the languages in our diverse workforce that have enriched my understanding of different cultures. (3)

_____

_____

6. We use the Internet daily for our research. (see the reference entitled "Online Search Procedures" for information about using search engines.) (2, 4, 6)

_____

_____

7. The *MLA Style Manual* gives suggestions for citing online resources. (4)

_____

8. Jenny Simpson said, "good listening supports effective relationships in the organization . . . " (5, 6)

_____

9. Important listening skills are: listening carefully; looking at the speaker and taking notes. (1)

_____

10. Do you have the go-get-'em attitude at work? (2)

_____

11. My supervisor said: "Take your time and tell me everything, but then she glanced at her watch, which indicated that she was really saying, "hurry up! I do not have all day". (2)

_____

_____

12. I read in the book "Being a Success on the Job" that distinguishing among the four types of language traps: dehumanization, stereotyping, categorization, and polarization—will improve career success. (3, 4)

_____

_____

_____

13. In one on one interactions, Jessicas communication style is: self confident, casual, and relaxed. (1, 3)

_____

_____

14. Josh stated on his résumé that "He was seeking a salary commiserate (sic) with his training and experience" and that he wanted to work party-time (sic). (3, 5)

_____

_____

15. The abbreviation RIM [Records and Information Management] was a well known expression to three fourths of the ARMA [Association of Records Managers and Administrators International] members surveyed in the 1990's. (3, 4, 5)

_____

_____

_____

Chapter 18

Numbers

OBJECTIVES

After you have studied this chapter and completed the exercises, you will be able to do the following:

1. Identify appropriate times to use words versus figures in expressing numbers.

2. Differentiate between cardinal and ordinal numbers.

3. Use numbers with addresses, ages, and dates correctly.

4. Use numbers in decimals, fractions, measurements, identification numbers, and financial quotes correctly.

5. Use numbers in amounts of money and percentages correctly.

6. Use numbers correctly in political divisions, publications, ratios, titles, inclusive sets of figures, and sizes.

7. Use numbers in telephone numbers, temperatures, time, and time periods correctly.

Workplace Applications:
Doing Business on the Internet

Most companies use the Internet to connect with their employees, their customers, and their suppliers. The term used to describe conducting operations online is *e-commerce,* which means electronic commerce. The most effective e-commerce sites provide the benefits of convenience, price, variety of offerings, and security.

Developing an Internet Presence

In order to attract customers and retain traffic to online sites, e-commerce merchants must develop e-marketing strategies. Successful companies doing business on the Internet must make certain that their sites are listed in online search results and directory listings. In addition, many businesses use banner advertisements, the most common advertising product on the Web. The most popular forms of direct marketing on the Internet are direct e-mail and newsgroup postings. The term for these unsolicited messages is "spam."

Online customers are demanding increased customer service. Many sites offer informational Web pages that anticipate customer questions, often referred to as FAQs (frequently asked questions). Most sites allow e-mail inquiries to be sent directly to customer service representatives (CSRs).

Credit cards are the dominant form of payment on the Internet, and the potential for identity theft and credit card fraud is high. To avoid fraud, security is an important component of doing business on the Internet. Online businesses use encryption technology to encode and decode information transmitted over the Internet so that only the sender and intended recipient can read the information.

Pretest

Instructions: *Underline the errors in number usage in the following sentences. Write the corrections in the space provided. Write **Yes** if the numbers in a sentence are written correctly.*

1. During an online sale, Leath Furniture sold its supply of 89 office desk lamps in 6 days. (1)

   1. _____

2. 37 financial institutions participate in our home-banking program. (1)

   2. _____

3. You are the 3d person to call us about the misplaced decimal point in our Web site advertisement. (2)

   3. _____

4. Lindfield, 32, left the company in August, 1998, to become part owner of an online retail sporting-goods store. (3)

   4. _____

5. Our accountant's fees increased 5 percent this year. (5)

   5. _____

6. We had to refund $300.00 to seventy-five customers. (1, 5)

   6. _____

7. The merger will give a pretax savings of $800 million to $1 billion a year. (5)

   7. _____

8. One e-commerce workshop begins at 8:30 a.m.; the other begins at 12 noon. (7)

   8. _____

9. The latest rough draft of our Web site copy was only 1/8 of a page. (4)

   9. _____

10. You will find the answer to your legal question on page eight of the document. (6)

    10. _____

11. We just completed our 8th year of doing business on the Internet. (2)

    11. _____

12. The online customer referred to model 264-9326 when he called for information on this product. (4)

    12. _____

13. I ordered a pair of Size six shoes, but I received the wrong size. (6)

    13. _____

14. Although we advertised the set of literary books, we had to delay the shipment of volume 5. (6)

    14. _____

15. Casey located a credit card company that charged only twelve percent interest on unpaid balances. (7)

    15. _____

Some people find numbers fascinating and enjoy working with them; others find numbers to be intimidating. Regardless of your feelings about working with figures, you should use them correctly in your written documents.

Numbers may be written in figures or in words. Figures are easier to read; however, numbers spelled out in words lend a formal touch to a document. The choice of using figures or words also may depend on whether the material is *technical* or *nontechnical.* The emphasis in this chapter is on numbers used in technical material, in business correspondence, and on business forms.

General Rules for Writing Numbers

Several rules are so general that they should be emphasized before studying specific applications and exceptions.

Numbers 1 Through 10

In general, use words to express the numbers one through ten.

> **At our last meeting, our speaker identified <u>eight</u> advantages of Web site advertising.**

> **Smart cards offer consumers flexibility because <u>one</u> card can be used for <u>three</u> or <u>four</u> functions.**

Do This

On a scale of <u>1 to 8</u>, our product was rated an <u>8</u>.

Do Not Do This

On a scale of <u>one to eight</u>, our product was rated an <u>eight</u>.

When numbers are referred to as numbers, use figures; for example, *scale of 1 to 8.*

Numbers Above 10

Use figures for numbers above ten.

> **I know that <u>20</u> states require business taxes to be paid electronically.**

> **We just received <u>914</u> leads for potential customers.**

Approximate Numbers

Approximate numbers are nearly exact numbers. Express approximate numbers from one through ten in words. Express approximate numbers above ten in figures.

> **About <u>ten</u> Internet service providers have offices in Tacoma.**

> **More than <u>30</u> firms a day are going into business on the Web.**

Numbers

Related Numbers

Adopt a consistent style for writing related numbers in a sentence. When related numbers, both above and below 10, are used in the same sentence, express all related numbers in figures. Do not express numbers ten and below in figures if the other numbers in the sentence are not related.

> **State Farm Insurance recently hired 3 new agents in Fort Collins, 4 in Colorado Springs, and 12 in Denver.**
>
> (When one number is above 10, the other related numbers are written in figures. In this sentence, the related items are the number of *new agents*.)
>
> **Out of the 15 questions on the product satisfaction questionnaire, only 5 questions gave us pertinent feedback.**
>
> (The numbers are related; both refer to *questions*.)
>
> **Experts say that questionnaires about product satisfaction should be limited to one page with no more than 15 questions.**
>
> (*One page* and *15 questions* are not related items. They should be written according to the general rules for writing numbers.)
>
> **Our bank's EasyPay accounting service has 900 clients, but only three employees monitor the transactions.**
>
> (The *900* clients and *three* employees are not related numbers. The general rules for writing numbers above and below 10 apply.)

Cardinal and Ordinal Numbers

The cardinal numbers are used in simple counting or in answer to *how many.* Write cardinal numbers as follows:

one	two	eleven	twenty-one
1	2	11	21

The ordinal numbers are used to show the order of succession. Write ordinal numbers as follows:

first	second	eleventh	twenty-first
1st	2d or 2nd	11th	21st

> **Third, duties should be divided so that one employee does not approve payments and also write checks.**
>
> (The ordinal number is *third,* and the cardinal number is *one.*)
>
> **The bank's latest home-banking software surpasses the expensive first generation of programs.**
>
> (The ordinal number is *first.*)

Commas in Numbers

Use commas to set off whole numbers with five or more figures in three-digit groups beginning at the right.

> **15,620   132,469   5,675,298**

Omit the comma in a whole number with only four digits. Use the comma if a number with only four digits is used in conjunction with numbers of five digits or more; for example, in a column.

> **3000   8500   2050**

(No commas are necessary in four-digit whole numbers.)

NOTES

Ordinal Numbers

The uses for ordinal numbers appear within the specific rules and exceptions that follow in the next section.

1,875

15,620

3,000

(In this column of numbers, commas are necessary in the numbers *1,875* and *3,000* because the number *15,620* requires a comma.)

Go to the
Web

Checkpoint 18.1
for more skills practice on this topic.

CHECKPOINT 18.1

*Instructions: Underline the errors in number usage in the following sentences. Write the corrections in the space provided. Write **Yes** if the numbers in a sentence are written correctly.*

1. All 4 of the Internet directory services offer fax numbers and 3 offer electronic mail addresses. _____

2. The online office supply store lists over eighty-five computer desks. _____

3. The bookkeeper made fifteen payments to fictitious companies before the 2 owners finally established some internal controls. _____

4. A brochure from Charter Bank listed 6 advantages of home-banking services. _____

5. We have sixteen online clients in Rochester and four in Alexandria. _____

6. Car rental rates advertised on the Internet should be checked fourteen, seven, and three days in advance to see if prices have been lowered. _____

7. As a 2d source of financial information, check the business and economic section of your newspaper. _____

8. As part of a pilot online program, People's Bank hopes to get one thousand customers and thirty merchants to participate. _____

Specific Rules for Writing Numbers

The type of writing that you do determines whether you use figures or words. Formal writing requires more numbers written as words. Most business correspondence includes material in which numbers require emphasis; therefore, more numbers are written as figures. The rules that follow involve those in general practice today.

Abbreviations

Use figures with abbreviations.

Bldg. **10**	**No. 2** pencil	Fig. **21**	**30** mph
5 in	2/10, n/**30**	**18** m	**20** gal

Addresses

House and Building Numbers. Write house and building numbers in figures except for those identified as *One*. Do not use commas in house or building numbers.

<u>152</u> Blanco Road   Building <u>118A</u>

<u>2531½</u> Dickens Drive   <u>18294</u> Oakwood Parkway

<u>One</u> Mankato Avenue

Street Addresses. Use words (ordinal format) to express street names that contain the numbers 1–10. Use figures (ordinal format) to express numbered street names above 10.

19 <u>Third</u> Street   209 <u>100th</u> Street

3545 <u>Tenth</u> Avenue   1201 North <u>62d</u> Street

Highway Numbers. Use figures to identify highway numbers.

Interstate <u>80</u> (or) I-<u>80</u>   State Highway <u>10</u>

U.S. Highway <u>1</u>   County Road <u>G12</u>

ZIP Codes. Use figures for all ZIP Codes. A nine-digit ZIP Code consists of the basic five digits followed immediately by a hyphen and another four digits. A nine-digit ZIP Code is also referred to as a ZIP+4 Code. Do not use commas with ZIP codes.

Flagstaff, AZ <u>86001</u>   Kansas City, MO <u>64195-0404</u>

Miscellaneous Address Numbers. Use figures for suite numbers, mailstop codes, and post office box numbers. Use exact user designated e-mail addresses.

Suite <u>27</u>, Plaza Building

21501 Oakhurst, Suite <u>27</u>

P.O. Box <u>4091</u> or Post Office Box <u>4091</u>

(A post office box may be used in place of a mailing address.)

MSC <u>42</u>

(Place the mailstop code above the addressee's name.)

Miller14@juno.com

(Use exact spacing, punctuation, and other characters exactly as they appear in e-mail addresses.)

Age

General Age. Use words to express general age.

I was <u>twelve</u> when I began looking at products offered for sale on the Internet.

(The word *twelve* is used in a general, nontechnical format.)

Now that Helen is in her <u>forties</u>, she is checking Web sites for retirement investment suggestions.

(The word *forties* is used in a general, nontechnical format.)

Precise Age. Use figures to express age when the age appears immediately after the person's name or when the age is expressed in years, months, and days.

Dan Kirkwood, <u>38</u>, is the new Web site design coordinator.

(The age is set off by commas when it appears after a name.)

Our oldest sales representative is <u>64</u> years <u>2</u> months old.

(Precise age requires figures.)

Legal Age. Use figures to express legal age.

My son applied for his driver's license at the age of <u>16</u>.

Pete did not want to retire at the age of <u>65</u>, but it was his company's mandatory retirement age.

Emphasis on Age. Use figures to emphasize age in general correspondence.

We are advertising a new line of computer products with <u>5</u>- and <u>6</u>-year-old children in mind.

(The ages *5* and *6* are in figures for emphasis.)

Anniversaries and Birthdays

Spell out ordinal numbers to express anniversaries that contain one or two words. (A hyphenated ordinal number counts as one word.) Use ordinal numbers in figures to express anniversaries that contain more than two words.

the firm's <u>tenth</u> anniversary (one word)

John's <u>thirty-fifth</u> birthday (one word)

the company's <u>150th</u> anniversary (three words [*one hundred fiftieth*])

CHECKPOINT 18.2

Instructions: *Underline the errors in number usage in the following sentences. Write the corrections in the space provided. Write* **Yes** *if the numbers in a sentence are written correctly.*

1. I requested the material from Mr. O'Brien at the following address:

   MSC 4,912

   Mr. Lance O'Brien

   Suite Nine, L.E. Phillips Building

   15,608 North 3d Street

   Columbia, SC 29,209-1560

   _____

2. Tim Collins, thirty-nine, decided that it was time to open his own online company.

   _____

3. We outgrew the storage space at 967 North Fifty-third Street and moved into new facilities on State Highway Eight.

   _____

4. The Money Store, a financial services company, says that it is the No. 1 lender of Small Business Association guaranteed loans.

   _____

Go to the
Web

Checkpoint 18.2
for more skills practice on this topic.

EDIT PATROL

From a doctor's report:
The patient is a 79-year-old widow who no longer lives with her husband.
Note: How can she live with her husband if she is a widow?

Copyright © by The McGraw-Hill Companies, Inc.

Numbers

567

5. According to a recent survey, twenty-eight-year-old Web surfers were the most uncomfortable about sharing personal information for online target audience advertisements.

_____

6. Please send all inquiries about online banking to 1 Plaza Boulevard.

_____

7. Through the years, accountants in their late 50s have seen many changes in the handling of accounts payable.

_____

8. We just celebrated our 2d successful year of online banking.

_____

Adjacent Numbers

Use a comma to separate adjacent numbers in a sentence when both figures are numbers or both are words.

> **By the year 2010, 45 percent of U.S. households may be shopping with debit cards.**

Beginning of a Sentence

Use words to express numbers that begin a sentence. Use hyphens with the numbers 21 through 99 expressed in words. Reword the sentence if the beginning number consists of more than two words. A hyphenated word counts as one word.

> **Twenty-four inquiries to our Web site advertisement surprised us.**
>
> (*Twenty-four* requires a hyphen. *Twenty-four* is written in words because it begins the sentence. *Twenty-four* counts as one word.)

Awkward:

> **Thirteen hundred twenty-eight people responded to our online personal information surveys.**

Improved:

> **We received 1328 responses to our online personal information surveys.**

Do This	Do Not Do This
Forty to fifty customers said that they thought our Web site was one of the best that they had seen.	Forty to 50 customers said that they thought our Web site was one of the best that they had seen.

Use words (*forty* or *fifty*) for related figures at the beginning of a sentence.

Consecutive Numbers

Generally, use words for the first number in consecutive numbers when one of the two numbers is part of a compound modifier.

four 12-story buildings   **twenty 5-page documents**

(The first numbers are written in words when they appear before compound modifiers.)

Use figures for the first of the consecutive numbers if the second number is shorter than the first when written out.

35 one-time hits   **900 two-page product reviews**

(The first numbers *35* and *900* are in figures; the second numbers *one* and *two* are shorter than *35* and *900* when written out in words.)

Dates

Months, Days, and Years. Use cardinal numbers to express dates in month-day, month-year, or month-day-year order. Use commas to separate the year from the month and day. Do not use commas to separate a month and year when used without the day.

May 2   **August 29, 2006**   **August 2007**

If you submit your payment by September 15, <u>2007</u>, you will be eligible for a discount.

(Commas separate the year from the month and day in this introductory clause.)

Bruce referred to an article on online commerce in the <u>November 2005</u> issue of the magazine.

(No commas are necessary when the date consists of a month and year only.)

Military and Foreign. Use cardinal numbers to express dates associated with military or foreign correspondence. Write dates in day, month, year sequence. Do not separate with commas.

2 May 2007   **29 August 2008**

Days Before Month; Days Alone. Use ordinal numbers when the day comes before the month or stands alone and the emphasis in the sentence is on the figure. Use ordinal words when the purpose of the writing is more formal. The intent of the sentence determines the use of figures or words.

Online registration must be completed by the <u>3d</u> of January.

(The emphasis in this sentence is on the date. Ordinal, not cardinal, numbers are necessary.)

Please contact us by the <u>21st</u>.

(The day *21st* is used alone. The day is emphasized and requires an ordinal, not a cardinal, number.)

You are cordially invited to a reception for the new president of OnlineAlert on the <u>third</u> day of October 2006.

(The formal tone of writing requires ordinal words rather than figures.)

Legal Documents. Use ordinal words to express dates appearing in legal documents.

NOTES

Legal Documents

Refer to a legal handbook or reference manual for information on number style in legal documents.

October twenty-first

or

the twenty-first day of October

Two thousand six

WITNESS WHEREOF I have hereunto set my hand and seal the twenty-first day of October, in the year two thousand six.

Decades and Centuries

Decades. Use words or figures to express decades.

the 1990s   the nineties   the '90s

during the years 2000–2010

Centuries. Use words or figures to express centuries.

the 1900s   the twenty-first century

Go to the
Web

Checkpoint 18.3

for more skills practice on this topic.

CHECKPOINT 18.3

*Instructions: Underline the errors in number usage in the following sentences. Write the corrections in the space provided. Write **Yes** if the numbers in a sentence are written correctly.*

1. 25 clients asked for assistance with personal finance planning in addition to tax planning this year.

   _____

2. I use the program Quicken to pay my bills on the fifth of each month.

   _____

3. I am responsible for 5 2-page articles for our Internet news magazine this year.

   _____

4. In the late '90s, many companies restructured to control their production costs.

   _____

5. Since July, 2005, nine hundred seventy-five thousand business taxpayers have been required to pay federal taxes electronically.

   _____

6. 220 people checked our Web site this week.

   _____

7. Consumer debt has grown much faster than wages since January 1 2000.

   _____

8. Do you have any predictions to make regarding online retail sales for the twenty-first century?

   _____

9. We received purchase orders dated 5 September 2006 from the military.

    _____

10. "I checked the original legal document, and it was dated the 'twenty-first day of October,'" responded the lawyer in his letter of October seven.

    _____

Decimals

Writing Decimals. Use figures to express decimals.

   1.326   **115.2**   **89.3926**

Using Zeros. Place a zero before the decimal point if the decimal appears by itself. The zero sets the decimal apart and makes it easy to recognize the decimal as less than a whole number.

   0.01   **0.00923**   **0.59**

Aligning Figures. Align figures at the decimal point. Add a zero or zeros at the end of a decimal to justify a column of figures on the right.

   9.5   **35.95**   **4.000**
   102.7   **2.50**   **12.500**
                        93.33

Financial Quotes

Use figures to express financial quotes.

   Home Depot stock was up 3/8 and closed at 68.

Fractions

Fractions on Their Own. Use words to express fractions that stand alone. Use a hyphen between the numerator (top number in a fraction) and denominator (bottom number in a fraction).

   two-thirds of our banking customers
   one-half of the assets
   one-eighth of a page

Fractions in Measurements. Use figures to express fractions in measurements. Do not use an *of* phrase after fractions written in figures. Write out the fraction in words if an *of* phrase must follow the fraction. Do not use *st, ds,* or *ths* after fractions expressed in numbers.

   7/8 ounce   *or*   **seven-eighths *of* an ounce**
   3/4 pound   *or*   **three-fourths *of* a pound**

   (Do not use *7/8ths of an ounce* or *7/8 of an ounce*. Do not use *3/4ths of a pound* or *3/4 of a pound*.)

Fractions and Whole Numbers. Use figures when a fraction is written with a whole number. Do not use a hyphen between the whole number and the fraction.

   2½ hours late   **5¼ pages**

Identification Numbers

Use figures to identify forms or items such as form numbers, model numbers, serial numbers, policy numbers, and invoice numbers. Do not use commas to separate the digits. The abbreviation *No.* is not necessary with most items identified by number if the item is preceded by a descriptive noun.

Form 940	**Diagram 1**
Policy 8342916429	**Model 203-S5**
Invoice 3213	**Chapter IX**
Part XJZ	**Item 614695-D**

(The abbreviation *No.* is not necessary with these items.)

Catalog No. 9640	**Serial No. 9640**
License No. KUP 874	**Social Security No. 384-63-5058**

(The abbreviation *No.* is necessary to identify these numbers.)

Go to the
Web

Checkpoint 18.4
for more skills practice on this topic.

CHECKPOINT 18.4

Instructions: Underline the errors in number usage in the following sentences. Write the corrections in the space provided. Write **Yes** if the numbers in a sentence are written correctly.

1. I just checked the Internet and learned that my favorite stock was at 56 and three-fourths, which was lower than yesterday's 57 and one-half.   _____

2. Consumer prices increased a moderate .3 percent with little sign of inflation.   _____

3. Bowman Nutrition Services submitted its Form 941 electronically this payroll period.   _____

4. Only 1/3 of the consumers are confident about buying mutual funds on their own.   _____

5. I knew that the only outstanding item on invoice 462 was for Catalog Number B6, 934.   _____
_____

6. By going online with my bank accounts, I save at least one half day a month working on bookkeeping tasks.   _____

7. The Web advertisement indicated that the material weighed just 1/4th of a pound.   _____
_____

8. By the time that I finished a draft of my Web site material, I had five and three quarters pages.   _____

Indefinite Numbers

Use words to express indefinite numbers and amounts. Indefinite numbers are not easily counted or determined.

many thousands of requests	**a few hundred debit cards**
dozens of online scams	**thousands of dollars**
hundreds of credit card delinquencies	

NOTES

Indefinite Numbers

Indefinite numbers are not easily counted or determined.

Large Numbers

Use a combination of figures and words to express numbers in the millions or above. If several large numbers appear in a sentence, be consistent in the format.

2 million people   **1.5 billion items**

9.5 million words

Real estate brokers used the Internet and major online services to list <u>975,000</u> of the approximately <u>4,100,000</u> homes available for sale.

(The number *4,100,000* [instead of *4.1 million*] is used because of the related number *975,000,* which is less than a million. The format should be consistent.)

Measurements and Dimensions

Measurements.   Use figures (including the numbers 1 through 10) to express measurements used in a technical sense. These measurements include items such as yards, inches, feet, acres, pounds, ounces, gross, dozen, gallons, quarts, computer measurements, and miles. Do not use a comma to separate a measurement that consists of two parts.

75 yards (yd)	**6 quarts (qt)**	**5 pounds 3 ounces**
8 dozen (doz)	**15 miles (mi)**	**5 feet 11 inches**
16 megabytes (MB)		**1.2 gigabytes (GB)**

Dimensions.   Use figures to express dimensions.

12- by 15-foot room   **a room 12 by 15 feet**

or

12- × 15-foot room   **a room 12 × 15 feet**

or

12' × 15' room   **a room 12' × 15'**

We need a 6- by 8-foot window for our office.

(Hyphens are necessary when the dimension precedes a noun.)

The window in our office is 6 × 8 feet.

(No hyphens are necessary in the dimension when the dimension does not precede a noun. The word *feet* is not repeated after both numbers; it is needed only after the last measurement.)

The window in our office is 6' × 8'.

(The symbol for feet ['] is necessary after both numbers.)

Metric Measurements.   Use figures to express metric measurements. Use a space to mark off groups of three digits.

a trip of 480 km (kilometers)

about 25 kg (kilograms)

a distance of 100 000 m (meters)

Go to the
Web

Checkpoint 18.5
for more skills practice on
this topic.

CHECKPOINT 18.5

Instructions: Underline the errors in number usage in the following sentences. Write the corrections in the space provided. Write **Yes** if the numbers in a sentence are written correctly.

1. Yahoo! Yellow Pages provides lists of local businesses and has 18,100,000 listings. _____

2. If you converted these figures to meter measurements, your answer would be 20,000,000 square meters. _____

3. The Internet advertisement indicated that the weight of the item was four pounds, six ounces. _____
_____

4. Each month 1000s of firms analyze the effects of advertising on the Web. _____

5. Forrester Research predicts that 3,300,000 jobs will move offshore by the year 2018. _____

6. The FTC estimates that scams can cause losses to consumers amounting to millions of dollars. _____

7. Dan submitted a preliminary Web site design that was seven inches by nine inches. _____
_____
_____

8. If you request a copy of our newsletter advertised on our Web site, you will receive a professional document printed on twenty-pound paper. _____

Money

Amounts Above $1.   Use figures to express amounts of money above $1. Do not use a decimal point or zeros after even dollar amounts within a sentence.

$2.98	$12.95	$429.63	$21,398.50
$25	$2000	about $50,000	

The invoice includes $2000 plus the sales tax of $100 for a total of $2100.

(No decimal points or zeros are necessary after the even amounts of money [*$2000* and *$100*]. The normal end-of-sentence period follows the last amount [*$2100*].)

Amounts in Columns.   Use zeros with even dollar amounts in a column of figures in which the other amounts contain cents.

$ 505.00

1015.22

95.95

Foreign Money.   Generally, place the abbreviated identification of foreign money before the amount.

MEX$10,000 (Mexican peso)   €10,000 (euro)

¥10,000 (Japanese yen)   £ 10,000 (British pound)

Large Amounts of Money.   Combine figures and words to express amounts of money of $1 million or more. Use the *dollar sign* or the word *dollars,* but do not use both with one figure.

Preferred	*Acceptable*
$2 million	**2 million dollars**
$5½ million	**5½ million dollars**
$5.5 million	**5.5 million dollars**

(Do not use the redundant forms *$2 million dollars, $5 million dollars,* or *$5.5 million dollars.*)

Related Amounts of Money.   Keep related amounts of money in the same format.

We paid $1,000,000 for the building on Main Street and $2,780,000 for the one on Central Avenue.

(Do not write *$1 million* and *$2,780,000* or *1 million dollars* and *$2,780,000.* Use the same format within the sentence.)

Amounts of Money Less Than $1.   Use figures to express amounts below $1. Spell out the word *cents* after the amount.

A stamp now costs <u>37 cents</u>, but the cost will likely increase.

The <u>70-cent</u> coupons add up at the grocery store.

Cents in a Series.   Do not use the dollar sign with an amount less than $1 unless it appears in a series or in a table in which the other figures require dollar signs.

The sales taxes on our purchases were $3.21, <u>$.80</u>, $12, and $6.25.

(The amount *$.80* should be written in the same format as the dollar amounts with cents.)

Range of Amounts of Money.   Repeat the dollar sign or cent sign with each amount when a range of prices is expressed. Do not repeat the word *dollars* or *cents* with each amount.

in the <u>$</u>25,000 to <u>$</u>40,000 range

an increase from 32 to 33 <u>cents</u>

Amounts of Money in Legal Documents.   Use words to express amounts of money in legal or formal documents. Write the amount in figures, and place it in parentheses after the written expression. Use the word *and* before the cents in written expressions of money.

Five Hundred Thousand Dollars ($500,000)

Three Thousand Two Hundred Twenty-nine <u>and</u> 83/100 Dollars ($3,229.83)

Percentages

Exact and Approximate Percentages.   Use figures to express exact or approximate percentages. Write the word *percent* after the number.

0.5 percent   10 percent   6.5 percent   6½ percent

nearly 65 percent   over 30 percent

Go to the
Web

Checkpoint 18.6
for more skills practice on this topic.

Series of Percentages. Write the word *percent* only at the end of the last number in a sentence with several percentages listed.

> **We offer trade discounts of 10, 20, and 30 <u>percent</u> to our long-term customers.**

CHECKPOINT 18.6

*Instructions: Underline the errors in number usage in the following sentences. Write the corrections in the space provided. Write **Yes** if the numbers in a sentence are written correctly.*

1. We just bought a book for $29.95 and found that the same book was advertised on the Internet for $25. _____

2. The product's cost of $839.00 included the five 1/2 percent sales tax. _____

3. I purchased an excellent personal finance software program for approximately forty dollars. _____

4. Prepaid phone cards may charge 2 cents, 5 cents, or $1.10 for each minute depending on whether the call is domestic or international. _____

5. A grocery item can cost $1.62 or $1.69; however, customers are usually in a rush and do not notice the seven-cent difference. _____

6. According to one statistic, sixty percent of online shoppers purchase once a month, and twenty-four percent of those shoppers plan to spend up to $100.00. _____ _____ _____

7. The machines to read smart cards cost merchants $500.00 to 1,000.00. _____

8. A Japan rail pass that is good for one week sold for ¥28,300 ($230.00) on Japanrail.com. _____

9. Someone told me that online telephone directories are only about seventy percent to eighty percent accurate. _____

10. Consumer spending probably rose .6% in July. _____

Political Divisions

Use words to identify political subdivisions such as congressional districts or precincts.

> **<u>Fifteenth</u> District representative**   **<u>Eighth</u> Precinct election**

Publications

Use figures to express pages, paragraphs, lines, steps, notes, and verses in publications. Do not capitalize the words *page, line, verse, step, note,* and *paragraph* before the numbers.

> **page <u>15</u>, line <u>2</u>**   **paragraphs <u>401–470</u>**

Ratios

Use figures to express ratios.

2-to-1 ratio   *or*   **2:1 ratio**

Roman Numerals

In Outlines and Reports.   Use roman numerals to subdivide items on outlines or reports. Align roman numerals at the right in an outline or list. Place a period after the numeral. You may see the word *roman* capitalized (*Roman*) in your workplace and in some reference manuals or dictionaries.

I. PRODUCTIVITY TOOLS
II. EFFECTIVE ADVERTISING DESIGN
III. SOFTWARE HIGHLIGHTS

As Literary Divisions.   Use roman numerals to indicate the major parts of complete literary works such as volumes or chapters.

Volume XII   **Chapter VI**

As Lowercase Roman Numerals.   Use lowercase roman numerals to indicate page numbers in prefaces or in other materials that precede text materials.

The mailing costs are on page ii of the introduction to the catalog.

In Seniority Titles.   Use roman numerals or arabic numerals for seniority titles depending on the individual's preference. Do not set aside seniority titles with commas unless the person referenced prefers the commas.

Robert Hamilton III   *or*   **Robert Hamilton 3d**
Lance Ford II   *or*   **Lance Ford 2d**

NOTES

Roman Numerals

Refer to a reference manual such as *The Gregg Reference Manual* for a list of roman numerals.

Inclusive Figures

Do not shorten the second number in an inclusive set of figures unless page numbers or dates are used frequently in a document.

pages 146-50 (frequent use)
or
pages 146-150 (general use)
1996-99 (frequent use)   *or*   **1996-1999 (general use)**

Do not shorten inclusive numbers under 100.

pages 46-50 (under 100)

Do not shorten the second number when the second number begins with a digit that is different from the first number.

1990-2005   pages 518-624

(Do not use the short forms of *1990-05* or *518-24.*)

Do not use a shortened form for the second number in any situation in which the first number ends in two or more zeros.

2000-2005   pages 300-306

(Do not use the short forms of *2000-5* and *300-6.*)

Go to the
Web

Checkpoint 18.7
for more skills practice on
this topic.

CHECKPOINT 18.7

Instructions: *Underline the errors in number usage in the following sentences. Write the corrections in the space provided. Write* **Yes** *if the numbers in a sentence are written correctly.*

1. Wallace L. Ingram the third referred to the advantages of the Internet on page ten in his handout.   _____

2. People in the 12th District voted against the sales tax referendum.   _____

3. A 2-to-1 ratio seems acceptable for our advertising purposes.   _____

4. You will find your answer in paragraph eight of the prospectus.   _____

5. For a more detailed explanation, refer to the information in Chapter ii, lines 63-8.   _____

6. This is the final outline for the seminar on small business technology: _____
    i   PRODUCTIVITY TOOLS FOR SMALL BUSINESSES
    ii NETWORKING SUGGESTIONS FOR SMALL BUSINESSES
    iii THE INTERNET TIPS FOR SMALL BUSINESSES

7. Companies became concerned with secure encryption methods in the years 1999-01.   _____

8. Check page VII in the table of contents for the chapter about online banking.   _____

Size

Use Figures to Express Size.   Do not capitalize the word *size* when it appears before the number.

Apparently, the only clothing items on sale were <u>size 8</u> or <u>size 18</u>.

Symbols

Use Figures with Symbols.

5 @ <u>$100</u> (5 items at $100 each)

<u>#10</u> (Number 10)

Telephone Numbers

Domestic Numbers.   Use figures for most telephone numbers. If a company uses combinations of letters and numbers or all words, follow the company's exact format. Use diagonals, parentheses, periods, or hyphens to separate the area code from the rest of the number.

212/555-1378   (212) 555-1378   212.555.1378   212-555-1378

International Numbers.   Use figures for international telephone numbers. Separate the international access codes, country codes, city codes, and telephone numbers with hyphens.

011-47-2-22-826-090

Extensions.   Use figures to identify an extension. Spell out *Extension* or abbreviate it (*Ext.*).

> 312-555-5476, <u>Extension 66</u>   *or*   312-555-5476, <u>Ext. 66</u>

Temperature

Use figures to express temperatures. Do not space between the number and the degree symbol or between the degree symbol and C (Celsius) or F (Fahrenheit).

> <u>80</u> degrees   <u>80</u> degrees Fahrenheit   <u>80</u>°F   <u>100</u>°C

Time

With *a.m.* and *p.m.*   Use figures with *a.m.* and *p.m.* Do not space within *a.m.* or within *p.m.* Do not use the word *o'clock* with *a.m.* and *p.m.*

> We expected our order to arrive by <u>4:30</u> p.m.

With Colons and Zeros Omitted.   Omit the colon and zeros with times that do not involve minutes (even when other expressions of time in the sentence include minutes).

> Express mail should arrive by <u>10</u> a.m. or by 3:30 p.m.

With the Word *O'clock.*   Use figures with *o'clock* to emphasize time. Use words with *o'clock* to set a formal tone.

> <u>5</u> o'clock   *or*   <u>five</u> o'clock
> <u>9</u> o'clock <u>at night</u> (for emphasis)
> <u>nine</u> o'clock <u>at night</u> (formal or social situations)

In Time Phrases.   Do not use the expressions *in the morning, in the afternoon, in the evening,* or *at night* with *a.m.* or *p.m.*

> Our office opens at <u>9 o'clock in the morning.</u>

(Using *9 a.m. in the morning* is redundant.)

With *Noon* and *Midnight.*   Express the terms *noon* and midnight in words. If other times in a sentence are written in figures, use *12 noon* or *12 midnight*.

> I plan to take a workshop on Internet security that begins at <u>noon.</u>

(The word *noon* may stand alone when no other time expressions are present.)

> I plan to take a workshop on Internet security that is scheduled from <u>12 noon</u> to <u>1:50 p.m.</u>

(The term *12 noon* is necessary because another time expression in figures is present.)

Time Periods

General Time Periods.   Use words to express general time periods such as years, months, weeks, and days except when the time period requires more than two words.

> During the past <u>twelve</u> years, I have seen many technological changes in the ways that <u>companies</u> transact business.

(The time period *twelve* consists of one word.)

By using the Internet, you can shop <u>365</u> days a year.

(The time period *365* would be more than two words if it were written in words.)

Business-Related Time Periods.   Use numbers to indicate time periods associated with payroll periods, discounts, mortgage periods, loan payments, credit terms, and interest payments.

I found it easy to compute the amount of interest that I would pay on a <u>15-year</u> mortgage.

(In this sentence, the term *15-year* is a business-related time period and requires numbers rather than words.)

To develop a global market for his products, Mike received a <u>4-year</u> loan from his bank.

(Even though the figure *4* is below *10*, it is a business-related time period and requires numbers rather than words.)

Go to the
Web

Checkpoint 18.8
for more skills practice on this topic.

 ## CHECKPOINT 18.8

Instructions: *Underline the errors in number usage in the following sentences. Write the corrections in the space provided. Write* **Yes** *if the numbers in a sentence are written correctly.*

1. Business Results is presenting seminars on November 19 and 20 at 8:30 a.m. in the morning, 12 noon, and 1 p.m. in the afternoon.

    _____

2. We had too many women's shoes in Size eight in our inventory.

    _____

3. These were the items ordered:

      5   #3078 @ $100.00

    12   #4853 @   88.98

      7   #2975 @   325.00

    _____

4. One car manufacturer says that its eight hundred number draws fewer leads for potential customers than its Web site.

    _____

5. A new Internet training center opened downtown, and its hours are 6 a.m. o'clock to 10 p.m. o'clock.

    _____

6. For a free catalog, call us at 1-800-555-6222, X922.

    _____

7. The computer malfunctions if the interior temperature exceeds eighty degrees.

    _____

8. We fill online orders from 7 a.m. in the morning until 12 o'clock midnight.

_____

9. Rincon Athletic Club developed a Web page over 15 years ago.

_____

10. The online calculator computed the cost of a thirty year mortgage.

_____

Diagramming Sentences

The following sentences for diagramming include a review of the rules you have studied in the previous chapters.

CHECKPOINT 18.9

Go to the
Web

Checkpoint 18.9
for more skills practice on this topic.

Instructions: *In the space provided, diagram the following sentences. All words may be diagrammed.*

1. Over the past few years, banks have promoted their home-banking services.

2. The directory *Venture Capital: Where to Find It* gives prospective business developers excellent ideas for sources of money.

3. Typical banner ads that appear on Web sites are quite expensive.

4. One company that advertised on the Web promised viewers a copy of its latest book on home health remedies.

5. Buying advertised Web site products requires some caution and common sense.

6. The job title of Web site designer sounds interesting, but I do not have an art background.

7. The Lane Elementary School uses SimCity in its social studies classes.

8. To start your own investment club, check these Internet sources.

Name _____ Date _____

PRACTICE 1

Using Numbers Correctly

*Instructions: Underline the errors in number and word usage in the following sentences. Write the corrections in the space provided. Write **Yes** if the numbers and words in a sentence are written correctly.*

1. Credit card interest payments ranging from 18 to 30 percent are not tax-deductible.

   1. _____

2. More than 67,000,000 Americans carry debit cards.

   2. _____

3. Most investors were surprised when the Dow Jones Industrial Average reached the eleven thousand mark.

   3. _____

4. Over a period of 10, 20, or 30 years, stocks seem to perform more effectively than other investments.

   4. _____

5. By the nineteen hundred and nineties, American manufacturers realized the impact that the Internet was having on their sales.

   5. _____

6. We received 3½ times the number of expected responses to our online advertising.

   6. _____

7. Printing costs for the brochure that we offered at our Web site increased $.16, and we can no longer send free copies.

   7. _____

8. Two-thirds of those responding to the survey indicated that they had not made purchases on the Internet.

   8. _____

9. By 2008, online advertisement spending will be more than $15,000,000,000.

   9. _____
   _____

10. I bought a forty dollar Windows utility program that removes old programs quickly and efficiently.

    10. _____

Choosing Correct Number Forms

Instructions: Select the correct form of the number, and write it in the space provided.

1. The product's cost of $839.72 included the (*6 percent, six percent*) sales tax.

   1. _____

2. Hutchinson Technology plans to expand its global operations to (*45, forty-five*) countries.

   2. _____

3. The next meeting of the Web site advertisement consulting group will be (*December, 2007, December 2007*).

   3. _____

Go to the
Web

Practice 1 Exercises
for more skills practice on this topic.

Name _____ Date _____

4. To mark our (*3d, third*) anniversary, we are offering several new products to our customers.

4. _____

5. Tonight's meeting of the Internet Marketing Club is at (*7:00 p.m., 7 p.m.*) in (*Building 5, Building Five*).

5. _____
_____

6. Some people have (*3 or 4, three or four*) major credit cards.

6. _____

7. (*30, Thirty*) years ago, Philips and Sony introduced CD-ROM players for PCs that sold for approximately (*$1000, $1,000.00, one thousand dollars*).

7. _____

8. Focus groups consisting of (*8 to 12, eight to 12, eight to twelve*) current customers are good sources of product information.

8. _____

9. Yields on (*30-year, thirty-year*) Treasury bonds were around (*4, four*) percent.

9. _____

10. As a sole proprietor, I file a Schedule C with my federal income tax (*Form 1040, Form No. 1040*).

10. _____

Go to the
Web

Practice 2 Exercises
for more skills practice on this topic.

PRACTICE 2

Identifying Errors

*Instructions: Underline the errors in number usage in the following sentences. Write the corrections in the space provided. Write **Yes** if the numbers in a sentence are written correctly.*

1. I bought a new computer for $900.00 for my daughter who is in her 1st year of college.

_____

2. The amount of Internet sales reached $37,000,000,000 dollars in 2,005 and was six to seven percent of all retail sales in the United States.

_____

3. Our team's Web site design placed 6th in the regional contest finals.

_____

4. We will be in Booth No. 1,920 at Internet World in Chicago in 6 months.

_____

5. Ninety percent of our home office sales come through personal contacts, not through the Internet.

_____

Name _____ Date _____

6. Members of the class of 06 bought their yearbooks on CD-ROM for forty dollars.

_____

7. A merger will result in an extra 80 cents to 90 cents per share in earnings for shareholders.

_____

8. How will small companies remain competitive in the 21st century?

_____

9. My favorite stock closed at fifty-six and three fourths yesterday.

_____

10. Roberto Hernandez, forty-eight, who has been our Texas manager for the past fifteen years, will be in charge of the plant on Thirteenth Street.

_____

11. For less than $1,000.00 of software and an Internet account, spammers can send e-mail to 1 person or to 1,000,000 persons.

_____

12. Features of the flat panel monitor include a sixteen-inch screen, a one-hundred and sixty degree vertical viewing area, and a five-hundred to one contrast ratio.

_____

13. If you pay off a $3,000 credit card debt at 18 percent over two years, you will make monthly payments that are around $149.00.

_____

14. 5 Hilton hotels have videoconferencing systems that show life-sized images on ninety-two-inch screens.

_____

15. The first McDonald's in our city opened thirty-eight years ago at 1,513 Hastings Way.

_____

16. Our agents contacted fifteen clients whose insurance policies had expired, but only eight of these clients renewed.

_____

17. The odds of winning the lottery this week are ten to one.

_____

18. We are offering Internet workshops for home business owners at 11 a.m. in the morning and 2:30 p.m. in the afternoon.

_____

Name _____ Date _____

19. The road signs indicated that we still had to travel 150 kilometers before we reached our destination.

_____

20. Some Internet merchants require buyers to call an eight hundred number to transmit credit card information.

_____

Go to the
Web

Practice 3 Exercises
for more skills practice on this topic.

PRACTICE 3

Proofreading

*Instructions: Proofread and compare the two sentences in each group. If they are the same, write **Yes** in the space provided. If they are not the same, write **No**. Use the first sentence as the correct copy. If you find errors in the second sentence, underline them. Insert any omitted words or marks of punctuation.*

1. The U.S. Small Business Administration's Web site (http://www.sbaonline.sba.gov) includes a section entitled "Financing Your Business," which provides information on all the SBA's funding programs.

   The U.S. Small Business Administration's Web site (http://www.sbaonline.gov) includes a section entitled Financing Your Business, which provides infomation on all the S.B.A.s funding programs.

   1. _____

2. Self-service online directories, which are offered free, help users find business or individual phone numbers by entering only a name or a partial address.

   Self-service online directories, which are offered free help users find business or person phone numbers by entering only a name or a partial address.

   2. _____

3. Funds Network offers access to more than 3300 funds and 300 fund families, including more than 700 with 4- or 5-star Morningstar ratings.

   Funds Network offers access to more than 3500 funds, and 330 fund families, including more than 700 with 4- or 5-star Morningside ratings.

   3. _____

4. Direct electronic access to social security records jumped from 3000 users a day to 8500 users after the introductory publicity, but access soon was suspended because of the invasion of personal privacy.

   Direct electronic access to social security records jumped from 3,000 users a day to 8,500 after the introductory publicity, but access soon was suspended, because of the invasion of personal privacy.

   4. _____

Name _____ Date _____

5. Most Internet transmissions are currently encrypted (electronically scrambled), which makes it very difficult for someone to intercept a message and use the personal information illegally.

5. _____

Most Internet transmissions are currently encrypted (electronically scrambled), which makes it very difficult for someone to intercept a message and use the personal information illegally.

Editing Copy

Instructions: Use proofreaders' marks to correct the following training announcement.

Join us for a series of free seminars to learn how new technology can help you meet your small buisness goals.

Internet Basics
Tuesday, April 21, 2007
    Learn the language of the internet.
    Identify the possibilities of the Internet.
    Save time and money in you research.
    Discover new solutions for your business problems
        9:30 a.m. - 12 o'clock noon
        1:30 p.m. - 4:00 p.m.
        5:30 p.m. - 8 p.m.
Networking Basics
Wed., April 22 2007
    Explore the many types of net works.
    Determine how networks function in different business envirnments.
    Identify networking solutions that will work for you.
        9 a.m. in the morning to 4 p.m.
Send your registration forms to Ideal Business Concepts, 1 South 10th Street, Bozeman, MT 59715, or call (406)-555-1380.

PRACTICE 4

Writing

Instructions: You received an unsolicited chain e-mail. You were asked to send $5 to the person's name at the top of the list. Your name would go on the list, and eventually people would start sending you $5. The e-mail claimed that people had made over $10,000. You think that this offer sounds too good to be true. Compose an e-mail to the Internet Fraud Watch describing the chain e-mail and ask this group for advice on handling the situation. Write at least two paragraphs and punctuate correctly. Answers will vary.

_____

_____

_____

_____

Go to the
Web

Practice 4 Exercises
for more skills practice on this topic.

Name _____ Date _____

PRACTICE 5

Using Numbers Correctly

*Instructions: Underline the errors in number and word usage in the following sentences. Write the corrections in the space provided. Write **Yes** if the numbers and words in a sentence are written correctly.*

1. During the past ten years, the use of the Internet has increased.

    _____

2. Our staff meeting is at 12 noon in the cafeteria.

    _____

3. Over 1/3 of online users store personal information with merchants.

    _____

4. Please call 707-555-3999, Ext. 78, for our pricing structure.

    _____

5. Order a 6" wrist support brace from an online orthopedic store.

    _____

6. If you read pages 121-34 of the HTML manual, you can probably troubleshoot the problem. (general use)

    _____

7. Please proofread pages five, eight, and 12 before posting this information on our Web page.

    _____

8. This was the third year that we increased our Web site advertising budget.

    _____

9. James Filmore the second financially supported our Internet venture.

    _____

10. Look on page II, immediately after the title page, to find the table of contents.

    _____

Choosing Correct Number Forms

Instructions: Select the correct form of the number, and write it in the space provided.

1. The number of men in our company outranks the number of women (*two to one, 2 to 1*).   1. _____

Name _____ Date _____

2. The technology coalition is working to defeat the   **2.** _____
(*10th, Tenth*) District representative.

3. We plan a (*.03, 0.03*) increase in the workforce   **3.** _____
next year.

4. Our first Web site advertisement was introduced   **4.** _____
in (*November 2001, November, 2001*).

5. The (*fifty-cent, 50-cent*) coupons were not   **5.** _____
incentives to cause me to switch phone cards.

6. We paid (*$1 million, $1,000,000*) to update our   **6.** _____
computers and our network.

7. Our Internet access costs (*$325.00, $325*) a   **7.** _____
month.

8. During the past (*ten, 10*) years, we have seen   **8.** _____
dramatic declines in the cost of computers.

9. Read page (*15, fifteen*) of the contract carefully.   **9.** _____

10. All (*twelve, 12*) Web site designs that we   **10.** _____
reviewed were excellent, but (*three, 3*) were
especially outstanding.

PRACTICE 6

Identifying Errors

*Instructions: Underline the errors in number usage in the following sentences. Write
the corrections in the space provided. Write* **Yes** *if the numbers in a sentence are
written correctly.*

1. A recent airline e-alert offered a round-trip Detroit-Seattle fare for
one hundred and seventy-nine dollars, a savings of forty-five
percent of the twenty-one-day advance purchase fare of $435.00.

_____

2. Chih-Yuan "Jerry" Yang, twenty-eight, and David Filo, thirty,
founders of Yahoo!, were the youngest philanthropists in Stanford
University history to give a $2,000,000 gift.

_____

3. Is one megabyte equivalent to one thousand kilobytes?

_____

4. Scott Oki, a retiree from Microsoft, is a member of twenty-three
nonprofit boards.

_____

5. 12 national high-tech companies performed poorly last quarter; of
the 12, only five have shown profits this quarter.

_____

Name _____ Date _____

6. The policies for a decentralized global communications network are targeted to be completed by January 1 2008.

_____

7. The stock fell four and three-quarters to seventy-six dollars.

_____

8. Call (800)555-3784, X38, to find out how the Massachusetts Department of Revenue eliminated two hundred tons of paper.

_____

9. American Airlines is increasing its 1st-class section from eight seats to fourteen.

_____

10. John was in his 20s when he began working at the plant that is located at 1 Ingram Circle.

_____

11. Model No. 40,500 is available at a price of $3099.00 if we order by March 30th.

_____

12. The computer listed on Page 92 weighs 3/4 of a pound and costs about two thousand dollars.

_____

13. Over 3/4 of home computers are infected with spyware.

_____

14. We stayed until after 12 a.m. midnight working on the computer problem.

_____

15. I am working this month from 6:00 a.m. until 2:00 p.m.

_____

16. If your ZIP Code is between 20,000 and 39,999, call (800) 555-4802 to reach Florist Express.

_____

17. New Century Network, located on 7th Avenue, sells advertising for about 100 newspapers.

_____

18. I paid ninety-nine cents to download mobile ring tones.

_____

19. 100 percent of Finnish young people aged 14 to 21 have mobile phones.

_____

Name _____ Date _____

20. During the 90's, the average budget to produce a video game was approximately $200,000.00; however, during the 21st century, the budget is approximately $2,000,000.00.

_____

PRACTICE 7

Proofreading

*Instructions: Proofread and compare the two sentences in each group. If they are the same, write **Yes** in the space provided. If they are not the same, write **No**. Use the first sentence as the correct copy. If you find errors in the second sentence, underline them. Insert any omitted words or marks of punctuation.*

1. More than four million people visit the National Consumers League Information Center (www.nclnet.org) Web site, whose goal is to assist fraud victims with reports on current issues.

1. _____

More than four billion people visit the National Consumers League Information Center (www.nclnet.com) Web site, whose goal is to assist fraud victims with reports of curent issues.

2. "Consumers lose between $10 and $10,000 in Internet scams," said National Consumers League president Linda Golodner. "Cybercrooks are in your wallet with a click of the mouse."

2. _____

"Consumers loose between $100 and $10,000 in Internet scams," said National Consumers League president Linda Goldner. "Cybercrooks are in you wallet with a click of the mouse.

3. Posting your name in a member directory, posting messages to a bulletin board, or participating in chat sessions will make your e-mail address available to strangers.

3. _____

Posting your name in a member directory, posting messages to a bulletin board, or participating in chat sessions will make your e-mail address available to strangers.

4. By the year 2008, interactive sales are forecasted to grow by 74.7 percent per year to reach $31.3 billion and to employ almost 200,000 workers.

4. _____

By the year 2025, interactive sales are forcasted to grow by 74.7 percent per year to reach $313 billion and to employ almost 200,000,000 workers.

_____

Numbers

Name _____ Date _____

5. The Direct Marketing Association has a Web site with industry news, upcoming events, membership tips, and marketing ideas.

5. _____

The Direct Marketing Association has a site with industry's news, upcoming events, membership ideas, and marketing tips.

Editing Copy

The Internet Fraud Complaint Center (IFCC) is a partnership between the Federal Bureau of Investigation (FBI) and the National White Collar Crime Center (NW3C).

IFCC's mission is to address fraud committed over the Internet. For victims of Internet fraud, IFCC provides a reporting mechanism that alerts authorities of a suspected criminal or civil violation.

Instructions: Underline the errors in the copy that follows. Key the document correctly.

Summary of Internet Fraud Crime Report
2003-2004
http://www1.ifccfbi.gov/index.asp

1. Internet fraud increased sixty-four percent from 2003 to 2004.

2. The total $ loss from Internet fraud was 68.14 million dollars with a medium dollar loss of $219 and 56 cents for each complaint.

3. Internet auction fraud consisted of 71.2% of all complaints.

4. Credit or debit card fraud consisted of 5.4% of fraud.

5. The highest median $ fraud was check fraud ($3,600.00), Nigerian letter fraud ($3,000.00), and confidence fraud ($1,000.00).

6. Of the people filing complaints, 67.2% were mail and the average age was thirty-eight.6.

7. Email and Web pages were the 2 primary mechanisms by which fraudulent contact took place.

_____

_____

_____

1. _____

2. _____

_____

3. _____

4. _____

5. _____

_____

Name _____ Date _____

6. _____
_____

7. _____
_____

PRACTICE 8

Writing

Instructions: *You have decided that you are going to do business on the Internet. The following are some criteria that successful marketers use to determine whether their products will sell on the Internet:*

- *The product appeals to the technologically savvy.*
- *The product appeals to a wide geographic audience.*
- *The product is an item otherwise difficult to locate.*
- *The product can be purchased over the Internet less expensively than otherwise.*

Select a product that you think would sell well over the Internet. In a paragraph, describe the product and indicate why you think this product is one that would sell well over the Internet. Write at least two paragraphs and punctuate correctly.
Answers will vary.

_____
_____
_____
_____
_____
_____
_____
_____
_____
_____
_____
_____
_____
_____
_____
_____
_____

Posttest

Instructions: *Underline the errors in number usage in the following sentences. Write the corrections in the space provided. Write **Yes** if the numbers in a sentence are written correctly.*

1. The Web site for the National Fraud Information Center won thirteen awards in just 1 year of operation. (1)

1. _____

2. Our Web site won 2nd place from Home Office Computing for our interactive ordering procedure. (2)

2. _____

3. Fred Tarkenton, 50, retired from Zipom in January, 1997, and started a Web design business. (3)

3. _____

4. After launching a Web page in January, we saw our sales increase twenty percent by December. (5)

4. _____

5. We paid $1,000.00 to a Web designer to modify our order form and link our site to twenty-five other sites. (5)

5. _____

6. By 2010, interactive marketing is expected to reach $31,300,000,000 a year. (5)

6. _____

7. 40 new clients requested assistance with Web site designs. (1)

7. _____

8. We must place the order by 2 p.m. in the afternoon. (7)

8. _____

9. James submitted his recommendations for developing a new Web page two and one-half days ahead of schedule. (3)

9. _____

10. Check paragraphs four and nine of the investment prospectus for your answer. (6)

10. _____

11. Research by the FBI shows that only 1 out of 10 people report Internet fraud. (6)

11. _____

12. Rhonda Brice, thirty-two, has an e-Bay account and conducted three-hundred and seventy-one transactions between January, 2005 and June, 2006, which generated approximately eighteen thousand dollars in revenue (1, 3, 5)

12. _____
_____
_____
_____

13. Our warehouse is located near the five-ten freeway at 1 North 62nd Street. (2)

13. _____

14. The IRS reported that 1/3 of U.S. taxpayers filed Form ten forty online and received an average refund of $836.00. (4, 5)

14. _____
_____

15. We have over $5,000,000.00 in revenue from online sales even though our office area is only 25 feet by 50 feet. (4, 5)

15. _____
_____
_____
_____

Glossary

A

absolute adjective: An adjective that does not allow for comparisons.

absolute adverb: An adverb that does not allow for comparisons.

accent mark: A stress mark indicating the syllable that requires emphasis when the word is pronounced.

acoustical panel: A suspension from a ceiling that controls sound.

acoustics: The characteristics of a building that improve reception to make sounds easier to understand.

action verbs: Verbs that indicate what someone or something does.

active voice: The subject of a sentence performs the action. Used for most business writing.

adjective clause: A group of words that modifies a noun or pronoun; has a subject and predicate but cannot stand by itself.

adjective phrase: A group of words that modifies a noun or pronoun but does not have a subject or predicate and cannot stand by itself.

adjectives: Words that modify (describe) nouns and pronouns. Adjectives answer the questions *What kind? How many? Which one?*

adverb clause: A group of words that modifies verbs, adjectives, and adverbs; has a subject and predicate but cannot stand by itself.

adverbs: Words that usually give additional information about the main verb but also modify adjectives or other adverbs. Adverbs answer the questions *In what manner? Where? When? To what extent?*

antecedent: The word or group of words to which a personal pronoun refers or that a personal pronoun replaces.

antonyms: Words that are opposite in meaning.

application software: Software that tells the computer how to accomplish specific tasks such as word processing.

appositive: A noun that explains or identifies a preceding noun or pronoun.

articles: The adjectives *a, an,* and *the.*

articulate: To pronounce distinctly and clearly.

articulating keyboard: Reshaping of a standard keyboard to improve hand and arm postures without requiring one to learn a new typing skill.

artificial intelligence: The capability of a machine to initiate intelligent human behavior, i.e., to reason, create, infer, and make decisions.

attrition: A normal decrease in the number of things or people.

autocratic style of management: All decisions flow from one person who wields ultimate authority within the organization.

auxiliary verbs: Verbs that assist and precede the main verb. Also called *helping verbs.*

B

banner ads: Rectangular boxes for Web page advertisements that are usually placed near the top or bottom of pages. The number of times that users click on the banner ads helps the advertiser evaluate the worth of this type of advertising.

blitz: An intense campaign (advertising war).

blogging: A running commentary on a Web page with links to other sites.

body language: Body movements and gestures observed as substitutes for verbal intent.

brainstorming: A group problem-solving technique characterized by unrestrained, spontaneous discussion.

bulleted lists: Material preceded by heavy dots used to bring attention to these items.

burnout: Exhaustion of physical or emotional strength as a result of prolonged stress or frustration.

business etiquette: The accepted requirements for proper professional behavior.

C

cardinal number: Any of the numbers that express an amount (e.g., *1, 2, 3*).

carpal tunnel syndrome: A nerve disorder resulting from pressure on the median nerve that travels through the wrist.

cash flow statement: A monthly accounting report that details the asset cash and its movement in and out of the firm.

cellular phone: A communications system that uses FM radio waves to transmit conversations.

circumstantial evidence: Facts offered as evidence from which other information is inferred. It is not direct evidence.

clause: A sequence of words with both a subject and a predicate.

clip art: A collection of computerized graphic art that can be electronically copied and inserted into documents.

collective antecedent: A group of people such as a committee, class, board, or jury to which a pronoun refers or that a pronoun replaces. Neuter in gender.

collective noun: A noun that refers to a group as one unit.

comma splice: An error in writing that results when a comma without a coordinating conjunction is placed between two independent clauses.

command sentences: Sentences that express direct commands or express courteous requests that imply action. The pronoun *you* is understood. Also called *imperative sentences.*

common nouns: Words that refer to general names and are not capitalized.

communication: To give information or to exchange thoughts with another.

comparative degree: A form of an adjective or adverb used to compare two things.

compensatory time: Time off or vacation with pay intended to compensate employees for extra hours worked.

complete predicate: Consists of a verb or verbs and all the modifiers that limit or describe the verbs.

complete subject: A simple or compound subject plus any of its modifiers.

complex sentence: A sentence with an independent clause and one or more dependent clauses.

complimentary closing: A parting phrase such as *Sincerely* at the close of a letter.

compound adjective: The combination of two or more words to form one thought when modifying a noun.

compound-complex sentence: A sentence with more than one independent clause and one or more dependent clauses.

compound noun: A noun composed of two or more words. A compound noun may be written as one word, a hyphenated word, or two words.

compound personal pronoun: Consists of a personal pronoun and the suffix *self* or *selves.*

compound predicate: Consists of two or more predicates that are connected by a coordinating conjunction and have the same subject.

compound preposition: A combination of words that is often considered as one preposition.

compound sentence: A sentence with two independent clauses connected by a coordinating conjunction.

compound subject: Two or more subjects connected by a coordinating conjunction.

conflict resolution: The process of solving a disagreement or problem.

conjunctions: Words that connect words, phrases, or clauses.

conjunctive adverbs: Adverbs that function as connectors and show a relationship between two independent clauses of equal weight.

consonants: All letters except the vowels *a, e, i, o,* and *u.*

consumer: A person who uses goods or services.

contact management software: Allows businesspeople to create a client/contact directory. It includes time management capabilities such as an appointment calendar and to do lists.

contraction: A word made up of two words combined into one by the omission of one or more letters. An apostrophe takes the place of the missing letter or letters.

contrasting expression: An expression that often begins with the word *not* or *never* and contradicts the preceding noun or idea.

coordinating conjunctions: Words (*and, or, but, nor*) that join two independent clauses.

coping strategies: Plans or methods for dealing with problems or responsibilities.

copyright: The exclusive right to use software (also literary, musical, or artistic works) protected by law for a specified period of time.

correlative conjunctions: Words such as *neither/nor* or *not only/but also* that appear in pairs and join words, phrases, and sentences of equal importance.

courteous request sentences: Sentences that require actions rather than answers in words. The pronoun *you* is understood.

cover letter: A letter describing one's education, experience, skills, and job qualifications that is submitted to a potential employer.

cultural diversity: Differences among people such as gender, physical size, age, ethnicity, or religion.

cultural heritage: The ways of living transmitted to succeeding generations.

cumulative trauma disorders (CTDs) or musculoskeletal disorders (MSDs): Injuries that occur because of mismatches between workers and the physical requirements of jobs. Also known as *repetitive motion injuries or illnesses, repetitive strain injuries or illnesses,* or *repetitive stress injuries or illnesses.*

curvilinear: A descriptive term for an item formed or characterized by curved lines such as a desk or table.

customer service: Providing help to someone who purchases goods or services.

cynicism: A distrustful, pessimistic disposition.

D

decision-making process: The steps followed in making up one's mind about a situation.

decision-making software: A software program that helps a decision maker organize thoughts, analyze multiple options, and make the best choice.

declarative sentence: A sentence that states a fact, an idea, or an opinion.

demographics: The statistical data of a human population such as age, income, and years of education.

demonstrative adjectives: The words *this, that, these,* and *those* that modify nouns. Answer the questions *Which one? Which ones?*

demonstrative pronoun: A pronoun that points out specific persons, places, or things (*this, that, these, those*).

dependent clause: A clause that must be joined to an independent clause to make sense; it cannot stand alone.

derogatory: Detracting from the character or standing of something; belittling.

descriptive adjective: An adjective that answers the question *What kind?*

direct address: A name of an individual who is being addressed directly.

direct object: A noun or pronoun that provides one way to complete the verb by answering the question *Whom?* or *What?* after the verb.

direct question: A question that is expected to have a reply and that ends with a question mark. Also called an *interrogative sentence.*

direct quotation: The exact words spoken or written by someone.

documentation: Written information and printed instructions that are helpful for using computer software or hardware.

double negative: A sentence construction in which two negative words are used in the same clause when one is sufficient.

download: To transfer data to the user's computer from another computer.

downsizing: Decreasing the number of employees due to production or economic conditions.

E

electronic mail: The exchange of computer-stored messages by telecommunications links.

ellipsis mark: A mark or series of marks (. . .) to indicate that part of a quoted sentence has been omitted.

e-mail: Short for *electronic mail.*

e-mail address: A code or series of letters, numbers, and/or symbols by which the Internet identifies a person or a location where information is stored.

emphatic tense: Adds emphasis to a verb when combined with the word *do.*

encryption: A process that converts data into unreadable text so that unauthorized users cannot access it. Only the designated recipient can use a key to read the message.

equal opportunity employer: A company that offers the same hiring policies and employment conditions for everyone.

ergonomics: An applied science that coordinates the design of devices and systems in the workplace with the requirements of the workers.

ethical decisions: Decisions made according to the principles of right and wrong.

ethical dilemma: A confusing situation that requires a choice of action based upon ethics.

ethics: A system of moral principles.

ethnicity: Traits of a group sharing a common cultural background.

etymology: The history of words.

exclamatory sentence: A sentence that expresses strong reactions and that ends with an exclamation mark.

expert system software: Software designed to address a specific company's needs and challenges.

eye point recognition: The use of retina scanning for security purposes.

F

fax machine: Abbreviation for *facsimile machine.* A device that can send or receive text or pictures over a telephone line.

Federal Communication Commission: United States government agency that certifies, regulates, and monitors communication systems and practices.

feedback: The return of evaluative or corrective information to the original sender.

first-person pronoun: A pronoun that refers to the one who is speaking.

flextime: A work environment in which each employee chooses his or her own hours of work (within designated limits).

future perfect progressive tense: The form of a verb tense that expresses a continuing action; used with *will have been* and the present participle of the main verb.

future perfect tense: Indicates an action or condition of a verb that will begin and end before a specific future time. Uses *will have* or *shall have* with the past participle of the verb.

future progressive tense: The form of a verb tense that expresses a continuing action; used with *will be* and the present participle of the main verb.

future tense: Indicates an action or condition of a verb that will occur in the future. Uses *will* or *shall* before the present part of the verb.

G

gender: 1. The sex of a person or an animal. 2. A set of grammatical categories applied to nouns such as masculine, feminine, or neuter.

gerund: A verb form ending in *ing* that functions as a noun.

gerund phrase: Includes a gerund (word ending in *ing*) and any modifiers that are needed to make the meaning complete.

global communications: Worldwide exchange of information.

global competition: A process in which products are manufactured and/or services performed by competing companies and are made available to customers throughout the world.

good faith: A manner of acting in an honest, sincere manner.

goodwill: A term representing the reputation of a business.

grant proposals: A request that is submitted to an organization or governmental agency for potential funding.

groupware: Software programs designed for small groups of coworkers in a network. An example is software to assist groups in collaborative writing tasks such as proposals or newsletters.

H

hassles: Irritations.

helping verbs: Verbs that assist and precede the main verb. Also called *auxiliary verbs*.

HMO: health maintenance organization.

homonyms: Words that sound alike but have different meanings.

honorarium: Payment for services when no designated amount of money was previously stated or agreed upon.

hypertext: The format for the World Wide Web, which provides links between related materials. This linkage or cross referencing of information allows Web users to search for information using key words.

I

idiom: An expression that has evolved from general usage through the years but which has no established rule for this usage.

imperative mood: A verb form used to give instructions and commands or to make courteous requests.

imperative sentences: Sentences that express direct commands or courteous requests that imply action.

indefinite numbers: Numbers that are not easily counted or determined.

indefinite pronoun antecedents: Third-person pronouns that do not refer to masculine or feminine nouns. May be singular or plural.

indefinite pronouns: Pronouns that refer to persons, places, or things in general ways (e.g., *all, any, more, most, none,* and *some*).

independent clause: A group of words that is a complete sentence and can stand alone.

indicative mood: A verb form used to state facts or to ask direct questions.

indirect object: A noun or pronoun that completes a verb by answering the question *To whom?* or *For whom?*

indirect question: A sentence that sounds like a question but does not require an answer; ends with a period.

indirect quotation: A restatement of the original material; does not require quotation marks.

inference engine: Component of expert system software that processes data and arrives at conclusions.

infinitive: A verbal that consists of the present part of a verb plus the word *to.*

infinitive phrase: The infinitive (*to* and a verb) and its modifiers.

information overload: Too much information is received to be able to effectively sort or use.

inside address: The name and address of the person to whom a letter is written.

insider trading: An illegal act of selling or buying stocks based on privileged information received before the purchase or sale.

integrity: Firm adherence to a code of ethics or morals.

intensive pronoun: A compound personal pronoun that adds emphasis.

interactive ordering: Placing an order for goods or services over the Internet.

interjections: One or two words that show emotions or strong reactions to events or things that have occurred.

Internet: A large computer system linking existing computer networks worldwide.

interrogative pronoun: A pronoun that is used to form direct and indirect questions.

interrogative sentence: A sentence that asks a question.

intransitive verb: An action verb that does not require an object to complete the thought.

irregular plurals: The plural forms change within the nouns or at the end of the nouns.

irritability: Easily annoyed.

J

jargon: A vocabulary that is unique to a group or profession.

job search: The process used in finding employment.

job targets: Specific occupational goals, kinds of industries, and/or places of employment determined by job candidates.

junk e-mail: Unwanted electronic messages. Also called *spam.*

K

kiosks: Open-ended structures similar to newsstands where products are sold in public locations.

Kiwanis and Rotary: International organizations that promote service in local communities and offer monetary assistance to local and international projects.

L

lateral move: Acceptance of a position equal in pay and prestige to the current one rather than a promotion.

leader: A person who influences the behavior of others.

leadership: The characteristics that a leader possesses which help influence the behavior of others.

limiting adjective: A number or word that indicates *how many;* limits the scope of the noun or pronoun.

linking verbs: Show a state of being or a condition and provide a "link" between the subject and a noun, a pronoun, or an adjective. Do not indicate action.

logo: A graphic symbol adopted by a company to identify its name, product, or service.

M

macro: A program of stored commands and keystrokes. Using a macro allows shortening tedious tasks such as rekeying paragraphs in form letters or legal documents.

mailbox: An electronic storage space where electronic messages are received or stored.

manila envelope: A light brown envelope that once was made from Manila hemp but is now made from other wood products.

master list: A time management technique that includes all possible tasks to be completed within a time period.

mediocre: A description of a plan or action that is neither good nor bad but just average.

mnemonic device: A memory device.

modem: An acronym derived from <u>mo</u>dulator/<u>dem</u>odulator. An electronic device or program that makes possible the transmission of data from a computer by telephone or other communication lines.

modifiers: Words that describe.

Morningstar: A financial rating service for stocks, bonds, and mutual funds.

multilingual: Using more than one language.

N

Net: Short for *Internet.*

netiquette: The proper behavior in sending and receiving electronic mail messages.

network: A group of two or more computer or telecommunications systems linked together to permit an exchange of information.

networking: The informal sharing of information among individuals, groups, or institutions.

neuter gender: A pronoun (*it, its*) used to refer to an antecedent that represents things.

newsgroup: An online discussion group.

nominative case: Nouns or pronouns used as subjects of sentences, as appositives, or as subject complements. Also called the *subjective case.*

nonrestrictive clause: A dependent clause that has a subject and predicate and does not add to the meaning of the sentence.

notary public: A person with authority to establish the authenticity of legal documents.

nouns: Words that name people, places, things, activities, ideas, or qualities.

O

objective case: Nouns or pronouns used as direct objects, indirect objects, objects of a preposition, or objects of infinitives.

Occupational Safety and Health Administration (OSHA): A federal government agency responsible for providing education, research, enforcement, and rule-making to combat injuries in the workplace.

off the record: Reference to an unofficial comment that should not be published or quoted.

online: One computer connected to another computer electronically to receive or send data.

operating system software: Software that tells the computer how to use its own components.

ordinal numbers: Numbers used to show the order of succession (e.g., *lst, 2d, 3d*).

P

pager: A small telecommunications device that receives short messages, typically a phone number, for the pager user to call. Also called a "beeper."

paralegals: People who work in law offices doing research for lawyers. Special training (not a law degree) is required.

parallelism: The linking together of similar grammatical parts in a sentence.

parenthetical expression: A side remark that interrupts a sentence and does not add to the clarity of a sentence.

participative management: A form of organizational governance that is shared by all personnel.

participial phrase: Consists of a present, past, or perfect participle plus any additional modifiers; functions as an adjective.

participle: May stand alone as an adjective or may be used with helping verbs to form different verb tenses.

passive voice: The subject of a sentence receives the action of the verb.

past participle: A verb part formed by adding *ed* to the base form.

past perfect tense: Shows that one action or condition of a verb began and was completed before another past action; uses past participle form with the helping verb *had*.

past progressive tense: Involves an action or condition of a verb that was in progress at a time in the past; uses the past tense of the verb *be* with the present participle of the main verb.

past tense: Expresses an action or condition of a verb that was started and completed in the past.

peripheral: A unit that operates outside the computer but is connected to it such as a CD-ROM drive or printer.

permanent record: Written information intended to last for a long, indefinite period.

personal digital assistant: A pocket-sized portable computer generally used as an organizer with communication capabilities.

personal information manager (PIM) software: A program that allows the storage and retrieval of information such as notes, addresses, appointments, and telephone numbers. PIMs may include calculators and schedules.

personal pronouns: Words that can substitute for nouns referring to persons or things.

phrase: A sequence of words with neither a subject nor a predicate that cannot stand alone.

plural nouns: Name two or more persons, places, things, activities, or ideas and qualities.

point-and-click interface: Clicking on a picture or words on an Internet Web page and being automatically connected to another Web page.

positive degree: The base form of an adjective to describe one person, place, thing, quality, idea, or one group of things; the base form of an adverb to describe a verb, adjective, or other adverb; cannot be used to make a comparison.

possessive adjective: A possessive pronoun such as *my, her, his, your, its,* and *our* that functions as an adjective; answers the question *Whose?*

possessive case: Shows that someone or something owns or possesses something else.

predicate: Adds meaning and clarity to the subject and tells what the subject is doing or what the subject is.

predicate noun: Follows a linking verb and renames the subject. Also called a *subject complement.*

prefix: A letter or word placed before a word (e.g., *self-confidence*).

prepositional phrase: A group of words that connects nouns and pronouns to other words.

prepositions: Words that connect nouns or pronouns to other words in the sentence.

present participle: A verb part formed by adding *ing* to the base form.

present perfect progressive tense: Describes a continuous action of a verb up to the present time; uses *has been/have been* with the present participle of the main verb.

present perfect tense: Shows that an action or condition of a verb that started in the past has just been completed or continues to take place up to the present; uses *has* or *have* with the past participle of a verb.

present progressive tense: Involves an action or condition of a verb that is in progress at the present time; uses the present tense of the verb *be* with the present participle of the main verb.

present tense: Expresses a general truth or an action of a verb that is occurring now.

procrastination: The postponement of action.

procrastinator: A person who postpones action.

project management software: Software that tracks all the tasks involved in a job and assists project managers in completing these tasks so that the entire project is finished by its deadline.

pronouns: Words that substitute for nouns.

proper adjective: A word derived from a proper noun that functions as an adjective; answers the question *Which?*

proper noun derivatives: Adjectives formed from proper nouns.

proper nouns: Words that refer to specific persons, places, or things.

Q

quality service: Excellent concern and care toward someone who purchases goods or services.

R

radius-edge: Trim that goes around the edge of a desk or table.

rapport: A close bond or relationship felt among a group of people.

reciprocal: Mutual satisfaction with all parties in agreement.

redundant: Repeating material unnecessarily.

referendum: A proposed item presented to the voting public for passage or rejection.

reflexive pronoun: A compound personal pronoun that refers to a previously named noun or pronoun.

relative pronoun: A pronoun that begins a dependent clause which cannot stand on its own.

repetitive stress injury (RSI): An injury that occurs because of a mismatch between the worker and the physical requirements of the job. Also known as *repetitive motion injury* or *illness, repetitive strain injury* or *illness,* or *cumulative trauma (or musculoskeletal) disorder.*

restrictive clause: A dependent clause that has a subject and predicate and is necessary to the meaning of the sentence.

résumé: A summary of one's education, experience, skills, and job qualifications submitted to a potential employer.

roman numerals: Any of the numerals in the ancient Roman system of notation (e.g., *I, II, III*).

rules of thumb: Plans or procedures grounded in experience rather than in a knowledge of science.

run-on sentences: Sentences in which two independent clauses run together. These sentences are not punctuated correctly. They may have comma splices, or they may lack periods, semicolons, or conjunctions.

S

salutation: The opening greeting of a letter (e.g., *Dear Ms. Miller*).

scams: Fraudulent schemes.

search engine: A service that helps organize various Internet sites into categories.

second-person pronoun: A pronoun that refers to the one spoken to.

self-managing teams: People who work together and manage themselves by sharing power, authority, and decision making.

sentence diagramming: Shows the parts of a sentence and the relationship of all the words to one another.

sentence fragments: Words, phrases, or dependent clauses that cannot stand alone.

sentences: Words correctly arranged so that the words comprise complete statements or ideas that make sense.

shareware: Copyrighted programs that are free on a trial basis. A fee to the author is expected if you continue to use the program.

silicon: A small piece of material on which computer chips are embedded.

simple predicate: A single verb in a sentence.

simple sentence: A sentence with one complete subject and one complete predicate.

simple subject: Main word of the subject in a sentence.

singular nouns: Words that name one person, place, thing, activity, or idea and quality.

smiley: A tiny picture on an e-mail message made using standard keyboard characters. It is meant to be looked at with the head tilted to the left [:-)].

software: Programs for directing the operation of a computer or processing electronic data.

software piracy: The unauthorized copying or use of software.

sole proprietor: Single business owner.

stereotypes: Images or beliefs formed about ideas or certain groups of people.

stress: Emotional tension caused by everyday events in our lives.

subject: Indicates who is speaking, who is spoken to, or who or what is spoken about in a sentence.

subject complements: Predicate nouns or predicate pronouns that follow linking verbs and rename the subject(s).

subjective case: See *nominative case.*

subjunctive mood: A verb used to express a condition that is contrary to fact or subject to an element of doubt.

subordinating conjunctions: Words that introduce a dependent clause and link it to an independent clause.

suffix: Letter(s) added to the end of a word.

superlative degree: A form of an adjective or adverb used to compare more than two things.

support staff: Office professionals who assist management personnel.

surf the Net: Looking at information on the Internet.

suspending hyphens: Hyphens that are used when a series of hyphenated adjectives has a common basic element and this element is shown only with the last item. A "suspended hyphen" is inserted after each incomplete adjective to indicate a relationship with the last term (e.g., *12- to 15-hour project*).

syllable: Represents distinct sound divisions in a word.

synonyms: Words that have the same or almost the same meaning.

T

tag question: A question that appears at the end of a sentence.

team: A number of persons working together.

teamwork: A cooperative effort by a group of persons acting together as a team.

telecommunications: The science and technology of transmitting all types of data, from voice to video, over great distances in the form of electromagnetic signals.

telecommuting: A term to describe working outside the traditional office or workplace on a computer and electronically transmitting information to a central office.

telemarketers: Employees hired by companies to sell goods and services by telephone.

tendinitus: An inflammation of the cord of tissue that connects a muscle with a bone.

tension: Mental or emotional strain.

testimonial letters: Written statements of recommendations about products or services.

thesaurus: A book that gives suggestions for similar substitute words as well as their parts of speech.

third-person pronoun: A pronoun that refers to the one spoken about.

time management: Identification and completion of tasks and projects within specified periods of time.

transitive verb: An action verb that needs an object to complete the thought.

traumatic: Upsetting or unsettling.

U

unilateral: Involving only one side of an issue when making a recommendation.

USPS: United States Postal Service.

V

value system: Determination of importance according to personal beliefs.

verb phrase: A helping (auxiliary) verb with a main verb.

verb tense: Identifies the time of an action or a state of being of a verb.

verbal: A gerund, participle, or infinitive that looks like a verb but functions as a noun, adjective, or adverb.

verbs: Words that show action, indicate a state of being, or help main verbs.

vision: A plan or direction for the future.

voice mail: A telephone system that can record and store human voices and play the recording back to the intended person on command.

voice recognition technology: A computer program with the ability to recognize spoken words as input.

vowels: The letters *a, e, i, o,* and *u.*

W

Web: Short for *World Wide Web.*

Web sites: Locations on the Internet with information about a person, organization, or business.

webcasting: Sending live programming to multiple Internet users at the same time.

work climate: The prevailing attitude, atmosphere, or condition of a place of employment.

workers' compensation: A compensation system of wage replacement benefits for and medical treatment of work-related injuries and occupational diseases.

workstation: A work area for one person; it often accommodates a computer.

World Wide Web: A graphical system on the Internet that supports links to other documents.

write-off: A reduction in or a cancellation of the value of something owned such as a bad debt or depreciation.

Z

ZIP Code: A system to facilitate mail delivery by assigning a numerical code to every postal area in the U.S. (*Zone Improvement Program*).

The **Spelling Review** correlates with exercises on the Instructor CD and on the Student Web page. The exercises are arranged by chapter and also cover material identified as **Commonly Misused or Confused Words and Phrases** (Appendix B) and **Frequently Misspelled Words** (Appendix C).

The number or numbers in parentheses after each rule indicate the chapter exercise on the Web where the rule applies.

ie/ei Words

The grade school rhyme *"i* before *e* except after *c* or when sounded like *a* as in *neighbor* and *weigh"* helps you spell many words. Study Rules 1–6 carefully.

Rule 1: Most words use *i* before *e*. (1)

friend	audience	variety
tier	patient	scientist

Rule 2: Use *i* before *e* except after the letter *c*. In many words, the *ie* sounds like *e* (as in *be*). (1)

achieve	brief	field
thief	wield	relieve

Exceptions:

either	neither	leisure
weird	seize	

Rule 3: Use *e* before *i* after the letter *c*. Note that the *ei* sounds like *e* (as in *be*). (2)

ceiling	conceive	deceit
perceive	receive	receipt

Rule 4: Use *e* before *i* when the *ei* sounds like *a* (as in *weigh*). (2)

freight	their	vein
reign	rein	neighbor

Rule 5: Use *e* before *i* when the *ei* sounds like *i* (as in *twice*). (2)

height	sleight

Rule 6: Use *e* before *i* when *ei* sounds like *i* (as in *fit*). (2)

foreign	forfeit	counterfeit

Adding Suffixes to Words

A *suffix* added to the *end* of a word changes the form of that word, the meaning of the word, and, in some cases, the spelling of that word. *Vowels* consist of the letters *a, e, i, o,* and *u.* The letters *w* and *y* sometimes act like vowels. All other letters are *consonants.* A *syllable* represents distinct sound divisions in a word.

Rule 7:   For words that end in a single consonant preceded by a single vowel, double the final consonant when adding a suffix that begins with a vowel or *y*. (3)

One-Syllable Word		Suffix	New Word
bid	+	er	bidder
stop	+	ed	stopped
wrap	+	ing	wrapping
bag	+	age	baggage
sad	+	en	sadden
fun	+	y	funny

Rule 8:   For words that end in *w, x,* and *y* preceded by a single vowel, do not double the final consonant when adding a suffix that begins with a vowel. (4)

One-Syllable Word		Suffix	New Word
draw	+	er	drawer
pay	+	able	payable
say	+	ing	saying
show	+	ed	showed
tax	+	ing	taxing

Rule 9:   Double the final consonant of a *two-syllable* word that ends in a *single* consonant preceded by a *single* vowel when you add a suffix that begins with a vowel. This rule applies when the accent falls on the last syllable of the root word. An accent mark (') is a stress mark and indicates the syllable that requires emphasis when the word is pronounced. (4)

Two-Syllable Word		Suffix	New Word
re fer'	+	ing	referring
oc cur'	+	ed	occurred
ex cel'	+	ing	excelling
trans fer'	+	ed	transferred
im pel'	+	ed	impelled
re mit'	+	ance	remittance

Rule 10:   If the accent falls on a syllable other than the last when a suffix is added, do not double the final consonant. Memorize these words. (4)

pre fer'	pref' erence *(The accent is on the first syllable.)*
re fer'	ref' erence *(The accent is on the first syllable.)*
con fer'	con' ference *(The accent is on the first syllable.)*

Exception:

ex cel'	ex' cellence *(Even though the accent is on the first syllable, the consonant doubles.)*

Rule 11: Do not double the final consonant when adding *any* suffix to words ending with two or more consonants. (5)

Word		Suffix	New Word
send	+	ing	sending
consent	+	ed	consented
conform	+	ed	conformed
earn	+	er	earner
back	+	ward	backward
harsh	+	ly	harshly
tempt	+	ed	tempted

Rule 12: Do not double the final consonant when adding *any* suffix to a word ending in one consonant and preceded by two vowels. (5)

Word		Suffix	New Word
mail	+	able	mailable
wear	+	ing	wearing
equal	+	ed	equaled
beat	+	en	beaten
retail	+	er	retailer
equip	+	ment	equipment

Exceptions:

equip	+	ing	equipping
equip	+	ed	equipped
quiz	+	ed	quizzed
quiz	+	ing	quizzing
quit	+	ing	quitting

Rule 13: Do not double the final consonant of a *one-syllable* word ending in *one* consonant and preceded by *one* vowel when adding a suffix beginning with a consonant. (6)

Word		Suffix	New Word
ship	+	ment	shipment
fret	+	ful	fretful
ten	+	fold	tenfold
bad	+	ly	badly
man	+	hood	manhood

Rule 14: Do not double the final consonant of a *multisyllable* word that ends in *one* consonant and is preceded by *one vowel* and is not accented on the last syllable when a suffix beginning with a vowel is added. (6)

Word		Suffix	New Word
can' cel	+	ed	canceled (preferred)
prof' it	+	ed	profited
of' fer	+	ed	offered
ben' efit	+	ed	benefited (preferred)
to' tal	+	ed	totaled (preferred)

Exceptions:

for' mat	+	ed	formatted
pro' gram	+	ed	programmed
hand' icap	+	ed	handicapped

Rule 15: With most words that end with *e*, drop the final silent *e* at the end of the word when adding a suffix beginning with a vowel. (7)

Word		Suffix	New Word
advise	+	able	advisable
reverse	+	ible	reversible
argue	+	ing	arguing
arrive	+	al	arrival
use	+	ed	used
please	+	ant	pleasant
scarce	+	ity	scarcity
hope	+	ing	hoping
procede	+	ing	proceding
base	+	ic	basic

Exceptions:

agree	+	ing	agreeing
mile	+	age	mileage
dye	+	ing	dyeing

Rule 16: With words that end with *e*, do not drop the final silent *e* when adding a suffix beginning with a consonant. See Rule 17 for the suffix *y* exception. (8)

Root Word		Suffix	New Word
absolute	+	ly	absolutely
advertise	+	ment	advertisement
care	+	less	careless
edge	+	wise	edgewise
enforce	+	ment	enforcement
entire	+	ty	entirety
nine	+	ty	ninety
sincere	+	ly	sincerely
use	+	ful	useful

Exceptions:

acknowledge	+	ment	acknowledgment (preferred)
judge	+	ment	judgment (preferred)
argue	+	ment	argument
true	+	ly	truly
nine	+	th	ninth
whole	+	ly	wholly
awe	+	ful	awful

Rule 17: With words that end with *e*, drop the final silent *e* before adding the suffix *y*. (8)

Root Word		Suffix	New Word
ease	+	y	easy
edge	+	y	edgy
ice	+	y	icy
spice	+	y	spicy

Exceptions:

price	+	y	pricey
smile	+	y	smiley

Rule 18: Do not drop the final silent *e* when a word ends in *ce* or *ge* and the suffix begins with an *a* or *o*. The *c* and *g* retain a soft sound.   (9)

Word		Suffix	New Word
advantage	+	ous	advantageous
change	+	able	changeable
manage	+	able	manageable
notice	+	able	noticeable
outrage	+	ous	outrageous
peace	+	able	peaceable
replace	+	able	replaceable

Rule 19: Drop the final silent *e* when a word ends in *ce* or *ge* and the suffix begins with *i*.   (9)

Word		Suffix	New Word
age	+	ing	aging
judge	+	ing	judging
mortgage	+	ing	mortgaging
finance	+	ial	financial
force	+	ible	forcible

Rule 20: Change the final *y* to *i* before adding a suffix to a word that ends in *y* preceded by a consonant.   (10)

Word		Suffix	New Word
envy	+	ous	envious
copy	+	er	copier
easy	+	ly	easily
try	+	ed	tried
heavy	+	est	heaviest
ordinary	+	ly	ordinarily
happy	+	ness	happiness
likely	+	hood	likelihood
merry	+	ment	merriment

Exceptions:

dry	+	ness	dryness
country	+	side	countryside
shy	+	ly	shyly

Rule 21: In most cases, retain the *y* in words ending in *y* preceded by a vowel when adding any suffix.   (11)

Word	Suffix		New Word
enjoy	+	ment	enjoyment
employ	+	ment	employment
play	+	er	player
display	+	ing	displaying
convey	+	ing	conveying
pay	+	er	payer
joy	+	ous	joyous

Exceptions:

day	daily	lay	laid
pay	paid	say	said

Words Ending in *able* and *ible*

Word endings are confusing. The lists that follow include words arranged in families according to their endings. When you are not certain about the correct spelling of a word, check your dictionary. (12)

Words Ending in *able* Most words end in *able*.

advis<u>able</u>	lik<u>able</u>	reason<u>able</u>
compar<u>able</u>	notic<u>eable</u>	receiv<u>able</u>

Words Ending in *ible* Some words end in *ible*.

collect<u>ible</u>	flex<u>ible</u>	sens<u>ible</u>
elig<u>ible</u>	leg<u>ible</u>	terr<u>ible</u>

Words Ending in *ence, ent, ant,* and *ance*

Words ending in *ant, ent, ance,* and *ence* do not have rules for spelling. Practice these words so that they become familiar. Use a dictionary whenever you are in doubt about a spelling. (13)

ence	**ent**	**ant**	**ance**
exist<u>ence</u>	incid<u>ent</u>	irrelev<u>ant</u>	attend<u>ance</u>
occurr<u>ence</u>	obsolesc<u>ent</u>	serge<u>ant</u>	hindr<u>ance</u>

Words Ending in *ize, ise,* and *yze*

Words ending with *ize, ise,* and *yze* do not have rules for spelling. Most words end in *ize,* but some commonly used words end in *ise.* Practice these words so that they become familiar. Use a dictionary whenever you are in doubt about a spelling. (14)

Words Ending in *ize*

amortize	economize	penalize	scrutinize
authorize	emphasize	realize	utilize

Words Ending in *ise*

advise	devise	merchandise	surmise
compromise	exercise	supervise	arise

Words Ending in *yze*

analyze	paralyze

Meanings of Suffixes

A suffix is a word part that is attached to the end of a word. A suffix added to a word may change the meaning of that word. (14)

Suffix		**Meaning**
ful	=	**full of**
useful		respectful
plentiful		thoughtful
ative	=	**inclined to**
demonstrative		talkative
creative		initiative
ous	=	**full of**
humorous		conscious
continuous		disastrous
envious		

Suffix		Meaning	
ly	=	**in the way or manner mentioned**	
undoubtedly		immediately	
obviously		patiently	

Adding Prefixes to Words

A prefix is a syllable that is attached to the beginning of a word. Misspellings often occur in words because a prefix is added incorrectly. The words below need extra review and practice. Use a dictionary whenever you are in doubt about a spelling. To avoid misspellings, analyze the word before you add a prefix; then add the prefix to the complete word. (15)

Prefix		**Word**		**New Word**
dis	+	satisfaction	=	dissatisfaction
dis	+	service	=	disservice
il	+	legal	=	illegal
il	+	legible	=	illegible
il	+	logical	=	illogical
im	+	mature	=	immature
mis	+	statement	=	misstatement
mis	+	spell	=	misspell
over	+	run	=	overrun
over	+	ride	=	override
un	+	necessary	=	unnecessary
un	+	natural	=	unnatural
under	+	rate	=	underrate

Meanings of Prefixes (16)

Prefix	Meaning
dis	**lack of, not**
disadvantageous	
distasteful	
im, in, ir	**not**
immeasurable	
inappropriate	
irreplaceable	
inter	**between**
intermission	
intersection	
mis	**wrong**
misinformed	
misinterpret	
pre	**before**
precaution	
prerecorded	
re	**again**
recover	
reemphasize	

Appendix B: Commonly Misused or Confused Words or Phrases

The list of **Commonly Misused or Confused Words or Phrases** below correlates with exercises on the Instructor CD and on the Student Web page. The exercises are arranged by chapter and also cover material from the **Spelling Review** (Appendix A) and from the **Frequently Misspelled Words** list (Appendix C).

The numbers in parentheses located in the right margin indicate the chapter exercises on the Web where the group of words will be found.

Use *The Gregg Reference Manual* or any other available reference manual to check the definitions of these commonly misused or confused words or phrases. You may also use your dictionary to look up these words.

insure	overdue	knew	fewer	irregardless	access	(1)
assure	overdo	new	less	regardless	excess	
ensure						
advice	etc.	loose	perspective	to	amount	
advise		lose	prospective	too	number	
		loss		two		(2)
allot	capital	recent	through	already	in regards	
a lot	capitol	resent	threw	all ready	in regard	
alot						(3)
addition	bases	council	device	of	set	
edition	basis	counsel	devise	have	sit	(4)
		consul				
adverse	cite	its	lessee	serve	stature	
averse	sight	it's	lesser	service	statue	
			lessor		statute	(5)
close	decent	apportion	cereal	bad	come/go	
clothes	descent	portion	serial	badly		(6)
cloths	dissent	proportion				
are	principal	quiet	their	among	kind of	
hour	principle	quit	there	between	kind of a	(7)
our		quite	they're			
accept	affect	coarse	rain	biannual	in	
except	effect	course	reign	biennial	in to	(8)
			rein	semiannual	into	
adapt	bring	lead	pole	precede	raise	
adept	take	led	poll	proceed	rays	(9)
adopt					raze	
defer	lessen	may be	passed	lie	may	(10)
differ	lesson	maybe	past	lay	can	
brake	detract	medal	shone	learn	let	
break	distract	meddle	shown	teach	leave	(11)
		metal				
		mettle				
disinterested	marital	miner	suit	anxious	doesn't	
uninterested	marshal	minor	suite	eager	don't	(12)
	martial		sweet			

foreword forward	hear here	later latter	respectably respectfully respectively	good well	real really	(13)
beside besides	interstate intrastate intestate	personal personnel	stationary stationery	every one everyone	than then	(14)
complement compliment	different from different than	leased least	plain plane	role roll	some time sometime sometimes	(15)
any one anyone	eminent imminent	moral morale	en route root route	cannot help but	could have should have would have	(16)
appraise apprise	last latest	precedence precedents	track tract	try and try to	vain vane vein	(17)
cent scent sent	disburse disperse	fiscal physical	reality realty	could hardly could not hardly	settle up settle	(18)

Commonly Misused or Confused Words or Phrases

The list of **Frequently Misspelled Words** below correlates with exercises on the Instructor CD and on the Student Web page. The exercises are arranged by chapter and also cover material from the **Spelling Review** (Appendix A) and from the **Commonly Misused or Confused Words or Phrases** section (Appendix B).

The number in parentheses after each word indicates the chapter exercise on the Web where the word will be found.

accommodate (8)	embarrass (18)	liaison (7)	San Francisco (8)
adjacent (11)	emphasize (13)	library (5)	satellite (9)
Albuquerque (9)	entrepreneur (15)	maintenance (3)	secretary (10)
analysis (14)	environment (17)	maneuver (1)	separate (2)
attendance (13, 14)	equally (5)	manila (18)	similar (12)
bankruptcy (2)	exaggerate (18)	mediocre (18)	simultaneous (13)
beneficiary (18)	exhibition (17)	miniature (18)	sponsor (15)
bureau (6)	exorbitant (12)	miscellaneous (12)	subpoena (16)
candidate (18)	extension (18)	misspell (9)	substantial (18)
category (3)	facilitate (18)	mortgage (10)	succeed (17)
collateral (18)	familiar (3)	necessary (1)	summary (18)
column (4)	fascinating (9)	negotiate (3)	surprise (14)
committee (18)	February (11)	ninety (5, 8)	thoroughly (3, 16)
conscience (7)	forty (5)	ninth (6)	unanimous (18)
conscientious (13)	fourth (6)	obsolescent (1, 13)	unique (4)
consensus (16)	government (18)	omission (8)	vicinity (18)
correspondent (9)	guarantee (8)	pamphlet (10)	warrant (11)
courtesy (10)	harass (9)	parallel (12)	Wednesday (17)
deductible (12)	hindrance (13)	patience (4)	withhold (11)
deficit (2)	impasse (17)	perseverance (13)	
definite (6)	inasmuch as (16)	persuade (2)	
Des Moines (15)	incredible (18)	potato, potatoes (7)	
develop (1)	indict (15)	practically (6)	
dilemma (16)	interim (13)	prerogative (14)	
disappoint (4)	itinerary (11)	pronunciation (3)	
dissatisfied (8)	jeopardy (14)	quantity (5)	
distinguish (18)	ledger (2)	questionnaire (1)	
eighth (10)	liabilities (18)	recommend (7)	
eliminate (14)	liable (4)	requisition (18)	

Photo Credits

Pages 1–3   Royalty Free/ CORBIS/ DIL
Pages 1, 30, 31   Chad Baker/ Ryan McVay/Getty Images/ DIL
Pages 1, 54, 55   PhotoDisc/ Getty Images/ DIL
Pages 89–90   Greg Kuchik/ Getty Images/ DIL
Pages 89, 120, 121   Matthew Flor/ Jason Reed/ Getty Images/ DIL
Pages 89, 148, 149   Royalty Free/ CORBIS/ DIL
Pages 89, 188, 189   Jason Reed/ Getty Images/ DIL
Pages 89, 222, 223   Royalty Free/ CORBIS/ DIL
Pages 255–257   Steve Cole/ Getty Images/ DIL
Pages 255, 286, 287   Keith Brofsky/ Getty Images/ DIL
Pages 255, 326, 327   Digital Vision/ Getty Images/ DIL
Pages 355–357   Royalty Free/ CORBIS/ DIL
Pages 355, 392, 393   Jason Reed/ Getty images/ DIL
Pages 355, 426, 427   R. Morley/ PhotoLink/Getty Images/ DIL
Pages 355, 456, 457   Digital Vision/ Getty Images/ DIL
Pages 489, 490, 491   Ryan McVay/ Getty Images/ DIL
Pages 489, 524, 525   Digital Vision/ Getty Images/ DIL
Pages 489, 560, 561   Chad Baker/ Getty Images/ DIL

Index

A

a/an, 241, 363–364
a number/the number, 338
Abbreviations
  of academic degrees, 161, 495, 496, 510
  apostrophes for, 536, 537
  capitalization of, 164, 165–166, 494–495
  of common nouns, 166
  of corporate names, 495
  in dictionary, 7, 8
  for foreign money, 574–575
  vs. foreign words, 497
  of geographic locations, 496
  identifying, at first use, 166
  for measurements, 103, 494
  for "number" *(No.),* 572
  with numbers, 565
  for parts of speech, 7
  periods for, 103, 164, 494–495
  of personal names, 495
  plurals of, 103, 537
  of professional identification, 496
  of proper nouns, 165
  in reference manual, 10
  vs. shortened words, 497
  small/lowercase letters for, 494–495, 536
  of states, 496, 509
  for time periods *(a.m., p.m.),* 164
  of titles, 496
-able/-ible endings, 399
Absolute adjectives, 369, 371
Absolute adverbs, 402, 404
Academic degrees, 161, 495, 496, 510
Accents
  marks, in dictionary, 7
  for regular verbs, 266
Action verbs, 36, 260–261, 292
  active *vs.* passive voice for, 301
  adjectives with, 401–402
  adverbs with, 401–402
Active voice, 301
Acts, titles of, 160–161
Addresses. *See also* Place/location
  capitalization of, 164–165, 170–171
  commas with, 509–510
  e-mail/Web site, 170–171
  on envelope, 171
  numbers in, 566
  ZIP Codes in, 496, 509, 565
Adjacent numbers, 568

Adjective clauses, 372–373
  commas with nonrestrictive, 506–507
  diagramming of, 375–376
  restrictive, 507
Adjective phrases, 372, 373
Adjectives, 33, 37–38, 356–377
  absolute, 369, 371
  vs. adverbs, 396, 397
  adverbs formed from, 399
  adverbs with, 39–40, 397–398, 402, 411
  articles as, 363–365
  clauses as, 372–373
  commas with independent, 502
  for comparisons, 369–371
  complete subject and, 62–63
  compound, 366–368, 538, 569
  demonstrative, 362
  descriptive, 360–361, 369–371
  diagramming of, 241
  independent, 502
  infinitive phrases as, 307
  irregular, 8, 370–371
  limiting, 360
  after linking verbs, 361
  nouns as, 362, 366–368
  numbers in compound, 367–368, 538
  phrases as, 367, 372, 373
  possessive nouns as, 128, 241, 361–362
  possessive pronouns as, 196, 361–362
  as predicate complements, 66
  prepositional phrases as, 433
  with pronouns, 38
  pronouns as, 241, 334
  proper, 362
  in *self-* words, 368
  series of compound, 368
  special, 374
  suspending hyphens with incomplete, 538
  types of, 360–362
  verbs as, 305–306 *(See also* Verbals)
Adverb clauses, 408
Adverbs, 33, 39–40, 392–412
  absolute, 402, 404
  vs. adjectives, 396, 397
  adjectives with, 39–40, 397–398, 402, 411
  adverbs with other, 397–398, 402, 411
  cautions for using, 405–406
  as clauses, 408

Adverbs—*(Cont.)*
  for comparisons, 402–404
  complete subject and, 62–63
  in compound adjectives, 366–367
  conjunctive, 467–468, 528–529
  diagramming of, 411
  double negatives as, 396, 405–406
  ending in *-ly,* 399, 400, 538
  formation of, 398–400
  formed from adjectives, 399
  functions of, 397–398
  here/there as, 67, 338
  identifying, 396–397, 400
  infinitive phrases as, 307
  irregular, 8, 403–404
  negative words as, 405–406
  not ending in *-ly,* 399–400
  prepositional phrases as, 433
  prepositions and, 432
  special, 409–410
  verbs as *(See* Verbals)
  verbs with, 39–40, 397–398, 401–402, 411
Age, numbers to express, 566–567
Agreement. *See* Pronoun/antecedent agreement; Subject/verb agreement
all, 235
almost/most, 409
a.m., 164, 579
Amendments, titles of, 160–161
among/between, 436
Ampersand, 500
and, 61, 71, 230, 461
  ampersand for, 500
  commas with, 463–464
  in series, 464
  subject/verb agreement and, 332
  use of, 463–464
Anniversaries, numbers for, 567
Antecedents, 225–242
  clarity of, 237–238
  collective, 232–233
  compound, 230–231
  indefinite pronoun, 233–235
Antonyms, in dictionary, 6, 8
any, 235
anyone/any one, 240
anywhere, 400
Apostrophes, 535–537
  for contractions, 197–198, 206, 405, 536
  possessive nouns and, 127, 129, 131–134, 536

Envelope address, 171
-*er* endings, 369–371, 403
Ergonomics, 357
Errors
  commonly misused words, 16
  with pronouns, 199
  in quotations, 544
  [sic] to indicate, 544
  spelling, 15–16
  "troublesome word list," 6
  to watch for in proofreading, 12
-*es* endings, 97, 329
Essential clauses, 203, 539. *See also*
    Restrictive clauses
-*est* endings, 369–371, 403
etc., 501
Ethics, 393
Ethnic designations, 162
Etiquette, 189, 392
Etymologies, 8. *See also* Word
    origins/history
every, 234, 333
every one/everyone, 240
Exclamation marks, 58, 60
  for interjections, 42–43
  with quotation marks, 534–535
Exclamatory sentences, 59, 60
Explanatory words/phrases
  antecedents and, 237
  asterisk to indicate, 545
  colons with, 531
  parentheses with, 542
  semicolons with, 529
Expression of wish, 303

F

-*f* endings, plurals of, 99
Family titles, 158–159
FAQs, 561
farther/further, 374, 409
-*fe* endings, plurals of, 99
Feminine pronouns, 227–228
few, 235
fewer/less, 374
-*ff* endings, plurals of, 99
Figures. *See* Numbers
Financial quotes, numbers in, 571
First-person pronouns
  nominative case, 192–193, 198
  objective case, 194–195, 198
  possessive case, 196, 198
  pronoun/antecedent agreement
    and, 225, 226
First-person subjects
  with *be,* 290
  with *do,* 291
  with *have,* 291–292
  with past tense verbs, 294–295
  with perfect tense verbs, 298
  with present tense verbs, 293–294

Footnotes, asterisks for, 545
for example (e.g.), 529, 531
Foreign dates, 569
Foreign money, 574–575
Foreign nouns, plural, 102
Foreign words, 497
Formal proposals, 303
Formal writing
  abbreviations in, 103
  dashes in, 540
  numbers in, 542, 565, 569
Format errors, proofreading of, 12
Fractional amounts
  decimal points with, 494, 571
  hyphens for, 538
  plural verb with, 337
  singular verb with, 337
Fragments, sentence, 72
further/farther, 374
Future perfect progressive tense, 300
Future perfect tense, 296, 297, 298
Future progressive tense, 299
Future tense, 292, 296

G

Gender, pronoun/antecedent
    agreement and, 225, 227–228,
    232–233
Geographic locations. *See*
    Place/location
Gerund phrases, 304–305
  diagramming of, 308–309
  subject/verb agreement and, 340
Gerunds, 304–305, 308–309
go and/go to, 471
good/well, 409
Government
  capitalization of titles relating to,
    157–158
  capitalization of
    units/departments of, 156
Grammar
  in dictionary, 6, 8
  parts of speech and, 33 (*See also*
    Parts of speech)
  proofreading for, 12, 13
  reference manual for, 10
Grammar checker, 13–14
Gregg Reference Manual, 10, 16,
    94, 435
Groups
  collective antecedents for, 232
  singular *vs.* plural verbs referring
    to, 335–336
Guide sheets, 11

H

had, 297–298
has, 297–298

have, 290, 291–292, 297
having, 305, 306
Helping verbs, 36–37, 262–263
  adjectives and, 39
  be/do/have as, 291–292
  with future tense, 296
  with past/present participles,
    264–265, 268
  with perfect tenses, 296–298
  with progressive tenses, 299–300
Here, sentences beginning, 67,
    338–339
Highway numbers, 566
his/her, 234
Holidays, capitalization of, 160
Hours of day, 531–532
Hyphenated numbers, 368,
    537–538, 539
  at beginning of sentences, 568
  for fractions, 571
  in legal documents, 171
Hyphens, 537–539
  changes in use of, 124, 537
  in compound adjectives,
    366–368, 539
  in compound nouns, 124–125
  in compounds without nouns, 125
  in dictionaries/reference
    manuals, 366
  in fractions, 538
  to indicate dual functions, 539
  to indicate range, 539, 577
  not used with -*ly* adverbs, 400, 538
  not used with some compound
    nouns, 538
  with numbers, 367–368, 573 (*See
    also* Hyphenated numbers)
  in *self-* words, 368, 539
  suspending, 538
  for syllabication, 7, 537
  in titles of people, 539
  in word division, 7, 537

I

-*ible/-able* endings, 399
-*ic* endings, 399
-*ics* endings, 339–340
Identification numbers, 572
Idioms, 439–441
i.e., 529
if, 303
Illustrations, colons with, 531
Imperative mood, 302
Imperative sentences, 59, 493, 499
in, 432
Inc., 510
Inclusive figures, 577
Indefinite numbers, 572

Indefinite pronouns, 201–202
  as antecedents, 233–235
  singular *vs.* plural verbs with,
    334–335
  as subjects *vs.* adjectives, 334
Independent adjectives, 502
Independent clauses, 69, 70, 460–462
  adverb clauses that follow, 408
  commas with, 498–499
  conjunctive adverbs with, 467–468
  coordinating conjunctions with,
    463, 498–499
  diagramming of, 511
  identifying, 499
  relative pronouns and, 203
  semicolons with, 528–529
  in sentence formations, 71–72
  two short, 499
Independent comments, 504
Indicative mood, 302
Indirect commands, 60
Indirect objects, 66, 96
  diagramming of, 134
  nouns as, 126
  pronouns as, 194
Indirect questions, 59, 202, 203, 494
Indirect quotations, 533
Infinitive phrases, 69, 304, 307–308
  as adjectives, 373
  commas with, 506
  diagramming of, 341
  introductory, 506
  prepositional *vs.*, 69, 431–432
Infinitives, 307
-ing endings, 264–265, 266, 304–305.
    See also Present participle
in/into, 437–438
Inititals, periods with, 495
Inside addresses, capitalization
    of, 170
Institutions. *See entries beginning*
    Company/organization
Instructions/directions
  parentheses for, 542
  quotation marks for, 534
Intensive pronouns, 199
Interjections, 33, 42–43
Internet, 91, 121. *See also* Web
    pages/sites
  e-commerce on, 561
  e-mail/electronic mail on, 91,
    170–171, 189
  references on, 3
  search engines on, 3, 121
  software piracy and, 287
  telecommuting and, 31
Interrogative pronouns, 202–203
Interrogative sentences, 59

Intervening words
  quotation marks and, 533
  subject/verb agreement and,
    331–332
Intransitive verbs, 260, 261, 269–270
Introductory clauses, to lists,
    530–531
Introductory expressions, 505–506
Introductory participial phrase,
    305–306
Introductory prepositional
    phrase, 304
Inverted sentences, 338–339
Irregular adjectives, 8
  comparison forms of, 370–371
Irregular adverbs, 8, 403–404
Irregular plural nouns, 8, 124,
    129–130
Irregular verbs, 8, 264, 266–268
  be, 36, 261–262, 264, 290–291
  do, 290, 291
  examples of tenses of, 294, 295
  have, 290, 291–292
  list of, 267
  special forms of, 269–270
it/its, 35, 232–233, 234, 237
Italics, 543–544
it's/its, 197

J

Job search, 491
Jr., 496, 510. *See also* Seniority
    designations

K

Keyboarding errors, proofreading
    of, 12

L

latter/later/last/latest, 374
Laws, capitalization of titles of,
    160–161
Laws, titles of, 160–161
lay/lie, 269
Leadership, 427
least/most, 370, 403
Legal documents
  capitalization in, 171
  money amounts in, 171, 575
  numbers in, 542, 569–570, 575
  reference manual for, 570
less/fewer, 374
less/more, 370, 403
Letters (business). *See* Business
    letters
Letters (of alphabet)
  hyphens to indicate range of, 539
  in lists, 497, 541–542
  following nouns, 166

Letters (of alphabet)—*(Cont.)*
  in outlines, 497, 542
  plurals of capital/lowercase,
    104, 536
like/as, 437, 471
Limiting adjectives, 360
Linking verbs, 36, 38, 261–262
  adjectives after, 361
  adjectives with, 401–402
  adverbs with, 401–402
  be/do/have as, 291–292
  plural verbs as, 330
  state of being, 261–262, 292
  subject complements and, 66,
    96, 330
  subject/verb agreement and, 330
Lists
  capitalization rules for, 168–169
  colons to introduce, 530–531
  numbers/letters in, 541–542
  periods in, 497
  sentence interruptions before, 531
  summary words following, 540
Literary works, titles of, 160
Location. *See* Place/location
Lowercase/small letters,
    494–495, 536
Ltd., 510
-ly endings, 399–400

M

Magazines. *See also* Publications
  capitalization of articles in, 160
  capitalization of names of, 159–160
  italics for names of, 543
  quotation marks for articles in, 533
many, 234, 235
many a/many an, 333
Masculine pronouns, 227–228
Measurements, 494, 565
  fewer/less and, 374
  fractions for, 571
  metric, 573
  numbers for, 571, 573
  plurals of, 103
  singular verb with, 337
merely, 406
midnight, 164, 579
Military documents, dates in, 569
million/billion, 573, 575
Minutes of day, 531–532
Minutes (of meetings)
  motions in, 303
  titles in, 158
Mnemonic devices, 15
Modifiers. *See also* Adjectives;
    Adverbs
  complete subject and, 62–63
  of gerunds, 304–305
  numbers in compound, 569

erbs—(*Cont.*)
  transitive, 260–261, 269–270
  voice of, 290, 301
versus, 171
Virtual assistants, 31
Virtual classes/education, 95
Vocabulary. *See also* Word usage
  for different fields, 33
  "troublesome word list" for, 6
Voice, 290, 301
vs., 171

W

was/were, 303
Web pages/sites, 91, 121, 170–171
well/good, 409
were/was, 303
West, capitalization of, 164–165
what, 202–203
where/that, 472
whether, to introduce questions, 533
whether . . . or, 464, 465
which, 202–203
  in adjective clauses, 372–373, 507
  vs. that, 203–204
who
  in adjective clauses, 372–373, 507
  vs. whom, 205
whom/whomever, 202, 203, 205–206
who's, vs. whose, 206
whose, 202, 203
  in adjective clauses, 372–373, 507
  vs. who's, 206
who/whoever, 205

who/whom/whose, 204–206
  as interrogative pronouns, 202–203
  as relative pronouns, 203
will have, 297–298
Wishes, subjunctive to express, 303
Word division/syllabication, 537
  dictionary for, 7
  reference manual for, 10
Word order, 67–68
Word origins/history, 6, 8
Word usage
  common mistakes in, 16
  in dictionary, 6
  parts-of-speech labels and, 7
  proofreading for, 12
  reference manual for, 10
  spell checker and, 16
  thesaurus for, 11
  tips on, 17
Words
  commonly misused, 16
  dashes for summary, 540
  introductory, 505
  italics to emphasize, 543
  shortened, 497
  slang, 534
  special-effect, 534
  substitute, 11
  summary, 540
World Wide Web, 121. *See also*
      Internet; Web pages/sites
Writing/style
  abbreviations in formal, 103
  consistency with numbers in, 564,
      565, 568, 573, 575

Writing/style—(*Cont.*)
  dashes in formal, 540
  ellipses in advertising, 544
  errors in, 12
  parallelism for clear, 460, 469
  proofreading for, 12, 13
  punctuation for clear, 493
  reference manual for, 10
  related numbers in, 564

X

-x endings, plurals of, 98–99

Y

-y endings, 265, 370, 399
  plurals of, 100
Years, numbers to indicate, 569–570,
      577, 579–580
you, 60, 237, 330
you're/your, 197

Z

-z endings, plurals of, 98–99
Zero
  in decimal numbers, 571
  in money amounts, 574
  in time expressions, 579
ZIP Codes, 496, 509, 565